How Things Work in Your Home (and what to do when they don't)

How Things Work in Your Home
(and what to do when they don't)

BY THE EDITORS OF TIME-LIFE BOOKS

HOLT, RINEHART AND WINSTON   NEW YORK

EDITORIAL STAFF
FOR "HOW THINGS WORK IN YOUR HOME"

EDITOR: John Paul Porter
Text Editors: William Frankel,
Robert M. Jones
Designer: Edward Frank
Assistant Designer: James Eisenman
Picture Editor: Rhea Finkelstein
Staff Writers: Simone Gossner, Lee Greene,
Lee Hassig, Myer Kutz, Don Nelson,
Jill Spiller, John von Hartz
Chief Researcher: Helen M. Hinkle
Researchers: Beatrice Combs,
Gail Cruikshank, Joyce Denebrink,
Jane Edwin, Tom Fitzharris, Sally French,
Ruth Kelton, Joel Legunn, Michael Luftman,
Joan McCullough, Brian McGinn,
Mary Carroll Marden, Joyce Pelto, Tanya Strage,
Scot Terrell
Design Assistants: Kaye Sherry Hirsh
Rosi Cassano, Carmen Mercadal
Editorial Assistant: Janet Hubbard

Published by Holt, Rinehart and Winston,
383 Madison Avenue, New York, New York 10017.
Published simultaneously in Canada by
Holt, Rinehart and Winston of Canada, Limited.

Library of Congress Cataloging in Publication Data
Main entry under title:
How things work in your home, and what to do when
they don't.
Bibliography: p.
Includes index.
1. Dwellings—Maintenance and repair—Amateurs'
manuals.   2. Plumbing—Maintenance and repair—
Amateurs' manuals.   3. Household appliances—Maintenance
and repair—Amateurs' manuals.   I. Time-Life Books.
TH4817.3.H677   1985   643'.7   84-25261
ISBN: 0-03-003672-0

Printed in the United States of America
10 9 8 7 6 5 4 3 2 1

ISBN 0-03-003672-0

CONTENTS

Small Appliances
How They Do
Routine Chores Better Than You Can

Appliances with Motors

Appliances That Heat

Large Appliances
Step-by-Step Methods
for Finding and Solving Problems

Heating

Cooling

Outdoors

CONSULTANTS

JACKSON HAND, as general consultant, read and commented on all parts of the original edition of this book. He is a freelance writer and editor of numerous articles and books in the field of home repair and maintenance.

MARK M. STEELE, consultant for the revised edition, operates a home-repair and maintenance business in the suburbs of Washington, D.C., and is a freelance editor of home-improvement articles and books.

Other consultants who have contributed in the areas of their specialization are:
HAROLD KAUNITZ, licensed master plumber and owner of a plumbing and heating firm in New York City.

THOMAS P. KONEN, Chief of the Building Technology Research Division, Davidson Laboratory, Stevens Institute of Technology, Hoboken, New Jersey.

RICHARD LLOYD served for more than 12 years on eight drafting panels for the National Electrical Code, then chaired the overall code-correlating committee for 10 years.

GEORGE OWENBURG, service manager and vice president of a company specializing in servicing major appliances in New York and New Jersey.

STANLEY H. SMITH, Associate Professor of Electrical Engineering, Stevens Institute of Technology, Hoboken, New Jersey.

MILTON Z. WALLACH, president of a New York City repair service specializing in small appliances.

CLIFFORD A. WOJAN, consulting engineer in thermal engineering; Professor of Mechanical Engineering, Polytechnic Institute of New York.

ARTISTS

ARTHUR DALE GUSTAFSON executed most of the illustrations in this book. Mr. Gustafson is a freelance artist specializing in technical and mechanical subjects.

Nicholas Fasciano, Fred Wolff and Jerry Wood also contributed major illustrations to this book. A complete list of credits will be found on page 358.

WRITERS

Charles G. Burck wrote the introductory chapter of this book. Other contributors to the text include Tony Chiu, Paul Duffy, Jonathan Norton Leonard and Henry Moscow.

INTRODUCTION

The modern American home is a humming and clanking complex of hydraulic, electrical and mechanical systems. It needs a lot of care to keep it running smoothly—and to keep the costs of running it from going out of sight. The purpose of this book is to help you achieve more comfort and convenience, at less cost, by taking over household maintenance and repair jobs that anyone can do safely and efficiently.

An understanding of how things work is fundamental to being able to fix them. Every article in this book begins with words and pictures that describe, with the aid of specially commissioned drawings, how the machines around you do their jobs: how air or liquid or electricity flows, how pipes or wires or gears fit together, how one part of a machine causes another part to move. Other illustrations and text explain how to disassemble things, replace parts and make adjustments. And troubleshooting charts provide a concise review of likely problems by listing symptoms, causes and solutions.

There are, of course, limits to the average homeowner's capacity for coping with the increasingly complicated devices of contemporary life. Radio, television and telephone repairs, for example, are not included in this book because they require expensive instruments and an intimate knowledge of electronic circuitry. But you will find that you can do certain essential, money-saving jobs even on some complex mechanisms, for even the most intricate contain relatively simple components. While only a qualified service technician should work on the oil burner in a furnace, the detailed description of how the burner works will help you make adjustments in other parts of the heating system. In every case, this book will tell you what you can do—and, equally important, it will also tell you what you should not do.

The Editors

The Machines in Your Home

Understanding Them:
The Key to Keeping Things Going

A prize for the all-time champion household mechanical mystery should probably go to Barbara Peters, who lives in California. Her new refrigerator apparently leaked—but only at night. When she came downstairs each morning, she would find a puddle of water on the floor in front of it, but she could never detect anything dripping. Twice she called in a repairman who studied the machine, tinkered a bit, expressed bewilderment and left. The puddles continued to appear—until the night Barbara went into the kitchen and discovered her Great Dane licking an ice cube on the floor.

Suddenly that little bulb lighted above Barbara's head. Her refrigerator had an automatic ice maker that dispensed ice cubes from a niche in the outside of the door. Her dog had learned that if it pressed a dispenser bar in the niche with its nose, out would tumble two refreshing ice cubes. The dog was satisfied with just one, leaving the other to produce an infuriating puddle. The solution? Keep the Great Dane out of the kitchen at night.

Most problems with household machines are far less exotic but no less baffling to the uninitiated. A faucet begins to drip. Why? And what to do? Why does the clothes washer go gurgle but not whir? What do you do about a fuse that keeps blowing? How do you prevent a flood when a pipe springs a leak at midnight and no plumber is to be found?

The truth is that mysteries of many kinds lie concealed among the everyday surroundings of your household. A house is a complex life-support system, and it has been growing more complex over the years. The typical American home today contains some 100 machines—using the term broadly, but accurately, to include such mechanical devices as light switches and sink-stopper mechanisms. It has far more wiring, plumbing and temperature controls than its predecessor of a generation ago. And the components of these major mechanical systems are themselves frequently more complex—fancy water-mixing valves replacing simple faucets, for example, or multiple chimes in place of old-fashioned buzzers.

Nowhere is the growing complexity more manifest than among electrical appliances. Take the refrigerator. Not many years ago it was an uncomplicated machine whose only moving parts were a motor and a compressor. The economy-model refrigerators today have seven operational components; the frost-free luxury model with a butter-storage drawer, automatic ice maker and other features may have 60 or more major components, including multiple motors, thermostats and heaters (yes, heaters—to melt frost and keep butter soft).

Other appliances follow a similar trend toward increasing complexity. And the average house has many more kinds of appliances—from dishwashers to electric carving knives—than it did a decade ago.

New materials that make repairs easier

To be sure, the growing complexity has been offset in part by other trends. Many systems and components have been simplified. It is easier, for example, to work with flexible copper tubing than with galvanized iron pipe—easier still to use plastic pipe that needs only glue.

The amateur electrician can handle plastic-coated electric cables with fewer tools and less effort than required for the older steel-armored cables. Devices like snap-on electrical plugs make certain minor repairs possible without the use of so much as a screwdriver.

Moreover, materials and parts are more readily available than they have ever been before. Many stores specialize in equipment for the home repairman, and some big supply houses that once dealt exclusively with professionals are now glad to serve the amateur.

Nevertheless, complexity and mystery are facts of domestic life, and many homeowners feel both frustrated and foolish in their inability to cope with everyday household machines. Paradoxically, everyday things become mysterious precisely because they are taken for granted. A refrigerator, for instance, does the routine job of keeping food cold, but its operations are so ordinary and its machinery is so well concealed that there is no obvious clue to how it works—or what steps should be taken when it mysteriously stops working.

Much of the mystery disappears once you understand the hows and whys of machinery. You cannot fix a faucet if all you know is that water goes in here and comes out there. But the details of the way a faucet controls the flow of water (pages 70-79) will help you to disassemble it, replace worn parts and put it back together in working order. With an idea of the basic principles, you will not be doing things by rote, but in the purposeful way that comes from understanding just how the things you do affect the machine as a whole.

Attacked this way, most household problems can become surprisingly straightforward. More important, they become responsive to the repair efforts of a homeowner who has no more than average mechanical skills.

No special knowledge or complex tools are needed to carry out the repairs described on the following pages. Safety precautions are given when necessary, but care and common sense are essential for even the simplest jobs. All procedures follow applicable electrical and plumbing codes, and none requires permits or licenses. When repairs need professional attention, the instructions say so.

Most of the machinery that is likely to be found in an American home—from water heater to attic fan—is included. But photographic and electronic equipment—television sets, cameras, telephones, stereos—are excluded because working on them requires rather costly test instruments, an investment hardly worthwhile for an occasional repair job. Nor are there instructions for working with equipment that is usually built into a house—in-the-wall wiring, doors or windows. With experience, you can go further in maintaining home machinery than the steps in this book. What follows is basic knowledge—but enough to make a big difference in keeping the things in your home working steadily, smoothly and economically.

Taking a calm and methodical approach

Fixing things does require a calm, purposeful survey and a systematic, organized approach to the task at hand. It is possible to storm into a job with both fists swinging and complete it successfully, but the most likely outcome of that approach is a botch. You have to establish not only what is wrong, but also what is not wrong; and you have to avoid tampering with parts that are doing their jobs. And when you run into a real crisis—water cascading down a staircase or smoke pouring from a clothes-washer motor—the calm, prepared approach takes emergencies out of the earthquake class. If you know where the water shutoff valve is, you can halt the flood; if you have circuits labeled, you can instantly know which fuse to pull or which circuit breaker to switch off. Then you have time for the essential process of analysis.

A case in point is the true story of Sam Halper, whose dishwasher broke down one evening. When it began to make horrible grinding sounds, he turned it off. Then he emptied the racks of dishes, looked for stray forks or pieces of china down in the bottom of the machine—there were none—and hopefully turned the washer on again. It still crunched and ground away.

At this stage, Sam Halper had to choose between unbolting things in the machine—and washing dirty dishes—or a big repair bill for something he himself might be able to fix. Sam gathered wrenches, screwdrivers, a trouble light and his dishwasher owner's manual, which contained a parts guide showing the whole machine in an exploded line drawing.

He knew his service panel, and started by unscrewing the dishwasher fuse. Then he reasoned with himself. The machine was getting water; he could hear it coming in. The water was draining; he could hear that, too. It crunched and groaned as the water sprayed about the interior with a familiar roaring sound. Something that moved the water inside the machine had to be the cause of the trouble. There was a rotating spray arm at the bottom, held in place by a single plastic nut. Sam unscrewed the nut, removed the spray arm, replaced the fuse, closed the door and started the washer. Still the noises.

Sam realized that he would have to go deeper. He removed the fuse again. Underneath the spray arm was a large plastic housing covering something that the diagram labeled "impeller." The impeller had fins, and after Sam had reflected for a moment, it became clear that it rotated too, forcing water through a series of slots in the housing. The diagram showed that two bolts held the housing in position. Carefully, Sam unscrewed the bolts and laid them next to the spray arm and its nut. (He put them all down in exactly the order in which he had removed them, so he would know how to put them back.) Out came the housing, exposing the impeller. It did not look broken. He probed with a finger between its blades.

Something small, hard and irregular was rattling between two blades. He fished it out—a fragment of china. Could that have been the cause of trouble? Scarcely daring to hope, Sam reassembled everything carefully. He screwed the fuse back in, drew a deep breath and turned the machine on. It worked.

Sam Halper glanced at his watch. He had envisioned hours of frustrating wrestling with the machine. Yet the entire business had taken 27 minutes. He calculated. A service call, he figured, would have run at least $35. "Let's see . . . that makes me worth better than seventy bucks an hour," he announced.

In one way, Sam was lucky: his owner's manual happened to have clear illustrations to guide him—and he had saved the manual.

But he had some acquaintance with the attitudes that make up the service technician's seemingly arcane knack. What had guided him through a potentially costly situation was a set of basic principles that can be stated as axioms:
■ Take precautions before working on anything: shut off water or electricity, or both.
■ Look first for the simple solution. A surprising number of machine failures result from nothing more serious than a loose plug, a blown fuse, tripped circuit breaker or broken cord. Many others are caused by doors that have not been fully closed, so that safety switches prevent the appliance from operating (driers, dishwashers, clothes washers and microwave ovens are among the machines so protected). Still other failures happen when dials are not quite turned to the on position, even though they appear to be.

It never hurts to jiggle a plug or a door, or to nudge a dial forward a fraction of a turn (but only a fraction—timing controls are easily damaged by manual turning when the power is on). There is even something to be said for giving a balky machine a swift kick or—if it is too small to kick—a sharp rap. The story still circulates that a manual supplied with an early British radar system of World War II gave

Pioneers of the New Housekeeping

Electrically powered appliances such as those pictured here transformed the lives of housewives, icemen, launderers—and nearly everyone else— in the decades of electrification that followed the founding of the nation's first public power company in San Francisco in 1879. A few of them, like the flip-down toaster and the piston-operated vacuum cleaner, worked by principles that—to the relief of those who remember using them—are now abandoned. But many others, including the complicated drum clothes washer at bottom right, pioneered basic systems that are still in use.

A two-way vacuum cleaner

The 1908-model vacuum cleaner above had a motor-powered piston that pushed a bellows in and out to generate a dust-eating air flow. If the electricity failed, or the power line had not yet reached the house, the bellows could be operated by hand with, as the cleaner's manufacturer advertised, "no tax on the strength."

Crude or complex, efficient or balky, all the ancestors of the sleek and shining appliances that are taken for granted today improved the quality of life in some way. Then as now, they eliminated much laborious drudgery and saved time for more enjoyable pursuits; they revolutionized marketing by permitting longer storage of perishable food; they banished the darkness of the night at the flick of a switch. And for all their lack of elegance, they pointed the way to the highly mechanized households that are now an accepted part of daily life in many parts of the world.

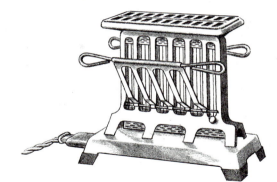

A toaster for one side at a time

You could brown—or burn—two slices of bread at once, one side at a time, in the 1913 electric toaster above. To turn a slice, you lowered the hinged rack away from the central heating element; the bread flipped over as it slid down.

When the coils were on top

The "monitor-top" electric icebox (left) had its condenser coil and compressor out in the open. It was noisy but amazingly durable; last made in 1938, some were still in use almost five decades later.

A light bulb with one filament

The single-filament lamp above, dating from about 1885, was better than Edison's 1879 model, which had no screw thread and a bamboo filament instead of this one's tougher osmium or tantalum. Today's tungsten lasts longer still.

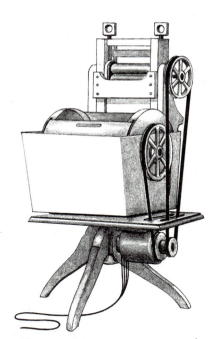

A washing machine with a wringer

This 1912 washer was run by a motor that turned both drum and wringer with belts. Hot water was poured in by hand and the wash was hand-fed to the wringer. But the device was a great advance over the old washboiler and scrubbing board.

one simple order as the last step in trouble-shooting: "Kick hard." The story may be apocryphal, but the point is well taken. Especially with machinery containing cams and gears, two moving parts may simply have become jammed during an operating cycle; freed by the impact of a kick or a rap, they may never jam again. If the problem recurs, however, the trouble lies deep within and needs genuine repair—perhaps a wire has broken loose and is making only intermittent contact.

■ Cultivate patience and try a systematic approach. Do not hurry: if you try to do a repair job too quickly, you may never get it done. Read all instructions, chart the job beforehand and lay out all the tools you will need.

■ Keep track of parts. Memorize the sequence in which they come out of the machine, and put them down in the same order. That way—and only that way—can you be sure of putting them back together exactly as they came apart. Watch for unexpected anomalies. Two neighboring bolts may not be quite the same length, though their threads are similar. There is probably a reason. Be sure each bolt goes back in exactly the place it came from.

■ Know your own limitations. Learn all you can about a machine's insides before you even begin to disassemble it. Otherwise, you may be unhappily surprised by odd objects that drop onto the floor or tiny springs that zing past your ear. You may never find those parts again; even more frustrating, you may find them but never figure out where they came from.

If a warranty *(page 19)* is in force, think twice before undertaking repairs yourself. Virtually all warranties warn that any unauthorized tampering will void the contract. Even if you are sure that your new electric drill is suffering from merely a defective brush you can easily replace, resist temptation. If the warranty clearly covers both parts and labor, take the drill back to the store at which you bought it. That is what warranties are for.

■ Keep all papers. Sales slips, warranties, manuals and bills from previous repairs are all potentially valuable solutions to future problems. If you have a taste for organization, put them in separate folders and file them alphabetically; if you cannot be bothered, stuff them in a big envelope. But keep them together.

When you do need help...

There comes a time, however, when all your understanding and skill prove to be inadequate and you are forced to call in a professional. On the average, service technicians make more than 100 million calls to American homes each year. Your difficulty, of course, is locating the right one. There is a genuine shortage of well-trained technicians, and the files of Better Business Bureaus and other consumer organizations throughout the country are crammed with complaints about shoddy service.

Obviously, your best guide to the right technician is the recommendation of a friend or neighbor who has had experience with a particular individual. Lacking that, start with the store that sold you the machine. It may have its own service shop or, more likely, it will give you the names of firms that do installation and warranty work for it.

Another good bet is any organization connected with the brand name of the machine: a factory-service outlet or an "authorized" agency will be answerable to the manufacturer whose wares it services.

There is always the unpleasant possibility, though, that you will not be able to find a technician just when your need is greatest—as on a hot Fourth of July when the whole family is coming for dinner. The refrigerator is full of food, beer and soft drinks; you open it to get a tray of ice cubes for iced tea before company

How Long Will It Last?

Some devices in the house last indefinitely (the 50-year span for a mercury switch is conservative), and as the graph below indicates, the lifetimes are not necessarily linked to cost. A sewing machine is little more expensive than a good power mower, but lasts five times as long; maker and buyer both know that a hardier power mower would have to cost more than many people would be willing to pay.

A few low-cost fixtures, bought for convenience—or quietness, like the mercury switch —offer a surprise bonus of great durability. And, of course, almost any appliance, whatever its cost, will last longer if cared for properly.

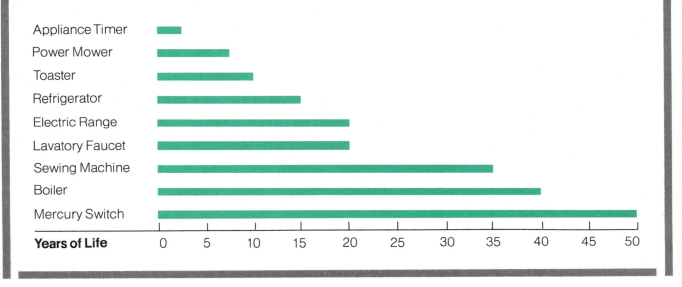

arrives, and the tray holds only water. The refrigerator has quit. No repair company answers the telephone and your dealer is closed.

For such plights, many major manufacturers maintain toll-free telephone lines, generally called "hot lines"—but in one case called a "cool line," presumably because it helps the customer keep his cool. When you call on a hot line, the employee on duty will give you the names and telephone numbers of service companies in your area that are available, as well as other information, such as where to get a service manual. Hot-line attendants are on duty 24 hours a day, seven days a week, for emergencies. In addition, some hot lines are manned during regular weekday working hours by experts who can answer technical questions— how to install machines and even make some repairs. Hot-line numbers appear in owner's manuals, in the pile of stuff you get when you buy your machine, and are often advertised in newspapers. If you cannot find the number, call—free—800-555-1212.

Some manufacturers and retailers offer a way to avoid the problem of finding and choosing a service technician. For a yearly fee, the company issues a service contract that commonly provides an annual maintenance checkup, and unlimited service calls and repairs, including parts and labor without additional charge. It sounds attractive, but the economics of such arrangements demand close appraisal. A typical clothes-washer contract offered by one retail chain costs 7 per cent of the machine's price in the first year after the warranty expires and increases yearly to a maximum of 25 per cent. By the eighth year, you have paid enough to cover the price of a new machine. A full discussion of the pros and cons of these "insurance policies" is on page 257.

Getting the best out of repair technicians

No matter how you choose a repair company, your own knowledge of the machine will help you to deal effectively with the person the company sends to your home. The more you know, the less likely you are to be deceived and victimized. Before the technician arrives, you may be able to get a pretty good idea of what is wrong and what is not. Of course, it can prove awkward or even disastrous to tell a technician his business: an untrustworthy or unquestioning individual may follow your instructions, whether they are right or wrong—then bill you for work that may not have solved the problem. But a technician will appreciate your attempts to be specific about symptoms.

Before the technician begins work, come to an understanding on four vital points:
■ Get an estimate of any major repairs—in writing, if possible—before authorizing the work. If the technician cannot provide an estimate without disassembling the machine or disconnecting pipes (and especially if the machine must be taken back to the shop), make sure the technician understands that you want a firm estimate before the job is begun.
■ Insist that the technician notify you immediately if the cost will exceed the estimate—doubly important if the estimate was not written.
■ Ask that replaced parts be given to you after the work is completed. They are evidence that the parts were replaced; unscrupulous technicians have been known to fix old parts and charge the customer for new ones. The only exception to this rule about return of defective parts should be made when the parts, under the warranty, must go back to the manufacturer.

■ When the job is done, request an invoice itemizing all new parts and the cost of labor.

You may feel reluctant about being firm in these matters. Maybe the technician is a pleasant individual who says, "Don't worry; we'll do the job right." You hate to hurt his or her feelings by seeming to be distrustful. But it is good business to keep the relationship cordially formal, particularly if the individual has never worked for you before. Then there will be no surprises when the bill is presented. And any repair service that values its reputation will not object; an unambiguous agreement benefits both parties in the long run.

You should also, of course, deal fairly: service technicians have complaints about customers, too, and many of them are justified. As a balance to shortcomings in service, consider some typical grievances voiced by repair companies:
■ "The cost of everything has gone up, but you expect me to fix your machine for less money than you spend taking the kids to the movies."
■ "You called me because your refrigerator stopped, and I postponed another appointment to get here in a hurry. Well, it was only a loose plug. But I can't charge you for the full value of my time without making you sore."
■ "I fixed the timer on your eight-year-old clothes washer. Three days later, you called me back, mad because the machine was broken again. It was, all right. But this time it was a valve that failed, and it didn't have anything to do with the timer I repaired. Your machine is getting old and the parts are wearing out. But who do you blame? Me, of course."
■ "Sure, the thermostats on your range conked out a week after I installed it. Sure, the retailer will give me a new part. But your warranty does not cover labor—you ought to know that, if you read the warranty when you bought the range. It's not my fault I have to charge you."

The Warranty: A Promise You Pay for

Everything you purchase, from the fanciest, fully accessorized appliance to the simplest mercury switch, has some kind of warranty that comes with it, even if there is nothing spelled out in writing. If there is a written warranty, look for it. Read it carefully. Know what it says. And take advantage of it.

The terms guarantee and warranty are used interchangeably to mean a promise relating to performance. There are two kinds: an implied warranty (also called a warranty of merchantability) and a written warranty. The first assures you that goods sold for a particular purpose will serve that purpose—that an appliance sold to wash dishes automatically will do so, and that a refrigerator will cool and safely store perishable foodstuffs. The written one generally states precisely what the supplier will do—and not do—for the purchaser over a specific period of time if the product breaks down.

Treat the written warranty just like a feature on the appliance itself. It costs the manufacturer money to fulfill warranty terms, and that cost is included in the price you pay. Therefore, it is important to determine exactly what you are getting for your money. The terms of the warranty should be clearly defined. The Major Appliance Consumer Action Panel (MACAP), an industry-sponsored, consumer-oriented liaison organization, has established a series of guidelines for warranties. To satisfy these requirements of MACAP, a warranty should clearly answer the following questions for the purchaser:

■ Who is the warrantor? Is the name and address included on the warranty?

■ Who is responsible for repairing the product? Is it the dealer? A service agency? The manufacturer? Where is the service agent located?

■ How long is the warranty in effect? Does it cover the entire product? Or only some of the individual parts or assemblies?

■ Who pays for what under the warranty? Parts? Labor? Shipping charges? Transportation expenses for the servicing agent?

■ If a product cannot be used or has to be removed from the home because of a service problem, will a substitute product or service be provided? By whom?

At the time of the sale you should complete and forward the product registration card that usually comes with your purchase. Although it is generally not necessary to mail the card to validate the warranty, doing so will supply proof —along with your sales slip—of the date of purchase if the product needs to be serviced. Read the warranty at once and become familiar with its terms; do not wait until something goes wrong to refer to it. And keep the warranty where you can find it.

Most written warranties distinguish between "defect" and "damage." A defect is the warrantor's responsibility; damage is the customer's.

A defect is any fault that exists in the product when it is sold, or that develops within a specified time limit; within this period, the guarantor accepts the responsibility for fixing a defective appliance, as long as the defect does not stem from improper use.

Damage is the result of improper treatment. For example, repeatedly overloading a clothes washer or neglecting to defrost the freezing compartment of a refrigerator can damage the appliance. Also, the effects of natural disasters such as flood, earthquake or fire, although beyond the control of either purchaser or warrantor, are always considered to be damage.

If, after carefully following the terms set forth in the warranty, you are still not completely satisfied with the treatment you and your appliance have received, you can start exerting your rights as a consumer through the various channels outlined on pages 20-23.

During recent years, there has been some improvement in the wording of many warranties, but still the best protection is careful scrutiny before putting your money on the line.

The technicians are caught in the middle, beset on one side by customers who expect their home machines to work, and on the other by machines that have become increasingly difficult and costly to fix.

More convenience, more complexity

The dimensions of the repair problem have only recently begun to be appreciated. For consumers look with delight on devices that become more complicated with each new model. The complexities make possible extra convenience and usefulness, and they have not been unreasonably costly. In dollar value, in fact, appliances have been one of the better bargains industrialism has to offer. For more than two decades, the prices of appliances in general have gone up less rapidly than the consumer price index; over the long run, most appliance prices have actually declined. Today's appliances turn out many years of useful service—a range should last for 20 years, a freezer for 21 years.

Yet there is much unhappiness in the land over the failure of machines to live out these hypothetical lifetimes—and the cost of coaxing them into doing so.

As the reliability of domestic machinery has become a public concern, the industry appears to be shifting slowly toward providing more of it. Modular components and systems for easy replacement have become widespread in the television industry, and this approach to design is finding its way into a variety of small appliances. Manufacturers are also beginning to experiment with other ways of making their machines easier to service. In one name-brand clothes washer, for example, all the wires to the timer are now incorporated in one block that is fitted with a jack and just plugs into the timer.

Meanwhile, machines fail, service technicians occasionally botch their work and, not infrequently, appeals to warranty protections are turned down on the basis of some phrase in the small print. Even then, there is no need to shrug and mutter about how much better things were in the good old days. You have many courses of action open.

First, of course, raise the problem with the people who serve you directly: the storekeeper who sold you the machine, the technician who fixed (or tried to fix) it. They are valuable allies, not antagonists, for they are generally interested in retaining your business. Yet the time may come when you cannot get satisfaction from the merchant who sold you a lemon, or from the plumber who did a terrible job. That is the moment to fight for your rights.

Like fixing a machine, getting your rights need not be an intimidating or baffling process. Calm down, to begin with; put aside the justifiable anger you may feel about having been victimized, and set about redressing your grievance systematically. Do not, for example, storm out of the store or repair shop shouting, "You'll be hearing from my lawyer!" Starting out with a lawsuit is expensive overkill, and a bluff simply undermines your credibility.

With an appliance, the correct first step is to get in touch with the manufacturer or the company's local service manager, if it has one. If the manufacturer maintains a hot line, call with your complaint. The hot-line attendant will pass it on to someone who can handle it.

Or write a letter. There are methods here, too, that many people have found useful:
■ Use a tone that indicates controlled determination. Abuse is likely to get your complaint nowhere except into a wastebasket.
■ Describe clearly the problem, and detail your attempts to get the machine repaired or replaced. Include copies (not originals) of sales slips, repair bills and correspondence.

■ Address the letter to the customer relations department or the service manager. If you get no satisfaction, write to the president of the company. (If the firm has a hot line, you should be able to get his or her name from the attendant. If there is no hot line, call the company headquarters and ask the switchboard operator. Or look up the name in a business directory in a library.) Send copies of your letter to as many officials—Better Business Bureau, consumer agencies—as you can think of, not forgetting the subordinate employee who failed to settle your complaint the first time.

■ Some people use their company's letterhead, feeling that the company they work for has more clout than they have as individuals.

When you get nowhere with the people directly involved—the dealer, the repair service, the manufacturer—you may have to seek outside help. You can try a variety of channels, most of which are of relatively recent origin:

■ VOLUNTARY CONSUMER GROUPS have sprung up throughout the United States and Canada in recent years. Such private citizens' organizations can bring the pressure of numbers and publicity to bear on all the people who have not listened to you; moreover, their staffs know whom to turn to in business or government to deal most efficiently with problems. Some organizations advertise in local newspapers and are easy to reach. You can also obtain their names from the Office of Consumer Affairs, Department of Health and Human Services, Washington, D.C. 20201.

■ GOVERNMENT CONSUMER OFFICES now exist at state or local levels in all of the 50 states. These official consumer offices are mostly set up as branches of the state attorney general's office, but many cities and counties run similar offices. They vary widely in responsibilities and powers; some are advisory only, others have enforcement powers and can put an unscrupulous dealer or service company out of business. In either case, however, you will be working with a government agency; prepare yourself for the paper work and delays that go with even a benign bureaucracy. To help you find the office that can handle your problem most directly, the Department of Health and Human Services' Office of Consumer Affairs compiles a directory of official consumer agencies and even of the toll-free telephone lines that some of them maintain for complaints. The directory is available from the Superintendent of Documents, U.S. Government Printing Office, Washington, D.C. 20402.

■ BETTER BUSINESS BUREAUS serve mainly as mediators between business and the consumer, and can usually do little more than warn you in advance if a firm has been the subject of complaints. For the record, though, and to help keep others from finding themselves in your particular predicament, you should call the local BBB if you have a serious complaint about a merchant or repair firm.

■ NEWSPAPER AND TV "ACTION LINES" in some communities investigate complaints of individuals who write to them. If an Action Line decides a complaint is justified, it asks the retailer, serviceman or manufacturer what he intends to do to correct the situation. Whether the customer wins or loses, the results of many such cases are publicized, and few businesses are willing to risk unfavorable notice. An Action Line often helps when other measures produce no satisfactory result.

■ MACAP, which stands for Major Appliance Consumer Action Panel, was set up by the manufacturers and retailers of major appliances as a court of last resort in disputes between appliance owners and the industry. MACAP has established a reputation as genuinely impartial; in its first few years of operation, it handled some 4,000 complaints annually and brought more than 85 per cent of them to a conclusion satisfactory to both sides. If you and the manufacturer cannot resolve your problem, write directly to MACAP at 20 North Wacker Drive, Chicago, Illinois 60606. Remember, though, that MACAP deals only with major appliances: washers, ranges, refrigerators and the like. It cannot help with small appliances.

If all else fails, two forms of last-resort action remain. Neither is a casual undertaking, but you may some day have no other recourse:

■ ARBITRATION is used to settle consumer disputes in most major metropolitan areas. An impartial arbitrator, approved by both sides from a list of volunteers supplied by the Better Business Bureau, holds a hearing, considers the evidence and arguments, and renders a decision. Almost all states recognize the process as binding. Often the very suggestion of arbitration ends the argument. As a Better Business officer in California said, "Both parties suddenly rethink their previously unmovable opinions." For more information, write the Council of Better Business Bureaus, 1515 Wilson Boulevard, Arlington, Virginia 22209.

■ SMALL-CLAIMS COURTS, found in most parts of the nation, are local courts in which people can sue without red tape or major expense. Such courts are limited to cases involving relatively small amounts—rarely more than $1,000. Neither party has to have a lawyer.

Before you go to court, try to find out how the law can help you—and when it cannot. Any agreement between yourself and a repair service, whether written or oral, falls into a legal gray area. If the service turns out to be unsatisfactory, you do not generally have any recourse unless you can prove that the technician worked without reasonable care, and that you suffered a monetary loss as a result. The mere

fact that the machine still does not work after you have paid the bill does not indicate the absence of reasonable care.

But if the plumber flooded the bathroom and ruined the ceiling of the room below, he has plainly failed to be reasonably careful, and you have strong legal grounds for refusing to pay; you may even be able to collect damages.

Less ambiguous are the laws governing purchases. Apart from formal warranty certificates, certain implied warranties hold both manufacturers and retailers accountable for quality. The consumer rarely has to prove that careless workmanship caused a product to fail prematurely; he has to prove only that it failed. These laws will generally cover advertising—printed or oral. Suppose, for instance, a salesperson tells you that the air conditioner you are about to purchase will function on the ordinary electric circuit in your house. You buy it and install it, only to blow fuse after fuse; it turns out, in fact, that the air conditioner requires a special heavy-duty circuit. Under the law, you have the right to demand a replacement that will work as represented.

With luck and practical knowledge—mainly the latter—you will never have to go to court. For understanding helps avoid unhappy situations that befall the mechanically innocent; you will know how to care for your household machines, when and how to fix them, when not to, and how to deal with professionals.

This kind of knowledge not only means money in your pocket but also offers you the pleasure of making your house a friend rather than an uncertain ally. You will find that working with your hands and with tools produces a special sense of accomplishment as you see the results of your own skill. Indeed, there are people who find these intangible satisfactions more valuable than the money they save.

A Troubleshooting Checklist

When household equipment fails, you will solve your problem more easily if you adhere to some simple rules of procedure. Here is a checklist for making repairs yourself, for dealing with a service company and, if necessary, for obtaining your rights as a consumer.

If you want to fix it yourself...

■ Consult your warranty. If it remains in force, you may render it void by working on the machine. Let the retailer or the manufacturer make any repairs that are needed.

■ Look first for the simple solution when you tackle any kind of trouble. The clothes-drier door may not be shut tight; the dishwasher dial may not be turned precisely to the "ON" setting; a fuse may have blown; or a plug may have worked loose in the socket.

■ Take safety precautions. Before you begin working on your appliance, be sure to shut off the electricity to the circuit, or shut off the water at the appropriate valve—or both, if necessary. Take it easy. An excited and hurried approach is very likely to result in a botched job.

■ Be systematic. Read all of the repair instructions carefully. Diagnose the probable cause of the trouble by determining what the machine is still doing right. Then chart a course of action. Lay out all necessary tools before beginning to take things apart.

■ Keep track of parts. Study the assembly before dismantling anything. Put each part down in the order in which it came out of the machine.

■ Know your limitations. If you are in doubt about your ability to repair an appliance, call for advice on the manufacturer's "hot line." To find out if the manufacturer has a hot line, call 800-555-1212.

If you need professional help...

■ Choose carefully. Call the retailer for a recommendation, or telephone the manufacturer's hot line for a list of good repair services in your area. Or ask the neighbors.

■ Reach agreement with the technician before he does anything. Make it clear that you will require an estimate of the cost in writing; your permission to proceed if the cost exceeds the estimate; a bill itemizing parts and labor when the job is completed; and return of all parts that have had to be replaced. A reliable service company will take the requests as a matter of course.

■ Be helpful but not bossy. Tell the technician how the machine has been behaving. If you think that you know what is wrong, suggest it to him. But do not tell him what to do.

■ Be firm, fair and friendly. If something the technician fixed does not stay fixed for a reasonable time, tell him so politely: a professional will be jealous of his reputation. But do not blame him if he fixes one thing and something else goes wrong; that is probably not his fault. And remember, a good technician can be a useful ally in obtaining redress for inherent defects.

If you have to demand your rights...

■ Telephone or write to the customer relations department of the manufacturer if the retailer fails to satisfy your complaints. Give the machine model and serial numbers, the retailer's name and address, and details of the problem. Enclose copies, not originals, of invoices and bills. If nothing happens, write to the company's president, by ordinary first class, not registered, mail. If he is away, registered mail may wait.

■ Consult voluntary or governmental consumer protection agencies if the manufacturer's response is unsatisfactory. You can obtain the addresses of such agencies by writing to the Office of Consumer Affairs, Department of Health and Human Services, Washington, D.C. 20201. Or appeal to the Action Line conducted by a local newspaper or broadcasting station.

■ Go to court. As a last resort, take your case to a small-claims court. You will not need a lawyer.

Buying, Using and Maintaining Tools

When you watch a professional craftsman at work, he seems quickly and effortlessly to accomplish tasks that you must strain to complete, less satisfactorily, in a much longer time. A few quick twists of the screwdriver and a whole panel comes free; you remember that it took you a half hour of turning, prying and jiggling with several tools the last time you tried to get the thing off. The secret advantage lies only partly in superior skill and knowledge, important as they are; the professional's tools make a big difference as well.

That much of the professional's secret you can buy at the hardware counter. You will not need everything in his tool box; a modest kit *(pages 26-33)* handles most general work, and a few extras are needed for plumbing *(pages 48-51)* and wiring *(pages 136-137)*. But any job is done better, faster and easier if you have tools that are of good quality, suited to the job at hand and well maintained.

Quality in a tool is determined by the process used to make it and by the material from which it is made. The shape of the tool and the care used in its assembly are also important; a screwdriver that is made of the best metal will not work well if the flat sides of its blade are not parallel, forcing it to jump out of a screw slot, or if the handle wobbles.

Most metal tools are made by either casting or forging. In casting, molten steel is poured into a mold where it cools and hardens. As it cools, it forms crystals that arrange themselves at random and are not bonded tightly enough to resist strong bending forces or heavy impacts. A hammer with a cast-steel head may chip easily. It can quickly become useless, and the chips can be dangerous as well. Those made by the the process called drop forging are more expensive than cast tools but are also stronger, longer-lasting and safer. They are made from steel ingots, heated and rolled so that their crystals are aligned in orderly fashion, then pounded to align the crystal grains to resist the forces of use. Most tools made by this process are stamped "drop-forged."

Another way you can recognize quality is to look for a tool that is well finished. If the appearance indicates the manufacturer was proud of his work, chances are he had reason to be. Sometimes this pride will be reflected in polished, even chrome-plated surfaces. Wood parts will be smooth and carefully enameled or varnished. Balance and "feel" are important; the tool should seem moderately heavy but comfortable to hold when you heft it, like a natural extension of your arm and hand.

There are also some specific things to look for in certain kinds of tools. The tip of a screwdriver blade should be square and the flat sides of the blade almost parallel; the shaft should extend well into the handle. The nut on an adjustable wrench should move easily, as should the drive on a ratchet. The more clicks a ratchet makes while turning, the easier it will be to use, because it can be moved through a wider arc in confined spaces. A saw blade ought to be thickest at its cutting edge so that it will not bind while cutting.

Handles must be fixed tightly. For hammers, they are best made of straight-grained hickory, tubular or forged steel, or fiberglass; cast handles, especially those lacking rubber grips, can transmit the hammering impact to your arm and give you the carpenter's version of tennis elbow. The handles of good pliers should curve to fit snugly into the palm of your hand when gripped.

Even the best quality tool is no good if it is unsuited to the job at hand. It must be the right type and, equally important, the right size.

The screwdriver *(page 26)* is the most fre-

quently abused tool in the kit. Using it on a screw that it does not fit can damage the screw and the screwdriver blade. It is made to withstand twisting force, not levering force, and the shaft will bend and the blade chip if it is used strenuously in place of a pry bar.

Pliers *(page 26)* are meant only to hold a part, not to turn it. Their rough-edged jaws chew up metal if you try to apply turning force.

Socket wrenches *(page 27)* are made up to fit nuts and bolts of specific sizes. A socket that is too small will not work at all, of course, but one too large is equally worthless. It will slip and round off the corners of the nut, making it impossible to remove. For nuts and bolts that do not fit your sockets, use an open-ended adjustable wrench. Always pull on the adjustable wrench in the direction of its jaw opening, so that most force is exerted on the fixed jaw, which is stronger than the adjustable jaw. And be sure that the jaws fit tightly around the nut or bolt; otherwise the tool may slip and show you why wrenches of this type are given the nickname "knuckle buster."

Storage and maintenance

Using the right tools with the right techniques is the best way to make tools last, but they also need careful maintenance. Keep unused tools covered with a thin coat of light oil by putting a few drops on a clean rag and wiping it over the tool. A couple of drops of oil should also be dripped on the moving parts of tools such as locking-grip pliers and adjustable wrenches. If rust does gain a foothold, it can be removed with steel wool and a few drops of oil. Protect the edges of cutting tools by storing them so that they will not bang against other tools. Hang them on nails or pegboards, or if you must keep them in a drawer, wrap each in a protective cloth. Finally, be sure to clean your tools thoroughly after using them.

A BASIC TOOL KIT

The equipment depicted and described on these and the next six pages will provide a maximum of versatility for a sensible expenditure. It includes only tools that are considered indispensable rather than merely desirable. A 16-ounce hammer of the quality recommended below, for example, will drive a cabinetmaker's small brads and a carpenter's tenpenny nails with sufficient facility for most household chores. But if you are going to build several cabinets, a 13-ounce hammer will be less clumsy, and for construction jobs involving big nails, a 20-ounce hammer speeds the work.

The wrenches, pliers, screwdrivers, chisel and nail set, as well as the electric drill shown on pages 32-33, are, similarly, of the types and sizes that give most people the most service. But for special tasks, a socket wrench, for example, for which seven sizes of sockets are suggested, has 200 optional parts. Buy them as you need them.

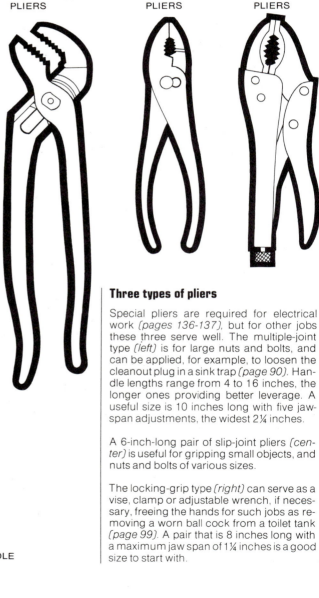

MULTIPLE-JOINT PLIERS   SLIP-JOINT PLIERS   LOCKING-GRIP PLIERS

Two types of screwdrivers

Screwdrivers come with either flat blades for single-slot screws or Phillips blades for the crossed-slot screws used in many appliances. You will want two blade lengths of each type. Short blades are for cramped areas; longer blades have bigger handles that allow a better grip and greater twisting power. Rubber-cushioned handles reduce wear and tear on your hands; a screwdriver's tip must match the screwhead—a tip too small or too large for the slot will damage the screw and possibly make it useless.

Two tip sizes for each screw type should suffice *(from left, below):* one Phillips screwdriver with a 6-inch blade and No. 3 tip, and one with a 3-inch blade and No. 1 tip; one flat-tipped screwdriver with a 3-inch blade and ³⁄₁₆-inch tip, and one with a 6-inch blade and ⁵⁄₁₆-inch tip.

Three types of pliers

Special pliers are required for electrical work *(pages 136-137),* but for other jobs these three serve well. The multiple-joint type *(left)* is for large nuts and bolts, and can be applied, for example, to loosen the cleanout plug in a sink trap *(page 90).* Handle lengths range from 4 to 16 inches, the longer ones providing better leverage. A useful size is 10 inches long with five jaw-span adjustments, the widest 2¼ inches.

A 6-inch-long pair of slip-joint pliers *(center)* is useful for gripping small objects, and nuts and bolts of various sizes.

The locking-grip type *(right)* can serve as a vise, clamp or adjustable wrench, if necessary, freeing the hands for such jobs as removing a worn ball cock from a toilet tank *(page 99).* A pair that is 8 inches long with a maximum jaw span of 1¼ inches is a good size to start with.

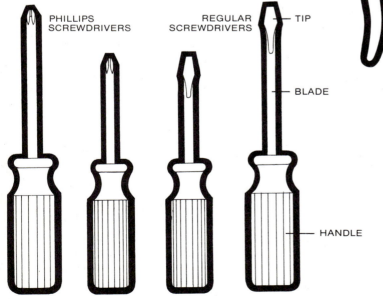

PHILLIPS SCREWDRIVERS   REGULAR SCREWDRIVERS   TIP

BLADE

HANDLE

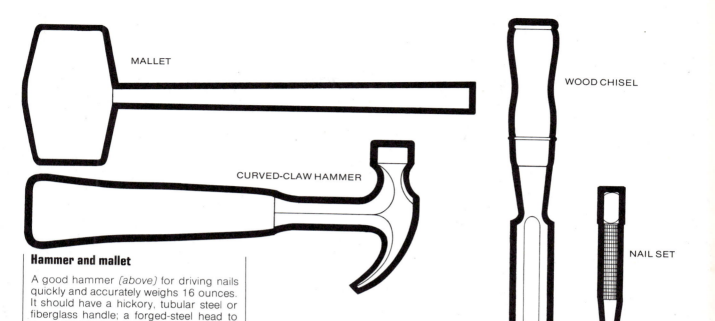

MALLET

CURVED-CLAW HAMMER

WOOD CHISEL

NAIL SET

Hammer and mallet

A good hammer *(above)* for driving nails quickly and accurately weighs 16 ounces. It should have a hickory, tubular steel or fiberglass handle; a forged-steel head to prevent chipping; and a slightly convex face, which drives well even if you do not hit the nail squarely. Its claw should have a finely beveled, sharp-edged, V-shaped slot for pulling out thin nails as well as big.

A 16-ounce rubber mallet *(above, top)* is handy for driving wood chisels *(right)* for loosening stuck windows and even for removing an electric-drill chuck *(page 33)*.

Three types of wrenches

A socket wrench *(left and below)* is especially useful in cramped areas because its ratchet handle and universal-joint assembly let you pump back and forth, and go around corners to reach hard-to-turn nuts. Choose one with a reversible ratchet handle 8 inches long that has a ⅜-inch drive, a ¼-inch drive adapter, a universal joint, and 3- and 6-inch extension shafts. For a start, get ⅞⅗-, ½-, ⁹⁄₁₆- and ⅝-inch sockets with ⅜-inch drive ends and ¼-, ⁵⁄₁₆- and ⅜-inch sockets with ¼-inch drive ends.

The open-end adjustable wrench *(below, right)* has smooth jaws. It is useful for such work as turning the packing nuts and locknuts on faucets. For those jobs, get one that is 10 inches in overall length.

The Allen wrench *(right)* turns screws that have hexagonal recessed heads—found, for example, on single-lever faucets *(pages 76-79)*, and clothes-washer and drier motors. Start with a set of eight, ranging in diameter from ¹⁄₂₀ to ⅜ inches.

Two woodworking aids

For such jobs as cutting recesses in a door and a frame to accommodate hinges, a good tool is a medium-thick, ½-inch-wide, 3-inch-long wood chisel *(above, left)*.

To conceal nailheads you need a steel nail set *(above, right)*. Its concave tip is placed on the nailhead and its top tapped by a hammer to drive the nail below the wood surface for covering with putty. A ²⁄₃₂-inch size works on the nails commonly used for window and door moldings.

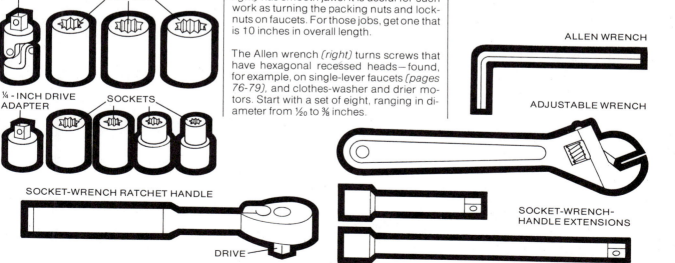

UNIVERSAL JOINT

SOCKETS

¼-INCH DRIVE ADAPTER

SOCKETS

SOCKET-WRENCH RATCHET HANDLE

DRIVE

ALLEN WRENCH

ADJUSTABLE WRENCH

SOCKET-WRENCH-HANDLE EXTENSIONS

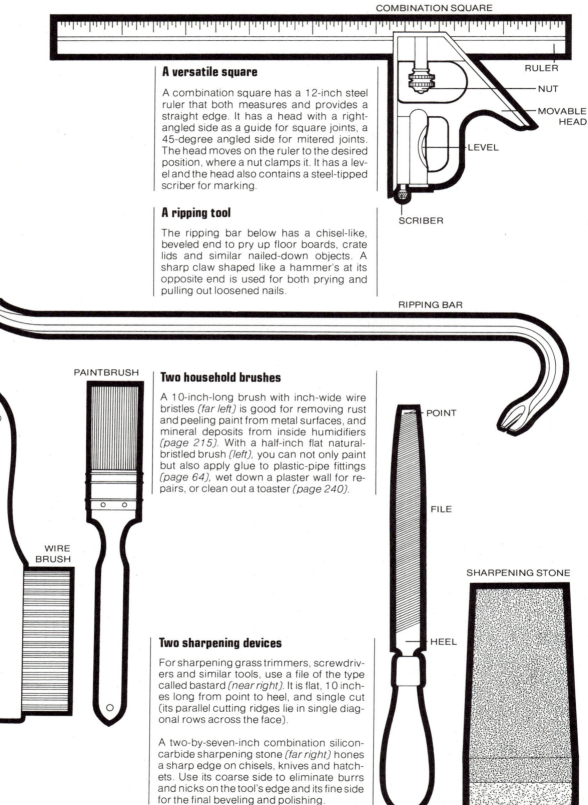

COMBINATION SQUARE

RULER

NUT

MOVABLE HEAD

LEVEL

SCRIBER

A versatile square

A combination square has a 12-inch steel ruler that both measures and provides a straight edge. It has a head with a right-angled side as a guide for square joints, a 45-degree angled side for mitered joints. The head moves on the ruler to the desired position, where a nut clamps it. It has a level and the head also contains a steel-tipped scriber for marking.

A ripping tool

The ripping bar below has a chisel-like, beveled end to pry up floor boards, crate lids and similar nailed-down objects. A sharp claw shaped like a hammer's at its opposite end is used for both prying and pulling out loosened nails.

RIPPING BAR

POINT

PAINTBRUSH

Two household brushes

A 10-inch-long brush with inch-wide wire bristles *(far left)* is good for removing rust and peeling paint from metal surfaces, and mineral deposits from inside humidifiers *(page 215)*. With a half-inch flat natural-bristled brush *(left)*, you can not only paint but also apply glue to plastic-pipe fittings *(page 64)*, wet down a plaster wall for repairs, or clean out a toaster *(page 240)*.

FILE

SHARPENING STONE

WIRE BRUSH

HEEL

Two sharpening devices

For sharpening grass trimmers, screwdrivers and similar tools, use a file of the type called bastard *(near right)*. It is flat, 10 inches long from point to heel, and single cut (its parallel cutting ridges lie in single diagonal rows across the face).

A two-by-seven-inch combination silicon-carbide sharpening stone *(far right)* hones a sharp edge on chisels, knives and hatchets. Use its coarse side to eliminate burrs and nicks on the tool's edge and its fine side for the final beveling and polishing.

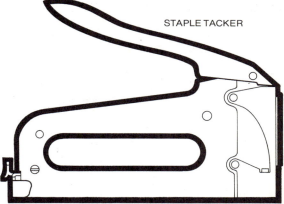

STAPLE TACKER

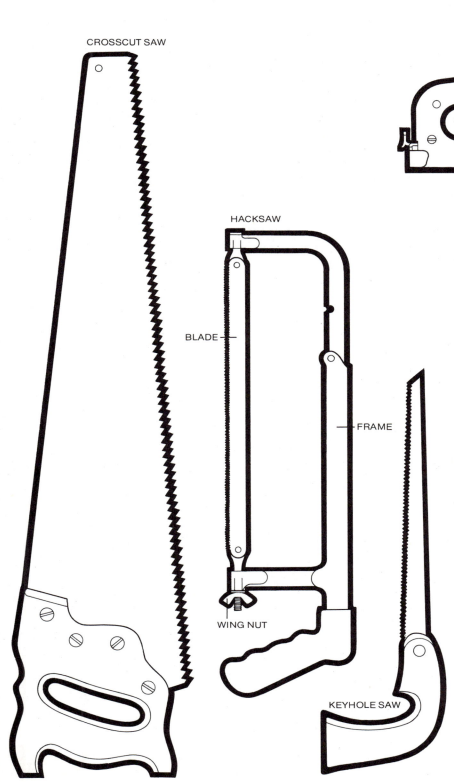

CROSSCUT SAW

HACKSAW

BLADE

FRAME

WING NUT

KEYHOLE SAW

A tacking tool

A staple tacker provides the best way to fasten light materials to wood. Most versatile is the type that takes .05-inch-thick wire staples for such heavy-duty jobs as anchoring carpets and pads, installing insulation and upholstering furniture. It also uses .03-inch-thick staples for lighter tasks like tacking shelf paper and covering valances.

Three types of saws

For cutting wood across the grain, a crosscut saw *(far left)* is the kind to use. Such saws have blades 16 to 26 inches long with, commonly, 8 or 10 tooth points per inch of blade. The more teeth, the finer the cut; fewer teeth provide a faster but rougher cut. A good-quality, all-round crosscut saw has a 10-point 26-inch blade—precision-set, taper-ground and bevel-filed.

The hacksaw *(center)* cuts metal and plastic in such jobs as sawing pipes *(page 63)*. A good hacksaw has a pistol-grip handle and an adjustable frame that can accommodate detachable blades a half inch wide and 8, 10 or 12 inches long. The blades are tightened into place with the wing nut. For such jobs as cutting bolts or pipe, use a flexible, high-speed, molybdenum-steel blade that is 10 inches long and that has 24 tooth points to the inch.

The keyhole saw *(near left)* is designed for making circular or straight "inside" cuts in wood paneling or thin boards to provide openings in floors, walls and ceilings for pipes, electrical outlets or vents. The keyhole saw has a nonremovable, tapered, tool-steel blade that is 10 or 12 inches long and has 10 tooth points per inch.

29

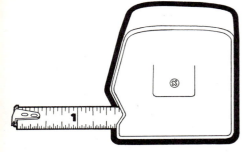

FLEXIBLE METAL RULE

A measuring tape

The flexible steel tape rule is pliable enough for measuring curved surfaces, yet rigid enough for measuring flat upright surfaces. The hook on its end can often fasten to one end of the object being measured. A good tape for home use extends to 12 feet, has a width of one half or three quarters of an inch, and is marked in feet and inches on one side and in inches on the other.

A portable light

When you repair wiring or plumbing in a dark area, or shut off the current in a circuit to change a ceiling fixture, you will need light from a distant circuit to work by. A trouble light with a 25-foot extension cord will provide it. The trouble light should have a strong, rigid handle, a hook on top for hanging, a switch, and a steel grid for protecting the bulb.

Two types of knives

A putty knife *(far left)* with a one-and-a-quarter-inch steel ground blade scrapes peeling paint from furniture and trim, and applies patching to small cracks in walls and ceilings. The utility knife *(near left)* is good for a wide range of cutting jobs, including those on carpeting and plasterboard. It has a retractable, razor-sharp, disposable blade that locks in four positions; extra blades store in the handle.

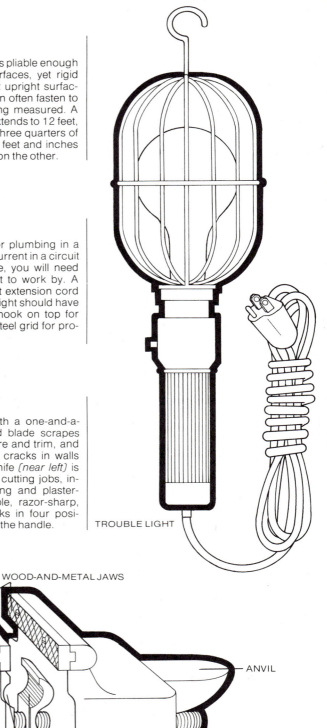

TROUBLE LIGHT

PUTTY KNIFE　　UTILITY KNIFE

WOOD-AND-METAL JAWS

ANVIL

A vise

The best way to hold work steady is with a vise. A heavy bolt-mounted model *(right)* with an anvil and a swivel base can be locked in place, enabling you to work in several different positions. The jaws should be four inches wide and should open four to six inches. Two pairs of detachable jaws are useful: one for holding wood and metal, one for pipe and other round objects.

WORKSHOP VISE

PIPE JAWS

SWIVEL BASE

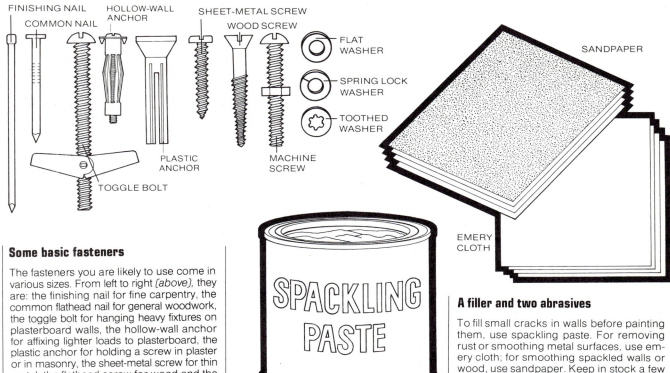

FINISHING NAIL

COMMON NAIL

HOLLOW-WALL ANCHOR

SHEET-METAL SCREW

WOOD SCREW

FLAT WASHER

SPRING LOCK WASHER

TOOTHED WASHER

PLASTIC ANCHOR

MACHINE SCREW

TOGGLE BOLT

SANDPAPER

EMERY CLOTH

Some basic fasteners

The fasteners you are likely to use come in various sizes. From left to right (above), they are: the finishing nail for fine carpentry, the common flathead nail for general woodwork, the toggle bolt for hanging heavy fixtures on plasterboard walls, the hollow-wall anchor for affixing lighter loads to plasterboard, the plastic anchor for holding a screw in plaster or in masonry, the sheet-metal screw for thin metal, the flathead screw for wood and the machine screw for bolting things together. The three kinds of metal washers help keep machine screws from loosening.

SPACKLING PASTE

A filler and two abrasives

To fill small cracks in walls before painting them, use spackling paste. For removing rust or smoothing metal surfaces, use emery cloth; for smoothing spackled walls or wood, use sandpaper. Keep in stock a few sheets of both abrasives in extra-coarse, coarse, medium and fine grades.

SILICONE CAULKING

ALL PURPOSE GLUE

EPOXY

EPOXY HARDENER

A sealant and two adhesives

To fill cracks between a fixture and a tile wall, or between tiles, use waterproof silicone caulking, which does not dry out. For permanent bonding of just about any material except rubber and some flexible plastics, use epoxy, whose resin and hardener come in separate tubes. Epoxy sets in five to six minutes and cures in two to 24 hours. All-purpose white glue bonds porous materials such as paper and wood; it dries in about 30 minutes.

Lubricants

To loosen machine screws that have rusted tight, use penetrating oil. For lubrication of close-fitting metal parts—hinges, shaver heads, some motor bearings—use a lightweight machine oil (if in doubt, you can ask for sewing-machine oil); it comes in both drip and aerosol cans. For loosening up stuck drawers or windows, use silicone spray. Unlike oils, it is not greasy.

SILICONE SPRAY

OIL

The Power Drill: A Versatile Tool

An electric drill represents a moderate investment and it is undoubtedly the most broadly useful of all power tools. Besides boring holes in anything from plywood to plaster, it can sand, ream, buff, brush, mix, and turn screws in or out.

Electric drills commonly come in three-eighths-inch and quarter-inch sizes; this refers to the diameter of the largest bit shank the jaws of the drill chuck can take, not directly to the sizes of the holes that can be bored—but the larger-sized drill generally can make bigger holes. For use at home, the quarter-inch size, once the most popular, is being displaced by the three-eighths size.

Although the two types often have the same kind of motor, the three-eighths size is geared to provide more twisting force for tough jobs like boring concrete, without reducing its capacity for fast drilling in wood or metal. The most useful is the reversible variable-speed type (below). Its trigger switch controls drilling speed to permit slow operation for boring hard materials and driving screws. When run in reverse, it backs out a jammed bit and pulls screws.

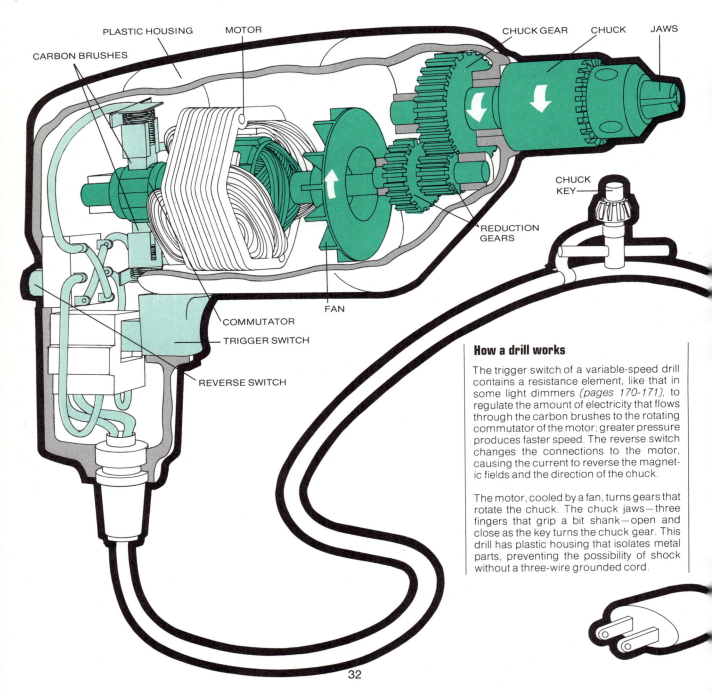

How a drill works

The trigger switch of a variable-speed drill contains a resistance element, like that in some light dimmers (pages 170-171), to regulate the amount of electricity that flows through the carbon brushes to the rotating commutator of the motor; greater pressure produces faster speed. The reverse switch changes the connections to the motor, causing the current to reverse the magnetic fields and the direction of the chuck.

The motor, cooled by a fan, turns gears that rotate the chuck. The chuck jaws—three fingers that grip a bit shank—open and close as the key turns the chuck gear. This drill has plastic housing that isolates metal parts, preventing the possibility of shock without a three-wire grounded cord.

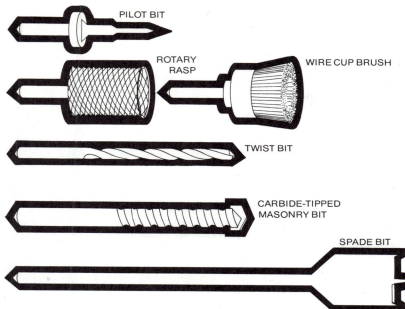

PILOT BIT

ROTARY RASP

WIRE CUP BRUSH

TWIST BIT

CARBIDE-TIPPED MASONRY BIT

SPADE BIT

Accessories for many jobs

The most practical attachments for a drill are sketched above and below. To make, in one operation, a hole that accepts a wood screw exactly, use a pilot bit. For smoothing curved surfaces or enlarging holes, use a rotary rasp. To remove rust or paint, use a wire cup brush. To drill holes in wood or metal, select a steel twist bit. To bore into masonry, use a carbide-tipped bit. To cut large holes in wood, a spade is best. An adapter pad *(below)* permits use of a polishing bonnet or sandpaper disc.

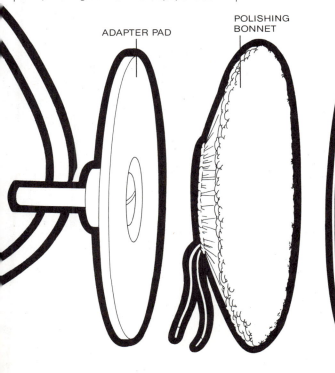

ADAPTER PAD

POLISHING BONNET

SANDPAPER
COARSE   FINE

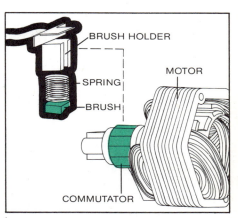

BRUSH HOLDER

MOTOR

SPRING

BRUSH

COMMUTATOR

Replacing the carbon brushes

Sparks seen through a drill's housing vents indicate that brushes need replacement. Remove the back, or one side, of the housing. Pull the old brushes and springs from their holders. Insert new brushes, matching the curves to the commutator.

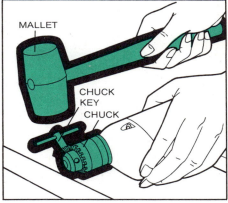

MALLET

CHUCK KEY

CHUCK

Cleaning the chuck

The chuck should be cleaned of sawdust and dirt when it slows down or binds. With the chuck key, open the jaws all the way. Then give the key, in place, a rap with a soft mallet to loosen the chuck. Unscrew it and clean it with paint thinner. Lubricate it with light machine oil, but take care to keep the oil out of the chuck jaws.

Plumbing

How New Materials and Proved Techniques Make Tough Jobs Easier

The kitchen faucet leaks. One of the toilets never stops running after you flush it. A bang wakes up the entire household when you turn off the water in the powder room. In the basement you notice water dripping from a mysterious pipe that disappears into the floor above. Only three streams of water come out of the shower head; the rest of the holes are clogged. It takes forever for the water to drain out of the lavatory basin, and just the other day you noticed a trickle of water seeping out from under the toilet. Suddenly you remember how the outdoor faucet froze and burst last winter when you forgot to close the shutoff valve inside the basement wall. And the memory of those plumbing bills! A visit from the plumber is never inexpensive, no matter how small or unimportant the job.

The solution, for more and more people, is to solve their plumbing problems themselves. Many plumbing repairs are quite simple, once you make up your mind to do them and roll up your sleeves. You can complete a repair quickly—while the plumber may not make it to your house for days. And even a dripping faucet can be a serious matter. It wastes water—and sooner or later it will stain or eat away the surface of the sink.

When you get started, you will find that modern plumbing equipment is designed to make repairs easier for the homeowner. The modern single-lever faucet *(pages 76-79)* is not only much more convenient to use than a pair of old-fashioned stem faucets, but is simpler to fix. While its action seems almost magical, when it needs fixing it can generally be made as good as new by replacing a single cartridge rather than an array of washers and O-rings.

As a result of such advances, relatively little physical effort is needed for plumbing work, and the techniques involved are readily mastered. What is more, there has been a shift of

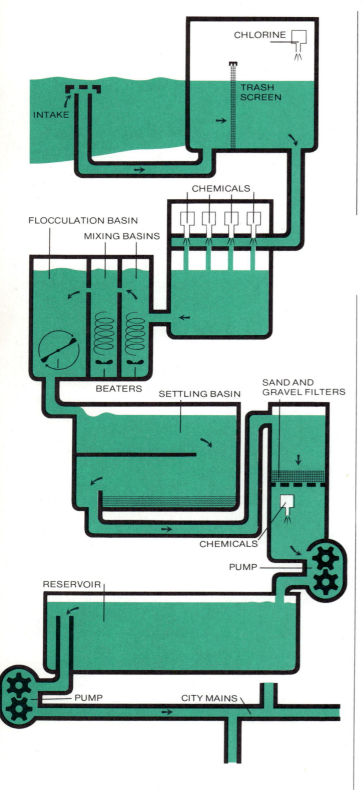

CHLORINE

TRASH
SCREEN

INTAKE

CHEMICALS

FLOCCULATION BASIN

MIXING BASINS

BEATERS

SETTLING BASIN

SAND AND
GRAVEL FILTERS

CHEMICALS

PUMP

RESERVOIR

PUMP   CITY MAINS

Making water fit to drink

All kinds of impurities from fish to invisible bacteria have to be removed in a treatment plant before water reaches your house plumbing. The water, generally from a lake or river, is drawn through an intake *(top)* and past a screen that blocks trash. Chlorine and other chemicals, to kill bacteria and eliminate off-tastes and odors, are blended into the water by beaters in the mixing basins. In the flocculation basin, a coagulant forms sticky globs to which impurities adhere. This floc sinks to the bottom of the settling basin. The water is filtered through sand and gravel, given another chemical dose, pumped to a reservoir and then sent to the central main.

attitudes among professional plumbers who, because they are so busy, appreciate it when you do some of the simpler jobs, leaving them time to tackle major work and emergencies. Some will give you advice over the phone on making minor repairs.

Despite encouragement from both plumbers and manufacturers, many people hold back from working on plumbing because they think it is prohibited by plumbing codes. In some cases the codes do establish requirements for certain work, such as the placement of new fixtures, that may exceed the amateur's resources. Rarely, however, will the plumbing codes prevent you from repairing and maintaining existing pipes and equipment, even if they forbid you to make additions to the system yourself. For the most part, codes prescribe the performance standards of a plumbing system and the materials used in it, not the person involved in making a repair.

Because plumbing codes vary from place to place, and because they are designed to protect you and your community from the dangers of faulty installations for water supply and waste disposal, you should know your local code—a copy of it is usually available at the local building inspector's office or health department. By observing code requirements, you can be sure that you are using the correct materials and methods. This chapter is confined to jobs you can do yourself, once you understand the operation of your plumbing system and its various components.

How a plumbing system works

You never see the major part of your plumbing system—the supply lines and waste pipes (300 feet of them, in an average house) that run through walls and under floors. Normally, you see nothing but the gleaming chrome-plated faucets and traps, and the smooth porcelain, vitreous china or stainless-steel sinks and lavatories and toilet fixtures. These parts are bewildering in their variety—designers make them that way deliberately, in order to meet individual tastes—but what goes on behind the walls and underneath the floors is pretty much the same in every house.

The supply lines carry fresh water to all the fixtures in your house, from garden-hose sillcocks to bathtubs. Behind your own system is a bigger one connecting you to a community reservoir or a well. In all of these supply systems, water is under high pressure—to force the water to the topmost story of the house. As much as 40 pounds of pressure per square inch is common; and big cities often require much more, in order to ensure having adequate pressure for fire hoses.

Many communities build up pressure by pumping water from wells or local reservoirs into a raised tank. Other towns draw their water from reservoirs in nearby hills, still others from rivers or lakes as much as 400 miles away. In all of these situations, gravity produces the required pressure, and the higher the "head" —that is, the vertical distance the water falls from its source to the house—the greater the pressure. As a general rule, water develops a pound of pressure for every 2.3 feet it falls.

If you have your own well, you probably use another method of establishing pressure: com-pression. Your pump forces water into a closed tank; as the water occupies more and more space, it compresses the air above it in the tank. The compressed air provides the pressure to send water throughout the system. (For the most modern methods of pressurizing the tank, see page 106.)

Wastes from the plumbing system are also drained off by gravity, but the head is much less—only that provided by the distance from a fixture to the main drainpipe. Within a house, all drainpipes have a downward pitch of at least one quarter of an inch for every foot they travel. Public drainlines, or sewers, run downhill as much as possible, though in some terrains sewage must be pumped over rises in the ground level. If your home is served by a public waste-disposal system, your most important—and, ideally, your only—concern is, of course, the drainage from your system into the main sewer lines.

If your home is not hooked into a public disposal system, your drains probably empty into your own septic tank (pages 118-121). In a septic tank, a natural chemical-biological process transforms much of the waste into liquids. Drained through perforated or open-jointed pipes into a drainage field, these liquids eventually filter into the soil. Periodically, however, the septic tank must be cleaned by a professional to remove the accumulation of materials not decomposed by this process.

A standard component of all waste systems is the "trap," a U-shaped dip in a line that remains filled with water at all times. The water seals off the waste line, preventing poisonous or combustible gases and foul odors from entering the house. There is a trap beneath or within every plumbing fixture. In addition, a main trap may seal the entire drain system of a house from the public sewer system.

Another component of the waste system that may go unnoticed is the roof vent, a pipe projecting through the roof above a vertical waste line, or "stack." Vents have three important functions. They dissipate gases into the atmosphere. They equalize air pressure throughout the drain system, preventing vacuums or back pressures that could interfere with the normal gravity flow of the system. And they protect the traps: if the system had no vents, the suction generated by flowing wastes would siphon the water out of the traps, destroying their usefulness as seals of the drainlines.

The relatively high pressure that delivers fresh water through the system and the relatively low pressure that takes wastes away are responsible for the vast majority of plumbing problems. That 40 pounds per square inch gives the pleasant spray effect of a warm shower and the power needed to sprinkle the lawn. But it also forces water through a leaky faucet or a defective pipe. It may cause the characteristic "water hammer" bang when a stream of fast-moving, high-pressure water is suddenly cut off *(page 67)*. It creates leaks in the hoses that connect washing machines and dishwashers to the system. Water under pressure is a restless captive, trying constantly to escape.

On the other hand, the relative weakness of the pressure in drains causes most of the problems in waste systems. The pull of gravity may not be strong enough to draw waste water through drains that are plugged with solid matter. People compound the problem by flushing foods, fats and coffee grounds down a kitchen sink, by using a toilet as a trash receptacle, or by permitting shower and lavatory-basin drains to clog. In all these cases, a pressure greater than that provided by the force of gravity may eventually be needed to open clogged drains *(pages 90-91, 101)*.

Other plumbing problems arise from the action of chemicals upon the metals of pipes and fixtures; corrosion can create leaks, and mineral deposits can clog pipes. And every system inevitably suffers wear and eventual disintegration from use and age. Thus, sooner or later, either you or your plumber will have to pick up tools and go to work.

Before taking on your share of the plumbing repairs, familiarize yourself with your own specific system, much as you might glance over a road map before setting out on a trip. Most home systems are similar to the one shown on pages 52-53, though there are many variations in arrangement and equipment. Concentrate, to begin with, on the standard elements you will find in every system:

■ MAIN WATER LINE. The water enters your house somewhere near the water meter; typically, the meter is on the street side of the house, and the incoming pipe enters a basement, a crawl space or, if you live in a house built on a slab, a utility center. This pipe is fairly large—probably at least three quarters of an inch in diameter, more commonly one inch. Normally, a shutoff valve is installed just inside the wall the pipe enters. This is the valve to close when you want to shut off the water supply to the entire house. If your water supply comes from your own well, the main water line starts at your supply tank.

■ BRANCH RUNS. Follow the main pipe and you will find "runs" of smaller pipe (one half or three quarters of an inch in diameter) branching off at several points. Each run serves a section of the system—possibly a section that serves fixtures in more than one room and on more than one floor. One of the branches from the main line always goes directly to the water heater. From the heater, pipelines carrying hot water run parallel to—but at least six inches

38

Why Plumbing Codes Vary

Plumbing codes have not been devised, as householders sometimes suspect, to protect plumbers' incomes by making procedures needlessly complex. They are intended to guard public health by requiring proper design, acceptable installation and adequate maintenance of plumbing systems *(page 36)*. The codes do not prevent you from doing the jobs described in this book, but you must use the materials and working methods that they specify.

You have to check specific requirements locally, however, because plumbing codes differ from place to place; there is no single national code as there is for electrical work *(pages 132-133)*. Regional discrepancies are due partly to conflicting opinions as to what materials and techniques to use. But sometimes there are considerations related to natural conditions. For example:

■ HARD WATER. Minerals contained in water—both the kind and the amount—often determine the kind of piping that must be used. In areas of the Southwestern United States, high concentrations of carbonate minerals leave heavy deposits that can quickly clog small-diameter copper tubing. Galvanized steel pipe is generally used instead of copper because it is less expensive in the larger sizes needed to avoid clogging.

■ SOFT WATER. Somewhat paradoxically, copper tubing may also prove troublesome in areas where there are very few minerals. A modest concentration of minerals produces a thin, protective coating inside the pipe. Without that protection, tubing erodes and then corrodes. Codes in these areas, too, prescribe galvanized piping.

■ CLIMATE. Where winters are fierce, codes require roof-top vents *(page 54)* to be extra large in order to prevent snow and ice from blocking the openings.

■ EARTHQUAKES. Localities in earthquake zones, such as those in California, require that plumbing be fastened very securely.

away from—the cold-water lines to fixtures such as sinks and bathtubs, which use both hot and cold water. (Not all fixtures need both of the lines; a toilet tank, for example, has only a cold-water line, a dishwasher only a hot one.)

■ RISERS. Plumbing facilities often lie directly over one another or back to back; thus, an upstairs bathroom may be located directly over a downstairs powder room, and a single "riser" —a vertical branch of pipe—serves them both.

■ BRANCH AND RISER SHUTOFFS. In a well-engineered plumbing system each branch or riser contains a shutoff valve at or near the point it leaves the main line. Thus, you can turn off an individual run, if necessary, without cutting off service to the rest of the house. Important: The shutoff valves are not designed for frequent use. Do not turn them off and on more often than necessary. When you must turn one off, open a faucet on the branch, then slowly turn the valve handle clockwise until the water stops running; do not turn the handle beyond this point.

■ FIXTURE SHUTOFFS. A branch of pipe usually disappears inside a wall or floor soon after it leaves the main line; you will not see it again until it emerges in a kitchen, bath or laundry. (At these points the size of the pipe usually changes to a still smaller diameter.) And once again, in a good system, shutoff valves control each fixture—one valve for hot water, one for cold. Some of these valves are visible directly below the fixture; others, particularly those for a built-in bathtub or shower stall, may be hidden behind removable panels in the wall, in a closet or even in an adjoining room. These shutoff valves enable you to deactivate a single fixture when you want to work on it, allowing the rest of the system to function normally.

■ THE SHUTOFF PLAN. If you have any doubts about which fixtures are controlled by which branch shutoff valves, there is a standard procedure to follow. First close the shutoff valve on one branch at the point where it leaves the main line. Then go around the house opening faucets and flushing toilets. A faucet that does not produce water when you open it must be controlled by that branch-line shutoff; a toilet tank that does not refill must be on that line too. Repeat the procedure with all the branches. Finally, hang a tag on each shutoff listing the outlets it controls. Now you will be able to shut off the correct line in a hurry when an emergency arises.

■ DRAINS. It is generally easier to chart the waste lines of your water system than the supply lines. The lines from sinks, lavatories and laundry tubs usually start out with a three-part assembly: a tailpiece fastened to the fixture, a U-shaped trap, and the fixture drain that disappears inside the wall. The three parts are easy to take apart when you must remove debris from the trap or when the trap itself must be replaced *(page 89)*. Waste lines from toilets, built-in tubs and shower stalls exit down through the floor.

■ STACKS. Either directly or by way of pipes that slant downward, all drainlines converge on "stacks"—vertical pipes that drop to the level of the outgoing sewer lines, and also project upward through the roof, where they serve as the vents mentioned on pages 52-54. In the lines and stacks, wastes and draining water move through the system and into a public sewer or a septic tank.

■ CLEANOUT FITTINGS. To provide access into drainlines, cleanout fittings are located at the points where vertical stacks connect with downward-slanted horizontal runs toward the main drain. The fitting has the form of an inverted Y or T, with the stack coming down into the stem, the horizontal run continuing from one arm, and the other arm sealed off with a removable plug. When a drainline clogs, you can unscrew the plug and go to work on the stoppage—up to a point *(page 91)*. A stoppage well beyond the cleanout fitting, or on the way to the public sewer or your septic tank, means the entire disposal system may be backed up—and that is definitely an emergency job for a professional plumber to handle.

The materials of modern plumbing

As a last step before you tackle any serious plumbing repairs, check into the materials that your water supply and waste lines are made of. A generation ago, iron, galvanized steel, brass and lead dominated the world of pipe and fittings. Today, the most common materials are copper and the increasingly popular plastics.

You can recognize copper easily; it has the color of a penny. Another clue is the fact that it may be joined with silver-colored solder, with "flare fittings" or with compression rings, all discussed in detail on pages 58-61.

Some homes may have threaded brass supply lines that look very much like their threaded galvanized-steel counterparts. After a few years of aging, even the colors may be similar. Professionals often scratch the pipe with a knife to see if it shows the yellowish color of brass or the silver color of the zinc used in galvanizing steel. Another way to tell them apart is with a magnet, which will stick to steel pipe but not to brass.

What difference does the piping material make? Quite a bit, in some situations. With a water heater, for example, steel plumbing elements should not be used in combination with copper or brass elements without certain precautions, because electrochemical reactions between steel and other metals cause serious corrosion. When you convert a section of steel pipe to one of copper—as you well might want to do, to gain the easy workability of copper in future repairs—you must use "insulating" fit-

Two Lost Legacies of Ancient Plumbing

Many concepts of modern plumbing originated in ancient times, in such civilizations as those of Babylon, India, the islands of the Mediterranean Sea, and Rome. There, thousands of years ago, men mastered the principles of hydraulics and applied them to the problems of sanitation.

One sophisticated plumbing system of antiquity served the palace of Knossos on the island of Crete, a center of Bronze Age civilization. At Knossos, archeologists have discovered 4,000-year-old remains of ingeniously designed terracotta piping used in the palace's water-supply system. The tapered sections of pipe, shown in the diagram above, were prefabricated, then interlocked and sealed at the joints with a clay cement. Their shape kept them clean. As water, moved by gravity, streamed through the narrow end of each section, its velocity increased. Thus the water traveled to its destination in a series of jetlike spurts, carrying with it sediment that might otherwise have clogged the pipes. The lobelike projections on the outer surfaces of some of the pipes were used in lashing the sections together with rope.

At the same Knossian site, archeologists also unearthed the remains of a drainage system that would meet the approval of a present-day board of health. Toilets, complete with wooden seats, were equipped with water-flushing devices and stone drains that ran into a main drainpipe. These drains had vents to release waste gases, and traps, remarkably similar to those used today, to seal off sewer odors.

Around 1400 B.C., much of Crete and all of the palace were destroyed, possibly by an earthquake or by a volcanic eruption. Whatever the cause, the achievements of Cretan plumbing were lost to mankind until the 20th Century, when archeologists began to dig away into the earth-covered ruins.

Plumbing's next great advance was among the Romans, who created a water-supply and drainage system built on a grand scale. By the Fourth Century A.D., the city of Rome had almost 900 public and private baths, over 1,300 public fountains and cisterns, and 144 public toilets (all water-flushed). To bring in 50 million gallons of water for the city's daily needs, the Romans built a 359-mile network of aqueducts, some of which are still in use today. Above ground, these aqueducts consisted of stone arches and spans carrying water down from hills and across valleys in covered conduits. Underground aqueducts also led into the city. Water was then fed into a network of buried pipes generally made of sheet lead, or *plumbum*—the Latin word from which "plumbing" acquired its name.

After Rome fell to the barbarians in the mid-Fifth Century A.D., its great plumbing system was abandoned for the lack of trained engineers and artisans to maintain it. In the centuries that followed, superstitions against bathing and other sanitary practices blocked the progress of plumbing—and for hundreds of years the people of Europe were generally unwashed and, what was far worse, beset by widespread plagues. Thus, with the skills of those old Cretan and Roman plumbers almost completely forgotten, generations of men and women endured squalor, suffering and needless death. Not until the 19th Century did European and American cities begin to plan and build the plumbing systems of our time.

tings to forestall corrosion at the connections between copper and steel.

By far the easiest material to work with, however, is the newest—plastic. Because it is so new, you will see it only in recently installed plumbing, but you will have no difficulty in identifying plastic. It comes in black, white and a variety of colors, and is usually labeled with an abbreviation of its chemical name —PVC, CPVC, ABS or the like *(page 65)*. What is far more important, you will discover that plastic is very nearly an ideal material for an amateur's repairs and replacements.

Plastic pipe is light in weight and easy to cut. You can join it with simple slip-together fittings, which are made fast and watertight by a solvent cement. Plastic comes in most of the sizes used for residential pipes and fittings, and can be combined with metal plumbing elements without danger of corrosion. In some sizes and types it is produced in a semiflexible form, easily bent into curves to avoid tedious fitting and joining.

Plastic plumbing's main drawback has been the slowness with which building codes in some areas have been authorizing its use. Day by day, however, its acceptance increases, and nearly all plumbing-supply outlets now handle plastic materials.

The basics of plumbing repairs

While it gets easier and easier to do a plumbing job, to do it right calls for care and a systematic routine. Here are some suggestions that will help you:

■ READ THE INSTRUCTIONS. On the pages that follow, you will find complete step-by-step instructions for repairing everything in your plumbing system that can be handled by an amateur without special skills or costly tools. Be sure you understand each step of a job before you start to do it.

■GET PROPER TOOLS. It is frustrating and pointless to start a repair job and then get hung up because you find that an essential tool is missing. Most plumbing tools are simple and not overly expensive; a useful kit is shown on pages 48-51. On the other hand, some tools are expensive and infrequently used; you can often rent them from a tool-rental outlet, or from the plumbing-supply dealer from whom you buy repair parts.

■ KEEP A SMALL STOCK OF PARTS. You may sometimes have to dismantle a plumbing element to find out what is wrong with it. In that case, there is nothing for you to do but take it apart, decide what replacement parts are needed, then go shopping for the parts. But you can stock some items ahead of time—parts that you know you will need some day. For less than a dollar you can buy a packet of washers that contains the sizes needed for most faucets. The same packet also contains screws to hold the washers in place, and may even provide a few of the packing washers that fit under the handles of some stem faucets *(page 75)*. Similarly, you can pick up cartridges or complete kits for some of the more modern faucets and keep them on hand. It is better to spend a few dollars ahead of time rather than find yourself helpless on that Saturday night when trouble arises and you will not be able to get into a shop before Monday morning.

■ TURN OFF THE WATER. Use the shutoff valve right at the fixture you will be working on, if there is one. Otherwise shut off the branch line—or as a last resort, the whole system. But always remember that you cannot break into a water-supply system without shutting off the water somewhere; if you forget, the result is a flood. Caution: Remember never to turn off a cold-water line into a bathroom while someone is in the shower, for the water of the shower will instantly turn scalding hot.

■CLOSE THE DRAIN. Before working over a sink or lavatory, trip the lever of a mechanical drain plug or set the rubber stopper in place. If there is no stopper, stuff a rag in the opening. This simple precaution prevents the loss of small screws or other parts down the drain. While you are at it, place a folded towel in the basin to cushion an accidentally dropped tool or part, thus preventing any damage to the surface of the fixture.

■PROTECT POLISHED SURFACES. It is wise to use a smooth-jawed monkey wrench, not a tooth-jawed pipe wrench, to work on chrome-plated surfaces. If the fixture nuts are not too large, their hexagonal shape will also permit the use of standard smooth-jawed adjustable wrenches. In either case, be sure the wrench's jaws are snug against the nut, so that they will not slip and cause damage. Many professionals further protect polished surfaces by wrapping them in friction, adhesive or plastic tape before applying a wrench.

■DON'T GIVE UP. Just disassembling a unit to get at the trouble is sometimes discouraging. Nearly all plumbing is held together by nuts or screws that are easy to take off but may not be easy to find, particularly on stylishly designed faucets. The secret to disassembling one handsome old faucet turned out to be a china button atop it, bearing the "H" symbol; actually, that button was the head of the screw holding the handle onto the faucet. Unless you already know how to disassemble your unit, you may have to do some detective work. First look hard for a visible fastener—many are tiny and inconspicuously located. If nothing seems made to accept a screwdriver or wrench, examine the unit closely for a concealed fastener. What seems to be a line in the design may be the seam where a fastener, or a plaque covering a fastener, joins the unit. Then try unscrewing or prying at the seam—but very gently, in case

Why Plumbers Charge So Much

A pipe springs a leak and a plumber comes to the rescue. In a little while he makes the pipe as good as new and you get a bill. In 1940 the bill might have been four to five dollars; in 1950, eight to ten dollars; in the late '70s, twenty to thirty dollars and in the '80s three times that or even more. The rapid rise in plumbing bills is due partly to inflation but more to the increasing complexity of the plumbing business.

For the master plumber—the person who sends you that bill—is not only an independent craftsman but is in a business with a large investment in specialized training and equipment, and a substantial overhead. Such a company must charge customers accordingly.

Before a plumber can hang out a shingle, he serves four to five years as an apprentice, while attending classes in subjects ranging from pipe fitting and welding to mechanical drawing and the physics of liquids and gases. At the end of this rigorous training period, and after scoring passing grades on a set of state or local examinations, the apprentice graduates to journeyman. To climb the last step up the professional ladder, he works from two to five more years, depending on his locality, and must pass a more severe set of exams. Only then is he a master plumber—that is, a businessman in his own right who possesses an official license that permits him to establish a contracting firm and to hire his own journeymen.

what seems to be a surface decoration turns out to be just that and nothing more.

■ DON'T USE TOO MUCH FORCE. Never pull or push too hard on a wrench. If a nut does not come loose under reasonable pressure, squirt a few drops of penetrating oil into the threads and let it soak in for two or three minutes; the oil will cut into any corrosion and lubricate the threads so that they will unscrew more easily. (Hardware stores sell penetrating oil in small squirt cans.)

■ KEEP TRACK OF PARTS. Plumbing elements are mechanically simple, as you will discover when you take one apart. Nevertheless, you may want to take advantage of an old mechanic's trick. As you disassemble a plumbing part, lay its components out in the exact order you removed them. Later, you can put the components back together in reverse order and be sure you are doing it right.

Shopping for plumbing supplies

Almost every day, as more homeowners do their own plumbing repairs, the shopping situation changes for the better. More and more different types of retail outlets now stock common repair items, and more and more outlets that were once professional-oriented have begun to welcome amateurs. No single shopping guide will make sense in every community, but here are some suggestions that will help you to obtain the best materials, the best service and probably the best advice.

An authentic, well-stocked plumbing-supply house, if you have one in your area, will always be the best place to shop. If it does not have exactly what you want, the man behind the counter will either order it for you or tell you of an outlet that does have it; and he will often give you suggestions for using or installing the item that you buy. The stock of a plumbing-supply house is generally of high quality, so you can

be sure the problem you are solving will not be back to plague you again in a few weeks. If you can, time your visit to a plumbing-supply house for midmorning or midafternoon. These are the times of day when professionals are ordinarily out on the job, rather than in the supply house picking up materials. Therefore, the salesman will have more time then to talk to you and help you with your problem.

If you do not have access to a professional plumbing outlet, a hardware store can fill most needs. Shop around, ask friends and neighbors for their recommendations and, if necessary, consult your own plumber to be sure of finding a genuine *hardware* store—not a *houseware* store that probably has more pots and pans than plumbing supplies. A good hardware store will have traps, toilet-tank units, replacement faucets and the like. Look there, too, for copper tubing, plastics and other items that are easy for the do-it-yourselfer to handle. But because of the wide merchandise assortment the hardware store stocks, the salesman will probably have less time and expertise to devote to your special problems.

A relatively new source of supply for the homeowner is the do-it-yourself superstore. These building-supply outlets are springing up all over the country—many in shopping centers—to meet the needs of people who want to do things themselves. They carry impressively large ranges of plumbing materials and repair items, but you generally have to wait on yourself; you will be lucky to find a salesman to talk to, and luckier still if he is knowledgeable enough to give you useful advice.

The large mail-order houses carry almost every plumbing item you will ever need, including major fixtures and special tools, but offer almost no assistance at all in choosing specific items; you must know exactly what you want before you order it. Another problem in shop-

The Peril of Back-Siphonage

A little-known precaution that is built into a plumbing system is the gap intentionally left between intake and outflow; there is never a direct connection between a supply pipe and a waste pipe. The reason is the possibility of back-siphonage—a suction of contaminated water into the fresh supply by a pressure drop in the line, such as when a street main breaks.

Accidental back-siphonage should always be guarded against. If an extension shower hose is left in a filled tub (right) with the faucet turned on, a pressure drop in the line could pull dirty water into the supply pipes (arrows, far right). Be sure to disconnect such attachments when they are not being used.

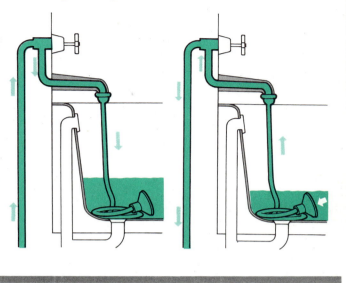

ping by mail is, of course, the inevitable delay. But if you live near one of the retail outlets of a mail-order house, you will have ready access to a good source of plumbing items, along with personnel qualified to give you advice.

Usually, the biggest problem in shopping for repair or replacement parts is to identify the specific item. The problem is compounded by an almost incomprehensible variation in design. There are standards for pipes and fittings, but almost none for other equipment. No two manufacturers make faucets exactly alike, and one company's catalog lists 150 different models for home use alone. For old equipment, parts may be impossible to find; the whole unit may have to be replaced.

If necessary, you can take the defective part to the store and show it to the salesman, but there is one drawback to this method. If you shut down an entire plumbing line to deactivate the outlet involved, that line will have to stay out of service until you get back from your shopping expedition.

On the other hand, if you can identify the part accurately, you can do the shopping before you shut down the line. Most manufactur-

ers are proud of their fixtures; if you examine a part carefully, you will find a brand name on it somewhere. It may be on the back or underneath, or hidden among "ON" and "OFF" or "HOT" and "COLD" labels—but it is almost always there, in fine stamped engraving or on an inconspicuous plaque.

Tell the plumbing-supply clerk the brand name, the place where the item is used (sink, lavatory, shower, tub and so forth), how many handles it has, whether the handles turn or lift, whether or not the spigot swings back and forth. Once you have that part in hand, the downtime on the water line will be no more than you take for the actual repair work.

One final recommendation. If many of the plumbing elements in your home are old, worn and inefficient, you may want to give some thought to replacement. It is not the purpose of this book to get you unnecessarily involved in new plumbing and high costs. But sometimes it is easier to replace, say, an entire set of ancient kitchen-sink faucets with a modern single-lever faucet than it is to keep patching the old ones with washers, gaskets and seats. You get a unit that looks and works better, and you will probably save money in the long run.

Working with Pipes and Fixtures

If you live in a typical American home, at least one of your faucets is leaking right now. If you are lucky, it is only a slow drip. But even that slow drip loses about 15 gallons of water down the drain every day—enough for a comfortable bath. If the faucet continues to drip at that rate, you will lose enough water in a year to fill a small swimming pool. But it will probably not continue at that rate; an unattended slow drip usually becomes a fast drip and eventually an unbroken stream that can waste as much as 400 gallons a day—almost double the amount an average family uses daily for drinking, cooking, bathing, laundering, toilet flushing and lawn sprinkling combined.

But a slow leak need not turn into a torrent, and it rarely will if you catch it at the outset. Replacing a 10-cent faucet washer *(pages 72-73)*, perhaps the simplest and most routine job in all household plumbing, may well do the trick. It is only one of the many tasks that a homeowner can carry out with inexpensive tools and easily mastered techniques. Except for the strange-sounding names, there is no mystery about such commonplace chores as sweating a joint *(pages 60-61)*, snaking a drain *(page 91)* or dressing a seat *(page 74)*.

But even elementary plumbing jobs are sometimes complicated by unexpected problems—the most frustrating being those that crop up the minute you start to take apart a pipe or fixture in order to repair or replace it. Many a dexterous homeowner has had the vexing experience of standing, wrench in hand, before an old, familiar faucet and realizing he does not know how to take it apart. The solution, once you figure it out, is generally quite simple: perhaps a screw is hidden behind the faucet, or a decorative escutcheon plate untwists rather than pries off.

Even after the faucet is apart there may be other surprises. Take, for instance, the case of the left-handed washer screw: to remove it you turn it clockwise instead of the usual counter-clockwise direction. (It is used, though rarely, by some manufacturers so that the closing of the faucet automatically tightens the screw.)

Problems such as these are no problems at all once you know about them. Nor are plumbing's inherent troubles—rust, corrosion and worn parts—which are readily remedied when you learn a few professional tricks of the trade. Among the more common stumbling blocks, and the ways around them:

■ The washer retaining screw will not budge. Try penetrating oil. Also, get more twisting power by using a screwdriver with a larger handle. You can also clamp locking-grip pliers on your screwdriver shank and push it with one hand while pressing the screwdriver handle with the other. If the screw slot is worn shallow or damaged, a couple of hacksaw strokes will deepen the slot for a better grip. A gentle hammer tap often does wonders in loosening a tight screw.

■ The head of the washer screw snaps off. Dig out the old washer with a penknife to expose the screw. Use pliers to twist the screw loose. If this does not work, replace the stem.

■ A pipe connection is rusted solid. Try penetrating oil, but it probably will not help on a badly rusted pipe. If it does not, clean off the exterior rust with a wire brush so you can get a good grip with a wrench, and try a technique called jolting. With the pipe or nut gripped tightly with a pipe wrench, give the end of the wrench a sharp rap with the heel of your hand. Do not use a hammer, however. Jolting is often more effective than simply pulling with both hands. If it does not work, slip a length of pipe, two to three feet long, over the wrench handle to get additional leverage. (NOTE: Use this method only with wrenches at least 18 inches long. Jolting can harm a smaller one.)

■ A piece of pipe has broken off inside a fitting. If enough of the broken pipe protrudes, try to remove it with a pipe wrench. Otherwise, use a pipe extractor. This ingenious tool, which looks like a large, stubby drill bit, can be purchased in a plumbing supply store. When tapped lightly into the embedded pipe, its grooves grip the inside surface of the pipe. A wrench can then be used on the square end of the extractor to unscrew the broken pipe. If this method fails, the entire connection can be cut off with a hacksaw and replaced by using the technique shown on page 63.

■ The wrong connection loosens. Unscrewing a locknut sometimes causes the pipe to turn with it, loosening the connection at the other end. To prevent this, use two wrenches (page 62), one to turn the locknut and the other to hold the pipe stationary. (NOTE: The double-wrench technique should always be used when removing pipe from the outlet side of a shutoff valve, as in the case of a faucet supply pipe. One wrench turns the pipe while the other holds the valve so that it does not loosen and release a spray of water from the inlet side.)

■ The drain-trap collar sticks. The slip nut at the top of the drain trap, called a collar, may be relatively fragile and thus difficult to grip both tightly and safely. It is often made of lightweight alloy that tends to crumble when gripped too hard with a smooth-jawed wrench. Switch to a tooth-jawed pipe wrench and grip the corners rather than the smooth surfaces. If that does not work, or if the nut has oxidized solidly onto the threads, it can usually be cracked loose with a few sharp strokes of a heavy hammer on a cold chisel.

The ability to overcome these problems and to perform your own plumbing maintenance can save you a lot of money and anguish. No longer need the drip-drip of a leaky faucet bring that doleful cry: "Call the plumber!"

A PLUMBING TOOL KIT

Plumbing jobs call for a few special tools. Basin and socket wrenches, for example, are handy for work in hard-to-reach places, and smooth-jawed wrenches should be used to protect the polished surfaces of certain plumbing fittings. Even a task as simple as clearing a blocked drain or toilet requires augers made for the purpose *(page 50).*

Some of these tools are expensive, especially since they may be needed only infrequently. Fortunately, many plumbing-supply outlets rent them out by the day. Before buying such tools as a seat dresser *(opposite, bottom),* a socket-wrench set *(below)* or a flaring tool *(page 51),* look into the possibility of rentals in your area. But if you do decide to buy these or any other plumbing tools, do not try to save money on cut-rate or bargain brands. High-quality tools cost more, but they pay for themselves because they make the job easier to accomplish properly.

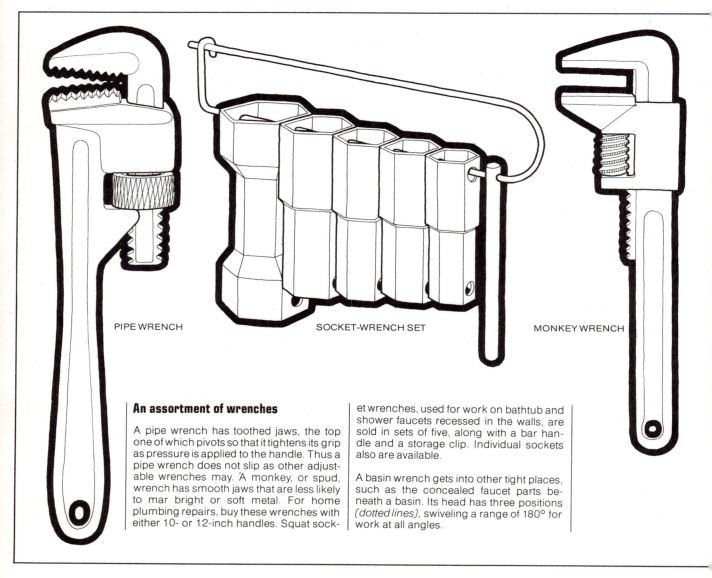

PIPE WRENCH · SOCKET-WRENCH SET · MONKEY WRENCH

An assortment of wrenches

A pipe wrench has toothed jaws, the top one of which pivots so that it tightens its grip as pressure is applied to the handle. Thus a pipe wrench does not slip as other adjustable wrenches may. A monkey, or spud, wrench has smooth jaws that are less likely to mar bright or soft metal. For home plumbing repairs, buy these wrenches with either 10- or 12-inch handles. Squat sock-et wrenches, used for work on bathtub and shower faucets recessed in the walls, are sold in sets of five, along with a bar handle and a storage clip. Individual sockets also are available.

A basin wrench gets into other tight places, such as the concealed faucet parts beneath a basin. Its head has three positions *(dotted lines),* swiveling a range of 180° for work at all angles.

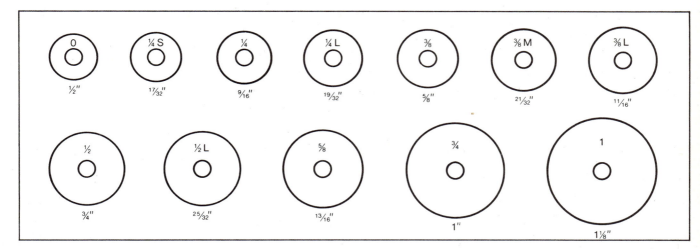

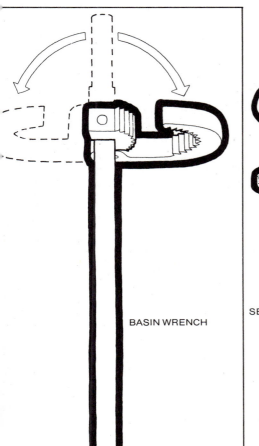

BASIN WRENCH

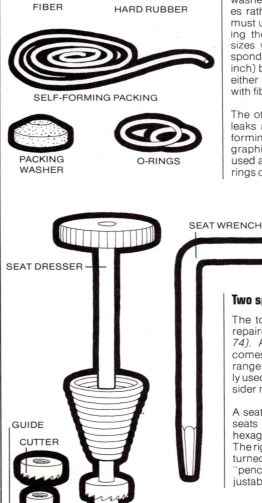

FAUCET WASHERS

FIBER   HARD RUBBER

SELF-FORMING PACKING

PACKING
WASHER   O-RINGS

SEAT DRESSER

GUIDE

CUTTER

SEAT WRENCH

Washers, packing and O-rings

Plumbing-supply outlets identify the faucet washers shown at left by arbitrary trade sizes rather than actual diameters, and you must use the trade-size numbers in ordering them. The chart above shows trade sizes within the washers and the corresponding diameters (in fractions of an inch) below. Hard-rubber washers may be either flat or beveled; a washer reinforced with fiber is usually flat.

The other materials shown at left prevent leaks at faucet stems and handles. Self-forming packing is usually sold in two-foot, graphite-impregnated coils, to be cut and used as needed. Packing washers and O-rings can be purchased individually.

Two specialized faucet tools

The tools at left are used exclusively for repairing or replacing faucet seats (page 74). A high-quality seat dresser, which comes with several guides and cutters in a range of sizes, is expensive and infrequently used; it is one of the tools you should consider renting rather than buying.

A seat wrench, used to remove old faucet seats and install new ones, has tapered hexagonal and squared ends to fit any seat. The right-angle wrench shown here can be turned by hand; an alternative straight, or "pencil," tool must be turned with an adjustable wrench.

Pipe and Drain Tools

The objects on this page are used mainly in emergencies; many homeowners buy them all and keep them readily available for the day when a drain clogs or a pipe springs a leak. Somewhat less essential are the materials and tools opposite, which are designed for permanent repairs; you may want to rent the more costly ones if you need them.

Tools for unclogging drains

The alternating suction and pressure of a rubber plunger—it is popularly known as a "plumber's helper" or "plumber's friend" —can unclog toilets, sinks and tubs.

If the plunger fails, a toilet, or closet, auger hooks and pulls out clogs in a toilet drain. For all other drains, use the drain and trap auger, or "snake."

Temporary seals for leaking pipes

A rubber-lined clamp will cover and seal a crack in a straight run of pipe. To stop a leak at a pipe joint, you will need a packet of epoxy seal, which can be molded like putty but dries to the hardness of metal. Both seals are temporary; the pipes or joints must eventually be replaced.

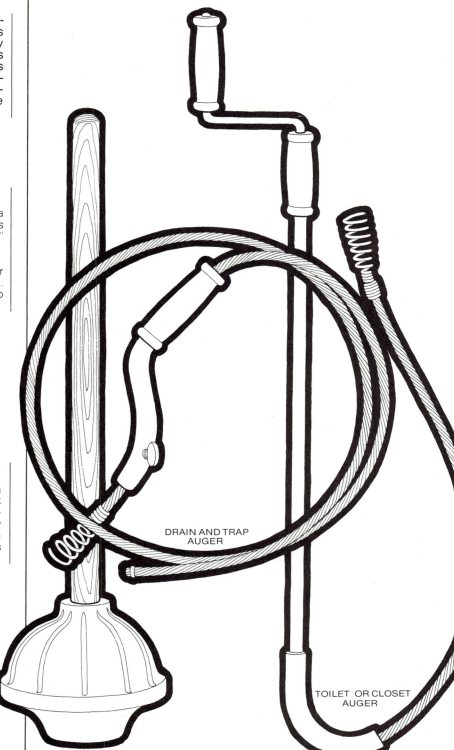

EPOXY SEAL

EPOXY RESIN

EPOXY HARDENER

PIPE CLAMP

RUBBER LINER

DRAIN AND TRAP AUGER

TOILET OR CLOSET AUGER

RUBBER PLUNGER

SOLVENT
CEMENT

PLUMBER'S SOLDER

FLUX

TUBE CUTTER

WIRE
CLEANING BRUSH

WICKING

PLASTIC
JOINT-SEALING TAPE

A comprehensive kit for pipe work

The tools and materials on this page will enable you to bend, cut, solder and seal pipes, particularly the copper tubing most often used in the home. A tube bender slips over the tube to prevent kinking. The tube cutter not only cuts the tube but provides a reamer that swings out *(dotted outline)* to smooth the inside of the tube end. For soldering, you will need a propane torch and an assortment of soldering paraphernalia: a wire cleaning brush, wire solder (be sure to get the plumber's solder, not electrician's) and a can of noncorrosive flux. A rather expensive option is a flaring tool, which permits you to connect copper tubes without solder. You will need solvent cement to join plastic piping together; be sure to get the kind that is compatible with the type of plastic pipe you are using.

The three remaining materials shown here are sealants. Pipe-joint compound, or pipe "dope," provides tight seals at points where threaded pipe enters fittings. Wicking is sometimes used with compound. A newer material, plastic joint-sealing tape, does the job of both wicking and compound.

PROPANE TORCH

TUBE BENDER

FLARING TOOL

PIPE-JOINT
COMPOUND

A HOME PLUMBING SYSTEM

The plan of the plumbing system in a typical three-bathroom house may look like a maze of pipes and fixtures—at first. It becomes easy to understand, however, when it is seen as a map of four separate but interrelated systems, one each for cold water, hot water, draining and venting.

Cold water enters the house through a service pipe *(bottom),* flows through a valve that can shut off all water, then goes through a meter and past a faucet that can drain the water supply lines *(page 67).* Between floors the water travels in riser pipes. Starting at a water heater, hot-water pipes parallel the cold. One system or the other (or both) runs to every water-using fixture and appliance.

In the pipes of these first two systems, water moves under pressure. The pipes can therefore be small, usually from three eighths to three quarters of an inch in diameter; they are generally straight, making right-angle turns with "elbows" and connections with "tees." Most fixtures have their own shutoff valves and some have check valves to prevent water from flowing backward into the wrong line. Near some fixtures, dead-end sections of pipe called air chambers forestall the noisy vibration known as water hammer *(page 67).*

The drain system begins with the water-filled traps that are under every fixture and inside every toilet bowl. Traps are U-shaped so that water always remains in the bottom of the U, sealing off the drain system; thus gases from the sewers are prevented from entering the house. From the traps, drainpipes carry waste water to a vertical pipe called a soil stack and thence to the main house drain. All these pipes must slope downward, since the supply system's pressure is absent and only gravity makes the waste water flow. To reduce the possibility of blockage and to ensure a fast, even flow in the absence of supply pressure, drainpipes have smooth interior surfaces with gentle bends, and are large, usually one and a half to four inches in diameter.

The fourth plumbing system consists of the vents: pipes connecting drains to open stack vents on the roof. Vent pipes contain no water, but carry gases outside and admit fresh air to maintain atmospheric pressure in the drains (without this pressure, the flow of waste water would suck the water from the drain traps).

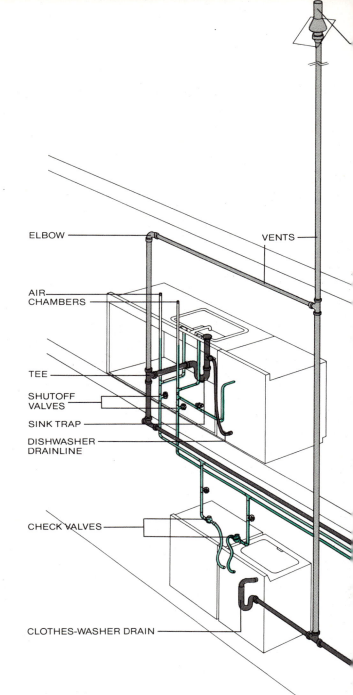

ELBOW

VENTS

AIR CHAMBERS

TEE

SHUTOFF VALVES

SINK TRAP

DISHWASHER DRAINLINE

CHECK VALVES

CLOTHES-WASHER DRAIN

The four plumbing systems

A home's four plumbing systems—one to supply cold water, another for hot, a third to drain wastes and a fourth to vent drains—are distinguished by colors *(key opposite).* Two special features in this diagram are a house trap—required in some communities to provide a seal between the house and the main sewer—and a fresh-air inlet needed with this kind of trap.

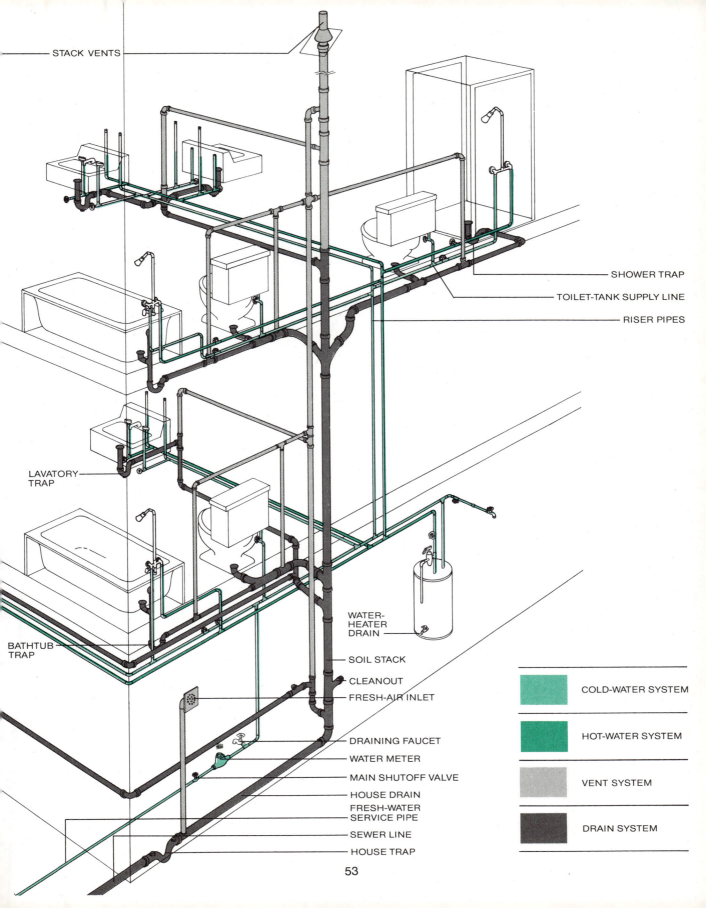

STACK VENTS

SHOWER TRAP

TOILET-TANK SUPPLY LINE

RISER PIPES

LAVATORY TRAP

WATER-HEATER DRAIN

BATHTUB TRAP

SOIL STACK

CLEANOUT

FRESH-AIR INLET

DRAINING FAUCET

WATER METER

MAIN SHUTOFF VALVE

HOUSE DRAIN

FRESH-WATER SERVICE PIPE

SEWER LINE

HOUSE TRAP

COLD-WATER SYSTEM

HOT-WATER SYSTEM

VENT SYSTEM

DRAIN SYSTEM

53

Some Vital Parts

Certain components of the plumbing system are regularly noticed by everyone but often misunderstood or misused. Few people associate the vent on a roof with plumbing at all; on the other hand, many seem to believe that sink traps are there to keep dropped rings and bobby pins from getting into the sewer.

Every component on these pages is vital to the operation of a plumbing system. Knowing what they look like and how they work will help you cope with the system in your home.

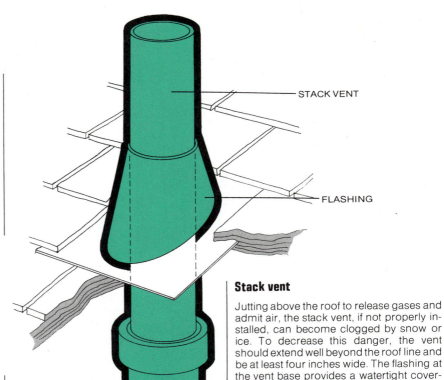

STACK VENT

FLASHING

Stack vent

Jutting above the roof to release gases and admit air, the stack vent, if not properly installed, can become clogged by snow or ice. To decrease this danger, the vent should extend well beyond the roof line and be at least four inches wide. The flashing at the vent base provides a watertight covering over the point where the vent pierces the roof; leaks in flashing should be sealed with roofing cement.

Two types of water meters

Water meters register either the number of gallons or, as shown here, cubic feet of water used. A direct-reading meter (bottom) gives the total at a glance. A cumulative-reading meter has several dials, each indicating a digit in the total figure. First read the dial showing the largest units (100,000 in this example), then successively smaller ones; disregard the smallest dial since it moves so fast that its digit is insignificant in the total. Both these meters register 60232. In computing usage, this figure would be compared with a previous reading.

CUMULATIVE-READING METER

DIRECT-READING METER

Fresh-air inlet

The primary function of this air inlet is to serve a main house trap, as shown on the preceding page. The inlet, set into an exterior wall and protected by a perforated metal plate, admits fresh air to maintain normal atmospheric pressure at the house trap. In harsh climates, the inlet serves an additional purpose. Warm air from a drain system tends to condense inside the stack vent on the roof (above), forming rings of frost that can turn into solid ice and seal the vent; the cold air admitted by a fresh-air inlet helps avert this condition.

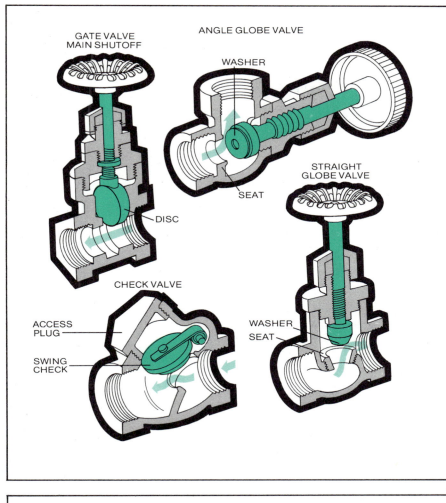

GATE VALVE
MAIN SHUTOFF

ANGLE GLOBE VALVE

WASHER

SEAT

DISC

STRAIGHT
GLOBE VALVE

CHECK VALVE

ACCESS
PLUG

SWING
CHECK

WASHER
SEAT

Basic valves

A gate valve *(top left)* is always used as the main shutoff valve, because in the open position, as shown here, it offers no resistance to the full flow of water. The gate valve should be set only fully open or closed; in the half-open position the valve will vibrate. Globe valves function smoothly even when partially closed. Two types are shown here: an angle globe *(top right)*, in which the water makes a right-angle turn, and a straight globe *(bottom right)*. In both types, water passes through the spherical chamber that gives the valve its name. A check valve *(bottom left)*, which prevents backflow of supply or drain water, cannot be controlled by hand. Water flows freely in the direction indicated by the arrow; water moving in the opposite direction forces the swing check shut. The access plug can be removed for cleaning or repair.

The valves shown here are threaded to accommodate steel or brass piping. Similar valves, with smooth inlets and outlets, are available to join with plastic or copper tubing.

Drain traps

The two traps shown below perform the same function, but in different parts of a plumbing system. The house trap *(right)* is located on the main drain; the P trap *(left)*, under sinks, tubs and showers. Both trap waste water in a U-shaped bend, creating a seal against sewer gases. They may be made of chrome-plated brass, copper or plastic and they may have cleanout plugs that provide access if the trap becomes clogged *(pages 90-91)*.

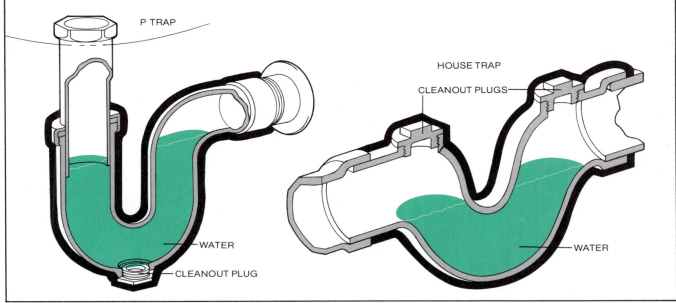

P TRAP

HOUSE TRAP

CLEANOUT PLUGS

WATER

CLEANOUT PLUG

WATER

WATER-TREATMENT DEVICES

Americans have the safest water in the world piped into their homes. Yet, one survey reported that 29 per cent of Americans complained about water appearance, taste, odor and—the greatest gripe of all—mineral-loaded hard water.

Fortunately, a number of water-treatment devices are readily available to eliminate such complaints. The simplest are water filters *(below)*, easily installed with the techniques described on pages 58-65. A porous cartridge traps particles of sand, silt or rust that cause cloudy water. If an activated-charcoal cartridge is used, the filter can remove the objectionable taste and smell left by chlorine purification treatments.

More complex is the water softener *(opposite)*, widely used where water is so hard that it reacts with bath soap to leave a ring of gray scum around tubs and lavatory basins. The softener removes the hardness from water by an exchange process. The hardness-causing minerals, magnesium and calcium, which react with soap, are exchanged for sodium, which does not react, as the water passes over sodium-containing plastic beads. The beads are replenished with sodium by bathing them with salt water—a sodium-chloride solution.

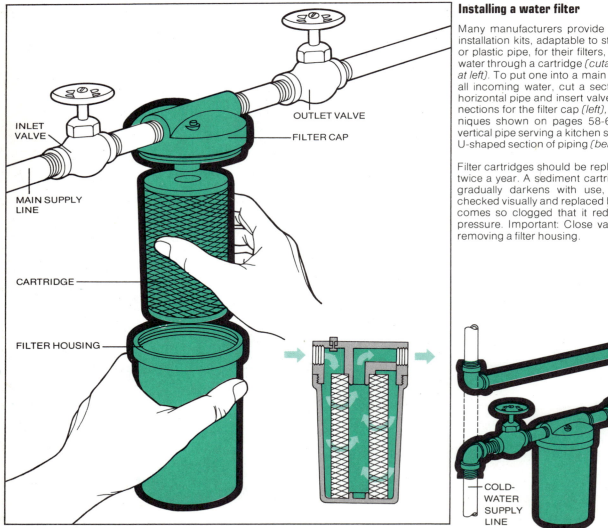

INLET VALVE

OUTLET VALVE

FILTER CAP

MAIN SUPPLY LINE

CARTRIDGE

FILTER HOUSING

COLD-WATER SUPPLY LINE

Installing a water filter

Many manufacturers provide easy-to-use installation kits, adaptable to steel, copper or plastic pipe, for their filters, which swirl water through a cartridge *(cutaway, below at left)*. To put one into a main line to treat all incoming water, cut a section from a horizontal pipe and insert valves and connections for the filter cap *(left)*, using techniques shown on pages 58-65. For the vertical pipe serving a kitchen sink, install a U-shaped section of piping *(below)*.

Filter cartridges should be replaced about twice a year. A sediment cartridge, which gradually darkens with use, should be checked visually and replaced before it becomes so clogged that it reduces water pressure. Important: Close valves before removing a filter housing.

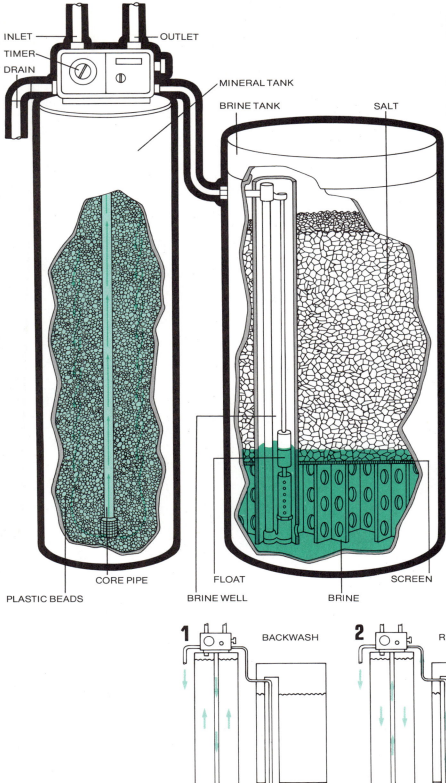

INLET

OUTLET

TIMER

DRAIN

MINERAL TANK

BRINE TANK

SALT

CORE PIPE

FLOAT

SCREEN

PLASTIC BEADS

BRINE WELL

BRINE

Softening hard water

In ordinary use, water flows only through the softener's mineral tank and does not enter the brine tank. From the inlet connected to the main supply line, water pours *(arrows)* over a bed of plastic beads that react with hardness minerals, replacing their calcium and magnesium with the beads' own sodium. The water, now containing sodium minerals instead of calcium and magnesium ones, goes up the core pipe to the outlet and the house plumbing.

As the beads lose their supply of sodium and build up calcium and magnesium, their activity must be regenerated *(diagrams, below)*. The timer temporarily disconnects the softener tank from the house supply and starts a cycle of washing the beads with sodium solution (salt water, or brine), which is then removed via the float-controlled brine well *(near left)*.

1 Reverse-flow backwash

The regeneration cycle begins as water flows down the core pipe and up through the plastic beads in a process that flushes dirt out through the drain.

2 Recharge

Salt water from the brine tank flows down through the beads, picking up their accumulated calcium and magnesium as it deposits its sodium on them. The solution, now laden with calcium and magnesium, passes up the core pipe and out the drain.

3 Rinse

Finally, water from the main supply line flushes unused brine from the mineral tank and flows through the brine well to dissolve salt in the brine tank for the next cycle.

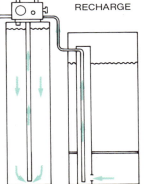

1 BACKWASH

2 RECHARGE

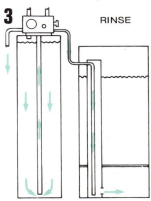

3 RINSE

FIXING PIPE

Every water supply pipe in your home will be one of three kinds: copper pipe (technically called tube or tubing); pipe made of other metals, usually steel or brass; or plastic pipe. Using proper tools, you can work with all three, as shown here and on the next pages.

Copper tubing carries water in more homes than any other kind of pipe. This lightweight, thin-walled pipe is versatile, durable and, in its flexible form, easy to cut or bend *(below)*. For some jobs, such as replacing a length of burst pipe, a copper tube should be soldered, or "sweated," at the joints *(pages 60-61)*. But for such jobs as adding a new shutoff valve to an existing line, the compression and flare fittings shown at right have self-sealing joints that can easily be disassembled and reassembled without the need for soldering tools and materials. And since flexible tube comes in standard sizes, many fittings are readily available.

Bending flexible copper tube

To prevent flexible copper tube from kinking as you bend it, slip a coiled, springlike tube bender along the tube until it covers the area to be bent. Then, using your thumbs or your knee as a fulcrum, bend the tube with your fingers or hands. When you have bent the tube to the desired curve, remove the tube bender.

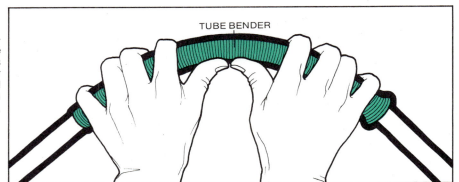

TUBE BENDER

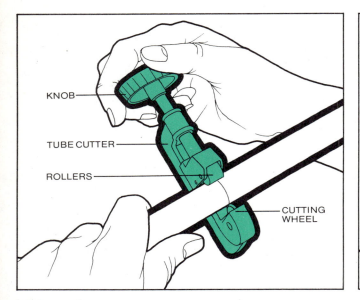

KNOB

TUBE CUTTER

ROLLERS

CUTTING WHEEL

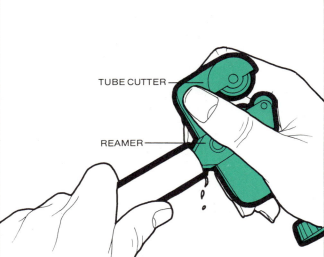

TUBE CUTTER

REAMER

Using a tube cutter

To cut rigid or flexible copper tubing, fasten a tube cutter on it and turn the knob until the cutter is snug. Rotate the cutter on its cutting wheel and rollers, tightening the knob slightly after each complete turn until the wheel cuts through the tube.

Reaming out the tube

A cutter leaves a rough burr inside a tube that reduces the tube's diameter. To remove the burr, swing out the reamer on the side of the cutter and insert it into the tube. Twist the reamer, applying enough pressure to cut the burr away.

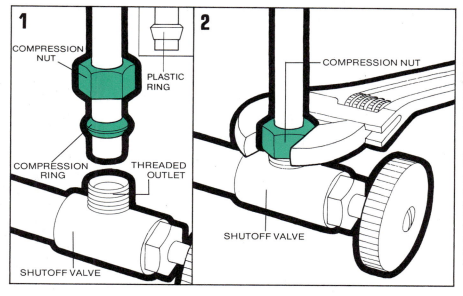

1 A fast fitting for flexible tube

One of the simplest devices for connecting sections of tubing is a compression ring. In the drawings at left it is used to join a tube to a shutoff valve. Over the tube slip the compression nut, then the compression ring, which is tapered at top and bottom for use on metal tubing, and on the bottom only for plastic tubing *(inset)*. Insert the tube into the threaded outlet of the valve.

2 Completing the connection

First tighten the compression nut onto the threaded outlet with your fingers; then, with an adjustable wrench, tighten the nut until it is just snug (overtightening will deform the compression ring and cause a leaky connection). The nut will squeeze the tapered compression ring between the tube and the outlet to form a watertight seal.

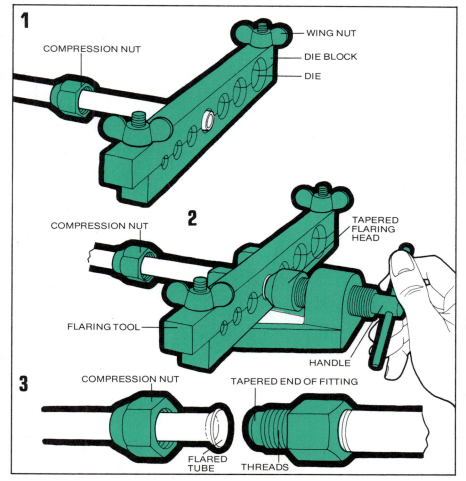

1 Preparing a tube for a flare fitting

An alternative method for connecting flexible copper tubing without using solder is the flare fitting, which requires a special flaring tool *(page 51)*. Open the die block of the flaring tool by unscrewing the wing nuts. Slip a compression nut onto the tube —and be sure to do it now; you won't be able to add the nut after the tube is flared. Insert the tube into the die that is exactly the tube's diameter. When the end of the tube projects just beyond the edge of the die, retighten the wing nuts.

2 Forming the flare

Attach the flaring tool to the die block so that the tapered flaring head is inside the end of the tube, then drive the head into the tube by slowly turning the tool handle clockwise. The tapered head should bend the tube's soft metal sides to an angle of about 45°. Withdraw the head by turning the handle counterclockwise.

3 Attaching the flared tube

Unscrew the wing nuts and lift up the top of the die block to remove the tube. The end of the flared tube should now fit snugly over the tapered end of any fitting designed for a flare connection. To complete the connection screw the compression nut onto the threads of the tapered fitting, using your fingers; then tighten the nut with an adjustable wrench until it is snug. Do not overtighten.

Soldering Copper

A soldered connection on flexible or rigid copper tubing will be stronger than the tube itself if you follow the basic steps on these pages. First, be sure that the tube ends are well cut and reamed, and perfectly round; remove squashed or dented ends with a tube cutter. Next, clean the surfaces to be soldered of moisture, dirt, grease and, above all, the film deposited on copper by oxidation. This film can be greenish, but often it is not even apparent to the eye. Always use flux, a pasty substance that keeps the working areas clean and bright by preventing oxidation. Finally, remember that the basic technique of soldering copper calls for heating the metal, not the solder. You should apply the flame of a torch to the copper connection until the metal is hot enough to melt solder; never aim the torch directly at the solder.

1 Cleaning the inside of a fitting

The soldering job shown on these pages consists of attaching a right-angle elbow fitting to a copper tube. Start the job by scouring the interior of both ends of the elbow with a wire brush. Twist or rotate the brush vigorously, inserting it deeply enough to reach all the areas you will solder.

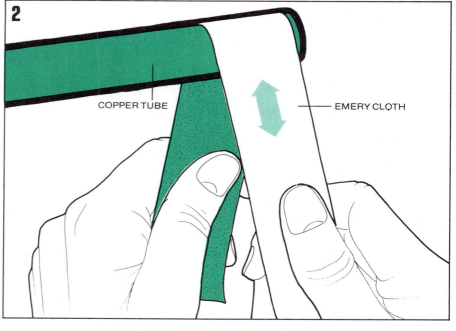

ELBOW FITTING   ELBOW SOCKET

WIRE CLEANING BRUSH

2 Cleaning the copper tube

Clean the end of the copper tube by rubbing it with emery cloth until the metal gleams brightly. Do not use a metal file or steel wool for this part of the job: a file will shave a thin layer of metal from the tube, while steel wool may leave almost invisible strands of steel clinging to the copper.

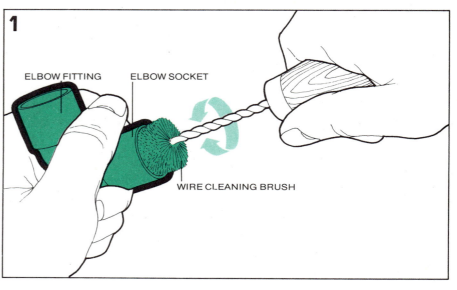

COPPER TUBE   EMERY CLOTH

3 Applying flux to the fitting...

After cleaning the copper surfaces, coat them with flux as soon as possible. The best flux is sold in paste form, and is applied with a small brush. Start this part of the job by brushing flux onto the inner surface of the fitting. A thin film is enough; too much flux can hinder the soldering process.

4 ...and to the tube

Brush a thin coating of flux onto the clean, bright end of the tube, following the procedure described for the fitting *(above)*. Insert the end of the tube into the socket of the elbow. When the tube is all the way in, give it a single full twist to spread the flux evenly over both copper surfaces. Wipe off excess flux with a clean rag.

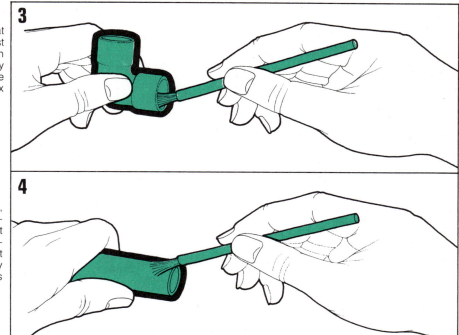

5 Heating the joint

Light a propane torch and heat the outside of the elbow socket, moving the flame slowly and evenly. Never direct the torch *into* the joint: you will burn away the flux and must then disassemble the fitting and start over. Test the temperature of the metal by touching the solder to the tube. When the solder melts, the connection is hot enough; go on immediately to the next step.

6 Soldering the heated joint

Divert the flame from the fitting and apply the solder to the outer end of the hot joint. You need not move the solder; by a process called capillary action, melted solder will be drawn into and around the entire space between the tube and the elbow *(insert)*. When solder spills from around the joint, the job is done. Wipe off excess solder with a clean rag.

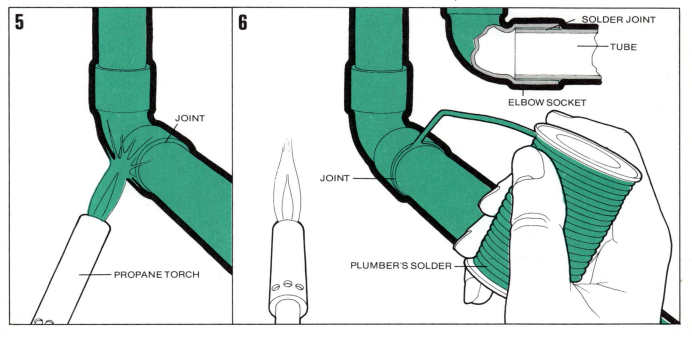

Threaded Pipe

Threaded pipe is easy to assemble with wrenches *(below)* and sealant, but removing a section presents a special problem. Since both ends of a pipe are threaded in the same direction, the pipe cannot turn; trying to unscrew it from a fitting at one end jams it tight against the fitting at the other. To avoid this problem, a length of threaded pipe may consist of sections joined by a coupling called a union, which comes apart to separate the two pipe sections; then each can be unscrewed from the fitting at its other end. When a pipe without a union must be replaced, it is cut in two and replaced by a pair of pipes with a union *(opposite)*.

FINE
WICKING

PIPE-JOINT
COMPOUND

PIPE-JOINT
TAPE

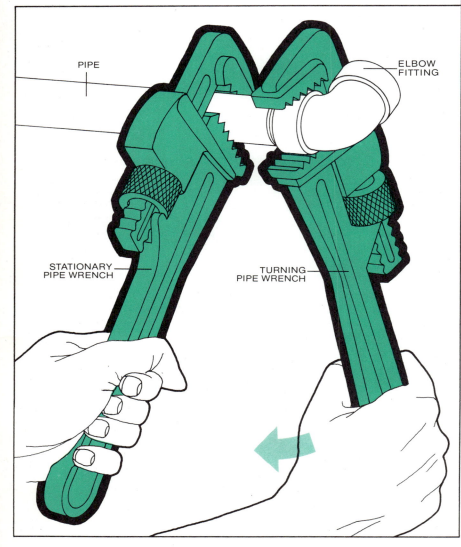

PIPE

ELBOW
FITTING

STATIONARY
PIPE WRENCH

TURNING
PIPE WRENCH

Sealing threaded connections

To make a watertight seal between threads on pipes and fittings, use either fine wicking and pipe-joint compound (also called pipe dope), or plastic joint-sealing tape. In the first method *(top)*, run a strand of wicking across the threads, then wind it clockwise into the threads. Coat the wicking and threads with a thin layer of compound.

Sealing tape *(bottom)* is more expensive than compound, but less messy. Wind one and a half turns of tape clockwise over the threads, exerting just enough tension to make the threads show through the tape.

Connecting threaded pipe

Two pipe wrenches should be used to put threaded pipe into a fitting (or to take it out): one to make the fitting turn, the other to hold the pipe stationary—if not held, the pipe will tend to turn with the fitting, straining all its connections. Always exert pressure on a pipe wrench in the direction of its jaw opening. In the picture at left, the pressure on the turning wrench is toward the user *(arrow)*; the pressure on the stationary wrench is away from the user. Allow a little play in the wrenches; when you start turning, the jaws will clamp tight.

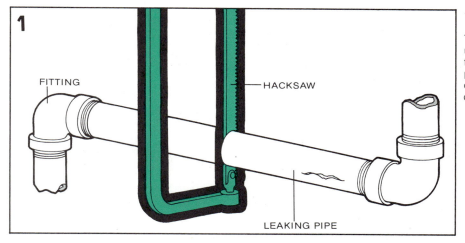

1 Removing a leaking pipe

To replace a threaded pipe that has no union coupling, turn off the water and cut the pipe with a hacksaw. Then, using two pipe wrenches—one to hold the fitting, the other to turn the pipe—unscrew each half of the severed pipe.

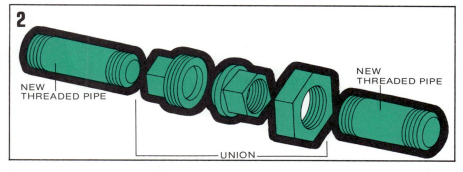

2 Preparing a replacement section

Take both halves of the old pipe to a plumbing supply store for a replacement, which consists of two new threaded pipes and a union. With the old pipe halves before him, the clerk can match their metal and diameter with new pipes, and gauge the length. Joined by a union, the two new pipes will be exactly the length of the old pipe.

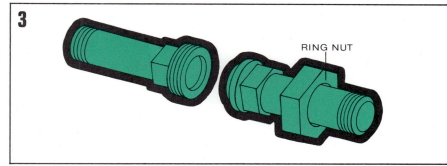

3 Assembling the union

Slip the large ring nut over one of the pipes. Apply sealing tape or wicking and pipe compound to the threads of the new pipes. Screw the two smaller parts of the union onto the new pipes by hand; then, using two wrenches, screw them tight.

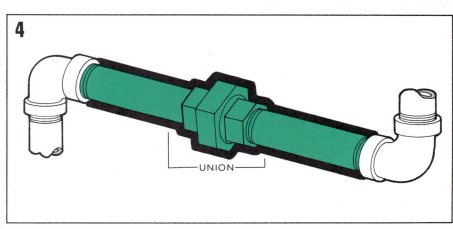

4 Making the connection

Screw the new pipes into the fittings and tighten them firmly with two wrenches. The two halves of the union should now just touch; if necessary, turn one of the fittings slightly to bring the union parts together. Screw the ring nut onto the exposed union threads with your fingers. Then with one wrench on the ring nut and the other holding the union piece facing the nut, tighten the union assembly firmly.

Plastic Pipe

Of all the different kinds of pipe, plastic is by far the easiest to work with. It is lighter than copper tube and far lighter than galvanized pipe. In addition, the plastic material will resist damage from corrosion, freezing and roots, and acts as an insulator to reduce condensation. One type is so flexible it can be snaked around almost like electrical wires. Of the four plastics *(table, opposite at bottom)*, only CPVC and polybutylene can withstand both pressure and hot water; the others have limitations that restrict their uses.

The rigid varieties are easily cut and assembled, and can be joined with solvent cement by the method shown below and at right; flexible pipe uses clamped insert fittings.

1 Preparing rigid pipe for a fitting

Cut rigid plastic pipe with a fine-tooth saw or a tube cutter equipped with a fine cutting wheel. Use a knife to remove ridges, burrs and loose strands of plastic from the inside of the cut end, and trim the outside to a bevel so that it slides into the fitting easily. Try out the fit. The end of the pipe should go into the fitting so snugly that the pipe will not fall out when it is pointed downward; if it comes out, try another fitting—they vary slightly in diameter.

2 Applying solvent cement

Make sure both parts are clean and dry. With this rigid type, remove the surface gloss on the outside of the pipe end and the inside of the fitting with fine sandpaper. For the cementing, use a small, natural-bristle brush; apply a liberal layer of solvent cement to the end of the pipe and a thin layer to the inside of the fitting. The cement dries very rapidly, so keep the can covered as much as possible. Important: Be sure to use the right cement for the plastic you are working with; check the label on the can.

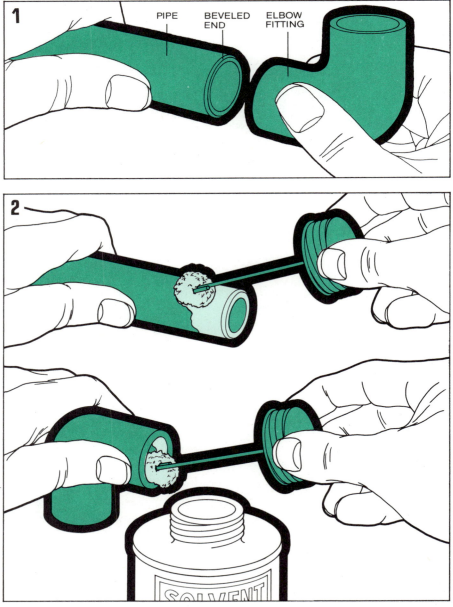

PIPE   BEVELED END   ELBOW FITTING

SOLVENT

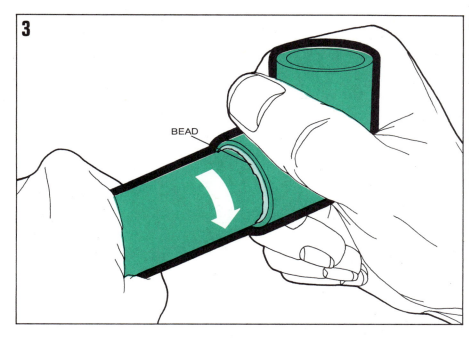

3

BEAD

3 Joining the parts

Within a minute after applying cement, slip the pipe into the fitting and give it a quarter turn *(arrow)* to spread the cement evenly. A well-made joint will show an even bead of cement between the pipe and the fitting. If it does not, separate the pieces—if the cement has not already bonded them together—and apply more cement. Quickly make sure the pipe and fitting form the angle you want—the cement sets in 15 seconds. Wipe away any excess cement and let the joint harden for at least an hour, but preferably overnight, before using it.

Joining rigid plastic to threaded metal

With the adapter shown at right, you can attach CPVC rigid plastic pipe to any female threaded fitting. Apply sealant to the pipe threads *(page 62)* and screw the threaded end of the adapter into the pipe. Then apply solvent cement to the plastic pipe *(opposite)* and the female end of the adapter, and bond them together.

Insert fittings for flexible plastic

Fittings for both hoses and flexible plastic pipe are made like the connector shown at right. An insert fitting—a ridged device made of rigid plastic or brass—fits tightly into the ends of two pipes being coupled and is held by clamps that are looped around the pipes and tightened by screws.

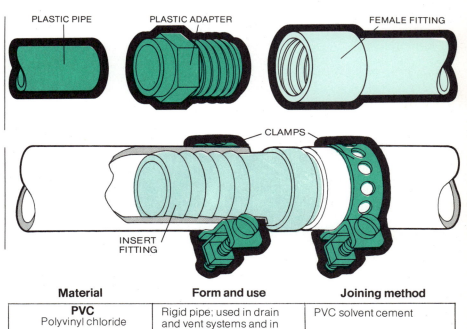

PLASTIC PIPE   PLASTIC ADAPTER   FEMALE FITTING

CLAMPS

INSERT FITTING

A guide to plastic pipe

The four kinds of plastic pipe listed at right are generally known by abbreviations of their chemical constituents, and these letters are usually printed directly on the pipe. Never mix one kind with another, and always be sure that you know which plastic—and also which corresponding joining method—you are working with.

Material	Form and use	Joining method
PVC Polyvinyl chloride	Rigid pipe; used in drain and vent systems and in cold-water supply lines	PVC solvent cement
CPVC Chlorinated polyvinyl chloride	Rigid pipe; used for hot- and cold-water supply lines	CPVC solvent cement
PE Polyethylene	Flexible pipe; used for outdoor cold-water supply lines	Insert-and-clamp fittings
POLY Polybutylene	Flexible pipe; used for hot- and cold-water supply lines	Insert-and-clamp fittings

Pipe Problems

Plumbing problems or emergencies can crop up at any time in the life of a house. Corrosion eats away at pipes and opens leaks. More dramatically, exposed pipes freeze; and when the pipes thaw, water spouts from cracks left by the expanding ice. Or your home may be plagued by the problem that is appropriately called water hammer: a thunderous bang that echoes through the house when a faucet is turned off.

All these problems are surprisingly easy to solve. You can thaw a frozen pipe (below), and then repair the leaks in it (right). The cause of water hammer is an abrupt stoppage of rushing water; shutting off the faucet generates shock waves along a run of pipe that create the characteristic clatter and bang. Most plumbing systems have air chambers to cushion the shock, but you must drain water from them periodically (opposite).

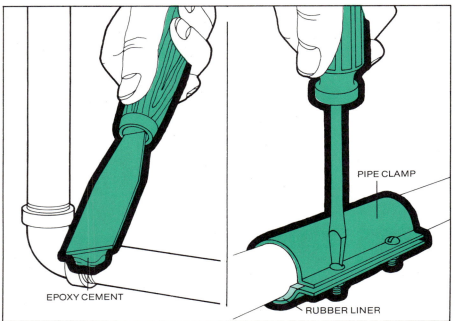

EPOXY CEMENT

PIPE CLAMP

RUBBER LINER

Patching a leak

Epoxy cement (above) or a pipe clamp (right) will temporarily seal leaks in pipes until a section or run can be replaced. Epoxy works best where pressure is low—on joints and drains. Before applying it, turn off the water to the pipe and wipe the crack clean and dry. Then spread the cement onto the joint or drainpipe with a putty knife. It will form a hard, watertight seal. On any straight run of supply pipe or drainpipe, a pipe clamp can be used. Obtain the right-sized clamp for your pipe, and be sure the clamp's rubber lining is fixed directly over the leak before you tighten the screws.

Thawing a frozen pipe

A frozen pipe is easy to detect: faucets will not yield water when turned on. Locate the frozen area by touch if possible, or thaw an entire run. (Caution: Be sure to open the faucet to let melted ice run out. And always work along a pipe starting from the faucet end; otherwise, ice could prevent steam from escaping and the pressure build-up could explode the pipe.) You can improvise a thawing implement; a hair drier or a heat lamp will do. The two methods described below are more efficient than others:

Affix a flame spreader to a propane torch (right), and place a heatproof pad behind the pipe to protect the wall. Play the torch along the pipe, beginning at the faucet. Important: Keep your torch moving, and do not get any part of the pipe so hot that you cannot touch it. Warm the pipe especially gently if it is made of plastic.

Alternatively (far right), wrap electric heating tape around the frozen area. To speed thawing, wrap insulating tape around the heating tape. Heating tape can also be used as a preventive measure in winter.

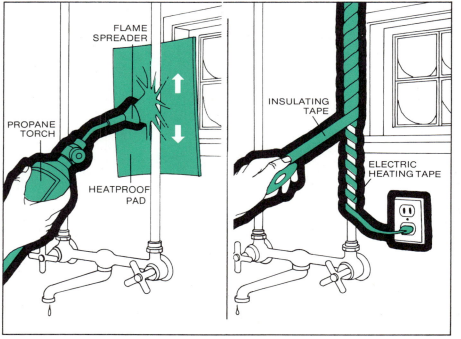

FLAME SPREADER

PROPANE TORCH

HEATPROOF PAD

INSULATING TAPE

ELECTRIC HEATING TAPE

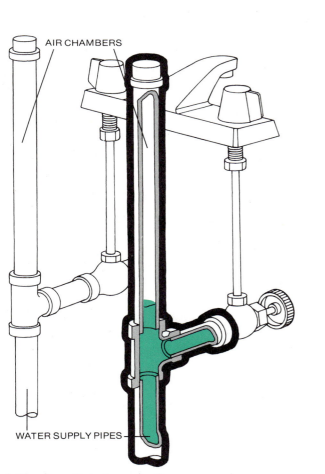

AIR CHAMBERS

WATER SUPPLY PIPES

Chambers that stop water hammer

To prevent the noise and damage of water hammer, most pipes leading to faucets and other fixtures are equipped with air-filled chambers—capped pipe sections *(above)* or special water-hammer arresters. The air trapped in these dead-end chambers provides a cushion for water shut off at a fixture—water that would otherwise rattle and loosen the pipes.

In time, the water level in an air chamber will slowly rise, as water absorbs the chamber's trapped air. When most of the air is gone, water hammer will recur. If your own plumbing system is equipped with air chambers but resounds with water hammer, you should drain the entire system, as explained in the box at right. The faucets you open in draining the system will admit fresh air to the chambers.

Draining Your Plumbing System

The plumbing system of a house could be drained for any of several reasons: to restore air to air chambers; to permit large-scale repairs; and, above all, to prevent pipes from freezing. If you plan to leave your house unheated during part of the winter, or if a power failure or fuel shortage cripples your heating system, you must drain your plumbing to avoid costly damage; freezing water can crack pipes, traps and even toilet bowls.

Begin the job by closing down the main shutoff valve to stop water from entering the system. Go through the house, opening every faucet and flushing every toilet. Then turn off the power to the water heater and—if you have hot-water or steam heat—to the furnace; drain them from their own drain faucets. If you have hot-water heat, first open the valves of every radiator, and then completely remove an air vent from a radiator on the top floor to maintain air pressure as the heating lines drain into the boiler.

Now open the drain faucet on the main supply line in the basement. This faucet is vital, for it releases any water that may remain in the system; but unfortunately, not all houses have it. If yours does not, it is definitely worth the money to have a plumber install one—and while he is in the house to do the job, ask him to see that all the supply pipes are pitched at the right downward angle to ensure fast, smooth drainage.

Next, use a cup and a sponge to bail the water left in the bottoms of the toilet bowls, and pour some antifreeze into the traps and toilet bowls. Automotive antifreeze is fine if you are hooked up to a city sewerage system; use the nontoxic antifreeze made for recreational vehicles and mobile homes if your house is served by a septic tank.

Finally, make a checklist of every pipe, fixture and trap that you drained, and every vent that you opened, so that next time the job will go quickly and even more easily.

Replacing Outmoded Fixtures

The most visible parts of any household plumbing system are its fixtures—the kitchen sinks, bathroom lavatories, bathtubs, showers and toilets. They are generally so sturdy they last for generations. Most of the older ones still in use are as plainly functional as the pipes that serve them. But in recent years there has been a trend to fixtures that are as attractive as they are utilitarian. In fact, not since the turn of the century, when English craftsmen adorned plumbing creations like the combination bathtub and shower stall illustrated at right, has there been such a widespread effort to beautify the once-lowly household plumbing fixture.

Manufacturers have turned to new materials—stainless steel, plastics and epoxy-enriched ceramics, for example—new designs and a palette of new colors to produce a generation of fixtures both esthetically pleasing and technologically superior to the old utilitarian fixtures. Yet, because basic plumbing systems are virtually the same today as they were a half century ago, it is possible to replace your old white lavatory with a decorative new one with little more effort than it takes to replace a faucet or a drain.

But before you go shopping for replacement fixtures, there are a few things you should know.
■ Sinks, tubs and lavatories are usually sold without such fittings as faucets and pop-up drains, which must be purchased separately. Bases for countertop lavatories also, as a rule, cost extra.
■ Although the location of the existing pipes will dictate where replacement fixtures may be installed, do not feel that you must replace an old unit with a new one of the same shape or type. Fixtures are available to suit special space require-ments. It is possible to fit two matching lavatories in the same space—and with the same pipes—formerly used by one. Or you might find that a four-foot-square bathtub—in which you can stretch out more than five feet diagonally—fits your space and taste better than the more familiar elongated shape.

With this general information in mind, here is what you can expect to find when you set out to replace one of your basic fixtures:

KITCHEN SINKS. The white-enameled cast-iron or steel sink that was the standby of American kitchens for decades is being replaced by counter-top units of stainless steel or epoxy-enriched porcelain. The stainless-steel sinks, which can be formed in any of a variety of sizes and shapes, are considered superior to the enameled types for durability, corrosion resistance and ease of cleaning.

But stainless steel can be dented and scratched. Also, a stream of running water tends to be noisy in a stainless-steel sink unless there is an aerator attachment on the faucet *(page 85)*. And stainless steel comes only in its natural silvery gray color. The new porcelain sinks are available in many colors as well as the traditional white. They are tough, durable and expensive.

All types of sinks can be fitted with either two-handled stem faucets or the newer single-lever faucets. Other popular options are spray attachments, dispensers for soap and hand lotion, and garbage disposers.

BATHROOM LAVATORIES. The old-fashioned vitreous china, with its glasslike, easily cleaned surface, is still a popular material for lavatories. But instead of the white, rectangular-shaped, free-standing basins of the past, you are more likely to find brightly colored round or oval units that are designed to be set into vanities or countertops. Some lavatories are sold already installed in cabinets. Lavatories are also available in enameled cast iron or steel, as well as in acrylic and cast-polyester plastics patterned to simulate fine marble. Some plastic types offer other unusual patterns and designs.

Lavatory fittings include a wide variety of faucets ranging from simple chrome-finished types to gold-plated units that cost more than the lavatory. Useful accessories include pop-up drains, shampoo sprays and soap dispensers.

BATHTUBS. Although more Americans bathe in enameled cast-iron or steel tubs than any other type, acrylic and fiberglass-reinforced plastic tubs are gaining in popularity. Not only do they feel pleasantly warm to the body, but their light weight—about 65 pounds each—makes it possible to install one without brawny helpers. Some manufacturers market a plastic tub-and-shower combination that can be assembled to form a watertight cubicle without the use of tiles or grouting on adjacent walls.

While a standard tub is about five feet long and some 30 to 32 inches wide, there are many longer and wider models to choose from—all the way to one maker's supertub, seven by five and a half feet. Most of today's tubs are connected only to a drain, with faucets and shower heads coming out of adjacent walls; thus they can be placed in a number of locations—free-standing, protruding, recessed, cornered or sunken.

Most modern bathtubs are fitted with a single set of controls for the tub spout and shower *(page 92)*. Some controls have mixing valves to assure desired water temperatures, and diverter valves that automatically switch water to the tub spout after you shower, preventing a wet surprise for a tub bather.

TOILETS. The three basic types of toilets—washdown, reverse-trap and siphon-jet—all resemble one another, with separate bowls of vitreous china and tanks of either fiberglass-reinforced plastic or vitreous china. But the reverse-trap type is superior to the old wash-down toilet, and the siphon-jet type *(page 101)* is even better. Best of all is the one-piece toilet, which combines bowl and tank in a single unit and can be mounted on the floor or hung from a wall. It is more attractive and much quieter than any of the others.

REPAIRING FAUCETS

Faucets come in so many different shapes and sizes that the only thing they seem to have in common is that water flows from all of them. Exterior appearances are deceiving, however. All faucets can be separated into two broad groups: stem faucets, shown here and on the following pages, and single-lever faucets *(pages 76-79)*.

Every stem faucet, no matter what the style of its handle or housing, contains three (or sometimes four) simple parts. There is the stem itself, a threaded metal shaft. A washer at the bottom of the stem plugs or opens a water supply line to control the flow of water. And a large packing washer or a doughnut-shaped band called an O-ring prevents water from seeping out at the handle or spout. The pictures at right and at the bottom of the opposite page show how these basic parts are arranged in three different stem-faucet systems.

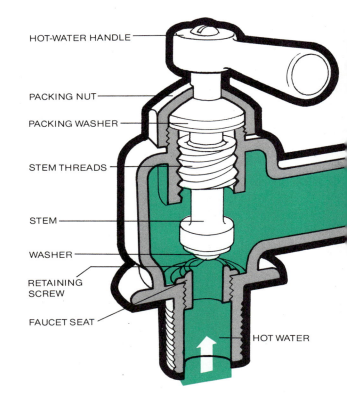

HOT-WATER HANDLE

PACKING NUT

PACKING WASHER

STEM THREADS

STEM

WASHER

RETAINING SCREW

FAUCET SEAT

HOT WATER

Troubleshooting Stem Faucets

Problem	Cause	Solution
Water drips from spout	Washer is worn	Replace washer *(pages 72-73)*
With new washer, water still drips from spout	Faucet seat is worn	Dress or replace faucet seat *(page 74)*
Water leaks around top of stem	Packing or O-ring is worn	Repack stem or change O-ring *(page 75)*
Water leaks around spout base	Spout O-ring is worn	Change O-ring on base of spout *(page 84)*
With new O-ring or packing, water still leaks from stem or spout	Stem assembly is worn	Replace entire stem assembly
Despite all repairs, faucet continues to leak	Faucet body is worn	Replace entire faucet *(pages 80-83)*

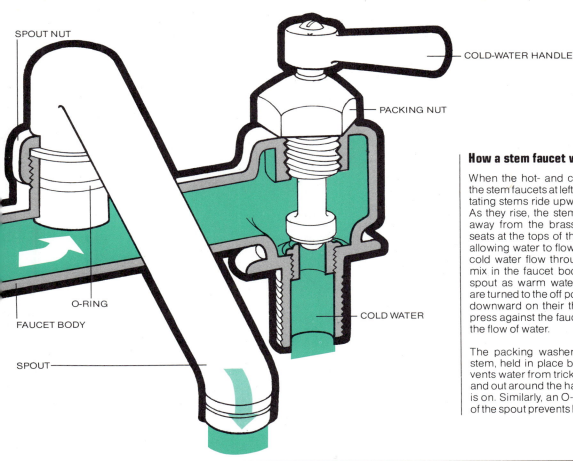

SPOUT NUT

COLD-WATER HANDLE

PACKING NUT

O-RING

FAUCET BODY

SPOUT

COLD WATER

How a stem faucet works

When the hot- and cold-water handles of the stem faucets at left are turned on, the rotating stems ride upward on their threads. As they rise, the stems draw the washers away from the brass rings called faucet seats at the tops of the water supply lines, allowing water to flow. When both hot and cold water flow through the faucets, they mix in the faucet body and run from the spout as warm water. When the handles are turned to the off position, the stems ride downward on their threads. The washers press against the faucet seats, shutting off the flow of water.

The packing washer at the top of each stem, held in place by a packing nut, prevents water from trickling up past the stem and out around the handle when the faucet is on. Similarly, an O-ring around the base of the spout prevents leaks at the spout nut.

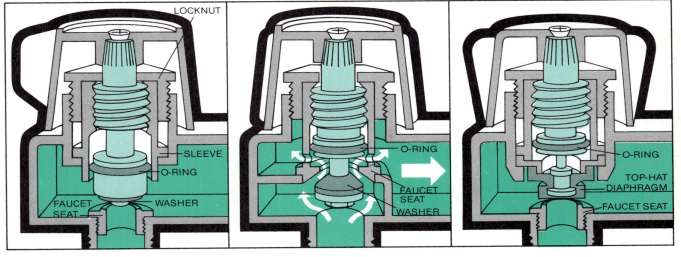

LOCKNUT

SLEEVE

O-RING

FAUCET
SEAT

WASHER

O-RING

FAUCET
SEAT
WASHER

O-RING

TOP-HAT
DIAPHRAGM

FAUCET SEAT

Standard stem

This modern design improves in two ways upon the stem faucet shown above: the stem is threaded into a sleeve, rather than into the faucet itself, reducing wear on the faucet body; and a locknut and O-ring replace the packing washer and nut. But with a standard stem, new or old, the washer is always under pressure and is therefore subjected to constant wear.

Reverse-pressure stem

Water pressure helps stop the flow of water through this faucet. With the handle turned on, the stem is lowered instead of raised, and water flows around the washer (arrows). At the off position the stem rises, bringing the washer up against the faucet seat to shut off water. Water pressure from below helps keep the washer firmly seated, giving a tight seal with little wear.

Top-hat stem

Developed in the 1960s, the top-hat stem is named for a diaphragm that resembles an inverted top hat and that takes the place of both washer and O-ring. The crown of the hat serves as a washer, covering the faucet seat; its brim prevents water from rising along the stem (the O-ring shown merely holds the stem steady). The entire device is replaced as a unit (page 73).

Replacing Washers

When a faucet spout drips, the likely cause is a worn washer. To replace one, you generally must first remove the faucet handle. It may be secured by a screw on top *(page 71),* a set-screw near the stem *(page 77),* or a screw under a threaded or a snap-on escutcheon *(below).* If the handle sticks, apply penetrating oil and wiggle gently upward; never bang the handle free—the stem might break.

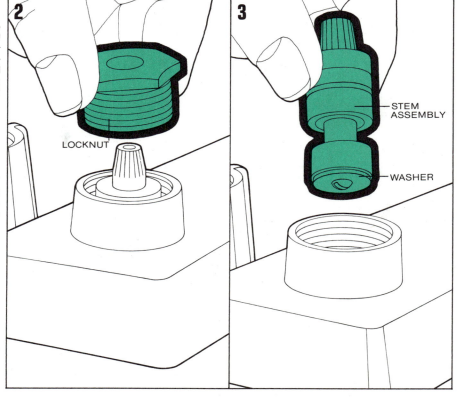

LOCKNUT

1

ESCUTCHEON

SCREW

1 Loosening the nut

After the faucet handle has been taken off, a nut underneath must be removed with an adjustable wrench to free the stem assembly. On the faucet above, it is a plain lock-nut, but older types have chrome-plated packing nuts *(page 71).* To avoid marring the chrome when you unscrew this kind of nut, wrap it in adhesive tape.

2 Lifting off the nut

When you have loosened the locknut or packing nut with your wrench, unscrew it by hand the rest of the way and lift it from the faucet as shown. Now you are ready to remove the stem assembly.

3 Withdrawing the stem assembly

A stem assembly held by a locknut fits snugly into the faucet, and you must draw it up firmly to remove it. If it resists, jiggle it slightly as you raise it. In faucets secured by packing nuts, the stem is threaded into the faucet. Unscrew it after removing the packing nut; if necessary, screw the handle back on to help you turn it.

2 LOCKNUT

3 STEM ASSEMBLY / WASHER

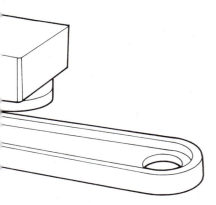

4 Replacing the washer

The procedure for removing an old washer and installing a new one depends on the type of stem assembly involved—standard, reverse-pressure or top-hat. In the standard assembly *(below, left),* unscrew the retaining screw. If the screwhead is so corroded that it crumbles when a screwdriver is used on it, use pliers to unscrew it. Pry out the old washer with the tip of a knife and insert the new washer into the stem cup with the beveled side facing toward the faucet seat. If your washer is not beveled, set the flat, smooth side facing downward. (Important: The washer must fit perfectly into the stem cup; if your plumbing supply store cannot provide the right-sized washer, reduce the diameter of a slightly oversized washer by rotating it against a file.)

Fasten the washer in place with a new retaining screw, tightening the screw until it compresses the washer slightly and holds it firmly in the cup.

To replace a washer in a reverse-pressure assembly *(below, center),* first remove the stem nut with an adjustable wrench. Disassemble all parts of the stem, then slip a new washer onto the threaded end of the stem. (Important: The replacement washer goes on with the beveled side facing the seat.) If the other parts are worn or rusted, replace them from a repair kit sold at plumbing supply stores. Complete the reassembly and tighten the stem nut with the wrench.

In a top-hat assembly *(below, right),* simply pull off the old diaphragm and slip a new one over the circular stem tip.

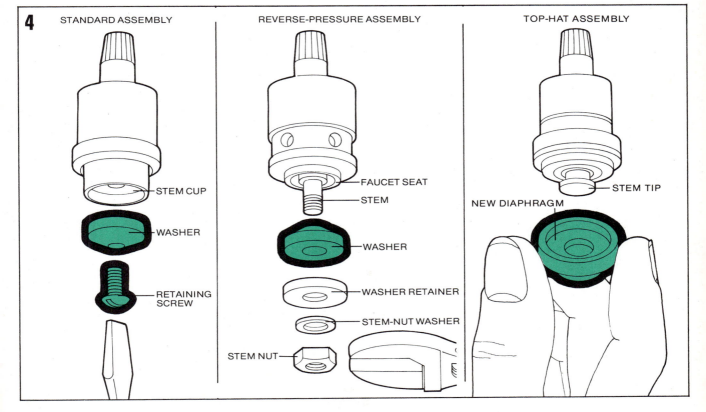

4

STANDARD ASSEMBLY

— STEM CUP
— WASHER
— RETAINING SCREW

REVERSE-PRESSURE ASSEMBLY

— FAUCET SEAT
— STEM
— WASHER
— WASHER RETAINER
— STEM-NUT WASHER
STEM NUT —

TOP-HAT ASSEMBLY

— STEM TIP
NEW DIAPHRAGM

Fixing Faucet Seats

If a faucet drips even after the washer has been changed, the trouble is probably the faucet seat—the rim of the opening that the washer press-es against. This problem is generally caused by sediments in the water, which wear the seat. A faucet seat that is only slightly cut or worn can be smoothed down, or dressed, with a seat-dressing tool. If the seat is too far gone, it must be replaced.

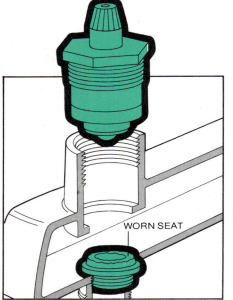

Checking seat wear

Remove the stem assembly (page 72) and stuff a rag or sponge inside the faucet body to soak up the water around the faucet seat. Examine the seat with a flashlight to check its condition; run a finger over its surface to feel for cuts or abrasions.

Dressing the seat

The tool that dresses a seat, smoothing out a worn edge, comes with a set of different-sized cutters and seat guides. Select a cutter that is exactly the size of the faucet seat and a guide that will fit snugly into the seat's center hole. (Several trials may be needed to determine the right sizes.) With the cutter and guide in place, screw the guide cone down into the faucet body until it holds the tool firmly in a vertical position. Using the palm of your hand, turn the knob at the top of the tool a few smooth, even strokes. Do not exert much downward pressure—the seat is soft brass, which of-fers little resistance. When the knob turns smoothly and easily the seat is dressed. Check again with your flashlight and finger for bumpy or uneven spots. If there are any, repeat the dressing procedure.

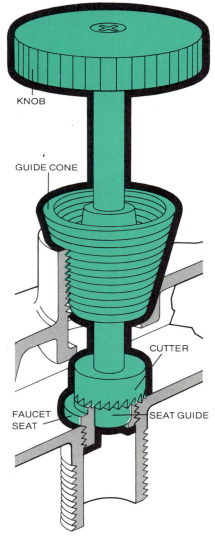

SEAT-DRESSING TOOL

KNOB

GUIDE CONE

CUTTER

FAUCET SEAT

SEAT GUIDE

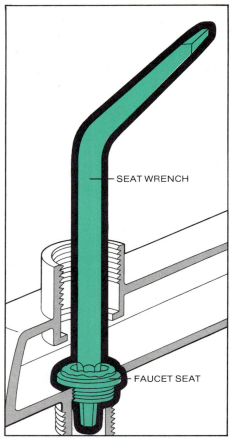

SEAT WRENCH

FAUCET SEAT

Replacing a faucet seat

Badly deteriorated faucet seats can be re-moved with a special seat wrench, square at one end and hexagonal at the other; use the end that matches the opening in the seat. (If your seat wrench is a straight, or "pencil," type, clamp an adjustable wrench on it for a handle; a seat wrench bent at an angle, like the one shown above, can be turned by hand.) After unscrewing the fau-cet seat, you may have to use needle-nose pliers to pull it out of the faucet. Before you install a new seat, coat its threads with pipe-joint compound to make a better seal.

Stopping Stem Leaks

When water seeps up around the top of a faucet stem, the cause depends upon the type of faucet. If the faucet has a packing nut, the fault may be in the nut itself, in a packing washer or in self-forming packing. In faucets with locknuts, stem leaks arise in the O-ring on the stem.

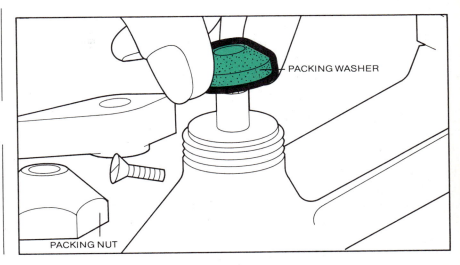

PACKING WASHER

PACKING NUT

Fixing faucets with packing

On a faucet with a packing nut, first check the nut. Cover it with tape and tighten it gently. Never overtighten this nut. If the leak persists, remove the nut entirely. If there is a packing washer underneath, slide it off, slip a new one over the stem, and reassemble the faucet. If you find self-forming packing, follow the procedure below.

Using self-forming packing

Some faucets with packing nuts are sealed by self-forming packing, which molds itself around the stem under the pressure of the nut. If tightening the nut *(above)* does not stop the leak on such a faucet, remove the nut and add two or three turns of packing to the old packing. If the existing packing is badly worn, dig it out with a knife and wind enough turns of packing around the stem to fill the packing nut, then add about half again as much; the nut will compress the packing when you screw it down.

SELF-FORMING PACKING

PACKING NUT

Changing O-rings

To repair a leaky stem that has an O-ring instead of packing, lift out the stem assembly *(page 72)*. Pinch the O-ring so that a section of it rises to provide a fingerhold, and pull it off. Take the O-ring to the store for an exact match, and buy several new ones to have a ready supply. Before slipping a new O-ring on the stem assembly, lubricate it with a bit of grease. Caution: New and slightly worn O-rings often look alike; do not pile them together or you may not be able to tell them apart.

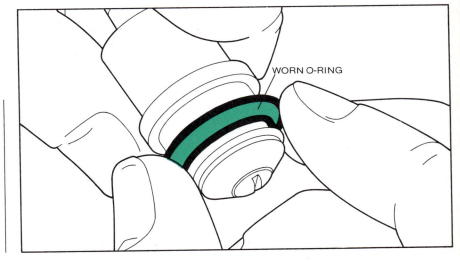

WORN O-RING

SINGLE-LEVER FAUCETS

Because of their intricate interior mechanisms, you might expect single-lever faucets to give more trouble than stem faucets. Just the opposite is the case. When a single-lever type begins to drip you can fix it quickly and easily with a replacement cartridge or a prepackaged repair kit. To be certain you get the right repair unit, jot down your faucet's brand name and model number before you head for the store, or take the worn parts with you. And

ON

LEVER

SPOUT NUT

ESCUTCHEON

O-RING

FAUCET BODY

COLD WATER

FAUCET SEAT

CENTRAL CAM

VALVE STEM

HOT WATER

Tipping-valve faucet

The lever of a tipping-valve faucet moves a tapered cam located between the hot- and cold-water valve stems. With the lever forward in the on position, the thick end of the cam tips the valve stems out of the faucet seats, and hot and cold water flow through the faucet *(arrows)*. Pushing the lever from side to side changes the proportions of hot and cold water; pushing it back to the off position slides the cam forward, and springs force the valve stems into the faucet seats *(dotted lines)*. Drips occur when this mechanical action wears the valve-stem assembly, or sediments cut into the faucet seats. To stop the leak, use a special tipping-valve-faucet repair kit containing new O-rings, strainer-plug gaskets, springs, stems and faucet seats.

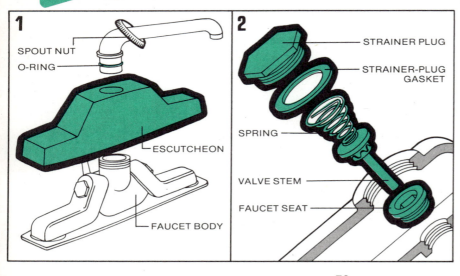

SPOUT NUT

O-RING

ESCUTCHEON

FAUCET BODY

STRAINER PLUG

STRAINER-PLUG GASKET

SPRING

VALVE STEM

FAUCET SEAT

1 Removing the cover

Shut off the water supply. Wrap adhesive tape around the knurled spout nut to guard its finish, then unscrew the nut with wide-mouthed pliers. Pull out the spout and replace the old O-ring with a new one from the repair kit, lubricating it with a daub of grease. Pry the escutcheon off the faucet body with the tip of a screwdriver.

2 Replacing valve-stem parts

Unscrew the strainer plugs with an adjustable wrench and remove all the parts beneath them. Unscrew the old faucet seats with a faucet-seat wrench, and spread pipe-joint compound (a sealant) on the new ones before screwing them in. Substitute the other new parts from the kit for the corresponding old ones, but reuse the old strainer plugs.

while you have the faucet apart, install *all* the new parts that come with the cartridge or kit, even if some of the old ones still look serviceable.

Like stem faucets, single-lever faucets come in a bewildering variety of exterior styles for kitchens and bathrooms. Many do not look exactly like any of the four shown here and on the following pages —but almost every single-lever faucet works on the principle of one or another of these four models.

Ball faucet

At the heart of this faucet is a hollow brass ball pierced by three holes; the lever rotates the ball in any direction. When you pull the lever forward to the on position, two holes in the ball line up over washer-like rubber faucet seats in the hot- and cold-water lines; the third hole faces the spout. Water runs into the first two holes, mixes inside the ball and flows out the third hole to the spout. Moving the lever back to the off position rotates the ball until the holes no longer line up with the seats and spout, and the ball's surface closes the water lines.

A repair kit provides new faucet seats, springs, a cam assembly, O-rings and an ingenious multi-purpose "key" tool.

ON

LEVER

BRASS BALL

HOLES

FAUCET SEAT

SPRINGS

HOT WATER

COLD WATER

O-RINGS

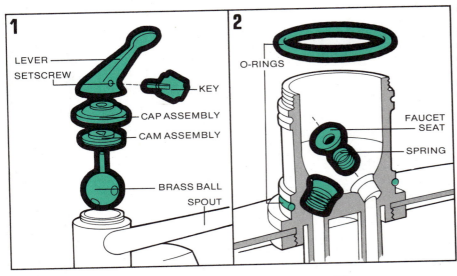

1

LEVER

SETSCREW

KEY

CAP ASSEMBLY

CAM ASSEMBLY

BRASS BALL

SPOUT

2

O-RINGS

FAUCET SEAT

SPRING

1 Taking the faucet apart

Loosen the setscrew at the base of the lever with the key from the repair kit, then pull off the lever. Unscrew the cap assembly, then lift out the two-piece cam assembly and the brass ball beneath it (the two assemblies fit together to hold the brass ball in place). Pull the spout from the faucet; if it resists, wiggle it gently.

2 Changing seats and springs

The faucet seats are pressed against the brass ball by small springs. Pull out the old seats and springs, and install the new ones from the repair kit. Replace the O-rings around the faucet body with new ones from the kit. (Do not apply grease to these O-rings; they are made of materials that never require lubrication.) Slip the spout into place and reassemble the faucet.

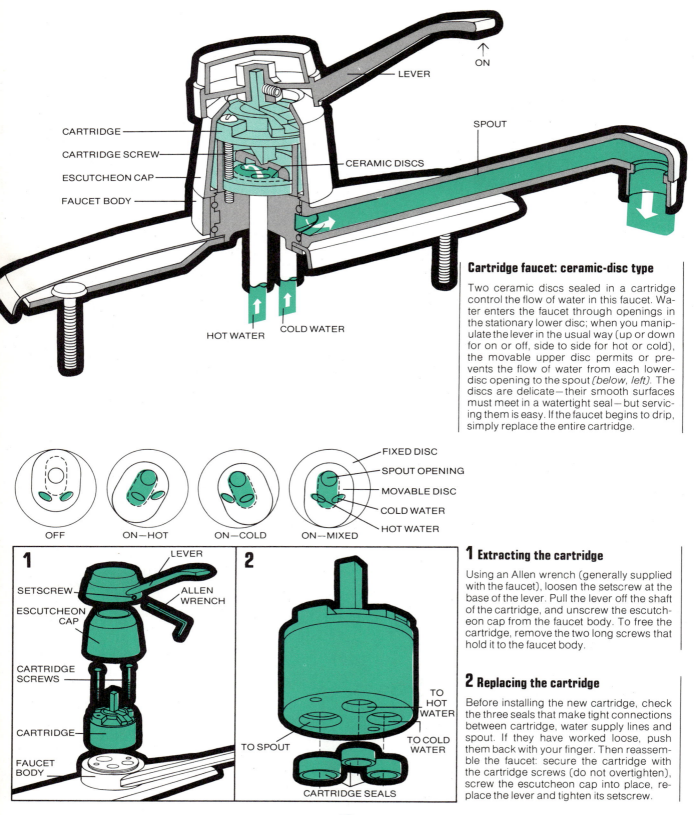

ON

LEVER

SPOUT

CARTRIDGE

CARTRIDGE SCREW

ESCUTCHEON CAP

FAUCET BODY

CERAMIC DISCS

HOT WATER   COLD WATER

Cartridge faucet: ceramic-disc type

Two ceramic discs sealed in a cartridge control the flow of water in this faucet. Water enters the faucet through openings in the stationary lower disc; when you manipulate the lever in the usual way (up or down for on or off, side to side for hot or cold), the movable upper disc permits or prevents the flow of water from each lower-disc opening to the spout *(below, left)*. The discs are delicate—their smooth surfaces must meet in a watertight seal—but servicing them is easy. If the faucet begins to drip, simply replace the entire cartridge.

FIXED DISC

SPOUT OPENING

MOVABLE DISC

COLD WATER

HOT WATER

OFF   ON—HOT   ON—COLD   ON—MIXED

1

LEVER

SETSCREW

ALLEN WRENCH

ESCUTCHEON CAP

CARTRIDGE SCREWS

CARTRIDGE

FAUCET BODY

2

TO HOT WATER

TO SPOUT

TO COLD WATER

CARTRIDGE SEALS

1 Extracting the cartridge

Using an Allen wrench (generally supplied with the faucet), loosen the setscrew at the base of the lever. Pull the lever off the shaft of the cartridge, and unscrew the escutcheon cap from the faucet body. To free the cartridge, remove the two long screws that hold it to the faucet body.

2 Replacing the cartridge

Before installing the new cartridge, check the three seals that make tight connections between cartridge, water supply lines and spout. If they have worked loose, push them back with your finger. Then reassemble the faucet: secure the cartridge with the cartridge screws (do not overtighten), screw the escutcheon cap into place, replace the lever and tighten its setscrew.

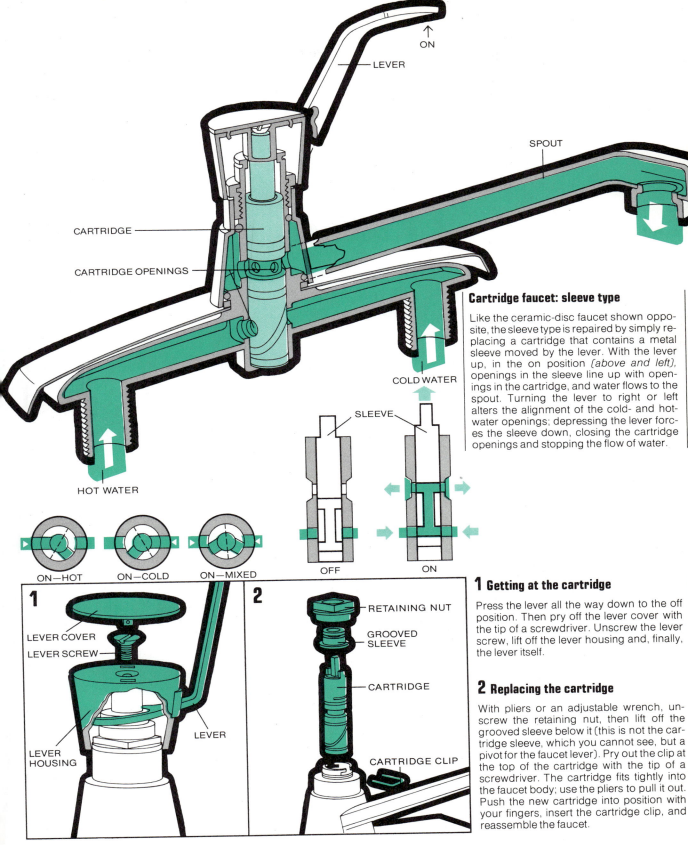

ON

LEVER

SPOUT

CARTRIDGE

CARTRIDGE OPENINGS

COLD WATER

Cartridge faucet: sleeve type

Like the ceramic-disc faucet shown opposite, the sleeve type is repaired by simply replacing a cartridge that contains a metal sleeve moved by the lever. With the lever up, in the on position *(above and left),* openings in the sleeve line up with openings in the cartridge, and water flows to the spout. Turning the lever to right or left alters the alignment of the cold- and hot-water openings; depressing the lever forces the sleeve down, closing the cartridge openings and stopping the flow of water.

HOT WATER

SLEEVE

ON—HOT   ON—COLD   ON—MIXED   OFF   ON

1

LEVER COVER
LEVER SCREW
LEVER HOUSING
LEVER

2

RETAINING NUT
GROOVED SLEEVE
CARTRIDGE
CARTRIDGE CLIP

1 Getting at the cartridge

Press the lever all the way down to the off position. Then pry off the lever cover with the tip of a screwdriver. Unscrew the lever screw, lift off the lever housing and, finally, the lever itself.

2 Replacing the cartridge

With pliers or an adjustable wrench, unscrew the retaining nut, then lift off the grooved sleeve below it (this is not the cartridge sleeve, which you cannot see, but a pivot for the faucet lever). Pry out the clip at the top of the cartridge with the tip of a screwdriver. The cartridge fits tightly into the faucet body; use the pliers to pull it out. Push the new cartridge into position with your fingers, insert the cartridge clip, and reassemble the faucet.

CHANGING FAUCETS

Homeowners will often tolerate outmoded kitchen faucets in the misconception that replacing them is a job for a plumber. Actually, substituting a new single-lever faucet for separate faucets is a job anyone can do. The main difficulty is the cramped work area beneath and behind the sink. To get some elbow room, use a long-handled, short-jawed basin wrench.

Before tackling the job, determine whether your water supply comes through threaded pipes or through plastic or copper tubing, which can be connected with solvent cement or solder, or with compression or flare fittings *(pages 58-61)*. The sink shown on these pages is supplied by threaded pipes, which are connected with adapters to the copper tubing attached to most single-lever faucets. If the supply lines were also tubing, either solder or compression fittings would make the connection. Be careful to bend tubing gently.

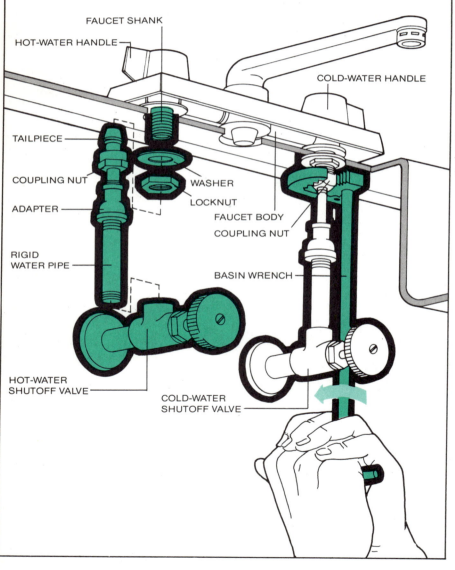

FAUCET SHANK

HOT-WATER HANDLE

COLD-WATER HANDLE

TAILPIECE

COUPLING NUT

WASHER

LOCKNUT

ADAPTER

FAUCET BODY

COUPLING NUT

RIGID WATER PIPE

BASIN WRENCH

HOT-WATER SHUTOFF VALVE

COLD-WATER SHUTOFF VALVE

Removing the old faucet

Turn the water off at both shutoff valves. With a basin wrench, remove the coupling nuts that secure the metal or plastic tailpieces connecting the faucet shanks to the shutoff valves. When the coupling nuts are loose, use the basin wrench to unscrew the corresponding locknuts on the faucet shanks. You can now pull the faucets up to free them.

Unscrew the rigid water pipe from the shutoff valves with two pipe wrenches *(page 62)*. The tailpieces will come off along with the pipe. Clean the top of the sink thoroughly before installing the new faucet.

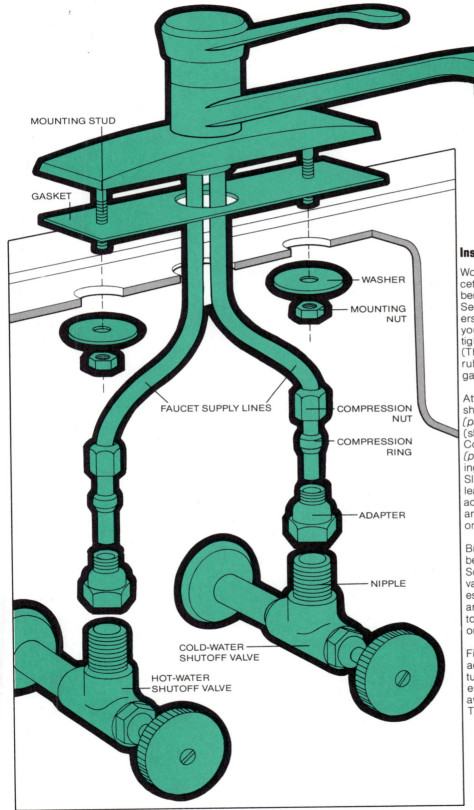

MOUNTING STUD

GASKET

WASHER

MOUNTING NUT

FAUCET SUPPLY LINES

COMPRESSION NUT

COMPRESSION RING

ADAPTER

NIPPLE

COLD-WATER SHUTOFF VALVE

HOT-WATER SHUTOFF VALVE

Installing the new single-lever faucet

Work the water supply lines of the new faucet through the center hole of the sink, bending them no more than necessary. Secure the faucet to the sink with the washers and mounting nuts, working first with your fingers, then using a basin wrench to tighten the nuts on the mounting studs. (The faucet shown comes with a watertight rubber gasket; if the one you install has no gasket, seal it with plumber's putty.)

Attaching the new faucet lines to threaded shutoff valves calls for compression fittings *(page 59),* adapters and brass nipples (short lengths of pipe with threaded ends). Coat both ends of the nipples with sealant *(page 62),* and screw on the adapters, using two pipe wrenches to make them fast. Slide the compression rings and nuts at least two inches up the faucet lines, slip the adapter-nipple assemblies onto the lines and hand-tighten the compression nuts onto the adapters.

Bring the assemblies to the shutoff valves, bending the lines as gently as you can. Screw the bottoms of the nipples into the valves and tighten them with two wrenches. While holding the adapters steady with an adjustable wrench, use another wrench to finish tightening the compression nuts onto the compression rings.

Finally, open the shutoff valves, remove the aerator from the spout and turn on a mixture of hot and cold water full force for several minutes; the running water will flush away any debris in the new connections. Then replace the aerator.

A New Faucet for an Old Lavatory

A bathroom lavatory often outlasts its faucets and its old-fashioned rubber drain stopper. The remedy is simple: discard the old fittings and replace them with a new faucet equipped with a pop-up drain. To some extent, the procedure resembles the one on pages 80-81; for example, you may need a basin wrench in tight places. The easiest way to attach the new faucet to the shutoff valves is with flexible water supply lines and compression fittings *(page 59)*.

Removing the old faucet

Turn off the water at the shutoff valves. Remove the handles and the stem covers. Using a wrench, remove the locknut and the washer under each stem cover.

Next, working underneath the lavatory, unscrew the packing nut at the bottom of the spout assembly; then pull off the metal washer and packing washer just above it. Unscrew the spout locknut, using a basin wrench if the working space is tight; pull down the washer above it, and lift the spout up out of the lavatory.

Still underneath the lavatory, loosen the coupling nuts that secure the tailpieces to their faucet shanks. Now you can remove the entire faucet assembly by lifting it slightly, angling it forward to clear the tailpieces and pulling it away from the lavatory.

If the new faucets fit the tailpieces, you will not need flexible water supply lines. If the shanks of the new faucets are too long or, as shown opposite, too short, remove the adapter-and-tailpiece units from the nipples with two pipe wrenches *(page 62)*.

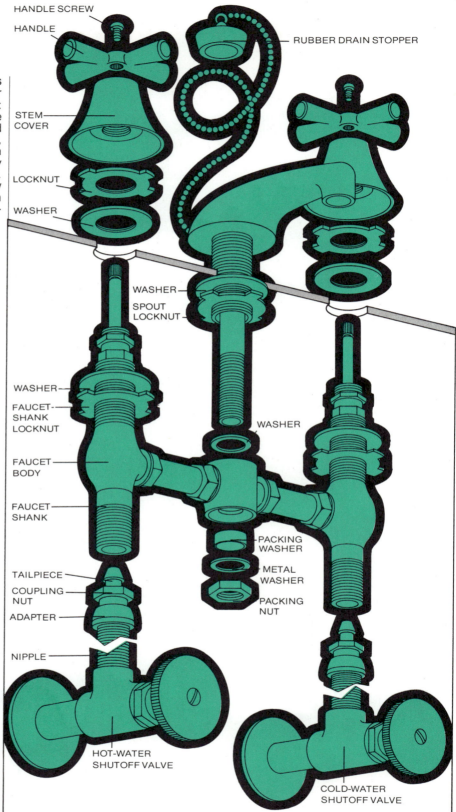

HANDLE SCREW
HANDLE
RUBBER DRAIN STOPPER
STEM COVER
LOCKNUT
WASHER
WASHER
SPOUT LOCKNUT
WASHER
WASHER
FAUCET-SHANK LOCKNUT
FAUCET BODY
FAUCET SHANK
PACKING WASHER
METAL WASHER
TAILPIECE
COUPLING NUT
ADAPTER
PACKING NUT
NIPPLE
HOT-WATER SHUTOFF VALVE
COLD-WATER SHUTOFF VALVE

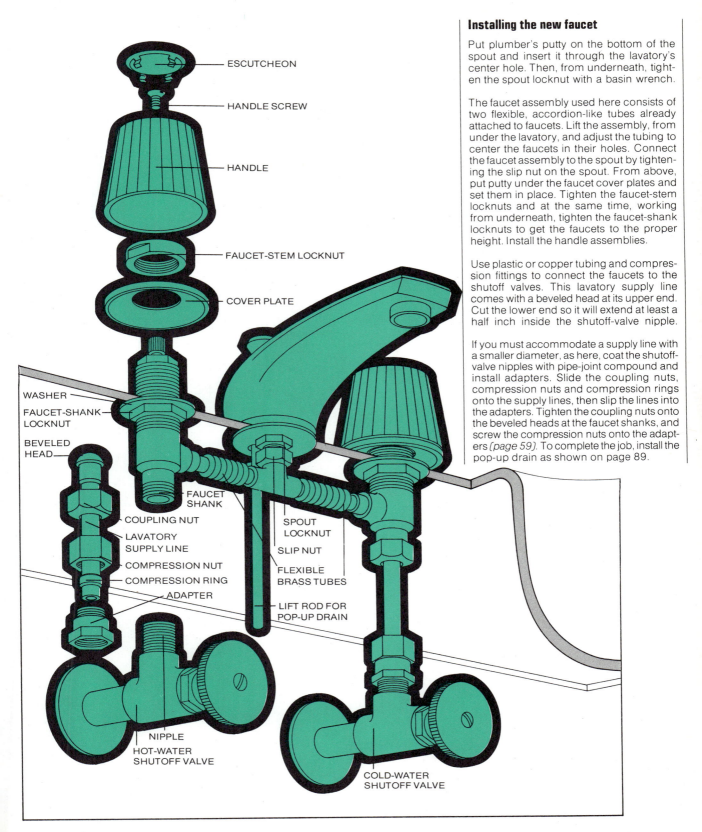

ESCUTCHEON

HANDLE SCREW

HANDLE

FAUCET-STEM LOCKNUT

COVER PLATE

WASHER
FAUCET-SHANK LOCKNUT

BEVELED HEAD

FAUCET SHANK

COUPLING NUT

LAVATORY SUPPLY LINE

COMPRESSION NUT

COMPRESSION RING

ADAPTER

SPOUT LOCKNUT

SLIP NUT

FLEXIBLE BRASS TUBES

LIFT ROD FOR POP-UP DRAIN

NIPPLE

HOT-WATER SHUTOFF VALVE

COLD-WATER SHUTOFF VALVE

Installing the new faucet

Put plumber's putty on the bottom of the spout and insert it through the lavatory's center hole. Then, from underneath, tighten the spout locknut with a basin wrench.

The faucet assembly used here consists of two flexible, accordion-like tubes already attached to faucets. Lift the assembly, from under the lavatory, and adjust the tubing to center the faucets in their holes. Connect the faucet assembly to the spout by tightening the slip nut on the spout. From above, put putty under the faucet cover plates and set them in place. Tighten the faucet-stem locknuts and at the same time, working from underneath, tighten the faucet-shank locknuts to get the faucets to the proper height. Install the handle assemblies.

Use plastic or copper tubing and compression fittings to connect the faucets to the shutoff valves. This lavatory supply line comes with a beveled head at its upper end. Cut the lower end so it will extend at least a half inch inside the shutoff-valve nipple.

If you must accommodate a supply line with a smaller diameter, as here, coat the shutoff-valve nipples with pipe-joint compound and install adapters. Slide the coupling nuts, compression nuts and compression rings onto the supply lines, then slip the lines into the adapters. Tighten the coupling nuts onto the beveled heads at the faucet shanks, and screw the compression nuts onto the adapters *(page 59)*. To complete the job, install the pop-up drain as shown on page 89.

SINK SPOUTS AND SPRAYS

The spouts and spray attachments of kitchen faucets sometimes present problems that seem serious but are easily solved. Leaks at the base of a spout, or low water pressure at either the spout or the hose nozzle are all malfunctions that can be remedied without even using the shutoff valves.

A spout that trickles rather than gushes may indicate that the aerator, the antisplash device at the opening, simply needs cleaning. Trouble in a spray attachment can start at the nozzle, the spray hose or the diverter valve that switches water between spout and spray. Buy nothing new until you have checked and cleaned such parts; then, if a new part is needed, take the old one to the store to be sure of getting the right type.

SPOUT NUT

O-RING

Working at the base of a spout

When water seeps out around the base of a spout, the O-ring in the spout base should be replaced. Cover the spout nut with tape and unscrew it with pliers. Lift off the spout to replace the O-ring.

In the faucet body beneath the spout base, a diverter valve directs water to either the spout or the spray attachment. Whenever the spray is off, the diverter directs water up into the spout. When you press the handle on the spray head, water begins to flow through the spray hose, the pressure at the base of the diverter drops and the valve changes position to direct water through the hollow attaching screw into the hose. If water does not switch quickly and easily from spout to spray, remove the diverter valve (some valves screw out, others can be pulled out by hand). Flush foreign materials out of the diverter area by gently opening one of the faucet handles, and wash the diverter at another faucet. If problems persist, replace the diverter valve.

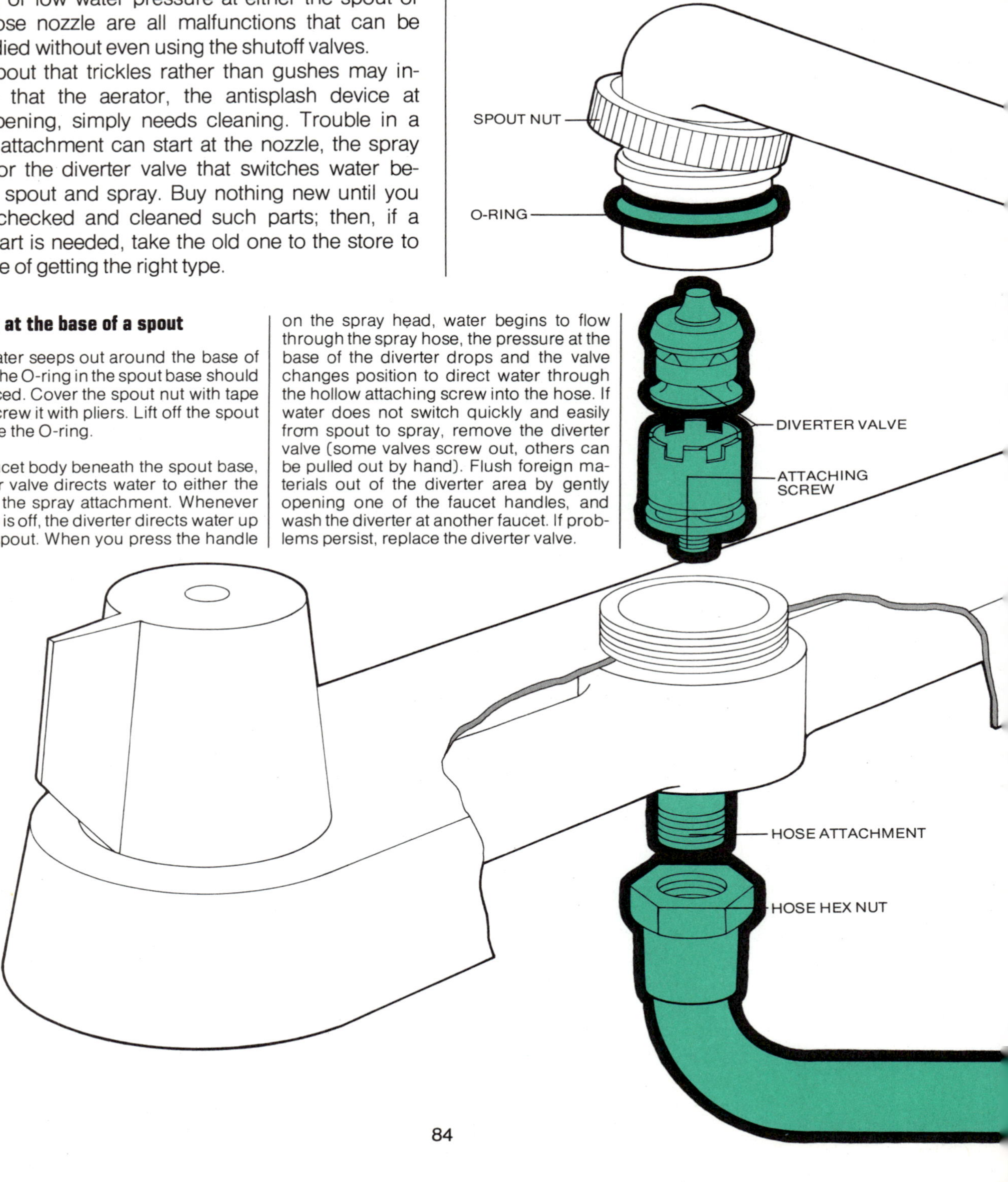

DIVERTER VALVE

ATTACHING SCREW

HOSE ATTACHMENT

HOSE HEX NUT

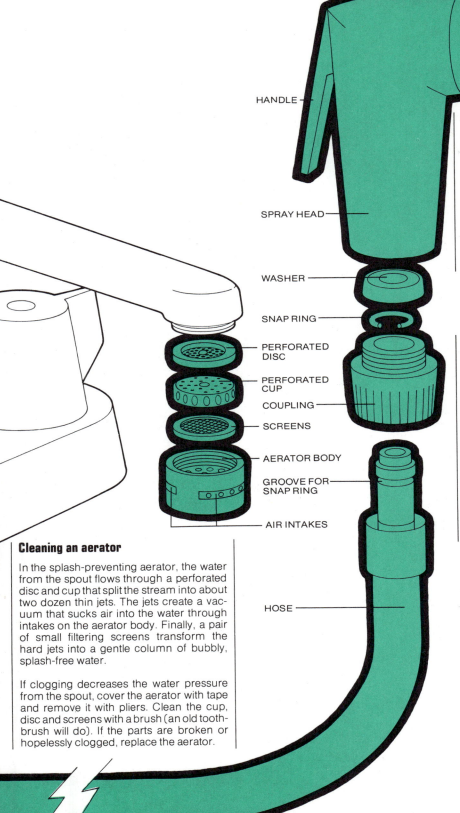

NOZZLE

HANDLE

SPRAY HEAD

WASHER

SNAP RING

PERFORATED DISC

PERFORATED CUP

COUPLING

SCREENS

AERATOR BODY

GROOVE FOR SNAP RING

AIR INTAKES

HOSE

Checking a spray head

When water flows from a spray head with less than normal force, unscrew the nozzle — by hand if possible. Turn on a faucet, then press the spray-head handle to permit water to cleanse the head's interior. If the head is cracked or badly worn, replace it. Unscrew the spray head from its coupling. A washer and the coupling itself, secured by a snap ring, will remain on the spray hose. Remove the washer, unclip the ring with the tip of a screwdriver and slip off the coupling. Then check the hose (below).

Checking the spray hose

A sharply kinked spray-attachment hose can permanently reduce water pressure at the spray head; a hose that is cut or worn through will, of course, leak. To replace a deteriorated hose, remove the spray head (above), then unscrew the hex nut at the base of the hose under the sink. If you cannot get at this hex nut with an adjustable wrench, use a basin wrench (page 49).

In choosing a new hose, make sure its hex nut — or an adapter — will fit the hose attachment in your sink. Hoses may be linked to this attachment in several different ways; match your new hose to the old one to be sure you have the right nut or adapter.

Cleaning an aerator

In the splash-preventing aerator, the water from the spout flows through a perforated disc and cup that split the stream into about two dozen thin jets. The jets create a vacuum that sucks air into the water through intakes on the aerator body. Finally, a pair of small filtering screens transform the hard jets into a gentle column of bubbly, splash-free water.

If clogging decreases the water pressure from the spout, cover the aerator with tape and remove it with pliers. Clean the cup, disc and screens with a brush (an old toothbrush will do). If the parts are broken or hopelessly clogged, replace the aerator.

REPLACING DRAINS

Designed to keep utensils and other objects from dropping into the drain, the sink strainer sometimes needs replacing, either because its metal facing has become worn and discolored or because it leaks around the edges. Leaks arise when the strainer body wears through or the putty that seals it to the sink dries out or becomes eroded.

To remove a marred or leaky strainer, follow the steps shown opposite. If a leak is the problem, you may need only fresh plumber's putty *(step 4)*. To reassemble the strainer, or to install a new one, simply reverse the steps used in removal.

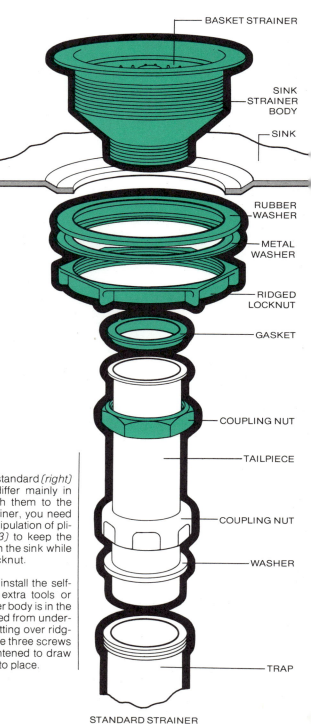

STANDARD STRAINER

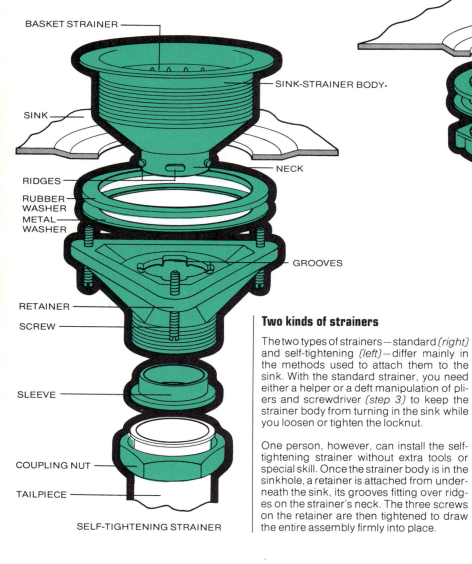

SELF-TIGHTENING STRAINER

Two kinds of strainers

The two types of strainers — standard *(right)* and self-tightening *(left)* — differ mainly in the methods used to attach them to the sink. With the standard strainer, you need either a helper or a deft manipulation of pliers and screwdriver *(step 3)* to keep the strainer body from turning in the sink while you loosen or tighten the locknut.

One person, however, can install the self-tightening strainer without extra tools or special skill. Once the strainer body is in the sinkhole, a retainer is attached from underneath the sink, its grooves fitting over ridges on the strainer's neck. The three screws on the retainer are then tightened to draw the entire assembly firmly into place.

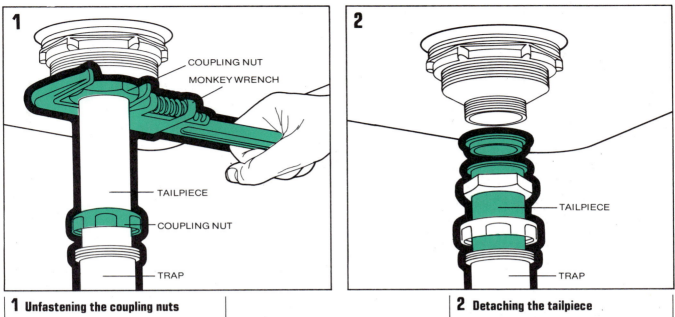

1 Unfastening the coupling nuts

To remove either type of strainer, loosen the two coupling nuts on the tailpiece with a monkey wrench. Slide the nuts clear of the threads. Remove the basket strainer that lifts out of the strainer body.

2 Detaching the tailpiece

If the old tailpiece is still serviceable, do not bother to remove it. Simply let it slip down into the trap and out of the way. If it shows signs of disintegration, take it to the store and buy a replacement.

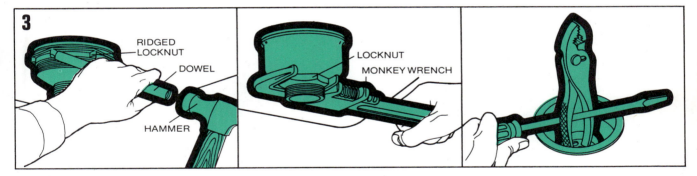

3 Removing the strainer body

To remove a standard strainer, you must unscrew a locknut. There are two kinds. One (above) has ridges. To unscrew it, place a wooden dowel or a blunt metal rod against each of the ridges in sequence, and tap the locknut loose with a hammer. The other kind of locknut (above, center) has no ridges. Use a monkey wrench or pipe wrench to remove it.

If the strainer body starts to turn in the sink while you loosen the locknut, stick the handles of a pair of pliers into the cross-members of the strainer, then place a screwdriver between them (above, right). If you, or a helper, hold the screwdriver steady, the pliers will be braced against the strainer so that they keep it from turning.

4 Installing a new strainer

Before placing a new strainer in the sink, put a one-eighth-inch bead of plumber's putty under its lip. NOTE: Some strainers come with adhesive-coated rubber gaskets, and need no putty. Peel the protective paper from the gasket and press the gasket under the lip of the strainer.

From underneath the sink, slip the rubber and metal washers over the neck of the strainer, then secure the locknut or retainer (opposite). Raise the tailpiece into place and tighten the coupling nuts.

A Lavatory's Pop-up Drain

The pop-up drain on a modern lavatory is neater than the old-fashioned rubber stopper, but it cannot open the drain as much and it rarely closes to make a completely watertight seal. However, it can be adjusted to work better than most people think, and alignment *(below)* requires no tools. Keeping it clean also helps. Although not all mechanical drains look alike, all work in much the same way and have similar basic parts. Even the type that does not seem to come apart for cleaning actually does, once you know how *(opposite).*

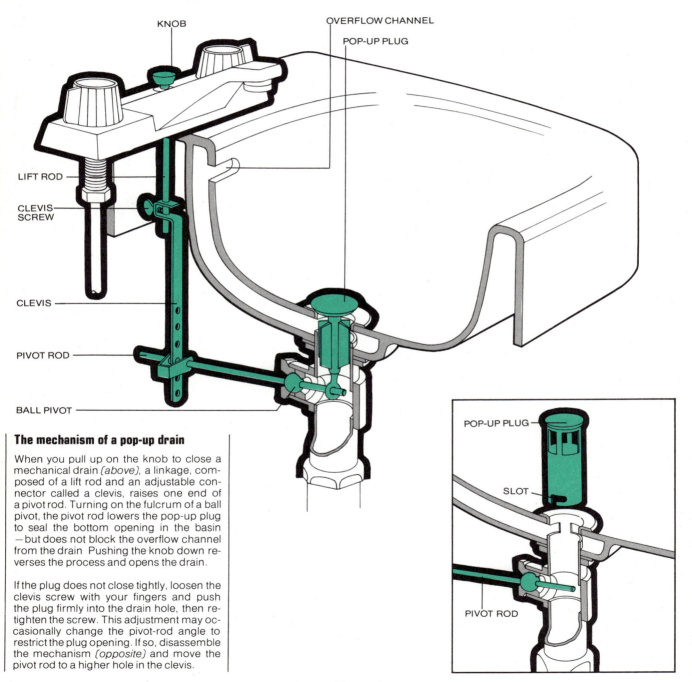

KNOB

OVERFLOW CHANNEL

POP-UP PLUG

LIFT ROD

CLEVIS SCREW

CLEVIS

PIVOT ROD

BALL PIVOT

POP-UP PLUG

SLOT

PIVOT ROD

The mechanism of a pop-up drain

When you pull up on the knob to close a mechanical drain *(above)*, a linkage, composed of a lift rod and an adjustable connector called a clevis, raises one end of a pivot rod. Turning on the fulcrum of a ball pivot, the pivot rod lowers the pop-up plug to seal the bottom opening in the basin —but does not block the overflow channel from the drain Pushing the knob down reverses the process and opens the drain.

If the plug does not close tightly, loosen the clevis screw with your fingers and push the plug firmly into the drain hole, then retighten the screw. This adjustment may occasionally change the pivot-rod angle to restrict the plug opening. If so, disassemble the mechanism *(opposite)* and move the pivot rod to a higher hole in the clevis.

Disassembling the drain

To install a new drain or replace worn parts in an old one, take the mechanism apart. Loosen the clevis screw, and then unfasten the compression nut with an adjustable wrench. Now pull the nut and pivot rod out of place; as you do so, the loosened clevis will slip off its lift rod. Lift the plug out.

For the next steps of the job use a monkey wrench. Loosen the slip nut, unscrew the drain tee from the flange (you can now unscrew the trap from the wall if you wish), and unscrew the flange locknut. Push the flange upward to remove it. When reinstalling the parts, coat all threads with pipe-joint compound, and apply plumber's putty under the lip of the flange. If necessary, replace gaskets and washers.

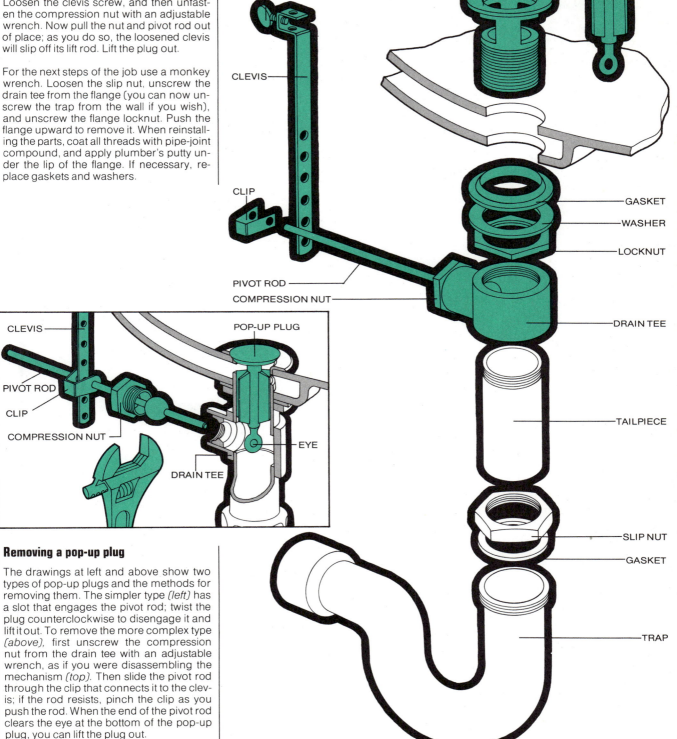

CLEVIS SCREW

FLANGE   POP-UP PLUG

CLEVIS

CLIP

PIVOT ROD

COMPRESSION NUT

GASKET

WASHER

LOCKNUT

DRAIN TEE

CLEVIS

POP-UP PLUG

PIVOT ROD

CLIP

COMPRESSION NUT

EYE

DRAIN TEE

TAILPIECE

SLIP NUT

GASKET

TRAP

Removing a pop-up plug

The drawings at left and above show two types of pop-up plugs and the methods for removing them. The simpler type *(left)* has a slot that engages the pivot rod; twist the plug counterclockwise to disengage it and lift it out. To remove the more complex type *(above)*, first unscrew the compression nut from the drain tee with an adjustable wrench, as if you were disassembling the mechanism *(top)*. Then slide the pivot rod through the clip that connects it to the clevis; if the rod resists, pinch the clip as you push the rod. When the end of the pivot rod clears the eye at the bottom of the pop-up plug, you can lift the plug out.

Unclogging Drains

Sink and lavatory drains will almost never clog if you observe one simple rule: do not use them for anything but waste water. Do not wash grease, coffee grounds or garbage down a kitchen drain; do not wash hair down a lavatory drain. A drain protected from such obstructions will last until it falls prey to old age.

Unfortunately, the rule for keeping drains open is almost impossible to observe strictly; drains do clog and must be opened. Before you start the job, locate the extent of the blockage by checking other drains. If all the drains in the house are blocked or sluggish, your problem is the main drain—and you need a plumber. If sinks along a single drain branch are clogged, clean out that branch with an auger *(opposite, bottom)*. If only one drain is blocked, try a liquid drain opener. Then, if necessary, follow the other instructions on these pages. For the special trick of using an auger on a bathtub drain, see page 93.

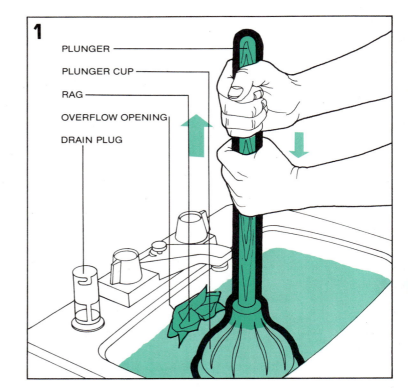

1 Using a plunger

Take off the pop-up plug of a lavatory *(pages 88-89)* or the strainer of a kitchen sink. Stuff a rag into the overflow opening of a lavatory; if necessary, have a helper hold the rag in place while you operate the plunger. Fill the basin with enough water to cover the plunger cup, place the cup over the drain, and work the plunger handle up and down. Press the plunger smoothly on the downstroke, which forces water down against the blockage, then jerk it sharply on the more important upstroke, which pulls the blockage from the drain. If five minutes' work with the plunger does not unclog the drain, go on to the next step.

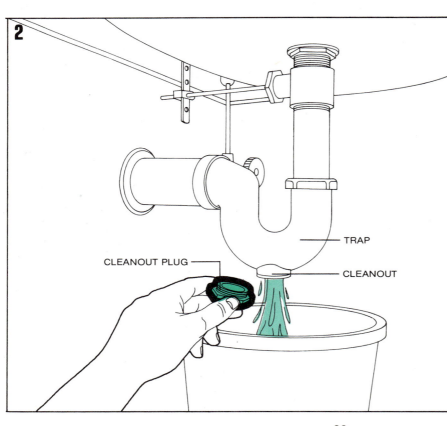

2 Clearing the trap

Set a bucket under the trap, unscrew the cleanout plug with an adjustable wrench and empty the contents of the trap into the bucket. Clear the pipe from the drain hole down to the cleanout with a drain and trap auger *(opposite);* when water flows freely from the basin to the bucket, any remaining blockage must be in the drainpipe going into the wall. Probe for it with the auger; if you fail to remove it, go on to step 3.

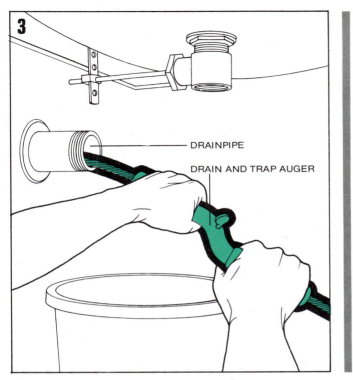

3

DRAINPIPE

DRAIN AND TRAP AUGER

3 Completing the job

Remove the trap *(page 89)*. Clear the drain-pipe with the auger, working down into the part of the pipe that runs beyond the wall. Be gentle with the auger. Ramming it too vigor-ously can loosen fittings behind the wall and could pierce an old, deteriorated pipe.

Chemical Cleaners: Worth a Try

Chemical drain cleaners offer a temptingly easy way to clear a clogged drain—just pour in the mixture and dissolve the blockage. Unfortunate-ly, the usefulness of these cleaners is limited, but they are worth a try because they allow you to avoid taking apart any plumbing and risking the damage that an auger can cause.

Take care both when buying and using a chemical drain cleaner. Choose a liquid rather than a powder, which generates heat and steam as it dissolves. The heat can damage pipes, and steam can spray the chemical right back out of the drain. Also, choose only an alkali product, one containing a form of hydroxide.

Remember that all chemical drain openers are dangerous. They can burn eyes and skin, and must be kept out of reach of children.

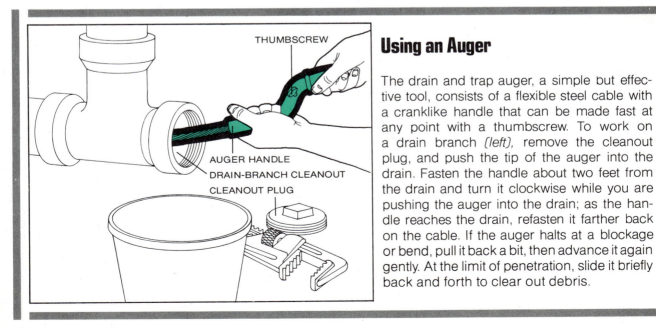

THUMBSCREW

AUGER HANDLE
DRAIN-BRANCH CLEANOUT
CLEANOUT PLUG

Using an Auger

The drain and trap auger, a simple but effec-tive tool, consists of a flexible steel cable with a cranklike handle that can be made fast at any point with a thumbscrew. To work on a drain branch *(left)*, remove the cleanout plug, and push the tip of the auger into the drain. Fasten the handle about two feet from the drain and turn it clockwise while you are pushing the auger into the drain; as the han-dle reaches the drain, refasten it farther back on the cable. If the auger halts at a blockage or bend, pull it back a bit, then advance it again gently. At the limit of penetration, slide it briefly back and forth to clear out debris.

TUB AND SHOWER PLUMBING

To most amateurs, repairs on bathtub and shower plumbing seem more difficult than they actually are because the faucets are usually hidden in the wall and the drain is hidden beneath the tub. You can work on these fixtures, however, once you understand how they function and how to get at their insides. For example, all bathtub drains, whether closed by a pop-up or trip-lever mechanism, or an old-fashioned stopper, have much the same overflow system—and the overflow tube is the best entry to a clogged drain (opposite, bottom) Techniques for stopping drips at a tub spout or a shower head are explained on pages 94-95.

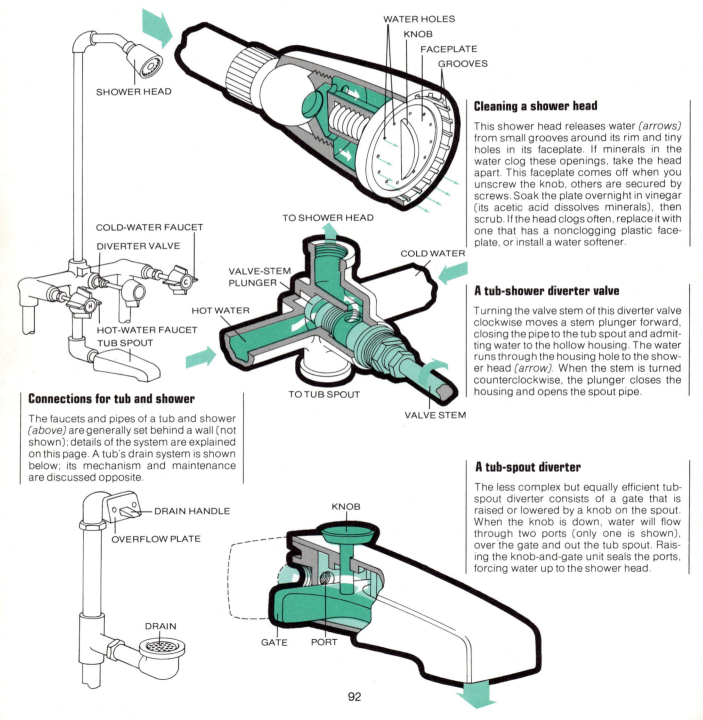

SHOWER HEAD

WATER HOLES
KNOB
FACEPLATE
GROOVES

Cleaning a shower head

This shower head releases water (arrows) from small grooves around its rim and tiny holes in its faceplate. If minerals in the water clog these openings, take the head apart. This faceplate comes off when you unscrew the knob, others are secured by screws. Soak the plate overnight in vinegar (its acetic acid dissolves minerals), then scrub. If the head clogs often, replace it with one that has a nonclogging plastic faceplate, or install a water softener.

COLD-WATER FAUCET
DIVERTER VALVE
HOT-WATER FAUCET
TUB SPOUT

TO SHOWER HEAD
VALVE-STEM
PLUNGER
HOT WATER
COLD WATER
TO TUB SPOUT
VALVE STEM

A tub-shower diverter valve

Turning the valve stem of this diverter valve clockwise moves a stem plunger forward, closing the pipe to the tub spout and admitting water to the hollow housing. The water runs through the housing hole to the shower head (arrow). When the stem is turned counterclockwise, the plunger closes the housing and opens the spout pipe.

Connections for tub and shower

The faucets and pipes of a tub and shower (above) are generally set behind a wall (not shown); details of the system are explained on this page. A tub's drain system is shown below; its mechanism and maintenance are discussed opposite.

DRAIN HANDLE
OVERFLOW PLATE
DRAIN

KNOB
GATE   PORT

A tub-spout diverter

The less complex but equally efficient tub-spout diverter consists of a gate that is raised or lowered by a knob on the spout. When the knob is down, water will flow through two ports (only one is shown), over the gate and out the tub spout. Raising the knob-and-gate unit seals the ports, forcing water up to the shower head.

A pop-up bathtub drain

The handle of a pop-up drain compresses or releases a spring to control the stopper. Turning the handle to the right compresses the spring and exerts pressure on one end of a rocker linkage; the other end of the rocker moves the stopper upward. Flipping the handle to the left releases the spring to let the stopper drop.

TUB WALL

OVERFLOW PLATE

HANDLE

OVERFLOW TUBE

SPRING

STOPPER

DRAIN

ROCKER LINKAGE

TUB WALL

OVERFLOW PLATE

HANDLE

LINKAGE

OVERFLOW TUBE

PLUNGER

DRAIN

A trip-lever drain

Pressing down the handle of this trip-lever drain raises a linkage and a hollow plunger inside the overflow tube to open the drain. Raising the handle drops the base of the plunger into the drain to close it off. Water in the tub that rises to the overflow plate flows down the overflow tube, through the hollow plunger and down the drain.

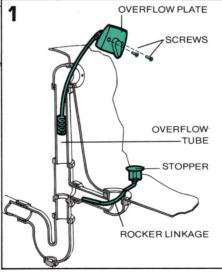

1 OVERFLOW PLATE
SCREWS
OVERFLOW TUBE
STOPPER
ROCKER LINKAGE

2 DRAIN AND TRAP AUGER
OVERFLOW TUBE
TRAP

1 Getting at a clogged drain

Whenever you must use an auger (page 91) on a tub drain, start by unscrewing the overflow plate. If the tub has a trip-lever or rubber-stopper drain, you are ready to go to work. If it has a pop-up drain (above), you must draw out the stopper and its linkage to avoid blocking the auger. Note the lineup of stopper and linkage so that you can replace them correctly.

2 Clearing the drain

Run a drain and trap auger down the overflow tube. (Important: If you have difficulty in making the auger turn the angles of the drain trap, do not try to force it through. Pull the auger back slightly, then push it forward again, turning it by its handle as you work it forward around the bend.) To complete the job, follow the instructions for unclogging a drain, given on page 91.

Tub-Shower Faucets

Tub and shower faucets are repaired the same way as sink faucets—but with a special trick. First turn on the faucets to see if there are any leaks around the stems; you may have to replace packing or O-rings *(page 75)*. If the stems do not leak but the tub spout or shower head drips, shut off the water.

Then, if you have stem faucets, you must replace their washers and, if necessary, their seats *(pages 72-74)*.

The trick is loosening the bonnet, a housing that screws into the faucet body behind the wall and encloses much of the stem assembly. To get a bonnet out, you may need a socket wrench *(page 48)*. Ball-type faucets *(page 77)* and cartridge faucets *(opposite, below)* are simpler; they slide out of the wall.

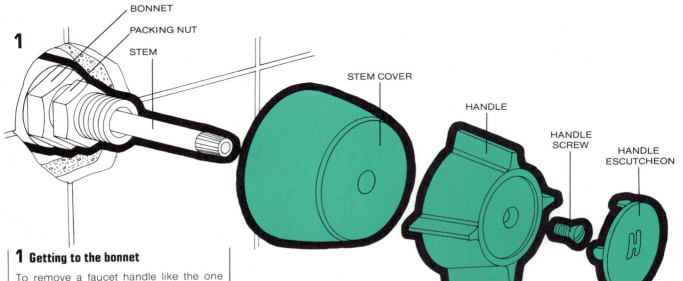

1

1 Getting to the bonnet

To remove a faucet handle like the one above, pry off the handle escutcheon with a screwdriver and unfasten the handle screw; other handles may be secured differently *(page 72)*. You can unscrew the stem cover to remove it. If the bonnet is encased in plaster or cement, chip this material away carefully with a hammer and chisel, clearing the bonnet on all sides to make room for the socket wrench.

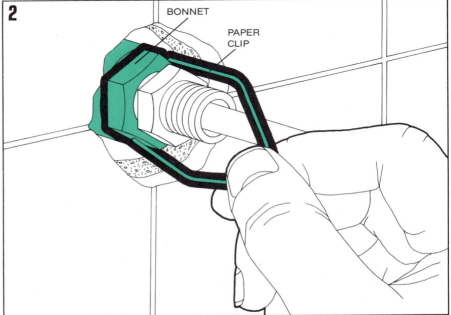

2 Measuring for a socket wrench

When you have to use a plumber's socket wrench to remove the bonnet of a stem faucet, you should consider renting a set or even an individual socket, for this is the only job in which you are likely to need this tool. Determine the size of the socket in the following way. Unbend a paper clip and place its ends on opposite sides of the bonnet, as shown at right. Compress the clip until it firmly holds the correct size; apply the clip several times to be certain it is not changing its shape. Take the clip to a plumbing supply store to use in selecting a socket.

3 Removing the stem assembly

The socket wrench should fit snugly over the bonnet. To get leverage in turning the wrench, slip a metal bar through holes at the outer end. If the end of the faucet stem extends as far as these holes, the bar cannot be used; in this case, grip the socket wrench with the jaws of a pipe wrench, and use the pipe wrench as the turning bar. The bonnet and the stem assembly will come out of the faucet body together.

4 Repairing the faucet

Proceed as you would with the faucet of a kitchen sink. Replace the worn-out washer (pages 72-73) and, if necessary, dress or replace the faucet seat (page 74). To loosen a packing nut, hold the bonnet with a pipe wrench and use an adjustable wrench on the nut. If the bonnet gasket is worn or broken, replace it with wicking (page 62). When you have replaced the bonnet, you should smooth plaster into the space between it and the wall to prevent shower water from seeping into the wall.

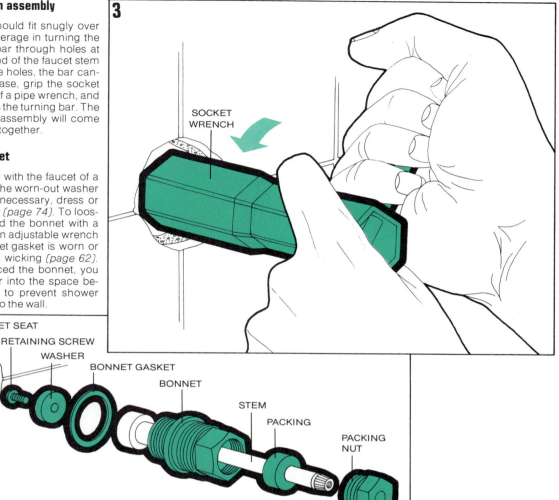

Repairing a cartridge faucet

Many modern tub and shower faucets are equipped with cartridges rather than conventional stems. To change these cartridges, follow exactly the same steps as with single-lever sink faucets (pages 76-79). For example, with the sleeve-cartridge faucet at right, remove the handle screw with a screwdriver, and slip off the handle and collar. Use pliers to pull off the retainer clip and draw out the cartridge. To get the right replacement, take the old cartridge to the plumbing supply store.

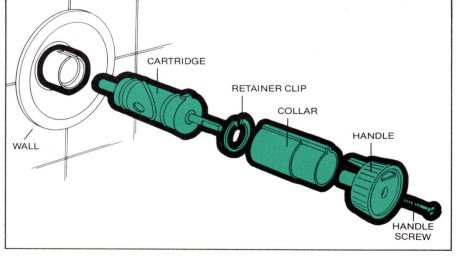

95

TOILETS: NEW AND OLD

Over the centuries, the extraordinary automatic device called the flush toilet has been invented and reinvented many times. In the 1400s, Leonardo da Vinci designed one that worked, at least on paper; and in 1596, Queen Elizabeth I had one in her palace at Richmond, complete with flushing and overflow pipes, a bowl valve and a drain trap. The toilet was first patented in England in 1775, appeared in the New World in the 1840s, and has since been standard in American plumbing.

In all versions, ancient and modern, the working principle is the same. Tripping a single lever sets in motion a series of actions. Water, generally from a tank, is suddenly released to swirl through the bowl into the waste line through a water-filled drain trap. Then the tank automatically shuts itself off from the bowl and begins to refill. When the tank is full, another automatic process shuts off the incoming water—and the cycle is complete.

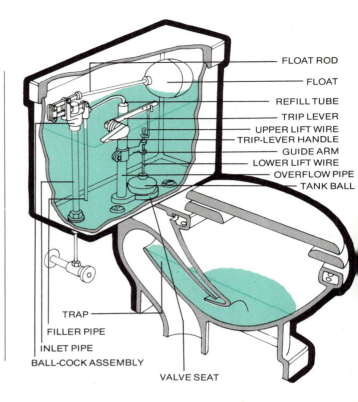

FLOAT ROD
FLOAT
REFILL TUBE
TRIP LEVER
UPPER LIFT WIRE
TRIP-LEVER HANDLE
GUIDE ARM
LOWER LIFT WIRE
OVERFLOW PIPE
TANK BALL

TRAP
FILLER PIPE
INLET PIPE
BALL-COCK ASSEMBLY
VALVE SEAT

Troubleshooting Tank Toilets

Problem	Possible Causes	Solution
Water runs continuously into bowl	Tank ball not seating properly Ball worn Valve seat needs cleaning Float or float rod faulty Ball cock leaking	Align lift wires and guide arm *(page 98)* Replace ball *(page 98)* Scour valve seat with steel wool *(page 98)* Replace float or bend rod down *(page 98)* Replace washers, packing or entire ball cock *(page 99)*
Inadequate flushing	Low water level in tank Ball seats too soon Bowl ports clogged	Bend float rod up *(page 98)* Replace ball or raise guide arm *(page 98)* Ream ports with brush or looped wire
Condensation on tank	Water runs constantly through tank House water unusually cold	Same as for first problem, above Insulate inside of tank with prepackaged sheets, available at plumbing-supply outlets
Water leaking outside from tank or bowl	Inlet-pipe gasket faulty Tank-and-bowl connection is bad Faulty seal between bowl and waste line	Replace gasket *(page 99)* Call a plumber Call a plumber

Parts of a toilet

A few simple mechanisms make a toilet work. The trip lever starts the flush cycle. A valve, opened and closed by the tank ball and its lift wires, releases water to the bowl. The float and its float rod control the ball-cock assembly, which both refills the tank through the filler pipe and adds water to the bowl through the refill tube. Fresh water enters the tank through the inlet pipe.

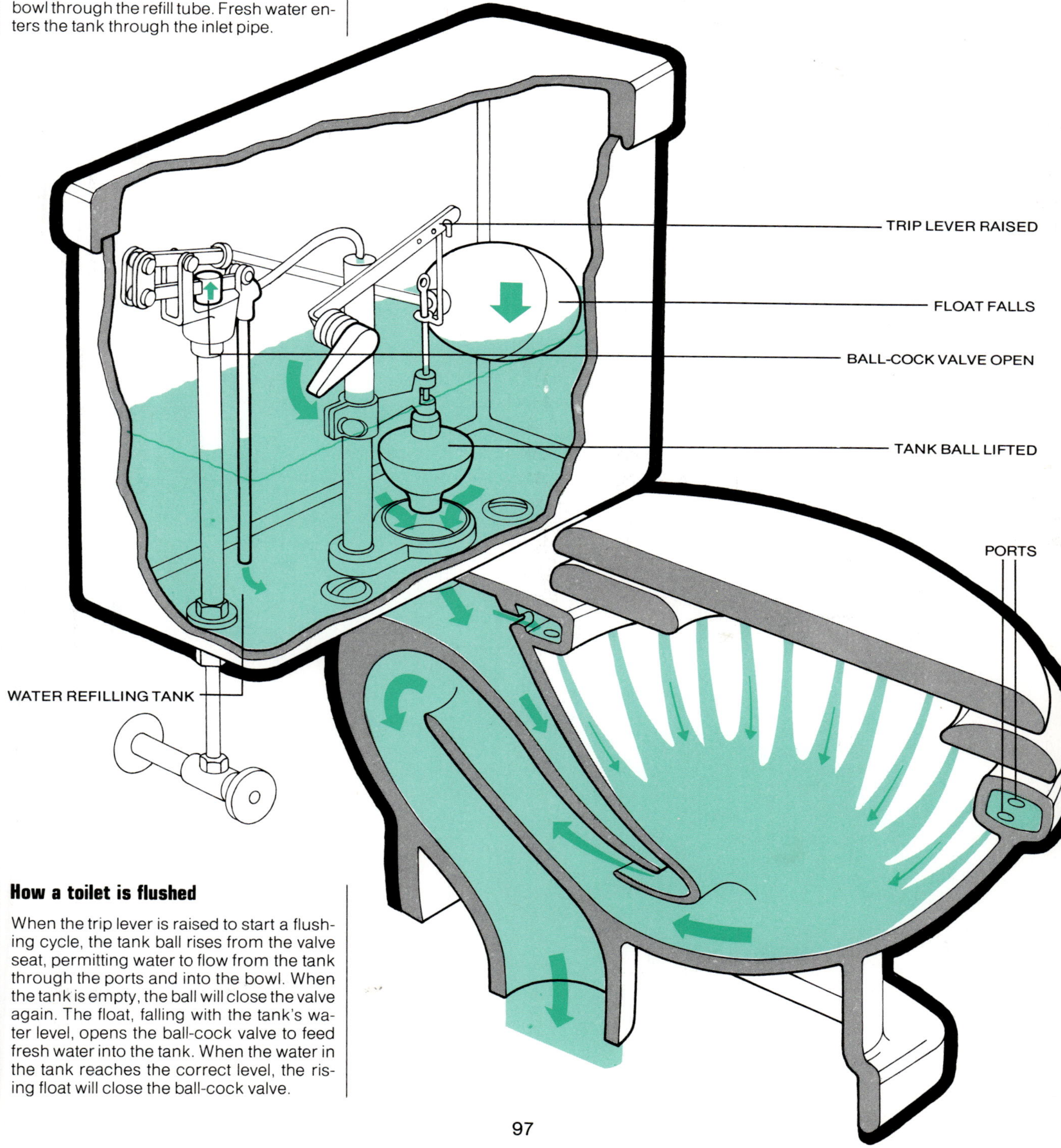

TRIP LEVER RAISED

FLOAT FALLS

BALL-COCK VALVE OPEN

TANK BALL LIFTED

PORTS

WATER REFILLING TANK

How a toilet is flushed

When the trip lever is raised to start a flushing cycle, the tank ball rises from the valve seat, permitting water to flow from the tank through the ports and into the bowl. When the tank is empty, the ball will close the valve again. The float, falling with the tank's water level, opens the ball-cock valve to feed fresh water into the tank. When the water in the tank reaches the correct level, the rising float will close the ball-cock valve.

Tank Repairs

The most common of all tank-toilet troubles is the running toilet: water leaks noisily and steadily into the bowl. To find the cause, lift the tank lid. If the water level is two or more inches below the top of the overflow pipe, the flush valve is not working properly; if water is spilling into the overflow pipe, the trouble must be in the float mechanism or in the intake valve of the ball-cock assembly.

You can make most tank repairs very easily, often without using tools. Even a leaky ball cock, the most complex component, usually needs only a new washer or leather packing, which you can buy in most hardware and all plumbing supply stores. A badly worn ball cock, however, will continue to leak and a broken one spurts water. Then you must replace the entire ball cock. In doing so, consider substituting the quiet, up-to-date model described at far right.

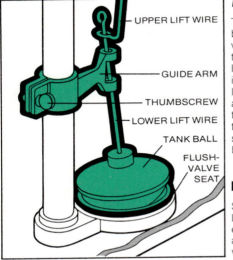

UPPER LIFT WIRE

GUIDE ARM

THUMBSCREW

LOWER LIFT WIRE

TANK BALL

FLUSH-VALVE SEAT

Aligning a tank ball

The most likely cause of a tank leak is a tank ball that does not fit snugly into the flush-valve seat *(left)*. Shut off the water supply, then flush the toilet and watch the ball drop. If the guide arm is askew so that the ball and its lift wires do not line up over the seat, loosen the thumbscrew that secures the arm, reposition the arm over the center of the seat and tighten the screw. If you see that one or both of the lift wires are bent, straighten gently with your fingers. If the ball is misshapen or badly worn, replace it.

Replacing a tank ball

Shut off the water supply and flush the toilet, then unscrew the ball from the threaded end of the lower lift wire *(right)*. Scrub all scum from the valve-seat rim with steel wool, then screw the new ball onto the wire.

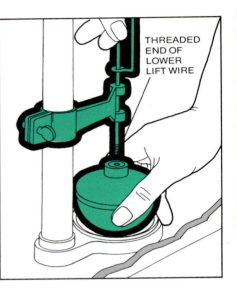

THREADED END OF LOWER LIFT WIRE

Adjusting a float mechanism

Water often runs into an overflow pipe because the float mechanism that controls the tank's water level fails to close the intake valve. Raise the float slightly with your hand. If the water still runs, the trouble is in the intake valve itself *(opposite);* if the flow stops, the fault is in the float.

To get the float to turn off the water flow at the proper point, bend the float rod down slightly with your fingers *(right)*. Flush the toilet; if you have bent the rod too far, water will stop running into the tank before it reaches the correct level, which is about one half inch below the top of the overflow pipe. In this case, bend the float rod upward; adjust it until the water stops running at exactly the right level.

While you are working on the float, check it for leaks. Shut off the water supply, flush the toilet, and unscrew the float from the float rod. Shake the float to see if it contains water; if it does, replace it.

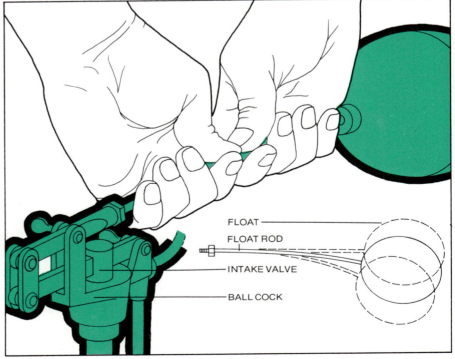

FLOAT

FLOAT ROD

INTAKE VALVE

BALL COCK

Repairing a ball cock

A ball-cock valve may leak when its plunger *(below)* needs a new washer or leather packing. Shut off the water supply and flush the toilet. Unfasten the two L-shaped thumbscrews with your fingers to remove the float mechanism and plunger. Slide the plunger off the lever. Remove the washer from the bottom of the plunger, then pull the leather packing from its groove. Install new parts and reassemble the unit.

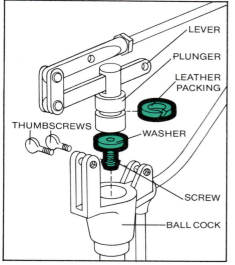

LEVER
PLUNGER
LEATHER PACKING
THUMBSCREWS
WASHER
SCREW
BALL COCK

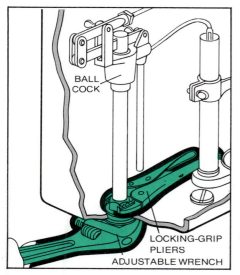

BALL COCK
LOCKING-GRIP PLIERS
ADJUSTABLE WRENCH

Replacing a ball cock

Shut off the water, flush the toilet, and unscrew the slip nut under the tank *(right)*. Hold the ball cock at its base with locking-grip pliers, then unscrew the locknut under the tank *(above)*. Pull out the ball cock, and reverse the procedure to install a new one.

BALL-COCK-VALVE ASSEMBLY

WATER-LEVEL LINE

SHANK

SHANK INLET SECTION

HEX NUT

SHANK BASE

INLET-PIPE GASKET

TANK HOLE

LOCKNUT

SLIP NUT

A new type of ball cock

The improved ball cock at left eliminates the most common cause of leakage by replacing the washer and packing with a two-section shank and a diaphragm valve stopper whose operation is diagramed in the cross sections below. The valve is closed by the pressure of the lever against a plunger and rubber diaphragm *(top)*. Flushing the toilet releases this pressure *(center)*, and water flows up the shank inlet section *(arrows)*, past a rubber vacuum-breaker seal, through ports into the shank filler section. If water pressure drops suddenly, the pressure drop in the inlet pipe sucks the seal against the ports *(bottom)*, preventing back-siphonage *(page 45)*.

When installing this or any other ball cock, screw the locknut slowly and carefully. Otherwise you may chip the vitreous china of which the tank is made.

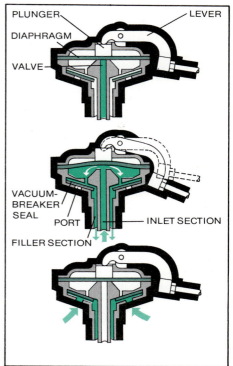

PLUNGER
LEVER
DIAPHRAGM
VALVE

VACUUM-BREAKER SEAL
PORT
INLET SECTION
FILLER SECTION

Two New Tank Parts

Though most flush toilets use conventional tank components, certain new designs work more quickly, quietly and efficiently than their older counterparts. Typical of such newer mechanisms are the ball cock and the flush valve on this page; they contain fewer moving parts and are especially easy to adjust and repair. The ball cock, made mainly of lightweight stainless steel and plastic, opens and closes the intake valve without a float and its tricky mechanism. The flush valve, called a flapper, replaces the tank ball; it works without a guide arm or lift wires.

An easy valve to work on

The intake valve of the new ball-cock unit is easily disassembled for cleaning or for replacement of the seals if the valve leaks. Pull off the snap ring to remove the cap. Pry the upper seal out of the cap and separate its sections for cleaning. Pull the lower seal from under the valve seat. Replacements for both seals come in a single repair kit.

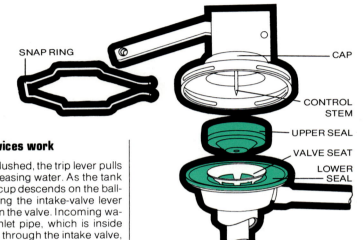

SNAP RING — CAP — CONTROL STEM — UPPER SEAL — VALVE SEAT — LOWER SEAL

The main parts of new tank devices

When the tank is full, the float cup of this new-style ball cock rests on the ball-cock shank, buoyed at the proper level by water in the upper part of the cup and a pocket of air underneath. Water level is adjusted by pinching the spring clip and moving the cup up or down the shank. Atop the shank is the intake valve, linked to the cup by a pull rod. A flapper, clipped on the overflow tube, seals the flush-valve opening.

How the new devices work

When the toilet is flushed, the trip lever pulls the flapper up, releasing water. As the tank empties, the float cup descends on the ball-cock shank, pulling the intake-valve lever downward to open the valve. Incoming water flows up the inlet pipe, which is inside the hollow shank, through the intake valve, and out the bottom of the shank (arrows) The float cup rises again as the flapper reseats and the tank refills.

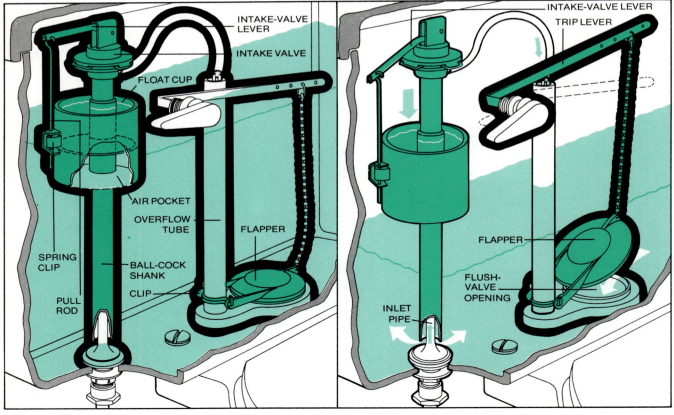

INTAKE-VALVE LEVER — INTAKE VALVE — FLOAT CUP — AIR POCKET — OVERFLOW TUBE — FLAPPER — SPRING CLIP — BALL-COCK SHANK — CLIP — PULL ROD

INTAKE-VALVE LEVER — TRIP LEVER — FLAPPER — FLUSH-VALVE OPENING — INLET PIPE

Unclogging Toilets

The trap of a toilet bowl is especially vulnerable to clogging. One object or another—a toilet article, toy, rag or whatever—falls or is tossed into the bowl. Flushing the toilet then forces the object into the trap and wedges it there, clogging the drain.

The remedy is generally simple. Bail excess water out of the bowl with a pan or a small pail. Then, wearing a rubber glove, reach into the trap through the outlet and pull out the object. If you cannot dislodge it, use the procedures below.

1 Using a plunger

Set the plunger's rubber cup over the outlet opening, press the handle down slowly, then pull it up quickly *(arrows)*. Repeat the process for about two minutes, then remove the plunger and pour water into the bowl. If the water level does not rise excessively, the trap may already be clear; test by flushing the toilet. If the water still backs up, do not use the plunger again; instead, bail out the excess water as before and proceed to step 2.

2 Using an auger

A toilet auger consists of a cable encased in a tubular shaft and ending in a coil. Insert the curved end into the outlet opening and crank the handle to work the cable into the trap. When the coil bites into the clog, try to draw out the obstruction without turning the handle. If you fail, crank the coil back and forth to break up the object. Remove the auger and try to flush down a wad of tissue. If it is still clogged, the trouble lies farther along the drain—call a plumber.

Unclogging a wash-down-toilet trap

Unlike the common jet toilet *(bottom)* with its outlet opening at the rear of the bowl, the wash-down toilet has this opening at the front, along with a smaller inlet opening at the rear. When you unclog a wash-down toilet, be sure to apply the plunger or auger to the outlet opening—located at the front of the bowl *(arrow)*.

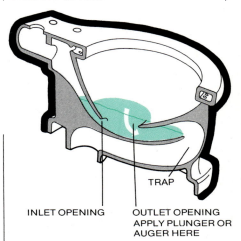

TRAP

INLET OPENING   OUTLET OPENING
APPLY PLUNGER OR
AUGER HERE

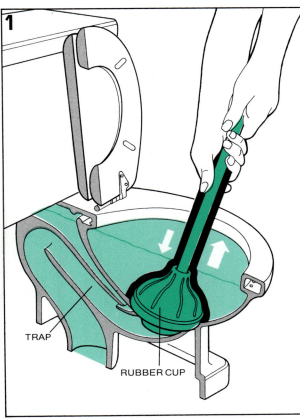

TRAP

RUBBER CUP

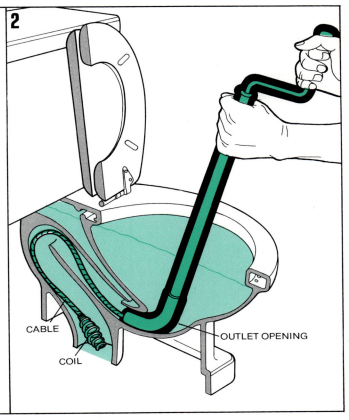

CABLE

COIL

OUTLET OPENING

Pressure Flush Valves

In many apartment houses, toilets have pressure flush valves instead of flush tanks. Hooked up between a water supply line and a toilet bowl, the valve sends water rushing under pressure from line to bowl. A control stop between line and valve regulates the water volume and pressure.

There are two types of pressure valves: the diaphragm *(below)*, relatively simple and easy to service; and the piston *(opposite)*, relatively complex but functional even with water laden with mineral or sediment. Both take little space and use less water than tank toilets. But they are noisy and must be served by water supply lines at least an inch in diameter. Because most single-family homes neither have nor need piping that large, pressure valves are not widely used; however, they are increasingly popular in new homes and in cooperative or condominium apartments.

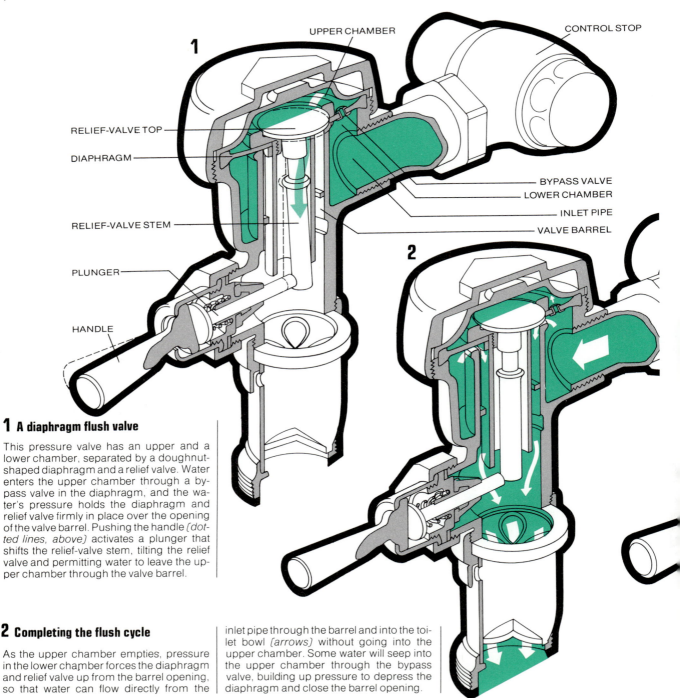

UPPER CHAMBER

CONTROL STOP

1

RELIEF-VALVE TOP

DIAPHRAGM

BYPASS VALVE
LOWER CHAMBER
INLET PIPE
VALVE BARREL

RELIEF-VALVE STEM

2

PLUNGER

HANDLE

1 A diaphragm flush valve

This pressure valve has an upper and a lower chamber, separated by a doughnut-shaped diaphragm and a relief valve. Water enters the upper chamber through a bypass valve in the diaphragm, and the water's pressure holds the diaphragm and relief valve firmly in place over the opening of the valve barrel. Pushing the handle *(dotted lines, above)* activates a plunger that shifts the relief-valve stem, tilting the relief valve and permitting water to leave the upper chamber through the valve barrel.

2 Completing the flush cycle

As the upper chamber empties, pressure in the lower chamber forces the diaphragm and relief valve up from the barrel opening, so that water can flow directly from the inlet pipe through the barrel and into the toilet bowl *(arrows)* without going into the upper chamber. Some water will seep into the upper chamber through the bypass valve, building up pressure to depress the diaphragm and close the barrel opening.

A piston flush valve

In the piston valve *(below)*, the two chambers are separated by a rubber cup that extends down inside a hollow piston; the bypass valve is located on the piston's side, and the relief valve seals the upper chamber from the lower one at the piston's bottom. When the handle plunger pushes against the relief-valve stem, the valve tilts momentarily, releasing water from the upper chamber. The water pressure above the relief valve drops, and high-pressure water from the inlet pipe forces the piston assembly up from the lower chamber.

Water will flow from the inlet pipe down the lower chamber until the smaller stream flowing through the bypass valve restores pressure inside the piston and forces the piston assembly down again.

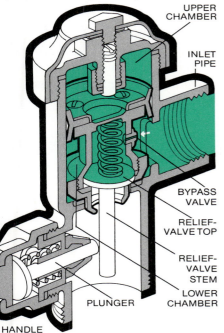

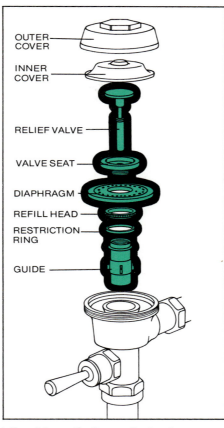

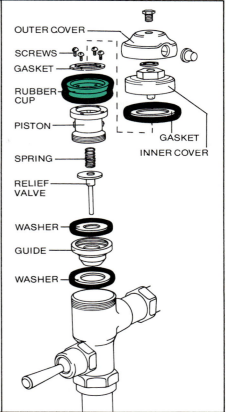

Repairing a diaphragm flush valve

Replacements for the relief valve, seat, diaphragm and guide assembly (guide, refill head and restriction ring) can be bought individually or in a single kit. Shut off the water supply, unscrew the outer cover from the valve top, take off the inner cover, then lift out the relief valve, seat, diaphragm and guide assembly as a unit. Replace worn parts. Reassemble the valve.

Repairing a piston flush valve

Only the rubber cup is replaceable. Shut off the water supply, unscrew the nut on the outer cover and remove the cover, then unscrew the inner cover from the valve top. Lift the entire assembly (gasket, cup, piston, spring, relief valve, guide and washers) out of the valve. Remove the screws holding the gasket and cup to the piston top. Install a new cup. Reassemble the valve.

Replacing the handle parts

To stop a leak at a pressure-valve handle, replace either the seal or the entire plunger unit, consisting of a plunger, spring, bushing, seal and gasket *(right)*. Remove the handle by unscrewing the coupling, and unscrew the plunger unit from the socket. Pull the seal from the plunger and substitute new parts.

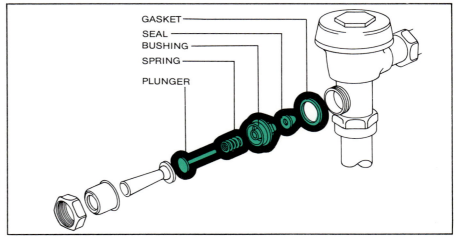

103

Independent Plumbing Systems

Not many years ago, outdoor plumbing was a term of derision. To city dwellers, served by municipal water and sewer lines, the phrase stood for the discomfort and inconvenience symbolized by two familiar sights in rural America: the long-handled well pump and the wooden privy. It was easy to ridicule a way of life in which water was toted inside in a bucket and wastes were dumped outside in a pit.

Today, more than 40 million Americans have their own private water supplies, and some 50 million use private waste-disposal systems—but no one jokes about these people or their way of life. For their homes have plumbing systems as sanitary and efficient as any home tied into a municipal system.

The outdoor plumbing is there, but it defies detection by the casual observer. The noisy, picturesque hand pump has been replaced by a quiet, unobtrusive automatic pump that may be concealed deep underwater in the well itself. The privy has given way to a septic tank and drainage field so well buried that even the homeowner sometimes has difficulty in locating them for inspection and maintenance. And independent plumbing systems—that is, systems lacking one or both of the customary municipal water and sewage connections—serve not only farm and country homes but many suburbs in which the development of new residential subdivisions has outstripped the extension of municipal lines. About 25 per cent of the homes now being built in the United States will use independent systems.

The essential element in any independent system is the same today as it was back in the old pump-and-privy days: a convenient and adequate supply of fresh underground water. In fact, plentiful water is more important than ever. Modern plumbing uses water not only for cleaning and cooking but also to flush away wastes—and the water that flushes wastes into a septic tank in the backyard must often come from a private well in the front yard.

Fortunately, there is fresh water under virtually every foot of the earth's surface—about 8.7 million billion tons of it, 97 per cent of the world's available supply. It occurs mainly as groundwater—the technical term for precipitation such as rain and snow that has seeped through the soil to a saturated layer of sand, gravel or broken rock. The top of this saturated zone, called the water table, may lie anywhere from ground level—at the edge of a pond—to several miles below ground.

Wells and water-supply systems

A well penetrates the water table and creates beneath it a space into which the surrounding water will flow in exactly the way that water fills the hole a child digs in wet beach sand. Wells that reach the water table in 25 feet or less are classified as shallow; they represent the practical limit for wells that a homeowner can dig himself with hand tools *(page 109)*. Virtually all deep wells—and many shallow ones —are drilled by professional well drillers with special rigs. They usually drill considerably deeper than the water table to guarantee ample water even when drought or overpumping lowers the table; some professionally drilled wells go down to 1,000 feet.

When the drill hole is deep enough, the well driller lowers welded or coupled lengths of steel or plastic pipe into the hole to form a well casing. The casing prevents the drill hole from caving in and is capped above the ground to protect the well from contamination by floods or vermin. Openings at the bottom of the casing permit water to enter and rise to the level of the surrounding water table; in a sandy area these openings must be screened to prevent sand from abrading submersible-pump parts or clogging the system. The well is completed by pouring a cement called grout between the casing and the drill hole to a depth of at least 10 feet and adding a wide cement seal around the top of the well. The seal prevents waste water and other potential pollutants on the surface from flowing down the outside of the casing directly into the water table.

In many localities, well drillers must provide copies of a "well log" to the well owner and the local government. The log records the location of the well, its depth and diameter, the ground formations penetrated, the water-table depth, the casing length and the potential yield in gallons per minute. Such information is valuable in calculating a well's capability and analyzing problems that may arise in using the well.

Most well problems fall into these areas:
- BACTERIOLOGICAL CONTAMINATION is often caused by the infiltration of sewage water into the water table from nearby disposal systems. This type of contamination is most likely to occur in shallow wells in areas where houses are crowded together. Wells should be tested at least once a year (most local health departments will test water samples submitted to them). Contaminated wells can be treated with chlorine or other chemicals recommended by health authorities, but the source of the contamination should also be found and eliminated.
- EXCESSIVE MINERAL CONTENT may occur when groundwater filtering into the water table carries with it large amounts of dissolved minerals, such as iron, picked up along the way. High concentrations of iron, particularly, can make water look dirty, taste bitter, and leave stains on laundry and fixtures. The remedy is an oxidizing filter.
- HARD WATER, the most common problem with well water, contains excess amounts of calcium and magnesium. These elements combine with soap to form a sticky curd—no long-

er a problem in the laundry, where detergents unaffected by water hardness are now generally used, but still a nuisance in the bathroom. The soaps used for personal cleansing combine with hard water to leave the bathtub "ring." In addition, hard water makes cooked green vegetables shrink and become tough, causes percolators and kettles to develop an internal scale, and leaves deposits on the insides of water heaters and tanks that reduce heating efficiency and thus increase heating costs. A water softener (pages 56-57) removes the calcium and magnesium—but the conventional process, which replaces these elements with sodium, may produce water harmful to patients on low-sodium diets because of heart or kidney disease.

■ ACID WATER, produced by carbon dioxide absorbed from the air or from organic matter in the ground, may corrode metal parts of an independent system, such as a well casing, a pump, a water-storage tank or a hot-water heater. To neutralize acid, you can either add an alkaline substance such as soda ash to the water or pass the water through a filter bed of limestone chips.

■ INSUFFICIENT YIELD may occur in old wells located in areas of heavy usage. Saturated zones of groundwater rarely run dry, but the water table may sometimes drop below the intake screen at the bottom of a well casing, leaving no water to be pumped. Such wells should be either redrilled to greater depths or replaced by new wells in better locations.

A well is only as efficient as the system that brings water to the surface and delivers it to the home. This system consists of a pump and a pressure tank, which function as a single unit even though they may be located some distance apart. The pump brings water up from the well and sends it to the tank; from there,

A Tank that Cannot Waterlog

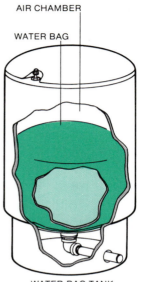

WATER-BAG TANK

The modern pressure tank shown above provides a surprisingly simple solution to the problem of waterlogged tanks—the plague of generations of well owners. As early as 1910, tank manufacturers were producing pressure tanks in which pumped water compressed trapped air; the compressed air then forced stored water through household pipes. The system has a drawback: the water gradually absorbs the air. In this condition, known as waterlogging, water rises nearly to the top of the tank and no air pressure is available to keep water flowing. Until recently, the only cure for waterlogging was draining and recharging the tank with fresh air (page 116).

A preventive instead of a cure is provided by precharged tanks, like the one above. It places an impermeable barrier between the stored water and an air chamber charged with pressurized air. The barrier, actually a tough plastic bag, eliminates waterlogging completely. The water is stored in the bag, which the compressed air squeezes to force water into the house lines.

106

air pressure forces it into the house supply pipes whenever a faucet is turned on, a toilet flushed or a washing machine started.

There are three basic types of pumps (described in detail in the pages that follow):

■ SUBMERSIBLE PUMPS *(pages 110-111)* work deep in the well and force water upward by centrifugal action. These pumps are increasingly popular because of their efficiency, silence and complete invisibility.

■ JET PUMPS *(pages 112-113),* the most widely used type, are operated from the surface and have no moving parts in the well. A jet pump recirculates much of the water it draws, using both centrifugal action and suction.

■ PISTON PUMPS *(pages 114-115),* the direct descendants of the old hand pumps, use suction to draw water from shallow wells, and both suction and pressure to draw water from deep ones. Piston pumps were the first electric pumps in wide use, and many older models still perform effectively.

The pressure tanks into which the well water is pumped use trapped air at pressures usually ranging from 20 to 40 pounds per square inch to force the water into the house plumbing. When the pressure drops to the low end of the range, the pump automatically sends more water into the tank; when the higher pressure is reached, the pump shuts down. In old pressure tanks, the water gradually absorbs the air in a process called waterlogging; these tanks may have valves to add new air or release excess air. Modern tanks eliminate waterlogging and maintain the correct air pressure without valves.

Waste-disposal systems

If today's independent water-supply system has come a long way from grandfather's hand pump and bucket, it can also be said that today's independent sewage-disposal system has come just as far from the privy pit. To dispose of raw sewage, most modern systems use a concealed septic tank and a drainage field. The septic tank, a concrete or metal box, separates raw sewage into three components: sludge, composed of solids that settle to the tank's bottom; scum, made up of grease and other lighter-than-water materials that rise to the surface; and effluent, sewage water that flows out of an opening in the end of the tank and into a system that lets the water seep out into the ground of a drainage field.

The trapped sludge and scum are gradually decomposed by bacterial action in the tank. This decomposition process is never complete, especially when the tank is subject to heavy use; to some extent, the septic tank serves as a storage area for gradually accumulating residues of sludge and scum. Therefore, the sludge and scum levels in the tank must be checked periodically *(page 121),* and the tank must be pumped out by professionals when necessary.

The effluent carried to the drainage field is fairly clear water but still contaminated. In the field—either a pit or perforated pipes buried about a foot underground—the effluent flows through a bed of gravel, which acts as a primary filter for the effluent before it seeps further. After passing through the gravel, some of the water enters the root systems of grass—a lush patch of lawn, nourished by the organic wastes in the effluent, often indicates the location of a drainage field—while the rest of the water is further filtered and purified by natural processes as it slowly seeps through the soil toward the water table.

Though overcrowded and overused sewage-disposal systems may create pollution problems in some locations, the system itself is effective. Normally, the effluent that passes into the water table has been transformed from sewage into fresh, drinkable groundwater.

WATER FROM A WELL

The well is only the beginning of an independent water-supply system—but it is the key element. Its productivity depends upon the underground layers from which it draws water, and these conditions determine the well and pump needed.

If there is a water-saturated layer of sand or gravel within 25 feet of the surface, one of the four relatively inexpensive wells on the opposite page will suffice. If the water-bearing layer lies deep beneath a layer of rock *(below)*, reaching it may require hundreds of feet of drilling. Depth and diameter of a well also determine the pump—submersible, jet or piston—best used *(pages 110-115).*

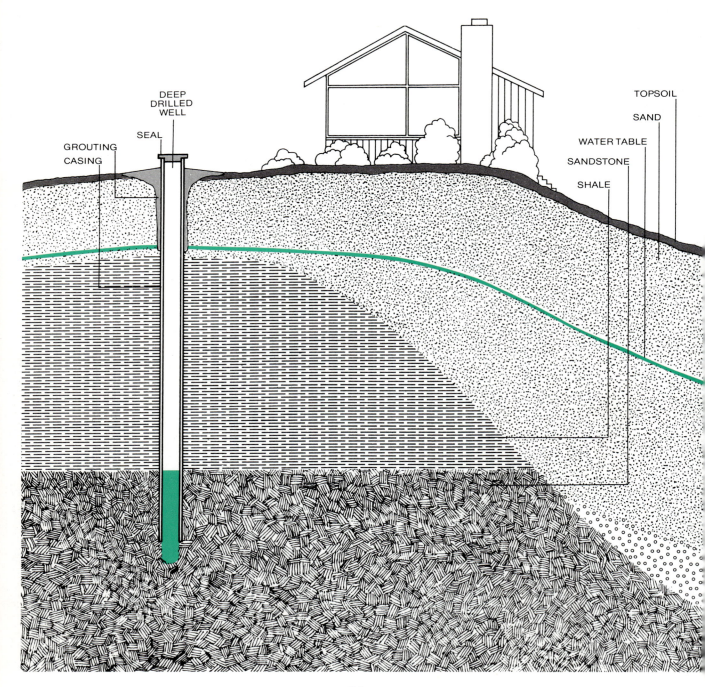

DEEP DRILLED WELL

SEAL

GROUTING

CASING

TOPSOIL

SAND

WATER TABLE

SANDSTONE

SHALE

Five kinds of wells

The geological cross section on these two pages shows the five types of wells in general use in the United States and Canada. (They are not drawn to scale.) When the water table, the uppermost level of groundwater, lies less than 25 feet below the topsoil, and when the formations that are directly below the table yield water readily, one of the four "shallow" wells sketched below will be adequate.

A so-called deep well *(opposite)* is needed when the water table is farther down or when, as in the rock formation shown here, the layer beneath the table consists of a rock such as shale, which absorbs water but does not yield it In this example, the well has been drilled through the shale into a deeper layer of water-bearing sandstone. Both the deep drilled well opposite and the shallow drilled well at far right require professional drilling equipment; they are expensive but reliable.

The other three wells, all shallow, can be constructed by using comparatively simple tools. The old-fashioned dug well, for example, calls for little more than a pick and shovel to dig the shaft, and a bucket and rope to lift out dirt—but the well cannot be dug more than a few feet below the water table; if the table drops, the well runs dry. The narrow (and therefore low-yield) driven well, especially suitable for sandy soils, consists of a series of pipes fitted to a drive point and coupled in succession as they are hammered into the ground. The bored well, often equipped with a sharp well point, is twisted into the ground with a hand or powered auger; it rivals the drilled well in dependability, but cannot be sunk through rock formations. Except for the driven well which consists solely of its own coupled pipes, all of these wells contain certain basic components. To protect against collapse, there are metal, masonry, ceramic or plastic casings; to prevent contamination from the surface, cement grouting fills the space around the upper part of the casings and the well openings are sealed.

The four shallow wells also contain devices for keeping out sand: a screen for the shallow drilled well, points that incorporate screens for the bored and driven wells, and a bed of crushed rock for the dug well. The deep drilled well needs no filter since it draws water from a rock formation.

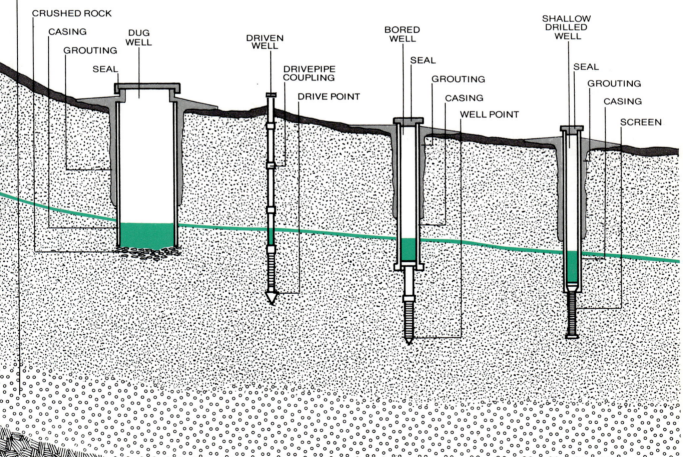

Submersible Pumps

The compact, ingenious submersible pump pushes water upward from a point deep in a well rather than pulling it up the way a suction pump does. This type, operating unseen, unheard and virtually without maintenance (cooling is provided by the well water in which the pump is submerged), is fast becoming the one most commonly installed for home wells. However, the popularity of the submersible pump is relatively recent, because it was not orginally designed for residential use. After decades of development for mines and oil wells, it was adapted to house water systems only in the late 1940s.

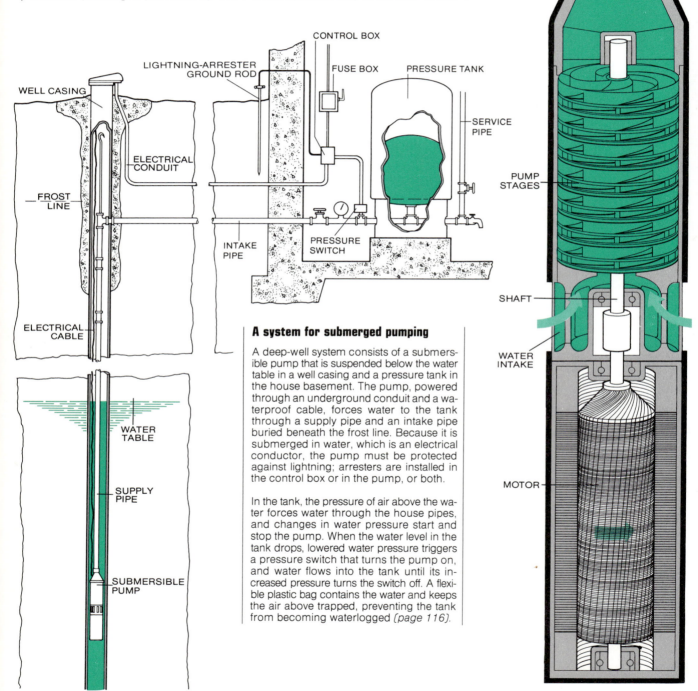

OUTLET TO SUPPLY PIPE

CONTROL BOX

LIGHTNING-ARRESTER GROUND ROD

FUSE BOX

PRESSURE TANK

WELL CASING

ELECTRICAL CONDUIT

SERVICE PIPE

FROST LINE

PUMP STAGES

ELECTRICAL CABLE

INTAKE PIPE

PRESSURE SWITCH

SHAFT

WATER INTAKE

WATER TABLE

SUPPLY PIPE

MOTOR

SUBMERSIBLE PUMP

A system for submerged pumping

A deep-well system consists of a submersible pump that is suspended below the water table in a well casing and a pressure tank in the house basement. The pump, powered through an underground conduit and a waterproof cable, forces water to the tank through a supply pipe and an intake pipe buried beneath the frost line. Because it is submerged in water, which is an electrical conductor, the pump must be protected against lightning; arresters are installed in the control box or in the pump, or both.

In the tank, the pressure of air above the water forces water through the house pipes, and changes in water pressure start and stop the pump. When the water level in the tank drops, lowered water pressure triggers a pressure switch that turns the pump on, and water flows into the tank until its increased pressure turns the switch off. A flexible plastic bag contains the water and keeps the air above trapped, preventing the tank from becoming waterlogged [page 116].

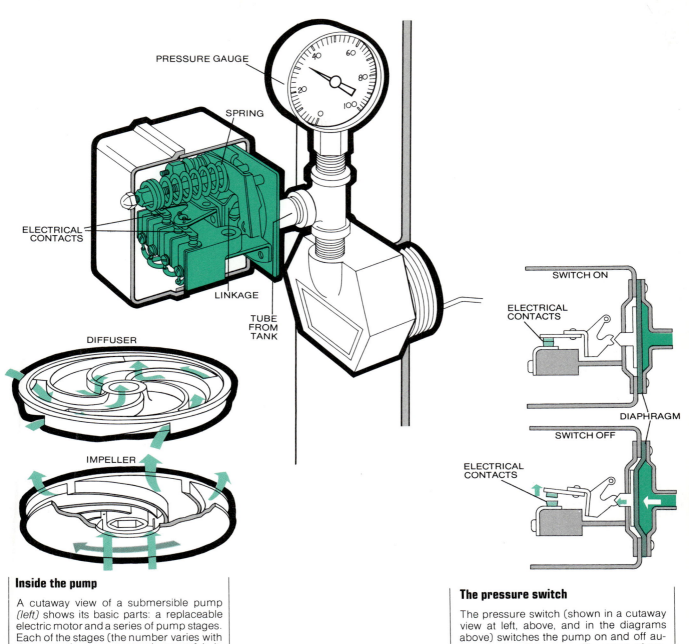

PRESSURE GAUGE

SPRING

ELECTRICAL
CONTACTS

LINKAGE

TUBE
FROM
TANK

DIFFUSER

IMPELLER

SWITCH ON

ELECTRICAL
CONTACTS

DIAPHRAGM

SWITCH OFF

ELECTRICAL
CONTACTS

Inside the pump

A cutaway view of a submersible pump
(left) shows its basic parts: a replaceable
electric motor and a series of pump stages.
Each of the stages (the number varies with
the system's pressure requirements) is itself a miniature pump. As shown in the
exploded view of a single stage *(above)*,
water enters the bottom of an impeller-
diffuser unit. It flows through the center of
the rapidly rotating impeller, is flung outward by the impeller blades, and passes directly into the stationary diffuser at its rim.
The diffuser baffles direct the water toward
the center, increasing its pressure and converting it into a single stream that enters the
center of the next impeller. As the water
moves outward, inward and upward, each
stage successively increases its pressure
until it eventually passes into the supply
pipe at the correct pressure level.

The pressure switch

The pressure switch (shown in a cutaway
view at left, above, and in the diagrams
above) switches the pump on and off automatically within a specific range of water pressure, usually 20 to 40 pounds per
square inch. Water from the storage tank
reaches the switch through a tube and
pushes against a watertight diaphragm inside the switch housing. The diaphragm
exerts pressure on a complex linkage held
in place by an adjustable spring. When
pressure drops to the low point of the pressure range, the spring forces the linkage to
close electrical contacts and start the pump
(above, top). The pump operates until the
upper limit of the range is reached; at that
point, the increased pressure on the diaphragm forces the linkage to open the contacts and stop the pump *(above, bottom)*.

Jet Pumps

The workhorse of private-home well systems is the jet pump, made in designs for either deep or shallow wells. Both types are suction pumps, but the deep-well pump shown on this page at right is the more intricate because it must lift water farther. It gets extra power by recirculating water back into its suction pipe through an ejector unit *(below)*. In this unit a high-velocity stream of the recirculated water acts as a booster, sucking well water up in a powerful flow.

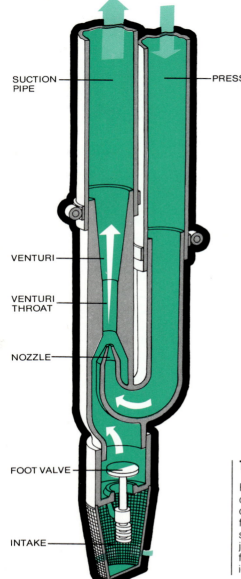

SUCTION PIPE

PRESSURE PIPE

VENTURI

VENTURI THROAT

NOZZLE

FOOT VALVE

INTAKE

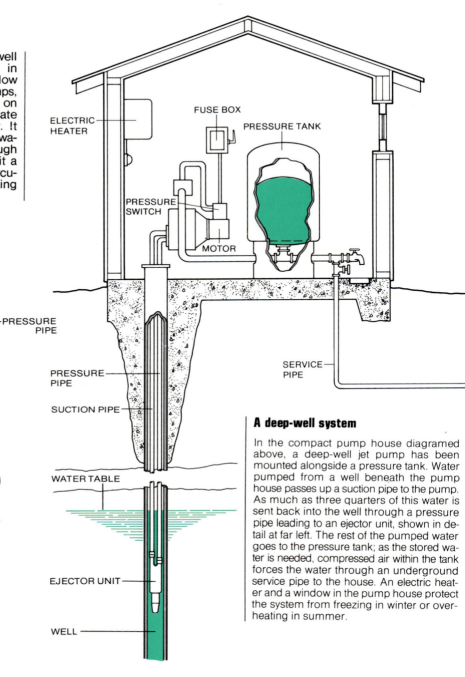

ELECTRIC HEATER

FUSE BOX

PRESSURE TANK

PRESSURE SWITCH

MOTOR

PRESSURE PIPE

SUCTION PIPE

SERVICE PIPE

WATER TABLE

EJECTOR UNIT

WELL

A deep-well system

In the compact pump house diagramed above, a deep-well jet pump has been mounted alongside a pressure tank. Water pumped from a well beneath the pump house passes up a suction pipe to the pump. As much as three quarters of this water is sent back into the well through a pressure pipe leading to an ejector unit, shown in detail at far left. The rest of the pumped water goes to the pressure tank; as the stored water is needed, compressed air within the tank forces the water through an underground service pipe to the house. An electric heater and a window in the pump house protect the system from freezing in winter or overheating in summer.

The deep-well ejector unit

Recirculated and freshly pumped water are combined in the Y-shaped ejector unit of a deep-well jet pump. The recirculated water, forced down the pressure pipe, turns to stream up and out a nozzle in a high-speed jet. As the jet enters the narrow throat of a flared tube called a venturi, the stream rapidly expands, creating a partial vacuum that sucks in well water. (The venturi principle can be observed in an ordinary shower bath; the jets lower pressure in the enclosure, thus sucking in the curtain.)

In the well, water enters the ejector through a screened intake and a foot valve that closes, keeping water in the system when the pump stops. The ejector's reinforcing suction can lift water from a depth of 120 feet.

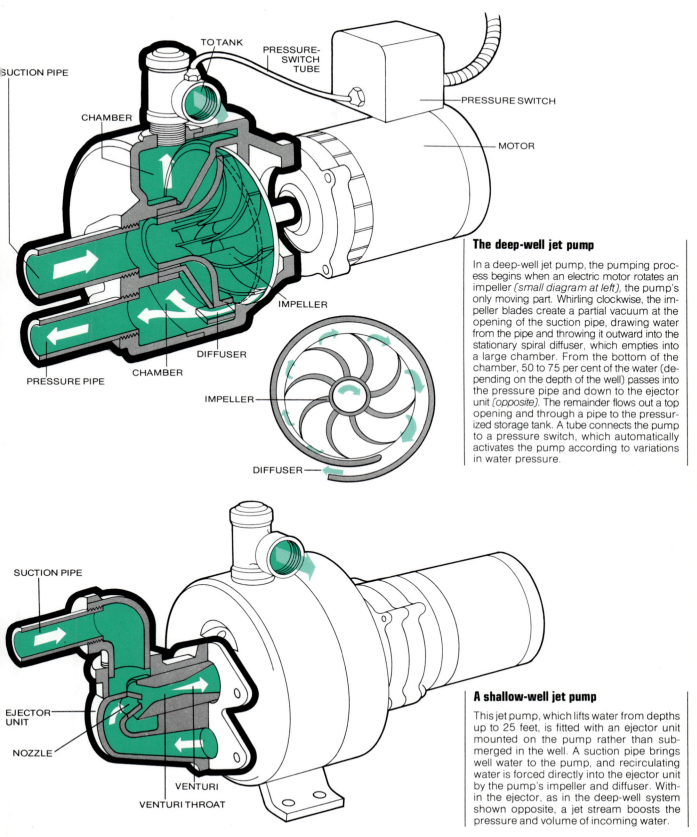

SUCTION PIPE

TO TANK

PRESSURE-SWITCH TUBE

PRESSURE SWITCH

MOTOR

CHAMBER

IMPELLER

DIFFUSER

CHAMBER

PRESSURE PIPE

IMPELLER

DIFFUSER

The deep-well jet pump

In a deep-well jet pump, the pumping process begins when an electric motor rotates an impeller *(small diagram at left)*, the pump's only moving part. Whirling clockwise, the impeller blades create a partial vacuum at the opening of the suction pipe, drawing water from the pipe and throwing it outward into the stationary spiral diffuser, which empties into a large chamber. From the bottom of the chamber, 50 to 75 per cent of the water (depending on the depth of the well) passes into the pressure pipe and down to the ejector unit *(opposite)*. The remainder flows out a top opening and through a pipe to the pressurized storage tank. A tube connects the pump to a pressure switch, which automatically activates the pump according to variations in water pressure.

SUCTION PIPE

EJECTOR UNIT

NOZZLE

VENTURI

VENTURI THROAT

A shallow-well jet pump

This jet pump, which lifts water from depths up to 25 feet, is fitted with an ejector unit mounted on the pump rather than submerged in the well. A suction pipe brings well water to the pump, and recirculating water is forced directly into the ejector unit by the pump's impeller and diffuser. Within the ejector, as in the deep-well system shown opposite, a jet stream boosts the pressure and volume of incoming water.

113

Piston Pumps

The lively veteran of motorized well pumps is the reciprocating piston pump, which became popular in the 1920s. Although many are still chugging away, replacement parts are becoming harder and harder to come by; in many cases, broken piston pumps must be replaced with modern jet pumps. Two types of piston pumps were common. One, for deep wells, pushes water to the surface; the other, for shallow wells, sucks—rather than pushes—the water up.

In a deep-well pump, the motor drives a single-acting piston up and down in a cylinder that is submerged in the well water, alternately sucking water into the cylinder and pushing it up in a powerful surge. In shallow wells, a double-acting piston at ground level simultaneously sucks up and discharges the water.

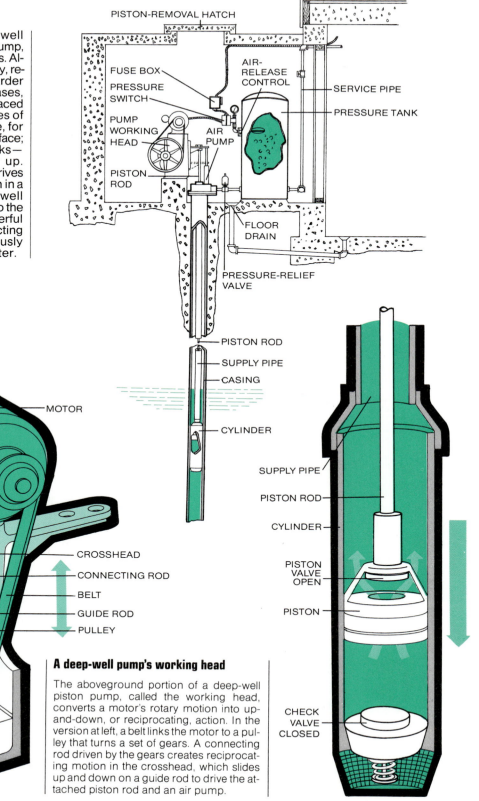

PISTON-REMOVAL HATCH

FUSE BOX

PRESSURE SWITCH

PUMP WORKING HEAD

PISTON ROD

AIR PUMP

AIR-RELEASE CONTROL

SERVICE PIPE

PRESSURE TANK

FLOOR DRAIN

PRESSURE-RELIEF VALVE

PISTON ROD

SUPPLY PIPE

CASING

CYLINDER

MOTOR

CROSSHEAD

CONNECTING ROD

BELT

GUIDE ROD

PULLEY

GEARS

SUPPLY PIPE

PISTON ROD

CYLINDER

PISTON VALVE OPEN

PISTON

CHECK VALVE CLOSED

DOWNSTROKE

A deep-well pump's working head

The aboveground portion of a deep-well piston pump, called the working head, converts a motor's rotary motion into up-and-down, or reciprocating, action. In the version at left, a belt links the motor to a pulley that turns a set of gears. A connecting rod driven by the gears creates reciprocating motion in the crosshead, which slides up and down on a guide rod to drive the attached piston rod and an air pump.

A deep-well piston-pump system

A deep-well piston pump drives a piston rod in a submerged cylinder at about 50 strokes a minute. Water moves up a supply pipe to a pressure tank—here the venerable type in which the air and water are not separated by a physical barrier *(page 110)*—along with air bubbles from an air pump. If excessive pressure builds up, a pressure-relief valve releases water, which goes down a floor drain.

Inside the submerged cylinder

The churnlike single-acting piston makes a downstroke and an upstroke for each delivery of water. When the piston rod forces the piston down in the cylinder *(below, left)*, water pressure closes the cylinder's check valve and opens the piston valve, forcing water into the upper part of the cylinder. On the upstroke *(below)*, the piston valve closes and the trapped water is pushed upward to the tank; at the same time, the piston sucks open the check valve and pulls more water into the lower part of the cylinder.

A shallow-well piston pump

Unlike the deep-well pump on the opposite page, a compact shallow-well piston pump raises water out of a well by suction alone. All the working parts are aboveground. The motor and a short piston rod drive a double-acting piston *(drawings, at bottom)* that both sucks in and discharges water on every stroke.

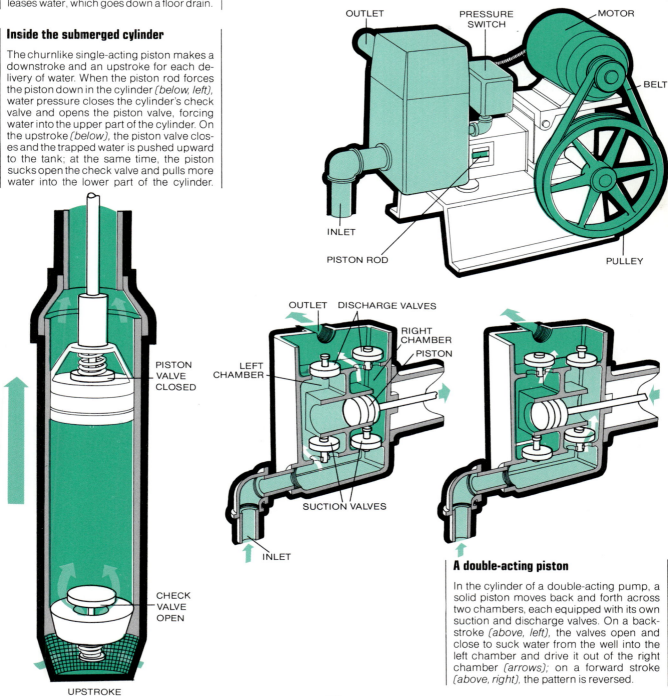

OUTLET PRESSURE SWITCH MOTOR

BELT

INLET

PISTON ROD

PULLEY

PISTON VALVE CLOSED

CHECK VALVE OPEN

UPSTROKE

OUTLET DISCHARGE VALVES

RIGHT CHAMBER

PISTON

LEFT CHAMBER

SUCTION VALVES

INLET

A double-acting piston

In the cylinder of a double-acting pump, a solid piston moves back and forth across two chambers, each equipped with its own suction and discharge valves. On a backstroke *(above, left)*, the valves open and close to suck water from the well into the left chamber and drive it out of the right chamber *(arrows)*; on a forward stroke *(above, right)*, the pattern is reversed.

Fixing Tank or Switch

Home pumping systems will usually provide at least 10 years of trouble-free service—and some last as long as 25 years without a major mishap. Even the most reliable system, however, occasionally fails. Two of the most common problems, malfunctioning pressure switches and waterlogged tanks, can be corrected by the procedures described on this page. Other simple repairs are listed in the chart on the opposite page.

Some troubles may require pulling submerged piping or pumping units from deep in the well; these jobs are best left to a serviceman.

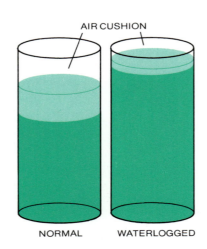

AIR CUSHION

NORMAL   WATERLOGGED

Repressurizing a waterlogged tank

Waterlogging, the absorption of air by water in a single-chambered pressure tank so that the essential air cushion at the top of a tank almost disappears, can be recognized by fluctuating water pressure or the sound of the pump turning on too frequently. The reason is indicated at left: this old-fashioned 42-gallon tank ordinarily delivers about seven gallons of water *(lightly tinted area)* before the falling pressure reactivates the pump. In a waterlogged tank, only a few pints are available and the pump will be starting and stopping almost constantly.

To replace the air cushion, cut off the electricity, then drain the tank by opening the drain valve and a house faucet. Air will enter the tank through the faucet. After the tank is drained, close the valve and faucet, and restart the pump; the air will then be trapped and compressed. If the tank becomes waterlogged often, it has developed an air leak and should be replaced with a modern model *(page 110)*.

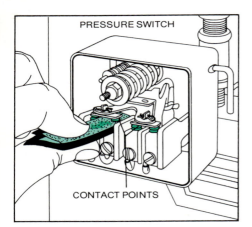

PRESSURE SWITCH

CONTACT POINTS

Cleaning pressure-switch contacts

If a pressure switch *(page 111)* chatters noisily or fails, shut off the electricity, remove the switch cover and check the surface of the contact points. Discoloration or unevenness—pitting—interferes with current flow. In an emergency, rub the points with fine sandpaper *(above)*. If trouble persists, replace the switch *(right)*.

Replacing the pressure switch

Turn off the electricity to the pump and drain the tank. Remove the switch cover, disconnect all wires and pull them out of the switch housing. Unscrew the hex nut behind the switch housing, then remove the switch from its mount. Reverse the procedure to install a new switch.

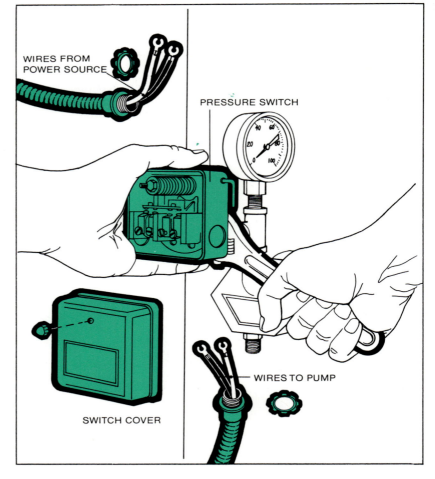

WIRES FROM POWER SOURCE

PRESSURE SWITCH

SWITCH COVER

WIRES TO PUMP

Troubleshooting Water-Supply Systems

Problem	Possible Causes	Solution
Pump will not start	Faulty electrical circuit	Check fuses, switches and wiring; replace worn or damaged components; tighten all connections
	Malfunctioning pressure switch	Clean contact points or replace switch (*opposite*)
	Inoperative pump motor	Have motor repaired or replaced
	Obstruction in tubing to pressure switch	Remove and inspect tubing; clean or replace plugged tubing
	Obstruction in piston- or jet-pump mechanism	Shut off power and turn pump mechanism manually to locate and remove obstruction
Pump will not stop	Incorrect pressure-switch setting	Adjust switch setting
	Defective pressure switch	Replace switch
	Obstruction in tubing to pressure switch	See same cause and its solution, above
	Loss of "prime" (full charge of water from pump to well) in jet or piston pump	Reprime by adding water through priming plug or opening; if problem persists, check valves and suction lines for leakage
Pump starts and stops often	Waterlogged pressure tank	Replace air-volume control; drain and refill tank (*opposite*)
	Malfunctioning pressure switch	Check switch settings and clean or replace switch (*opposite*)
	Air leak in pressure tank	Coat upper tank surface with a film of soapy water; if bubbles form, have leaks repaired or tank replaced
	Leak in house plumbing	Check house outlets, especially faucets and toilets; repair or replace leaky units
Pump motor overheats and shuts down	Inadequate ventilation	Improve ventilation or move pump
	Worn-out motor	Have motor repaired or replaced
	Pump overworked by heavy water consumption	Install more powerful motor
Little or no water	Inadequate prime	Reprime pump (*see above*); if problem persists, check valves and suction lines for leakage
	Inadequate well capacity	Shut off pump until well refills; if possible, extend pump intake to lower level
	Blockage at pump intake	Have pump or intake cleaned
Water spurts from faucets	Excess air in pressure tank	Check air-volume control and have it replaced if necessary
Excessive noise	Worn motor bearings	Grease bearings; if necessary, have motor replaced
	Poor motor mount	Insulate motor from concrete floor with rubber mat or washers
	Sticking valves in piston pumps	Inspect and clean around valves; if they do not close tightly have them replaced

DISPOSAL SYSTEMS

The septic tank and drainage system that make up an independent sewage-disposal unit are generally designed to perform efficiently for 20 years or more—but many of them never reach anything near that age. Instead, they fail prematurely because of overuse or neglect, or both. Yet a few simple precautions will ensure maximum life for either of the two basic arrangements shown on these pages: be sure the septic tank is large enough for household needs; conserve water, which makes up 99 per cent of the material the system must handle; inspect the tank regularly *(page 121)* and clean it out before trouble begins, not after.

A drainage-field system

This cutaway view shows the preferred set-up for independent disposal, in which sewage moves from the house through a pipe to a concrete septic tank for treatment *(page 120)*. Inside the tank, the sewage separates into four components: sludge and scum, which are trapped in the tank; gas, which escapes back through the sewer pipe to the house drain vent; and liquid sewage, called effluent.

The effluent flows through an outlet pipe to a drainage field composed of perforated pipes that are set into gravel *(cross section, bottom left)*. As the effluent trickles from the pipes and seeps down into the earth, its impurities are neutralized.

The chart on the opposite page indicates the capacities of septic tanks that are required for homes of various sizes.

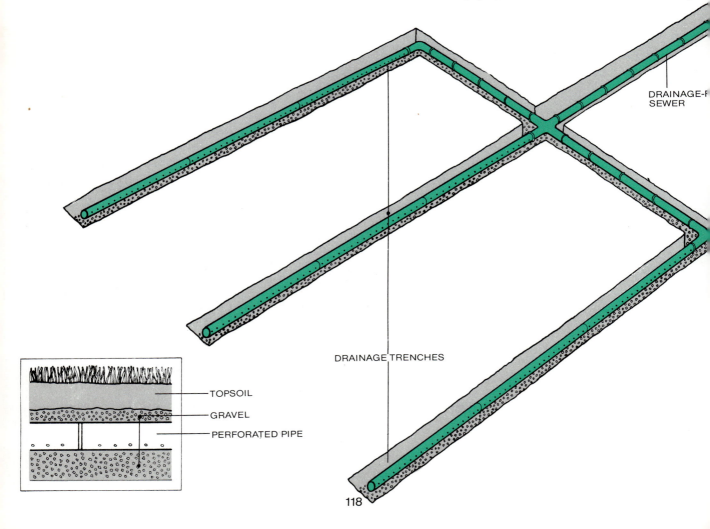

DRAINAGE-F
SEWER

DRAINAGE TRENCHES

TOPSOIL

GRAVEL

PERFORATED PIPE

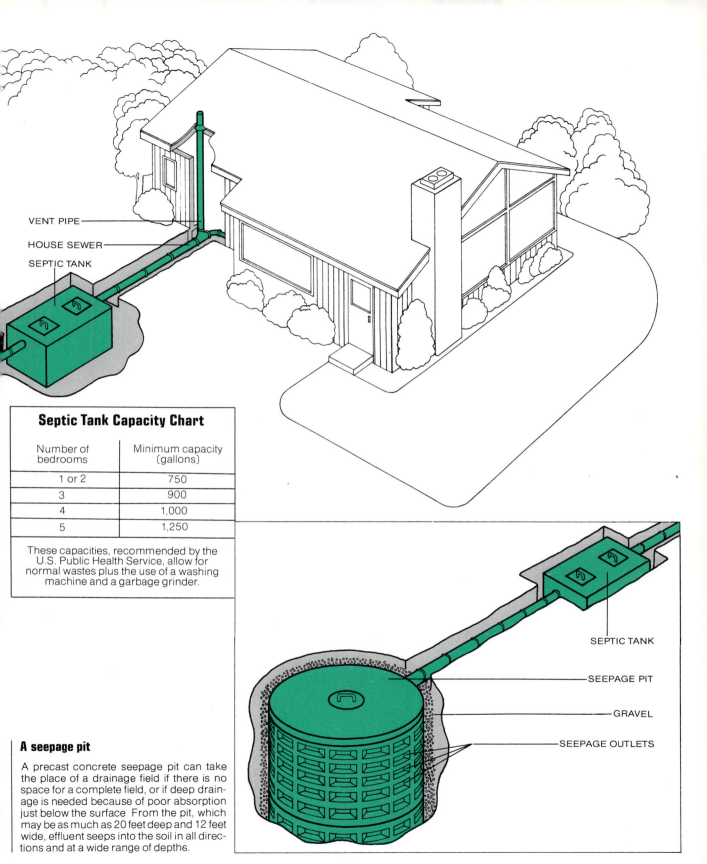

VENT PIPE

HOUSE SEWER

SEPTIC TANK

Septic Tank Capacity Chart

Number of bedrooms	Minimum capacity (gallons)
1 or 2	750
3	900
4	1,000
5	1,250

These capacities, recommended by the U.S. Public Health Service, allow for normal wastes plus the use of a washing machine and a garbage grinder.

SEPTIC TANK

SEEPAGE PIT

GRAVEL

SEEPAGE OUTLETS

A seepage pit

A precast concrete seepage pit can take the place of a drainage field if there is no space for a complete field, or if deep drainage is needed because of poor absorption just below the surface From the pit, which may be as much as 20 feet deep and 12 feet wide, effluent seeps into the soil in all directions and at a wide range of depths.

The Septic Tank

To many homeowners, septic tanks are out of sight and out of mind. Because the buried tank rarely requires maintenance, some people do not bother to place a landmark, such as the birdbath in the drawing below, to pinpoint its location for the time when maintenance is needed.

Though lightly used tanks survive neglect for years, most tanks require cleaning every two or three years to remove the build-ups of sludge and scum. At least once a year, inspect your tank for such build-ups, following the procedures opposite.

The workings of a septic tank

Raw sewage enters a concrete septic tank through a submerged inlet pipe. Within the tank, biochemical action converts some of the sewage solids to liquids and gases. Three levels of sewage result: solids sink to the bottom as sludge, oily substances float to the top as scum, and the remaining liquid, called effluent, fills most of the tank.

When the tank's liquid level rises above the point shown in the drawing, effluent flows through the outlet pipe and on to a drainage field. The covered opening above the outlet pipe enables you to inspect the levels of sludge and scum. The opening at the left is used by a professional tank cleaner to pump out the tank's contents.

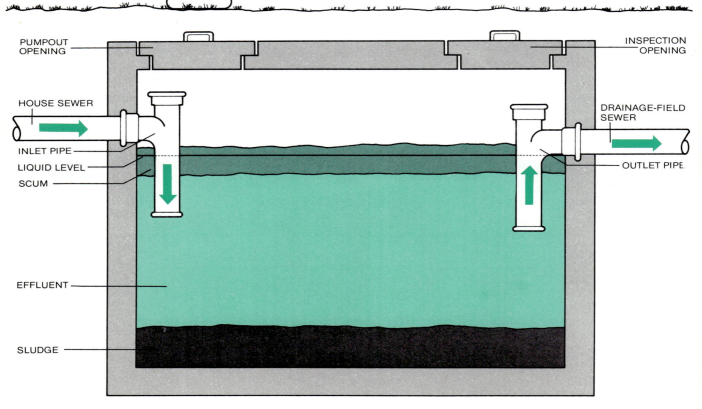

LOCATION MARKER

PUMPOUT OPENING

INSPECTION OPENING

HOUSE SEWER

DRAINAGE-FIELD SEWER

INLET PIPE

LIQUID LEVEL

SCUM

OUTLET PIPE

EFFLUENT

SLUDGE

120

1 Measuring the scum level

Uncover the inspection opening and insert a scum stick—a six-foot pole with a six-inch wooden square or disc secured to its end. Lower the stick deep into the tank, then raise it slowly until you feel resistance from the scum *(below, left)*. Holding the stick at this position, mark point A where the stick is even with the ground.

Lower the stick along the outlet pipe until you feel the end reach the pipe bottom *(below, right)*; mark ground level at B on the stick. If the distance from A to B is three inches or less, the tank requires professional cleaning.

2 Measuring the sludge level

Make a sludge stick: a long pole with white toweling tacked tightly around the lower three feet and a nail driven through the pole near the base. Uncover the inspection opening and lower the stick through the outlet pipe until the nail catches the bottom rim of the pipe. Holding the stick at that level, mark point A on the stick even with the ground. Now lower the stick to the bottom, and mark ground level at B on the stick.

Raise the stick slowly and measure the length of toweling blackened by sludge. Measure the distance between A and B to get the distance from the bottom of the outlet pipe to the bottom of the tank. From this distance, subtract the length of sludge accumulation to determine the distance between the sludge and the outlet pipe.

Finally, determine the depth of the liquid in your tank by measuring the moistened portion of the sludge stick. You can now use the table below to decide if the sludge build-up calls for a tank cleaning.

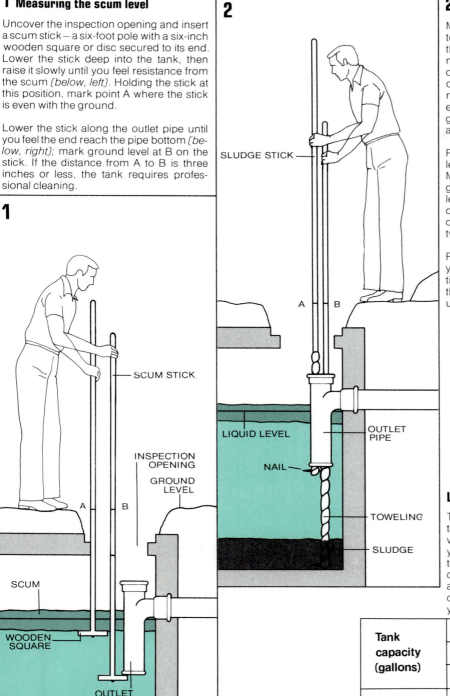

Limits for sludge build-up

This chart indicates the minimum safe distance between sludge and outlet pipe for various tank sizes and liquid levels. Use your septic tank's capacity and liquid level to find the correct minimum in your own case. If the tank's sludge-to-outlet distance, as determined in step 2, is less than the chart figure, then it is time for you to have your tank pumped out.

Tank capacity (gallons)	Tank liquid level		
	3 feet	4 feet	5 feet
	Sludge-to-outlet distance (inches)		
500	11	16	21
600	8	13	18
750	6	10	13
900	4	7	10
1,000	4	6	8

Electricity

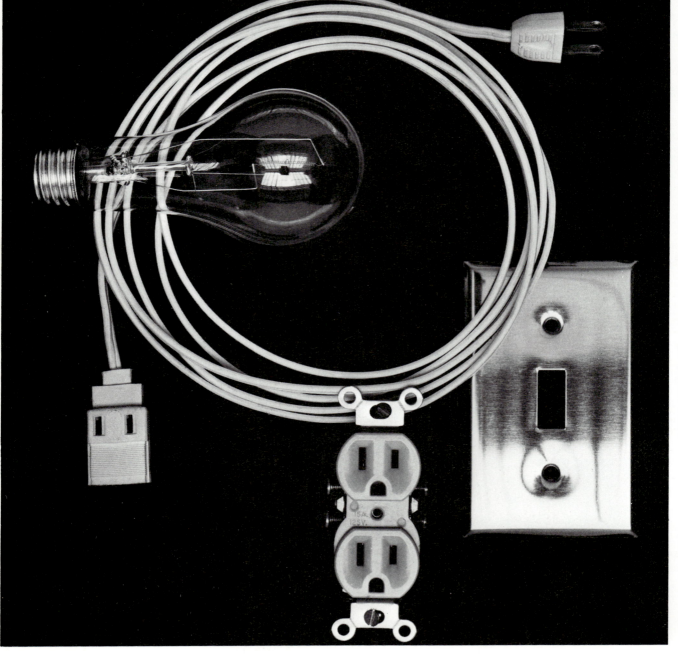

Taking the Guesswork
Out of Home Wiring

Nobody invented electricity. This natural phenomenon was around for billions of years before man arrived on this planet and for another couple of million years before he tried to do anything with it. Then, after timid and slow beginnings—the first light bulb in 1879, the first electric fan in 1882—the use of electricity gained momentum. This momentum has never been greater than in recent decades. On the one hand, new technology developed novel products and improved old ones; on the other, increasingly sophisticated life styles provided an ever-widening and eager market. The result has been a dramatic surge in electricity's application in the home: more than one billion electrical appliances are in use in America.

Since World War II, the consumption of electric power in the United States has doubled every 10 years, and the wiring installed in American homes has been beefed up accordingly. An average house built in the 1950s was provided with electrical capacity that could, in effect, light seventy 100-watt bulbs simultaneously. New houses now are generally built with up to 10 times that capacity.

Today, electric power keeps homes warm in winter, cool in summer and well lighted at all times. Labor-saving electrical appliances can be had for almost any task, from brushing teeth to running a cement mixer. Electricity has become the most useful, most convenient and most versatile servant humanity has ever known—and people are finding still more uses for it every day. At the same time, its cost increases constantly, and it represents a steadily growing portion of the family budget.

You can get the most effective—and economical—help from this versatile, ever-ready servant if you know something about the way electricity works, and how to keep it working. Take lighting, for example: is it more efficient to replace incandescent light fixtures with flu-

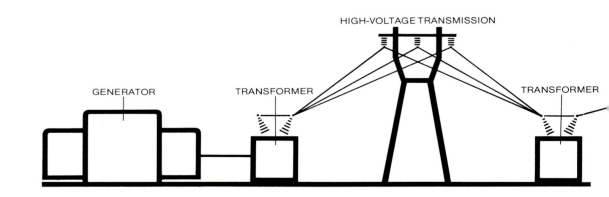

HIGH-VOLTAGE TRANSMISSION

GENERATOR   TRANSFORMER   TRANSFORMER

orescent ones? (It is—and what is more, you can do the job yourself, as shown on pages 156-157.) Do "long-life" electric bulbs represent a saving over ordinary bulbs? (Not always, as you will see on page 157.) Are modern dimmer switches worth the extra money that they cost? (They are, for they save electricity by permitting you to lower the lighting level to fit your mood and your needs; they are described on pages 170-171.)

Clear rules for safe and easy work

More important, an understanding of electrical fundamentals will enable you to do basic repair and maintenance work yourself. There is nothing difficult in any phase of the work itself, nor is there any legal barrier to keep you from doing it. Yet many homeowners who cheerfully tackle complex repairs on their cars, boats and plumbing shy away from electrical work. The reason, usually, is ignorance of basic electrical principles. Once the ignorance is dispelled, the ease of electrical maintenance and repair becomes clear.

Once you turn off the current at its source —as you must do before starting any electrical job—working with electricity is in some respects safer than working with plumbing. It is always less messy; you may find some fittings a little dusty, but they will never dump water or wastes on the floors of your home.

Part of the ease of electrical work comes from the standardization of parts. The manufacturers of plumbing supplies offer their pipes, fittings and fixtures in a bewildering va-

riety of shapes and sizes; a part that works in one plumbing system often fails to fit another. Not so with electrical materials. No matter where you shop or what you shop for—a switch, a socket, a wall or ceiling light fixture —the part you buy is going to fit into the electrical system that is in your home.

The work itself is astonishingly easy. A plumber who "sweats a joint" calls upon perfected skills and years of experience—and a homeowner doing the same job *(pages 60-61)* may find his own skills taxed. A home electrician has only to assemble a few wires and connect them according to a standardized color code. Since every electrician follows the same wiring rules, your house will be wired in much the same way whether you live in Miami or Vancouver. With standardized parts and standardized installation methods, making replacements or minor additions to house wiring becomes almost as simple as the assembling of your child's Erector set.

With only a few simple tools you can replace a malfunctioning switch or a broken socket, install or repair a doorbell or chime, change your lighting fixtures, or change over entirely from incandescent to fluorescent light. But whatever you do will be done better if you prepare yourself with a fundamental knowledge of electricity. When you know how an electric current flows, the wiring of a light fixture becomes logical and meaningful. When you understand why the fixture is "grounded"—that is, has a direct connection to the earth—some of the safety rules that apply to all electrical

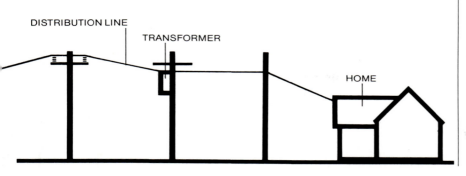

Electricity's up-and-down path

On its way from generator to home, power is repeatedly raised or lowered in electrical pressure, or voltage, at the expense of amperage, the rate of flow. Transformers, like those in doorbells *(page 177)*, step up voltage from perhaps 15,000 at a generator to as much as 765,000 for high-voltage transmission, then down to about 13,000 volts for distribution, and finally to 120 volts for your home. The reason for making these changes in the voltage is economy: transmission losses are least at low amperage and correspondingly high voltage.

work will become obvious. And you will find a fund of directly useful information once you learn the meanings of a small group of terms: amperes, volts, watts and cycles. The same words, stamped by manufacturers on light bulbs and most appliances, give you essential facts about these products.

The characteristics of electricity

In one sense, electricity is what the world is made of. Every speck of matter, including the substance of your own body, contains small particles of electricity. Some particles are said to carry a "positive" electric charge, others a "negative" one; the terms positive and negative are arbitrary labels, and only the negative ones matter to you as a user of electricity. The flow of these particles (called electrons) between two points of a wire constitutes a current. All the measurements of electricity refer to this stream of electrons. An ampere measures its volume of flow, a volt measures the force that makes it flow, and a watt measures its power to do work.

An electric current travels with lightning speed—20,000 miles per second along a copper wire—but individual electrons do not: they amble along at less than an inch per second. The current streaks through the wire because the electrons jostle each other all the way.

The phenomenon can best be understood by imagining a pipe completely filled with golf balls. If an additional ball is pushed in at one end of the pipe, a ball will pop out almost instantly at the other end. Similarly, when a dis-

tant power plant forces electrons into one end of a wire, other electrons almost immediately come out at the other end—to light a lamp, perhaps, or start the coffee.

Electrons more than make up in quantity what they lack in speed; their volume of flow in a current, as measured in amperes, is astonishingly great. To light an ordinary 100-watt light bulb, which requires a current of about one ampere, some six million million million electrons must flow through the bulb each second. In a 15-ampere house circuit used at full capacity, the current consists of 94,200,000,000,000,- 000,000—nearly 100 million million million —electrons per second. The amperage does not measure just a number of electrons, but the number of electrons that flow past any point in a wire each second, just as gallons per second measure the flow of water through a pipe.

The water analogy also helps to explain the units called volts, for voltage is to electricity what pressure is to water. The higher the pressure at the source, the greater the flow of water that is forced through a pipe; similarly, the higher the voltage, the greater the flow of electrons through a wire. For lights and most appliances, homes in the United States and Canada use approximately 120 volts. But for large appliances requiring very heavy currents —for cooking, heating, centralized air conditioning—240 volts are generally used.

Watts, the third major measure of electricity, generally concern you most of all; for watts measure the rate at which you consume electrical energy, and energy is what you pay for when you use electricity. The power consumption of many devices—lamps, irons—will be marked on them in watts. Other devices—fuses, motors—are rated by the current they carry; that is, by amperes. The units are related, however, so if you know one you can always figure out the other. The power in watts is equal to the voltage multiplied by the number of amperes. Thus an 8-ampere air conditioner on a 120-volt circuit consumes 960 watts; or, conversely, a 1,000-watt steam iron on a 120-volt circuit draws 8.3 amperes.

Total energy consumption, of course, depends on how long an appliance is kept running, and is calculated by multiplying the power (expressed in 1,000-watt units called kilowatts and usually abbreviated to kw) by the time in hours. The result is a composite figure called kilowatt-hours (kwh). If you use a 1,000-watt iron for an hour, it will consume exactly one kilowatt-hour, which will be tallied on your electric meter (pages 150-151) and will eventually figure in your electric bill.

AC and DC: two kinds of current

These measures—volts, amperes, watts and kilowatt-hours—apply to all forms of electricity, whether from a battery or from a wall outlet. But the source of the current does make a crucial difference. The current produced by batteries, used to power such appliances as flashlights, toothbrushes and grass clippers, is a direct current (DC), flowing in one direction; for house wiring, power plants generate alternating current (AC)—a current that rapidly and repeatedly changes its direction. In the United States and Canada—but not in most of the world (page 128)—it is a 60-cycle current: that is, it flows in one direction, then in the opposite direction, and completes this two-part cycle 60 times a second.

Why alternating current? In the 1880s, that question was bitterly debated. Thomas Edison, for one, could see no need for it. He had perfected a generating and transmission system that could power anything from a light bulb to a trolley car—with direct current. Its only drawback was that the power plant had to be within a mile or two of the appliance; according to one critic, most families would need generators in their backyards if they wanted to make use of Edison's electric light. But a new generation of inventors and engineers, particularly those employed by Edison's chief rival, George Westinghouse, insisted that they could transmit electricity over miles or hundreds of miles—if they sent it out in alternating current at 2,000 volts. (Their plans were modest; today, current travels at voltages in six figures.) To Edison, the idea seemed utterly preposterous. "The use of alternating current," he snorted, "is unworthy of practical men."

Thomas Edison eventually lost what his contemporaries called the War of the Currents (an outrageous and vicious propaganda campaign that led many newspapers, influenced by Edison, to refer to the execution of a criminal by alternating current as "sending him to the Westinghouse"). Although DC continued to be supplied to some homes until after World War II, all electricity for homes is now AC because of the necessity of locating central power stations far from the point of use. The device that makes long-distance transmission possible and also provides a useful variety of voltages within the home is a transformer. It does what its name suggests: transforms the voltage and amperage of electricity passing through it. It contains no moving parts, just coils of wire, plus in some cases pieces of iron, but it works only with alternating current.

The transformation of alternating current is made possible because of the relationship between electricity and magnetism. When cur-

Picking the Right Extension Cord

An extension cord obviously has to carry enough current to supply the needs of the appliance it serves. What is not so obvious is whether it can. If the wire is too thin, the current will overheat and damage the cord—and even start a fire. Moreover, a long cord may waste power, for resistance of the wire causes the voltage to drop—the longer and thinner the wire, the greater the loss of voltage. This drop can have serious effects.

An extension cord that receives 120 volts at the outlet but delivers only 108 volts at its other end causes a 10 per cent voltage drop; but that drop costs a motor almost 20 per cent of its normal power and costs a lamp 30 per cent of its normal light. Severe voltage drop so weakens a motor it may burn out.

Fortunately, increasing the thickness of a wire reduces the loss in voltage, just as it lessens heating. Some voltage drop is inevitable and acceptable; a decrease of 2 per cent or less is unimportant. To keep voltage loss within this limit in a long cord, pick one with wire large enough for the length as well as the current consumption marked on the appliance nameplate. The chart below matches wire sizes to length and amperage. (If consumption is expressed in watts, divide by 120 in order to get amperes.)

Matching wire size to length and amperage

Appliance current consumption (amperes)	Length (feet)	Wire size (gauge no.)
Up to 7	50	16
	100	14
8 to 14	Up to 25	16
	50	14
	100	12
15 to 18	Up to 25	14
	50	12
	100	10

rent moves through a wire, the wire produces a magnetic force. And conversely, when a magnetic force is moved near a wire, a current is produced in the wire. This principle is used in generators to produce power and in motors (pages 190-193) to produce mechanical motion. In the transformer, it is applied to two separate coils of wire, one coil connected to a power source, the other coil connected to the power-using device or devices. A current flowing through the first, or primary, coil generates magnetism in the space nearby. If the current changes—as alternating current does, rapidly reversing its direction—the magnetism will change similarly, reversing the direction of its north and south poles. The result is a moving magnetic force. It causes current to flow in the second coil, the secondary, since current is induced in any wire that is subjected to a moving magnetic force.

The new current that is magnetically induced in the secondary need not be exactly the same as the power-supply current in the primary. Its voltage and amperage depend on the number of windings in each coil. If the secondary has more turns of wire than the primary, the secondary voltage will be greater—and its amperage will be correspondingly less. Such a "step-up" transformer is employed at the generating station to create very high voltages and relatively low amperage for transmission. This voltage-amperage combination is the secret of economical transmission of electricity, because it reduces the inevitable loss of power along the way to where it is consumed.

Whenever electricity passes along a wire, some power is wasted, mostly in heat that is generated by electrons moving against the wire's resistance. At high amperages, with correspondingly high numbers of electrons passing through the wire, the heat loss makes long-distance transmission impractical.

By reducing the amperage, the transformer cuts the transmission loss; it does not change the total power, which remains constant because the voltage is simultaneously increased. This economizing trick of the transformer is the reason alternating current is now universally supplied by power lines—transformers require changing currents and magnetism, which are not provided by the constant flow of direct current but are the essential characteristics of alternating current.

Between the generating station and your home, a number of transformers trade volts and amperes, stepping voltage up at the generator, then down in successive stages as the distribution network divides and subdivides to deliver power to individual consumers (drawing, pages 124-125). The end of the network is visible on a pole near your house: a metal container, about the size of a garbage can, that houses a step-down transformer to reduce the local distribution voltage (usually about 13,000 volts) to two separate supplies of approximately 120 volts each.

Most homes built within the last two decades are connected to both supplies. The two separate voltages not only can be used independently to give 120-volt power but also can be added together to provide electricity of 240 volts—an arrangement called 240-volt power. A very few older homes, however, are still connected to only one of the two supplies that are available from the neighborhood transformer; they are said to have 120-volt power.

How current is distributed through a house

Whether the house is wired for 120 or 240 volts, the connections from the power company's transformer go to a "service panel." Here, in a metal box equipped with safety devices to shut off electricity automatically if something goes wrong, the incoming electricity is divid-

A World of Assorted Volts and Cycles

Americans, accustomed to a continent-wide standardization of electric power that enables them to plug shavers and hair driers into receptacles from Montreal to Kansas City to Houston, are often dismayed when they travel overseas. For there is no worldwide standardization, but rather a frustrating variety of plugs, receptacles, voltages and frequencies—the result of attempts by early manufacturers to design systems that would prevent the use of a competitor's products. In many countries, American and Canadian appliances cannot even be plugged in—their plugs do not fit the receptacles.

The biggest variation is in voltages, which may be almost anything from 100 volts in Japan to 600 volts in Bombay, India. While a combination of 220 and 380 volts is standard in most of Europe, England uses 240 and 415, while France offers a bewildering assortment of voltages that range from 110 to 380 volts. Paris is one of the few places in the world that provides electricity at 115 and 230 volts.

As with voltage, so with frequency. The 60-cycle alternating current of North America is unknown almost everywhere else. Most foreign countries generate alternating current at a frequency of 50 cycles.

For an unwary traveler who carries a small appliance in his luggage, differences in voltage and frequency can be bothersome at best, dangerous at worst. A motor or heating element designed for 120 volts will almost instantly burn out at 220. Some manufacturers offer appliances that can be converted to a higher voltage. More adaptable is a plug-in device that transforms high voltages to low. The frequency difference is less easily overcome. Most 60-cycle hair driers and shavers will run at 50 cycles, though somewhat slower. In an electric clock or a phonograph, the difference in speed is crucial—and the appliance had better be left at home.

ed up into separate circuits (pages 146-147). A circuit is a closed path along which current may pass. The circuits are generally out of sight, consisting of heavy cables that snake through walls and ceilings to outlets—metal or plastic boxes that contain switches, attachments for lighting fixtures, or receptacles that you can plug lamps and appliances into.

Some circuits serve only one outlet (the one for the dishwasher, for example), while others supply a whole string. A well-equipped modern home contains several dozen circuits, some of them providing their outlets with 120 volts, others furnishing 240 volts. The difference in voltage calls for somewhat different wiring arrangements, which become visible when you open an electrical outlet box to make a repair or replacement.

The 120-volt circuits are the simpler of the two types. Their cables generally consist of several layers of insulation surrounding three separate wires: one bare, one coated with white plastic and one coated with black plastic (pages 138-139). The black wire in the cable provides the electric current when a circuit is switched on to light a bulb or start an appliance. It is often called the hot wire because it carries electrons "under pressure"—at 120 volts—and is therefore ready to perform work. In the analogy to the plumbing system, the black wire is the equivalent of the supply pipe, which carries water under pressure.

The white wire in the house cable has an opposite function. Because electric systems, like water systems, require complete circuits, there has to be a path carrying electrons from a using device back to the generator at the power plant. It is the white wire that provides the return path. It runs continuously through each circuit, bypassing all switches to ensure an uninterrupted return flow. The white wire is the equivalent of the plumbing drain. Just as wa-

ter in a drain is under extremely low gravity pressure, so the electrons flowing through the white wire are at close to zero volts. They have given up virtually all of their energy in operating whatever device they have passed through.

Because a black wire inside the house is always hot unless power is shut off at the service panel, it is dangerous; if you touch the wire itself, you will get a shock. By contrast, the white wire is neutral. By the time the current reaches this wire, the energy of its 120 volts has been expended; the wire is then at the same voltage as the earth. It cannot force a current to flow through your body or anything else. Thus, theoretically, it is safe to touch. But do not. Sometimes electricians make mistakes or take shortcuts and use the white wire as a hot wire. In a few cases, such as in a switch loop (page 167), this is perfectly permissible. So do not consider a white wire or any other part of a circuit safe to work on until you have disconnected the power at the service panel.

The purpose and importance of grounding

To ensure that the white wire is at the same voltage as the earth, it is installed with direct connections to the earth, that is, it is "grounded." Grounding of the white wire—by connecting it in the service panel to a metal bar that is bonded to a plumbing pipe leading to underground water or connected directly to a pipe or stake driven deep into the ground—also ensures that it will always be at the same voltage that you are, and thus keeps it neutral.

The bare—or sometimes green-covered—wire in the house cables is an extra safety device. It guards against mistakes in installation, and also against deterioration. All fixtures, appliances and other electrical apparatus gradually become worn, and when they are worn they are potentially dangerous. After repeated use, their parts break and their insulation crumbles or wears thin; current that should pass through them can leak from its normal path. The leak may cause a spark or generate intense heat, raising the possibility of fire. It also may put 120 volts into something you might touch. To ensure that the leak does not become dangerous, the bare wire is connected to a grounded wire of the power company's incoming line (thus, it is grounded itself), and it is securely fastened to every possible point of leakage—that is, to every box in every circuit, and in many modern installations, to the metal frames of switches, receptacles, light fixtures and many small and large appliances.

Suppose, for example, that a switch is incorrectly installed, or that the insulation on its black wire wears through; in either case, an exposed hot wire may make contact with the inner surface of the box. Immediately, the entire box, including the visible metal plate that covers it, can become hot and a potential source of shock or fire. The bare grounding wire protects the house and its inhabitants by completing a new circuit that leads from the exposed black wire to the ground. This new circuit is a "short circuit." It contains no lamp or appliance; thus it transmits—instead of using up—the energy of incoming electrons. A great surge of current will pass through the black and bare wires directly to the service panel. A fuse will blow or a circuit breaker will trip (pages 148-149); they are simply switches that interrupt current whenever it exceeds a specified limit. What is more, a replacement fuse will also blow and a circuit breaker will continue to trip until the fault in the wiring—or in an appliance—is found and corrected.

An extra hot wire for 240-volt circuits

Most of the elements of the 120-volt circuit—safety shutoff devices as well as ground and hot wires within the cables—are also present in a 240-volt circuit. The difference is in the cable (and in the design of plugs and receptacles, to prevent anyone from plugging 120-volt machinery into 240-volt outlets and vice versa). The 240-volt cable usually contains three wires, coded in one of two ways: bare for grounding, black and white for hot; or white for grounding, and black and red for hot. When the current is at 120 volts in one hot wire, it is also at 120 volts—but flowing in the opposite direction—in the other hot wire. The total voltage carried by the two wires is thus 240. To deliver these 240 volts, both hot wires are hooked to the terminals of a receptacle. There is no neutral wire in such a circuit; the return to the power source is, in fact, over one of the hot wires. The bare or white wire provides grounding for the entire circuit.

Occasionally, a four-wire cable is used in a 240-volt circuit: a white neutral wire, a bare ground wire, and red and black hot wires. Although the total voltage of the black and red hot wires is 240 volts, the voltage obtained by hooking together either hot wire and the neutral wire is 120 volts, just as in an ordinary 120-volt circuit. Such a cable would serve an outlet that contains both a 120-volt receptacle and a 240-volt receptacle, as might be the case with an electric range that draws 240 volts, while a receptacle on the range for plugging in small appliances requires only 120 volts.

Either one of the hot wires—red or black—and the neutral white wire can be connected to a receptacle to provide 120 volts. The hot wire on the 120-volt receptacle plus the other hot wire can then be connected to the terminals of a 240-volt receptacle to provide 240 volts. The bare wire serves, as in the case of the three-wire system, as a ground for both of the receptacles as well as for the box.

The bulk of house-circuit wiring, whether 120 or 240 volts, is beyond the reach of the av-

Watching the Costs of Your Current

As the costs of producing energy continue to soar, the efficient use of electricity has become every homeowner's concern—these costs, after all, turn up in your utility bill. The information in this chart can help you decide where it may be possible to cut down on current usage—and when it is not worth worrying about.

The chart lists the approximate number of kilowatt-hours consumed in a year under normal conditions by a variety of commonly used electrical appliances. A quick-recovery water heater uses the most—nearly 5,000 kwh annually; a toothbrush the least—a meager 0.5.

To find the approximate cost to you of operating any of these appliances, multiply the appliance's kilowatt-hour figure by the average price you pay for a kilowatt-hour as determined by the method described on page 151. Then focus your personal electricity-conservation program on those appliances you own that use the most energy. Giving up an electric clock or shaver would hardly put a dent in your bill; but you could make real savings by turning off a color television when you are not watching it or running a dishwasher only once a day at full capacity. It also pays to consider the energy requirements of appliances you plan to buy. Some manufacturers place a higher priority than others on energy efficiency. Thus two refrigerators with substantially the same features may vary significantly in operating costs. Check the wattage rating when choosing an appliance to estimate and compare annual operating costs.

Appliance	Estimated kilowatt-hours consumed annually
Air conditioner (room)	1,389
Blender	15
Broiler	100
Clock	17
Clothes drier	993
Clothes washer	103
Coffee maker	106
Dehumidifier	377
Dishwasher	363
Fan	
attic	291
circulating	43
rollaway	138
window	170
Food mixer	13
Freezer (15 cu. ft.)	1,761
Frying pan	186
Garbage disposer	30
Grill	33
Hair drier	14
Heater (portable)	176

Appliance	Estimated kilowatt-hours consumed annually
Humidifier	163
Iron	144
Microwave oven	300
Radio	86
Range	
standard	1,175
self-cleaning oven	1,205
Refrigerator-freezer (14 cu. ft.)	1,829
Roaster	205
Sewing machine	11
Shaver	1.8
Television	
black-and-white	362
color	502
Toaster	39
Toothbrush	0.5
Trash compactor	50
Vacuum cleaner	46
Water heater	
standard	4,219
quick-recovery	4,811

erage nonprofessional. Making connections at the service panel can be hazardous, and this task is best left to a licensed electrician. Most of the cables themselves are out of sight, inside walls and ceilings where they are not simple to get at. But the ends of the cables, where they are attached to the things you use, are easily reachable—and there you can do many jobs safely and efficiently.

Wherever electricity is tapped in your home, you will find a rectangular or octagonal steel or plastic box containing a small end section of a house-circuit cable. The boxes serve as mounts for light fixtures, switches, receptacles and the like. All of these parts contain screw terminals or wires for making connections to the cable wires; when you have connected the wires, you screw the part to the box. The simplicity of installation makes it easy for anyone to replace a defective part with a new one, or to replace an outmoded part with a modern one.

For work of this type, neither a professional electrician's license nor a special permit is required, but common sense and prudence are always essential. Some old houses may contain wiring that does not follow present standards, and many modern homes contain complex circuitry that calls for a professional. You should not attempt any job you do not completely understand; never guess.

Generally the connections at the box are safe to work on provided that you follow the rules. There are only two that must never under any circumstances be dodged:

■ Turn off the electricity reaching the box before opening it. Disconnect power at the service panel by removing the fuse or tripping the circuit breaker controlling that circuit. It is not necessary—or, generally, even desirable—to turn off the main switch and disconnect all circuits; not only will you lack lights you may need, but you may have to go around unplugging appliances so that you do not put a strain on the system later by starting everything up simultaneously. After you have disconnected power to the circuit, make sure that you have turned off the right circuit by testing as shown on pages 142-143.

■ Follow standard procedures in making connections, never deviating. Black wires are connected only to black or red wires, or to brass-colored terminals. White wires are connected only to silver-colored terminals or to other white wires, unless they are part of a switch loop, in which case they must be recoded black with tape or paint (pages 166-169). Bare wires are connected only to ground: other bare wires, ground terminals or, on some new fixtures, green-coded ground wires. After all connections have been securely fastened and the power has been turned on again at the service panel, retest as shown on pages 142-143 to make sure you have made no mistakes.

The National Electrical Code

The standard procedures for electrical work are so simple to follow partly because they are standard throughout the United States. Electrical codes, unlike plumbing codes, vary little from community to community. Nearly all local codes follow the National Electrical Code, which dates back to the early 1890s, when fire insurance companies began to concern themselves with the hazards of faulty electrical wiring. In 1897, the first edition of the code was published under the sponsorship of the National Fire Protection Association. Revised every three years or so since that time, it has become the basic guide to electrical installation.

You can buy a copy of it from the National Fire Protection Association, Batterymarch Park, Quincy, Massachusetts 02269. But under normal circumstances you will never need to read the code; its closely packed, highly technical pages are not very helpful to the nonprofessional. The explanations and instructions in this volume, and the many handbooks on home wiring, incorporate all of the code data that you are likely to need.

You should, of course, use components of quality rather than bargain-bin specials. Look for the UL symbol of the Underwriters' Laboratories on every part you buy; for eight decades this not-for-profit organization has led the electrical industry toward the manufacture of better and safer products (box, right).

When you observe these precautions, you may be surprised by your success in electrical work. The average electrical repair job is not only simpler and cleaner than most plumbing jobs, but also needs to be done less often. Electrical maintenance problems are generally minor. The metal wires do not deteriorate much inside walls or ceiling, for electrons do not wear out the materials they pass through. Insulation may harden and become brittle over a period of years, but this seldom matters unless the wires are disturbed in such a way that the insulation breaks off.

On the other hand, switches, receptacles, light fixtures and extension cords do call for work that the homeowner can perform. All are subject to constant handling, to switching on or off, to occasional movement and to accident. And all of them are likely to become victims of obsolescence. New and better switches, fixtures and receptacles appear periodically. New ideas in safety, like the three-prong grounded plug, make replacements and improvements wise if not necessary.

The tools for such jobs are few, inexpensive and easy to use (pages 136-137). The procedures are simple and easy to follow. Within the limits of an average homeowner's skills, you can be your own electrician.

UL: Safety's Watchman

When President Grover Cleveland pressed a button in the White House on May 1, 1893, the Chicago World's Fair suddenly glowed in the night as no spectacle ever had: the President had flicked on Thomas A. Edison's new electric light bulbs in their grandest display. But the public wonderment turned to dismay as wires began to sputter and crackle—among the buildings they set afire was, embarrassingly, the Palace of Electricity.

Overwhelmed by damage claims, the fair's insurance companies sent to Boston for William H. Merrill, a troubleshooting electrical engineer. He found poorly insulated wires, bare wires, crossed wires and overloaded circuits. The new electrical industry needed standards. To provide them, Merrill set up shop with two helpers and $350 worth of testing equipment above a Chicago firehouse.

Thus was born Underwriters' Laboratories, Inc. (or UL), an independent testing organization whose charter requires that it be operated "for service and not for profit," and whose governing board includes government scientists, insurance officials, consumers, bankers and industrialists. In its four laboratories, 325 engineers annually test the safety of thousands of products ranging from dolls' hair to roof tiles and fire doors. At one lab, whole houses are set ablaze to determine the fire resistance of building materials.

Most of the UL's work—about two thirds of the products tested—is concerned with electricity. A new electric iron is dropped six times from ironing-board height to ascertain any effect on its thermostat. Products are submitted voluntarily by some 17,000 manufacturers in 45 countries, who pay for the tests; a product that passes gets the UL symbol indicating it meets minimum safety standards, and 400 inspectors visit factories unannounced to ensure that standards do not slip. UL does not judge the price or quality—only safety—and guarantees nothing. But the UL symbol is looked for by wise consumers.

Basic Steps in Electrical Work

Doing nearly any kind of work on a household electrical system is reasonably simple because the procedures have all been rigidly formalized, requiring that every step be done by the rules laid down in the nationwide code. Unfortunately everyone does not always follow the rules faithfully. Even professionals have been known to get careless, and you may be surprised by the things you find when you open an outlet in your house for any one of the jobs described on the following pages. The diagrams on those pages show typical electrical circuits, switches, fixtures and receptacles the way they should look if they have been installed properly. But it is entirely possible that you may discover that a unit has wiring of the wrong color code or even wiring that has been improperly attached.

Spotting a botched job

Certain errors and omissions are frequent. Among those you should watch out for (and correct as soon as possible) are:

■ Ground wires missing or left unconnected. Make certain that the ground wire from the cable is attached to the box. If the fixture has a ground terminal, be sure that a wire connects it both to the box and to the ground wire. Exception: Ground connections to the box are not necessary if the box is made of plastic rather than metal.

■ Reversed connections. A receptacle, for example, may not have the black, or hot, wire attached to the brass-colored terminal, and the white wire may not be on the silver-colored terminal, as it is supposed to be.

■ Switches connected to white wires. If this installation is an out-and-out mistake, rewire the switch—the code requires that neutral wires never be interrupted by a switch. But there are circuits in which a white wire is quite correctly used as a hot wire (pages 167-169), and what seems like an error in installation may be nothing more than an electrician's failure to provide the black identifying coating of paint or tape at the end of the wire that such a connection requires.

Even if the wiring you see looks correct, it is always best to be suspicious. Every wire should be considered to be potentially hot—and dangerous to touch—no matter what its color. Make certain you know what you are working with by testing all wiring with the methods outlined on pages 142-143.

Tracing problems from the service panel

Since a circuit must be deactivated before you work on it, it is convenient to know which circuit breaker or fuse controls it: the alternative is to try each one in turn and scurry around the house to determine which devices no longer work. Generally, each circuit is labeled at its origin in the service panel by the electrician who installs it. If he did not do so, it is worth finding out which fuse or circuit breaker protects what circuit, and labeling accordingly.

The easiest way to trace circuits is to borrow a child's walkie-talkie—and the child. Stand at the service panel with one walkie-talkie, tripping each circuit breaker (or removing each fuse) in turn. Your assistant uses the other walkie-talkie to report the results from the rooms around the house, telling you which lamp or appliance goes dead. Remember that at least two circuits generally serve each room, and a kitchen may have four or more. Test each room, receptacle by receptacle, fixture by fixture, to find which area is on which circuit. Write this information on adhesive labels, which then can be displayed prominently on the panel.

Labeling circuits on the service panel makes it easier not only to isolate a problem but also to find its cause, especially if your panel uses circuit breakers instead of fuses. A blown fuse reveals by its appearance whether failure arose from an overload or a short circuit (page 148); a circuit breaker will give you no such clues. But if your service panel has complete circuit information, some rough calculations can help you to diagnose the problem when a breaker trips. Just compare the capacity of the circuit—marked in amperes on the circuit breaker—with the total load on the circuit to see if it is overloaded.

Totting up amperes

To compute the load on a circuit, check every light bulb and appliance that draws current from that circuit and note the current consumption of each device in amperes. If the device is marked in watts, divide the wattage by the voltage (120, unless marked otherwise); the resulting number indicates consumption in amperes. Add the amperage of all of the devices on the circuit in question; if it exceeds the amperage of the fuse or the circuit breaker, your problem is probably an overloaded circuit. Unplug enough appliances to reduce amperage consumption to a total below the rated capacity.

If the circuit breaker still switches off—or if a fuse of the correct capacity still blows—suspect a short circuit. To trace its source you must first disconnect every fixture and appliance that draws current from the circuit and reset the circuit breaker—or install a new fuse. If it fails when no appliances are turned on, the short circuit is in the circuit breaker, in the wiring between the service panel and an outlet, or in something connected to an outlet. Check lamps, lighting fixtures, appliances, switches and receptacles; repair if necessary (pages 155-173). If none of these components are faulty, the trouble may lie in the service panel or house wiring; call an electrician.

AN ELECTRICAL TOOL KIT

A handful of special tools is needed for electrical work. Although some—particularly the pliers—may resemble items found in an all-purpose tool kit, these tools are designed and shaped to ensure the safety, neatness and precision that electrical jobs require. An electrically heated soldering iron, for example, is used instead of the plumber's propane torch because it delivers even, controlled heat that will not damage insulation. The solder itself is a special compound.

Safety is a major consideration in choosing the tools to buy. The voltage tester should be at the top of your priority list. A fuse puller is needed only if cartridge fuses are used in your house.

Soldering gear

A pencil-type soldering iron with an electrically heated tip is necessary for some connections, such as those involved in the repair of certain small appliances or in the emergency splicing of an extension cord *(page 141)*. Be sure that you use electrical rosin-core solder, which provides a surface free of corrosion while you solder; the acid-core solder used in plumbing is unsuitable for electrical work because it causes corrosion that hampers the flow of current across the connection.

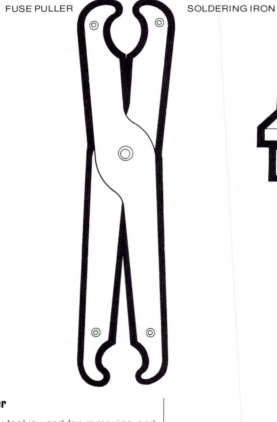

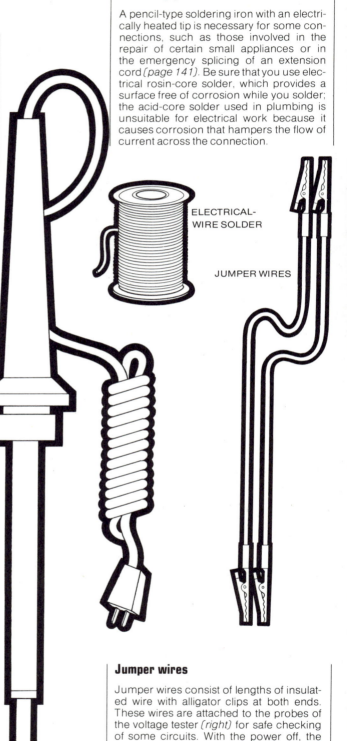

FUSE PULLER SOLDERING IRON

ELECTRICAL-WIRE SOLDER

JUMPER WIRES

Fuse puller

This handy tool is used for removing and for replacing cartridge fuses *(page 148)* such as the main fuses often found in the service panels of older houses. The fuse puller is made entirely of fiber or some other nonconducting material, without any metal parts, to protect you against shocks. Jaws at both ends accommodate cartridges of various diameters.

Jumper wires

Jumper wires consist of lengths of insulated wire with alligator clips at both ends. These wires are attached to the probes of the voltage tester *(right)* for safe checking of some circuits. With the power off, the tester is clamped by jumper wires to the appropriate terminals; the power can then be turned on and the circuit checked without touching the tester *(page 262)*.

Continuity tester

A break in a wire (in an extension cord, for example) can be pinpointed with a continuity tester. This device is connected by an alligator clip to one end of the cord and its probe is touched to the other end. If the cord is intact, electricity generated by a battery in the tester handle will flow through the cord and turn on a small bulb in the tester. If the bulb fails to light up, there is a break in the circuit. The continuity tester may be used in a similar manner to locate loose connections in an appliance circuit.

Insulating materials

A roll of plastic electrical tape and some wire caps are the only insulating materials you are likely to need in house wiring. Use a strong, self-adhesive tape to cover exposed splices and to reinforce wire connections. Wire caps in assorted sizes will enable you to connect two or more wires together without solder *(page 140).*

Wire stripper and crimper

This tool will strip insulation from wires quickly and without damaging the wires. Its graduated stripping holes accommodate standard wire sizes. The tool's overlapping jaws attach solderless connectors, frequently used in small appliances *(page 187),* to wires by crimping them on.

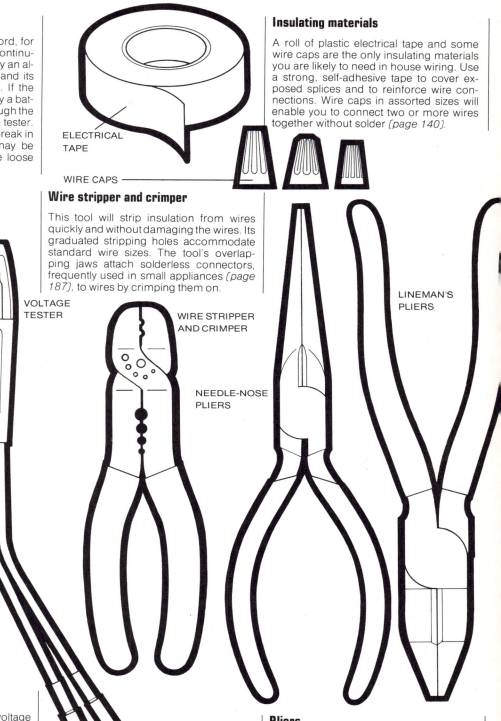

ELECTRICAL TAPE

WIRE CAPS

CONTINUITY TESTER

VOLTAGE TESTER

WIRE STRIPPER AND CRIMPER

NEEDLE-NOSE PLIERS

LINEMAN'S PLIERS

Voltage tester

The inexpensive, yet indispensable, voltage tester reveals whether electricity is flowing between two points of a circuit: a built-in neon lamp glows when the tester prods are touched to those two points. Most testers are designed to function in the 90- to 500-volt range; special models are available for the checking of low-voltage devices such as doorbells and chimes.

Pliers

Needle-nose pliers twist wire around a terminal screw *(page 140)* and do other jobs in cramped places. Lineman's pliers are a stronger tool for making splices and bending heavy-gauge wire. Both have blades for cutting wire and waffle-like surfaces on their jaws to keep wires from slipping.

WIRE TO FIT THE JOB

Among the wires carrying electricity through your home, there are three essential differences: where they are used, the way they are sheathed and the diameter of the metal that conducts current. Sheathing varies with the ruggedness needed. The size of wire varies with the amount of current that must be carried. These variations, plus the job to be done, distinguish two common classes of wiring materials: cords and cables.

Cords, which connect lamps and appliances to wall outlets, are flexible and most are made for light duty. Cables, usually running inside walls to bring current to outlets and built-in lighting fixtures, are difficult to replace and carry large currents; they are heavily sheathed and relatively large in diameter. (A third type, the conduit [opposite], is used for some special purposes.)

Wires for house cables

Wire diameter, shown here actual size, is indicated by gauge number—the larger the number, the smaller the wire. The smallest wire in house cable is No. 14, used to connect a circuit of built-in lighting fixtures or wall outlets. For heavier duty, as in kitchen and laundry, No. 12, No. 10 or No. 8 is installed. These wires are single, solid conductors. The larger, twisted wires are used chiefly at the service entrance.

Types of cord

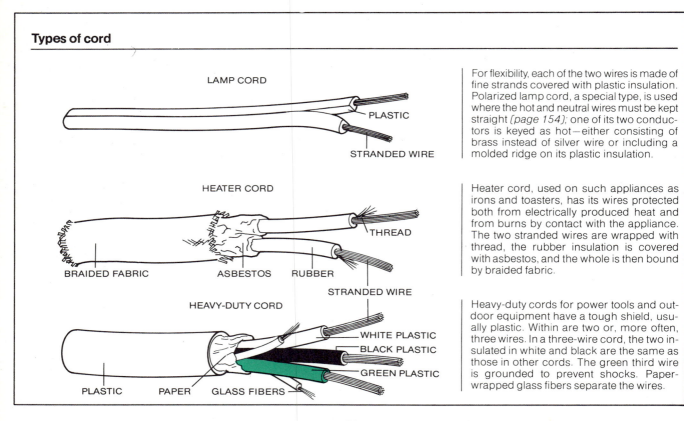

LAMP CORD
PLASTIC
STRANDED WIRE

HEATER CORD
THREAD
BRAIDED FABRIC   ASBESTOS   RUBBER
STRANDED WIRE

HEAVY-DUTY CORD
WHITE PLASTIC
BLACK PLASTIC
GREEN PLASTIC
PLASTIC   PAPER   GLASS FIBERS

For flexibility, each of the two wires is made of fine strands covered with plastic insulation. Polarized lamp cord, a special type, is used where the hot and neutral wires must be kept straight (page 154); one of its two conductors is keyed as hot—either consisting of brass instead of silver wire or including a molded ridge on its plastic insulation.

Heater cord, used on such appliances as irons and toasters, has its wires protected both from electrically produced heat and from burns by contact with the appliance. The two stranded wires are wrapped with thread, the rubber insulation is covered with asbestos, and the whole is then bound by braided fabric.

Heavy-duty cords for power tools and outdoor equipment have a tough shield, usually plastic. Within are two or, more often, three wires. In a three-wire cord, the two insulated in white and black are the same as those in other cords. The green third wire is grounded to prevent shocks. Paper-wrapped glass fibers separate the wires.

Types of cable

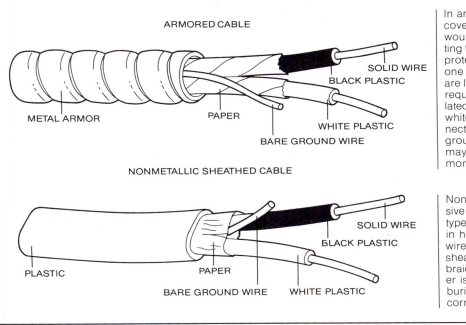

ARMORED CABLE

METAL ARMOR

PAPER

BARE GROUND WIRE

SOLID WIRE

BLACK PLASTIC

WHITE PLASTIC

NONMETALLIC SHEATHED CABLE

PLASTIC

PAPER

BARE GROUND WIRE

WHITE PLASTIC

SOLID WIRE

BLACK PLASTIC

In armored cable, two insulated wires are covered with paper and encased in spirally wound, interlocking steel that while permitting the cable to flex provides strength and protection. This cable, usually known by one of its brand names, BX, is the type you are likely to find in an older house; it is still required in some cities. The wires are insulated with plastic and are colored black and white for identification so they can be connected to the proper terminals. A bare wire grounds the circuit, although older cable may lack this ground. The sheathing of armored cable must be cut with a hacksaw.

Nonmetallic sheathed cable, less expensive and easier to install than the armored type, is the kind now most widely employed in homes. The insulated black and white wires, along with a bare ground wire, are sheathed in plastic, as shown, or in a fabric braid. A tougher type without the paper layer is used outdoors where wire must be buried in the ground and in other damp or corrosive locations.

Conduit: Wires in a Pipe

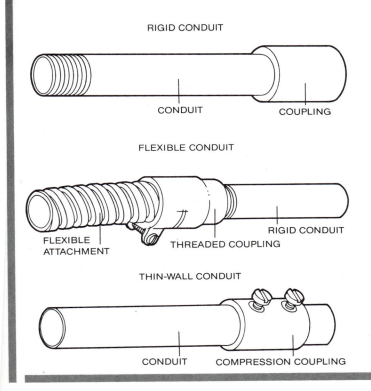

RIGID CONDUIT

CONDUIT

COUPLING

FLEXIBLE CONDUIT

FLEXIBLE ATTACHMENT

THREADED COUPLING

RIGID CONDUIT

THIN-WALL CONDUIT

CONDUIT

COMPRESSION COUPLING

Not all the pipes in your cellar necessarily carry water. Some may hold electrical wires. This pipe, called conduit, is used where wires need extra protection against moisture and physical damage—at the service entrance, outdoors and in the basement or utility room. It is versatile because the piping is installed empty; the wires, as many as needed within the limits of the conduit size, are threaded through later and are easily replaced.

Rigid conduit *(top)* needs threaded couplings for straight connections and elbows for corners, but can be joined to a flexible attachment *(center)* at terminal points. The thin-walled type *(bottom)* is joined by compression fittings and can be bent like the tubing used for plumbing.

MAKING CONNECTIONS

Almost every home-wiring job, from the making of an extension cord *(pages 152-153)* to the replacement of a lighting fixture *(pages 156-157)*, involves such basic steps as stripping insulation, connecting wires together and attaching wires to terminals. Except for splicing, the techniques are the same for the heavy wire of cables that supply receptacles, switches and fixtures, and for the lightweight wires used in lamp and extension cords.

The solid supply wire is easily spliced with wire caps *(below)*, but the connection is always made inside a junction box equipped with clamps to prevent tension on the splice. Flexible cord is not meant to be spliced—it pulls apart too easily; the technique opposite is for emergencies only.

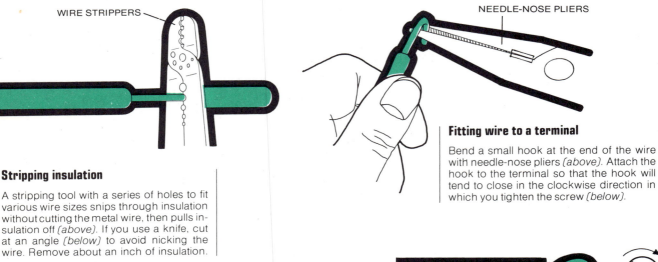

WIRE STRIPPERS

NEEDLE-NOSE PLIERS

Stripping insulation

A stripping tool with a series of holes to fit various wire sizes snips through insulation without cutting the metal wire, then pulls insulation off *(above)*. If you use a knife, cut at an angle *(below)* to avoid nicking the wire. Remove about an inch of insulation.

Fitting wire to a terminal

Bend a small hook at the end of the wire with needle-nose pliers *(above)*. Attach the hook to the terminal so that the hook will tend to close in the clockwise direction in which you tighten the screw *(below)*.

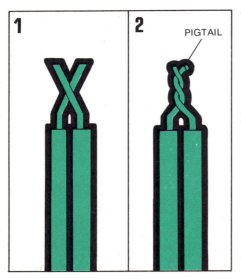

PIGTAIL

1 Starting a solid-wire splice

Strip about three quarters of an inch of insulation from the end of two solid wires. To ensure good electrical contact, scrape the bare wires lightly with the back of a knife until they are shiny. Set the wires side by side and cross the bare ends.

2 Making a pigtail

Holding the insulated part of the wires in one hand, grasp the bare ends with pliers and twist them together two or three turns.

3 Attaching a wire cap

Slip the cap over the end of the pigtail and twist it *(top)* until it covers the bare wires completely. When the cap is fully twisted on, its springlike metal threading will bind the wire ends securely *(cutaway, at bottom)*, while the plastic cover insulates them.

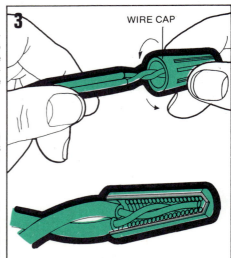

WIRE CAP

Lamp-Cord Splices — Inadvisable but Sometimes Necessary

The National Electrical Code prohibits splices in all flexible cord, such as lamp and tool cord. The reason for the ban is simple: even the best of splices — and amateur splices are often far from the best — weakens the wire and increases the danger of a short circuit that could start a fire. Yet home electricians go on splicing, arguing that emergencies do arise in which a damaged cord for a lamp or radio has to be spliced because no replacement cord is available and the device must be pressed into service immediately. If you must make such an emergency splice, do it right.

The strongest splice for stranded wire is the Western Union splice, so named because it was apparently developed a century ago by telegraph linemen. With the wires correctly twisted, soldered and taped, your splice will last until the emergency is over. Then you can repair the damage the right way — with a continuous replacement cord.

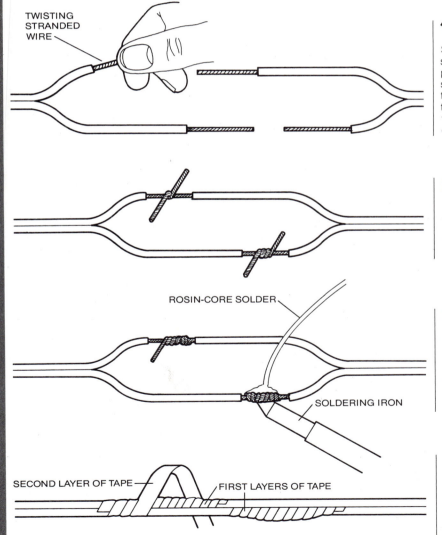

TWISTING STRANDED WIRE

ROSIN-CORE SOLDER

SOLDERING IRON

SECOND LAYER OF TAPE

FIRST LAYERS OF TAPE

1 Preparing the lamp cord

Separate both ends of the cords to be spliced, then cut the cords in the staggered pattern shown at left, so that the completed splices will not lie next to each other. Strip two inches of insulation from the ends of the wires. Then scrape the stripped wires with the back of a knife, and twist the end of each wire into a tight string.

2 Fastening the splices

Form a bend in the middle of each bare end of wire and link each pair of ends together as shown in the upper part of the drawing; twist the remainder of the ends tightly around the opposite wires.

3 Soldering the splices

For a good electrical contact and a strong coupling, solder both splices. Hold a hot soldering iron to the splices — not to the solder — until the wires are hot enough to melt the solder, then let the solder flow along and into each splice. Important: Use rosin-core solder for this job.

4 Taping the completed splices

When the wires and solder have cooled, wrap each splice separately with a layer of electrical tape, covering about an inch of insulation at each end. Finally, tape both wires together with a second layer of tape.

STRAIGHTFORWARD RULES FOR ELECTRICAL SAFETY

Using electricity and working on electrical wiring or appliances can be—and should be—safe. Yet several hundred people are killed each year in household electrical accidents. And many fires are blamed on faulty electrical devices of one kind or another. These tragedies are unnecessary, for a few common-sense rules and simple tests afford good protection.

Electricity can cause a fire when its normal passage is inadvertently impeded—by a break in a wire or a faulty connection—so that it generates intense heat. It can cause a shock only when it is permitted to flow from a supply wire, which in a house circuit carries 120 or 240 volts, to a neutral wire or to ground *(pages 144-145)*, where there is no voltage. This difference in voltage is what gives a jolt to anyone who touches the voltage-carrying wire and at the same time touches the neutral wire or any object, such as a cold-water pipe, that allows electricity to flow into the earth; he makes himself, literally, a part of the electrical circuit. Current passes through his body, whose moist internal tissues are good electrical conductors, just as it would flow through a copper wire.

It is, obviously, impossible to get a shock if no electricity is present. You can make electrical repairs in safety if you follow the cardinal rule for electrical work of any kind: make absolutely sure that the appliance or section of house wiring you are working on contains no current. To ensure that the completed job introduces no shock or fire hazards, follow established procedures to the letter:

■ When working on your house wiring, turn off current to the circuit by pulling the fuse or tripping the circuit breaker. Use the test on the opposite page to be sure you have turned off the circuit containing the receptacle, switch or light fixture you intend to replace.

■ Use a fuse puller *(page 136)* to remove cartridge fuses. Use only one hand to remove screw-in fuses, and touch only the knurled glass rim of the fuse. Do not touch anything with your other hand.

■ Use the techniques that are described on page 140 when fastening wires together with wire nuts and when connecting wires to terminals.

■ Check your work. With the power on, connect the voltage tester to the voltage-supply wire, which is black, and the ground, then connect it to the voltage-supply wire and the neutral wire, which is white—the tester should light in both cases. Connect the tester to the neutral wire and the ground —it should not light. Test a receptacle after completely installing it *(opposite)*. The connections of voltage-carrying, neutral and ground wires in switches and light fixtures are tested similarly, but with the box open. Turn on the power for the tests; turn it off before mounting the switch or fixture.

■ Always unplug an appliance before working on it. If you must plug in the appliance to test it, unplug it again before proceeding with the repair or reassembling the appliance.

A shock can occur during the use of an electric appliance whose exterior metal parts have accidentally become electrically charged. A few modern appliances, mainly power tools, are double insulated *(page 32)* to prevent such accidents. In other appliances, a ground wire runs through the cord that is connected to the housing. When it is grounded through the house wiring *(page 144)*, this ground wire carries away electricity that reaches the appliance housing—and blows the circuit fuse. To guard against shock when using appliances:

■ Use the tests on the opposite page to make sure the receptacles in your home are grounded and safe to plug appliances into.

■ Ground every appliance that has a ground wire, using either a three-slot receptacle or a grounding adapter *(page 173)*.

■ When using an appliance, be sure your hands are dry. (Dry skin resists electricity 500 times better than damp skin.) Do not use an electrical device while touching a good ground: a water faucet or a pipe; the water in a tub, sink or toilet; a wallswitch or receptacle cover plate; a radiator or storm drain; another grounded appliance.

■ Periodically examine your appliances for worn parts. Replace any frayed cords or broken plugs *(pages 186-187)* promptly.

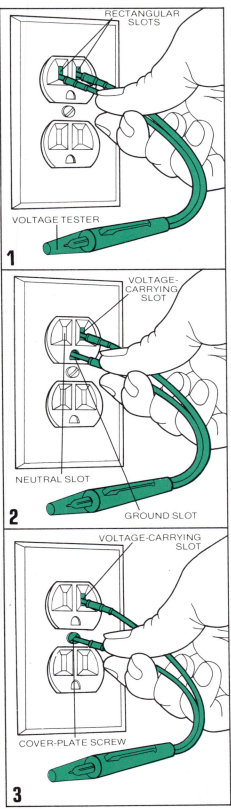

1 Testing for voltage in a receptacle

These tests show if a receptacle is correctly connected. First, insert leads of a voltage tester into the rectangular slots. If current is on, the neon bulb will glow.

2 Testing the ground slot

Connect one tester probe to the arched ground slot and the other to each rectangular slot in turn. When the probe is in one of the rectangular slots (the smaller of the two in modern receptacles), the tester glows if the receptacle is grounded.

3 Checking the cover plate's ground

Connect the voltage tester between the cover-plate screw and the voltage-carrying rectangular slot found in step 2. If the plate is properly grounded, the tester will glow.

Making sure the current is off

Use the voltage tester to make sure the electricity to a circuit has been turned off before you work on it. If you are working on a receptacle [below], take off the cover plate and touch the voltage-tester probes to the brass-colored and silver-colored terminals; on a switch [page 164], touch the two brass terminals; on a light fixture, lower the canopy [page 156] and touch the tester probes to the fixture's voltage-carrying (black) and neutral (white) wires. In all cases the tester will not glow if the current is off. If it does glow, you have disconnected the wrong fuse or circuit breaker. When you finish replacing the device, follow the procedure illustrated at left to be sure you have hooked up all wires correctly.

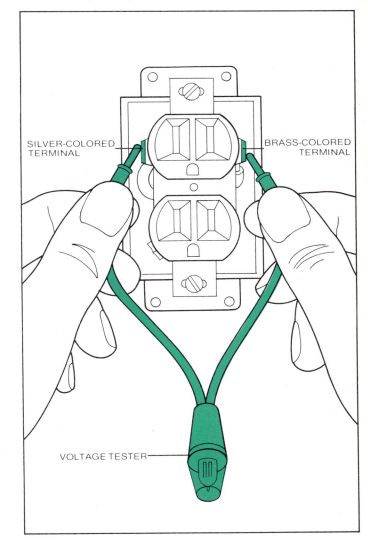

How Grounding Protects You and Your Home

By the end of the 18th Century, several experimenters had been accidentally electrocuted in trying to duplicate Ben Franklin's famous kite experiment, and scientists were well aware of the dangers of electricity. An accumulation of charge could cause a shock, or create a spark or heat to start a fire. But these hazards endangered few people until electric lighting and appliances put the problem into almost every home.

Among the kinds of protection now employed, one method — applied to doorbells, for instance — is to use only low voltages so that sparks and shocks are insignificant. Another approach is to insulate every part of a wiring system or appliance so thoroughly that sparks are contained and it is virtually impossible to touch anything carrying an electrical charge. Some new power tools *(page 32)* are built on this principle.

A third possibility, and the one most widely practiced, is to ground everything that could conceivably leak any electricity. Grounding prevents charge accumulations by connecting exposed parts directly to earth. Any charge that builds up flows to the ground; if hazardous, it blows a fuse or trips a circuit breaker, turning off current.

From accidental grounds to grounding systems

Provisions for grounding have grown elaborate over the years. The men who first formulated the National Electrical Code in the early 1890s had neither the knowledge to write recommendations for adequate grounding nor the materials with which to achieve it: no wiring was ever grounded except by accident. The first grounding that was by design appeared in 1899 with armored cable *(page 139)*, which houses the "hot" and neutral wires inside a steel sheath. With this cable, grounding was (and in old houses still is) accomplished by using the metal sheath as a conductor. One end of the sheath was firmly attached to the metal outlet box, the other to an established ground connection at the service panel.

The flaw in this scheme was its dependence on the metal armor as an electrical conductor. If the contact between the armor and the metal box was poor, or if it deteriorated, the intended link to ground was interrupted. In newer cable, whether sheathed in metal armor or in plastic, a separate uninsulated ground wire, alongside the hot and neutral wires, was connected to every box in the house *(middle drawing, opposite)*.

Connecting the third wire to each box only half solved the grounding problem, however. It did ground the box but it did not ground appliances plugged into a receptacle. The next step in electrical safety was the grounding of heavy-duty machinery by switching to a three-prong plug on major appliances and on most power tools. The third prong (the rounded one) is connected by a separate wire in the cord to the metal housing of the machine. When the plug is put into a receptacle, that prong fits a slot connected to ground.

The introduction of the three-prong plug focused attention on a weakness in the electrical defensive system. Although boxes were securely grounded, the devices in the boxes sometimes were not. A switch, and more important a receptacle, still was connected to ground not by wires but by metal-to-metal contact with the box through mounting screws. If a sloppy paint job destroyed this contact the receptacle would be ungrounded, as would any appliances with three-prong plugs, which depend on the receptacle for grounding. This defect was remedied in 1974, when the

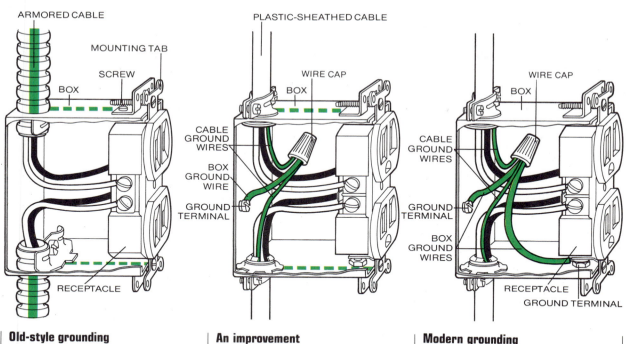

ARMORED CABLE
MOUNTING TAB
SCREW
BOX
RECEPTACLE

PLASTIC-SHEATHED CABLE
WIRE CAP
BOX
CABLE GROUND WIRES
BOX GROUND WIRE
GROUND TERMINAL

WIRE CAP
BOX
CABLE GROUND WIRES
GROUND TERMINAL
BOX GROUND WIRES
RECEPTACLE
GROUND TERMINAL

Old-style grounding

Although special ground wires are lacking, this receptacle is grounded. Metal fasteners connect it to the metal box, which is in contact with the metal armor of the cable. The armor is connected to ground at the service panel.

An improvement

Two wires ground this receptacle. One wire attached to the box is connected by a wire cap to ground wires in both cables entering the box. The receptacle still depends for its ground on screws and tabs fastening it to the box.

Modern grounding

To eliminate the danger of a faulty contact between the receptacle and the box, a short wire is connected from a special terminal at the receptacle base to the box ground wire and then to both of the cable ground wires.

Code recommended that a second short length of wire be run from the wire cap directly to a special grounding connection on receptacles, switches and some lighting fixtures *(drawing at right, above)*. The devices illustrated in this book include the extra connection, and such devices are recommended; however, devices without these connections are still widely available.

The latest development in shock prevention is the ground-fault circuit interrupter (GFCI), a device that detects the flow of minute currents to ground. It turns off the circuit so fast that a hazardous current never develops. Also, it does not require a separate, third, ground wire. Thus it can be used to improve safety in old houses where no reliable ground is available in many boxes *(page 173)*.

Such interlocking protective systems would eliminate almost all electrical hazards if electrical codes were rigidly followed. Often, however, boxes and their receptacles are not grounded. Connections may have deteriorated. New wiring using cable with a built-in grounding wire, especially if it is an extension of an older system that lacks this extra wire, might not be grounded. Electricians have been known to save time by not installing ground connections, so that even the wiring of a new house could be inadequately grounded.

The only way to be sure your system is completely protected is to check outlets with a voltage tester *(page 143)*. You can add ground wires to switches, receptacles and fixtures that have ground connections, or you can improve the electrical contact between boxes and the devices in them by cleaning the mounting tabs and screws. If, after such attention, an outlet still is ungrounded, consider installing a GFCI, particularly in damp locations.

HOME CIRCUITS

A modern home depends on electricity for light, heat (with almost any heating system) and the power to run dozens of appliances. This electricity is distributed throughout the house by a number of separate circuits—independent stretches of wiring that run inside the walls and ceilings.

A generation ago a typical home might get by with four 120-volt circuits and a total of 60 amperes' service for the house. Today, in an age of enormously increased electrical consumption, a home may need from 150 to 300 amperes, both 120 and 240 volts, and as many as three dozen circuits.

To supply these circuits, electricity from a utility company's wires passes through a meter and a service panel *(below, left),* which divides the power among the separate circuits. The floor plan opposite shows how 18 circuits might serve a compact, two-story home; the plan indicates circuit arrangement, not the actual location of wires or outlets. The color code *(bottom, far right)* identifies the voltage and amperage, which together determine the power capacity of each circuit.

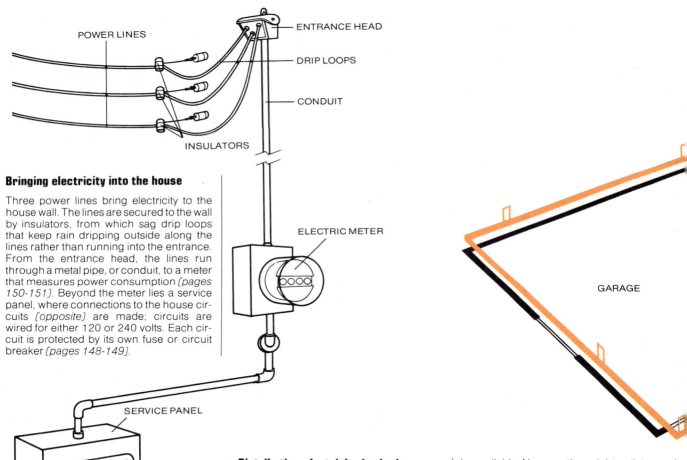

POWER LINES

ENTRANCE HEAD

DRIP LOOPS

CONDUIT

INSULATORS

ELECTRIC METER

GARAGE

SERVICE PANEL

Bringing electricity into the house

Three power lines bring electricity to the house wall. The lines are secured to the wall by insulators, from which sag drip loops that keep rain dripping outside along the lines rather than running into the entrance. From the entrance head, the lines run through a metal pipe, or conduit, to a meter that measures power consumption *(pages 150-151).* Beyond the meter lies a service panel, where connections to the house circuits *(opposite)* are made; circuits are wired for either 120 or 240 volts. Each circuit is protected by its own fuse or circuit breaker *(pages 148-149).*

Distributing electricity in the house

The house sketched here contains 18 electrical circuits to serve all of the lighting fixtures, wall receptacles and major appliances. Relatively low-capacity—120-volt, 15-ampere—circuits *(orange)* will suffice for most of the lamps, TV sets and small appliances used in the family room, living room, bedrooms and bathrooms. Outlets in any one room are divided between two circuits, so that if one fails, power will still be available. No more than eight outlets are installed on any one circuit to reduce the chance of overloading. Heavier-capacity—120-volt, 20-ampere—circuits *(purple)* will serve kitchen, workshop, storage room and dining room for such appliances as refrigerator, toaster and power tools. For each appliance that uses large amounts of power, such as a clothes drier or electric range, there is a separate 240-volt circuit of either 30-ampere *(light blue)* or 50-ampere *(dark blue)* current capacity.

BEDROOM

BEDROOM

BEDROOM

MASTER BEDROOM

BATHROOM

BATHROOM

WORKSHOP

CENTRAL AIR
CONDITIONER

LIVING ROOM

DINING ROOM

FAMILY ROOM

LAVATORY

ENTRANCE

REFRIGERATOR

STORAGE ROOM

CLOTHES
WASHER

WATER
HEATER

KITCHEN

CLOTHES
DRIER

RANGE

DISHWASHER

CIRCUIT CAPACITIES

120 VOLTS, 15 AMPS.

120 VOLTS, 20 AMPS.

240 VOLTS, 30 AMPS.

240 VOLTS, 50 AMPS.

Circuit Protectors

To protect you against fire or shock, every circuit in your house includes one or the other of two types of safety device: a fuse or a circuit breaker. They operate differently but serve the same purpose—to shut off electricity when the circuit carries more current than it is intended to.

Fuses *(below)* destroy themselves —"blow"—to interrupt circuits when excess current flows, and must be re-

placed before current can flow again. Many modern circuits are protected by circuit breakers *(opposite),* which function as switches with contacts that automatically snap open when current exceeds their ratings; after danger has passed, the circuit breaker can be reset manually.

The excess current that makes fuses blow and circuit breakers open can arise in two ways. An overload —usually the result of plugging too many appliances into a single circuit —draws so much electricity that re-

sistance in the wire could produce enough heat to start a fire. A short circuit—perhaps caused by worn insulation that lets bare wires touch each other or the grounded frame of an appliance—introduces the danger of shock—and produces a heavy, heat-generating surge of current.

Though circuit protectors will protect you from these consequences, they cannot cure an overload or a short circuit. Before replacing a fuse or resetting a circuit breaker, find the cause of trouble and correct it.

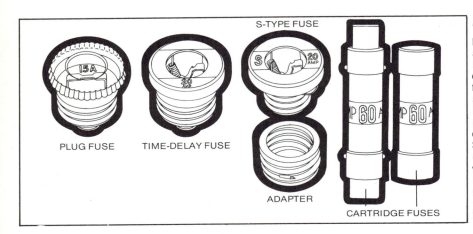

PLUG FUSE   TIME-DELAY FUSE   S-TYPE FUSE   ADAPTER   CARTRIDGE FUSES

A fuse for every circuit

Fuses are marked with the maximum in amperes ("AMP" or "A") they permit. All have metal strips that melt when heated by excess current. The plug type is the most familiar. A time-delay fuse has a spring to support the strip and keep it from breaking if softened by a brief surge (such as an appliance carries on starting); only if the excess lasts will the strip melt to blow the fuse. S-type fuses have ring adapters—in different threads for different capacities—to prevent use of a fuse of the wrong rating. Cartridge fuses—capped for currents up to 60 amperes, knife-edged for 60 or higher —protect an electric range and link circuits to the main power line.

The telltale face of a fuse

A glance at a plug fuse tells the condition of the circuit it protects. If the metal strip is intact *(above, left)*, both fuse and circuit are in good order. In a blown fuse, a cleanly parted strip *(center)* indicates an overload; a discolored window *(right)*, a short circuit.

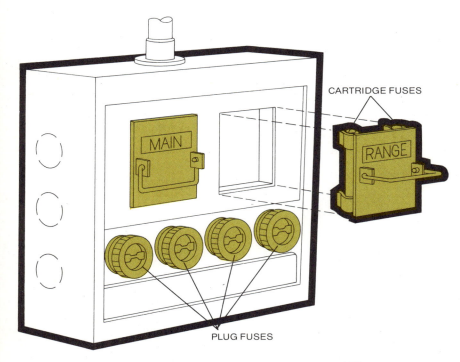

CARTRIDGE FUSES   MAIN   RANGE   PLUG FUSES

A fuse panel

The old-style service panel at left serves a relatively small home. Its main switch, fitted with two cartridge fuses, monitors current in four appliance-and-light circuits, each protected by a plug fuse. The similar range switch passes current directly to an electric range. Pulling out the main and range switches takes their fuses out of their circuits, so that you can then handle these cartridge fuses safely with your fingers. In replacing a plug fuse, stand on a dry surface and touch only the fuse rim.

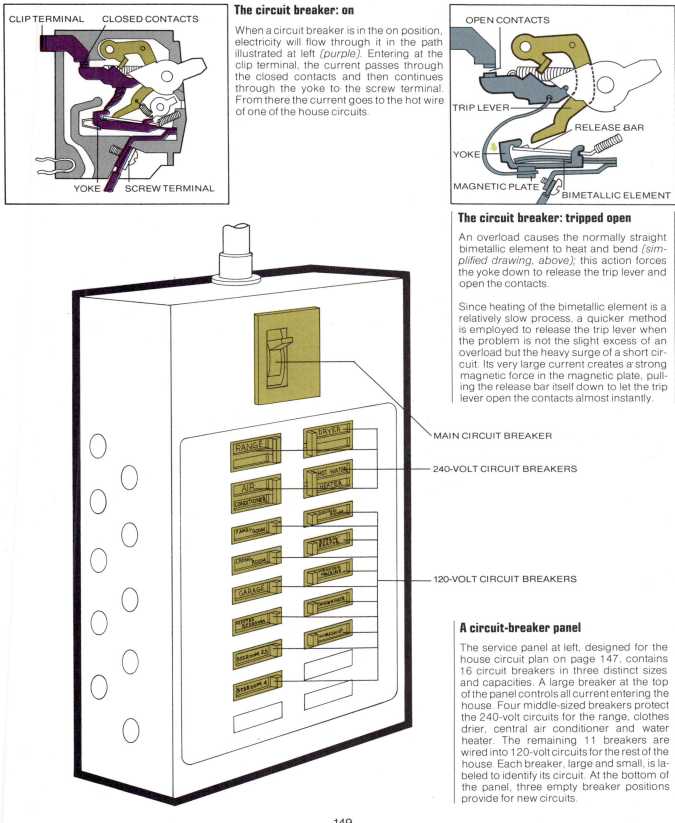

The circuit breaker: on

When a circuit breaker is in the on position, electricity will flow through it in the path illustrated at left *(purple)*. Entering at the clip terminal, the current passes through the closed contacts and then continues through the yoke to the screw terminal. From there the current goes to the hot wire of one of the house circuits.

CLIP TERMINAL   CLOSED CONTACTS

YOKE   SCREW TERMINAL

OPEN CONTACTS

TRIP LEVER

RELEASE BAR

YOKE

MAGNETIC PLATE

BIMETALLIC ELEMENT

The circuit breaker: tripped open

An overload causes the normally straight bimetallic element to heat and bend *(simplified drawing, above)*; this action forces the yoke down to release the trip lever and open the contacts.

Since heating of the bimetallic element is a relatively slow process, a quicker method is employed to release the trip lever when the problem is not the slight excess of an overload but the heavy surge of a short circuit. Its very large current creates a strong magnetic force in the magnetic plate, pulling the release bar itself down to let the trip lever open the contacts almost instantly.

MAIN CIRCUIT BREAKER

240-VOLT CIRCUIT BREAKERS

120-VOLT CIRCUIT BREAKERS

RANGE   DRYER

AIR CONDITIONER   HOT WATER HEATER

FAMILY ROOM   DINING ROOM

LIVING ROOM   REFRIGERATOR

GARAGE   WASHING MACHINE

MASTER BEDROOM   DISHWASHER

BEDROOM 2,3   WORKSHOP

BEDROOM 4

A circuit-breaker panel

The service panel at left, designed for the house circuit plan on page 147, contains 16 circuit breakers in three distinct sizes and capacities. A large breaker at the top of the panel controls all current entering the house. Four middle-sized breakers protect the 240-volt circuits for the range, clothes drier, central air conditioner and water heater. The remaining 11 breakers are wired into 120-volt circuits for the rest of the house. Each breaker, large and small, is labeled to identify its circuit. At the bottom of the panel, three empty breaker positions provide for new circuits.

ELECTRIC METERS AND BILLS

Wise consumers regularly check their electric meters and bills to catch errors made by the meter reader or by the company in computing charges. The meters used in the United States and Canada *(below)* measure the consumption of electricity in kilowatt-hours, or kwh (a single kwh represents the consumption of 1,000 watts for one hour). Inside each meter, a small electric motor, its speed determined by the flow of electricity into the house, drives a disc whose edge is visible at the meter face. The disc and its shaft, floating in air on a magnetic suspension system to reduce drag, drive a train of gears that advance number wheels or dial pointers. Periodic readings of the numbers are used to draw up your bill *(opposite)*.

Pointer-type electric meters

The common pointer-type electric meter *(below)* looks somewhat like a set of one-handed clocks, with alternate hands turning clockwise and counterclockwise. (The method for reading the meter is described on the opposite page.) The cryptic figures below the dials tell the following story: CL200—the meter will measure current up to 200 amperes; 240V—the meter is designed for a 240-volt power supply; 3W —three wires are used to conduct electricity to the meter; FM25—the manufacturer's code for the meter's internal wiring scheme; TA30—the meter's accuracy was checked under a 30-ampere current.

Cyclometer-type electric meters

The easiest electric meter to read is the cyclometer type *(above)*, which displays a kwh count on number wheels like those of an automobile odometer. The numbers are read directly across the face, giving a cumulative consumption figure, which is converted into monthly consumption as shown opposite. A relatively modern design, this meter is more expensive than the pointer type *(right)* and less widely used.

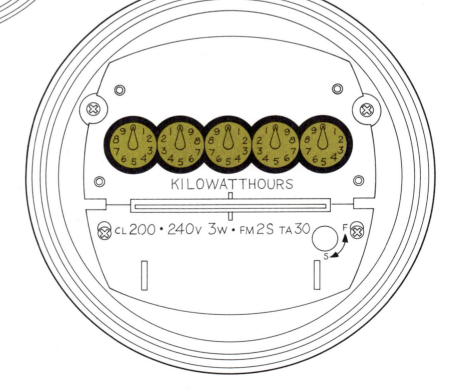

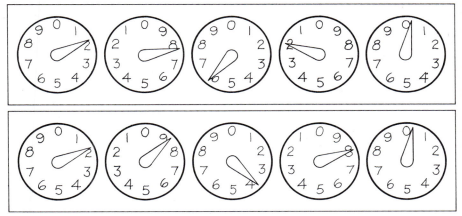

Reading a pointer-type meter

Since all electric meters indicate a cumulative kwh figure, it takes two separate readings to calculate the consumption over a given period of time. Both readings, usually made one or two months apart, will appear on your electric bill. The top meter face at left, recorded as the March 12 reading on the bill shown below, is read from left to right in the following way. The first pointer (turning clockwise) reads 1, the second (counterclockwise) reads 7, and so on, for a complete reading of 17620. When checked on April 12, the meter had advanced to the bottom reading, 18380.

Unscrambling an electric bill

Though their formats differ, most electric bills show the same basic information. On a typical bill this includes, starting at top left, an account number and the dates of the period covered by the bill. On the line below are the rate class for the kind of service supplied, two meter readings, the total kwh consumed (the difference between the two readings), and the amount of the bill. You can verify consumption figures by taking regular meter readings yourself; to check the dollar amount of the bill, multiply your consumption by the rates listed on a rate card, which is available at the power company office.

The rate structure of most electric companies follow graduated scales in which cost per kwh decreases as usage increases. For the bill shown here, the following rates were in effect: the first 25 kwh cost $6.75, the next 75 kwh cost 11.4¢ each ($8.55), the next 200 kwh cost 7.5¢ each ($15.00) and the remaining 460 kwh cost 6.3¢ each ($28.98), for a total of $59.28. A supplemental charge added to this basic amount is local tax—on this bill, $1.77. In addition, there may be a fuel adjustment, a charge or deduction that varies as the fuel costs paid by the power company fluctuate. In this example, fuel costs had gone up slightly during the month covered, and $2.10 was added to the bill. The grand total: $63.15, or just about 8.3¢ per kwh.

Keene Power

Mail payment to
Box 20
Keene, Colorado 80000

Account Number				From	To
41	1422	0585	0004 1	3/12	4/12

Rate	Previous Reading	Present Reading	Kwh used	Amount
1	17620	18380	760	59:28

PREVIOUS BALANCE	
TAX 3.0%	1:77
FUEL ADJUSTMENT	2:10

Next reading date	Amount due
MAY 12	63:15

Keep this part

Keene Power

Box 20
Keene, Colorado 80000

JANET HUBBARD
729 LARCH ROAD
KEENE
COLORADO 80000

Account number			
41	1422	0585	0004 1

Amount due
63 15

Return this portion with your payment

EXTENSION CORDS

The methods for repairing or assembling an extension cord involve basic wiring skills, which are also used, for example, in replacing broken plugs and repairing lamps *(pages 154-155)*. But extension cords present certain special problems. A cord for an appliance that stays in one place should be cut to the exact length needed to reach the wall outlet;

no loops should clutter the floor. Use lightweight two-channel cord and components *(below and right)* for most small nonheating appliances.

However, for larger appliances such as air conditioners and power tools, use heavy-duty three-channel extension cord *(opposite, bottom)*. The size of wire required in a heavy-duty extension depends on its length and the current it must carry (see page 127 for a chart showing how to select the right-sized wire for your needs).

SHELL

PLUG BODY

TERMINAL SCREWS

A two-wire, light-duty extension cord

Make extension cords for lamps, radios and other small appliances of No. 16 two-channel cord, a two-terminal plug and a two-terminal connector. To wire the connector *(right)*, remove the securing screw, separate the parts and loosen the terminal screws. Strip insulation from one half inch of cord, twist the bare wires and loop them around the terminals in the direction the screws tighten. Tighten the terminal screws and reassemble the parts.

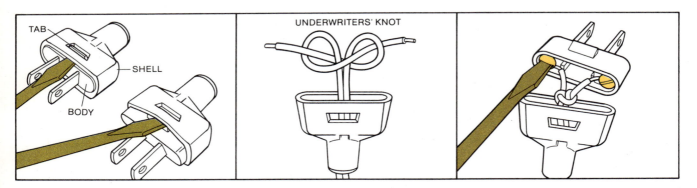

TAB

SHELL

BODY

UNDERWRITERS' KNOT

1 Splitting the plug's case

Push the tip of a wide-bladed screwdriver into the joint between the outer shell of the plug and the body of the plug *(above, left)*. Using a prying and twisting motion, gently force the shell away from the body of the plug far enough to free the retaining tab *(above, right)*, which locks together the two parts of the plug. Turn the plug upside down and repeat the procedure to free the second tab. Pull the body of the plug free of the shell.

2 Tying an Underwriters' knot

Thread the cord into the shell of the plug and separate the channels for about two inches from the end. Strip approximately one half inch of insulation from each channel, and tie the two channels in the Underwriters' knot (people often pull the cord instead of the plug, and this knot will take up the strain, preventing the wires from coming loose). Pull the cord back until the knot lies snug in the shell.

3 Connecting the wires

Twist the stripped wire into tight strands and wind each strand around a terminal, clockwise, so that the screws will draw the wires up securely when tightened. In the type of two-terminal plug shown here, a wire can be attached to either terminal; in a polarized plug, the coded wire should be attached to the brass terminal, the uncoded wire to the silver. Tighten the screws and push the body of the plug back into the shell to lock the tabs.

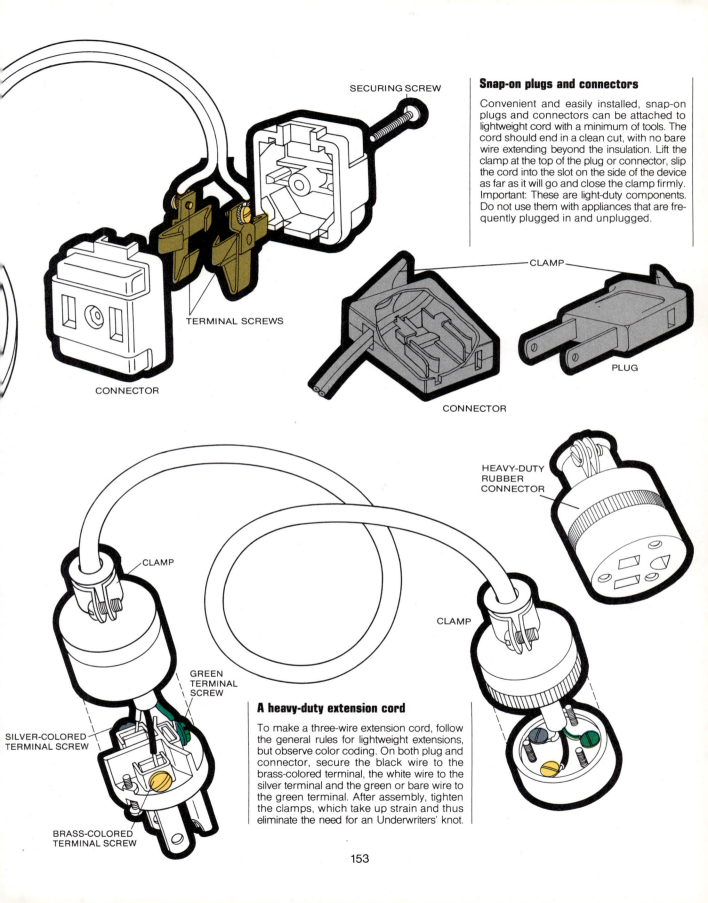

SECURING SCREW

TERMINAL SCREWS

CONNECTOR

Snap-on plugs and connectors

Convenient and easily installed, snap-on plugs and connectors can be attached to lightweight cord with a minimum of tools. The cord should end in a clean cut, with no bare wire extending beyond the insulation. Lift the clamp at the top of the plug or connector, slip the cord into the slot on the side of the device as far as it will go and close the clamp firmly. Important: These are light-duty components. Do not use them with appliances that are frequently plugged in and unplugged.

CLAMP

CONNECTOR

PLUG

HEAVY-DUTY RUBBER CONNECTOR

CLAMP

CLAMP

GREEN TERMINAL SCREW

SILVER-COLORED TERMINAL SCREW

A heavy-duty extension cord

To make a three-wire extension cord, follow the general rules for lightweight extensions, but observe color coding. On both plug and connector, secure the black wire to the brass-colored terminal, the white wire to the silver terminal and the green or bare wire to the green terminal. After assembly, tighten the clamps, which take up strain and thus eliminate the need for an Underwriters' knot.

BRASS-COLORED TERMINAL SCREW

153

REWIRING LAMPS

You need never throw out a lamp that does not work, once you know how to fix it. Unplug the lamp and examine the plug and the cord; if either is broken or shows signs of wear, replace it. (Never splice a worn lamp cord; replace it completely, as shown below.) If both plug and cord are in good shape, move on to the socket. You may want to consider replacing a one-way socket with a three-way type, which offers several lighting levels. The wire connections to such a socket are identical with those of the one-way type. In either case, keep the hot and neutral sides of the wiring separate so that current is fed only to the small button at the bottom of the socket rather than to the more accessible shell, where it could cause a shock.

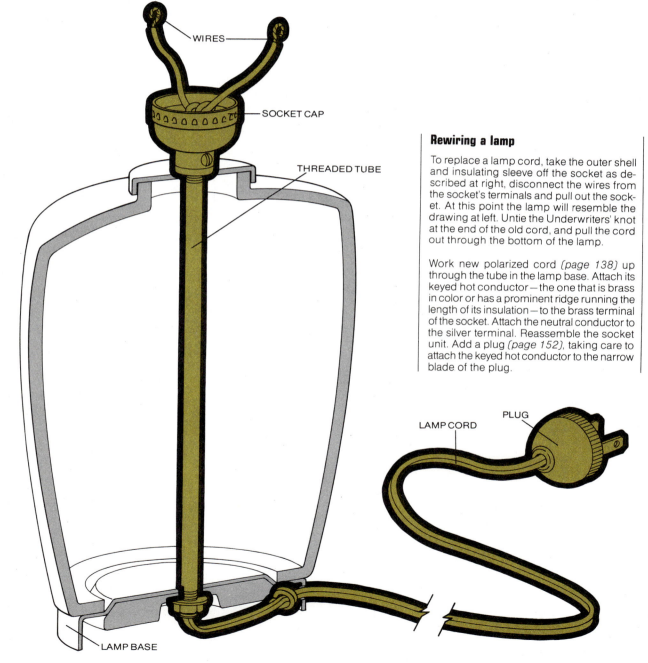

WIRES

SOCKET CAP

THREADED TUBE

LAMP BASE

LAMP CORD

PLUG

Rewiring a lamp

To replace a lamp cord, take the outer shell and insulating sleeve off the socket as described at right, disconnect the wires from the socket's terminals and pull out the socket. At this point the lamp will resemble the drawing at left. Untie the Underwriters' knot at the end of the old cord, and pull the cord out through the bottom of the lamp.

Work new polarized cord *(page 138)* up through the tube in the lamp base. Attach its keyed hot conductor—the one that is brass in color or has a prominent ridge running the length of its insulation—to the brass terminal of the socket. Attach the neutral conductor to the silver terminal. Reassemble the socket unit. Add a plug *(page 152)*, taking care to attach the keyed hot conductor to the narrow blade of the plug.

OUTER SHELL

Replacing a lamp socket

Disassemble a worn-out lamp socket by working from top to bottom. Push the tip of a screwdriver against the point marked "PRESS," and lift off the shell. Remove the insulating sleeve. Loosen the terminal screws, and pull off the wires. Untie the Underwriters' knot only if the cord must be replaced, as shown opposite, or if a new socket cap is needed.

If the old socket cap is reusable, simply leave it in place and assemble the new socket in it. Install the new socket by reversing the disassembly procedure.

INSULATING SLEEVE

How a three-way bulb works

A three-way bulb provides a choice of three levels of illumination from two filaments. The bulb at top right is typical: one filament provides the light of a 50-watt bulb, a second filament that of a 100-watt bulb, and both filaments together that of a 150-watt bulb. The socket (center) contains contacts for two separate circuits. With the switch in its first on position, a circuit passes through the socket's screw shell, the bulb's threaded base and the bulb's ring contact, thus lighting the 50-watt filament (bottom). In the switch's second position, the first circuit is disconnected while a second circuit passes through the screw shell and the bulb's tip contact to light the 100-watt filament. In the third position, both circuits are used and both filaments light.

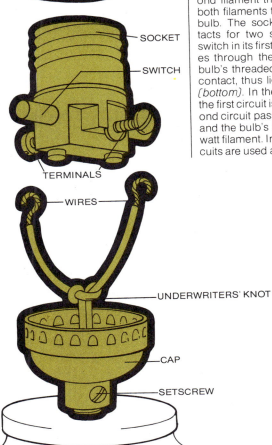

SOCKET

SWITCH

TERMINALS

WIRES

UNDERWRITERS' KNOT

CAP

SETSCREW

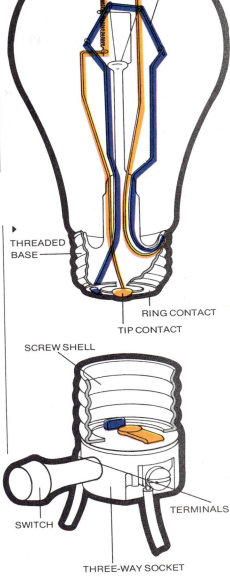

100-WATT FILAMENT 50-WATT FILAMENT

THREADED BASE

RING CONTACT

TIP CONTACT

SCREW SHELL

SWITCH

TERMINALS

THREE-WAY SOCKET

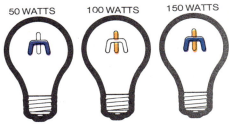

50 WATTS   100 WATTS   150 WATTS

REPLACING LIGHT FIXTURES

Although neither incandescent- nor fluorescent-light fixtures require repair very often, they sometimes become so outmoded a replacement is necessary. Whether a new light fixture is a matter of taste or necessity, the wiring is easy: in most cases, you simply connect the black wire to the brass-colored terminal on the fixture, and the white wire to the silver-colored terminal. The only slight difficulty you may encounter will be with the hardware for holding the fixtures in place.

The size and weight of the fixture determine how it is installed. The smallest fixtures are screwed directly to tabs of the metal box in the ceiling or wall (below, left). Fixtures with mounting holes too far apart to fit the box tabs are attached with fixture straps (below, right). A heavy chandelier is attached to the house structure by an assemblage of oddly named pieces (right): threaded rods called a stud and a nipple, a connector called a hickey, and a fastener called a collar.

When you replace an old fixture, turn off the power and remove the light bulbs. You will need two hands; have a helper hold the fixture while you work, or shape hooks from clothes hangers to suspend the fixture from the ceiling box.

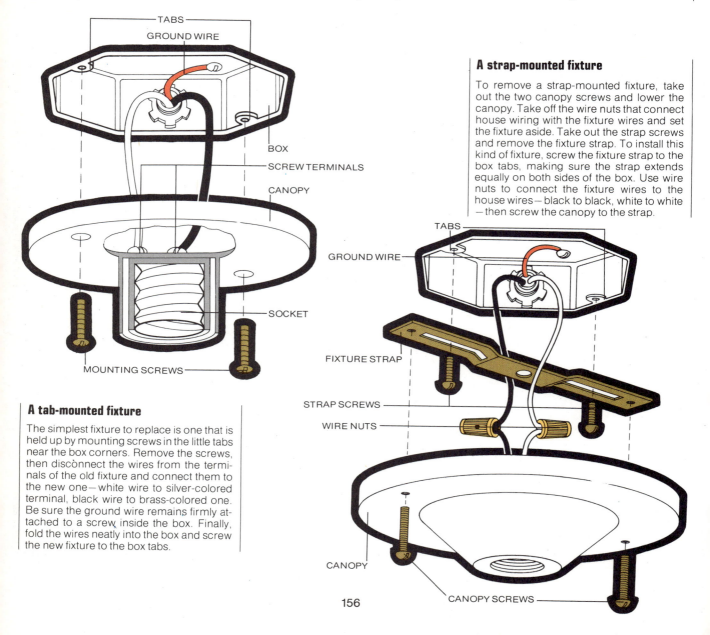

A strap-mounted fixture

To remove a strap-mounted fixture, take out the two canopy screws and lower the canopy. Take off the wire nuts that connect house wiring with the fixture wires and set the fixture aside. Take out the strap screws and remove the fixture strap. To install this kind of fixture, screw the fixture strap to the box tabs, making sure the strap extends equally on both sides of the box. Use wire nuts to connect the fixture wires to the house wires—black to black, white to white—then screw the canopy to the strap.

A tab-mounted fixture

The simplest fixture to replace is one that is held up by mounting screws in the little tabs near the box corners. Remove the screws, then disconnect the wires from the terminals of the old fixture and connect them to the new one—white wire to silver-colored terminal, black wire to brass-colored one. Be sure the ground wire remains firmly attached to a screw inside the box. Finally, fold the wires neatly into the box and screw the new fixture to the box tabs.

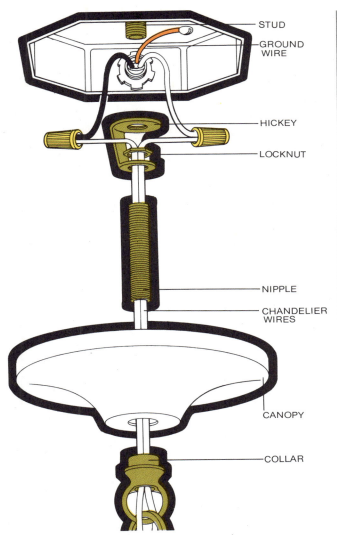

STUD

GROUND WIRE

HICKEY

LOCKNUT

NIPPLE

CHANDELIER WIRES

CANOPY

COLLAR

Long-Life Bulbs: A Bargain?

Light bulbs that "last three times as long" are hard to resist. They do reduce the inconvenience of changing burned-out bulbs. And though a long-life bulb costs slightly more, it may be less expensive in the long run than replacing a regular bulb three times. There is a catch, however.

A long-life bulb lasts longer than a regular bulb because its filament is designed to operate at a lower temperature. But lower temperatures also mean less light. Tripling the life of a bulb makes it 25 per cent dimmer than a regular bulb that uses the same amount of electricity. Put another way, to get the same amount of light you need a long-life bulb of higher wattage—which, of course, will mean a higher cost for electricity.

So, are long-life bulbs worth the higher cost of the light they produce? You should decide according to your needs. If you want maximum illumination per dollar, regular bulbs are probably the better buy. On the other hand, the less frequent need to replace hard-to-reach bulbs—particularly in hallways and stairwells—might well be worth the extra cost of long-life bulbs.

A stud-mounted fixture

Remove a chandelier by unscrewing the collar. Then lower the chandelier and canopy, and disconnect the wires. To hang a chandelier, assemble nipple, hickey and stud so their combined length will allow the collar to hold the canopy to the ceiling. Do not attach the collar yet. Tighten the locknut on the nipple. Thread the chandelier wires through canopy, nipple and hickey bottom, and connect them to the house wires. Screw the collar onto the nipple to secure the canopy.

A wall-mounted fixture

To replace a wall-mounted fixture, unscrew the center nut from the nipple and then follow the wiring procedures described for other fixtures. When installing the new unit, adjust the nipple so the center nut holds the fixture snug against the wall.

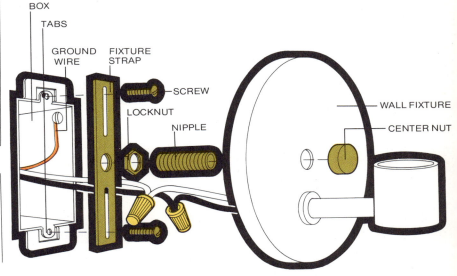

BOX

TABS

GROUND WIRE

FIXTURE STRAP

SCREW

LOCKNUT

NIPPLE

WALL FIXTURE

CENTER NUT

Saving Electricity with Fluorescents

As far back as 1896, Thomas A. Edison built a primitive fluorescent-light fixture that worked, after a fashion; however, fluorescent light remained commercially impractical until it reappeared in its modern form in 1938.

By the early 1960s, it accounted for more than half the electric illumination in the United States; in a recent year, America produced more than 300 million fluorescent bulbs.

This rise in popularity is due mainly to fluorescent lighting's economy. This type of bulb produces more than five times as much light per watt of power consumed as an incandescent. And although it costs more to buy, its longer life means it is a less expensive investment in the long run. Recent advances have made fluorescent lights more versatile and attractive. The color of the light cast, once a cold blue-white, can today be almost any shade desired. Along with the familiar straight tubes, there are now also circular bulbs *(page 162)*, U-shaped bulbs, and special plant-growing and germ-killing bulbs.

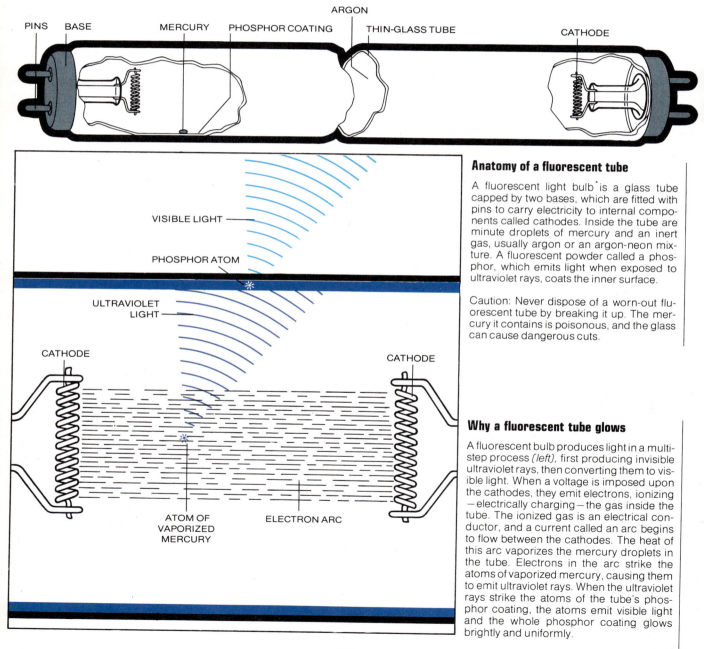

Anatomy of a fluorescent tube

A fluorescent light bulb is a glass tube capped by two bases, which are fitted with pins to carry electricity to internal components called cathodes. Inside the tube are minute droplets of mercury and an inert gas, usually argon or an argon-neon mixture. A fluorescent powder called a phosphor, which emits light when exposed to ultraviolet rays, coats the inner surface.

Caution: Never dispose of a worn-out fluorescent tube by breaking it up. The mercury it contains is poisonous, and the glass can cause dangerous cuts.

Why a fluorescent tube glows

A fluorescent bulb produces light in a multi-step process *(left)*, first producing invisible ultraviolet rays, then converting them to visible light. When a voltage is imposed upon the cathodes, they emit electrons, ionizing —electrically charging—the gas inside the tube. The ionized gas is an electrical conductor, and a current called an arc begins to flow between the cathodes. The heat of this arc vaporizes the mercury droplets in the tube. Electrons in the arc strike the atoms of vaporized mercury, causing them to emit ultraviolet rays. When the ultraviolet rays strike the atoms of the tube's phosphor coating, the atoms emit visible light and the whole phosphor coating glows brightly and uniformly.

The ballast and the starter

In every fluorescent fixture, an essential component called a ballast regulates the flow of electricity to the tube cathodes. The ballast is essentially a small transformer, no different in principle from the one that adjusts the voltage entering your house *(page 125)*. The ballast steps up voltage to start the lamps. It also contains components that interact magnetically with current flow to limit current to the cathodes to keep them from burning out prematurely. In older fixtures, ballasts lower the required starting voltage by preheating the cathodes with a small current channeled through a starter *(below)*. New fixtures produce starting voltage without starters *(page 161)*.

A ballast should last about 12 years. When replacing one, follow the wiring diagram pasted to the housing.

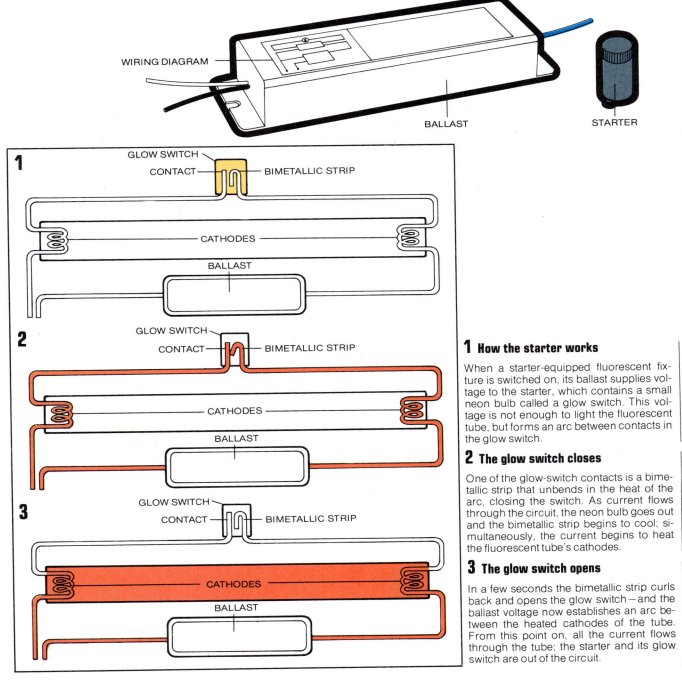

WIRING DIAGRAM

BALLAST

STARTER

GLOW SWITCH
CONTACT — BIMETALLIC STRIP
1
CATHODES
BALLAST

GLOW SWITCH
CONTACT — BIMETALLIC STRIP
2
CATHODES
BALLAST

GLOW SWITCH
CONTACT — BIMETALLIC STRIP
3
CATHODES
BALLAST

1 How the starter works

When a starter-equipped fluorescent fixture is switched on, its ballast supplies voltage to the starter, which contains a small neon bulb called a glow switch. This voltage is not enough to light the fluorescent tube, but forms an arc between contacts in the glow switch.

2 The glow switch closes

One of the glow-switch contacts is a bimetallic strip that unbends in the heat of the arc, closing the switch. As current flows through the circuit, the neon bulb goes out and the bimetallic strip begins to cool; simultaneously, the current begins to heat the fluorescent tube's cathodes.

3 The glow switch opens

In a few seconds the bimetallic strip curls back and opens the glow switch—and the ballast voltage now establishes an arc between the heated cathodes of the tube. From this point on, all the current flows through the tube; the starter and its glow switch are out of the circuit.

Three Fluorescent Starting Systems

Early fluorescent lamps had one major disadvantage: the few seconds of darkness or flicker between the moment you flicked the switch and the moment the light went on. Modern engineering has solved the problem. New ways of striking an arc in the fluorescent tube are embodied in two starting systems that can set lamps aglow with little or no delay.

Your own fluorescent fixtures may be the old-fashioned preheat type described on page 159 and shown below. With a pair of new lamp holders, a new ballast and the appropriate tube, you can convert a preheat fixture to a newer system *(opposite)*.

Installing a completely new fluorescent fixture is even simpler. The new fixture will come with the ballast already mounted and correctly connected to the lamp holders; all you need do is turn off power to the old fixture, then disconnect it from the house wiring and hook up the new one. Important: Make sure that the fixture is well grounded. Fixtures of the rapid-start type *(opposite, bottom)* may malfunction if their tubes are more than one half inch from a grounded metal strip.

A fluorescent fixture is generally built around a metal box that holds all the components. Screws secure the box to wall or ceiling; the shallow lid is the base for the ballast, lamp holders and all the wiring. (Fixtures with more than one bulb are of similar design, with additional wiring for the bulbs.) As in an incandescent-light fixture *(pages 156-157)*, electrical connections are made between the fixture leads and the house wiring—black to black, white to white, and ground wire to a terminal on the fixture. The lid conceals the ballast and wiring. A fluorescent tube that matches the starting system and ballast completes the installation.

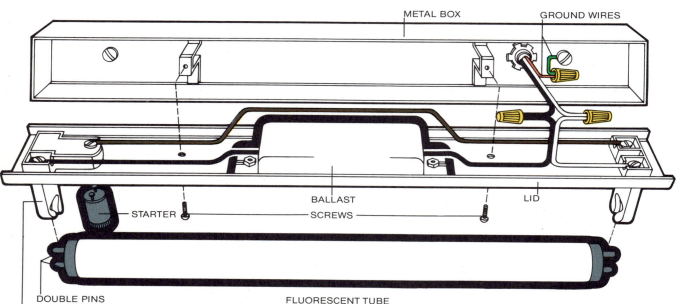

METAL BOX   GROUND WIRES

BALLAST   LID

STARTER   SCREWS

DOUBLE PINS
LAMP HOLDER   FLUORESCENT TUBE

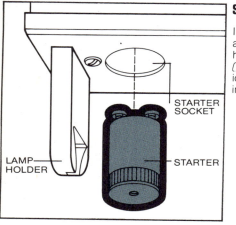

STARTER
SOCKET

LAMP
HOLDER   STARTER

Starter-equipped preheat fluorescents

In the preheat fluorescent starting system above, there is a special starter circuit to heat the tube cathodes and strike an arc *(pages 158-159)*; such systems are easily identified by the aluminum starter protruding from the fixture next to one of the lamp holders *(left)*. A starter usually lasts up to 10 years. Replacing one that shows the signs of malfunction *(chart, page 163)* is as simple as replacing a light bulb. Remove the fluorescent tube, twist the starter counterclockwise and pull it out of its socket. Insert a new starter into the socket, twist it clockwise and replace the tube.

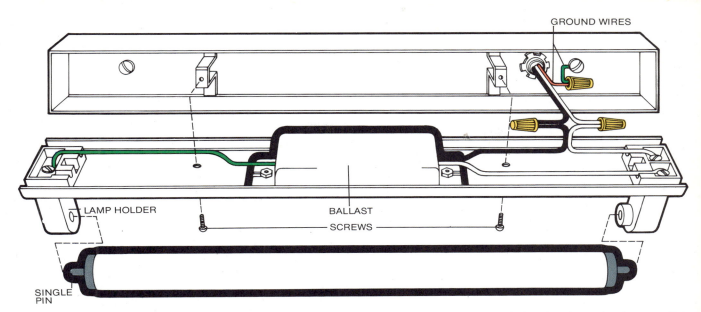

GROUND WIRES

LAMP HOLDER

BALLAST

SCREWS

SINGLE PIN

Instant-start fluorescent lights

An instant-starting system, generally identified by a tube with only a single pin at each end, has no starter circuit to preheat the tube's cathodes. When the light is turned on, a special ballast containing a transformer bigger than other types provides a high voltage—as much as four times the bulb's operating voltage—across the cathodes, immediately ionizing the gas in the tube. As the cathodes heat up and emit more electrons, the arc needs less voltage to sustain it. At this point the ballast reduces its output voltage to the normal operating level. The high voltage used to strike the arc in an instant-start bulb can be dangerous; most lamp-holder designs incorporate a switch at the tube socket that cuts off all power to the ballast as the tube is removed, reducing the hazard of shock to anyone who is changing a tube. Instant-start systems create their high voltage by using bulkier, more expensive ballasts than other fluorescent starting systems; for this reason, they have been giving way to the rapid-start system described below.

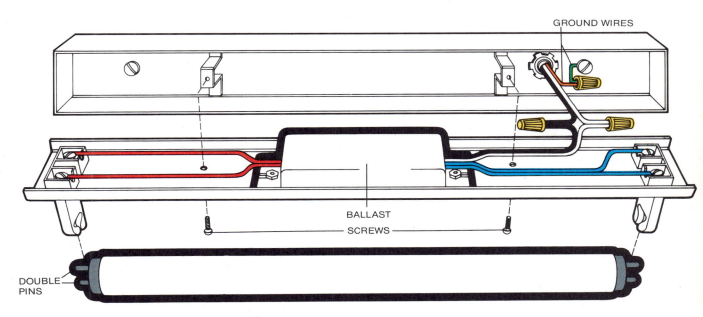

GROUND WIRES

BALLAST

SCREWS

DOUBLE PINS

Rapid-start fluorescent lights

As in a preheat system, a rapid-start tube has two pins at each end, and the tube's cathodes are heated to strike an arc—but there is no starter circuit. Instead, the rapid-start ballast supplies a relatively low voltage directly to special, quick-heating cathodes. The tube lights up without the delay of a starter's glow-switch cycle [page 159]; in fact, the starting time of a rapid-start light approximates that of an instant-start light. The only drawback of the system is its slightly greater consumption of power—so long as the light stays on, a small current from the ballast continues to heat the cathodes. Offsetting the extra power used by these continuously heated cathodes is a slightly greater output of light than provided by a tube of the same size in a preheat or an instant-start system. The combination of quick starting, bright light and compact ballast has made the rapid-start type today's most popular fluorescent light.

161

Circline Fixtures

Imagine an ordinary fluorescent tube bent into a circle, with its ends touching each other. What you are seeing in your mind's eye is the doughnut-shaped tube called a circline lamp, a useful light for special purposes.

Circline tubes fit attractively into small spaces such as bathrooms and some kitchens, where a long straight fixture would look awkward; and the circular tube concentrates its light, making it ideal for small work areas that need high-intensity illumination. To gain these advantages, the tube and fixture have special features.

A single plastic collar at the ends of the tube contains all of the four pins that normally protrude from the ends of a preheat or rapid-start tube *(pages 160-161)*. This arrangement of pins makes the wiring of a circline fixture *(below)* somewhat different from that of an ordinary one, and calls for a special bulb-changing procedure *(opposite)*.

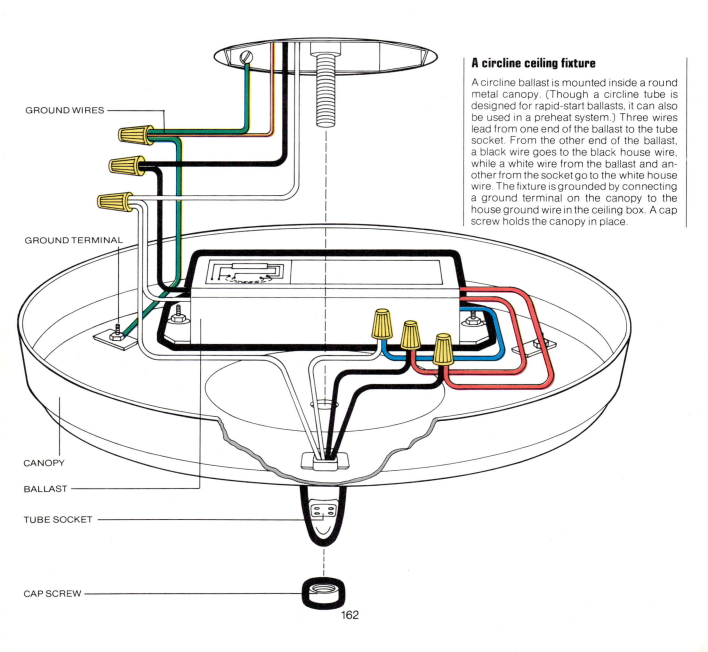

GROUND WIRES

GROUND TERMINAL

CANOPY

BALLAST

TUBE SOCKET

CAP SCREW

A circline ceiling fixture

A circline ballast is mounted inside a round metal canopy. (Though a circline tube is designed for rapid-start ballasts, it can also be used in a preheat system.) Three wires lead from one end of the ballast to the tube socket. From the other end of the ballast, a black wire goes to the black house wire, while a white wire from the ballast and another from the socket go to the white house wire. The fixture is grounded by connecting a ground terminal on the canopy to the house ground wire in the ceiling box. A cap screw holds the canopy in place.

162

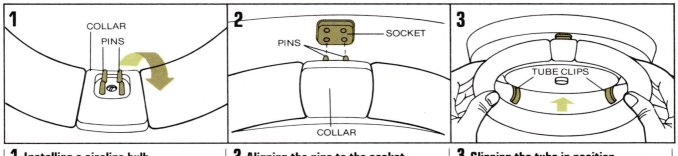

1 Installing a circline bulb

To make it easier to insert the pins of a circline tube into the socket of a fixture, the plastic collar on the tube rotates *(arrow)*. Caution: The collar is delicate and vulnerable. Turn it slowly and gently in order to avoid damaging the tube.

2 Aligning the pins to the socket

Holding the tube in one hand, rotate the collar until the pins line up with the holes in the socket. Then, grasping the tube firmly in both hands with your thumbs on the collar, push the pins into the socket holes as far as they will go.

3 Clipping the tube in position

Grasp the tube near the metal tube clips that are located on either side of the fixture. Push the clips slightly toward the center of the fixture with your middle fingers. Swing the tube upward into position until the clips snap onto it.

Troubleshooting Fluorescent Lights

Problem	Possible Causes	Solution
Light fails to start	Bulb burned out Bulb dirty Incorrect bulb for ballast Defective starter Broken lamp holder Fixture wired incorrectly Line voltage too low Air temperature below 50°	Replace bulb Remove bulb and clean with damp sponge; dry tube before reinstalling it Check ballast label for correct bulb Replace starter Replace lamp holder Check wiring diagram on ballast label Call electrician or power company Warm the room; if necessary, install special low-temperature ballast
Ends of bulb glow but center does not	Defective starter Fixture wired incorrectly Fixture grounded inadequately	Replace starter Rewire according to ballast wiring diagram Check ground wires on fixture
Ends of bulb are black	Bulb nearly burned out	Replace bulb
Bulb flickers or blinks	Tube pins making poor contact Bulb nearly burned out Defective or incorrect starter Air temperature below 50°	Tighten tube in lamp holder Replace bulb Replace starter Warm the room; if necessary, install special low-temperature ballast
Fixture hums	Ballast incorrectly installed Incorrect ballast	Refer to ballast wiring diagram and check ballast mounting Replace with correct ballast for fixture

SWITCH INSTALLATIONS

Everyone uses switches dozens of times each day to turn lights on and off, and they all seem much the same. Yet behind their look-alike cover plates, household wall switches conceal a wide variety of ingenious mechanisms. Some switches can gradually reduce the amount of current that flows through a circuit *(pages 170-171)*; others delay breaking a circuit for several seconds after the switch is thrown, so that you can leave a garage or basement without plunging yourself into darkness *(opposite, bottom)*. Some modern switches are amazingly durable—the silent mercury switch opposite is guaranteed for 50 years; but all switches wear out eventually, and you will sometimes find a different type of switch more desirable than an existing one. Replacing them is a simple job, requiring no skill and only a screwdriver and pliers.

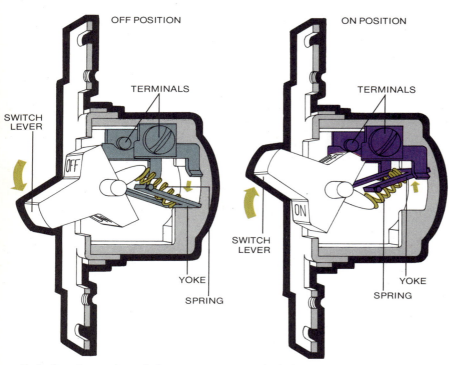

A single-pole toggle switch

The ubiquitous single-pole, on-off switch—the most common of all switches—generally has four basic working parts: a lever, a spring, a U-shaped metal yoke and a pair of brass-colored terminals. With the switch off *(above, left)*, the slightly compressed spring holds the yoke away from the terminal brackets. As the lever is raised to turn the switch on *(large arrow, right)*, it compresses the spring and pushes it to the other side of the yoke; in turn, the spring expands again to force the yoke upward into contact with the terminal brackets *(small arrow)*, completing the circuit. When the switch is turned off again, the reverse spring action moves the yoke away from the terminals.

1 A delayed-action toggle switch

When a delayed-action switch is turned on, a foot on the switch lever depresses a V-shaped assembly. As the assembly moves, one arm forces air out of a chamber at the bottom of the switch, while the other arm fits into a notch in the yoke.

2 The delay

When the switch is turned off, the arm in the notch continues to hold the yoke against the terminals—but the chamber gradually refills with air through a hole in its top.

3 Breaking the circuit

In about 45 seconds, the expanding chamber will push the V assembly upward, forcing the arm out of the notch. The spring then snaps the yoke from the terminals, breaking the circuit.

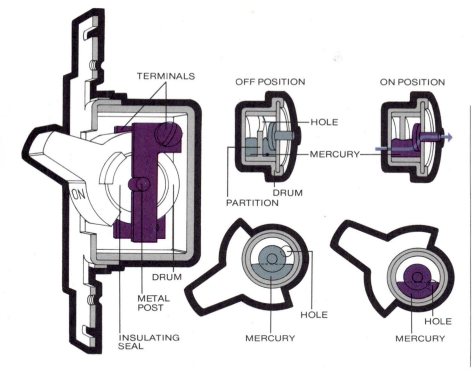

TERMINALS

OFF POSITION

ON POSITION

HOLE

MERCURY

DRUM

PARTITION

DRUM

METAL POST

INSULATING SEAL

HOLE

MERCURY

HOLE

MERCURY

A silent mercury switch

A small drum partially filled with mercury, a good conductor of electricity, turns current on or off with no snapping action — or noise — in this switch *(far left)*. One side of the drum's metal case makes contact with one switch terminal; a metal post, projecting into the drum but insulated from the case by a seal, makes contact with the other. When the switch is off *(center)*, a nonconducting partition divides the mercury into two separate pools. One pool is in contact with a terminal through the drum case, and the second pool is in contact with the other terminal through the post — but current cannot flow through the partition.

Turning the switch on rotates the drum and moves a hole in the partition below the mercury level; now the two pools of mercury merge, creating an electrical path through the hole and completing the circuit.

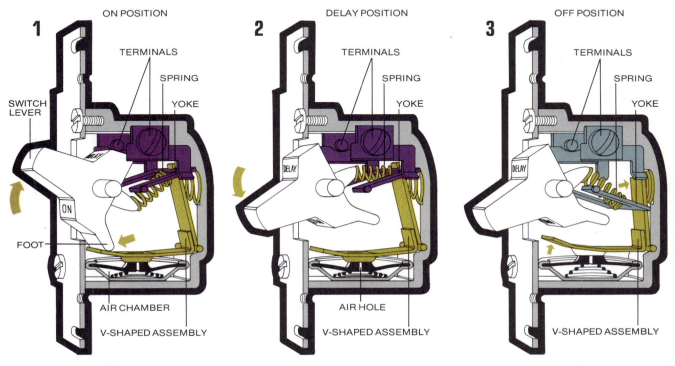

1 ON POSITION

TERMINALS

SPRING

YOKE

SWITCH LEVER

FOOT

AIR CHAMBER

V-SHAPED ASSEMBLY

2 DELAY POSITION

TERMINALS

SPRING

YOKE

DELAY

AIR HOLE

V-SHAPED ASSEMBLY

3 OFF POSITION

TERMINALS

SPRING

YOKE

DELAY

V-SHAPED ASSEMBLY

Replacing Switches

When the flick of a switch fails to turn on a light, and both the light bulb and the fuse or circuit breaker are in order, the problem is usually a faulty switch. Installing a new one requires only a screwdriver and pliers. Before beginning work on any switch, turn off the power to the entire circuit at the service panel. Then remove the switch cover plate, take out the switch and study the connection carefully; you must hook up the new switch like the old one. There will certainly be a black hot wire leading to the switch. But there will also be a white wire in the box, and there may be a bare wire, a green one, a red one and, sometimes, a white wire tipped with black. The color arrangements indicate what lights the switch controls and how; and they should be your guide in connecting the new switch.

Use the slots at the top and bottom of the switch to align it so that the cover plate returns to its original position.

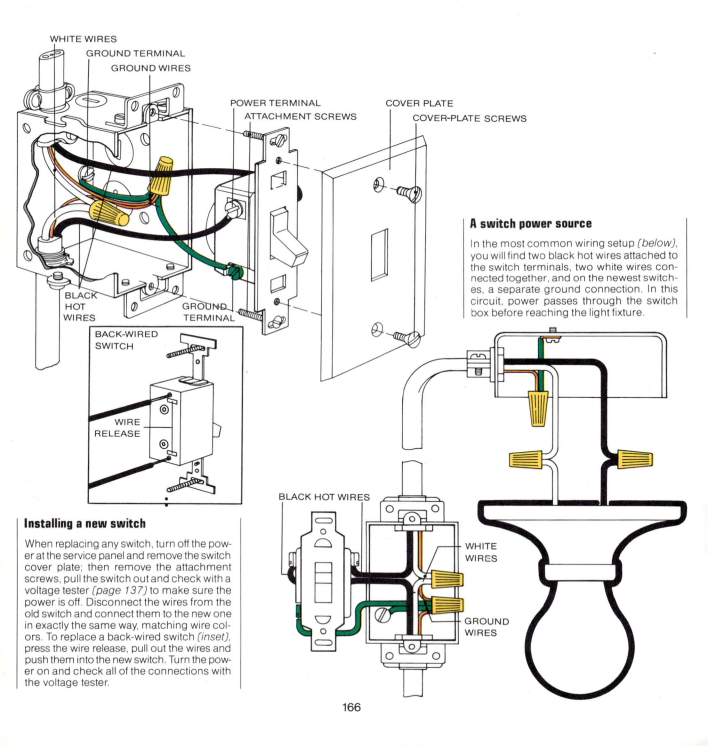

WHITE WIRES
GROUND TERMINAL
GROUND WIRES
POWER TERMINAL
ATTACHMENT SCREWS
COVER PLATE
COVER-PLATE SCREWS
BLACK HOT WIRES
GROUND TERMINAL
BACK-WIRED SWITCH
WIRE RELEASE
BLACK HOT WIRES
WHITE WIRES
GROUND WIRES

A switch power source

In the most common wiring setup *(below)*, you will find two black hot wires attached to the switch terminals, two white wires connected together, and on the newest switches, a separate ground connection. In this circuit, power passes through the switch box before reaching the light fixture.

Installing a new switch

When replacing any switch, turn off the power at the service panel and remove the switch cover plate; then remove the attachment screws, pull the switch out and check with a voltage tester *(page 137)* to make sure the power is off. Disconnect the wires from the old switch and connect them to the new one in exactly the same way, matching wire colors. To replace a back-wired switch *(inset)*, press the wire release, pull out the wires and push them into the new switch. Turn the power on and check all of the connections with the voltage tester.

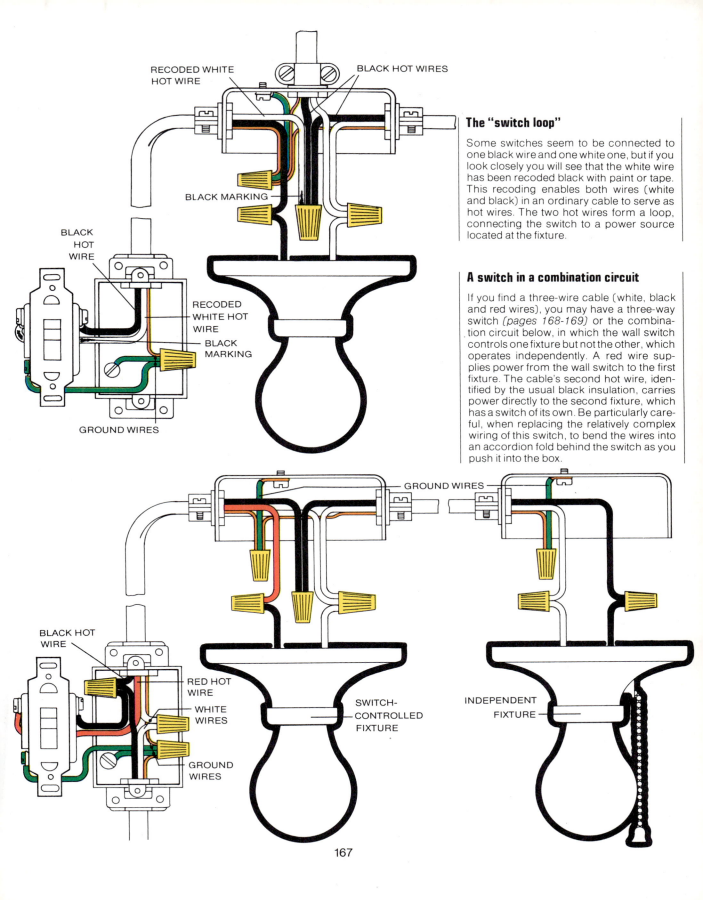

RECODED WHITE
HOT WIRE

BLACK HOT WIRES

BLACK MARKING

BLACK
HOT
WIRE

RECODED
WHITE HOT
WIRE

BLACK
MARKING

GROUND WIRES

The "switch loop"

Some switches seem to be connected to one black wire and one white one, but if you look closely you will see that the white wire has been recoded black with paint or tape. This recoding enables both wires (white and black) in an ordinary cable to serve as hot wires. The two hot wires form a loop, connecting the switch to a power source located at the fixture.

A switch in a combination circuit

If you find a three-wire cable (white, black and red wires), you may have a three-way switch *(pages 168-169)* or the combination circuit below, in which the wall switch controls one fixture but not the other, which operates independently. A red wire supplies power from the wall switch to the first fixture. The cable's second hot wire, identified by the usual black insulation, carries power directly to the second fixture, which has a switch of its own. Be particularly careful, when replacing the relatively complex wiring of this switch, to bend the wires into an accordion fold behind the switch as you push it into the box.

GROUND WIRES

BLACK HOT
WIRE

RED HOT
WIRE

WHITE
WIRES

GROUND
WIRES

SWITCH-
CONTROLLED
FIXTURE

INDEPENDENT
FIXTURE

167

Three-Way Switches

For reasons of safety or convenience you may have "three-way" switches that control a single light from two different locations—from the top and bottom of stairs, for example. The switches that do this job are distinctive; they do not contain markings for on and off, they contain three main terminals rather than two, and they are always connected to a cable containing three insulated wires. The diagrams on this page show the principle by which either of two three-way switches can turn a light on or off. The ones on the opposite page show two common methods of wiring these switches—the method chosen depends on the home wiring layout. Different manufacturers locate the three switch terminals in different positions and use different color codings. But—as on other types—there is always a copper-colored terminal for a black wire; the other terminals may be either brass- or silver-colored, and are easy to distinguish from the copper-colored one.

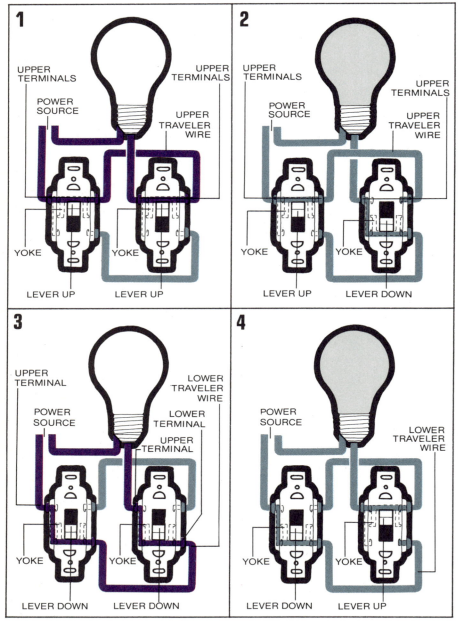

1 Both switch levers up

This and the following drawings show how a pair of three-way switches permit a flow of electricity *(purple lines)* or prevent the flow *(gray lines)*, so that either switch can turn a light on or off. The lines in the diagrams indicate paths of current, not wiring as shown at right.

Each switch lever moves a metal yoke. When both levers are up, electricity passes across the yoke through the upper terminals of the first switch, then through an upper "traveler" wire to the second switch, through its yoke and upper terminals, and thence to the bulb.

2 First lever up, second one down

Pushing the second lever down swings its yoke down, breaking the connection between its two upper terminals, and no current reaches the bulb.

3 Both levers down

With both levers down, the yokes establish a circuit inside each switch between one of the upper terminals and a terminal on the lower part of each switch. The current enters the first switch, makes a zigzag down a leg of the yoke and across the yoke to the lower terminal. The current then flows through the lower traveler wire to the second switch, follows a zigzag path through this switch and relights the bulb.

4 First lever down, second one up

Flipping the second switch lever back up disconnects the yoke from the lower traveler terminal. Again, as in drawing 2, the circuit is interrupted at the second switch, and the current cannot reach the bulb.

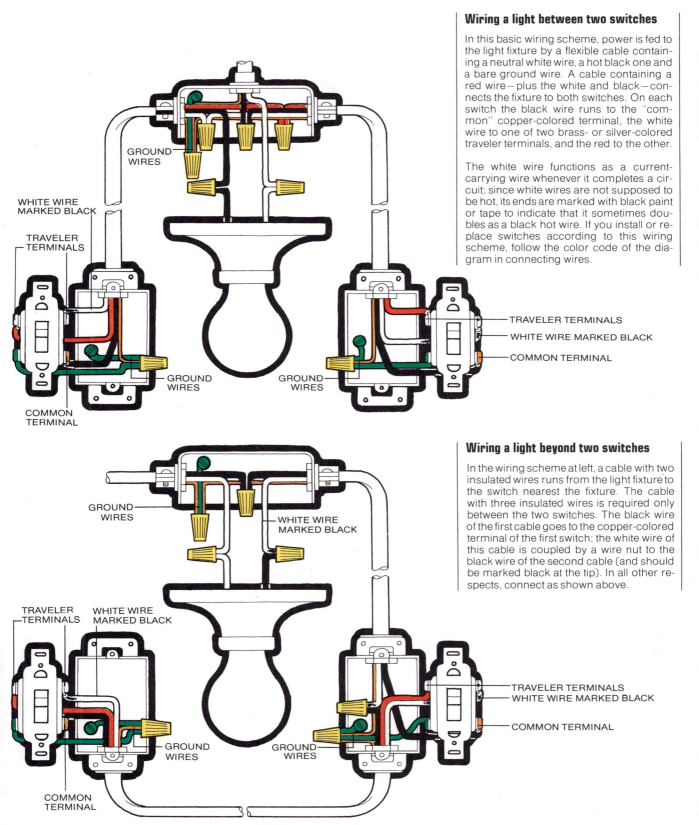

Wiring a light between two switches

In this basic wiring scheme, power is fed to the light fixture by a flexible cable containing a neutral white wire, a hot black one and a bare ground wire. A cable containing a red wire—plus the white and black—connects the fixture to both switches. On each switch the black wire runs to the "common" copper-colored terminal, the white wire to one of two brass- or silver-colored traveler terminals, and the red to the other.

The white wire functions as a current-carrying wire whenever it completes a circuit; since white wires are not supposed to be hot, its ends are marked with black paint or tape to indicate that it sometimes doubles as a black hot wire. If you install or replace switches according to this wiring scheme, follow the color code of the diagram in connecting wires.

GROUND WIRES

WHITE WIRE MARKED BLACK

TRAVELER TERMINALS

GROUND WIRES

GROUND WIRES

COMMON TERMINAL

TRAVELER TERMINALS

WHITE WIRE MARKED BLACK

COMMON TERMINAL

Wiring a light beyond two switches

In the wiring scheme at left, a cable with two insulated wires runs from the light fixture to the switch nearest the fixture. The cable with three insulated wires is required only between the two switches. The black wire of the first cable goes to the copper-colored terminal of the first switch; the white wire of this cable is coupled by a wire nut to the black wire of the second cable (and should be marked black at the tip). In all other respects, connect as shown above.

GROUND WIRES

WHITE WIRE MARKED BLACK

TRAVELER TERMINALS

WHITE WIRE MARKED BLACK

GROUND WIRES

GROUND WIRES

COMMON TERMINAL

TRAVELER TERMINALS
WHITE WIRE MARKED BLACK

COMMON TERMINAL

Power-saving Dimmer Switches

Dimmer switches are easy to install and enable you to adjust lighting to suit your mood. But older types wasted power at low settings because they contained what amounted to electrical heating elements—current not wanted for the lights was diverted and converted into heat. New ones *(below and opposite)* interrupt current to dim lights—but so briefly that the interruption is not visible. They draw only as much power as is needed for the desired illumination.

The high-low switch below, which provides for two illumination levels, uses a diode, an element that passes electricity in one direction only. Since alternating current regularly reverses its direction, completing a cycle 60 times a second, the diode can cut off power for half a cycle—1/120 second—reducing power consumption by 50 per cent and light output by 70 per cent.

The dimmer opposite provides a continuously variable light level from full brightness to off. Its key component is a triac, a transistor-like device that turns current off whenever its direction changes—twice each cycle, or 120 times a second—but turns current on only when a specified voltage is reached. The time required to reach that voltage—and the duration of each on period—is adjusted by setting the rate at which the voltage builds up in an electricity-storing element called a capacitor. Thus the power to the lamp can range from almost zero to 100 per cent.

Dimmer switches will fit standard boxes and, like other switches, they are connected to the black wire of household circuits (switch-wiring instructions are on pages 166-167). But observe two cautions: the total wattage of lights controlled by a dimmer must not exceed the switch rating; and dimmers can be used only with incandescent lights—motor appliances or fluorescents connected to them can be damaged.

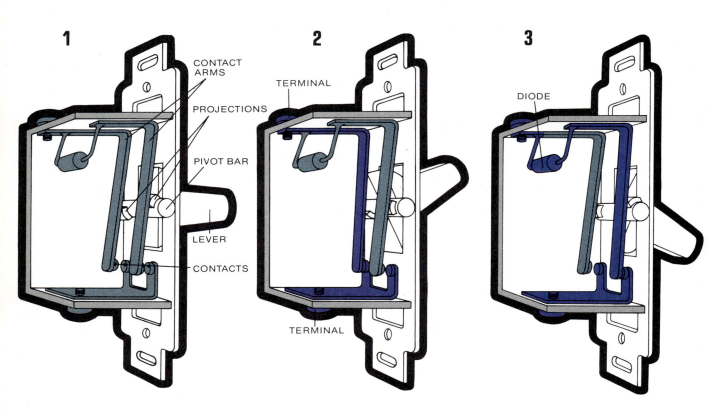

1 The high-low switch: off

A high-low switch is off when the lever is centered. Projections on the lever pivot bar then press both contact arms away from the contacts. No current can flow and lamps connected to it remain off.

2 The high-low switch: high

With the lever up, the pivot turns so that one projection holds one contact open; the other projection is out of the way. The contact arm directly connecting the terminals *(purple)* can close; full current flows.

3 The high-low switch: low

With the switch lever down, the pivot-bar projections now open the full-power contact and close the other. Electricity then flows, via the purple path, through the diode, which blocks half the power.

Inside a triac full-range dimmer

The triac interrupts current 120 times a second, but transmits current only when delivered a minimum voltage from its firing capacitor; the control knob regulates this voltage build-up *(bottom right)*.

With the control knob set low, little current flows into the firing capacitor, and its voltage accumulates slowly, delaying firing of the triac. Since the triac turns off at a fixed, regular rate, lighting current flows for a short time — perhaps 1/1,000 second — before the sequence begins again. With the knob set high, the capacitor builds voltage faster, the triac fires sooner, and lighting current flows longer before the triac goes off again — and the light is brighter.

The interference capacitor and choke filter out triac signals, which cause static on radios or streaked pictures on TV sets.

A full-range dimmer control

A round control knob on the continuously variable dimmer brightens or dims the light to any desired level as it is turned. Some knobs have a click on-and-off point on their turning circumference; others push in and out for on-off control. The heat sink, a button of heat-conducting metal, absorbs heat from the elements inside the switch to dissipate it outside.

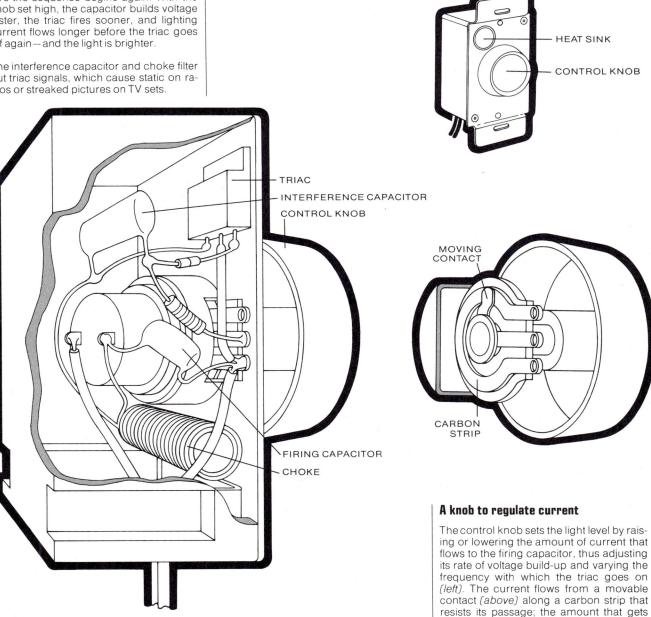

HEAT SINK

CONTROL KNOB

TRIAC

INTERFERENCE CAPACITOR

CONTROL KNOB

MOVING CONTACT

FIRING CAPACITOR

CHOKE

CARBON STRIP

A knob to regulate current

The control knob sets the light level by raising or lowering the amount of current that flows to the firing capacitor, thus adjusting its rate of voltage build-up and varying the frequency with which the triac goes on *(left)*. The current flows from a movable contact *(above)* along a carbon strip that resists its passage; the amount that gets through depends on the contact position.

PLUG-IN RECEPTACLES

Receptacles eventually wear so much that they do not hold a plug securely. Do not try to repair them; replace them. If there is a proper grounding conductor in the box, you should replace two-slot receptacles with three-slot grounded ones.

Before starting to work on any receptacle, turn off the power to that circuit by tripping its circuit breaker or removing its fuse at the service panel. Then test as explained on pages 142-143; remove the cover plate and unscrew the receptacle. The wiring should conform to one of the three types diagramed here. Disconnect the wires and connect the new receptacle, observing the color code. If some of the ground connections are missing, add them if the box is grounded *(page 143, Step 3)*. If it is not, consider installing a ground-fault circuit interrupter, especially if the receptacle is in a damp or outdoor location.

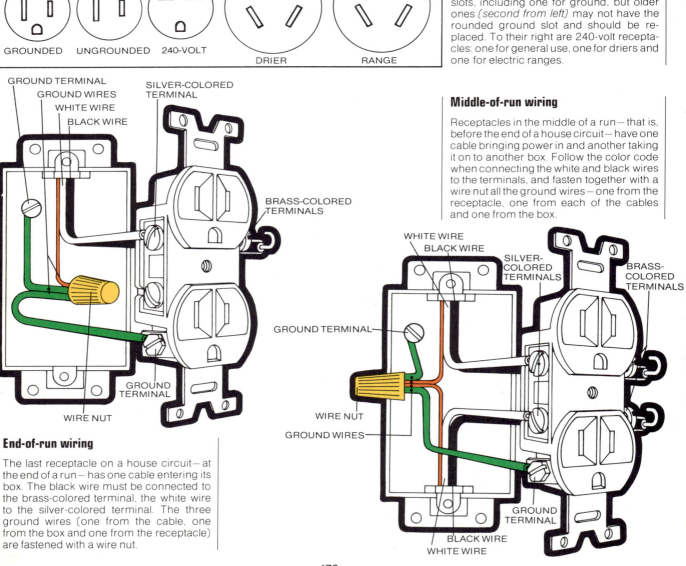

Common electric receptacles

The slot arrangements of five common receptacles are diagramed at left. The standard 120-volt receptacle *(far left)* has three slots, including one for ground, but older ones *(second from left)* may not have the rounded ground slot and should be replaced. To their right are 240-volt receptacles: one for general use, one for driers and one for electric ranges.

Middle-of-run wiring

Receptacles in the middle of a run—that is, before the end of a house circuit—have one cable bringing power in and another taking it on to another box. Follow the color code when connecting the white and black wires to the terminals, and fasten together with a wire nut all the ground wires—one from the receptacle, one from each of the cables and one from the box.

End-of-run wiring

The last receptacle on a house circuit—at the end of a run—has one cable entering its box. The black wire must be connected to the brass-colored terminal, the white wire to the silver-colored terminal. The three ground wires (one from the cable, one from the box and one from the receptacle) are fastened with a wire nut.

172

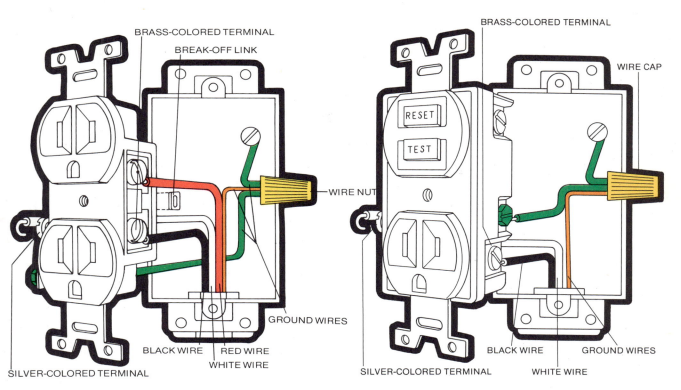

BRASS-COLORED TERMINAL
BREAK-OFF LINK
WIRE NUT
BRASS-COLORED TERMINAL
WIRE CAP
RESET
TEST
GROUND WIRES
BLACK WIRE
RED WIRE
WHITE WIRE
SILVER-COLORED TERMINAL
BLACK WIRE
GROUND WIRES
SILVER-COLORED TERMINAL
WHITE WIRE

Split-circuit wiring

A receptacle connected in a split circuit has extra flexibility. Since each half of the receptacle has its own power supply, one can be wired to a switch for remote control of a lamp, while the other can provide a constant supply of electricity for an appliance. The split circuit has a cable with a red wire in addition to the black and white ones. Connect the extra red wire to the receptable along with the black and white wires, which are connected as usual; the red wire goes to the brass-colored terminal on the switch-controlled section of the receptacle. Remove the break-off link in the brass-trimmed strip by twisting with pliers.

A ground-fault circuit interruptor

If one black and one white wire enter the box, connect the black to a brass-colored terminal and the white to a silver-colored terminal. If there are four wires, connect the two black ones to brass-colored terminals, the two white ones to silver-colored terminals. If a separate ground wire is available, connect it to the GFCI's green terminal.

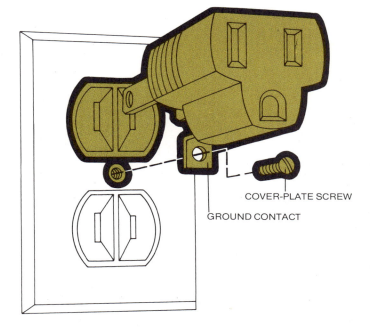

COVER-PLATE SCREW
GROUND CONTACT

Grounding adapter plugs

If you have two-slot receptacles, appliances with three-prong grounding plugs, such as air conditioners, can be plugged in if you install a grounding adapter *(right)*. First test to make sure that the box is properly grounded *(page 143, Step 3)*. If it is, remove the screw in the receptacle cover plate, plug the adapter into the receptacle and replace the screw through the hole in the adapter's ground contact. If the box is not grounded, install a GFCI *(above, right)*.

Extra Receptacles with Surface Wiring

When you need extra electrical receptacles there are three choices. Extension cords are not expensive, but since they lie unprotected on the floor they are liable to damage that may create fire hazards. The best choice is an addition to your in-the-wall wiring. This wiring is both safe and permanent, but the cost may be high if the work has to be done by an electrician. The third option, surface wiring, is safe and relatively inexpensive, since you save money by installing it yourself.

Two kinds of surface wiring are shown here. The plastic type *(below),* which consists of interlocking two-wire units that just snap together, is a very simple way to extend the circuits and keep cords safely off the floor. But it does not provide grounding and is thus suitable only for small things like lights, radios and clocks.

The metal type *(opposite),* which you must cut and wire to size, can be fitted to provide the grounding needed for any appliance, such as a heater or electric typewriter.

As with all wiring jobs, turn off the electricity before connecting additions to the house circuit.

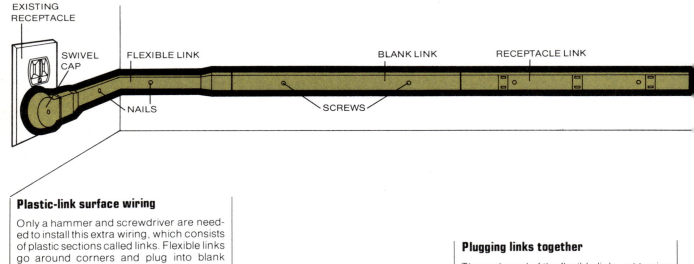

Plastic-link surface wiring

Only a hammer and screwdriver are needed to install this extra wiring, which consists of plastic sections called links. Flexible links go around corners and plug into blank links that connect to receptacle links. The flexible link can be cut to the desired length and nailed to the wall. It plugs into an existing outlet through a swivel cap that turns in any direction. Blank and receptacle links come only in one-foot lengths and are screwed to the wall.

Plugging links together

The male end of the flexible link, cut to size with a special tool available from electrical supply stores, is protected by a plastic cover *(below, far left)* that slips on over the metal prongs. This is the only link that can be plugged into the swivel cap for connection to the house circuit. The female connection of the flexible link *(below, left)* accepts the male connection of either a blank or receptacle link *(right).* Blank and receptacle links can be plugged together in any sequence desired.

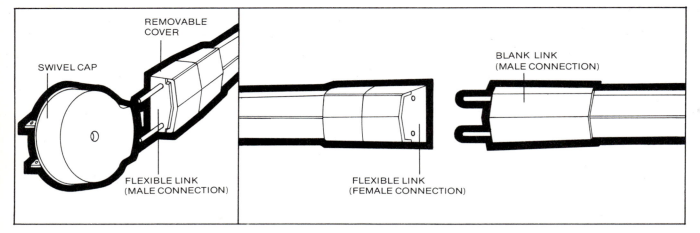

174

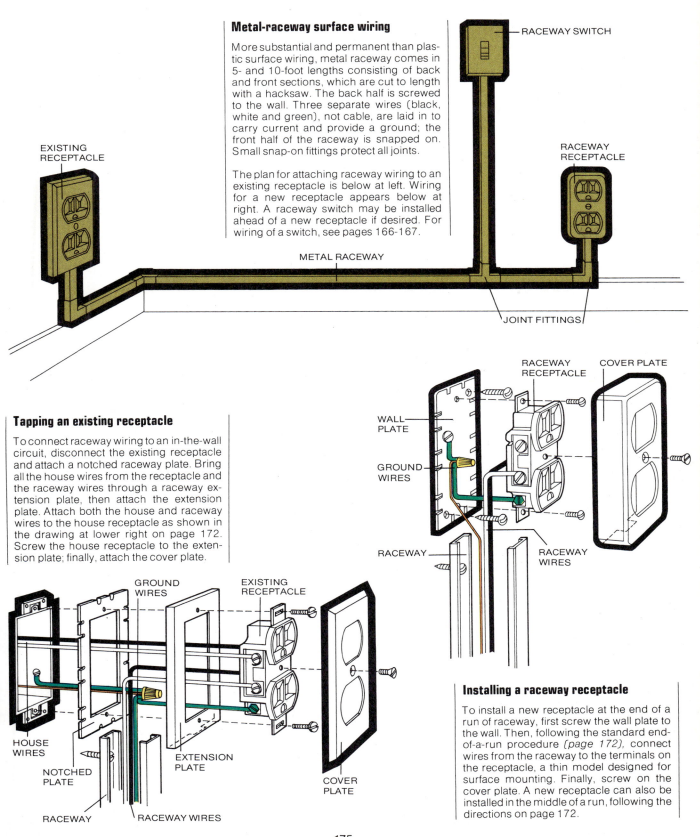

Metal-raceway surface wiring

More substantial and permanent than plastic surface wiring, metal raceway comes in 5- and 10-foot lengths consisting of back and front sections, which are cut to length with a hacksaw. The back half is screwed to the wall. Three separate wires (black, white and green), not cable, are laid in to carry current and provide a ground; the front half of the raceway is snapped on. Small snap-on fittings protect all joints.

The plan for attaching raceway wiring to an existing receptacle is below at left. Wiring for a new receptacle appears below at right. A raceway switch may be installed ahead of a new receptacle if desired. For wiring of a switch, see pages 166-167.

EXISTING RECEPTACLE

RACEWAY SWITCH

RACEWAY RECEPTACLE

METAL RACEWAY

JOINT FITTINGS

Tapping an existing receptacle

To connect raceway wiring to an in-the-wall circuit, disconnect the existing receptacle and attach a notched raceway plate. Bring all the house wires from the receptacle and the raceway wires through a raceway extension plate, then attach the extension plate. Attach both the house and raceway wires to the house receptacle as shown in the drawing at lower right on page 172. Screw the house receptacle to the extension plate; finally, attach the cover plate.

RACEWAY RECEPTACLE

COVER PLATE

WALL PLATE

GROUND WIRES

RACEWAY

RACEWAY WIRES

GROUND WIRES

EXISTING RECEPTACLE

HOUSE WIRES

NOTCHED PLATE

EXTENSION PLATE

RACEWAY

RACEWAY WIRES

COVER PLATE

Installing a raceway receptacle

To install a new receptacle at the end of a run of raceway, first screw the wall plate to the wall. Then, following the standard end-of-a-run procedure *(page 172),* connect wires from the raceway to the terminals on the receptacle, a thin model designed for surface mounting. Finally, screw on the cover plate. A new receptacle can also be installed in the middle of a run, following the directions on page 172.

DOORBELLS AND CHIMES

The 19th Century scientists Hans Oersted and Michael Faraday should get a share of the credit for every doorbell, buzzer and electric chime in use today. They demonstrated the interrelationship of electricity and magnetism—an electric current moving along a wire creates a field of magnetic force around the wire, and conversely, a changing magnetic field generates a current in a wire. These are the working principles of the interrupter, the transformer and the solenoid, which are the electromagnetic devices at the heart of doorbells and chimes. Though their sounds and their styling may vary, all household signaling systems, even the most complex, consist of combinations or variations of the basic installations explained here and on the following pages.

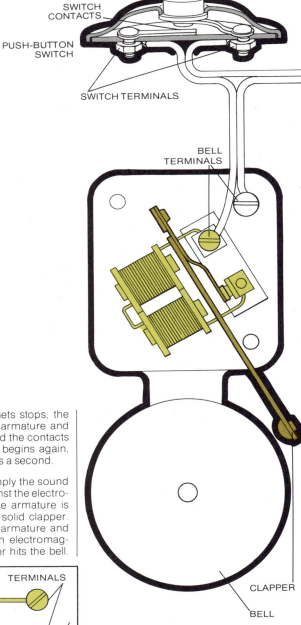

SWITCH CONTACTS

PUSH-BUTTON SWITCH

SWITCH TERMINALS

BELL TERMINALS

CLAPPER

BELL

How bells and buzzers work

An interrupter *(below)* is an electromagnetic switch that turns itself off and on, repeatedly and automatically. Whenever the switch circuit is closed, current will flow through the coils of wire, forming two electromagnets and generating a magnetic field around them. The magnetism attracts an iron armature—but as the armature moves toward the magnets *(arrow, left)*, it opens the circuit by pulling a movable contact arm from a stationary contact. The flow of electricity to electromagnets stops, the magnetism disappears, the armature and contact arm spring back, and the contacts meet *(right)*—and the cycle begins again, repeating itself up to 30 times a second.

The sound of a buzzer is simply the sound of the armature clicking against the electromagnets. In a bell *(right)* the armature is longer and ends in a small, solid clapper. Once in each cycle, as the armature and contact arm shuttle between electromagnets and contact, the clapper hits the bell.

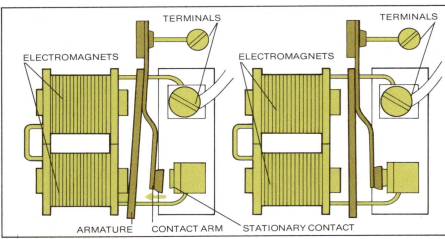

TERMINALS

TERMINALS

ELECTROMAGNETS

ELECTROMAGNETS

ARMATURE   CONTACT ARM   STATIONARY CONTACT

176

How a doorbell is wired

In addition to a bell and its interrupter, the circuit of any doorbell system includes a push-button switch and a transformer. The switch closes the circuit to activate the interrupter. The transformer, hooked into the house wiring and grounded at a junction box, adjusts voltage (as explained at right) from the 120-volt house supply to 10 volts for the doorbell. This low voltage permits the use of thin wire—usually 18-gauge—to link the system's components. In the typical doorbell installation at left, wires run from the transformer to the bell and the switch, and a third wire runs directly from the switch to the bell.

How a transformer works

Every transformer contains two coils of wire, called the primary and the secondary, wound around a piece of iron. Alternating current—which is constantly changing —flows through the primary and sets up a changing magnetic field, which is intensified by the iron; the varying magnetism generates an alternating current in the secondary. The current characteristics depend on the relative number of windings in the coils. In this transformer, a secondary coil with one fifth the windings of the primary steps down voltage to one fifth that of the primary—while simultaneously increasing amperage to five times that of the primary.

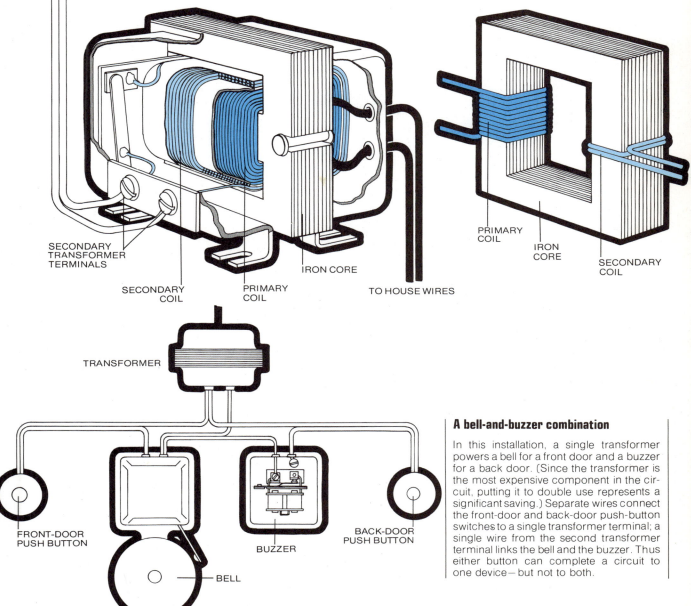

TRANSFORMER

SECONDARY TRANSFORMER TERMINALS

SECONDARY COIL

PRIMARY COIL

IRON CORE

TO HOUSE WIRES

PRIMARY COIL

IRON CORE

SECONDARY COIL

TRANSFORMER

FRONT-DOOR PUSH BUTTON

BUZZER

BACK-DOOR PUSH BUTTON

BELL

A bell-and-buzzer combination

In this installation, a single transformer powers a bell for a front door and a buzzer for a back door. (Since the transformer is the most expensive component in the circuit, putting it to double use represents a significant saving.) Separate wires connect the front-door and back-door push-button switches to a single transformer terminal; a single wire from the second transformer terminal links the bell and the buzzer. Thus either button can complete a circuit to one device—but not to both.

Chimes: Sounds Made by a Magnet

Many homeowners consider mellow-toned door chimes a great improvement over raucous bells and buzzers. The modern device is also versatile: most chimes sound a double tone for the front door (elaborate models may sound four or more) and a single one for the back. These tones are produced by the moving core of an electromagnetic device called a solenoid rather than by an interrupter.

In other respects, chimes are similar to buzzers and bells. Chimes are wired in much the same way and, like a bell-and-buzzer combination, require only a single transformer to reduce the house voltage. In many cases an old bell transformer will operate a new set of chimes, so that replacing a bell and buzzer calls for no more than transferring wires from the old components to the appropriate terminals on the chimes. But check the voltage requirement of your chimes first; if your old transformer supplies the wrong voltage, you will have to replace it as well.

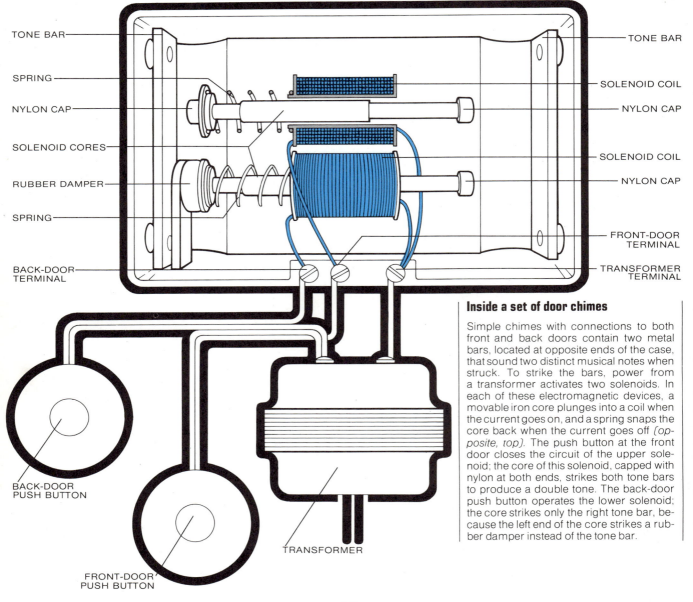

TONE BAR

SPRING

NYLON CAP

SOLENOID CORES

RUBBER DAMPER

SPRING

BACK-DOOR TERMINAL

TONE BAR

SOLENOID COIL

NYLON CAP

SOLENOID COIL

NYLON CAP

FRONT-DOOR TERMINAL

TRANSFORMER TERMINAL

BACK-DOOR PUSH BUTTON

FRONT-DOOR PUSH BUTTON

TRANSFORMER

Inside a set of door chimes

Simple chimes with connections to both front and back doors contain two metal bars, located at opposite ends of the case, that sound two distinct musical notes when struck. To strike the bars, power from a transformer activates two solenoids. In each of these electromagnetic devices, a movable iron core plunges into a coil when the current goes on, and a spring snaps the core back when the current goes off (opposite, top). The push button at the front door closes the circuit of the upper solenoid; the core of this solenoid, capped with nylon at both ends, strikes both tone bars to produce a double tone. The back-door push button operates the lower solenoid; the core strikes only the right tone bar, because the left end of the core strikes a rubber damper instead of the tone bar.

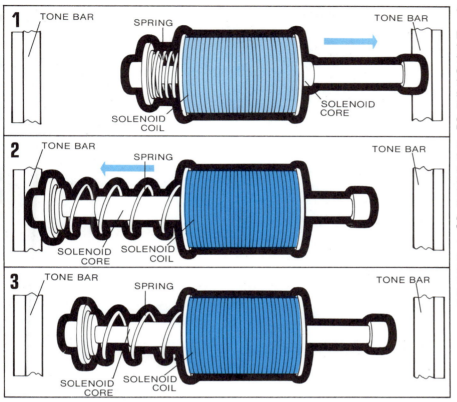

1 How a chime works: Bing!

Pressing a push button completes an electrical circuit between solenoid and transformer. Current flows through the solenoid coil, creating a magnetic field, which pulls the iron core through the coil *(arrow)* to strike the right tone bar. As the core moves, it compresses the spring.

2 Bong!

Releasing the button opens the circuit, and the current stops flowing; the coil ceases to act as a magnet. Now the spring expands, snapping the core back *(arrow)* to strike the left tone bar. At this point the spring is slightly extended.

3 ....

The spring now contracts slightly, but not enough to pull the solenoid core all the way back to the right bar. The core thus comes to rest between the tone bars; the chime is silent and ready for another push of the button to begin a new cycle.

Troubleshooting Doorbells and Chimes

Problem	Possible Causes	Solution
Bell or chime does not sound	Fuse blown or circuit breaker tripped	Replace fuse or reset circuit breaker
	Push-button contacts corroded or dirty	Clean contacts with fine sandpaper
	Push button broken	Replace push button
	Defective transformer	Check transformer output terminals with low-voltage tester *(page 137)*; if tester lamp does not glow, replace transformer
Bell does not ring	Interrupter contacts fail to make electrical connection	Clean contacts with fine sandpaper
	Interrupter contacts stuck shut	Gently bend contact arm until contacts open
Chime does not sound	Solenoid core jams in coil	Clean core with small brush, and lubricate with silicone spray
	Short circuit in push button	Examine opened button for contacts between bare wires; separate them or rewire
Bell does not stop ringing	Short circuit in push button	Examine opened button for contacts between bare wires; separate them or rewire

Small Appliances

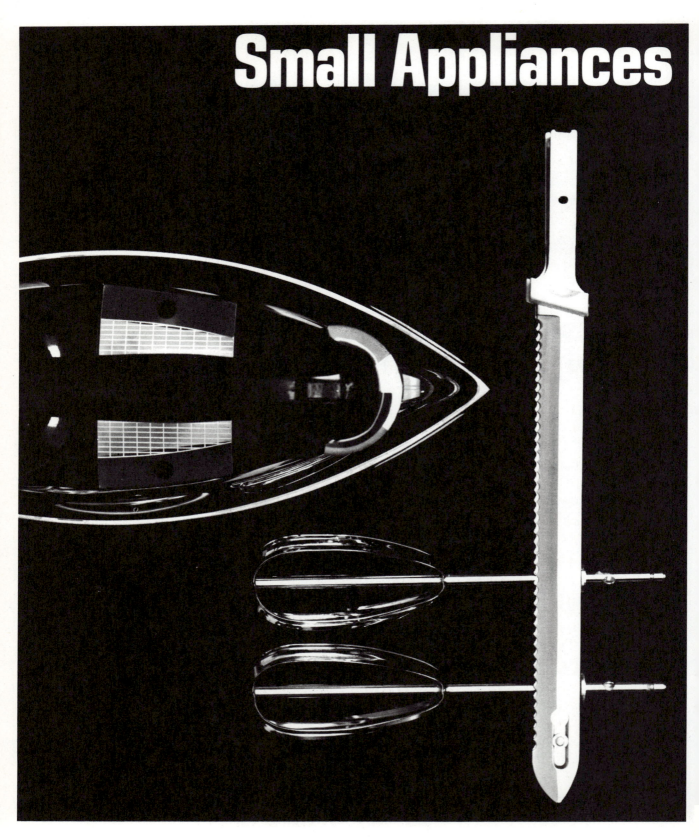

How They Do Routine Chores Better Than You Can

The clusters of small machines in kitchens, bathrooms and broom closets are devices most homeowners could get along without—but few would dream of doing so. These appliances have won a well-deserved popularity because they have taken over many monotonous tasks and perform them very well—better, in fact, than human hands can do them:

■ An electric food mixer can easily stir the heaviest batters. And it can stir thinner liquids with lightning speed: be careful when you whip cream with one or the cream will turn to butter before you flip the switch off.

■ No razor can duplicate the smooth, gliding action of an electric shaver, primarily because the shaver has hundreds of cutting surfaces and a screen so fine that its tolerances are measured in thousandths of an inch.

■ An electric coffee maker starts brewing seconds after it is turned on because only a very small amount of water is boiled at a time; no watching of the kettle is needed.

Ingenuity characterizes all these devices—not only in the harnessing of small motors and heating elements to do a job better, but also in clever employment of drive shafts, gears, mechanical linkages, switches, thermostats and timers. Some appliances do not need such accessories: the fan is just a motor with blades attached to the shaft. But most of them include extra devices to help them work better.

Reduction gears transform a fast rotating motion into a slower one that exerts a stronger turning force. It also makes possible useful combinations such as the can opener and knife sharpener, both powered by a single motor that gives high speed to the sharpener, slow speed to the opener.

Such gears may be part of a drive train that changes the direction of the motion; a food mixer, for example, has a horizontal motor driving beaters that point vertically downward into the mixing bowl. In some drive trains, mechanical linkages transform rotary motion into the back-and-forth motion of blades for an electric knife or a shaver.

More intricate are the automatic controls in heating appliances. Most of these appliances include, at the very least, thermostats that keep their heating elements at a preselected temperature. In a coffee maker, however, the thermostat not only cuts off the brewing element when the coffee is ready, but turns on a low-temperature warming element to keep the brew at serving temperature. Better yet, a clock-timer can be added to switch on the electricity in the morning and have the coffee ready when you get up.

Understandably, all these convenient refinements are not without their drawbacks. By adding to the complication of modern appliances, they increase the ways in which the appliance can break down. In general, however, these additional features are no harder to fix than more conventional parts, and they add greatly to the versatility of a device.

Basic rules of care and safety

Like all machinery, small appliances last longer and work better if you take care of them. A few rules apply both to appliances with motors (pages 188-231) and to those employing heating elements (pages 233-253):

■ Operate appliances directly from a wall receptacle whenever possible. Avoid extension cords, which waste some electricity and may provide insufficient current for good performance. Extension cords are particularly unsuited for use with heating appliances since these devices draw much more current than most extension cords are designed to carry.

■ Disconnect appliances by grasping the plug; tugging on the appliance cord could break its wires or the connections inside the plug.

■ Keep appliances clean; accumulations of dust, grease or food particles clog motors, drive trains and even switch contacts.

■ Never immerse an appliance in water unless the manufacturer's instructions specifically state that you may; water seeping into a motor or coil can cause a shock or a short circuit when the appliance is plugged in again.

Why home repairs make good sense

Even with good care, parts sooner or later wear or break. If the warranty is still in effect (box, page 19), let the manufacturer or his service agent do the fixing.

If the warranty has expired, you will find that it is always less expensive, and usually quite simple, to make the repairs yourself. In fact, professional repairs on some small appliances may be so costly, in a relative sense, that the only economic alternative to fixing the thing yourself is buying a new one.

Parts for a new model generally fit an older one, and ordinarily, the parts most likely to break or wear out are kept in stock at appliance service centers. If there is no service center nearby, write or call the manufacturer at the address given on the warranty.

As simple and inexpensive as the home repair of small appliances may be, it does present some hazards for the uninformed and the unwary. The fast spinning action of blender blades or mixer beaters can mangle a finger; the high temperature of a steam iron can inflict serious burns; and a toaster can give a severe shock if you touch a live wire in the heating element. Such accidents are readily avoided if a few precautions are taken:

■ If the appliance runs on house current, be sure to disconnect it from the wall receptacle before you do anything else.

■ Remove all detachable units such as cutting

blades, beaters and bowls. Only then remove the housing (pages 184-185).

■ If the appliance runs on batteries, you may not be able to remove them; in appliances such as electric toothbrushes, they are usually sealed or soldered to connections inside the housing. But proceed cautiously: after you open up an appliance, it can be activated as long as the batteries are in place. Do not touch the switch, which could start the motor.

In undertaking a repair, your first task will be to determine the cause of the trouble. Without even removing the appliance housing, it is often possible to make an educated guess:

■ An unusual grinding or uneven sound during operation is of mechanical origin: either a part —such as the motor shaft—has broken or shifted out of alignment, or something in the mechanism is binding.

■ If the speed of the motor or the temperature of the heating element does not correspond to the selected setting, the source of the trouble most probably is electrical.

The appliance cord and its plug are particularly vulnerable parts, especially in appliances, such as irons and vacuum cleaners, that are moved about frequently during use. Inspect the plug prongs for signs of corrosion or other damage. If the prongs appear clean and intact, there could be a broken wire inside the cord or a loose connection between a wire and the plug; find out by checking the cord with a continuity tester (page 186).

The next step is an inspection of the contacts and wiring inside the appliance. Open the housing carefully, particularly if the device includes mechanical linkages that could be jarred loose in the process; check the circuit with a continuity tester.

If, on the other hand, you suspect a mechanical problem in the motor, you usually can pinpoint it easily, once the mechanism is exposed. Turn the motor drive shaft slowly with your fingers while observing the transfer of motion. You should be able to see if a gear is slipping or broken, a drive shaft is out of alignment, or other moving parts are not meshing properly.

Once you have determined the cause of the problem, you may find that it can be solved merely by refastening a loose connection, by coaxing a displaced mechanical part back into position or, especially in the case of a motor, by applying a few drops of lubricant (pages 194-195). If you discover a broken or worn part, inspect all others for signs of wear, and if necessary, replace them at the same time.

Some parts are designed to break for safety's sake when trouble develops: a gear in a food mixer, for example, snaps automatically when the beaters jam, in order to prevent more serious damage to the rest of the mechanism. These "fail-safe" parts are always inexpensive and are meant to be replaced rather than repaired. Keep in mind, however, that the circumstances that caused the part to break in the first place should be determined and corrected; otherwise, the newly replaced part will break again—and again.

After you have completed the repair, take advantage of the fact that the appliance is still out of its housing to give it some preventive maintenance: clean or lubricate as recommended by the manufacturer. The appliance is then ready to be reassembled and put to a final running test before it is returned to duty.

Although you may approach the first repair with some trepidation, you will soon discover that all makes of a given type of appliance are built much alike (the pages that follow describe typical models), and that even different types share a relatively small number of basic principles. The knowledge you gain by doing one job will make each successive one easier.

BASIC REPAIRS

Even simple repair jobs, such as replacing a cord *(pages 186-187)* or cleaning hair and dust from a hair drier *(page 251),* can be accomplished only by first removing the housing. Often, when all the obvious fasteners have been removed, the casing still clings together. Designers have streamlined small appliances by concealing fasteners, and the machines have become increasingly difficult to get apart when they need repairs. Retaining screws are ingeniously placed under nameplates and pads, and behind latches on attachments.

When you are stymied by such a diabolically sealed fastener, resist the impulse to reach for a hammer. An appliance should be sent back for repair if it is still under warranty. If it is not, look for indentations, seams or detachable sections that may be clues to fastenings. But if professional repair of an appliance would cost more than replacement, disregard caution. You have nothing to lose.

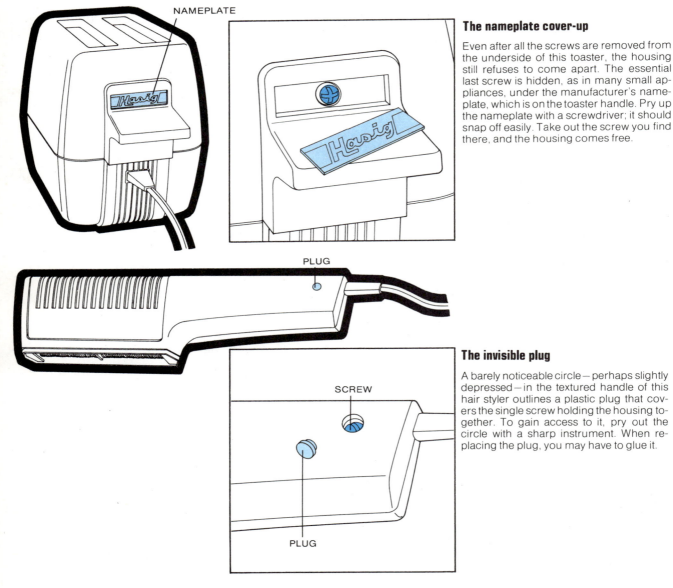

NAMEPLATE

PLUG

SCREW

PLUG

The nameplate cover-up

Even after all the screws are removed from the underside of this toaster, the housing still refuses to come apart. The essential last screw is hidden, as in many small appliances, under the manufacturer's nameplate, which is on the toaster handle. Pry up the nameplate with a screwdriver; it should snap off easily. Take out the screw you find there, and the housing comes free.

The invisible plug

A barely noticeable circle — perhaps slightly depressed — in the textured handle of this hair styler outlines a plastic plug that covers the single screw holding the housing together. To gain access to it, pry out the circle with a sharp instrument. When replacing the plug, you may have to glue it.

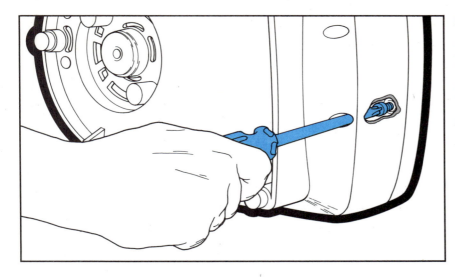

Recessed screws

Screws that fasten parts of a plastic appliance housing to each other often are hidden in deep cavities molded into the parts themselves. Like shallow recesses *(opposite)*, these deep cavities may be concealed by a plastic plug. After prying out the plug, use a screwdriver with a long shaft to loosen the recessed screw. Then turn the appliance upright to drop the screw out of the cavity.

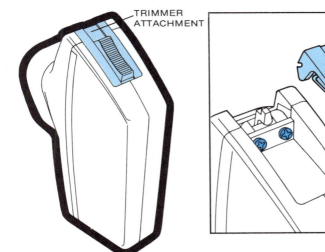

TRIMMER ATTACHMENT

The attachment cover

The housing on an electric shaver like this one will not come apart unless two hidden screws are removed. Look for them under the sideburns trimmer. Push up and back on the front of the trimmer with your thumb, and it should snap right off, revealing two screws that hold the front and back of the shaver together.

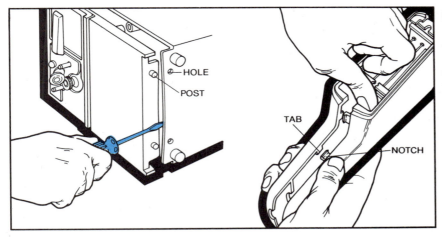

HOLE

POST

TAB

NOTCH

Self-fastening parts

Look closely at the appliance for plastic protrusions, called posts, that project from one part of the case into holes in the other. Insert a screwdriver into the seam near the posts *(far left)* and pry the housing apart gently, releasing the posts from their holes. Concealed tabs and notches are harder to detect. Try to look inside a vent or opening in the appliance to spot them, or press down along the housing seam with your thumb. The housing half with the tabs will give slightly. Press the housing down at a tab location and pull the halves of the housing apart *(left)*.

Appliance Cords

One of the most common reasons a small appliance stops functioning or works intermittently is that electricity cannot get to it—meaning that the cord, the plug, or the motor or heating-element may be faulty. All are simply repaired or replaced.

The cord is composed of two separately insulated wires, sheathed together, that carry the electricity from a wall receptacle through a plug to the appliance and back. Most of the time a visual inspection will determine where the break in the circuit has occurred: a broken or wobbling plug prong, a partially severed cord, or a loose connection at the cord sleeve. Check the receptacle also; to be sure it is good, plug in a lamp that you know is working properly.

Shaking the appliance sometimes briefly re-establishes a lost connection and, even before the housing is opened, may point to trouble in the internal wire terminals. If it does, repair them—loose interior connections can cause fire.

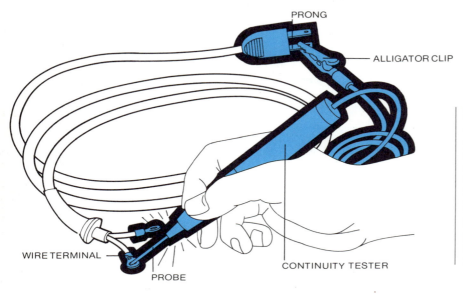

PRONG

ALLIGATOR CLIP

WIRE TERMINAL

PROBE

CONTINUITY TESTER

Testing the cord for continuity

To determine whether a cord and plug are in good order, set up a flow of current by attaching the alligator clip of a battery-powered continuity tester to a plug prong, and touch each of the wire terminals with the probe. Then move the clip to the other prong and test both terminals again. If the light does not go on when you touch one terminal in each test, cut off the plug and re-test the cord. If the cord is good, attach a new plug to it (opposite, below). Otherwise replace both cord and plug.

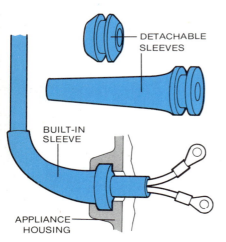

DETACHABLE SLEEVES

BUILT-IN SLEEVE

APPLIANCE HOUSING

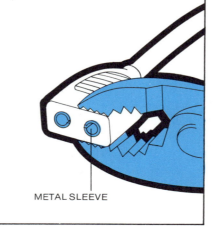

METAL SLEEVE

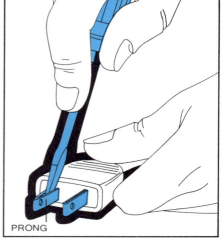

PRONG

Protecting the cord from stress

A pliable rubber sleeve added to an appliance cord at the point it enters the housing — where the cord is subject to the greatest stress—protects and assures it of a longer life. Some such sleeves are permanent parts of cords, designed for a specific appliance; other sleeves are separate units that can be slipped onto wires and then snapped into any housing.

Adjusting a female plug

Many hand-held appliances have detachable cords that are connected to built-in prongs by a female plug—a molded plastic unit that has two internal metal sleeves. If the cord repeatedly falls out of its socket, squeeze firmly on the plug with a pair of pliers. The pressure will reduce the diameter of the metal sleeves and produce a tight fit and good electrical contact.

Adjusting plug prongs

If a plug makes poor or intermittent contact, it may have the type of split prongs shown here. When such a plug will not stay tight in the receptacle, its prongs may be compressed. Insert the tip of a screwdriver into the center of each of the prongs, and twist slightly in order to spread the sides. If the plug has solid prongs, bend the prongs slightly farther apart.

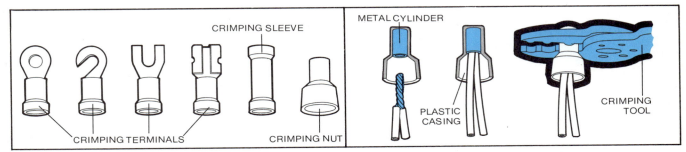

METAL CYLINDER

CRIMPING SLEEVE

CRIMPING TERMINALS

CRIMPING NUT

PLASTIC CASING

CRIMPING TOOL

Solderless crimping connectors

These connectors, used in many small appliances, are simply squeezed onto wires with a crimping tool. The bottom part of a terminal, a metal sheath cased in plastic, holds the wire and the tip attaches to a screw post, bolt or tab. The sleeve and nut connect two wires—the sleeve for wires coming from opposite directions.

How to crimp a connection

To connect two wires coming from the same direction, twist the ends together *(left)*, insert them into a crimping nut *(center)* and squeeze the top of the nut firmly with a crimping tool *(right)*. The inner cylinder collapses and anchors the wires. The crimping sleeve requires two presses—one at each end—to secure the wires.

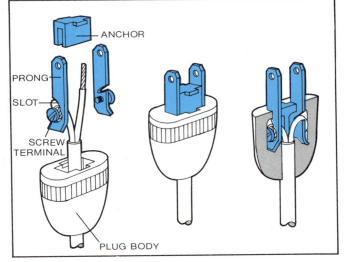

ANCHOR

PRONG

SLOT

SCREW TERMINAL

PLUG BODY

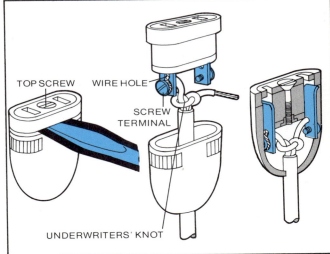

TOP SCREW   WIRE HOLE

SCREW TERMINAL

UNDERWRITERS' KNOT

Replacing a male plug

Appliance plugs, being frequently inserted and removed, are apt to get hard usage. While a snap-on plug *(page 153)* is adequate for light-duty purposes such as lamp cords, the type shown here, with screw terminals, is preferable for appliances. To attach this type, use a small screwdriver to pry out the anchor that sits between the prongs, then lift out the prongs. As is shown in the diagrams at the left above, push a prepared cord *(page 140)* through the plug body. Place the end of one of the wires in the slot on a prong, wrap it clockwise around the screw and tighten *(left)*. Repeat for the other wire. Pull the cord gently, easing the prongs into position *(center)*. Replace the anchor *(right)*.

Replacing a female plug

To get at the screw terminals in a female plug, pry apart the top and bottom with a screwdriver *(above, left)*. It is not necessary to remove the top screw. Run the cord through the plug body and tie the wires in an Underwriters' knot *(page 152)*. Push each wire through a hole in the metal plate, turn it clockwise around its screw and tighten *(center)*. Rejoin the two sections *(right)*.

Appliances with Motors

The first electric power ever consumed in American homes—except for lighting—was probably used to run a crude—and short-lived—sewing-machine motor. The motor, which the Curtis, Crocker, Wheeler Company began to manufacture in 1886, ran on six-volt batteries; too few residences were wired for electricity to offer a mass market for any appliances that worked on house current.

Those early motors were direct ancestors of the universal motor *(pages 190-191)*, which now powers many small appliances. It is an extremely reliable device, its principal weakness being the brushes—the sliding contacts that transmit the electric current from the power source through a rotating part called a commutator, and thence to the rotating motor coils.

Early brushes were literally that—bundles of copper wires bound at one end—and they quickly wore out the commutator by abrasion. Universal motors became more durable with the introduction in 1888 of brushes made of small blocks of carbon. They are curved to match the shape of the commutator, making better contact with it to reduce wear.

But brushes remain the weak part of the motor. Constant friction during operation gradually wears them down. When they no longer maintain close contact with the commutator, the motor stops. Because brushes do wear out, they are always mounted so that they are accessible and easy to replace *(pages 190, 195)*.

In spite of the occasional nuisance of changing brushes, the universal motor is preferred for many appliances because it uses electricity more efficiently than other kinds of motors; its speed is easily regulated, and it runs on either alternating current from the house supply or direct current from batteries.

Universal motors do not monopolize the appliance market, however. The Curtis, Crocker, Wheeler Company had barely surfaced with its electric sewing-machine motor when a revolutionary change in motor design was proposed by Nikola Tesla, then a Westinghouse engineer. Tesla discovered that a rotating magnetic field could be created without any mechanical moving parts by using alternating current, and he showed that the rotation of this field could be employed to turn a rotor (page 193). This method of making the magnetism spin does away with the need for brushes. No part connected to electricity has to move; all the motion is produced magnetically.

A number of motor types in use today derive from the Tesla discovery. A low-power, compact version of this brushless motor, called a shaded-pole motor (pages 192-193), is used in appliances such as can openers and dental irrigators, which require only limited turning speed. For these uses, the shaded-pole motor is chosen rather than the universal motor because the absence of brushes renders it nearly maintenance-free, and its simpler construction makes it less expensive to manufacture.

Protecting an appliance motor

Except for the routine replacement of brushes in the universal type, motor repairs require professional skill. But the need for repairs should seldom arise, because both types of motors rarely fail unless they have been mishandled. Their care is simple:

■ Oil a motor regularly if it is not permanently lubricated at the factory. Save instructions, which indicate the location of the oil ports where oil is to be placed.

■ Never impose undue strain on the motor. A knife is no more designed to slice thick bones than a garbage disposer is meant to grind them.

The requirements for care that apply to the motors of small appliances hold for other parts: considerate use and lubrication as necessary

will prolong their life. But unlike the motor, the other parts are vulnerable to wear and damage. Breakdowns are most likely in the drive mechanisms, the ingenious combinations of gears, shafts, cams or pivots that connect the motor to fan blades, beaters or whatever device actually gets the desired job done.

The simplest drive mechanism is a direct one: the working tool is attached directly to the motor shaft—the cutter of a blender, for example, or the fan in a hair drier. When switched on at full speed, the cutter or fan spins at the same rate the motor does.

Many jobs require more turning force than the motor normally provides. For them, a series of alternately large and small gears driven by a small gear on the motor shaft is used. The drive wheel of a can opener, for example, is attached to the last gear in line; the gear's speed, and that of the drive wheel, is 72 times slower than that of the motor, but its torque is nearly 72 times greater than the motor's.

By using specially shaped gears to turn drive shafts set at right angles to each other, the power from the motor can be made to turn a corner. This principle is used in appliances such as food mixers—it makes the beaters point downward into the mixing bowl.

Adding a special linkage to a drive train —such as a gear with an off-center pin (page 206)—can transform a motor's rotary action into reciprocating motion, as in the back-and-forth movement of electric-knife blades.

Drive gears occasionally wear out. Some are even designed to break under stress, so that more expensive components are saved from damage. Replacing drive trains of most machines is simply a matter of opening the appliance housing (pages 184-185), removing a retaining screw or two and dropping a new part into place.

HOW MOTORS WORK

Among electric motors, the universal motor has proved to be the most practical for use in small appliances such as blenders, carving knives, food mixers and vacuum cleaners. Those appliances require great power over a wide speed range, a combination the universal type of motor can sup-

ply. In food mixers and blenders, for example, the speed can be varied as desired by means of a selector switch. A vacuum cleaner draws on the motor's strength rather than its versatility. The motor is called universal because, as a rule, it works equally well on alternating or on direct current, making it equally suitable for devices that run on batteries or on house current; or those that are powered by either interchangeably.

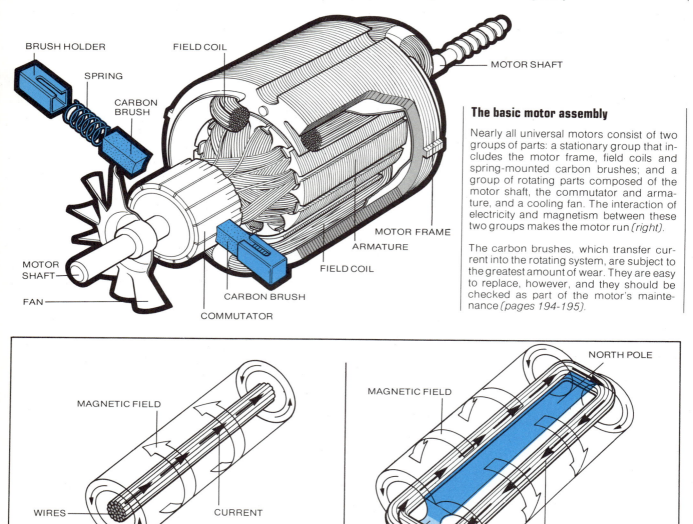

BRUSH HOLDER

SPRING

CARBON BRUSH

FIELD COIL

MOTOR SHAFT

MOTOR SHAFT

FAN

COMMUTATOR

CARBON BRUSH

FIELD COIL

ARMATURE

MOTOR FRAME

The basic motor assembly

Nearly all universal motors consist of two groups of parts: a stationary group that includes the motor frame, field coils and spring-mounted carbon brushes; and a group of rotating parts composed of the motor shaft, the commutator and armature, and a cooling fan. The interaction of electricity and magnetism between these two groups makes the motor run (right).

The carbon brushes, which transfer current into the rotating system, are subject to the greatest amount of wear. They are easy to replace, however, and they should be checked as part of the motor's maintenance (pages 194-195).

MAGNETIC FIELD

WIRES

CURRENT

NORTH POLE

MAGNETIC FIELD

COIL

SOUTH POLE

Coiled wires to create magnetic poles

When a current passes through a wire, a field of magnetic force—represented symbolically in the picture above by the outlined cylinder—is generated around that wire. Several parallel wires bundled together, all with current flowing in the same direction, intensify the force. When the current flows in the direction of the thin arrows, the resulting magnetic lines of force run circularly around the wires as indicated by the broad arrows. If the current is made to flow in the opposite direction—by passing it through a coiled wire (above, right)—two magnetic forces of opposing direction are generated, and the coil acts like a bar magnet with north and south poles. The fact that opposite magnetic poles attract each other is the principle that governs the design of electric motors.

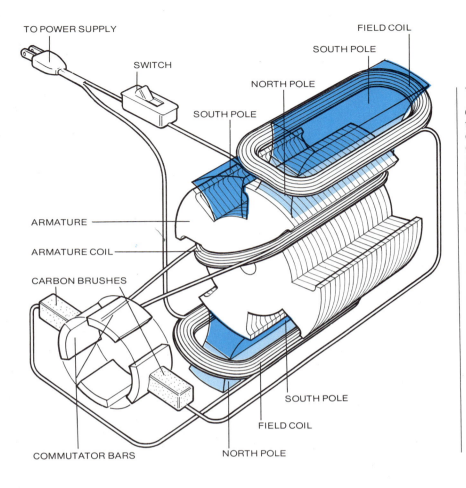

TO POWER SUPPLY
SWITCH
FIELD COIL
SOUTH POLE
NORTH POLE
SOUTH POLE
ARMATURE
ARMATURE COIL
CARBON BRUSHES
SOUTH POLE
FIELD COIL
COMMUTATOR BARS
NORTH POLE

The electrical circuit

Operation of the motor involves two stationary, or field, coils, wired so that they carry current in opposite directions. One end of each field coil is connected to the power supply, the other to a carbon brush. Between the brushes, the circuit continues on into the rotating, or armature, coils through a number of commutator bars.

The wire ends of each armature coil are connected to two adjacent commutator bars as shown at left (for clarity, only one armature coil has been drawn). When the motor is switched on, the current flows from the power source through the first field coil and on to the first carbon brush. Contact between the brush and one of the commutator bars sends the current simultaneously through the two armature coils that are wired to that bar, then consecutively through each remaining armature coil on both sides of the brush.

The second brush, with a bar on the opposite side of the commutator, picks up the current and sends it through the second field coil and back to the power source. The north and south poles created by the passage of current through the various coils make the motor turn (below).

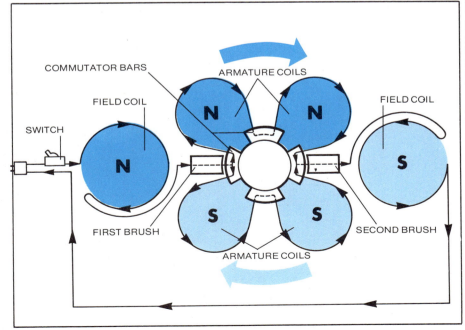

COMMUTATOR BARS
FIELD COIL
ARMATURE COILS
FIELD COIL
SWITCH
N
N
N
S
FIRST BRUSH
S
S
SECOND BRUSH
ARMATURE COILS

How the motor turns

In this diagram, the black arrows trace the path of current through the motor to illustrate how the attraction of north and south magnetic poles for each other will make the motor turn. The current, coming in through the switch at far left, establishes a north pole in the first field coil it encounters. As the current divides at the first brush to flow in opposite directions, it creates north poles in the upper armature coils and forms south poles in the lower ones. After the current has recombined at the second brush, it goes on to the second field coil, creating a south pole. As a result, the poles of the stationary field coils attract and repel those of the rotating armature to turn it in the direction the broad arrows indicate.

After a fraction of a turn, the armature coil at upper right straddles the commutator bar connected to the second brush; the current briefly bypasses that coil, temporarily erasing its magnetic field. But adjacent armature coils remain magnetized and momentum carries the demagnetized coil beyond the brush.

Shaded-Pole Motors

The small, compact motors known as shaded-pole motors are generally used in place of universal motors *(pages 190-191)* in appliances that require little power, such as small fans, can openers and hair driers.

Shaded-pole motors work on alternating current alone. The motor's rotating assembly—or rotor—is made to turn by currents the magnetic action of the field coil induces in the rotor. For that reason, the rotor itself needs no direct electrical connections and so does not require either a commutator or brushes.

Two factors, the absence of brushes, which wear down, and the fact that the rotor is cast in a single solid piece, considerably simplify maintenance since there are fewer parts to wear out. The shaded-pole motor can generally be counted on to have the same life expectancy as the appliance that it serves.

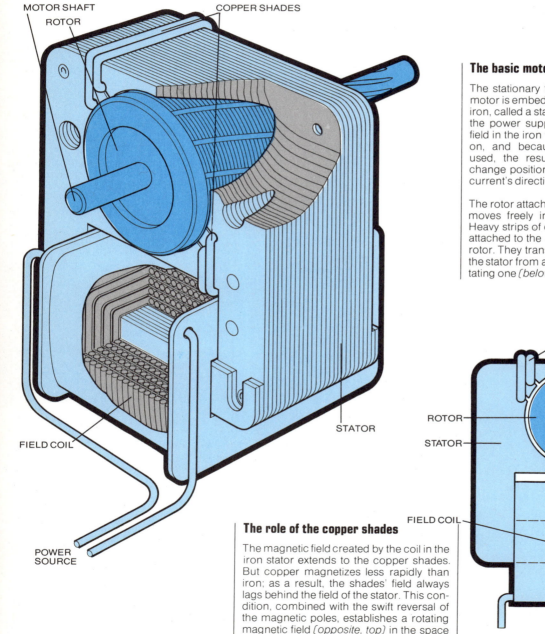

MOTOR SHAFT
ROTOR
COPPER SHADES
FIELD COIL
POWER SOURCE
STATOR

The basic motor assembly

The stationary field coil of a shaded-pole motor is embedded in a laminated block of iron, called a stator. The coil, connected to the power supply, generates a magnetic field in the iron when the current is turned on, and because alternating current is used, the resulting magnetic poles exchange position with each reversal of the current's direction.

The rotor attached to the shaft of the motor moves freely in the hollowed-out stator. Heavy strips of copper, called shades, are attached to the stator on either side of the rotor. They transform the magnetic field of the stator from an alternating field into a rotating one *(below)*.

COPPER SHADES
ROTOR
STATOR
FIELD COIL

The role of the copper shades

The magnetic field created by the coil in the iron stator extends to the copper shades. But copper magnetizes less rapidly than iron; as a result, the shades' field always lags behind the field of the stator. This condition, combined with the swift reversal of the magnetic poles, establishes a rotating magnetic field *(opposite, top)* in the space the rotor occupies.

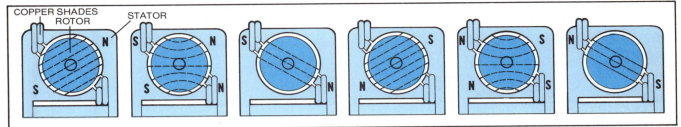

How the magnetic field rotates

When the power is turned on, magnetism induced by the field coil creates a north and a south pole in the iron stator *(left, above)*; magnetic lines of force *(dotted lines)* extend between the two poles, across the space occupied by the rotor. A fraction of a second later, north and south poles arise in the copper shades *(second diagram from left)*; these poles interact with the iron stator's poles to deflect the lines of force. As the alternating current reverses its direction, it temporarily blanks out the iron stator's poles. Because the copper shades' magnetism lags behind that of the iron, the shades are still magnetized and the only lines of force present are those between the shades' poles *(third diagram from left)*. As soon as the current has reversed, north and south poles reappear in the stator, but their positions *(fourth diagram from left)* are now the opposite of those that they had occupied before. Except for this reversal of the poles, the sequence continues *(remaining two diagrams)* in exactly the same order that it had previously.

The squirrel-cage rotor

The rotor of a shaded-pole motor is cast in one piece. Evenly spaced strips of copper are embedded in a solid metal cylinder and connected at the edges of the cylinder by two end rings, usually made of copper. The general appearance of the copper strips and end rings suggests that of a squirrel cage—a term commonly used to designate this type of rotor.

As the motor is switched on, magnetic poles arise in the stator, on opposite sides of the rotor (only the north pole is shown in the drawing at right). The subsequent rotation of the stator poles, described above, turns the rotor as explained below.

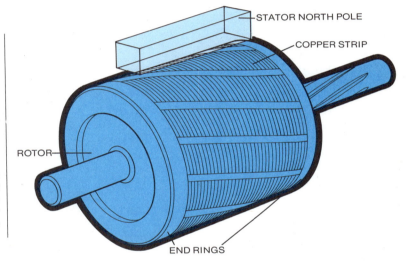

STATOR NORTH POLE

COPPER STRIP

ROTOR

END RINGS

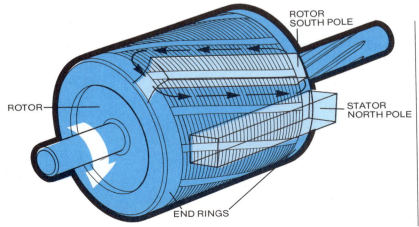

ROTOR SOUTH POLE

ROTOR

STATOR NORTH POLE

END RINGS

How the motor turns

When the poles of the stator field pass over a section of the rotor they constitute a moving magnetic field and thus generate electricity in nearby wires *(pages 346-347)*—in this case, the nearest copper strips and adjoining segments of end rings (only the stator's north-pole side is depicted at left). These induced currents *(small arrows)* create a magnetic force of their own. But its polarity is opposite to that of the stator. A south pole forms in the rotor a fraction of a second after the stator's north pole has gone by; since north attracts south, the rotor's pole will continually seek to catch up with the stator's, and the motor will turn in the direction shown by the broad arrow.

Bearings and Motor Maintenance

A small appliance will last longer if its motor and bearings get a little simple attention. Inspect regularly for accumulations of grime and debris: lint, for example, building up in a vacuum cleaner or flour accumulating on the inside of a food mixer.

Much foreign matter can be wiped away by running a damp cloth around the inside of the appliance housing. Take care not to wet any wires. Deeper cleaning can be accomplished by lightly vacuuming the motor, making sure there are no loose parts to be sucked into the vacuum cleaner.

After a motor has been used for a while, oil that had been put on by the manufacturer may dry or cake, causing the shaft to freeze in its bearings. A few drops of light motor oil or sewing-machine oil in the right place *(below and bottom)* will correct the difficulty. But use the oil sparingly. Excess oil dripping onto motor coils may start a fire.

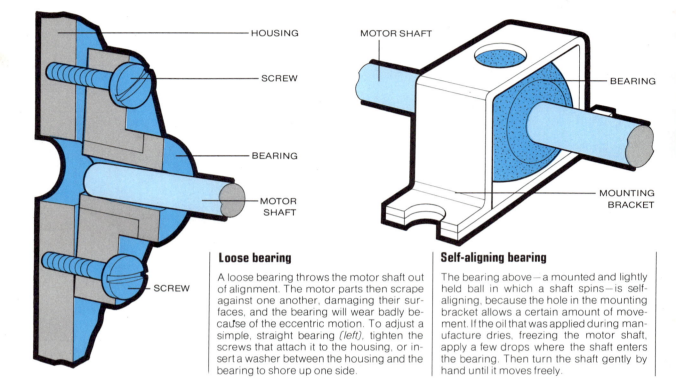

HOUSING

SCREW

BEARING

MOTOR SHAFT

SCREW

MOTOR SHAFT

BEARING

MOUNTING BRACKET

Loose bearing

A loose bearing throws the motor shaft out of alignment. The motor parts then scrape against one another, damaging their surfaces, and the bearing will wear badly because of the eccentric motion. To adjust a simple, straight bearing *(left)*, tighten the screws that attach it to the housing, or insert a washer between the housing and the bearing to shore up one side.

Self-aligning bearing

The bearing above—a mounted and lightly held ball in which a shaft spins—is self-aligning, because the hole in the mounting bracket allows a certain amount of movement. If the oil that was applied during manufacture dries, freezing the motor shaft, apply a few drops where the shaft enters the bearing. Then turn the shaft gently by hand until it moves freely.

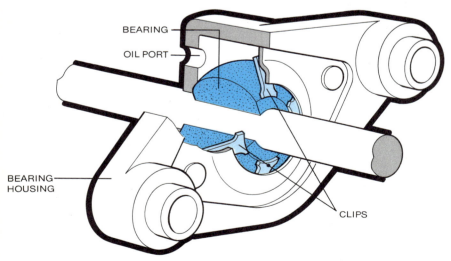

BEARING

OIL PORT

BEARING HOUSING

CLIPS

Clip-held bearing

A common variant of the self-aligning bearing described above is hung by clips in its own housing and usually has oil ports for lubrication. In some models, the ports hold a felt wick that feeds oil as it is needed; in others, the port merely channels oil directly to the bearing. In either case, periodically apply a few drops of oil at the port.

Troubleshooting Small Motors

Problem	Possible Causes	Solution
Motor does not run	Power not reaching motor	Check fuse or circuit breaker; receptacle *(page 143)*; cord *(pages 186-187)*
	Loose connection	Correct as explained on pages 186-187
	Worn brushes (universal motor only)	Replace brushes if brush length has worn to less than twice the width of brush holder
	Weakened brush springs (universal motor only)	Replace springs if they no longer hold brushes firmly against commutator
	Faulty switch	Replace switch with one of same type
Motor runs continuously	Shorted switch	Replace switch with one of same type
Motor runs erratically	Defective cord or plug Loose connection Worn brushes (universal motor only) Weakened brush springs (universal motor only) Faulty switch	See solutions above, under "Motor does not run"
Motor overheats	Dirty motor or clogged air intake Tight bearings	Clean with vacuum cleaner If rotor or armature cannot be turned freely by hand, lubricate bearings *(opposite)*
Motor blows fuses	Rotor jammed in frozen bearings Defective cord	Lubricate bearings *(opposite)* Replace cord *(pages 186-187)*
Motor is noisy	Worn bearings	Tighten and lubricate bearings *(opposite)*
	Dirty motor Bent fan blades	See above, under "Motor overheats" Straighten blades to clear housing
Universal motor sparks	New brushes	Condition normal until brushes wear to fit contour of commutator
	Worn brushes	See above, under "Motor does not run"
	Worn brush springs	Replace springs

BLENDERS AND MIXERS

Nearly half the homes with small appliances have a food blender or processor, descendants of a laboratory device for pureeing cultures that was moved to the kitchen. Blenders and direct-drive processors are similar in operation, but disassembly varies—sometimes in different models of the same make.

The universal motor, used because its speed is easily regulated, is discussed on pages 190-191; it rarely breaks down. More vulnerable are the couplings linking the motor to the cutter blades. Two types of coupling are common: toothed-wall (right) and stud (opposite, bottom).

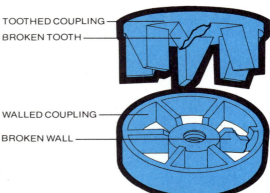

TOOTHED COUPLING
BROKEN TOOTH

WALLED COUPLING
BROKEN WALL

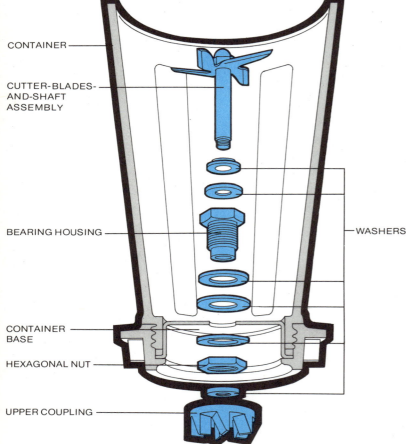

CONTAINER

CUTTER-BLADES-AND-SHAFT ASSEMBLY

BEARING HOUSING

WASHERS

CONTAINER BASE

HEXAGONAL NUT

UPPER COUPLING

Detaching a motor coupling

Lifting the container before the motor stops can damage the couplings between motor and cutter assembly. In most blenders the couplings (above) are plastic, with a toothed part fitting one with spokelike internal walls. In the model sketched, the lower, or motor, coupling is walled and the upper, or shaft, coupling toothed, but the positions may be reversed in your own blender. To remove a damaged motor coupling (below), use a screwdriver to keep the motor shaft from turning. Then unscrew the coupling, usually clockwise but counterclockwise in some models.

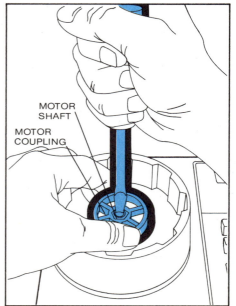

MOTOR SHAFT

MOTOR COUPLING

The cutting mechanism

The business end of a food blender—the cutting mechanism that is whirled rapidly by the motor and bites into the food—is disassembled above. A shaft links the cutter blades to the coupling at the bottom of the container; a bearing housing that is se-cured by a hexagonal nut holds the shaft in place; and a series of washers provide tight seals. Each one of these parts can be replaced separately if it wears out. The cutting mechanism disassembles easily, but in order to get at a defective part you must first detach the coupling from the shaft assembly (opposite, top).

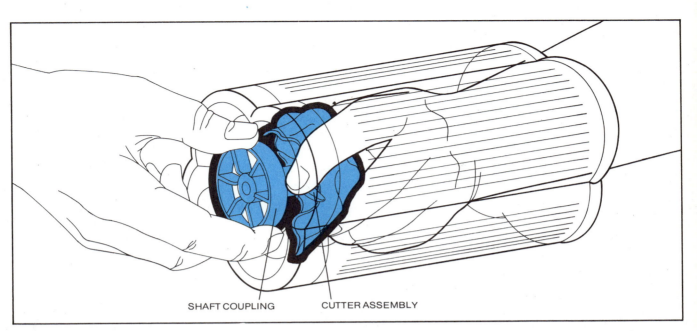

SHAFT COUPLING   CUTTER ASSEMBLY

Detaching a walled shaft coupling

Using a cloth to protect your fingers, grasp the blades firmly to keep them from rotating. Then unscrew the walled shaft coupling, turning it gently clockwise. If it does not budge, however, the coupling on your model may come off counterclockwise; do not use force until you have made sure of the proper direction for disassembly.

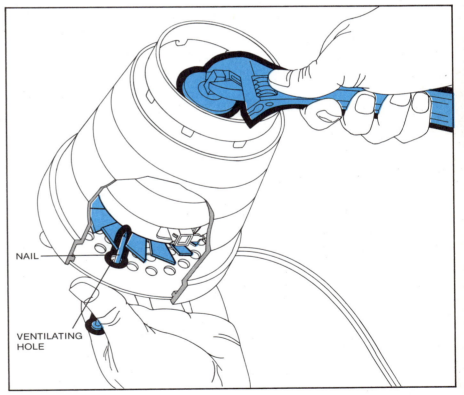

NAIL

VENTILATING HOLE

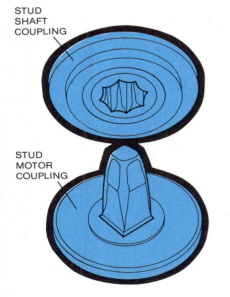

STUD SHAFT COUPLING

STUD MOTOR COUPLING

Detaching a stud motor coupling

In some blender models the motor coupling consists of a metal stud that fits into a corresponding shaft coupling *(left)*. These parts wear rather than break, but they too must be replaced occasionally. The shaft coupling is removed by the method shown at top; the stud motor coupling calls for a different procedure because it completely covers the end of the motor shaft. Hold the motor stationary by thrusting a nail through a ventilating hole in the base and bracing it against one of the fan blades *(above)*; then unscrew the coupling—clockwise (or counterclockwise, depending on model).

Food Mixers

An electric food mixer, whether the pedestal type shown here or the portable type discussed on pages 200-201, is basically an egg beater fitted with a motor. Of the two, the pedestal type is the more versatile but is heavier and more expensive.

Some pedestal machines have as many as 12 different speeds—from slow for stirring up thick dough and heavy batters to fast for whipping cream or egg whites. The action of the beaters also will turn the mixing bowl for more thorough blending. On the more elaborate pedestal mixers, the motor shaft can be connected to a variety of accessories—ice crushers, meat grinders, knife sharpeners, juicers. They fit an opening on the housing face or top.

The most common problems that develop in these sturdy machines are damaged beater gears (pages 200-201) and a bowl that fails to turn; both are easy to correct.

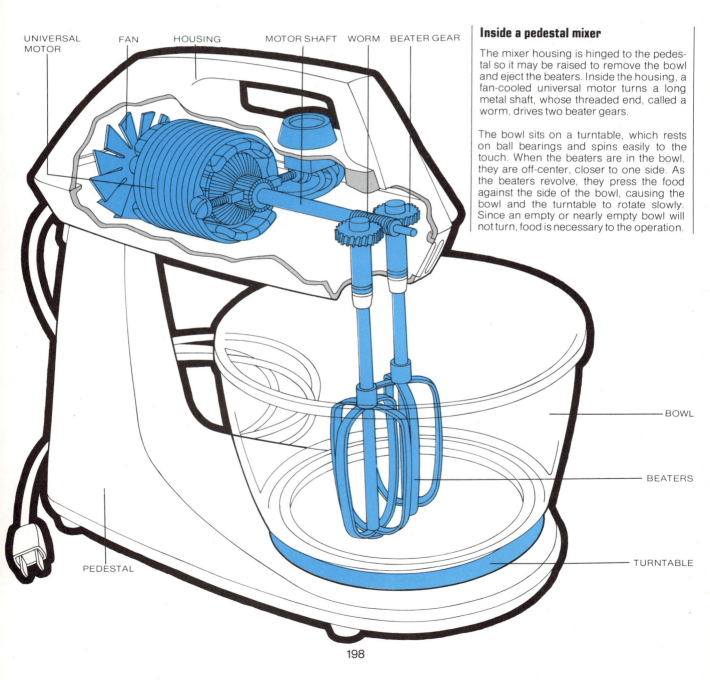

UNIVERSAL MOTOR FAN HOUSING MOTOR SHAFT WORM BEATER GEAR

BOWL

BEATERS

TURNTABLE

PEDESTAL

Inside a pedestal mixer

The mixer housing is hinged to the pedestal so it may be raised to remove the bowl and eject the beaters. Inside the housing, a fan-cooled universal motor turns a long metal shaft, whose threaded end, called a worm, drives two beater gears.

The bowl sits on a turntable, which rests on ball bearings and spins easily to the touch. When the beaters are in the bowl, they are off-center, closer to one side. As the beaters revolve, they press the food against the side of the bowl, causing the bowl and the turntable to rotate slowly. Since an empty or nearly empty bowl will not turn, food is necessary to the operation.

Mixers with slow-speed attachments

Mixers that accept accessories at the front of the housing are designed to reduce the motor's rapid rotations into the slower, more powerful revolutions required by a meat grinder [below] or an ice crusher. The reduction is achieved by a secondary gear train. A spiral worm sits atop one of the beater gears; meshing with it is a wheel with a shaft leading to a coupling. The accessories have a shaft that fits the coupling.

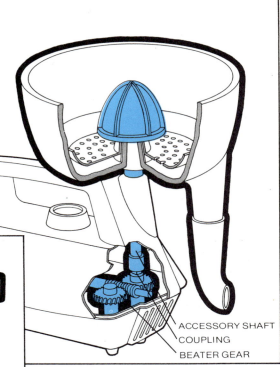

ACCESSORY SHAFT
COUPLING
BEATER GEAR

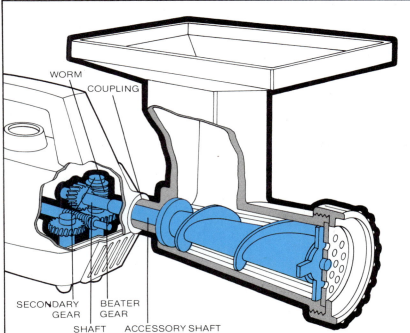

WORM
COUPLING

SECONDARY GEAR
BEATER GEAR
SHAFT
ACCESSORY SHAFT

Mixers with high-speed attachments

Mixers with an accessory fitting atop the housing accept attachments, like a juicer [above] and a knife sharpener, that operate at high speeds and do not require additional power. Consequently, there is only a coupling atop one of the beater gears. The accessory shaft fits into this coupling.

The top mounting calls for care in use. After using a juicer, wipe around the opening. If sticky liquids drip into it, they can interfere with the smooth operation of gears.

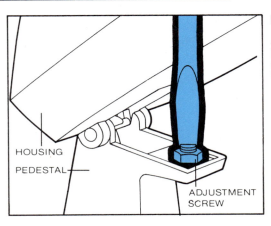

HOUSING
PEDESTAL
ADJUSTMENT SCREW

Making the bowl turn automatically

A bowl that does not turn when the mixer is in use can easily be set right with a screwdriver. The problem is the distance of the beaters from the bowl bottom. If you hear metal striking the bowl, the beaters are too low; if you cannot hear any noise and the bowl does not turn, they are too high.

To adjust, tilt the housing up and reset the adjustment screw on top of the pedestal. Turning the screw counterclockwise will have the effect of raising the beaters; turn it clockwise to lower them. Adjust the screw so the beaters touch the bowl bottom; then, make one full turn counterclockwise.

Replacing a Food Mixer's Gears

What breaks down most often on a food mixer are the gears that connect the beaters to the motor. They are meant to. If they do not give way during a blockage of the beaters—a spoon or a spatula caught in the blades—the sudden stress can twist the beaters or burn out the motor.

To provide fail-safe protection, the beater gears are made of soft plastic; thus they are easily worn or broken, and are inexpensive and simple to replace. The procedure shown on these pages works equally well with either hand or pedestal mixers.

Getting at the gears

To reach the beater gears of a mixer, remove the beaters and take the housing apart—most models, like the one at right, have retaining screws that hold the top and bottom together. If the switch is attached to the top, remove the switch-mounting screw so that you can lay the top aside. Toward the front of the bottom housing, a metal retaining plate holds the beater gears in place and serves as a guide for the ejector shafts. Loosen the screws that secure this plate and put aside both the plate and ejector mechanism. You can now lift the beater gears out of the bottom housing.

What the gears do

A food mixer's motor shaft is machined in the form of a screwlike gear called a worm, which meshes with the two beater gears to turn the beaters. This simple arrangement accomplishes three distinct purposes: the power from the horizontal motor shaft turns a corner to spin vertical beaters; the beaters rotate in opposite directions; and the difference in size between the worm and beater gears serves to change the high speed of the motor shaft to a slower beater speed with a greater turning force.

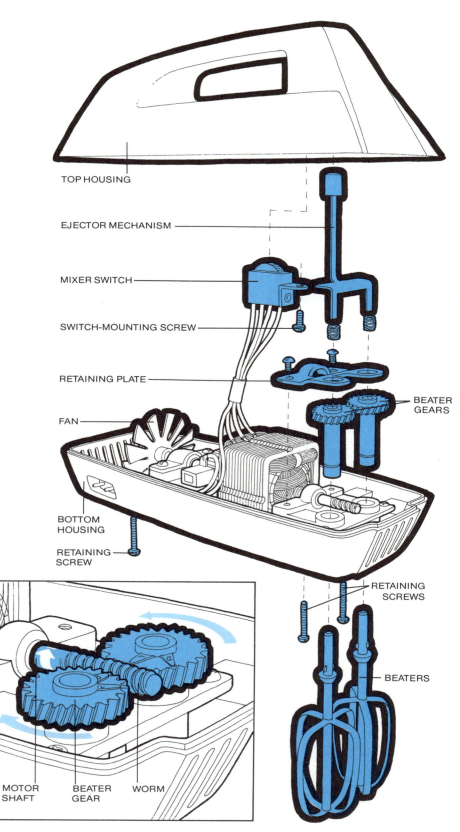

TOP HOUSING

EJECTOR MECHANISM

MIXER SWITCH

SWITCH-MOUNTING SCREW

RETAINING PLATE

FAN

BEATER GEARS

BOTTOM HOUSING

RETAINING SCREW

RETAINING SCREWS

BEATERS

MOTOR SHAFT

BEATER GEAR

WORM

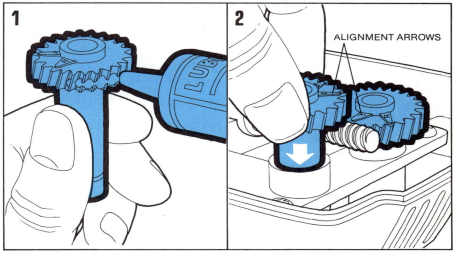

WORN TEETH

FRACTURED SHAFT

BROKEN TOOTH

ALIGNMENT ARROWS

Signs of gear defects

Concave grooves in the beater gear teeth *(above, left)*, worn by friction between the metal worm and the plastic beater gears, may become so deep that the worm and the beater gears no longer mesh. More common is a broken gear tooth or a fractured shaft *(above, right)* that are caused by sudden stress.

1 Getting the right replacements

Note the mixer's make and model number, and take the old gears to the store. It is best to replace both, even if only one is defective. Before installing new gears, lubricate them slightly with silicone gear grease.

2 Installing the new gears

Slip the gears into place, with the arrow marked "L" on one gear pointing to the arrow marked "R" on the other. If there are no arrows, turn the motor shaft by its fan; if the beaters clash, reposition the gears.

Troubleshooting Food Mixers

Problem	Possible Causes	Solution
Motor does not run, runs continuously, runs erratically, overheats, blows fuses, or sparks	Motor defective	These problems are discussed in the troubleshooting chart for small electric motors on page 195
Motor runs but beaters do not turn	Beater gears worn or damaged Beater shafts worn	Replace beater gears Replace beaters
Pedestal-mixer bowl does not rotate	Beaters too far from bottom of bowl	Adjust beater clearance *(page 199)*
Motor runs slowly	Load too great for mixer	Avoid stirring very stiff mixtures
Mixer is noisy	Beater gears dry or defective Beaters bent	Lubricate or, if necessary, replace beater gears Straighten beaters

Food Processors

Food processors differ from blenders and mixers in the higher speed of their shaft rotation. Interchangeable blades and cutting discs—which require the higher speed to function properly—allow the machine to mix, blend, slice and shred a wide variety of foods.

The first processors had motors connected directly to their blade shafts. The blades thus turned at the same speed as the motor. This type of processor, some models of which are still made today, relies on a relatively high-powered motor. More recently designed models, however, incorporate a lower-powered, higher-speed universal motor *(pages 190-191),* which runs with less strain. It is linked to a separate blade shaft by combinations of belts and gears that boost the power of its rotation.

Because most processors operate for only a few seconds at a time, they typically last a long time and require little maintenance. Manufacturers supply replacement kits for belts and pulleys on belt-driven processors, as well as replacement gears, shafts and motors.

BOWL COVER

BOWL

BLADE SHAFT

MOTOR SHAFT

SWITCH

MOTOR

SAFETY SWITCH

MOTOR SHAFT

A direct-drive processor

The motor is positioned underneath the bowl in this model, its shaft directly interlocked with the blade shaft. Most processors of this type run only at a single speed but have no belts or gears to break.

BOWL COVER

SAFETY SWITCH

BOWL

BLADE SHAFT

MOTOR PULLEY

SWITCHES

SHAFT PULLEY

A belt-driven processor

In this type of food processor, a ribbed belt connects the motor, via a small motor pulley, with a larger shaft pulley. Reduction gears, which are shifted depending on the position of a control switch, permit the appliance to be operated at two speeds. The processor also has a pulse switch for short, manually controlled bursts of power. A safety switch prevents the motor from operating until the bowl cover is tightly closed.

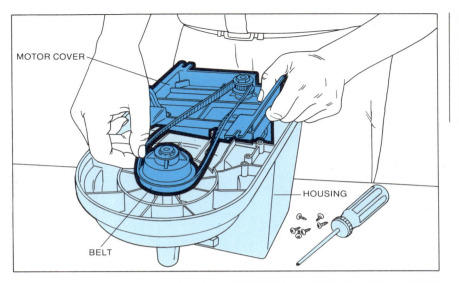

MOTOR COVER

HOUSING

BELT

Replacing a belt

Unplug the processor, detach the blade and bowl, and turn the body of the machine upside down. Remove the screws holding the bottom of the housing and lift it off. Remove the screws from the motor cover and lift the motor and its pulley up enough to slacken the belt. Slip off the old belt and replace it with a new one.

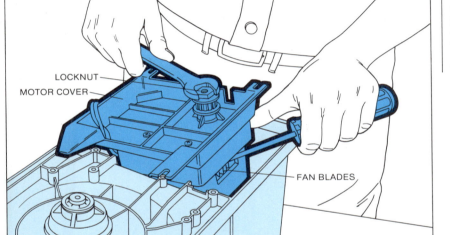

LOCKNUT
MOTOR COVER

FAN BLADES

Changing the small pulley

With the belt removed and the motor cover lifted slightly, insert a screwdriver between the motor fan blades to keep the motor shaft from rotating. Use a wrench to remove the reverse-threaded locknut. Slip the pulley off the motor shaft and replace it with a new one.

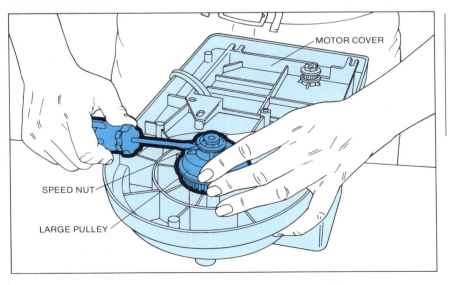

MOTOR COVER

SPEED NUT

LARGE PULLEY

Removing the large pulley

To pry off the speed nut that secures the large pulley and shaft, lightly tap a screwdriver in under the nut, then twist. Repeat this action at several locations around the edge of the nut. Once the nut is free of the shaft, slide the large pulley off and replace it. Finally, tap on a new speed nut and reassemble the food processor, replacing the belt, motor cover and housing base.

CAN OPENERS

While a motor-driven can opener may not be indispensable, it makes one of the most monotonous and frequent kitchen chores a great deal easier—and at a modest cost. Its motor, though small and frugal in energy consumption, develops great cutting power by means of ingenious gears *(below, left)*.

The major problem with these appliances is accumulations of food that jam the cutting mechanism. Some cutter wheels must be unscrewed for cleaning *(below, right)*; others simply slip off *(opposite)*. The cutter eventually dulls; it cannot be sharpened but is easy and inexpensive to replace.

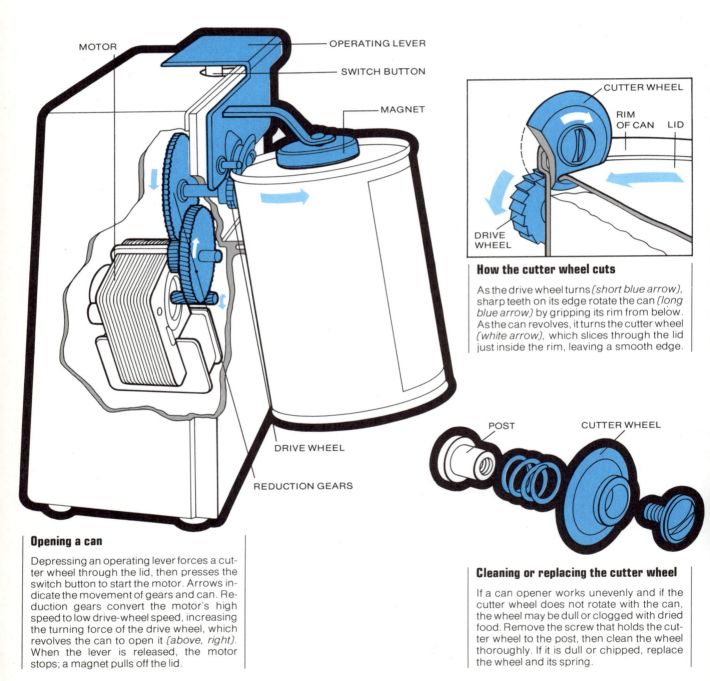

MOTOR

OPERATING LEVER

SWITCH BUTTON

MAGNET

DRIVE WHEEL

REDUCTION GEARS

CUTTER WHEEL

RIM OF CAN   LID

DRIVE WHEEL

How the cutter wheel cuts

As the drive wheel turns *(short blue arrow)*, sharp teeth on its edge rotate the can *(long blue arrow)* by gripping its rim from below. As the can revolves, it turns the cutter wheel *(white arrow)*, which slices through the lid just inside the rim, leaving a smooth edge.

POST   CUTTER WHEEL

Opening a can

Depressing an operating lever forces a cutter wheel through the lid, then presses the switch button to start the motor. Arrows indicate the movement of gears and can. Reduction gears convert the motor's high speed to low drive-wheel speed, increasing the turning force of the drive wheel, which revolves the can to open it *(above, right)*. When the lever is released, the motor stops; a magnet pulls off the lid.

Cleaning or replacing the cutter wheel

If a can opener works unevenly and if the cutter wheel does not rotate with the can, the wheel may be dull or clogged with dried food. Remove the screw that holds the cutter wheel to the post, then clean the wheel thoroughly. If it is dull or chipped, replace the wheel and its spring.

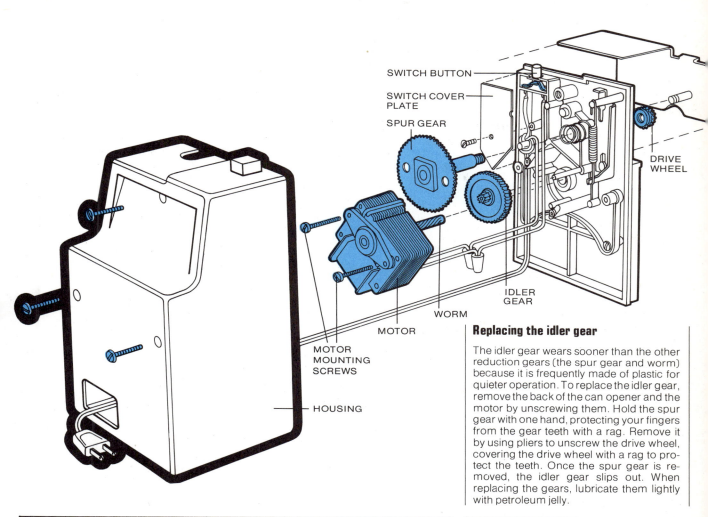

SWITCH BUTTON

SWITCH COVER PLATE

SPUR GEAR

DRIVE WHEEL

IDLER GEAR

WORM

MOTOR

MOTOR MOUNTING SCREWS

HOUSING

Replacing the idler gear

The idler gear wears sooner than the other reduction gears (the spur gear and worm) because it is frequently made of plastic for quieter operation. To replace the idler gear, remove the back of the can opener and the motor by unscrewing them. Hold the spur gear with one hand, protecting your fingers from the gear teeth with a rag. Remove it by using pliers to unscrew the drive wheel, covering the drive wheel with a rag to protect the teeth. Once the spur gear is removed, the idler gear slips out. When replacing the gears, lubricate them lightly with petroleum jelly.

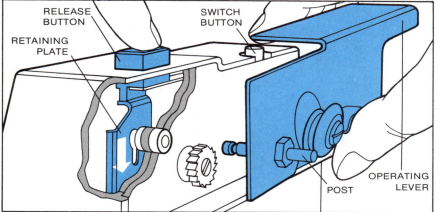

RELEASE BUTTON

SWITCH BUTTON

RETAINING PLATE

POST

OPERATING LEVER

An easier-to-remove cutter wheel

Some can openers have a release button that lowers a retaining plate *(arrow)*, freeing the pivot post so the operating lever and the cutter wheel can be removed as a unit and washed with the rest of the dishes. Before replacing the lever, apply petroleum jelly to the cutter-wheel shaft.

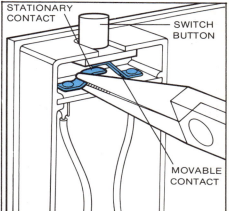

STATIONARY CONTACT

SWITCH BUTTON

MOVABLE CONTACT

Repairing the switch button

When the can opener does not work, its switch button may be at fault. Unplug the can opener and remove the contact cover plate *(top)*. If the movable contact does not touch the stationary contact when the button is pressed, gently bend the stationary contact up with needle-nose pliers.

ELECTRIC KNIVES

An electric knife makes neat carving effortless by combining power, speed and a special cutting action. Through an ingenious arrangement of a simple gear, a motor drives two serrated blades in a back-and-forth motion that reverses itself as fast as 50 times per second. Each blade acts as a small saw; together, they produce a high-speed sawing and shearing action that enables a novice carver to turn out professional-looking slices.

Despite a wide variety of switch styles, blade-release mechanisms, housings and handles, all electric knives—including the cordless, battery-powered ones—operate on the same principles. The parts most vulnerable to damage or wear can easily be replaced (opposite).

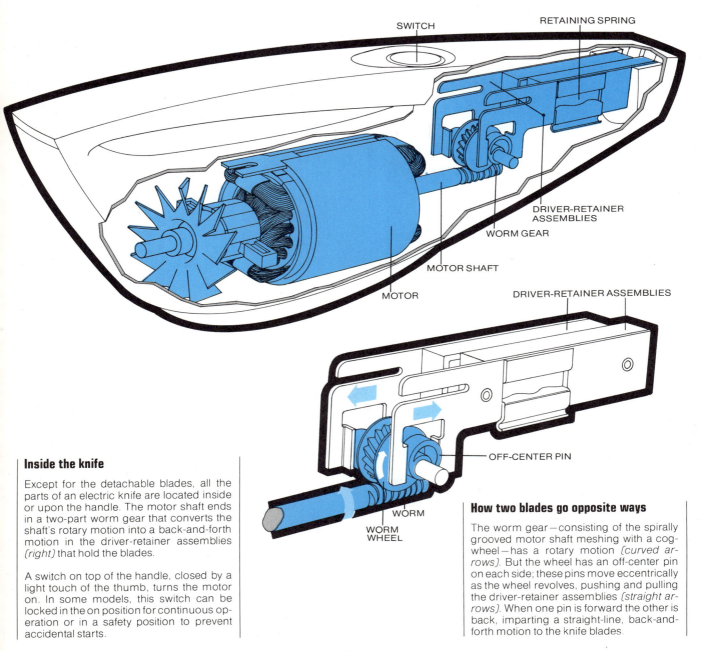

SWITCH

RETAINING SPRING

DRIVER-RETAINER ASSEMBLIES

WORM GEAR

MOTOR SHAFT

MOTOR

DRIVER-RETAINER ASSEMBLIES

OFF-CENTER PIN

WORM

WORM WHEEL

Inside the knife

Except for the detachable blades, all the parts of an electric knife are located inside or upon the handle. The motor shaft ends in a two-part worm gear that converts the shaft's rotary motion into a back-and-forth motion in the driver-retainer assemblies (right) that hold the blades.

A switch on top of the handle, closed by a light touch of the thumb, turns the motor on. In some models, this switch can be locked in the on position for continuous operation or in a safety position to prevent accidental starts.

How two blades go opposite ways

The worm gear—consisting of the spirally grooved motor shaft meshing with a cog-wheel—has a rotary motion (curved arrows). But the wheel has an off-center pin on each side; these pins move eccentrically as the wheel revolves, pushing and pulling the driver-retainer assemblies (straight arrows). When one pin is forward the other is back, imparting a straight-line, back-and-forth motion to the knife blades.

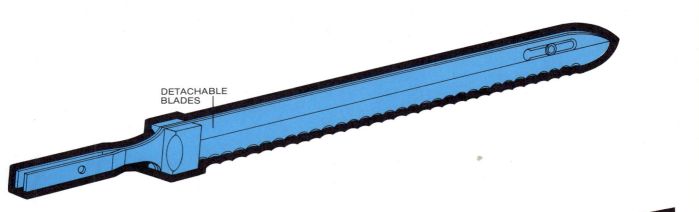

DETACHABLE
BLADES

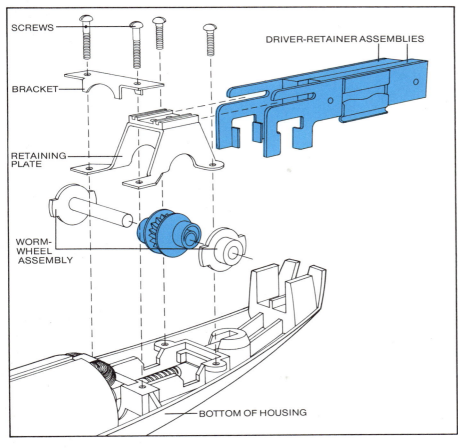

SCREWS

DRIVER-RETAINER ASSEMBLIES

BRACKET

RETAINING
PLATE

WORM-
WHEEL
ASSEMBLY

BOTTOM OF HOUSING

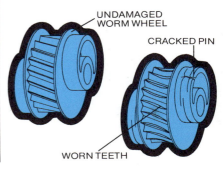

BROKEN
RETAINING
SPRING

CRACKED SLOT

UNDAMAGED
WORM WHEEL

CRACKED PIN

WORN TEETH

Checking the driver-retainer assembly

Subjected to constant and rapid vibration, a driver-retainer assembly rarely lasts as long as the blades or motor. Cracks may develop around the slot in which the off-center pin rotates, and the spring that secures the end of a blade may break. You must replace the entire assembly because its components are riveted together.

Disassembling the knife

In the exploded view above, an electric knife has been dismantled for the replacement of damaged parts. (Motor problems are discussed on page 195.) In disassembling, note the order in which you remove parts. First, unplug the knife. Take off the blades; then remove the screws securing the top of the handle and lift this part of the

housing off. (If your knife is the battery-powered type, do not disconnect the battery; avoid touching wires, however, and lock the switch in the safety position.) Remove the four screws from the bracket that fits over the worm-wheel and the driver-retainer assemblies. Lift off the bracket and the retaining plate that holds down the bearing through which the motor shaft runs. The remaining parts lift out.

Checking the worm wheel

The designers deliberately make the worm wheel the most fragile part in an electric knife. Formed of plastic or fiber, it will give way if the blades meet sudden stress, thus protecting the motor. Even under normal operation the wheel's teeth wear down and its off-center pins crack. Replace the wheel only; reuse the other parts of the assembly.

Cordless Appliances:
New Convenience from Improved Batteries

Batteries are the oldest source of useful electric current, but they never have been so busily employed as they are now. From electric tooth brushes and hearing aids to grass clippers and carving knives, battery-powered cordless electric appliances are increasing in diversity and usefulness, principally because of the development of small, long-lived and efficient batteries, and improved devices to use with them.

The principle of the battery was discovered in the late 1780s, when Luigi Galvani, professor of anatomy at the University of Bologna, noticed that dissected frogs' legs twitched when hung by copper hooks against an iron railing. Galvani's observation led to the harnessing of an electrochemical process called ionization. This process depends on the fact that the atoms of many metals, such as copper, iron and zinc, will, if in a chemical solution like that in a frog's body, readily give up electrons, the negatively charged atomic particles that make up electric currents. The zinc atom, having lost a negative charge through the departure of an electron, becomes electrically unbalanced—it is a charged atom, also called an ion. If metal atoms ionize continuously, the steady stream of electrons they release can flow through a conductor as an electric current. This continuous ionization of atoms is what makes a battery produce electricity.

All batteries have two electrodes, or electrical contacts, one called the cathode and one called the anode. Zinc, for example, makes a good anode. The electrodes are immersed in an electrolyte, a liquid or paste composed of highly active ions. When the electrolyte ions touch the zinc anode, the zinc atoms ionize and combine with the electrolyte ion, forming a neutral compound. The electrons that are left over from this chemical reaction accumulate on the anode, giving it a negative charge. At the same time, the positive electrolyte ions are attracted to the cathode, giving it a positive charge.

The secret of making a good battery is this: one of the electrodes must give up many more electrons than the other. Two zinc electrodes would produce no current since the charges would be the same on both. But one electrode of zinc and one of copper generate a current since the charge on the zinc is less than on the copper. Some kinds of batteries are made to be thrown away when their electrodes are consumed and the batteries no longer generate power. Throwaway cells by the billions have powered flashlights since about 1900. But there is another type of battery that can be recharged. Its chemical reactions can be reversed by sending a current through the cell in a direction opposite to that in which current flows when the battery produces power. The recharging rejuvenates the electrodes, and the battery is ready for work again.

While old-style storage batteries are too large for portable use, the new generation of storage batteries is small, powerful and easily recharged hundreds of times. For cordless appliances such as the ones described on the following pages, the nickel-cadmium battery is almost always the power source. Although nickel and cadmium are expensive materials, several recent technological developments have made nickel-cadmium batteries suitable for small appliances. Ways have been found to make them small enough for hand-held appliances and inexpensive enough

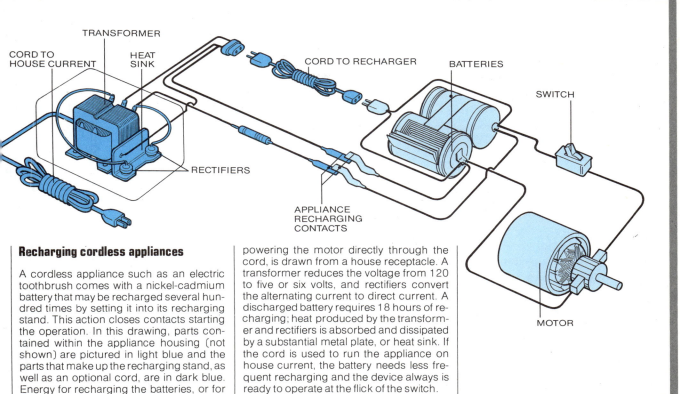

TRANSFORMER

CORD TO HOUSE CURRENT

HEAT SINK

CORD TO RECHARGER

BATTERIES

SWITCH

RECTIFIERS

APPLIANCE RECHARGING CONTACTS

MOTOR

Recharging cordless appliances

A cordless appliance such as an electric toothbrush comes with a nickel-cadmium battery that may be recharged several hundred times by setting it into its recharging stand. This action closes contacts starting the operation. In this drawing, parts contained within the appliance housing (not shown) are pictured in light blue and the parts that make up the recharging stand, as well as an optional cord, are in dark blue. Energy for recharging the batteries, or for powering the motor directly through the cord, is drawn from a house receptacle. A transformer reduces the voltage from 120 to five or six volts, and rectifiers convert the alternating current to direct current. A discharged battery requires 18 hours of recharging; heat produced by the transformer and rectifiers is absorbed and dissipated by a substantial metal plate, or heat sink. If the cord is used to run the appliance on house current, the battery needs less frequent recharging and the device always is ready to operate at the flick of the switch.

to be practical for cordless toothbrushes, grass clippers, shavers and electric knives.

But even the improved nickel-cadmium batteries are not, in small sizes, powerful producers of electricity. Their popularity depends on two developments of recent years. One is motors that run effectively on little power. They are small and light, but more important, they get by without the electrical field coils in other motors *(page 190);* to create the essential magnetism ordinarily produced by field coils, they have permanent magnets. Dispensing with the field coils, of course, dispenses with the electricity field coils consume.

Even the small amount of power that such a motor demands drains a battery fairly quickly. The development that solves this problem is a recharging device. Recharging requires running current through the battery backward, that is, in a single direction. If house current is to be used; it must be converted from the back-and-forth flow of AC to the steady flow of DC. The accessories, called rectifiers, that achieved this conversion used to be substantial gadgets containing large vacuum tubes. But the electronics revolution that brought the transistor also provided an equally small and cheap silicon rectifier—a chip of treated silicon with the convenient property of transmitting electricity in one direction only.

The silicon rectifier made recharging easy. The appliance is simply plugged into a stand connected to house current and containing a transformer to regulate voltage *(page 177)* and a silicon rectifier to change AC to DC. While the appliance waits to be used again, its battery rejuvenates.

A major disadvantage in many cordless appliances is that they are manufactured in such a way that they cannot be taken apart economically and repaired; when anything, including the long-lived battery, fails, the whole device must be replaced. But cordless devices are convenient and where a live cord would be limiting or dangerous, they are preferable to appliances using house current.

GARBAGE DISPOSERS

Garbage disposers that attach to the kitchen sink and grind up food wastes are nearly as common nowadays as the kitchen sink itself. They have become standard equipment in many new houses where local sewage lines are large enough to handle the load. (If you have a septic tank, check the chart on page 119 for the extra capacity a disposer requires.) Some disposers have built-in overload devices that cut the motor off whenever it jams or overheats.

The unit is suspended from the sink bottom by a flange and secured by heavy screws. Garbage drops through the mounting into the hopper, which, in this typical installation, is also connected to the dishwasher outflow. Garbage from the sink and food particles from the dishwasher fall onto a turntable where they are ground up and then flushed out the drainpipe with water from the tap, as indicated by the arrows in the drawing at right. Disposers are durable; the most frequent problem is failure of a motor seal *(below)*, which requires the unit to be removed *(opposite)* and disassembled *(following pages)*.

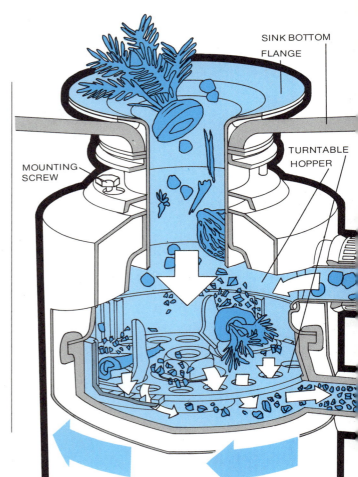

SINK BOTTOM
FLANGE

TURNTABLE
HOPPER

MOUNTING
SCREW

How the disposer works

There are two general kinds of disposers; one runs continuously when the switch is turned on, the other is activated by twisting the cover after each batch of garbage is fed into it. Both of them need running cold water to flush the material through, and both function in the same way.

The turntable does the main work of the disposer. It is simply a perforated metal disc, with two impeller blades, that is fastened to the motor shaft by a locknut. As garbage reaches the turntable, centrifugal force flings it outward where it is caught between the impeller blades and the cutting edges of the grind ring. This process shreds and grinds food wastes into particles that are small enough to pass with the cold water through the holes in the turntable and out the drain.

If water drips from the disposer, the fault is usually a worn seal, which lets water seep out a weep hole and onto the floor. The unit should be removed and the seal replaced *(pages 212-213)* promptly, or water may get into the motor and damage it.

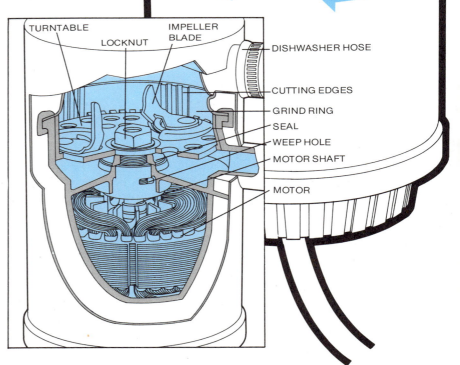

TURNTABLE
LOCKNUT
IMPELLER
BLADE
DISHWASHER HOSE
CUTTING EDGES
GRIND RING
SEAL
WEEP HOLE
MOTOR SHAFT
MOTOR

210

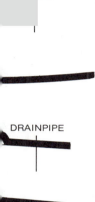

HWASHER HOSE

DRAINPIPE

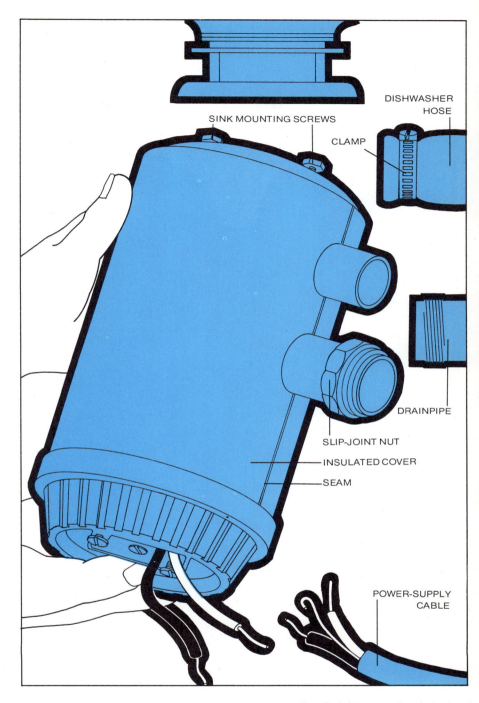

SINK MOUNTING SCREWS

DISHWASHER HOSE

CLAMP

DRAINPIPE

SLIP-JOINT NUT

INSULATED COVER

SEAM

POWER-SUPPLY CABLE

Disconnecting the disposer

After turning off power to the disposer circuit at the service panel, disconnect the wires at the disposer's bottom. Keep in mind that they must be reconnected according to color — black to black, and white to white, with the ground wire securely attached. Next, loosen the screw on the clamp around the dishwasher hose and

unscrew the slip-joint nut on the drainpipe connection. As you loosen the screws from the sink mounting, keep a firm hand under the disposer so it will not fall.

Once the unit is free of the sink, use a screwdriver to pry open the insulated cover at the seam; it should snap off easily. Then dismantle the machine by the method described on the following pages.

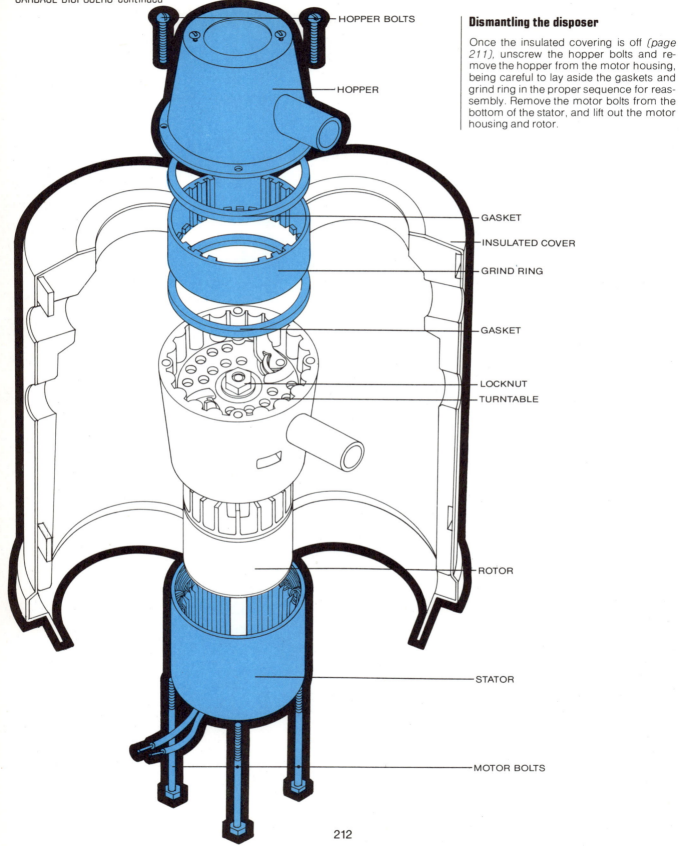

HOPPER BOLTS

HOPPER

GASKET

INSULATED COVER

GRIND RING

GASKET

LOCKNUT

TURNTABLE

ROTOR

STATOR

MOTOR BOLTS

Dismantling the disposer

Once the insulated covering is off *(page 211)*, unscrew the hopper bolts and remove the hopper from the motor housing, being careful to lay aside the gaskets and grind ring in the proper sequence for reassembly. Remove the motor bolts from the bottom of the stator, and lift out the motor housing and rotor.

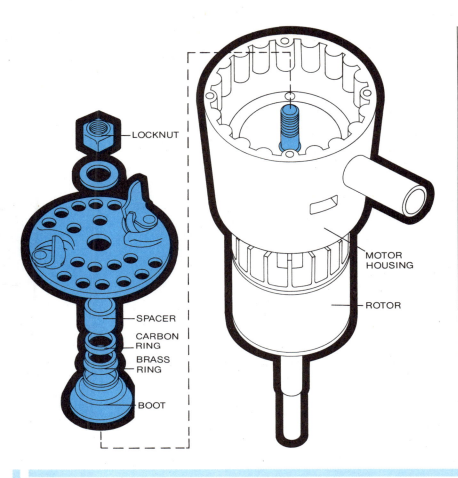

LOCKNUT

SPACER

CARBON RING

BRASS RING

BOOT

MOTOR HOUSING

ROTOR

Replacing the seal unit

Because the rotor and the turntable revolve together, you will have to immobilize the rotor with one hand before unscrewing the locknut. You can now take off the turntable, exposing the spacer and the seal unit directly beneath it *(far left)*. Take off the spacer, and lift out the seal unit.

The typical seal unit consists of three parts: a carbon ring, a flexible boot, and a brass ring that fits into the top of the boot. Inside the boot is a spring that pushes the rings together. The highly polished surfaces of the two rings enable the carbon ring to rotate on top of the stationary brass ring without letting water seep between them.

Examine the surfaces of the rings to determine whether dirt has come between them and unseated the seal. Also, look over the rings for nicks or scars, and inspect the boot for tears. If there is any evidence of damage, the entire seal unit should be replaced. Remember that the seal is delicate and that its ring surfaces must be perfectly smooth. In reseating the seal, handle the rings with care because even new parts can be damaged by rough treatment.

Troubleshooting Garbage Disposers

Problem	Possible Causes	Solution
Disposer does not run	Power not reaching disposer Circuit breaker or overload protector tripped	Check fuse or circuit breaker Push reset button or let motor cool
Leaks at sink flange	Loose mounting Defective gasket	Tighten nuts Replace gasket
Leak from weep hole	Unseated or worn seal	Replace seal *(above)*
Slow grinding	Undisposable matter in hopper Damaged impeller Dull cutting edges Insufficient water flow	Remove matter Replace turntable Replace grind ring Open faucet fully
Jammed	Object stuck between impeller and grind ring	Manually move impeller backward to free debris
Excessive noise or vibration	Undisposable matter Broken impeller Damaged motor bearings	Remove clogged matter Replace turntable Take disposer to service center

HUMIDIFIERS

In winter, you may have a dry throat, feel chilly even though your heating system is working fine, and find that your wood furniture is warping. The reason is simple: heated air absorbs moisture from the objects it surrounds. The cure is also simple: a humidifier, which adds moisture to the air.

If you heat your home with forced warm air, you can incorporate a humidifier in the central heating system. If you have steam, hot-water or electric heat, you can use portable one-room humidifiers like the two on these pages. Both pull air through a wet pad, evaporating moisture from the pad to increase the amount of water vapor in the room. Most portable humidifiers are turned on and off manually, but a few have automatic controls.

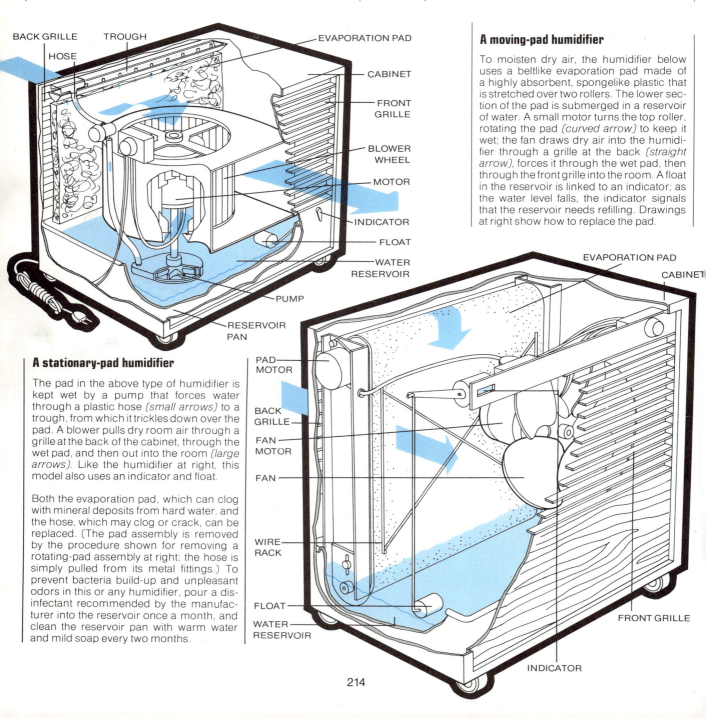

A moving-pad humidifier

To moisten dry air, the humidifier below uses a beltlike evaporation pad made of a highly absorbent, spongelike plastic that is stretched over two rollers. The lower section of the pad is submerged in a reservoir of water. A small motor turns the top roller, rotating the pad *(curved arrow)* to keep it wet; the fan draws dry air into the humidifier through a grille at the back *(straight arrow)*, forces it through the wet pad, then through the front grille into the room. A float in the reservoir is linked to an indicator; as the water level falls, the indicator signals that the reservoir needs refilling. Drawings at right show how to replace the pad.

A stationary-pad humidifier

The pad in the above type of humidifier is kept wet by a pump that forces water through a plastic hose *(small arrows)* to a trough, from which it trickles down over the pad. A blower pulls dry room air through a grille at the back of the cabinet, through the wet pad, and then out into the room *(large arrows)*. Like the humidifier at right, this model also uses an indicator and float.

Both the evaporation pad, which can clog with mineral deposits from hard water, and the hose, which may clog or crack, can be replaced. (The pad assembly is removed by the procedure shown for removing a rotating-pad assembly at right; the hose is simply pulled from its metal fittings.) To prevent bacteria build-up and unpleasant odors in this or any humidifier, pour a disinfectant recommended by the manufacturer into the reservoir once a month, and clean the reservoir pan with warm water and mild soap every two months.

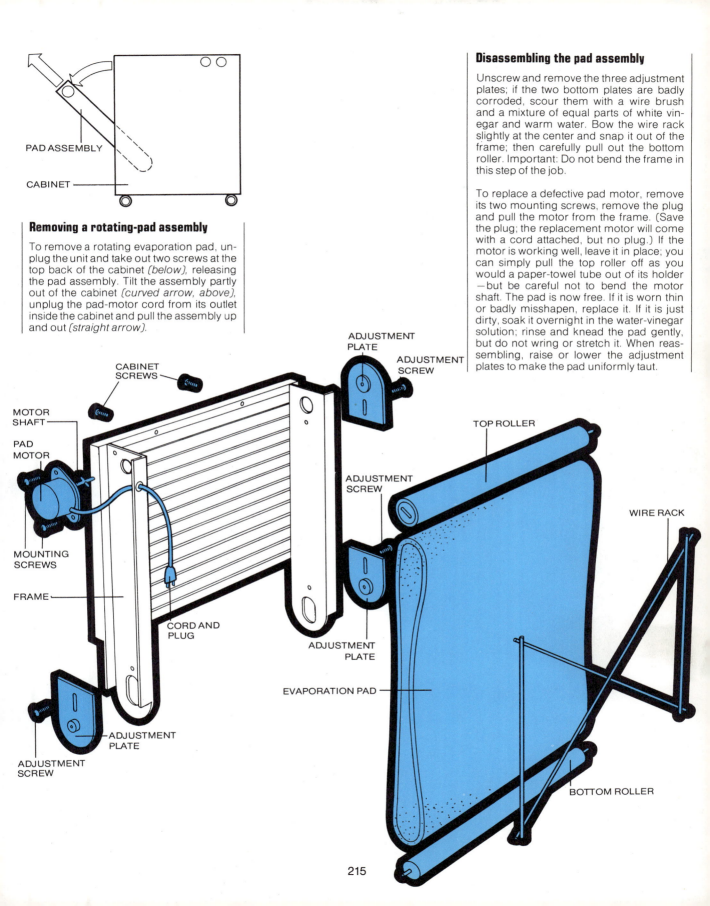

PAD ASSEMBLY

CABINET

Removing a rotating-pad assembly

To remove a rotating evaporation pad, un-plug the unit and take out two screws at the top back of the cabinet *(below)*, releasing the pad assembly. Tilt the assembly partly out of the cabinet *(curved arrow, above)*, unplug the pad-motor cord from its outlet inside the cabinet and pull the assembly up and out *(straight arrow)*.

Disassembling the pad assembly

Unscrew and remove the three adjustment plates; if the two bottom plates are badly corroded, scour them with a wire brush and a mixture of equal parts of white vinegar and warm water. Bow the wire rack slightly at the center and snap it out of the frame; then carefully pull out the bottom roller. Important: Do not bend the frame in this step of the job.

To replace a defective pad motor, remove its two mounting screws, remove the plug and pull the motor from the frame. (Save the plug; the replacement motor will come with a cord attached, but no plug.) If the motor is working well, leave it in place; you can simply pull the top roller off as you would a paper-towel tube out of its holder —but be careful not to bend the motor shaft. The pad is now free. If it is worn thin or badly misshapen, replace it. If it is just dirty, soak it overnight in the water-vinegar solution; rinse and knead the pad gently, but do not wring or stretch it. When reas-sembling, raise or lower the adjustment plates to make the pad uniformly taut.

CABINET SCREWS

MOTOR SHAFT

PAD MOTOR

MOUNTING SCREWS

FRAME

CORD AND PLUG

ADJUSTMENT PLATE

ADJUSTMENT SCREW

ADJUSTMENT SCREW

ADJUSTMENT PLATE

ADJUSTMENT PLATE

ADJUSTMENT SCREW

TOP ROLLER

WIRE RACK

EVAPORATION PAD

BOTTOM ROLLER

CLOCKS AND TIMERS

Electric clocks and timers have motors or microchips that operate in exact synchronism with the 60-per-second alternations of AC power—as long as the powerhouse generator runs on time, so does the clock. Some timekeepers, such as the digital clock shown opposite, top, are sealed in capsules; if they fail, they must be discarded. Others, such as the clock and timer below, have accessible workings.

In a clock that is not completely sealed, the rotor unit—which is susceptible to wear because it runs constantly at high speed—can be taken out easily and a new one installed. Other repairs demand professional skill.

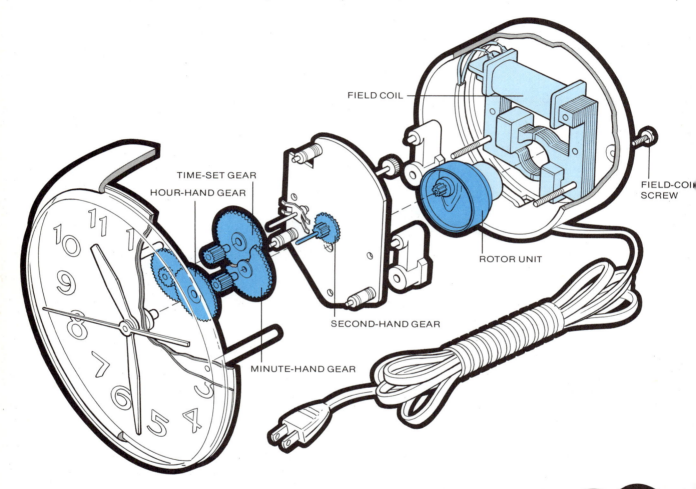

FIELD COIL

TIME-SET GEAR

HOUR-HAND GEAR

FIELD-COIL SCREW

ROTOR UNIT

SECOND-HAND GEAR

MINUTE-HAND GEAR

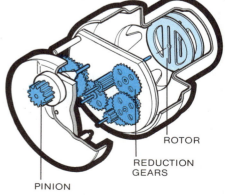

ROTOR

REDUCTION GEARS

PINION

How electric clocks operate

The motor of a clock keeps step with current alternations because the magnetism induced by current in the field coil keeps step. The motor turns a rotor *(right)* that, through reduction gears, rotates a pinion. The pinion moves gears behind the clock face to rotate the second hand once a minute, the minute hand hourly, the hour hand every 12 hours. The time-set gear disengages the hands so that they can be reset.

Replacing a rotor

When a clock's hands do not move but the motor hums, the trouble likely is in the rotor unit. To replace the unit, unplug the clock and remove the field-coil screws. The field coil and the rotor unit will come out together. Separate them and insert a new rotor unit; be sure the pinion engages the teeth of the second-hand gear. An odor of charred insulation signals a rare field-coil failure. Coils are not readily replaced.

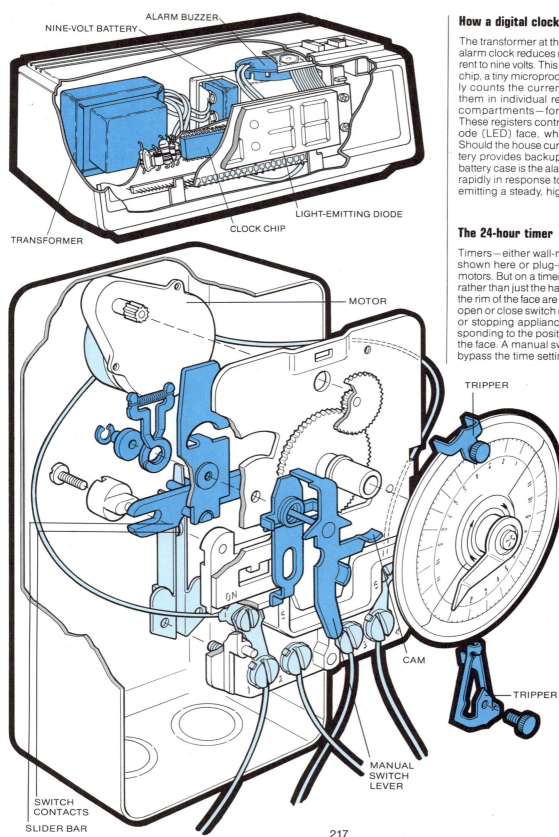

ALARM BUZZER

NINE-VOLT BATTERY

LIGHT-EMITTING DIODE

CLOCK CHIP

TRANSFORMER

MOTOR

TRIPPER

TRIPPER

CAM

MANUAL
SWITCH
LEVER

SWITCH
CONTACTS

SLIDER BAR

How a digital clock works

The transformer at the back of this compact alarm clock reduces normal household current to nine volts. This current flows to a clock chip, a tiny microprocessor that automatically counts the current cycles and records them in individual registers—or electronic compartments—for minutes and hours. These registers control the light-emitting diode (LED) face, which displays the time. Should the house current fail, a nine-volt battery provides backup power. On top of the battery case is the alarm, a disc that vibrates rapidly in response to an electrical current, emitting a steady, high-frequency buzz.

The 24-hour timer

Timers—either wall-mounted ones like that shown here or plug-in models—use clock motors. But on a timer, the entire face rotates, rather than just the hands, as on a clock. On the rim of the face are adjustable trippers that open or close switch contacts, thus starting or stopping appliances at the times corresponding to the positions of the trippers on the face. A manual switch can be flipped to bypass the time settings.

VACUUM CLEANERS

When the electric vacuum cleaner was introduced in 1908, it weighed 60 pounds. Since that first model, which looked much like the modern upright below, vacuum cleaners have become lighter, sleeker and more efficient. They have taken new shapes *(opposite)*. Mechanical parts have been refined. But, basically, vacuum cleaners work as they have from the beginning. A universal motor *(pages 190-191)* drives a fan that blows air through the appliance, creating a partial vacuum that sucks up dust and debris, and deposits them in a bag. The air flows through the bag's porous walls back into the room. How the three types of household vacuum cleaners—upright, canister and tank—achieve their results is explained on these two pages. What to do when the air stops flowing is detailed on the following pages.

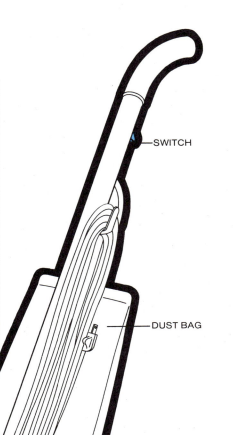

SWITCH

DUST BAG

The upright cleaner

The upright, which is shown here with its hood cut away, is especially effective for cleaning rugs because it is equipped with a spinning beater brush. When the motor is turned on by the switch on the handle, it activates the fan and a rubber drive belt that rotates the brush in the nozzle *(small arrows)*. The whirling bristles loosen up dirt and whisk it out of the rug into the air flow *(large arrow)* created by the fan. The air stream pulls the dirt in through the nozzle and up into the dust bag on the handle.

Air flow in an upright cleaner

In the cross-section drawing below, air and dirt drawn through the nozzle travel under the motor housing and fan to the dust bag *(dark blue arrows)*. The bag traps the dirt but its pores *(light blue arrows)* permit the air to escape. Accumulated dust and debris in the bag impede the air flow, so the bag should be emptied when half full.

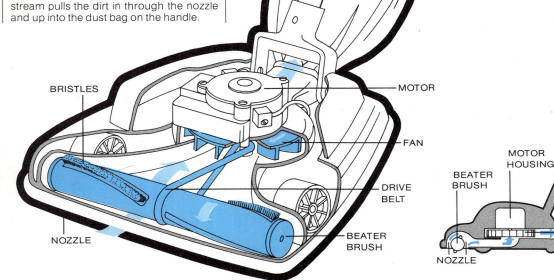

BRISTLES

MOTOR

FAN

DRIVE BELT

NOZZLE

BEATER BRUSH

BEATER BRUSH

MOTOR HOUSING

DUST BAG

NOZZLE

FAN

The canister cleaner

The canister (right) employs suction that is stronger than in an upright because the motor is more powerful. The canister's detachable parts are less cumbersome than an upright's for cleaning drapes, window sills, and other above-floor areas.

For floors, one end of a flexible hose is snapped into the canister inlet port; its other end fastens to a metal wand and floor nozzle, which on some models contains its own small motor and a set of beater brushes. When the cleaner is on, air and dirt are pulled directly into a dust bag inside the canister top. Air escaping from the bag flows past fan and motor housing, and out through a side exhaust port (arrows).

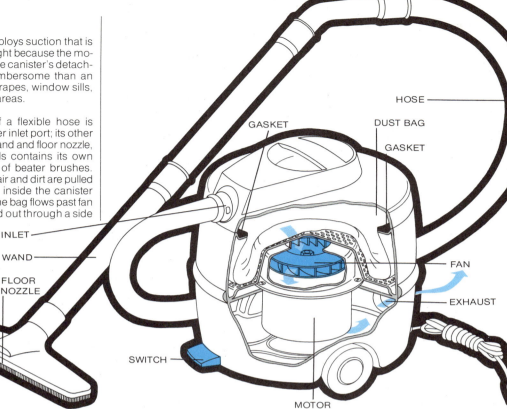

GASKET

HOSE

DUST BAG

GASKET

INLET

WAND

FLOOR NOZZLE

FAN

EXHAUST

SWITCH

MOTOR

The tank cleaner

Except for its different shape and the horizontal, rather than vertical, grouping of its internal parts, the tank cleaner below is basically the same as a canister type.

With its attachments, the tank cleaner, like the canister, can penetrate the nooks and crannies that an upright cannot reach. Its special advantage is that its shape permits it to be perched on staircases for easy cleaning of stairs and stair runners.

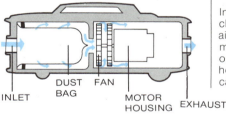

INLET

DUST BAG

FAN

MOTOR HOUSING

EXHAUST

Air flow of a canister or tank cleaner

In the cross-section drawing of the tank cleaner (left), the arrows indicate the path air travels. Because the dirt is trapped immediately upon entry into the cleaner and only the air moves past the fan and motor housing, these parts stay relatively clean. A canister cleaner works the same way.

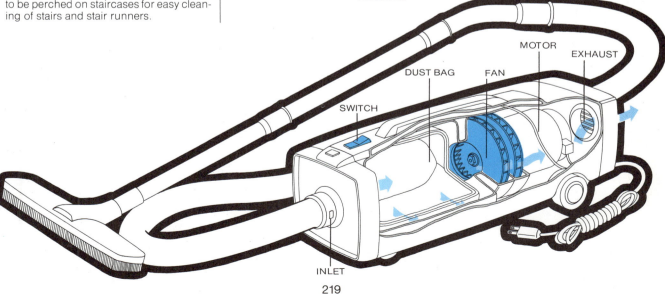

DUST BAG

MOTOR

EXHAUST

FAN

SWITCH

INLET

Cleaner Repairs

Most vacuum cleaners get a lot of abuse. They are hauled about mercilessly by their electric cords, to the cords' damage. They are allowed to swallow hairpins and buttons, which clog nozzles and hoses. They are used on newly shampooed—and still damp—rugs, and so pick up moist dirt that gets into motors. Yet, when a cleaner malfunctions, the problem is often easily solved.

The most common complaint is inadequate suction, which is generally the result of failure to empty or replace the dust bag. A nearly full bag reduces the air flow. If the bag is not the source of the trouble, a clogged hose may be. To check a hose for blockage, disconnect it, turn on the cleaner's motor, and place a hand over the air intake. If the pull on your hand is strong, the hose is the problem. To clear a hose, attach it to the cleaner's outlet port, take the machine outdoors and turn it on to blow out the debris. Pins and paper clips caught crosswise are almost impossible to dislodge—check for them by dropping a quarter through the hose.

If blowing fails, you can carefully poke either a broom handle or a length of heavy plastic-coated wire through the cleaner's hose.

If clogging recurs frequently, you probably need a new hose, which is simple to install (right). If neither dust bag nor hose is at fault, check the gaskets for holes or brittleness. Replace worn gaskets.

If the motor will not start, the cord may be faulty. To check or repair it, see pages 186-187. On an upright, the drive belt may stretch or beater-brush bristles may wear—replacing may be necessary (below).

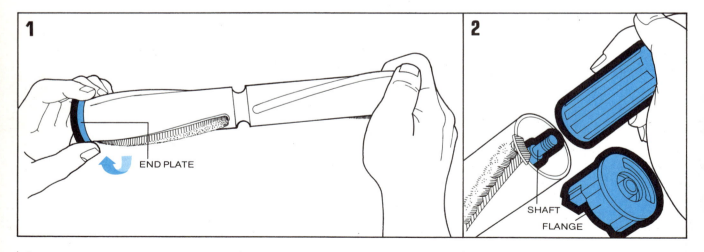

1 DRIVE BELT / BEATER BRUSH

2 METAL SURFACE — MOTOR-SHAFT PULLEY

1 Removing a stretched drive belt

Lay the cleaner on the floor, bottom up. Remove the belt cover plate. Note whether the belt is stretched flat, or is twisted; a new one must go in the same way. Lift the belt from the motor-shaft pulley, remove the beater brush and slide the belt off.

2 Inserting a new drive belt

Place a new belt in the center groove of the beater brush; snap the brush into place. Remove bits of old rubber from the pulley and stretch the belt around it; align the side nearest the metal surface with the arrow on that surface. Replace the cover.

1 END PLATE

2 SHAFT / FLANGE

1 Taking apart a worn beater brush

Brushes of some beaters unscrew; others snap out of the nozzle cavity. A metal plate covers each end of the beater brush. Grasp the plates and twist them in opposite directions (arrow). One of the metal plates will unscrew and come off.

2 Loosening the second end plate

At the end where the plate has unscrewed, use a screwdriver to pry off an inner metal flange. With the screwdriver's handle, tap the protruding end of a shaft housed in the beater-brush core. This releases the plate at the other end of the beater brush.

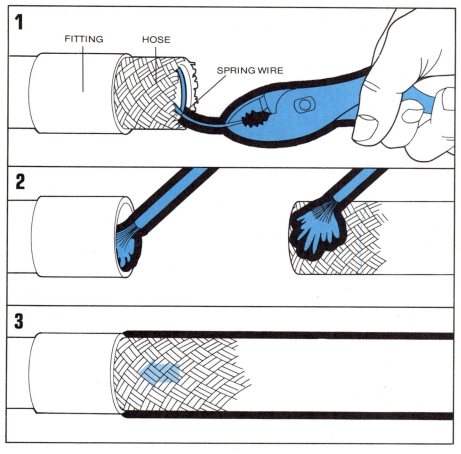

1 Removing hose fittings

If a hose must be replaced, you can generally reuse the old fittings. Rubber fittings can be twisted off. To remove metal or plastic ones, use a knife to cut through the hose about two inches from each fitting end. With pliers, pull out loose ends of spring wire from hose and fittings. Remove any bits of fabric clinging to the fittings.

2 Gluing the hose and fittings

Buy a new hose without fittings at an appliance repair shop. Brush white glue on the inside of each fitting and on the outside of the hose at the ends where they will join. Spread the glue on the hose a distance equal to the length of the fitting collar *(dotted line)*. Coat the hose ends with glue to prevent frayed fabric edges.

3 Joining the hose and fittings

At the points where they have been coated with glue, firmly push the ends of a fabric-type hose into the fittings *(arrow)*. If the hose is of the plastic corrugated type, screw it into the fitting. Let the glue dry for 24 hours before using the hose.

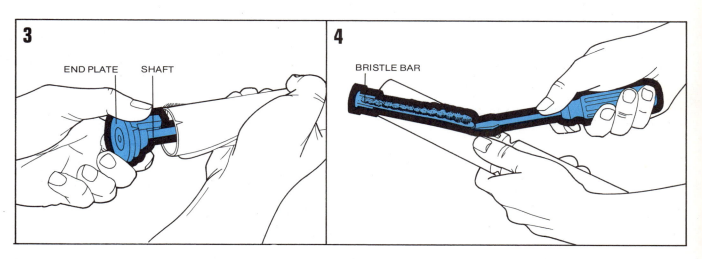

3 Removing the plate and shaft

Carefully pull the newly loosened end plate and the attached shaft from inside the beater brush. They lock the brushes on and, once removed, permit their replacement. Upend the beater-brush core to shake out dirt, then wipe it clean with a damp cloth.

4 Changing the bristles

With a screwdriver, carefully push the bristle bars off the brush channels. Slide new bristle bars into the channels. Lubricate bearings at the beater's ends with sewing-machine oil. Replace worn washers and reassemble the beater brush.

SEWING MACHINES

If any one machine verifies Yankee ingenuity, it is the sewing machine. American inventors of the 19th Century, improving on one another's improvements, devised a machine so fast in operation, it outstitched the swiftest hand-seamstress; so precisely built, its tolerances were measured in thousandths of an inch; so durable, it could last a lifetime; and so easy to use, it found markets in primitive lands. Most important, it did something quickly and easily that before had been done only laboriously—it used two threads in each stitch, locking them together for durability.

The improvements did not stop there. Engineers of this century contributed the useful and decorative zigzag stitch—in machines built so solidly they all but defy the assaults of amateur repairmen. In fact, except for an easy resetting of thread tension, repairs are better left to specialists. But oiling is still needed once every three or four sewing hours.

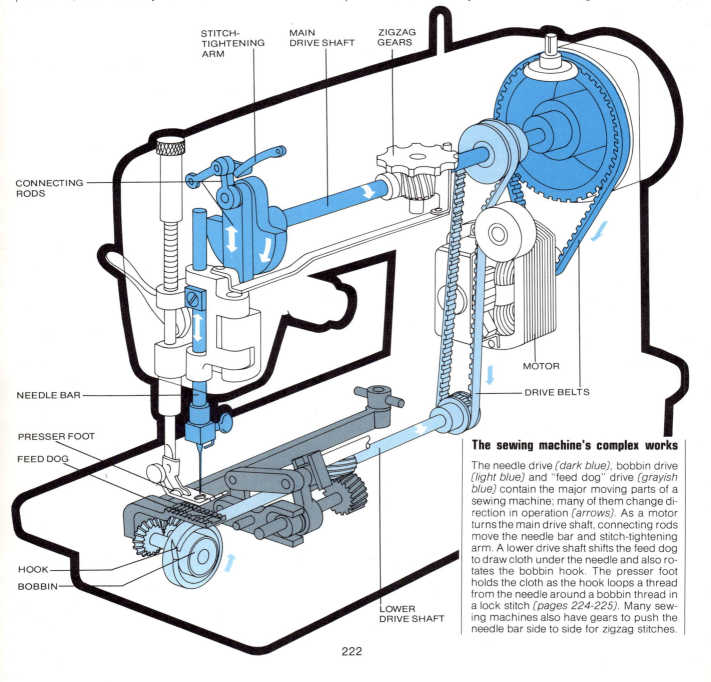

STITCH-TIGHTENING ARM

MAIN DRIVE SHAFT

ZIGZAG GEARS

CONNECTING RODS

NEEDLE BAR

PRESSER FOOT

FEED DOG

HOOK

BOBBIN

LOWER DRIVE SHAFT

MOTOR

DRIVE BELTS

The sewing machine's complex works

The needle drive (dark blue), bobbin drive (light blue) and "feed dog" drive (grayish blue) contain the major moving parts of a sewing machine; many of them change direction in operation (arrows). As a motor turns the main drive shaft, connecting rods move the needle bar and stitch-tightening arm. A lower drive shaft shifts the feed dog to draw cloth under the needle and also rotates the bobbin hook. The presser foot holds the cloth as the hook loops a thread from the needle around a bobbin thread in a lock stitch (pages 224-225). Many sewing machines also have gears to push the needle bar side to side for zigzag stitches.

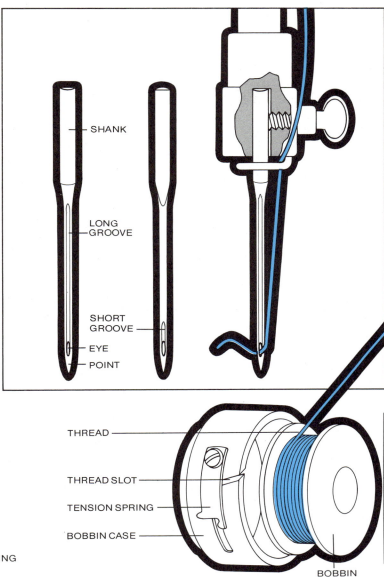

A special needle for machine stitches

A sewing-machine needle differs significantly from ordinary needles. Not only is the eye near the point, but into the blade are cut two grooves, one long and one short. As the needle lifts, the thread fits into the long groove located on one side of the needle; the short groove on the other side forces the thread to form the loop needed for a lock stitch. One side of the needle shank may be flattened to make proper installation easy. The relationship of the needle eye to the hook surrounding the bobbin case is so precise that a needle too long will break off, and one that is too short will not meet the hook to form a stitch.

SHANK

LONG GROOVE

SHORT GROOVE

EYE

POINT

THREAD

THREAD SLOT

TENSION SPRING

BOBBIN CASE

BOBBIN

The bobbin: a second spool of thread

The bobbin, a small spool that fits in the base of the machine below the needle, is the source of the second thread needed for a lock stitch. It is wound (and rewound, when it becomes empty) with the same kind of thread as that on the spool that feeds the needle. After the bobbin is put in the bobbin case, its thread is passed through a diagonal slot and under a spring that presses it against the case to keep it taut as the sewing machine stitches.

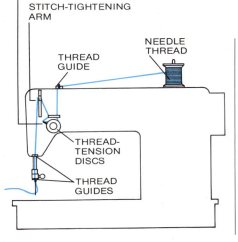

CHECK SPRING

STITCH-TIGHTENING ARM

THREAD GUIDE

NEEDLE THREAD

THREAD-TENSION DISCS

THREAD GUIDES

The path of the needle thread

The needle thread follows a circuitous path from spool to needle, going first through a thread guide, then between adjustable thread-tension discs, and under the check spring. Pressure on the thread at the tension discs determines how taut it will be; the wrong tension can break the needle thread or cause snarled, loopy stitches.

The stitch-tightening arm, which pulls the stitches snug, is the next station. One or two more thread guides lead the thread to the needle, which it enters from front or side, depending on design. Bobbin thread remains under the base.

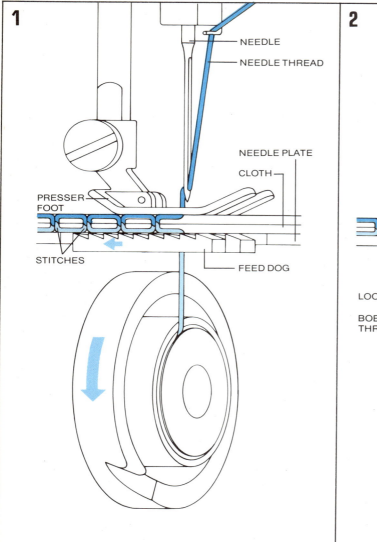

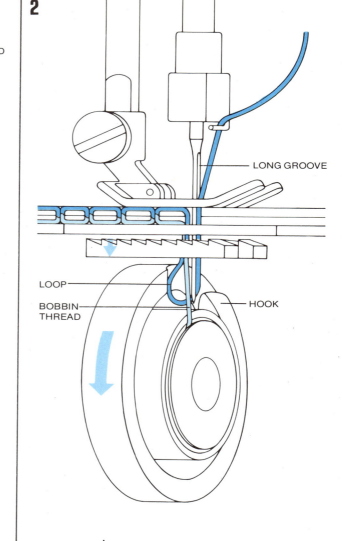

1 Start of a sewing-machine stitch

A sewing machine loops one length of thread around another in a lock stitch, which derives its strength from the tight grip the interlocking threads have on each other in the seam. Even if one thread breaks, adjacent stitches will not unravel.

The machine moves needle, cloth and feed dog (small arrows) while the bobbin spins (broad arrow). First the needle pushes the thread through two pieces of cloth that the feed dog has advanced. As the needle starts down, the feed dog retracts. The presser foot holds the cloth taut so the needle can easily pierce it, and the hook rotates or oscillates into position.

2 Forming a loop

As the needle begins to rise, the thread on the short-groove side of the needle remains beneath the cloth, and forms a loop. There is no loop on the opposite side of the needle because the thread fits snugly into a long groove in the needle blade and rises with the needle.

As the loop appears, the hook moves to catch it behind the bobbin thread. The retracted feed dog begins its shift to advance the cloth for the next stitch.

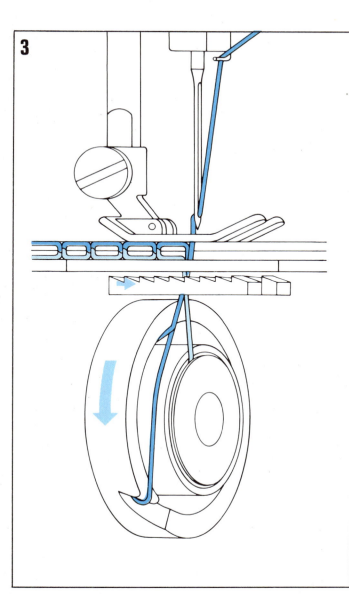

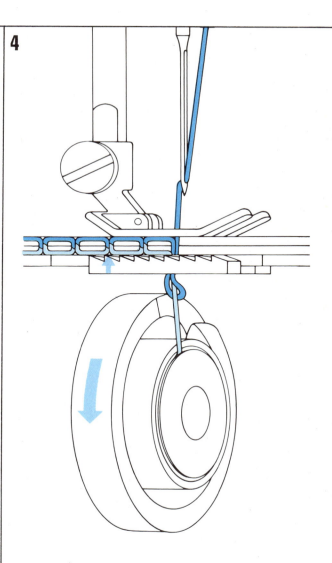

3 Making the loop bigger

As the needle, rising toward the top of its stroke, comes out of the cloth, the hook continues to enlarge the loop by pulling the needle thread down from the needle's eye. Moving a little farther, the hook passes one side of the enlarged loop of needle thread over the bobbin and the other side under it, thus trapping bobbin thread inside a loop of needle thread.

As the sewing machine completes a stitch, the feed dog is raised, and becomes ready to bite into the cloth again.

4 Pulling the stitch tight

To complete the stitch, the stitch-tightening arm near the top of the sewing machine pulls up on the needle thread. It tightens the loop of needle thread around the bobbin thread and pulls the stitch up into the pieces of cloth. The hook turns or oscillates behind the bobbin thread, but there is no loop this time for it to catch (a loop for the next stitch will be ready and waiting for the hook the next time it comes by).

The feed dog has now gripped the fabric again. When the loop is pulled tight, it will shift the fabric, and the needle can come down once more to start another stitch.

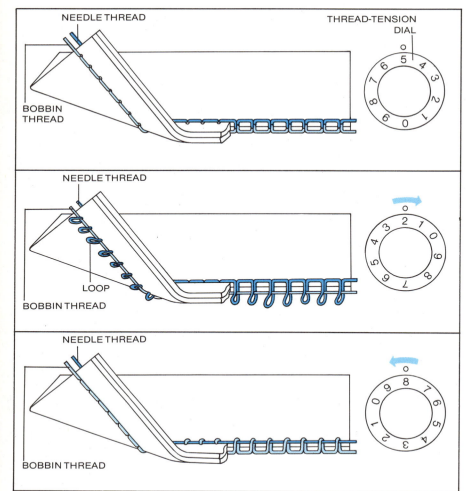

Correct needle-thread tension

A middle setting of the thread-tension dial provides the right needle-thread tension for many combinations of fabric, thread and stitch. It should make a seam that looks like the one at left: needle thread and bobbin thread locked tightly together part way into the fabric, and a strong row of stitches between the two pieces of cloth.

Too little tension

The appearance of loops on the underside of a seam signals insufficient needle-thread tension, which allows too much needle thread to go into the stitch. This kind of stitch is little better than no stitch at all, since the bobbin thread can easily be pulled out of the needle-thread loops. To correct such a loose stitch, turn the dial clockwise to increase tension.

Too much tension

Too taut a needle thread pulls the bobbin thread all the way up through the seam. Besides causing the cloth to pucker, this tension also makes a weak stitch, as the needle thread can be pulled from under the bobbin thread loops. To adjust, turn the dial counterclockwise to a lower setting that will decrease the tension.

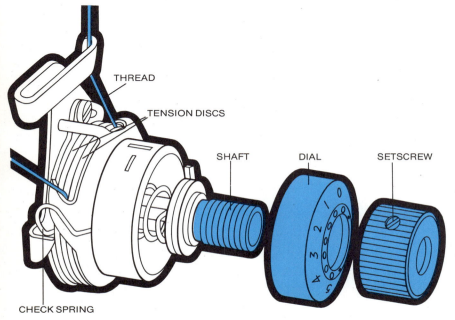

Thread tensioner calibration

If adjusting the tension dial does not improve the stitches, the thread tensioner may need calibrating. Loosen the setscrew and unscrew the knob; then pull the dial off the shaft. Thread the sewing machine through the tension discs, but do not pass the thread under the check spring.

With the presser foot down, turn the tension shaft back and forth until there is just the slightest drag on the thread when you pull it. To test the tension, raise the presser foot to release all tension, then lower it and pull the thread. As the foot moves down, you should feel only slightly increased resistance in the thread. Push the dial onto the shaft and turn it counterclockwise; it will stop at zero with almost no tension on the thread. Screw on the knob, tighten the setscrew and reset the dial.

Troubleshooting Sewing Machines

Problem	Possible Causes	Solution
Machine will not run	Power not reaching machine	Check fuse or circuit-breaker; receptacle *(page 143)*; cord *(pages 186-187)*
Motor runs but machine does not	Machine set to wind bobbin Drive belt slips Loose motor pulley	Reset winding control Have a serviceman replace drive belt Tighten pulley setscrew
Motor hums and machine will not run	Thread tangled around bobbin or bobbin case Machine lacks oil	Clean thread out of bobbin area Oil the machine
Machine runs but will not stitch	Machine threaded incorrectly Needle too short or too long Needle bent Needle inserted incorrectly Empty bobbin Bobbin case inserted incorrectly Thread too heavy	Rethread the machine Replace the needle with one made for the machine Replace the needle Reinsert the needle correctly Rewind the bobbin Reinsert the bobbin case Use lighter thread or heavier needle
Needle breaks	Needle too long Bent needle Needle inserted incorrectly Loose presser foot or wrong type for stitch Needle plate loose or wrong type for stitch Bobbin case inserted incorrectly	Replace with a needle made for the machine Replace the needle Reinsert the needle Tighten foot or use a different one Tighten needle plate or use a different type Reinsert the bobbin case
Needle thread breaks	Machine threaded incorrectly Needle inserted incorrectly Needle thread tangled Poor quality thread Needle-thread tension too high Wrong-sized needle Bent needle or burred needle eye Burred or pitted thread guides or presser foot	Rethread the machine Reinsert the needle Untangle thread and rethread Use better thread Decrease tension Select a different needle Replace the needle Have a serviceman repair the machine
Bobbin thread breaks	Bobbin damaged Bobbin wound too tightly or bobbin thread knotted Damaged bobbin case Bobbin case inserted incorrectly Bobbin thread of poor quality	Replace the bobbin Rewind the bobbin Replace bobbin case Reinsert the bobbin case Use better thread
Thread loops or bunches	Machine threaded incorrectly or thread tangled Needle-thread tension too low Bobbin thread too heavy	Rethread the machine Increase thread tension Use lighter thread
Fabric does not feed	Presser foot raised Stitch length set at zero	Lower presser foot Adjust stitch-length setting
Noisy machine	Machine dirty or lacks oil	Oil and clean machine
Machine runs slowly	Bobbin winder engaged Machine lacks oil	Disengage the bobbin winder Oil the machine

SHAVERS

The various types of shavers—curved-head, flat-head and rotary-head—all shave the same way. Hairs penetrate holes in a thin metal shield, called the head, and are sheared off by rapidly moving cutters. The motor and drive mechanisms are so durable that most shavers have a tightly sealed housing; only head and cutters are detachable.

A poor performance is generally the outcome of clogged cutters. After every shave, remove all hairs, using the brush that is supplied with the shaver. And once a month, detach the head and cutters and rinse them under hot water. The lubricant necessary for smooth action between the cutter and the head is washed off in this procedure, so after you reassemble your shaver, place two drops of clear, light oil on the head while the shaver's motor is running.

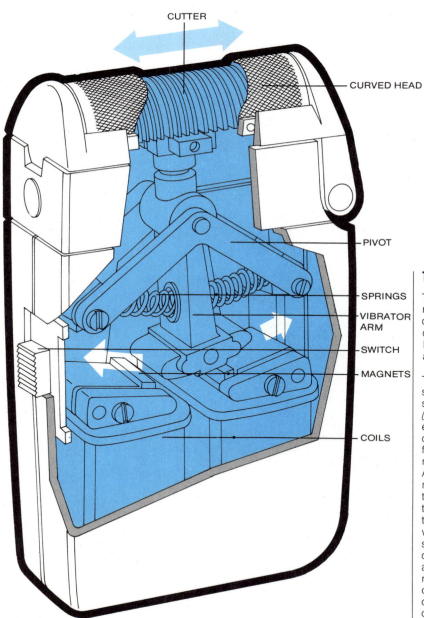

CUTTER

CURVED HEAD

PIVOT

SPRINGS

VIBRATOR ARM

SWITCH

MAGNETS

COILS

The curved-head shaver

The curved head is made of thin, flexible metal that can be pressed in to follow facial contours. Beneath the head lies a single cutter with some three dozen individual blades driven back and forth *(arrow)* by a vibrator motor.

The cutter is connected to a pivoted T-shaped arm that is flanked by a pair of springs. At rest, the arm sits off center *(above, left)*. When you switch on the shaver, alternating current passes through the coils, producing an alternating magnetic force. Because the arm is closer to one magnet it is first pulled toward it *(arrows)*. As one cycle of the current ends and the magnetism alters in step with the current, the magnet releases the arm. The spring then pushes the arm back past center, so that on the next current cycle it will move toward the other magnet. The vibrator arm swings through a complete stroke for each cycle of current and magnetism—60 times a second. The two-coil arrangement permits the shaver to be used on either 120- or 240-volt power—a control switch sets circuits so that each of the coils never receives more than 120 volts.

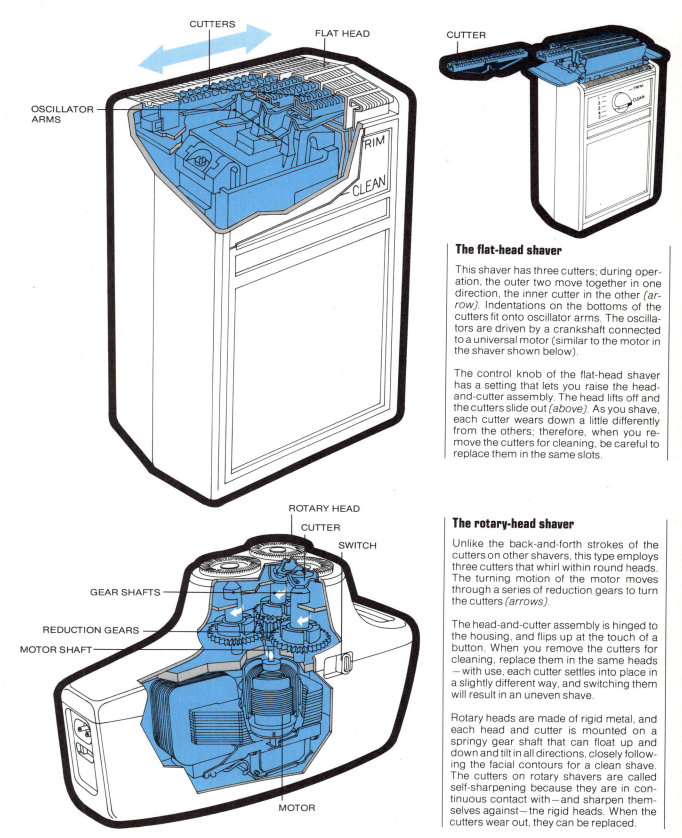

CUTTERS

FLAT HEAD

OSCILLATOR
ARMS

TRIM

CLEAN

CUTTER

TRIM

CLEAN

The flat-head shaver

This shaver has three cutters; during operation, the outer two move together in one direction, the inner cutter in the other (arrow). Indentations on the bottoms of the cutters fit onto oscillator arms. The oscillators are driven by a crankshaft connected to a universal motor (similar to the motor in the shaver shown below).

The control knob of the flat-head shaver has a setting that lets you raise the head-and-cutter assembly. The head lifts off and the cutters slide out (above). As you shave, each cutter wears down a little differently from the others; therefore, when you remove the cutters for cleaning, be careful to replace them in the same slots.

ROTARY HEAD

CUTTER

SWITCH

GEAR SHAFTS

REDUCTION GEARS

MOTOR SHAFT

MOTOR

The rotary-head shaver

Unlike the back-and-forth strokes of the cutters on other shavers, this type employs three cutters that whirl within round heads. The turning motion of the motor moves through a series of reduction gears to turn the cutters (arrows).

The head-and-cutter assembly is hinged to the housing, and flips up at the touch of a button. When you remove the cutters for cleaning, replace them in the same heads —with use, each cutter settles into place in a slightly different way, and switching them will result in an uneven shave.

Rotary heads are made of rigid metal, and each head and cutter is mounted on a springy gear shaft that can float up and down and tilt in all directions, closely following the facial contours for a clean shave. The cutters on rotary shavers are called self-sharpening because they are in continuous contact with—and sharpen themselves against—the rigid heads. When the cutters wear out, they can be replaced.

TOOTHBRUSHES AND CLEANERS

Early in this century, Edmund Kells made one of the first dental irrigators by converting a blowtorch gas tank to pump mouthwash, and the first electric toothbrush was made in Scandinavia as early as the 1930s. But the modern versions of both appliances appeared only when better techniques allowed precision internal parts—gears, pumps and tubing—to be made accurately from plastic.

The cordless toothbrush uses a rechargeable battery to power its DC motor. Its charger—like the one on page 209—has a transformer to change AC from a wall receptacle to DC before it enters the battery. The irrigators and toothbrushes with cords use an AC motor and can be plugged directly into a wall receptacle.

If the tubing in an irrigator springs a leak, it is simple to replace *(opposite)*. But toothbrushes are sealed to keep moisture out of the motor. If an internal part breaks, the entire unit must be replaced.

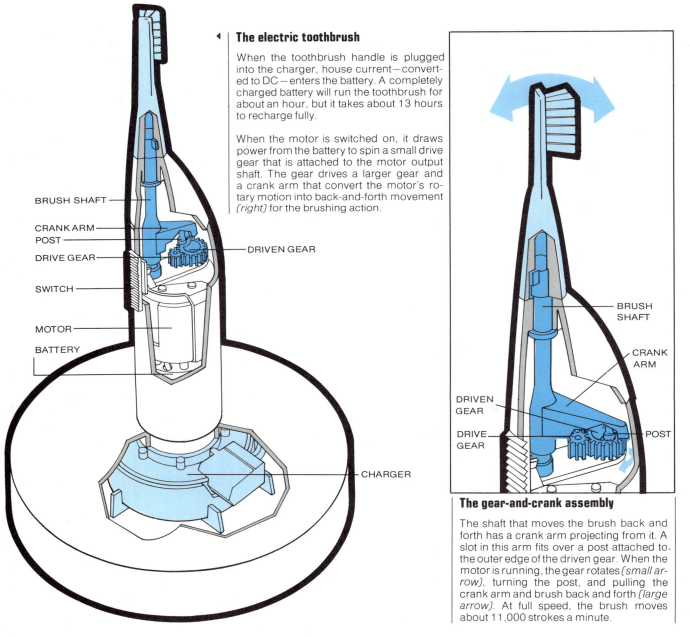

The electric toothbrush

When the toothbrush handle is plugged into the charger, house current—converted to DC—enters the battery. A completely charged battery will run the toothbrush for about an hour, but it takes about 13 hours to recharge fully.

When the motor is switched on, it draws power from the battery to spin a small drive gear that is attached to the motor output shaft. The gear drives a larger gear and a crank arm that convert the motor's rotary motion into back-and-forth movement *(right)* for the brushing action.

BRUSH SHAFT

CRANK ARM

POST

DRIVE GEAR

SWITCH

MOTOR

BATTERY

DRIVEN GEAR

CHARGER

BRUSH SHAFT

CRANK ARM

DRIVEN GEAR

DRIVE GEAR

POST

The gear-and-crank assembly

The shaft that moves the brush back and forth has a crank arm projecting from it. A slot in this arm fits over a post attached to the outer edge of the driven gear. When the motor is running, the gear rotates *(small arrow)*, turning the post, and pulling the crank arm and brush back and forth *(large arrow)*. At full speed, the brush moves about 11,000 strokes a minute.

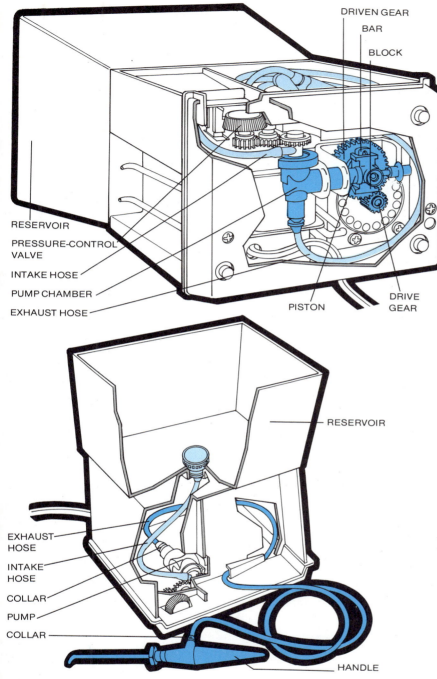

DRIVEN GEAR
BAR
BLOCK

RESERVOIR
PRESSURE-CONTROL VALVE
INTAKE HOSE
PUMP CHAMBER
EXHAUST HOSE

PISTON
DRIVE GEAR

RESERVOIR

EXHAUST HOSE
INTAKE HOSE
COLLAR
PUMP
COLLAR

HANDLE

The dental irrigator

The irrigator, shown here on its side, uses a tiny piston pump to spurt over 1,000 jets of water per minute from a handle at the end of its exhaust hose. A block that is attached to a bar on the gear of the motor shaft moves the pump piston back and forth. One full turn of the gear pushes the piston through one back-and-forth stroke. Water from the reservoir enters the pump chamber through the intake hose, and the piston forces it out the exhaust hose at a pressure of as much as 85 pounds per square inch. Motor and pump are separated by a plastic housing that protects the motor wiring from water damage.

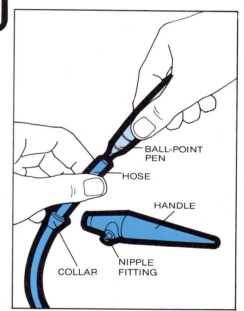

BALL-POINT PEN
HOSE
HANDLE
COLLAR
NIPPLE FITTING

Installing a new hose

To install a new exhaust hose, first put a new collar over one end of the replacement hose and enlarge the hose opening by forcing and twisting a ball-point pen into it. Push the hose over the handle's nipple fitting and slide the collar up over the hose end and fitting. Repeat the procedure for the pump end of the hose. A new intake hose can simply be pressed over the fittings without enlarging the end openings.

Removing leaky hoses

If your irrigator has an internal leak, the problem may be a broken pump or a cracked exhaust or intake hose. To replace a leaking hose, you will need only a knife and a ball-point pen.

Remove the irrigator's bottom plate and make sure that the exhaust and intake hoses fit tightly to the pump. Put some water in the irrigator's reservoir and turn the motor on. If the pump is leaking, it must be fixed professionally. If the problem is a leaking hose, remove it. The intake hose is usually made of soft rubber and is pressed lightly over the reservoir-valve and pump-intake fittings. It can be pulled off easily. The exhaust hose is heavy plastic and is held to the exhaust and handle fittings with plastic collars. Pry the collars back and cut the hose from the fittings with a knife.

Appliances That Heat

Since James Joule discovered in 1841 that heat was produced by the resistance of a wire to the passage of electricity, the principle has been applied to cook food, press clothes and dry hair. The wire that helps perform these minor miracles must be able to get hot enough to do the job without burning itself up—the best material is a nickel-and-chromium alloy, generally used today in the many appliances that contain heating elements.

Since such resistance wire is used for so many different chores, it is made in different forms, each suited to a special task. In a waffle cooker, it is strung in a few loose coils and secured with insulators. In a toaster-oven, it is sealed in a stiff, insulated-metal or glass tube, which protects it from spilled food. Because the surfaces of frying pans must often be scoured after use, the wire in them is enclosed permanently in their metal bodies so that the pan can be immersed for cleaning. In a toaster, the wire is made flat to be wound around a flat mica sheet just a bit bigger than a slice of bread (since heated air rises, temperature over the area is equalized by using fewer turns of wire at the top than at the bottom).

Before thermostats were added to control the heat created by the resistance wire, some appliances such as electric irons had to be unplugged or switched off manually every few minutes to maintain an even temperature. Now, thermostats keep heat uniform in a frying pan, for example, more accurately than the most watchful cook can—and nobody has to watch the pan. The thermostat also saves electricity—it turns power on only intermittently.

Two kinds of thermostats are used. The blade type *(page 237)* controls all appliances that need to have adjustable temperatures, because the blade action of the thermostat can be varied with a tension adjustment. Disc thermostats *(page 236)* are used in some single-temperature appliances because these thermostats are inexpensive to make and easy to replace; blade types are used in others.

Tracing a Problem

When one of your heating appliances breaks down, the failure is usually the result of a malfunctioning thermostat or a break in the electrical circuit. But before you delve into the appliance itself, make sure that the problem is not a blown fuse or tripped circuit breaker. Most appliances with heating elements draw tremendous amounts of current for their size —a toaster or iron uses more than a medium-sized air conditioner. Turning them on can easily add enough load to the circuit to blow a fuse or trip a circuit breaker.

If the fuses or circuit breakers are in order, the next thing to check is the power cord (pages 186-187), which gets heavy wear in this type of appliance. A defective cord should be replaced, not repaired. Cords for heating appliances carry large amounts of electricity, so be sure to buy a replacement that meets the same specifications as the old cord.

If the cord is intact, suspect a broken resistance wire in the heating element. You can visually check appliances in which elements are exposed, such as the common hot plates and waffle cookers, or those that have their elements enclosed in heat-resistant glass, such as some toaster-ovens. If the wiring in an enclosed element breaks, the entire element must be replaced. Exposed wires, however, can be temporarily repaired with a splicing sleeve or electrical flux (page 239). These repairs will only tide you over until you replace the entire element, for they create a high-resistance "hot spot" that will burn out again.

But there are many appliances, like frying pans and irons, in which the heating element is hidden and a visual check is not possible. In such cases, you can find out if the element is broken by using a continuity tester. A battery-powered tester works on a heating element only if its batteries are new; the element has such a high resistance—in order to do its job —that a battery can barely push current through it. Even fresh batteries produce only a faint glow in the tester bulb, and it is best to test in a darkened room to be certain you can see the glow and are not fooled into thinking the element is damaged when it really is not. Be sure to replace the element with one that is identical, not just of the same wattage.

If the cord and resistance wires are intact, the problem is usually a malfunctioning thermostat. This problem is indicated if the appliance seems to work properly but fails to reach or maintain the desired temperature.

Often, the fault in a thermostat is caused by an easily removed obstruction. In a toaster, crumbs get between the thermostat blades and block their movement; hair causes a similar problem in a drier. If you suspect the thermostat, clean it and check the blade alignment before putting in a new one.

Thermostats in coffee makers are simple to replace, but those in other appliances, such as some waffle cookers, are best left to a serviceman—they are held with rivets that must be drilled out for removal, and a replacement must be either riveted or welded in.

Because of the large currents drawn by heating appliances and the high temperatures they generate, it is imperative to unplug them before working on them. When you disassemble one, be sure to keep track of all screws, nuts and washers; a loose bit of metal can cause a short circuit if it drops into a thermostat or electrical connection. Similarly, never work on cords, plugs or wiring over an appliance, for bits of wire might drop inside.

HEATING ELEMENTS, CONTROLS

The simplest way to use electricity in an appliance is to convert it into heat. No moving parts or complicated construction is necessary for heating, and many such appliances—waffle cookers, skillets, irons—contain no mechanisms except controls.

Heat is generated when an electric current flows through a wire or ribbon made of a metal that is resistant to this electric flow: the metal heats up as if by friction, like a surface subjected to vigorous rubbing. In small appliances, the metal most commonly used for this purpose is an alloy containing nickel and chromium, usually referred to as nichrome, that can operate at temperatures up to 2200° without sustaining heat damage. Nichrome is employed only for the heating element; the rest of the circuitry is usually made of copper, aluminum or nickel wire.

In order to protect adjoining parts of the appliance from direct contact with the electrical circuit, the heating element is supported on mica or ceramic insulators *(below and opposite, bottom),* or encased in a sheath such as the ceramic-and-steel combination at right. The temperature range is selected and regulated by one of the thermal controls described on pages 236-237.

Simple heating coil

One of the oldest, and still widely used, heating elements found in small appliances is a simple coiled length of resistance wire *(below)*. Compared to a straight wire, the coil provides greater efficiency by concentrating the heat within a smaller space.

In the waffle cooker at right, one coil is mounted beneath the lower of two detachable grills while an identical coil—hidden in this drawing—is located behind the upper grill. The coils are supported by ceramic insulators; their straightened ends are connected to terminals of the electric circuit.

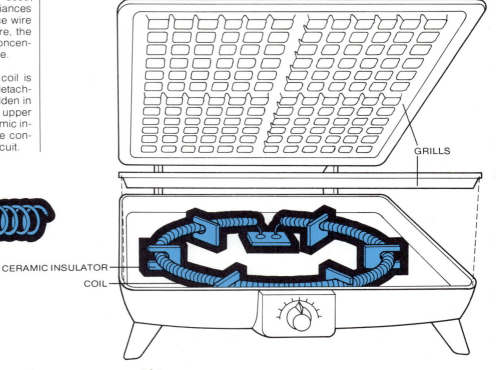

COIL

GRILLS

CERAMIC INSULATOR

COIL

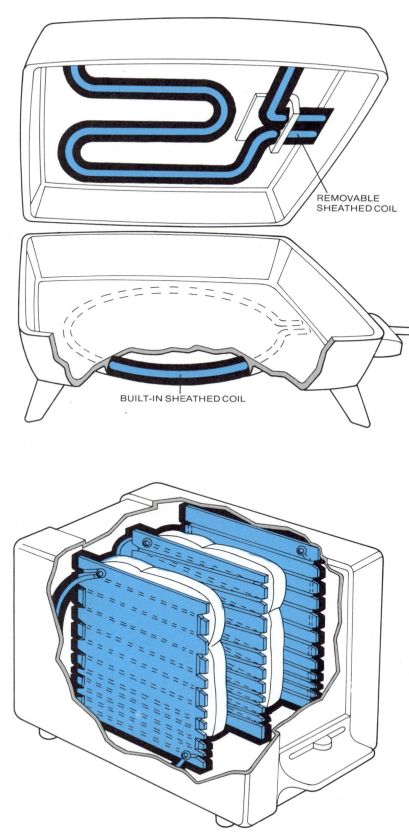

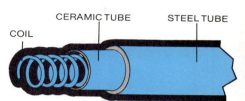

Sheathed coil

In appliances like the combination broiler-skillet at left, the heating coils must be protected from splattering grease and liquid spills as well as electrical contact with the appliance's metal housing. For this reason, the coil is encased in a double sheath consisting of a ceramic inner tube, which provides electrical insulation, and a steel outer tube, which guards against chipping and breakage of the ceramic (above).

In the broiler, or top, part of the appliance, the sheathed coil may be mounted on the inside of the lid. In the skillet, or bottom, part, which requires a smooth cooking surface, the coil is embedded in the bottom.

Flat-wire element

Heating elements in toasters must provide even heat over the entire surface of the bread slice. This uniformity is achieved in two steps. First, a flat wire is substituted for the coil so that all parts of the wire are equidistant from the bread. Second, the wire is wound on a sheet of mica in such a way that the number of windings decreases from bottom to top; as a result, more heat is generated at the bottom than at the top, but since hot air rises, the temperature is equalized over the entire surface of the element.

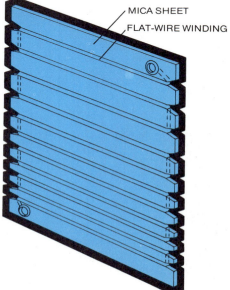

Temperature Controls

An appliance using heat, whether a skillet or a percolator, must operate within a fairly narrow range of temperatures. The task of maintaining this range is handled by a thermostat, which is simply a switch operated by heat, turning the current on when temperature falls below a set level and off when it rises above the level. All thermostats depend on two characteristics of metals: they expand when heated, and each expands at a different rate. So if a blade or disc is made of two different metals bonded together (a "bimetallic" unit), it will bend when heated because the expansion of the metal on one side is greater than on the other. This bending separates the switch contacts.

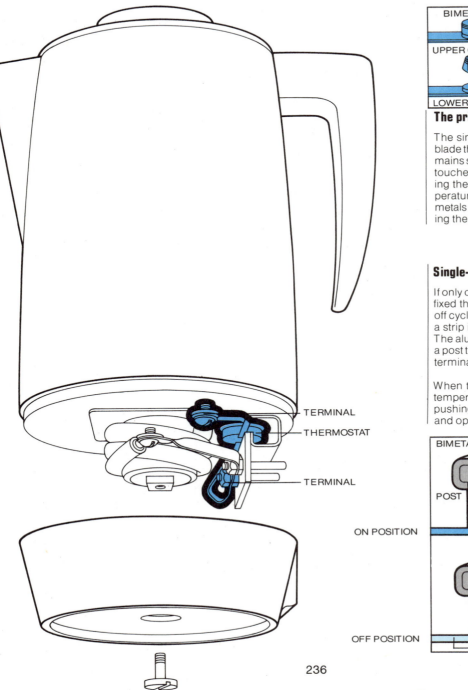

TERMINAL

THERMOSTAT

TERMINAL

The principle of thermostats

The simplest thermostat uses a bimetallic blade that, while the appliance heats up, remains straight *(top)*. Its upper contact point touches the lower contact point, thus keeping the circuit closed. At the selected temperature, unequal expansion of the two metals bends the blade *(bottom)*, separating the two contact points.

Single-setting thermostats

If only one temperature setting is needed, a fixed thermostat is used to control the on-off cycle. It is also bimetallic, but instead of a strip it may be a disc as in this coffeepot. The aluminum-covered disc is attached by a post to a metal connector that bridges two terminals in the up, or on, position.

When the appliance reaches the required temperature, the disc warps downward, pushing down on the post and connector, and opening the circuit.

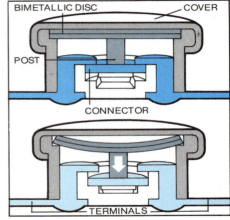

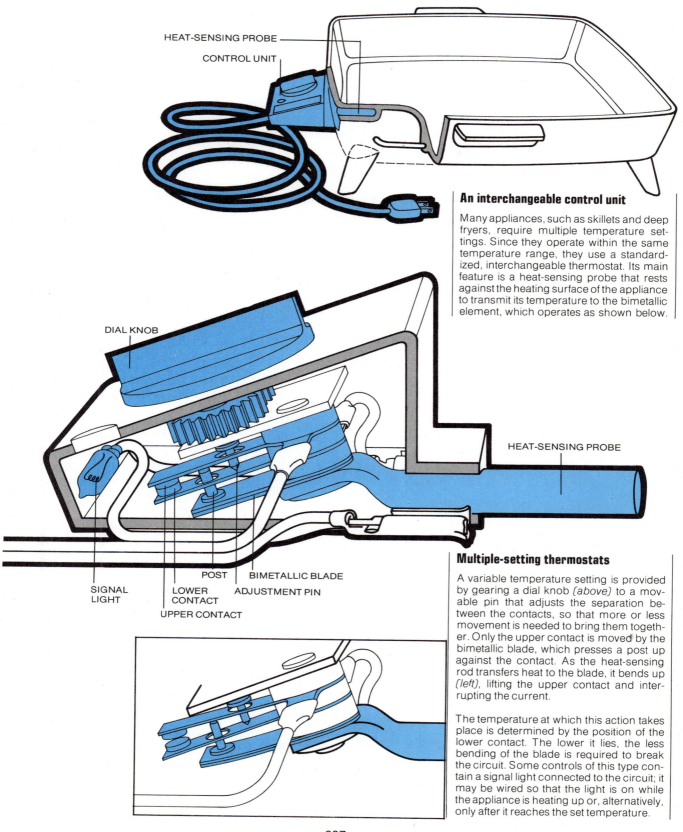

HEAT-SENSING PROBE

CONTROL UNIT

An interchangeable control unit

Many appliances, such as skillets and deep fryers, require multiple temperature settings. Since they operate within the same temperature range, they use a standardized, interchangeable thermostat. Its main feature is a heat-sensing probe that rests against the heating surface of the appliance to transmit its temperature to the bimetallic element, which operates as shown below.

DIAL KNOB

HEAT-SENSING PROBE

POST   BIMETALLIC BLADE

SIGNAL
LIGHT

LOWER   ADJUSTMENT PIN
CONTACT

UPPER CONTACT

Multiple-setting thermostats

A variable temperature setting is provided by gearing a dial knob (above) to a movable pin that adjusts the separation between the contacts, so that more or less movement is needed to bring them together. Only the upper contact is moved by the bimetallic blade, which presses a post up against the contact. As the heat-sensing rod transfers heat to the blade, it bends up (left), lifting the upper contact and interrupting the current.

The temperature at which this action takes place is determined by the position of the lower contact. The lower it lies, the less bending of the blade is required to break the circuit. Some controls of this type contain a signal light connected to the circuit; it may be wired so that the light is on while the appliance is heating up or, alternatively, only after it reaches the set temperature.

237

REPAIRING HEATING ELEMENTS

Some of the handiest electrical kitchen appliances are the simplest in design and construction. Most small cooking devices, for example, consist basically of a power cord, a heating element *(pages 234-235)* and a container or surface for cooking the food. But variations on this theme seem limitless. There are frying pans, stew pots, waffle cookers, slow cookers, broilers, fondue pots, egg cookers and, of course, all-purpose hot plates.

Most are fairly rugged appliances that with regular cleaning and reasonable handling last indefinitely. But sometimes heating elements will break down. When the unit's design permits you to get to the elements, as in the examples on this page, they are easily repaired *(opposite, bottom)* or replaced *(below)*. But when the elements are sealed inside metal enclosures *(opposite, top)*, repair is usually impractical or impossible.

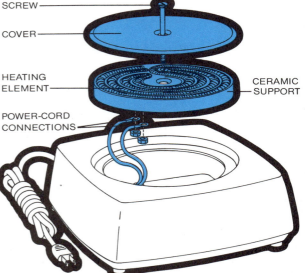

SCREW

COVER

HEATING ELEMENT

POWER-CORD CONNECTIONS

CERAMIC SUPPORT

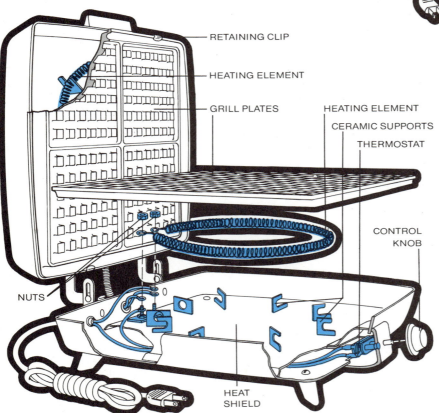

RETAINING CLIP

HEATING ELEMENT

GRILL PLATES

HEATING ELEMENT

CERAMIC SUPPORTS

THERMOSTAT

CONTROL KNOB

NUTS

HEAT SHIELD

A cooking appliance's basic design

A simple hot plate, as useful for cooking soup as popping corn, consists of a heating element mounted on a nonconducting ceramic support, a protective cover, connections to the power-supply cord, and a base. If the heating element breaks, remove the screw to reach the element for replacement or repairs *(opposite)*.

Repairing a waffle cooker

When a waffle cooker will not heat, disconnect the power cord, then remove the grill plates by pulling back the retaining clips. To remove a broken heating element, unscrew the nuts connecting it to the power-supply wires, and then unwrap it from the ceramic supports that hold it up above the heat shield. Be careful not to kink the new element as you install it, or to fasten it too tightly to the supports. It must be free to move as the wire heats and expands.

A temporary repair can be made by either of the methods on the opposite page, but if the heating elements are not broken, the thermostat is most likely the culprit. Take the appliance to a repair shop.

Sealed Elements for Even Heat, Easy Cleaning

Many electric cooking appliances have heating elements permanently sealed inside. This type of construction has its advantages: in a frying pan with a heating element embedded in the bottom of the pan, heat is evenly distributed. And if you disconnect the power cord and thermostat, the pan can be immersed in water for cleaning. But there is a disadvantage: the element cannot be repaired.

The slow cooker shown at right is a veteran example of these sealed appliances. Its cooking surface is an inner ceramic pot. Wrapped around the pot in this model are two heating elements, one for low heat (about 200°) and another one for high heat (about 300°), controlled by a two-level switch. The pot and heating elements are sealed together inside an insulating outer case that protects both of them. But as with the frying pan, this construction puts the heating elements beyond the reach of any repairman.

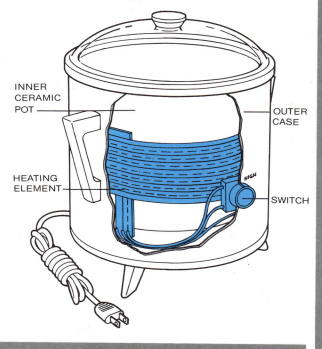

INNER CERAMIC POT

OUTER CASE

HEATING ELEMENT

HIGH

SWITCH

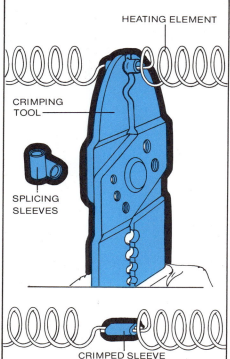

HEATING ELEMENT

CRIMPING TOOL

SPLICING SLEEVES

CRIMPED SLEEVE

Splicing a broken heating element

A temporary repair on a broken heating element is easy with a splicing sleeve, an open-ended cylinder of nickel alloy. Disconnect the power cord, and without removing the element, gently straighten the two broken ends with pliers. Scrape both ends with a knife until the metal is shiny, and insert them into a splicing sleeve. For the best repair, use the smallest sleeve the wires will fit into. Then squeeze the sleeve with a crimping tool over its full length. If the connector can be moved at all, a hot spot will develop and burn out the wire.

Soldering a broken heating element

Broken ends of a heating element can also be soldered together. Prepare a material called electrical flux powder by mixing it with water in a lid. Then, with the power cord disconnected, straighten the element ends with pliers and scrape them with a knife. Place the ends so they lie correctly in the appliance, and also touch and overlap one quarter inch or so. Surround the ends with a small glob of flux. Then plug in the appliance and turn it on high. (Caution: Do not touch the element.) The heat will weld the flux and element ends firmly together.

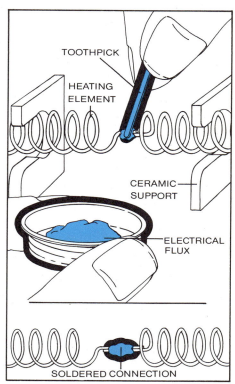

TOOTHPICK

HEATING ELEMENT

CERAMIC SUPPORT

ELECTRICAL FLUX

SOLDERED CONNECTION

TOASTERS AND BROILERS

Of all small appliances that warm or cook food by radiant heat—toasters, toaster-ovens and tabletop rotisseries—the most common is the deceptively simple-looking toaster. Some toasters have motors that automatically lower bread placed on the rack. In others, the carriage is lowered manually, but everything else is automatic. In some toasters a spring and cylinder combination called a dashpot pops the carriage up; others have a spring under the front panel to pull up the carriage.

The complex internal parts of toasters made since the mid-1960s are welded or riveted in place and cannot be replaced at home. They do, however, require periodic cleaning, but before beginning—even emptying the crumb tray—unplug the cord: a push on the handle can send current to the heating element and cause burns or shock.

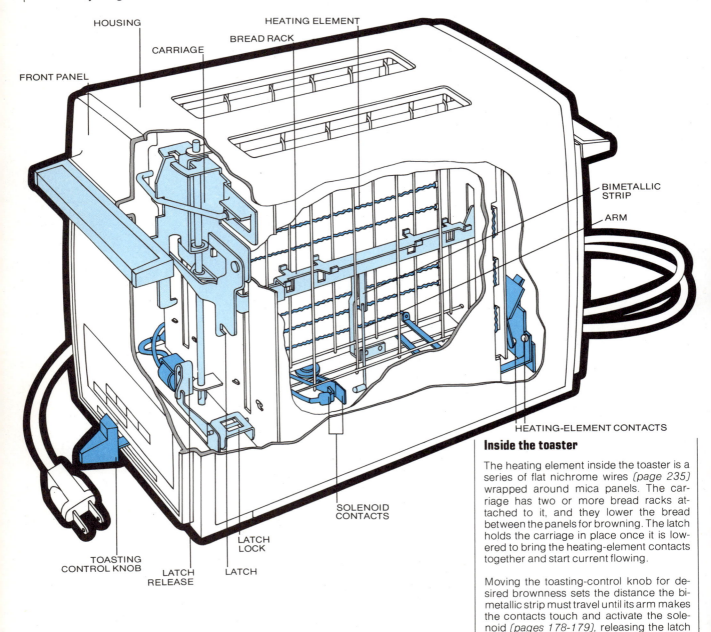

HOUSING
HEATING ELEMENT
BREAD RACK
CARRIAGE
FRONT PANEL
BIMETALLIC STRIP
ARM
HEATING-ELEMENT CONTACTS
SOLENOID CONTACTS
LATCH LOCK
LATCH
TOASTING CONTROL KNOB
LATCH RELEASE

Inside the toaster

The heating element inside the toaster is a series of flat nichrome wires *(page 235)* wrapped around mica panels. The carriage has two or more bread racks attached to it, and they lower the bread between the panels for browning. The latch holds the carriage in place once it is lowered to bring the heating-element contacts together and start current flowing.

Moving the toasting-control knob for desired brownness sets the distance the bimetallic strip must travel until its arm makes the contacts touch and activate the solenoid *(pages 178-179)*, releasing the latch and letting the toast rise *(opposite, top)*.

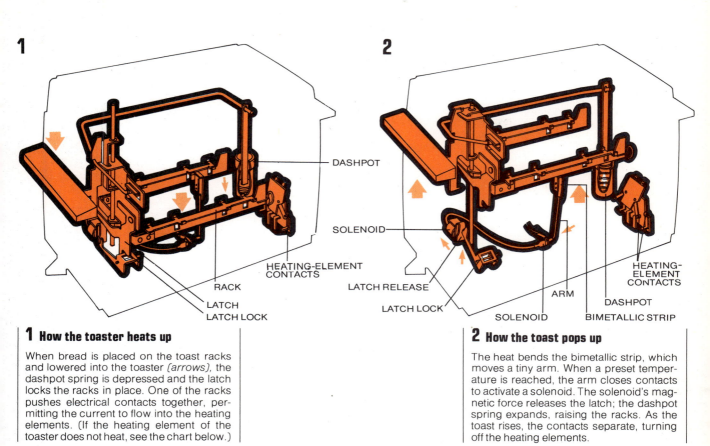

1

1 How the toaster heats up

When bread is placed on the toast racks and lowered into the toaster *(arrows),* the dashpot spring is depressed and the latch locks the racks in place. One of the racks pushes electrical contacts together, permitting the current to flow into the heating elements. (If the heating element of the toaster does not heat, see the chart below.)

2

2 How the toast pops up

The heat bends the bimetallic strip, which moves a tiny arm. When a preset temperature is reached, the arm closes contacts to activate a solenoid. The solenoid's magnetic force releases the latch; the dashpot spring expands, raising the racks. As the toast rises, the contacts separate, turning off the heating elements.

Troubleshooting Toasters

Problem	Possible Causes	Solution
Toaster does not heat	Power not reaching toaster	Check fuse or circuit breaker; check cord and repair if necessary *(pages 186-187)*
	Heating-element contacts obstructed	Brush off, straighten or realign heating-element contact points
Toast browns only on one side	Defective heating element	Take to repair shop
Toast does not pop up	Solenoid contacts obstructed or out of line	Brush off or straighten solenoid contact points
	Main spring loose or broken	Reconnect or replace main spring
Toaster smokes	Crumbs caught inside	Empty crumb tray, blow out with vacuum cleaner

Tabletop Ovens

Together, a toaster-oven and broiler-rotisserie are as versatile as a regular oven. They are especially handy for preparing small amounts of food.

The toaster-oven, in addition to browning bread, bakes casseroles, sandwiches and ready-made foods such as frozen dinners and breakfast pastries. One variation on the basic toaster-oven, sketched below, has a slot in the top for toast. Otherwise, all makes and models are essentially the same. The oven has a glass front door that opens for placement of food on a metal tray. Inside, there are shields to reflect the heat that is produced by several heating elements and regulated by a thermostat and the control knobs.

The broiler-rotisserie functions as a broiler, and has a motor-driven spit to turn meat and poultry for even cooking and easy basting.

Both appliances must be cleaned after every use, but newer models can be easily disassembled to facilitate that chore.

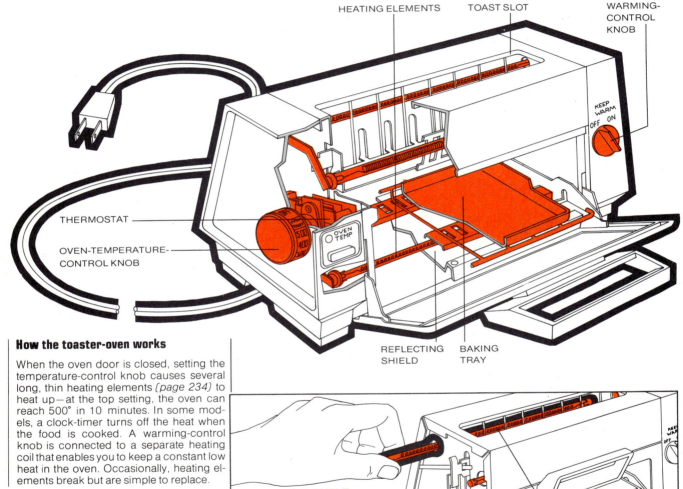

HEATING ELEMENTS TOAST SLOT WARMING-CONTROL KNOB

THERMOSTAT

OVEN-TEMPERATURE-CONTROL KNOB

REFLECTING SHIELD BAKING TRAY

How the toaster-oven works

When the oven door is closed, setting the temperature-control knob causes several long, thin heating elements (page 234) to heat up—at the top setting, the oven can reach 500° in 10 minutes. In some models, a clock-timer turns off the heat when the food is cooked. A warming-control knob is connected to a separate heating coil that enables you to keep a constant low heat in the oven. Occasionally, heating elements break but are simple to replace.

Replacing the elements

Unplug the oven and unscrew the bottom plate; then pull off the end panel containing the temperature control. Slide out each element and inspect it. If it is enclosed in glass, a break in the coil of nichrome wire will be visible. For metal-covered elements, use a continuity tester (page 137). Replace broken elements with new ones made for your model. In reassembling the end panel, be sure the heating element sockets fit securely over the element ends.

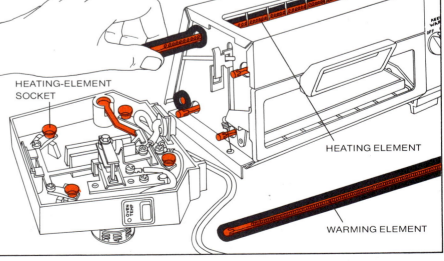

HEATING-ELEMENT SOCKET

HEATING ELEMENT

WARMING ELEMENT

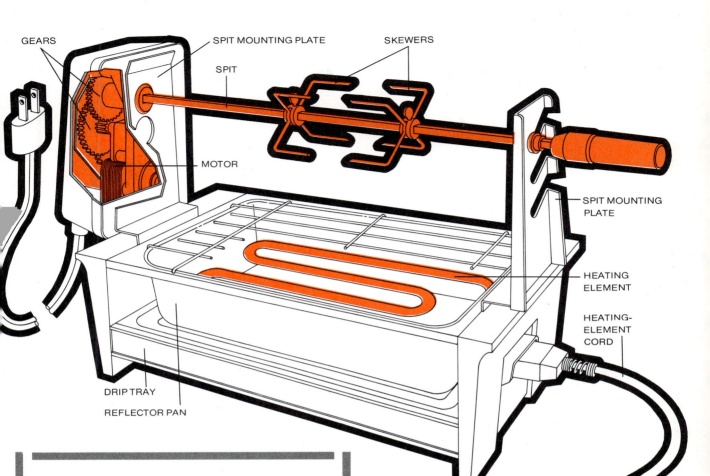

GEARS

SPIT MOUNTING PLATE

SKEWERS

SPIT

MOTOR

SPIT MOUNTING
PLATE

HEATING
ELEMENT

HEATING-
ELEMENT
CORD

DRIP TRAY

REFLECTOR PAN

Broiler-Rotisseries, Old and New

The first portable broiler-ovens, introduced about 30 years ago, were generally cumbersome closed units with exposed coils of heating wire that became red-hot during cooking. The servicing you can perform on such an appliance is limited to repairing the heating-element coils *(page 239)*. If it is fitted with a rotisserie, replacement gears and motors are nearly impossible to find.

Modern broiler-rotisseries are available in two versions: open *(above)* and closed. The open model usually comes with a grill for barbecuing, and some have a detachable hood to speed cooking. The closed model resembles a scaled-down version of yesteryear's broiler-oven. The working parts of both models are the same, and repairs are made in the same way on each.

A modern rotisserie

An open rotisserie is a simple sturdy appliance. The basic unit consists of a sheathed heating element over a reflector pan and drip tray. The element, which has two prongs jutting from an opening in the reflector pan, attaches to its own power cord for operation as a grill without the spit. During use, the element gets hot enough to burn off most food residues; still, it can be unhooked for cleaning—or replacement, in the rare event that it breaks.

Above the basic unit is the spit assembly, which has its own power cord. Mounting plates fit into the ends of the reflector pan. One plate supports a motor and gears to drive the spit; the other plate holds the free end of the spit. The housing can be unclipped, or unscrewed, and separated for inspection of the motor. If the gears are clogged with grease, clean them with a commercial degreaser. But if the sealed motor burns out, or if the gears break, the entire unit must be replaced.

COFFEE MAKERS

Virtually all electric coffee makers, including the modern drip types *(below and opposite)* and older percolators *(page 247),* contain the same basic parts: a brewing element that heats water nearly to boiling, a system that delivers the hot water to the ground coffee, a thermostat that turns off the brewing element at the end of its cycle and a warming element to keep the finished brew hot. Though analogous parts may look different, their purpose generally is self-evident and repairs are straightforward.

The most common coffee-maker problems are not actual breakdowns but stem from inadequate maintenance. Drip machines are particularly prone to clogged plumbing from mineral deposits; these clogs cause longer brew times and heavy steaming. To forestall trouble, at least once a month (every two weeks in regions with hard water), you should run a full reservoir of white vinegar or commercial deliming solution through the entire brew cycle.

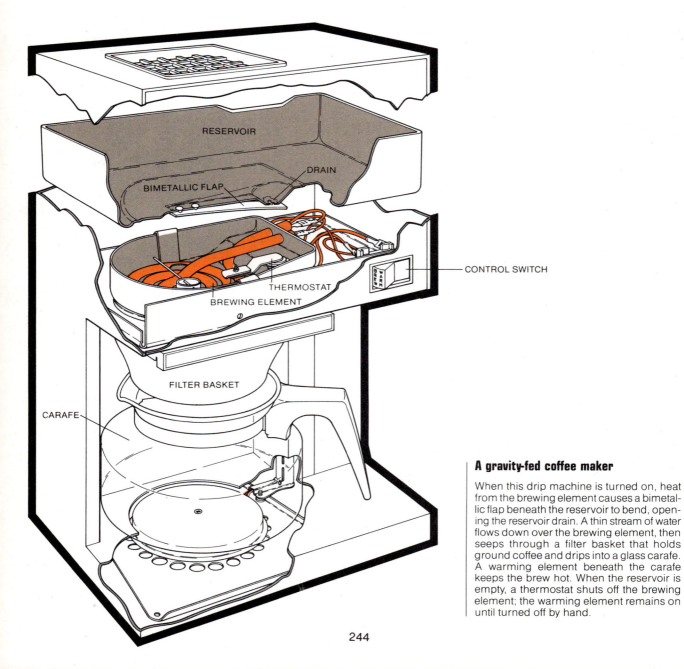

RESERVOIR

DRAIN

BIMETALLIC FLAP

CONTROL SWITCH

THERMOSTAT

BREWING ELEMENT

FILTER BASKET

CARAFE

A gravity-fed coffee maker

When this drip machine is turned on, heat from the brewing element causes a bimetallic flap beneath the reservoir to bend, opening the reservoir drain. A thin stream of water flows down over the brewing element, then seeps through a filter basket that holds ground coffee and drips into a glass carafe. A warming element beneath the carafe keeps the brew hot. When the reservoir is empty, a thermostat shuts off the brewing element; the warming element remains on until turned off by hand.

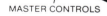

RESERVOIR

HEATING WELL

MASTER CONTROLS

A steam-pump coffee maker

The brewing element heats water in a pump similar to that in a percolator *(page 247)*. Water from the reservoir flows into a heating well. Steam generated in the well pushes a column of hot water up, across and down a pipe to the filter basket. (In some steam-pump machines the heating chamber is bracketed between one-way valves that prevent hot water from flowing backward.) When the reservoir and heating well run dry, a thermostat turns off the brewing element; the warming element remains on.

Replacing a warming element

The most common coffee-maker breakdown is a burned-out warming element. If the coffee will not stay hot, unplug the machine and remove the screws or bolts that fasten the base plate of the machine to the housing. Unscrew the warming element from the base plate and unplug its wires from the switch terminals in the upper part of the housing. Position a new warming element on the base plate, plug its wires into the switch and reassemble the coffee maker.

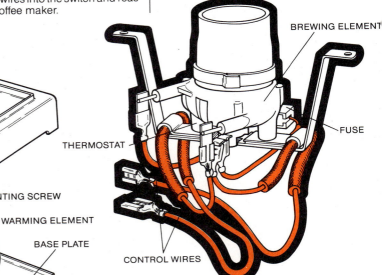

BREWING ELEMENT

FUSE

THERMOSTAT

CONTROL WIRES

MOUNTING SCREW

WARMING ELEMENT

BASE PLATE

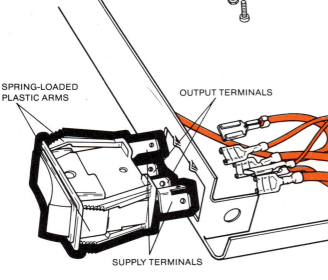

SPRING-LOADED
PLASTIC ARMS

OUTPUT TERMINALS

SUPPLY TERMINALS

Remedies for the brewing element

If the warming element works but the brewing element does not, the fault may lie in the brewing element fuse, its thermostat or the element itself. If the fuse and thermostat can be replaced separately, check them with a continuity tester *(page 137)* and replace the faulty part. If all three parts must be replaced as a unit, as here, do not bother with continuity tests. Unplug the machine and remove the bottom or back to gain access to the element. Unfasten the nuts that hold the element and install the new element. Finally, disconnect the old wires from the control switch one by one and plug the new ones in their places.

Removing a defective switch

If the coffee maker does not work at all, the trouble probably lies in the control switch. Unplug the machine and remove the back or bottom to gain access to the switch terminals. Turn the switch on and test for continuity *(page 137)* across its supply and output terminals. If the switch is defective, remove any screw clips that fasten it from behind. Then pinch or break off the notched, spring-loaded plastic arms that lock it into position. Slide the switch out the front of the housing, transfer the wires one by one to a new switch and snap the new switch into the housing.

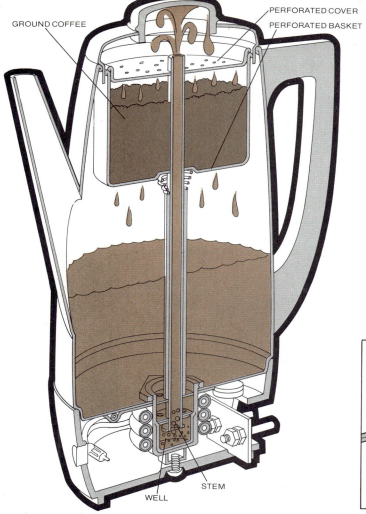

GROUND COFFEE

PERFORATED COVER

PERFORATED BASKET

WELL

STEM

How a percolator works

Hot water, brought to a boil a little at a time in a heating well, is forced up a center stem. The water is deflected at the top of the container and drips down through a perforated cover that spreads it over coffee in the basket. Perforations in the base of the basket let the brew drip into the pot; it then returns to the well to be pumped up again.

The heating well

The flow of water into the well and up the stem is regulated by a valve that is a movable ring around the stem bottom. When the coffee maker is turned on, the ring rests on the stem's bottom flange [1]. Water can enter the well through holes in the two plates above the ring. A brewing element surrounding the well quickly boils its small amount of water. Steam pushes the ring up, closing off the well and forcing hot water up the stem [2]. As steam escapes, the ring drops and more water can enter.

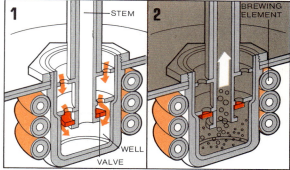

Troubleshooting Coffee Makers

Problem	Possible Causes	Solution
Coffee maker does not function at all	Fuse blown or circuit breaker tripped in house circuit	Replace fuse or reset circuit breaker
	Defective line cord	Repair cord
	Defective brewing element	Replace brewing element
Water heats up but coffee does not brew	Clogged valve	Scour pot or delime drip system
	Bent or broken valve	Replace valve
Coffee boils	Defective warming element	Replace warming element
	Defective thermostat	Replace thermostat
Coffee brews but is not kept warm	Defective warming element	Replace warming element
	Burned-out signal light	Replace signal light
Coffee is weak	Insufficient ground coffee	Check directions and use proper amount
	Warm water was used at the start	Start again with cold water
Coffee tastes bitter	Coffee or mineral deposits in pot	Scour pot or delime drip system
	Too much ground coffee	Check directions and use proper amount

STEAM AND SPRAY IRONS

The steam iron makes its own steam, which it shoots out of ports, but the press of a button on the handle closes the steam valve and converts the steam iron temporarily into a dry iron. Many steam irons are equipped also to spray water for erasing deep wrinkles in fabric.

The base, or soleplate, used to be of iron but now has been replaced by stainless steel or aluminum, sometimes with a nonstick coating. Stainless steel resists scratches better than aluminum, but is slightly heavier, heats more slowly and costs more. The aluminum soleplate heats and cools quickly and evenly but, besides being susceptible to scratches, accumulates starch that can stain fabrics. Nonstick coatings are easily damaged when the iron runs over zippers and buttons, and cannot be satisfactorily restored.

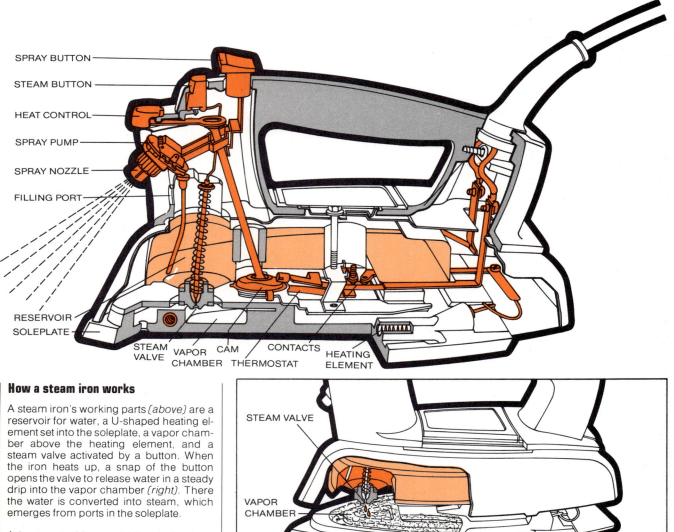

SPRAY BUTTON
STEAM BUTTON
HEAT CONTROL
SPRAY PUMP
SPRAY NOZZLE
FILLING PORT
RESERVOIR
SOLEPLATE
STEAM VALVE
VAPOR CHAMBER
CAM
THERMOSTAT
CONTACTS
HEATING ELEMENT

STEAM VALVE
VAPOR CHAMBER
STEAM PORTS

How a steam iron works

A steam iron's working parts *(above)* are a reservoir for water, a U-shaped heating element set into the soleplate, a vapor chamber above the heating element, and a steam valve activated by a button. When the iron heats up, a snap of the button opens the valve to release water in a steady drip into the vapor chamber *(right)*. There the water is converted into steam, which emerges from ports in the soleplate.

A heat-control lever, which sets the temperature, rotates a cam that regulates the opening between contacts on a thermostat. The thermostat keeps the iron within a few degrees of the setting. A thumb-operated pump sucks water out of the reservoir and sprays it through a nozzle.

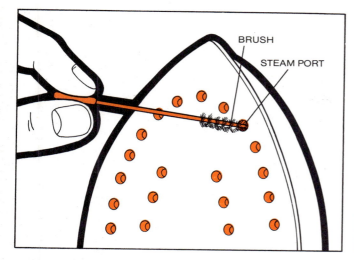

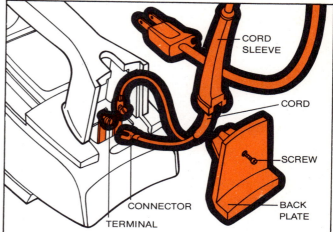

Maintaining the iron

Most problems with a steam iron happen when the iron has been dropped, the cord has been abused or minerals from the water supply have been allowed to accumulate. If deposits block steam ports, remove them by filling the reservoir with white vinegar; heat the iron to transform the vinegar into steam. Rinse the iron thoroughly afterward, and use a small brush to clean out the steam ports. If deposits are a frequently recurring problem, use only distilled or demineralized water to fill the iron. To clean an aluminum soleplate, use a rag dipped in a solution of one part of baking soda to two parts of water. For stainless steel, apply a damp, soapy scouring pad. In either case, rinse and dry thoroughly. Then set the heat-control lever at a low temperature, and run the iron over wax paper and then over a dry cloth. If a soleplate snags fabrics because it has been nicked, buff it with emery cloth. To clean nonstick coatings, use only a damp cloth or sponge to avoid marring the coating.

If the iron does not work after a fall, it needs professional attention; once the housing is removed, reassembly is difficult.

Replacing the cord

If the iron does not heat, the cord, plug or connectors may be frayed or broken. Remove the screw holding the back plate to expose the cord terminals. Detach the cord and test it for continuity (page 186). If the cord is good, tightly reconnect the terminals. If the test discloses a broken cord, you can buy a new one at an electrical supply store (be sure to get one with the same kind of terminals). Adding a cord sleeve will relieve stress. If the cord is in good condition but the iron still does not heat, the iron requires professional servicing.

Troubleshooting Steam Irons

Problem	Possible Causes	Solution
Iron does not heat	Power not reaching iron	Check fuse or circuit breaker; check receptacle (page 143); repair or replace cord or plug (above and pages 186-187)
	Faulty heating element or thermostat	Needs professional service
Iron does not heat enough or gets too hot	Faulty thermostat	Needs professional service
Iron does not steam	Clogged steam ports	Clean with vinegar and brush out steam ports
	Reservoir empty	Refill reservoir
Iron spits or leaks water	Dial not fully in steam position Steam button turned on too soon Reservoir overfilled	Set dial exactly on steam position Wait two to five minutes Empty out some water

HAIR DRIERS AND STYLERS

Whether a hair drier is a compact blowgun *(below),* a drier-styler combination *(page 252)* or a salon-style hood *(page 253),* its parts are similar. The appliance will contain, in some form or other: a fan — or impeller — to circulate air, a heating element to warm it and a housing to channel it in the right direction.

The key to keeping any kind of drier in good working order is to make sure that a steady stream of air flows through the housing and that the flow is not impeded. Unless the heat generated by the element is carried away, the appliance will overheat.

To keep air flowing, intake vents, through which the fan draws air, must be kept clear of dirt, hair accumulations and other obstructions; also, the impeller itself must rotate freely.

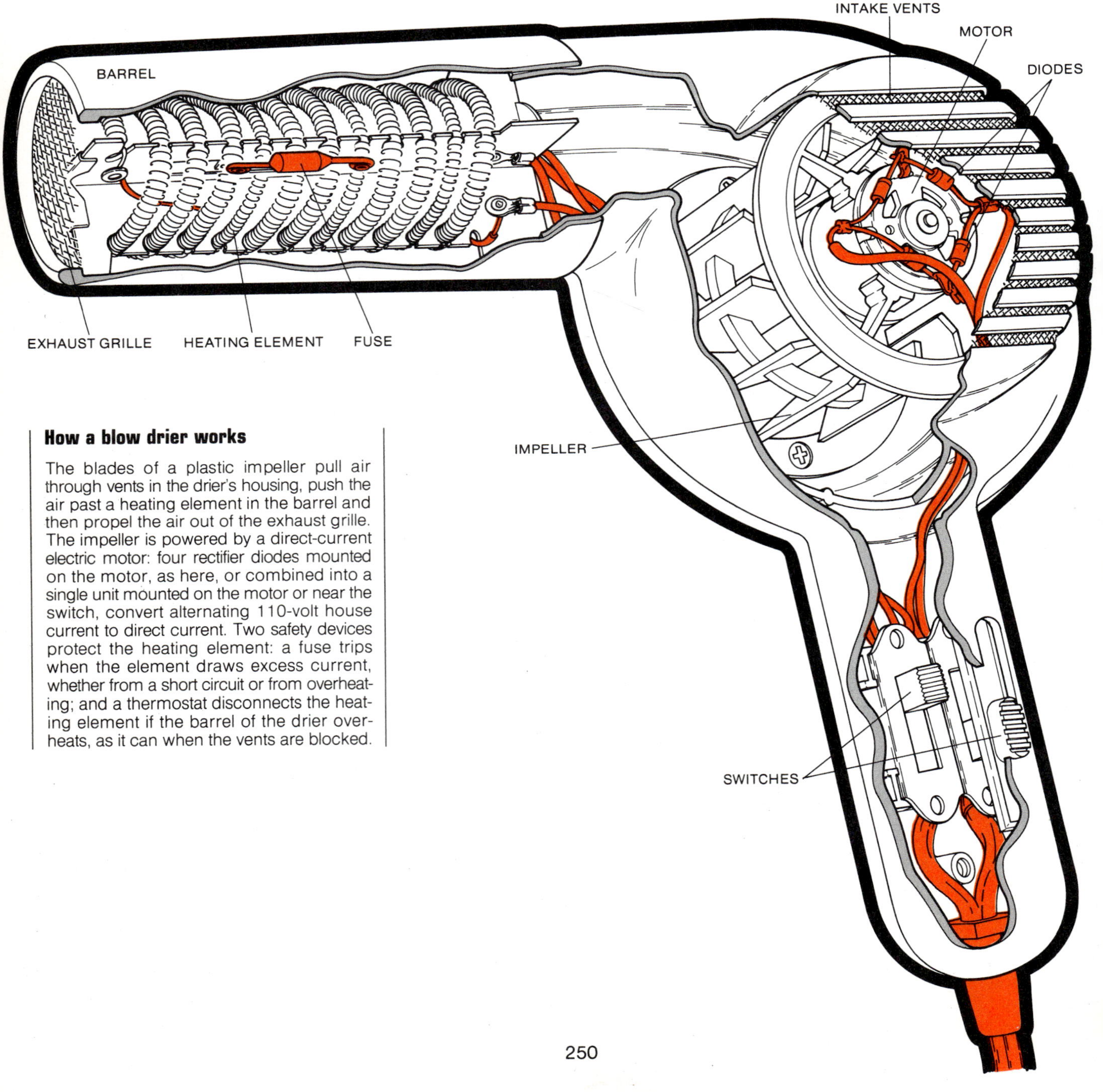

INTAKE VENTS

MOTOR

DIODES

BARREL

EXHAUST GRILLE   HEATING ELEMENT   FUSE

IMPELLER

SWITCHES

How a blow drier works

The blades of a plastic impeller pull air through vents in the drier's housing, push the air past a heating element in the barrel and then propel the air out of the exhaust grille. The impeller is powered by a direct-current electric motor: four rectifier diodes mounted on the motor, as here, or combined into a single unit mounted on the motor or near the switch, convert alternating 110-volt house current to direct current. Two safety devices protect the heating element: a fuse trips when the element draws excess current, whether from a short circuit or from overheating; and a thermostat disconnects the heating element if the barrel of the drier overheats, as it can when the vents are blocked.

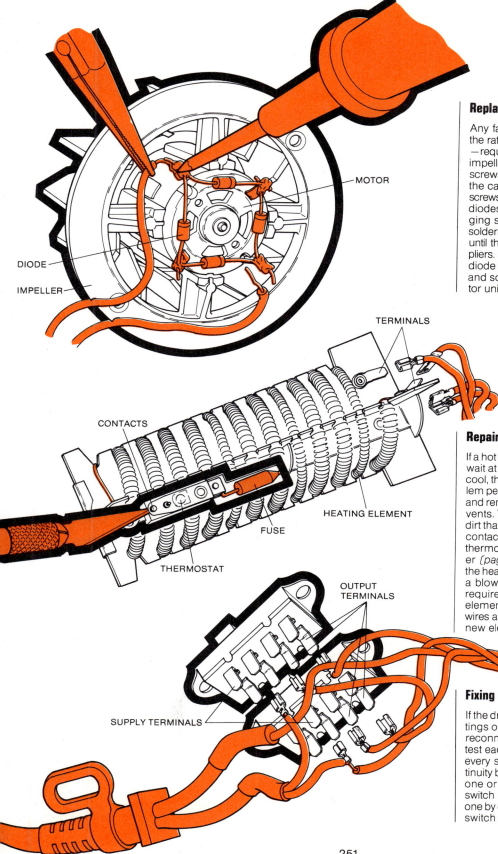

Replacing the motor and impeller

Any fault in the motor or impeller—typically the rattling sound of a broken impeller blade—requires replacement of the whole motor-impeller unit. Unplug the drier, remove the screws holding the split case together, open the case and remove the motor mounting screws. Lift out the motor unit and remove the diodes from the motor—either by unplugging spade-type connectors or by using a soldering iron to heat soldered connections until the diode wires can be pulled loose with pliers. One by one, slide the wires from each diode into their terminals on the new motor and solder them in place. Set the new motor unit in place and reclose the drier's case.

MOTOR

DIODE

IMPELLER

TERMINALS

CONTACTS

HEATING ELEMENT

FUSE

THERMOSTAT

Repairing a balky heating element

If a hot drier suddenly stops or blows cold air, wait at least 10 minutes for its thermostat to cool, then test the machine again. If the problem persists, unplug the drier, open the case and remove any obstructions from the intake vents. Then use a knife to scrape away any dirt that might prevent the thermostat switch contacts from closing *(left)*. Next, check the thermostat and the fuse with a continuity tester *(page 137)*. Finally, look for breaks in the heating element itself. A broken element, a blown fuse or a defective thermostat all require replacement of the entire heating-element assembly: simply free the supply wires and solder them to the terminals of the new element, then reassemble the drier.

OUTPUT
TERMINALS

SUPPLY TERMINALS

Fixing a faulty switch

If the drier does not work at some switch settings or at all, unplug it, open the case and reconnect any loose or broken wires. Then test each switch for continuity *(page 137)*; every setting except OFF should yield continuity between the supply-cord terminal and one or more of the output terminals. If the switch proves defective, reconnect its wires one by one to a new switch. Emplace the new switch and reassemble the drier case.

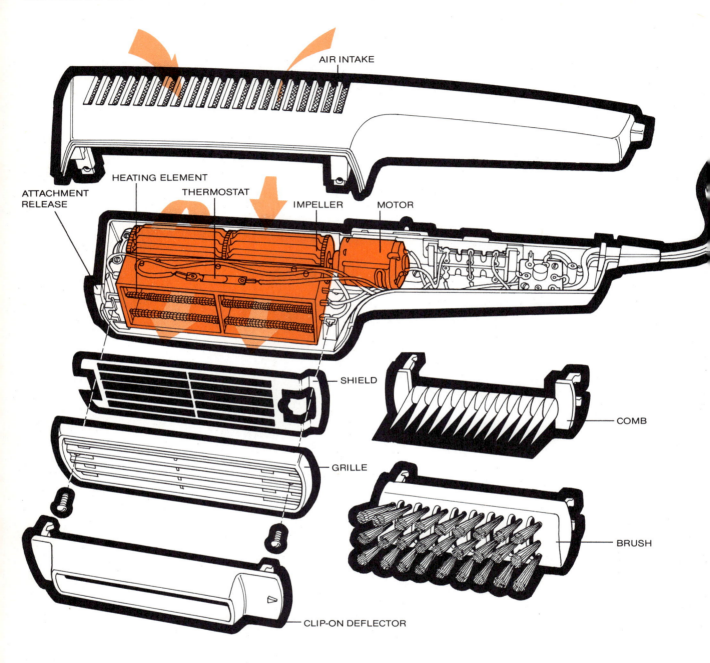

AIR INTAKE

ATTACHMENT
RELEASE

HEATING ELEMENT

THERMOSTAT

IMPELLER

MOTOR

SHIELD

COMB

GRILLE

BRUSH

CLIP-ON DEFLECTOR

The hair styler: hand-held versatility

Although it does not look much like a gun-type blow drier, the hair styler is basically a blow drier fitted with combs, brushes and similar attachments. In operation, the styler's impeller sucks air through intake vents into the housing and channels it past the heating element *(arrows)*. The warm air then passes through a shield and a grille as it leaves the machine. The shield and grille protect the hair from direct contact with the element. Attachments—typically, a deflector for rapid drying, and a comb and brush for styling—snap over the grille and are held in place by a clip that is controlled by a button. A thermostat prevents overheating of the appliance.

Important: Never use any drier over a filled sink or tub. If you drop it into the water, it may be ruined permanently; if you reach into the water to retrieve it, you risk shock.

252

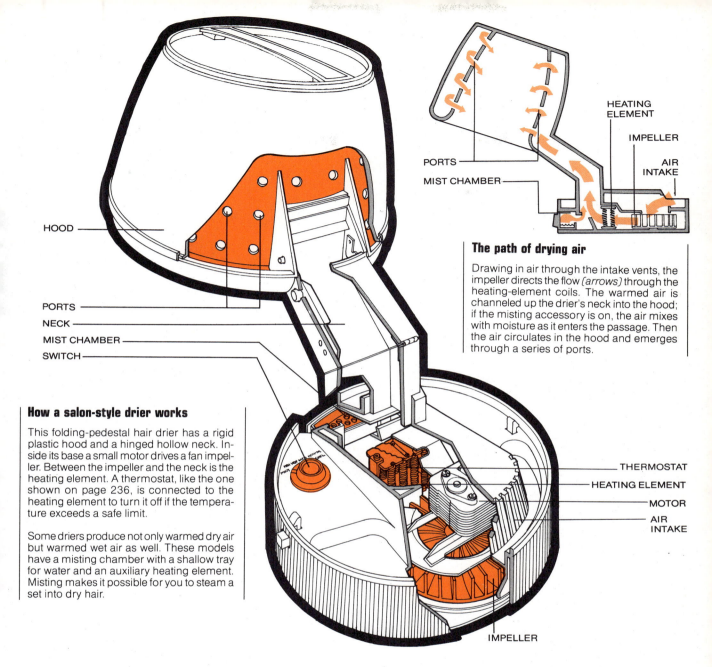

HOOD

PORTS

NECK

MIST CHAMBER

SWITCH

HEATING ELEMENT

IMPELLER

AIR INTAKE

PORTS

MIST CHAMBER

THERMOSTAT

HEATING ELEMENT

MOTOR

AIR INTAKE

IMPELLER

The path of drying air

Drawing in air through the intake vents, the impeller directs the flow *(arrows)* through the heating-element coils. The warmed air is channeled up the drier's neck into the hood; if the misting accessory is on, the air mixes with moisture as it enters the passage. Then the air circulates in the hood and emerges through a series of ports.

How a salon-style drier works

This folding-pedestal hair drier has a rigid plastic hood and a hinged hollow neck. Inside its base a small motor drives a fan impeller. Between the impeller and the neck is the heating element. A thermostat, like the one shown on page 236, is connected to the heating element to turn it off if the temperature exceeds a safe limit.

Some driers produce not only warmed dry air but warmed wet air as well. These models have a misting chamber with a shallow tray for water and an auxiliary heating element. Misting makes it possible for you to steam a set into dry hair.

Troubleshooting Driers and Stylers

Problem	Possible Causes	Solution
Drier switches on and off by itself	Air intake blocked Impeller sticking	Remove blockage Remove impeller and clean
Drier rattles	Impeller loose, broken or obstructed	Remove impeller and clean; if necessary, replace
Cool air emerges	Defective heating element	Replace heating element
Housing becomes hot	Thermostat stuck in closed position	Free thermostat; if contacts are fused, replace thermostat and heating element as a unit

Large Appliances

Step-by-Step Methods for Finding and Solving Problems

Large appliances are a separate category of household machines, not so much because they are bigger and more complex than small appliances, but because the breakdown of a large appliance is more serious than any small-appliance problem. Small appliances generally do their jobs faster and more efficiently than the jobs can be done without electric power, and keeping them in good working order is important to a smoothly running household.

But these devices are not really essential to the maintenance of a modern life style even in an affluent society. A household can get along without any of them (except, perhaps, for a vacuum cleaner) with surprisingly little inconvenience or lost time. If you have to, you can always beat eggs with a fork instead of an electric mixer and the omelet will not taste different; or you can revert to using a muscle-powered toothbrush without danger that you will need to see a dentist any more often.

Large appliances, on the other hand, are indispensable servants in a modern household. The energy they consume, derived from gas or electricity, substitutes for the energy that hard manual labor once demanded of almost all families—washing and drying clothes and dishes, hauling ice in and meltwater out, and chopping wood or shoveling coal to feed cooking ranges and water heaters.

But while large appliances have freed people from time-consuming household drudgery, people, in turn, have become dependent on them. A modern home no longer contains the old-fashioned equipment that the appliances have replaced; when the clothes washer grinds to a halt, dirty clothes pile up until it is back in action, because there are few washtubs left (and even fewer people willing to use them). More important, the time once spent in major household chores is now devoted to other activities. And however the time is used, it seems valuable to anyone robbed of it by the breakdown of a large appliance.

So the real cost of such a breakdown—in money *and* time—comes to more than the cost of replacement parts or repair work. The shorter the interruption in service, the lower its real cost to the family. Often the fastest way to get one of these essential robots back on the job is to diagnose the trouble and—if you are able —to fix it yourself.

Detecting appliance breakdown

Dealing with a failure involves practical considerations: knowing what each important part of the machine looks like, how it functions, where it is located, and how the parts are mechanically or electrically linked together. But failures are generally detected in a quite down-to-earth way, through the evidence of the senses—by smelling a motor burnout, for example, or by hearing a funny sound (an abnormal sound, really). You become attuned to the characteristic noises of large household appliances; the first indication of trouble is often an unfamiliar sound, such as the clanking of a loose object in the innards of a dishwasher, or the absence of a familiar sound, such as the rhythmic whumping of a dishwasher's spray.

Noises and smells may point to the trouble. But the systematic analysis used by engineers can help to isolate the problem faster. Any large appliance can be dissected into two interrelated sets of subsystems that are partly mechanical, partly electrical.

In the first set, the subsystems consist of components such as motors, pumps, compressors, valves and heaters, all of which provide movement and mechanical energy—and, in some, control the supply of fuel—as the appliance runs through its cycle of operations. The subsystems of the second set include devices such as timers, water-level switches, door in-terlocks and thermostats, that control the components of the first set; as the machine progresses through its cycle, these devices automatically start and stop the motors, pumps and heaters in accordance with a predetermined sequence that is fed into the appliance through push buttons, knobs and dials.

If one of the power subsystems fails, the machine does not do all its jobs. Breakdown of one of the control subsystems can also stop an operation (or make it occur at the wrong time in the operating cycle), but this kind of failure is generally distinctive.

Soon after you start a clothes washer, for example, you expect to hear water splashing into the tub. If you do not, you know that something is wrong. But where do you look for the cause of failure? The best way is to start going through the power and control subsystems in a logical way, step by step, until you find one that does not work (or work at the proper time). In a clothes washer, the power subsystem is made up of the household water supply lines, the faucets, the hoses, the inlet valves and screens; and the motor, gears and belts. Always start at the beginning, for simple things are most often troublemakers. Is there pressure in the water pipe? Are the faucets turned on? Is there a kink in a hose? Are the inlet valves working? Are the inlet screens clogged?

The second, or controlling, subsystem consists of the timer, which signals magnetic devices to start and stop the operations, the water-level switch, which shuts off water, and safety switches. Is the timer failing to send an "open" signal to the inlet valves? Is the fill switch sending a "close" signal, even though the water level is down to zero?

Because you do not have sophisticated test equipment, you cannot hope to isolate the defective part in every situation. But understanding how an appliance works is a powerful tool,

The Pros and Cons of Service Contracts

In addition to the protection of an appliance warranty *(page 19),* many manufacturers, dealers and service shops offer service contracts. Their worth depends on the kind of machine to be covered, its age and reliability, and your own ability to maintain it or to find a repair service when you need one. Before you sign up, however, make sure that you understand exactly what you are getting. These contracts are not standardized, and generally their terms depend on the machinery involved — whether it is an appliance or a permanently installed home system. There are two basic kinds of contracts.

MAINTENANCE CONTRACTS can be useful for complex installations like an oil or gas heating plant. For an annual fee, the dealer who sold you the system, an independent service representative or a fuel supplier will provide a yearly tune-up and inspection. These experts have specialized testing instruments and tools for checks and adjustments, and should some major repair be necessary, the know-how to do it.

REPAIR CONTRACTS usually run a year. The premium rate, low at first, rises as the appliance ages. Most fit into three categories:

■ The unlimited contract — the most expensive — covers repairs, parts and labor charges. It may also include annual inspections.

■ The fixed-call contract allows a set number of service calls per year. If your machine needs more service, you pay for it.

■ The deductible contract, usually the least costly, requires you to pay for repairs up to a fixed yearly sum. If you exceed that sum, the contractor absorbs the cost.

Service contracts offer convenience and insurance against big bills; if you have a lemon, you save a lot. But if your repair needs are normal, using your own repair shop may cost much less over a machine's lifetime.

because what an engineer calls defect isolation often consists of an elimination process in which a troubleshooter locates failures in either one of the subsystems by checking its elements in a logical sequence.

Suppose, for example, an electric water heater supplies water, but not hot water. That fact automatically rules out all the subsystems that involve the water supply; the trouble lies with those concerning heat and electricity. After you have checked the elementary things — the main power supply, the circuit breaker or fuse, the thermostat settings — the next step is the first control subsystem, the two thermostats. A simple continuity test *(page 263)* tells you whether one of them is keeping electricity from reaching the power subsystem — the heating element. If both thermostats are operating properly, go on to examine the element.

Or suppose, for another example, that the refrigerator is warm. It could be that a thermostat is defective and is failing to signal the compressor to start working. The first thing to do is to take out the thermostat carefully *(page 284).* Then bypass it by connecting and taping together the wires that lead to it. If the compressor still does not go into action, you have eliminated the thermostat as the cause of the problem and can start looking elsewhere.

Both your checklist and your efforts of analysis may fail; you cannot always avoid calling a repair service. But you can make your call more effective by describing the appliance's failure symtoms — usually by reporting on the evidence of your senses — to give a service technician a head start.

Once you understand how a large appliance works (and all makes of a particular appliance operate according to the same general principles), you will be ready to use your knowledge, your skill and the contents of your toolbox effectively and efficiently.

WATER HEATERS

The water heater, once a reservoir on the kitchen stove, has evolved into an efficient, self-contained appliance. A typical heater, like the gas-fired unit at right, routinely heats about 100 gallons of water each day to as much as 150° to provide for an average family's cleaning, laundering and bathing. If the heater is overdrawn by heavy demand, it can provide a new supply of hot water within minutes.

Heaters do their work automatically with the aid of ingenious controls, illustrated on these pages for gas heaters and on following pages for oil-fired and electrical units. These controls range in complexity from the thermocouple, which converts heat into electricity for an electromagnetic safety valve (opposite), to the "sacrificial" anode, a rod suspended inside the tank (right); the rod is made of magnesium, which enters chemical reactions more readily than steel, and it serves simply to be eaten away by corrosion that otherwise would attack exposed metal of the tank.

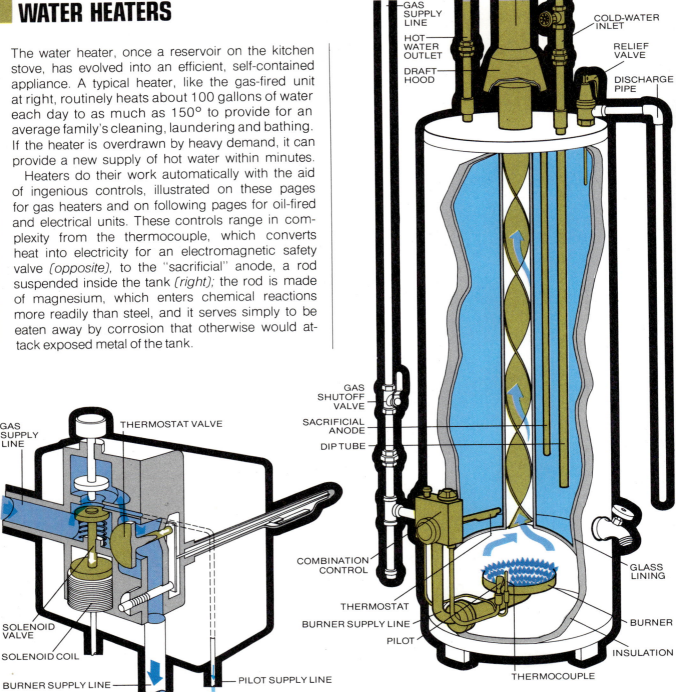

A gas-heater combination control

The flow of gas to the burner and pilot supply lines (blue arrows) is regulated by the movement (white arrows) of two valves —one of them is linked to a thermostat, the other to a solenoid, thermocouple and reset button (opposite).

Inside a gas water heater

When a hot-water faucet is turned on, hot water is forced up in the heater into the hot-water outlet as cold water enters and flows down through the dip tube. The thermostat reacts to the resulting temperature drop by opening a valve that sends gas to the burner, where it is ignited by the pilot light, as shown here, or by an electric ignition spark. Hot gases (arrows) are then vented through the flue and its heat-retaining baffle to the draft hood and vent pipe. A relief valve (page 261) vents excessive pressure through the discharge pipe. The anode and the glass lining will prevent corrosion of the tank walls.

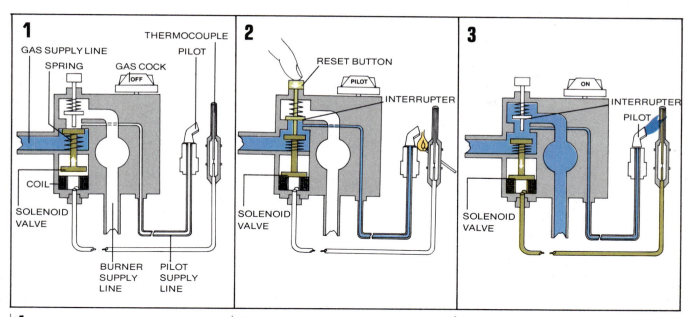

1 Protecting against pilot failure

If the pilot light goes out, the thermocouple, deprived of heat, stops generating its heat-produced electricity. Without current, the solenoid coil loses the magnetism that pulls down on the solenoid valve. A spring then forces the valve upward to block an opening, preventing gas from entering either the burner or pilot supply lines.

2 Igniting the pilot light

To relight the pilot, turn the gas cock to the "PILOT" setting and hold down the reset button. This action forces the interrupter to close the burner supply line, at the same time forcing the solenoid valve down to open the pilot supply line. The pilot can now be safely relit without the danger of accidentally igniting the burner as well.

3 Activating the solenoid

As the pilot flame heats the thermocouple, it becomes a tiny electric generator by converting heat energy into electric current. That current produces magnetism in the solenoid coil to hold the solenoid valve open. With the reset button released and the gas cock turned to "ON," gas is now able to enter both supply lines.

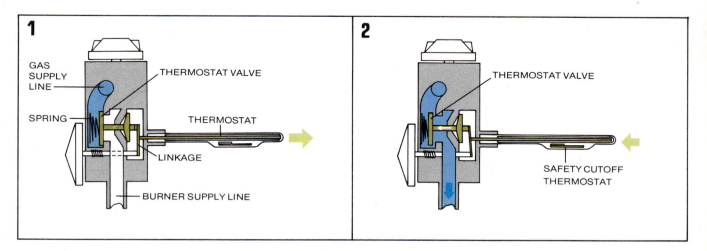

1 How a thermostat stops a burner

The gas heater's primary control is a thermostat—a two-part bar—linked to a valve on the burner supply line. The bar expands (arrow) as water temperature rises, releasing tension until a spring closes the valve and shuts off the gas flow.

2 How a thermostat starts a burner

Cooling water causes the outer part of the thermostat to contract (yellow arrow) and squeeze the inner part against the valve linkage, pushing the valve open (white arrow) so that gas flows to the burner (blue arrow). A smaller thermostat, wired to the solenoid, will function as an emergency cutoff switch if heat rises excessively. It is not mechanical like the main thermostat, but electrical—a bimetallic element that, when heated beyond safe limits, cuts off current going to the solenoid. The solenoid valve then closes and stops all gas flow, as illustrated at top left.

Troubleshooting Gas Water Heaters

Problem	Possible Causes	Solution
No hot water	Pilot flame out	Relight pilot *(page 259)*; make sure pilot is protected from strong drafts
	Pilot does not stay lit	Make sure gas shutoff valve and gas cock are turned fully on; with gas turned off, see that thermocouple is correctly positioned so that pilot flame heats it and so that it is firmly connected to solenoid
	Burner does not light	Check gas-cock setting; have a serviceman clean burner ports
	Thermocouple defective	Replace thermocouple *(page 309)*
Insufficient hot water	Incorrect thermostat setting	Reset thermostat
	Faulty thermostat	Have serviceman replace the combination control
	Long runs of exposed pipe between heater and major points of hot-water use	Insulate pipes, move heater or have second heater installed
	Insufficient heater capacity	Have larger heater installed
	Slow heater recovery	Have serviceman clean burner ports and combustion chamber
	Scale and sediment in tank	To prevent build-up of scale and sediment, drain tank monthly until water runs clear
	Leaky hot-water faucet	Repair faucet *(pages 70-73)*
Insufficient hot water, accompanied by rumbling noises	Scale and sediment in tank	Drain tank until water runs clear; if noises persist, call serviceman to clean tank interior
Water too hot	Incorrect thermostat setting	Reset thermostat
	Faulty thermostat	Have serviceman replace the combination control
	Check for a blocked vent by placing your hand near the draft hood; an outflow of air indicates blockage	Inspect flue outlet for obstruction and remove it
	A leaky faucet may be causing tank stratification (adjoining layers of hot and cold water)	Repair faucet *(pages 70-73)*
Water leaks	Leaky drain valve	Tighten or replace drain
	Relief valve is operating	Place bucket under discharge line; if valve operates frequently, call a plumber
	Tiny holes in tank caused by internal corrosion	Have heater replaced

Oil-fired Heaters

Although separate oil-fired units like the one below represent less than 1 per cent of water heaters used in American homes, using oil as fuel to get hot water is not rare. In the cold-weather Northern states and Canada many homes have integrated oil systems that use a single burner to provide both heat and hot water *(page 317)*. These systems work so efficiently that few require the addition of a separate water heater.

In places where a separate oil-fired water heater is desired, it performs remarkably well. A typical unit can heat a tank full of cold water to piping hot about three times faster than a gas heater can do it, and about five times faster than an electrical heater can normally function.

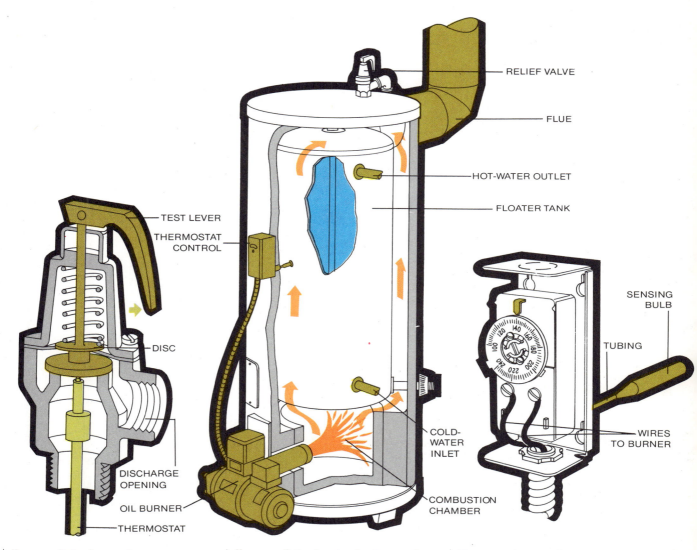

TEST LEVER
THERMOSTAT CONTROL
DISC
DISCHARGE OPENING
OIL BURNER
THERMOSTAT

RELIEF VALVE
FLUE
HOT-WATER OUTLET
FLOATER TANK
COLD-WATER INLET
COMBUSTION CHAMBER

SENSING BULB
TUBING
WIRES TO BURNER

How a relief valve works

A double safeguard for oil-fired and other types of water heaters, the temperature-pressure relief valve is activated when the water pressure on the disc exceeds 150 pounds per square inch or when a temperature of 210° causes the thermostat element to expand. In either case, the disc is forced up and water escapes through the discharge opening. A lever manually operates the valve for testing.

How an oil-fired water heater works

Triggered by the thermostat control, an oil burner ignites a mixture of fuel and air with an electric spark in the water-heater combustion chamber, exactly as it does in an oil-burning home heating system *(pages 304-305)*. The water heater shown here holds the water in a "floater tank"—one suspended so that hot gases flow over the entire tank surface *(arrows)* before being vented through the flue.

Thermostat control

The thermostat control of an oil-fired water heater is regulated by a vapor-filled sensing bulb, much like those used in gas ranges *(page 288)*, that protrudes into the water in the tank. As the water heats, the vapor expands, passing through tubing to push open an electrical contact and shut off the burner circuit. The vapor will contract as the water cools, allowing the contact to close and restart the burner.

Electric Water Heaters

The tank and plumbing of an electric water heater are basically the same as those of gas units. But electric heating elements and their controls are much less complicated than the burners and valves of other kinds of water heaters: they contain no moving parts other than slowly curling bimetallic strips in the thermostats.

This simplicity lets you test the water heater and repair it on the rare occasions when it breaks down. Before you begin, check the fuse or circuit breaker. If the fuse is blown or if the circuit breaker has tripped, then test the heating elements *(page 264)*. But first be sure there is no power going to the water heater *(step 1, below)*. If the fuse is all right, start your troubleshooting with the tests presented on these and the next two pages.

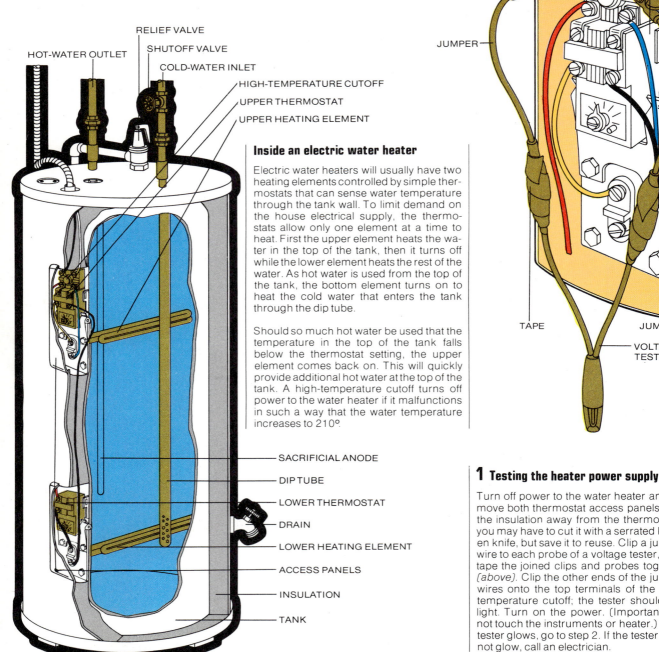

HOT-WATER OUTLET

RELIEF VALVE

SHUTOFF VALVE

COLD-WATER INLET

HIGH-TEMPERATURE CUTOFF

UPPER THERMOSTAT

UPPER HEATING ELEMENT

SACRIFICIAL ANODE

DIP TUBE

LOWER THERMOSTAT

DRAIN

LOWER HEATING ELEMENT

ACCESS PANELS

INSULATION

TANK

Inside an electric water heater

Electric water heaters will usually have two heating elements controlled by simple thermostats that can sense water temperature through the tank wall. To limit demand on the house electrical supply, the thermostats allow only one element at a time to heat. First the upper element heats the water in the top of the tank, then it turns off while the lower element heats the rest of the water. As hot water is used from the top of the tank, the bottom element turns on to heat the cold water that enters the tank through the dip tube.

Should so much hot water be used that the temperature in the top of the tank falls below the thermostat setting, the upper element comes back on. This will quickly provide additional hot water at the top of the tank. A high-temperature cutoff turns off power to the water heater if it malfunctions in such a way that the water temperature increases to 210°.

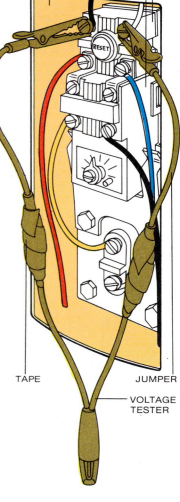

INSULATION

HIGH-TEMPERATURE CUTOFF

THERMOSTAT

1

JUMPER

TAPE

JUMPER

VOLTAGE TESTER

1 Testing the heater power supply

Turn off power to the water heater and remove both thermostat access panels. Pull the insulation away from the thermostats; you may have to cut it with a serrated kitchen knife, but save it to reuse. Clip a jumper wire to each probe of a voltage tester, then tape the joined clips and probes together *(above)*. Clip the other ends of the jumper wires onto the top terminals of the high-temperature cutoff; the tester should not light. Turn on the power. (Important: Do not touch the instruments or heater.) If the tester glows, go to step 2. If the tester does not glow, call an electrician.

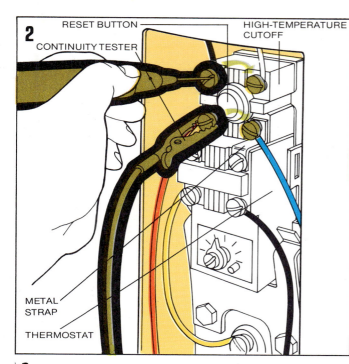

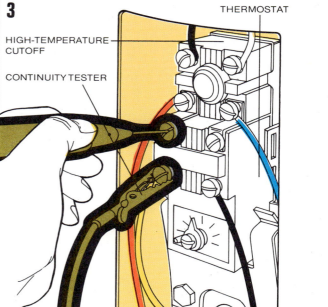

2 Testing a high-temperature cutoff

Disconnect power to the heater at the main house panel. If the cutoff-reset button has popped out, push it in. Connect a continuity tester between the terminals on the left of the cutoff, then connect it between the terminals on the right. If the tester does not light in both cases, replace the cutoff. Make a diagram showing what color wire goes to each cutoff terminal. Then disconnect the wires and the metal straps, and remove the cutoff by pulling it upward. Push a new cutoff into place; connect the wires and metal straps as they had been previously.

3 Testing the upper thermostat

With the power disconnected, make sure the heater has cooled off and attach a continuity tester to the left terminals of the upper thermostat. If the tester does not light, replace the thermostat. Make a wiring diagram and disconnect the wires from the thermostat and from the bottom terminals of the high-temperature cutoff. Remove the cutoff, then pull on the thermostat to snap it out of the spring clips that hold it to the tank. Install a new thermostat, push the cutoff into place and connect the wires as they had been previously.

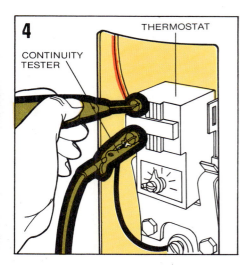

4 Testing the lower thermostat

With the power disconnected, attach a continuity tester to the thermostat terminals. If the tester does not light, replace the thermostat as in step 3.

5 Testing thermostat heat response

With the power disconnected, remove both thermostats Connect a continuity tester to the terminals on the right of the upper thermostat and hold it over a candle. After no more than 15 seconds you should hear a click, and the tester should light. (Caution: Remove the candle quickly; excess heat causes damage.) Repeat the test on the lower thermostat; the tester should now light at first, and go out at the click. If either thermostat behaves differently, replace it.

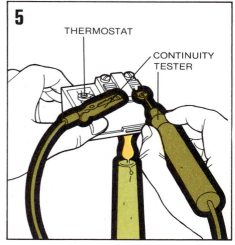

1 Heating-element short circuits

To find faults in electric-water-heater elements, first test for a short circuit. Disconnect the power at the main house panel. Remove access panels and pull away insulation from around the thermostats *(page 262)*. Attach a continuity tester to a heating-element mounting bolt and an element terminal. If the tester lights, there is a short circuit. Replace the element *(opposite)*.

A short circuit caused by a heating-element wire coming in contact with the surrounding metal sheath will blow the water-heater fuse. But a short resulting from water seeping into the heating element will either blow the fuse or make the heater overheat, activating the high-temperature cutoff.

2 Testing heating-element continuity

If there is no short, and the heater produces insufficient hot water, the wire inside an element may be broken. After disconnecting power to the heater, attach a continuity tester between the terminals of each heating element. The tester should light. If it does not, the wire is broken. Replace the element *(opposite)*.

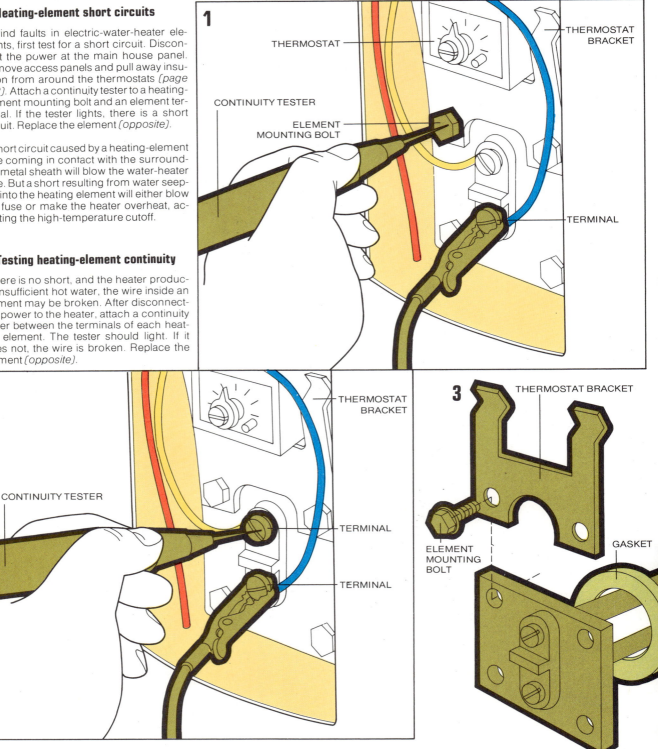

1
THERMOSTAT
CONTINUITY TESTER
ELEMENT MOUNTING BOLT
THERMOSTAT BRACKET
TERMINAL

2
CONTINUITY TESTER
THERMOSTAT BRACKET
TERMINAL
TERMINAL

3
THERMOSTAT BRACKET
ELEMENT MOUNTING BOLT
GASKET

Troubleshooting Electric Water Heaters

Problem	Possible Causes	Solution
No hot water	Power not reaching water heater	Check fuse or circuit breaker; if it fails repeatedly, call an electrician
	High-temperature cutoff activated	Push in reset button; if it activates again, test thermostats and elements *(pages 263-264)*
	Thermostat fails to turn on element	Check thermostats *(page 263)* and replace if necessary
	Heating elements defective	Replace elements *(left)* if necessary
Insufficient hot water	Incorrect thermostat setting	Reset thermostat
	Heating element burned out	Check elements for continuity *(left)*
	Insufficient heater capacity	Have larger heater installed
	Long pipe runs between heater and major points of hot-water use	Insulate pipes, move heater or have second heater installed
Insufficient hot water accompanied by hissing or sizzling noises	Sediment in tank; scale on tank or elements	Drain tank until water clears; soak elements in vinegar; scrape off scale
Water too hot	Incorrect thermostat setting	Reset thermostats
	Defective heating elements	Replace elements *(left)* if necessary
	Faulty thermostat	Check thermostats *(pages 263)* and replace if necessary
	Loose insulation around thermostats	Pack insulation tighter
Water leaks	Faulty heating-element gasket	Replace gaskets; see chart on page 260 for other leaks

Always turn off power to an electric water heater before removing thermostat-access panels

HEATING ELEMENT

3 Replacing a heating element

After disconnecting power to the heater, turn off the water inlet to the heater and open a nearby hot-water faucet to start emptying the tank. Remove remaining water from the tank drain with a hose or a bucket. Disconnect the wires from the element. Unscrew the bolts that secure the element, remove the thermostat bracket — let the thermostat hang by its wires — and pull the element out of the tank. When installing a heating element, always use a new gasket. Bolt the element and the thermostat bracket to the tank. Connect the wires to the element and clip the thermostat into place. Close the tank drain and turn on the water to refill the tank. When water runs from the open hot-water faucet, the tank is full.

Restore power to the water heater only after it has been filled and only when you have finished repacking the insulation around the thermostats and screwed the access panels into place.

CLOTHES WASHERS

Ever since human beings first wore clothes, women have cleaned those clothes by beating them against rocks along riverbanks. It was hard on clothes—and women. The first laundry machines, invented in 18th Century England, were muscle-powered contraptions that at least kept hands out of the water part of the time. From that modest beginning, the washer has evolved into a complex machine that, once started, fills and empties itself, washes, rinses, spins fabrics damp-dry, regulates water temperature, and adds detergent, bleach and rinse agents on cue—all automatically.

This automation has turned the washing machine into a very complicated appliance, one that can quickly be damaged by unknowledgeable tinkering. (Nor has human operating error been eliminated: when a machine damages fabrics one of the most likely causes is overloading.) But there are a few repairs, such as replacing a faulty water pump or freeing a clogged water hose, that are simply managed—and doing even them yourself can save the fees servicemen charge simply for coming to the house.

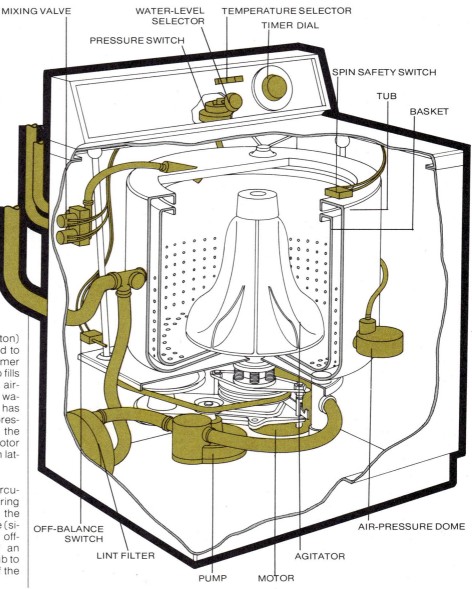

MIXING VALVE

WATER-LEVEL SELECTOR

TEMPERATURE SELECTOR

TIMER DIAL

PRESSURE SWITCH

SPIN SAFETY SWITCH

TUB

BASKET

OFF-BALANCE SWITCH

LINT FILTER

PUMP

MOTOR

AGITATOR

AIR-PRESSURE DOME

What goes on in a washing machine

Turning the timer dial (or pushing a button) starts the timer, a clock motor attached to switches that control operation. The timer first opens a mixing valve. While the tub fills up with hot, warm or cold water, an air-pressure dome senses the increasing water pressure; when it indicates water has reached the preset level, it signals a pressure switch (page 111) that closes the valve. The timer also controls the motor that works the wash-cycle agitator, then later spins the basket to whirl out water.

A pump, driven by the same motor, circulates wash water through a lint filter during washing and rinsing. During the spin, the pump pushes water out of the machine (simultaneously cleaning the filter). An off-balance switch stops the washer if an unevenly distributed load causes the tub to wobble; a spin safety switch operates if the lid is raised during the spin cycle.

How a mixing valve works

Mixing valves fill the washer with hot, cold or warm water depending on which valve has been opened.

When a valve is closed *(cold-water valve, at right in drawing)*, a solenoid plunger *(pages 178-179)* blocks a pilot hole in a flexible diaphragm, and water from the valve port enters a cavity above the diaphragm through a bleed hole. Water pressure on both sides of the diaphragm is the same, but the total force on top is greater because the pressure there affects a greater area, and the valve is held closed.

To open a valve *(hot-water valve, at left in drawing)*, the solenoid raises the plunger to unblock the pilot hole. Water flows from the cavity, lowering the force over the diaphragm. Water below the diaphragm lifts it and flows into the tub.

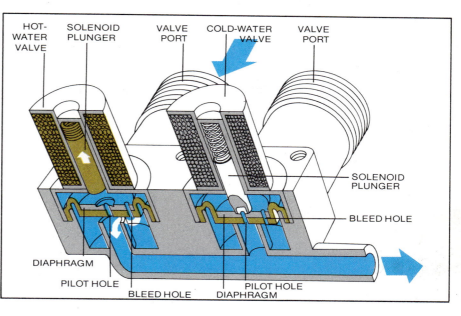

Why the agitator rocks

Whenever the washer motor runs, it moves a belt that rotates two pulleys, one on the basket shaft and the other, called the main pulley, at one side, where a small gear on its shaft turns the drive gear. As this drive gear revolves, a connecting rod causes a wedge-shaped gear and the agitator gear it meshes with to swing back and forth. The washer spins or agitates depending on whether or not this agitator gear is locked to the agitator shaft. During agitation, the agitator gear is pushed down onto a pin jutting from the agitator shaft so the gear can rock the agitator back and forth.

How the washer basket spins

To shift from agitate to spin, the timer releases a solenoid, moving the agitator cam bar upward and left, raising the agitator gear free of the drive pin on the agitator shaft. The same signal sets the pump to drain water from the machine. Then another solenoid moves the spin cam bar to the left. The yoke spring pulls down on the brake yoke to engage the basket's clutch plate with the rotating basket pulley; the basket starts to spin. When the spin cam bar is moved out again by the timer, it disengages the clutch and puts on the brake to stop the basket, thus resetting the mechanism so the machine will be ready to agitate when it is again filled with water.

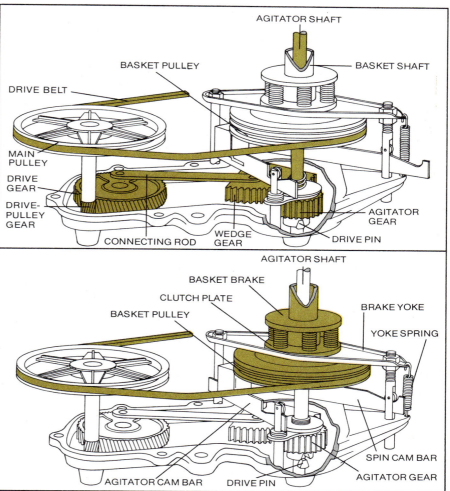

Simple Clothes-Washer Repairs

The parts of an automatic washer that circulate water usually require repair or replacement more often than other parts. But their problems also are fairly simple to diagnose and fix.

If the washer fills up more slowly than usual, for example, and the water pressure at other faucets around your house appears normal, check the washer hoses. If they are kinked, straighten them. If they are leaking, replace them. Otherwise, you may be able to speed filling by removing and rinsing the strainer screens in the inlet hoses and valves.

If the tub does not drain properly, you can install a new water pump yourself on many kinds of washers. But washer malfunctions involving the electrical system are difficult to troubleshoot and hard to fix without special equipment; they are best left to a serviceman.

Cleaning water-inlet strainer screens

Turn off the water at the faucets, unplug the machine, move it out from the wall, and unscrew the hoses from the water-inlet valve ports on the back of the washer. Pry the domed strainers out of these ports with the blade of a small knife, being careful not to damage the mesh. Rinse the screens clean and put them back, domed side out. Screw on the hoses finger-tight, then use pliers to tighten one third of a turn more. If there are similar strainers in the faucet ends of the hoses, clean them too.

Check that the machine is level when it is back in place. If it is not, adjust the leveling feet with a wrench. An off-level washer will wobble when spinning, actuating the off-balance switch and turning itself off.

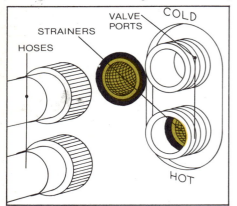

1 Replacing a clothes-washer pump

In a machine like the one illustrated on page 266, you need access from the bottom to replace an ailing pump (on other washers, the pump is reached from the back). Siphon the water out of the tub. Turn off the water and detach the water-supply hoses. Then disconnect the washer. When the tub is empty, carefully tip the washer forward onto a spread-out blanket. If the pump is leaking or has a worn bearing (it rumbles when you turn the pump with the drive belt), replace the pump. First loosen the motor mounting bolt that penetrates a slotted hole. Push the motor aside to slacken the drive belt.

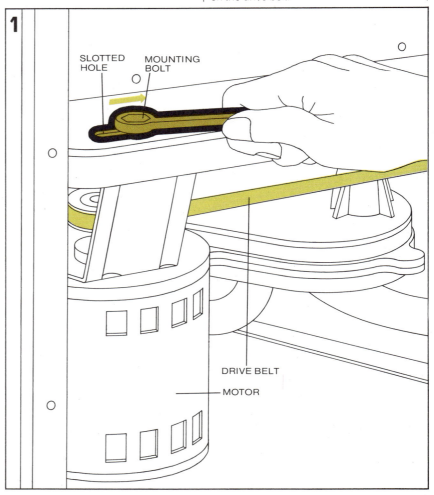

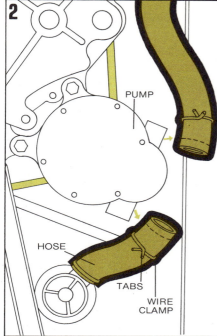

2

PUMP

HOSE

TABS

WIRE
CLAMP

2 Disconnecting the pump hoses

Spread an old towel under the pump to soak up any water trapped in the hoses that might drain onto the floor. To loosen the pump hoses, use a pair of locking-grip pliers to squeeze and hold open the tabs of the wire clamps that hold the hoses on the pump. Then slide the clamps, one at a time, along their hoses away from the pump. Set the pliers aside and then twist the hoses manually off the pump.

3 Unbolting the pump

Support the pump with one hand and remove the mounting bolts with a socket wrench; lift the pump off. To install a new pump, attach the two hoses. Engage the projecting pump lever with the bar that directs the water flow, and bolt the pump on. Attach the drive belt, then tighten it by bracing a hammer handle between motor and washer frame to push on the motor; keep the belt taut and tighten the mounting bolt.

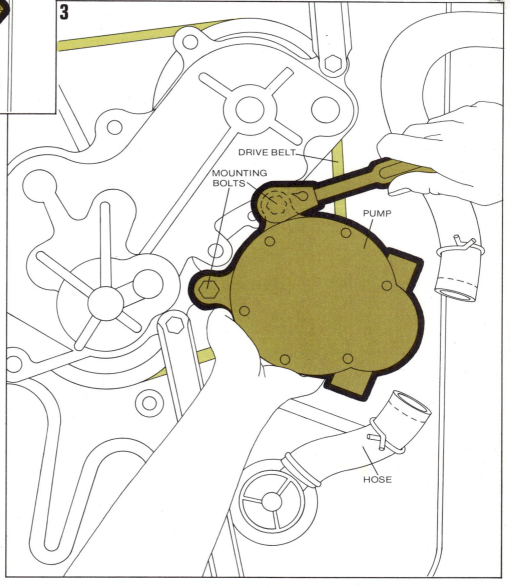

3

DRIVE BELT

MOUNTING
BOLTS

PUMP

HOSE

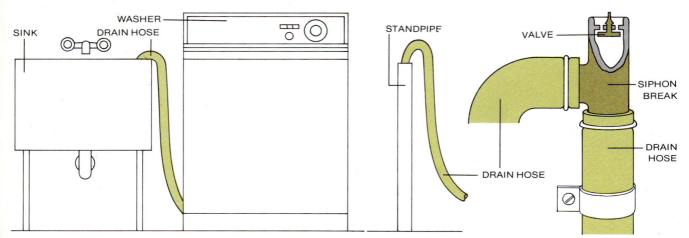

Positioning the drain hose

One very common way of disposing of wash water is simply to empty the clothes washer into a large sink. The rim of the sink must be high enough—generally about three feet above the floor—for the drain hose to discharge at a point above the level of the water inside the washer. Otherwise the water might siphon out of the clothes-washer tub at the wrong time.

Draining the washer into a standpipe

Instead of a sink, a pipe with a diameter a bit larger than that of the drain hose can be installed directly over a floor drain and the drain hose then hooked into it. Such a standpipe should be tall enough to prevent any siphoning action while the washer is operating but no taller than four to six feet —the maximum height that the washer pump can lift water as it empties out the tub.

Connecting the washer to a floor drain

If you must empty the washer directly into a floor drain, or if you cannot place the hose discharge above the water level in the machine, install a device called a siphon break on the back of the washer four inches above the machine's maximum water level. This accessory, inserted in the drain hose, has a valve that lets air into the hose, preventing the water from siphoning out.

The Problem of Replacing Drive Belts

Clothes-washer manufacturers use drive belts made of reinforced rubber to let the expensive parts of a washer last longer. By stretching or even breaking as it absorbs stress, the drive belt lessens wear on other parts.

On most machines, a stretched belt can easily be tightened by loosening one or two motor mounting bolts and forcing the motor in the direction that takes up slack in the belt. Replacing a broken belt can be another matter. On some types of washers *(below, left),* installing a new belt is easy; on other types *(below, right),* a considerable amount of disassembly is needed to get other parts out of the way so that you can fit a new belt around the pulleys.

If you decide to replace a worn or broken belt, buy or borrow a service manual for your washer. It will give detailed instructions for putting a new belt on your model and can save you hours of needless frustration.

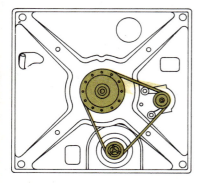

A simple drive-belt arrangement

The motor, pump and drive pulleys all extend through the bottom of the washer at left. Once it is tipped on its side, replacing the belt is a simple chore.

A less accessible drive belt

Pulleys of the washer on the right are inside the washer cabinet. To install a new belt you must unhook a spring, remove several bolts and reposition three braces. A service manual is essential.

Troubleshooting Clothes Washers

Problem	Possible Causes	Solution
Washer does not run	Power not reaching washer	Make sure washer is plugged in; check to see if fuse is blown or circuit breaker tripped
	Safety switch activated	Be sure clothes are evenly distributed in the basket and washer door is closed
Water does not enter tub	Water supply turned off	Turn on the water
	Strainers in mixing valve clogged	Remove and rinse strainers
	Water-supply hoses pinched or kinked	Move the washer if it is pinching hoses, or untwist kinks
	Washer not turned on	Rotate the timer dial a bit farther, or push control button firmly
Motor hums but will not run	Too large a load	Wash smaller loads
	Too much suds	Use less detergent or a low-sudsing one
Washer does not agitate	Loose or broken drive belt	Tighten or replace the belt
Water does not drain out	Kinked or clogged drain hose	Unkink the hose; remove hose and flush out with water from a garden hose
	Suds blocking water flow	Dip excess suds out of washer and flush tub with cold water
	Loose drive belt	Tighten the belt
	Drain hose too high	Lower the hose so it discharges less than six feet above the bottom of the washer
Basket does not spin	Loose drive belt	Tighten the belt
	Broken drive belt	Install a new belt
	Load unevenly distributed in the basket	Reposition the load
Washer leaks	Water-inlet hoses loose	Tighten hose connections
	Pump hoses loose	Tighten hose clamps or replace with new ones
	Hoses broken or split	Replace with new ones
Washer vibrates excessively or "walks" across the floor	Washer not level	Adjust washer's leveling feet
	Load unbalanced	Redistribute the load
Washer damages fabrics	Too large a load	Wash smaller loads
	Too little water	Use more water
	Too much bleach	Use less bleach
Water is not hot enough	Inadequate supply of hot water	Check water-heater thermostat; set at 140° to 160°
	Water hoses connected to wrong mixing-valve ports	Reverse the hoses
Pump makes rumbling noise	Defective pump	Replace the pump

CLOTHES DRIERS

A typical drier has a heat source (gas flame or electric coils), motor, drum, fan and controls; and even the controls are not complex. They depend on bimetallic thermostats like those in coffee makers *(page 236)*. A dial or button selects one of the thermostats to control the duration of the drying cycle (some driers have several operating thermostats to provide a choice of temperatures as well as different drying cycles).

Each thermostat is wired to both the heat source and timer-clock motor, turning the timer on only after the selected thermostat shuts off the heat source. Linking timer to thermostat automatically controls the length of the drying cycle, since the temperature rises enough to operate the thermostat only after the desired amount of water has been evaporated.

How a drier functions

Setting the timer and operating the starting switch turns on a motor that drives both the drum and a fan located in the exhaust duct. At the same time, the heat source goes on. In an electric drier *(right)* the timer lets current flow through heating coils. The burner in a gas drier *(below)* fires when the timer activates a valve like the solenoid safety valve in a gas water heater *(pages 258-259)*. Warm air is thus drawn through the clothes in the drum *(opposite)*.

The operating thermostats are mounted in the top of the exhaust duct. The one selected with the temperature-control buttons monitors air entering the duct, and controls cycling of the timer and heat source until the clothes are dry. If the operating thermostat fails or if the temperature near the heat source goes much above 200°, a safety thermostat in the intake duct shuts off the heat. A trap in the exhaust duct keeps lint from blocking air flow.

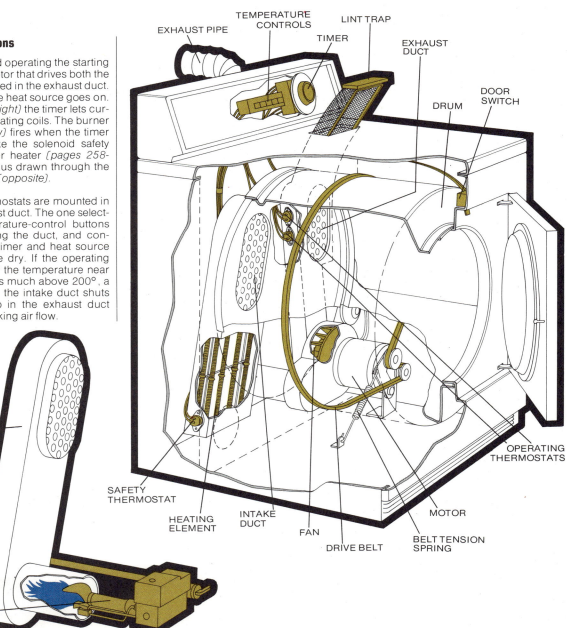

EXHAUST PIPE
TEMPERATURE CONTROLS
LINT TRAP
TIMER
EXHAUST DUCT
DOOR SWITCH
DRUM
SAFETY THERMOSTAT
HEATING ELEMENT
INTAKE DUCT
FAN
DRIVE BELT
MOTOR
BELT TENSION SPRING
OPERATING THERMOSTATS
INTAKE DUCT
SAFETY THERMOSTAT
GAS BURNER

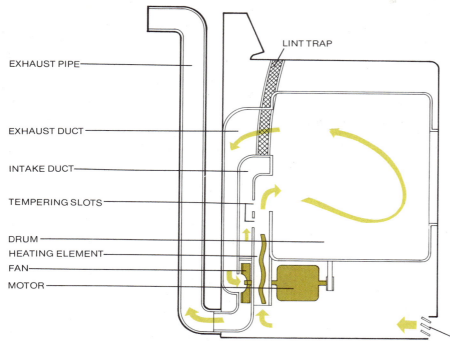

EXHAUST PIPE

LINT TRAP

EXHAUST DUCT

INTAKE DUCT

TEMPERING SLOTS

DRUM
HEATING ELEMENT
FAN
MOTOR

INTAKE GRILLE

Air flow through the system

Air for drying the clothes is pulled into the machine by a fan located in the exhaust duct and driven by the main motor. Since the ducts and drum are sealed from the surrounding air, starting the fan causes air to be drawn through the intake grille at the front of the machine and into the intake duct. Here it is heated above 150° and mixed with a small amount of outside air drawn in through the tempering slots to prevent scorching the clothes.

The hot, dry air is pulled into the drum, passed through the clothes, and is drawn into the exhaust duct and lint trap. Here, particles that might block the system are caught for a later removal. The moisture-laden air, its temperature by now reduced to perhaps 135°, is expelled through the exhaust pipe to the outside air.

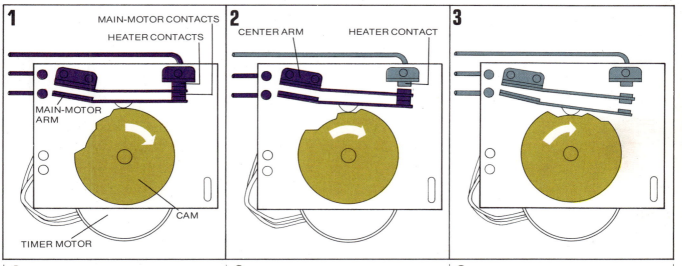

1

MAIN-MOTOR CONTACTS

HEATER CONTACTS

MAIN-MOTOR ARM

CAM

TIMER MOTOR

2

CENTER ARM   HEATER CONTACT

3

1 Starting the drying cycle

When the timer is set, the main-motor arm is forced up onto the high part of the cam. The arm presses both the main-motor contacts and the heater contact together to turn on both the motor and the heater, starting the drying cycle. The cam begins to rotate when the operating thermostat, previously selected by pushing a button or turning a knob on the control panel, lets the timer motor go on.

2 Timing the cool-down period

As the drying cycle continues, the rotating cam allows the main-motor arm to fall into the first of two notches in the cam circumference. Both the main-motor arm and the center arm drop from the upper contact, breaking the heater circuit and shutting it off. But the downward movement does not separate main-motor arm and center arm; the main-motor contacts stay together to operate fan and drum as the clothes cool.

3 Turning off the drier

The cam continues to rotate during the cool-down period as the clothing temperature drops to a comfortable range. The cam then lets the main-motor arm drop into the deepest notch in the cam. Now the main-motor arm separates from the center arm, breaking the circuit to the motor and stopping fan and drum. More complex driers may have additional contacts to control panel lights and cycle signals.

Repairs

Before you take apart a malfunctioning drier, check the simple but often overlooked trouble spots. If the machine will not start, look for either a blown fuse or a loose plug. If you find the clothes are not being adequately dried, the lint trap or the exhaust duct may be clogged.

When these faults have been ruled out, proceed in the order indicated on these pages. Check the thermostats *(below)* and the door switches *(page 277)* with a continuity tester, then look for obvious failures in electric heating elements, or if you have a gas drier, call a service man. If the drum does not turn even though all electrical circuits are working, the drive belt may be broken; how easy it is to replace one depends on the type of machine *(page 276)*.

All these tasks require the removal of one or more of the drier's outer panels. Most are secured with clips or with sheet-metal screws. Important: Unplug the drier before starting any tests or repairs.

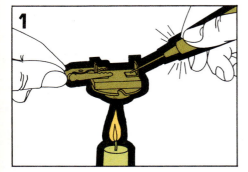

1 Testing thermostats

If a drier will not produce heat, check the heating element *(opposite)* and thermostats. Most drier thermostats have contacts that are closed at room temperature and open when hot. To check such a thermostat, remove it from the machine (for typical locations, see drawing on page 272), clip a continuity tester to one of its terminals and touch the tester's probe to the other; the tester should light. Then hold the thermostat briefly near a flame—intense heat for more than a moment will damage it. A click should be heard and the tester light should go out. If the thermostat is the type that is closed when hot and open when cool, the tester light should be off during the cold test, on during the flame test.

2 Getting at the heating element

If an electric drier's thermostats all work, check the heating element in the intake duct. (For a gas drier, call a serviceman.) Take off the rear panel, pull the wires off the terminals of the element and safety thermostat; take the intake duct off its brackets.

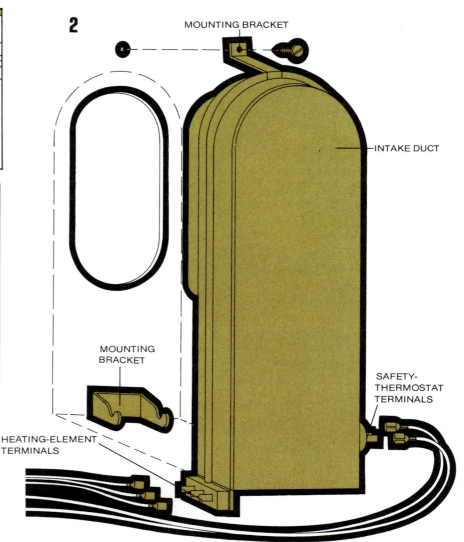

MOUNTING BRACKET

INTAKE DUCT

MOUNTING BRACKET

SAFETY-THERMOSTAT TERMINALS

HEATING-ELEMENT TERMINALS

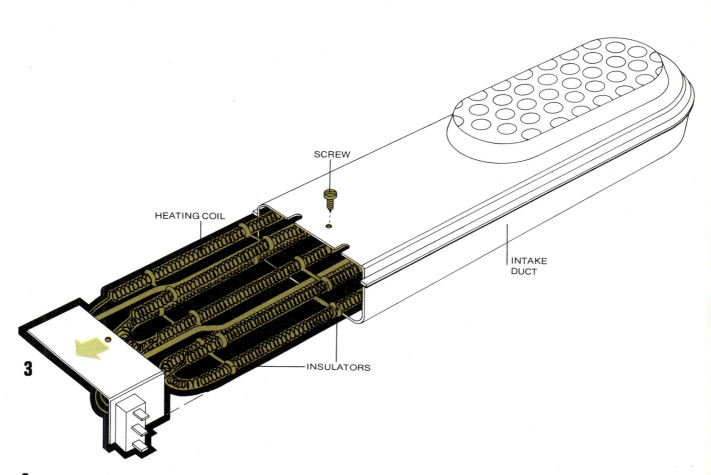

SCREW

HEATING COIL

INTAKE
DUCT

INSULATORS

3

3 Removing the element from the duct

The heating element is attached to the intake duct by a screw located at the bottom of the duct. Once the screw is removed, the element easily slides out for inspection. Handle it gently; it is easily damaged.

4 Inspecting the element

Look for broken or sagging coils, or broken insulators. An element with a broken coil cannot conduct electricity and create heat. Sagging coils or a broken insulator can impair the ability to produce heat. If you find any of these defects, replace the element. A sagging coil cannot be stretched back into position, cracked insulators cannot be replaced, and twisting broken coil ends back together makes a connection that will quickly burn out.

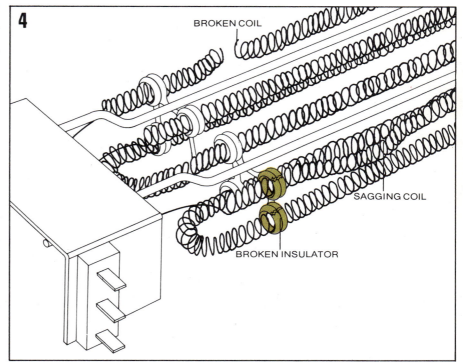

4

BROKEN COIL

SAGGING COIL

BROKEN INSULATOR

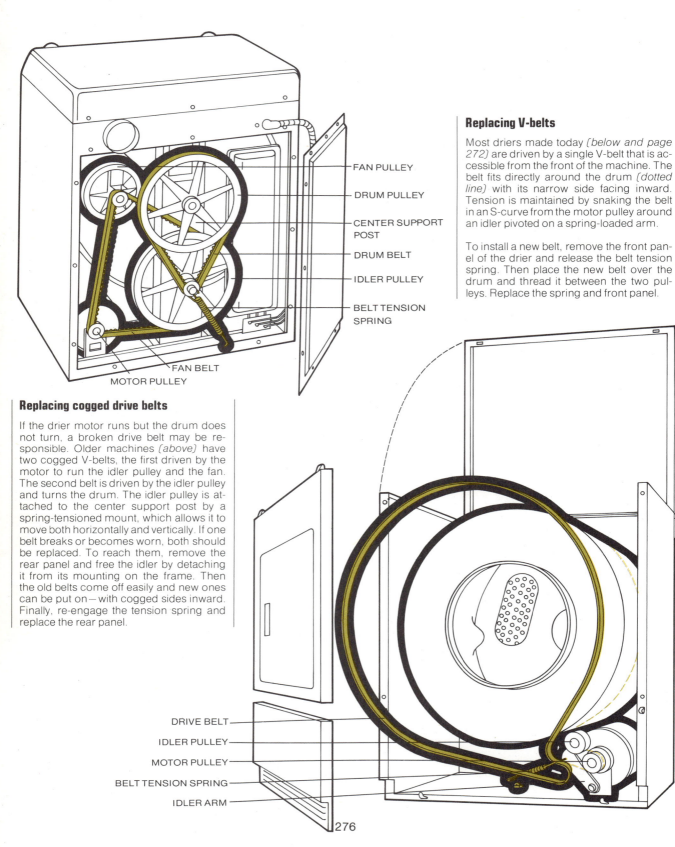

FAN PULLEY

DRUM PULLEY

CENTER SUPPORT POST

DRUM BELT

IDLER PULLEY

BELT TENSION SPRING

FAN BELT

MOTOR PULLEY

Replacing V-belts

Most driers made today *[below and page 272]* are driven by a single V-belt that is accessible from the front of the machine. The belt fits directly around the drum *[dotted line]* with its narrow side facing inward. Tension is maintained by snaking the belt in an S-curve from the motor pulley around an idler pivoted on a spring-loaded arm.

To install a new belt, remove the front panel of the drier and release the belt tension spring. Then place the new belt over the drum and thread it between the two pulleys. Replace the spring and front panel.

Replacing cogged drive belts

If the drier motor runs but the drum does not turn, a broken drive belt may be responsible. Older machines *[above]* have two cogged V-belts, the first driven by the motor to run the idler pulley and the fan. The second belt is driven by the idler pulley and turns the drum. The idler pulley is attached to the center support post by a spring-tensioned mount, which allows it to move both horizontally and vertically. If one belt breaks or becomes worn, both should be replaced. To reach them, remove the rear panel and free the idler by detaching it from its mounting on the frame. Then the old belts come off easily and new ones can be put on—with cogged sides inward. Finally, re-engage the tension spring and replace the rear panel.

DRIVE BELT

IDLER PULLEY

MOTOR PULLEY

BELT TENSION SPRING

IDLER ARM

276

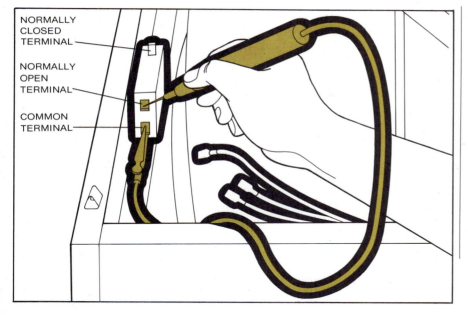

NORMALLY
CLOSED
TERMINAL

NORMALLY
OPEN
TERMINAL

COMMON
TERMINAL

Testing the door switch

The door switch, located behind the front panel, is a safety device that shuts the drier off when the door is opened. If the motor runs when the door is open, or will not run at all when the door is closed, check first for a jammed switch. Jiggle the button or lever—usually located in the door recess.

If jamming is not the problem, make a continuity test. Remove the drier's top panel and unclip the three leads that go to the switch. The terminals on most driers are marked "com" (common), "n.c." (normally closed) and "n.o." (normally open). With the door closed, clip the tester to the common terminal and touch its probe to the normally open terminal. The tester light should go on. When the door is opened, the tester light should go off. If the switch does not respond properly, replace it.

Troubleshooting Clothes Driers

Problem	Possible Causes	Solution
Drier will not run	Drier not receiving power Door open or door switch defective Timer or motor defective	Check fuses and circuit breakers Test door switch *(above)* Call a repairman
Drier runs but will not heat	Defective thermostat Defective heating element (electric models) Defective burner (gas models)	Test thermostats *(page 274)* Check element for broken or sagging coil, or broken insulators *(page 275)* Call a repairman
Drier runs and heats but will not dry clothes	Blocked lint trap or exhaust duct	Clean lint from trap and duct
Drum will not rotate	Broken belt Broken tension spring	Replace belt *(opposite)* Replace spring
Drier runs with door open	Defective door switch	Test switch and replace if necessary *(above)*

DISHWASHERS

The automatic dishwasher is in many ways an economical machine. It saves time for whoever in the family has to clean up after meals—every year there is an average of 40,000 glasses, dishes, pots and pans to do. Dishwashers are water misers besides, using about 15 gallons per full load, less than the amount generally required by a hand-wash job. The operating cost is low, too—the electricity used is less than you use in making waffles and bacon for the family breakfast, and even lower if you select an "air-dry" option, which dries the dishes without switching on the heating element.

Although dishwashers are complex machines, many failures are relatively simple to fix, and most parts can be replaced as units *(pages 280-281)*.

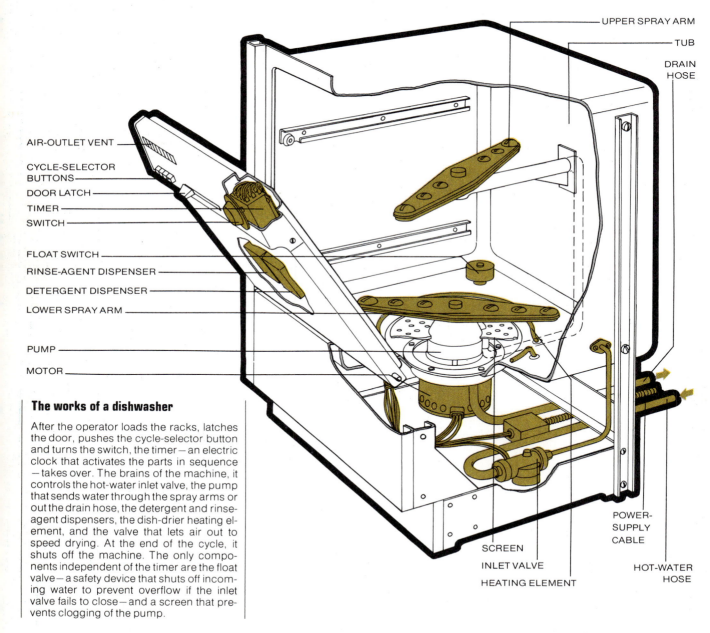

The works of a dishwasher

After the operator loads the racks, latches the door, pushes the cycle-selector button and turns the switch, the timer—an electric clock that activates the parts in sequence—takes over. The brains of the machine, it controls the hot-water inlet valve, the pump that sends water through the spray arms or out the drain hose, the detergent and rinse-agent dispensers, the dish-drier heating element, and the valve that lets air out to speed drying. At the end of the cycle, it shuts off the machine. The only components independent of the timer are the float valve—a safety device that shuts off incoming water to prevent overflow if the inlet valve fails to close—and a screen that prevents clogging of the pump.

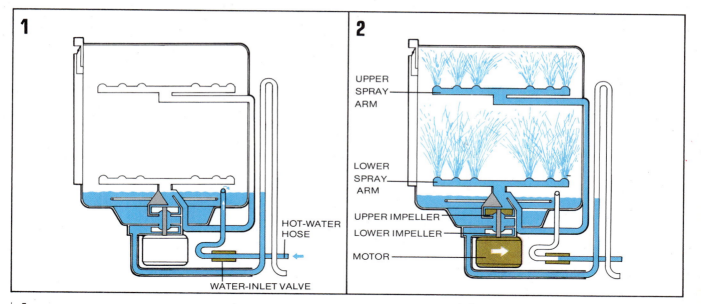

1 Filling the dishwasher

At the beginning of each wash or rinse cycle, the timer opens the inlet valve to bring hot water—ideally at about 150°—into the dishwasher *(arrows)*. The timer shuts off the water flow when the proper level is reached in the tub.

2 Washing or rinsing the dishes

The timer starts the motor *(arrow)* that turns the pump impellers. Water pumped through the spray arms by the upper impeller turns the arms and hoses dishes at 50 gallons a minute. The lower impeller pumps no water in this part of the cycle.

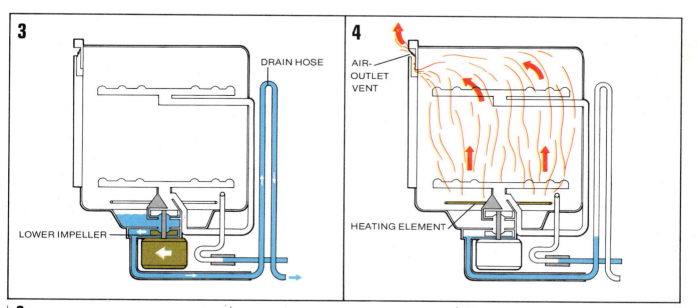

3 Draining the dishwasher

At the end of a wash or rinse, the timer reverses the direction of the motor *(broad arrow)*, so that the lower impeller pumps water out of the tub through the drain hose *(small arrows)*. After the final rinse, the timer starts the drying stage.

4 Drying the dishes

After the tub has been pumped dry, the timer opens the air vent, allowing the hot, moist air to escape *(arrows)*. If the faster drying of a "heated dry" cycle has been selected, the timer also turns on the heating element, raising the temperature to around 180°.

Dishwasher Repairs

Many problems with dishwashers are caused by clogging and are remedied by cleaning trapped debris out of the screen *(right)* or drain hose. Getting inside the pump to unclog it or replace corroded parts *(below)* requires a bit more patience, but offers no great difficulties. However, if you must replace a timer *(opposite),* take extra care to make sure you hook up the numerous wires—they are color coded—to the new timer exactly the same as they were on the old one.

Before starting any work suggested here, remember to turn off power to the dishwasher circuit by either removing the fuse or tripping the circuit breaker at the service panel.

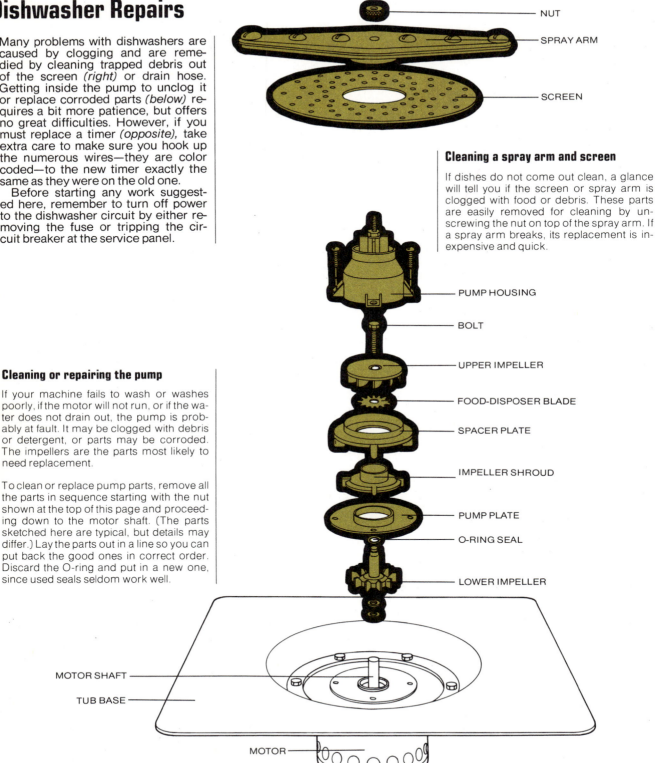

Cleaning a spray arm and screen

If dishes do not come out clean, a glance will tell you if the screen or spray arm is clogged with food or debris. These parts are easily removed for cleaning by unscrewing the nut on top of the spray arm. If a spray arm breaks, its replacement is inexpensive and quick.

Cleaning or repairing the pump

If your machine fails to wash or washes poorly, if the motor will not run, or if the water does not drain out, the pump is probably at fault. It may be clogged with debris or detergent, or parts may be corroded. The impellers are the parts most likely to need replacement.

To clean or replace pump parts, remove all the parts in sequence starting with the nut shown at the top of this page and proceeding down to the motor shaft. (The parts sketched here are typical, but details may differ.) Lay the parts out in a line so you can put back the good ones in correct order. Discard the O-ring and put in a new one, since used seals seldom work well.

NUT

SPRAY ARM

SCREEN

PUMP HOUSING

BOLT

UPPER IMPELLER

FOOD-DISPOSER BLADE

SPACER PLATE

IMPELLER SHROUD

PUMP PLATE

O-RING SEAL

LOWER IMPELLER

MOTOR SHAFT

TUB BASE

MOTOR

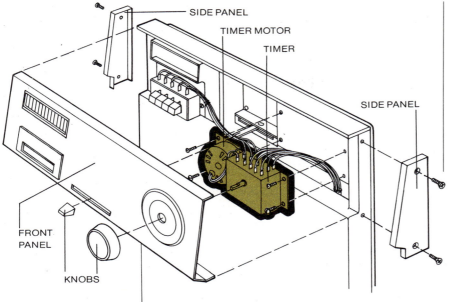

SIDE PANEL

TIMER MOTOR

TIMER

SIDE PANEL

FRONT PANEL

KNOBS

Replacing a timer

If the timer does not advance—after you have made sure the door is latched, the switch is on, and the fuse or circuit breaker is operative—the timer motor is probably defective. The whole unit must be replaced. Pull off the knobs, and remove the side and front panels. Hold the new timer next to the old one and transfer the wire connectors one by one to their correct positions on the new timer. (They slide on, requiring no screwdriver or solder.) Remove the old timer from the door and attach the new one. Replace the panels and knobs.

Troubleshooting Dishwashers

Problem	Possible Causes	Solution
Dishwasher does not run	Power not reaching dishwasher Door not latched Cycle-selector button not fully depressed Defective door-latch switch Defective timer	Check fuse or circuit breaker Latch door securely Push selector button all the way in Test switch with continuity tester (page 137) and replace if necessary Turn timer slightly; if it does not advance, replace it
Dishwasher does not fill or overfills	Defective float switch	Lift float to check for freedom of movement; if switch does not click on and off, check continuity with a tester and replace if defective
Dishes are not satisfactorily cleaned	Spray arm clogged Spray arm not rotating Water temperature too low	Clean holes in spray arm Make sure nothing obstructs spray-arm rotation Adjust water-heater setting
Water does not drain	Drain hose kinked Either impeller jammed or lower impeller broken	Straighten drain hose Disassemble pump, and clear or replace impeller
Motor hums but does not run	Impeller jammed	Disassemble pump and clear impellers
Motor does not run	Defective timer Defective motor	Replace timer Have motor replaced

REFRIGERATORS

The refrigerator is the one major appliance that Americans cannot do without: 99.9 per cent of all United States homes with electricity have refrigerators. The machine's popularity as a food preserver is a surprisingly recent phenomenon, however. The principles were known as early as 1748: a liquid absorbs heat from its surroundings when it evaporates into gas; a gas releases heat when it condenses to liquid. But it was not until the mid-1920s that the availability of small motors, widespread power distribution and mass production combined to bring a refrigerator to every home.

In addition to keeping foods cool or frozen, a refrigerator may have many convenient extras: a fan to ensure that chilled air is evenly distributed through the compartments, a device to make ice cubes automatically, even a small heater to keep butter spreadable. But the most convenient improvement of recent years was the introduction of devices that defrost the machine automatically —either by constant evaporation (a "frost-free" type) or at intervals *(below)* so that frost melts and drains into a pan.

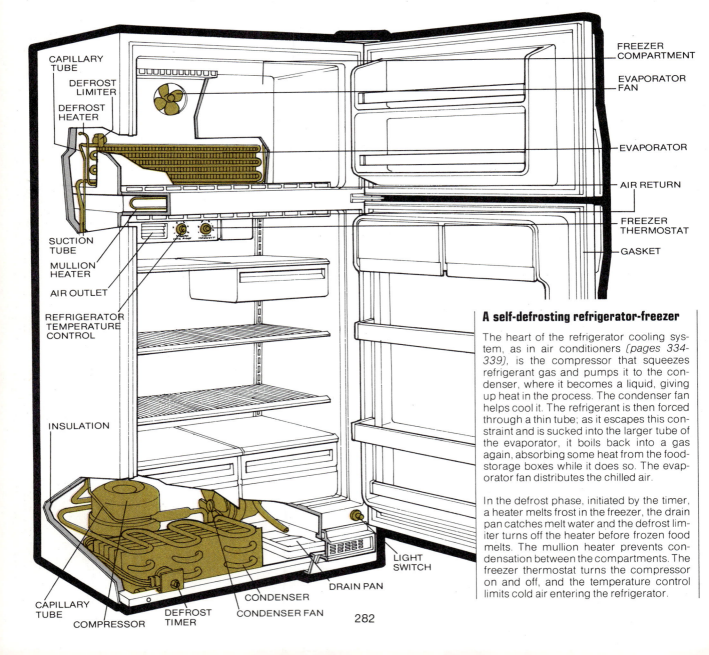

CAPILLARY TUBE
DEFROST LIMITER
DEFROST HEATER
SUCTION TUBE
MULLION HEATER
AIR OUTLET
REFRIGERATOR TEMPERATURE CONTROL
INSULATION
CAPILLARY TUBE
COMPRESSOR
DEFROST TIMER
CONDENSER FAN
CONDENSER
DRAIN PAN
LIGHT SWITCH
FREEZER COMPARTMENT
EVAPORATOR FAN
EVAPORATOR
AIR RETURN
FREEZER THERMOSTAT
GASKET

A self-defrosting refrigerator-freezer

The heart of the refrigerator cooling system, as in air conditioners *(pages 334-339)*, is the compressor that squeezes refrigerant gas and pumps it to the condenser, where it becomes a liquid, giving up heat in the process. The condenser fan helps cool it. The refrigerant is then forced through a thin tube; as it escapes this constraint and is sucked into the larger tube of the evaporator, it boils back into a gas again, absorbing some heat from the food-storage boxes while it does so. The evaporator fan distributes the chilled air.

In the defrost phase, initiated by the timer, a heater melts frost in the freezer, the drain pan catches melt water and the defrost limiter turns off the heater before frozen food melts. The mullion heater prevents condensation between the compartments. The freezer thermostat turns the compressor on and off, and the temperature control limits cold air entering the refrigerator.

282

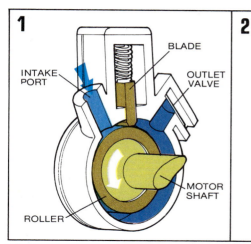

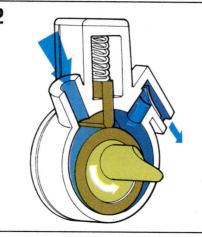

1 The compressor ready to pump

Inside the compressor cylinder is a roller mounted off-center on a motor shaft. In the schematic drawing, the roller, which is turning counterclockwise, pushes against gas *(dark blue)* trapped in front of the roller, forcing the gas through an outlet valve into the condenser. Other types of compressors have blade- or piston-operated pumps that achieve the same purpose.

2 The roller in mid-cycle

The compressor's roller continues to rotate, forcing more gas through the outlet valve. As the roller rotates, the space behind it grows larger and gas from the evaporator *(light blue)* is sucked through the intake port *(left)* into the compressor cylinder. A blade, held continuously pressed against the roller by a spring, keeps the gas in the intake and outflow areas separated.

3 The roller at the cycle's end

The roller has now forced all of the original charge of gas through the outlet valve, which closes to prevent any backflow. In the meantime, the space behind the roller has expanded to its maximum size and is filled with gas from the evaporator. Finally, as the roller continues to turn, it will force the new charge of gas around the cylinder to the outlet valve.

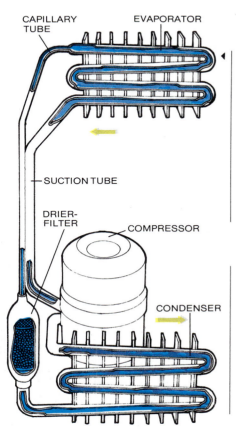

The refrigeration cycle

As a refrigerant is alternately vaporized to absorb heat and liquefied to give it up, it follows the path shown at left. In liquid form, it is pushed by the compressor through the capillary tube and evaporates, soaking up heat. The warmed gas is sucked back into the compressor and pumped through the condenser, losing heat as it changes back to a liquid. The drier-filter removes any moisture and impurities that get into the system during manufacture. This system is sealed, so problems here require the attention of a serviceman.

Distributing chilled air

In a self-defrosting refrigerator, a fan draws air over the evaporator, where it is chilled, and then blows it through ducts to cool food stored in the freezer and refrigerator compartments. Moisture condenses into frost on the cold evaporator coils; it is evaporated or melted and drained away when the coils are warmed during the defrosting cycle. An adjustable baffle partially blocks the air flow into the refrigerator so it does not get as cold as the freezer.

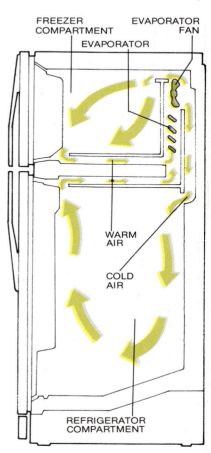

Checking Out Controls

Temperature control is the key to economical food preservation in a refrigerator. The thermostat controls freezer temperature directly and automatically, while cold coming from the freezer chills the other compartments. Check temperatures with a thermometer. The freezer compartment should be 5° or less. In a self- defrosting refrigerator there will also be an automatic or manual control to regulate cold-air flow to the refrigerator compartment, where the temperature should be near 35°, and a timer to run the defrosting heaters.

To operate efficiently, refrigerators must be tightly sealed to keep heat out. Close the door on a dollar bill; the door gasket should grip it as you try to pull it out. If it comes out easily, check the gasket *(page 286)*.

Two temperature controls

All refrigerators come with one thermostat *(right)* that keeps storage compartments cold by turning the compressor motor on and off to chill coils alongside a wall of the freezer. In some models, a second control adjusts the temperature in the refrigerator compartment by opening or closing a duct bringing in cold air.

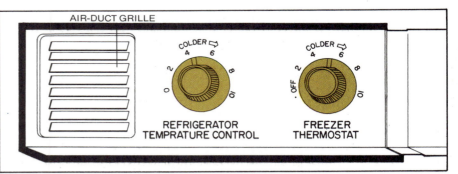

Checking the refrigerator control

If the refrigerator is too warm and the freezer is normally cold, and adjusting dials does not help, make sure air ducts are unobstructed. Then check the refrigerator control; set it at midrange, take off the knobs and snap off the front panel. Measure the opening of the air-duct door *(right)*. Turn the freezer thermostat off and open the refrigerator. If the air-duct door does not open wider as the refrigerator warms up, the control needs replacement.

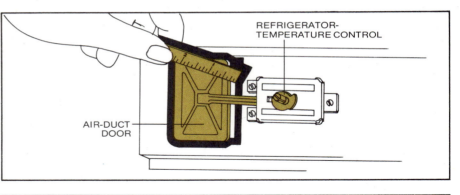

Checking the freezer thermostat

If the freezer is too warm or the compressor runs erratically, and adjusting the thermostat dial does not help, then check the thermostat. Unplug the power cord. Unscrew the thermostat and gently pull it out. Disconnect its wires and tape their ends together with electrical tape. Then plug in the power cord. If the refrigerator then operates normally, or if it does so when you turn the defrost timer *(opposite)* with a coin until it clicks out of the defrost setting, the thermostat will need replacement. For any other temperature problem, consult the chart on page 287.

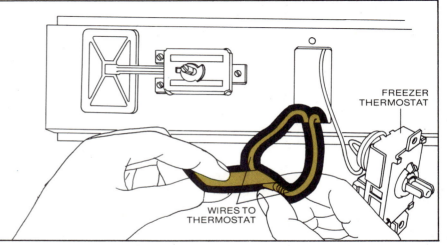

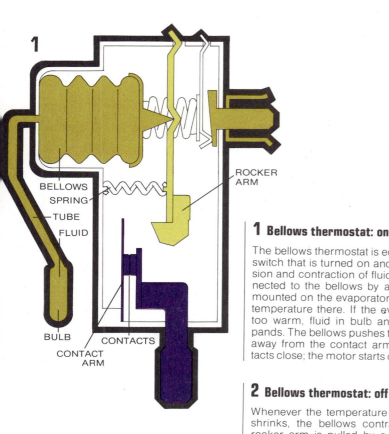

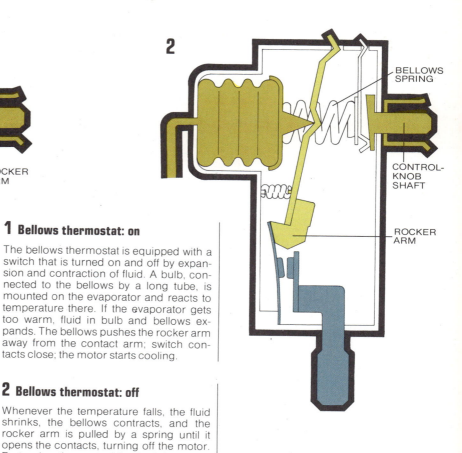

1 Bellows thermostat: on

The bellows thermostat is equipped with a switch that is turned on and off by expansion and contraction of fluid. A bulb, connected to the bellows by a long tube, is mounted on the evaporator and reacts to temperature there. If the evaporator gets too warm, fluid in bulb and bellows expands. The bellows pushes the rocker arm away from the contact arm; switch contacts close; the motor starts cooling.

2 Bellows thermostat: off

Whenever the temperature falls, the fluid shrinks, the bellows contracts, and the rocker arm is pulled by a spring until it opens the contacts, turning off the motor. By turning the control knob, tightness of the bellows spring can be varied so the thermostat will turn the compressor on and off to maintain a selected temperature.

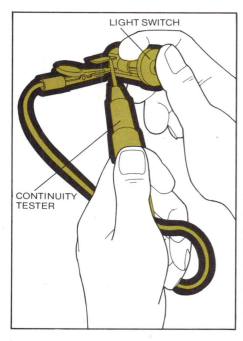

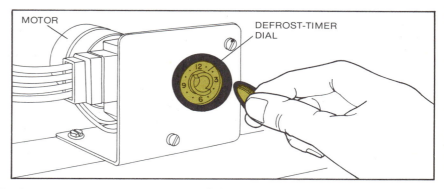

Testing the light switch

If the refrigerator light does not turn on, check the bulb. If it is good, unplug the power cord, pry out the light switch gently and disconnect its wires. Test the switch with a continuity tester (page 137). The tester light should be on with the plunger out, off with the plunger in. If the switch is defective, replace it. There may be a similar switch to control the air-circulating fan; a continuity tester checks it, too.

Checking the defrost timer

If a frost-free refrigerator does not defrost, check the defrost timer. If its motor is noisy or the timer knob does not advance, the motor is defective. Have the timer replaced. If the motor works, turn the timer dial with a coin (above). Normally, the timer should click and the unit should begin defrosting. If it does not, either a switch inside the timer, or the heating elements, may be defective. Call a serviceman.

285

GASKET

GASKET-RETAINING
STRIP

RETAINING SCREWS

Replacing a defective door gasket

A door gasket so worn or dirty that it lets
cold air leak out is wasteful. Dirt and grease
can be removed with detergent and water.
To replace a defective gasket, at first remove only the top section of gasket retainer and the top couple of screws on each
side. Strip out the top of the gasket, replace
it with the new one, and replace the top retainer. One at a time, do the same with the
other three sides. On most refrigerators,
the gasket overlaps the gasket-retaining
strip *(below)*, so you will have to peel back
the gasket to reach the retaining screws.
The job is easier if two people work together. Do not remove all retainers at once; the
door shelving might come off or the door
might warp out of shape.

Most door gaskets have magnets enclosed
in the rubber on all but the hinge side to
hold the door snugly closed and keep the
cold air from leaking out. The magnets are
used in place of the latches found on older
refrigerators and eliminate the danger that
a child may lock himself inside.

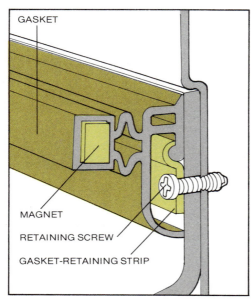

GASKET

MAGNET

RETAINING SCREW

GASKET-RETAINING STRIP

Troubleshooting Refrigerators

Problem	Possible Causes	Solution
Refrigerator does not run and light is out	Power not reaching refrigerator	Check fuse or circuit breaker; receptacle *(page 143)*; cord *(pages 186-187)*
Refrigerator does not run and light is on	Defective thermostat Overheated compressor Timer at defrost setting Defective compressor	Have thermostat replaced Clean condenser coils; check condenser fan, allow adequate ventilation Adjust timer *(page 285)*, have it replaced if necessary Call serviceman
Compressor runs but light is out	Burned-out bulb Defective light switch	Replace bulb Check switch *(page 285)*; replace if necessary
Compressor starts and immediately stops	Low power-line voltage	Remove other appliances from the circuit
Refrigerator runs but does not cool	Temperature controls set too warm Defective temperature controls Door open too often Faulty door seal Air ducts blocked Room too warm Dirty condenser Defroster always on Defective evaporator fan Defect in sealed system	Adjust temperature controls Check controls *(page 284)*; have replaced if necessary Open less often Adjust latch; make sure refrigerator is level; check gasket and replace if necessary *(opposite)* Remove obstructions Reduce room temperature or move refrigerator to a cooler room Clean condenser coils. Check timer *(page 285)*; have it replaced if necessary Make sure fan is on with all door-operated switches depressed; call serviceman Call serviceman
Refrigerator too cold	Temperature controls set too warm Defective temperature controls	Adjust controls Check temperature controls *(page 284)*; have replaced if necessary
Excessive frost accumulation	Door open too often Faulty door seal Defective defrost timer Air humidity too high Defective defrost heater or defrost wires	Open door less often Adjust latch; make sure refrigerator is level; check gasket and replace if necessary *(opposite)* Check timer *(page 285)*; have it replaced if necessary Consider dehumidifier if condition persists Call serviceman
Refrigerator noisy	Machine not level	Adjust leveling screws in base

COOKING RANGES

The modern kitchen range, whether it has gas burners *(below)* or electric elements *(pages 291-293)*, can boil a quart of water in less than six minutes. But the electric range heats more efficiently than a gas range, because about 75 per cent of the electric energy reaches the food as heat —cooking utensils sit directly on top of the heating element. Only 40 per cent of a gas burner's heat reaches the food; its open flame dissipates the rest to the surrounding air. Electric ranges, on the other hand, cost more to operate, and they cost more to buy than comparable gas ranges because they require more expensive materials and labor.

Replacing an electric-range element *(pages 292-293)* is an easy job. So is adjusting a gas burner *(right)*. But before adjusting a burner, make sure it is not tilted or loosely connected to the manifold, and is not affected by drafts; such faults often make flames burn inefficiently.

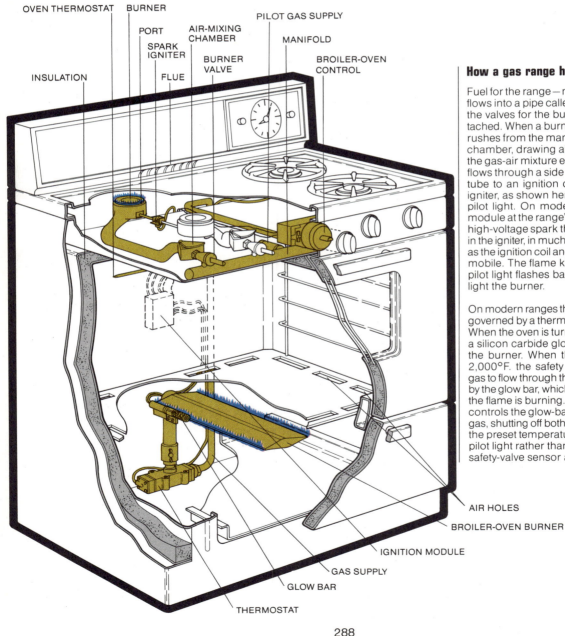

OVEN THERMOSTAT   BURNER
PORT   AIR-MIXING
CHAMBER
SPARK
IGNITER
BURNER
VALVE
FLUE
PILOT GAS SUPPLY
MANIFOLD
BROILER-OVEN
CONTROL
INSULATION

AIR HOLES
BROILER-OVEN BURNER
IGNITION MODULE
GAS SUPPLY
GLOW BAR
THERMOSTAT

How a gas range heats

Fuel for the range — natural or bottled gas — flows into a pipe called a manifold, to which the valves for the burners and oven are attached. When a burner valve is opened, gas rushes from the manifold into an air-mixing chamber, drawing air into the chamber. As the gas-air mixture enters the burner, some flows through a side port and an open flash tube to an ignition device—either a spark igniter, as shown here, or an old-fashioned pilot light. On modern ranges an ignition module at the range's back generates a tiny high-voltage spark that jumps across a gap in the igniter, in much the same arrangement as the ignition coil and spark plug of an automobile. The flame kindled by the igniter or pilot light flashes back through the tube to light the burner.

On modern ranges the broiler-oven burner is governed by a thermostat and a safety valve. When the oven is turned on, electricity heats a silicon carbide glow bar, or coil, beneath the burner. When this bar reaches about 2,000°F. the safety valve opens, allowing gas to flow through the burner and be ignited by the glow bar, which remains hot as long as the flame is burning. The burner thermostat controls the glow-bar circuit and the flow of gas, shutting off both when the oven reaches the preset temperature. Older ranges use a pilot light rather than a glow bar to heat the safety-valve sensor and light the burner.

Adjusting the gas burner

When a burner control knob is set on "HIGH," the outer flame should be blue with a blue-green inner cone about three quarters of an inch long. If the flame does not meet this description, the gas-air mixture may need re-adjusting. Use a wrench to turn the adjusting nut clockwise to increase gas flow, counter-clockwise to decrease it.

To vary the amount of air, loosen the air-mixer adjusting screw and slide the mixer plate to change the size of the opening to the mixing chamber. Improper flame conditions—and how to recognize and cure them—are outlined in the troubleshooting chart on the next page.

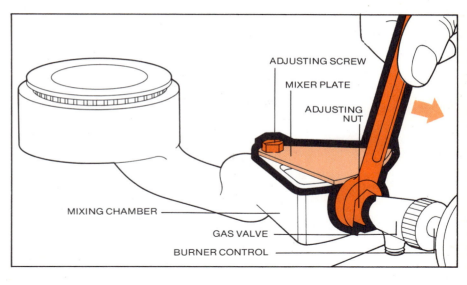

ADJUSTING SCREW

MIXER PLATE

ADJUSTING NUT

MIXING CHAMBER

GAS VALVE

BURNER CONTROL

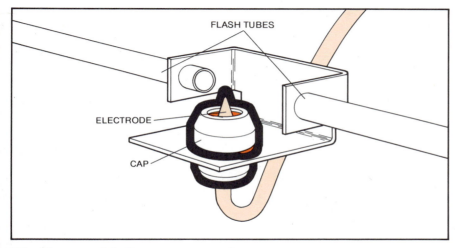

FLASH TUBES

ELECTRODE

CAP

Checking a spark igniter

If the igniter does not spark visibly and emit a rapid clicking sound when the control knob is turned to "LITE," inspect the igniter electrode and cap for dirt. If necessary, clean the parts gently with a soft cloth. Caution: The igniter parts are delicate. Never clean them with liquids or abrasives. If the igniter still does not spark, turn off the power to the range and carefully inspect the wires between the control knob, the ignition module on the back of the range and the igniter. If none appears loose or burned, unplug the igniter and the ignition module and take them to a repair shop for testing.

Adjusting a pilot light

Pilot flames should be three sixteenths of an inch high and blue with a yellow-tinged tip. If one is too small or goes out easily, pull off the pilot shield and clear the opening with a pin. If the flame is still small, turn the adjusting screw counterclockwise.

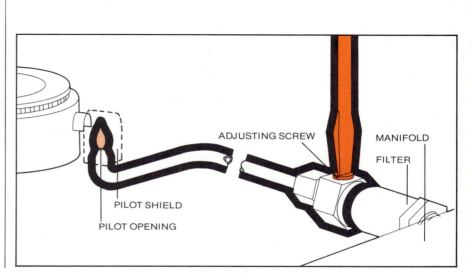

ADJUSTING SCREW

MANIFOLD

FILTER

PILOT SHIELD

PILOT OPENING

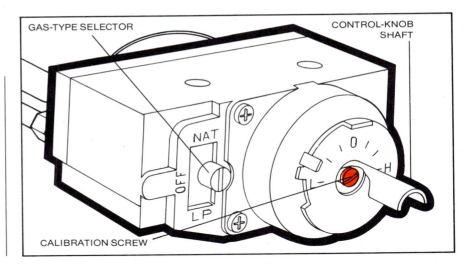

GAS-TYPE SELECTOR

CONTROL-KNOB SHAFT

NAT

OFF

LP

CALIBRATION SCREW

Adjusting the oven thermostat

If the oven bakes too fast or too slow, its thermostat may need recalibration. Place a mercury-filled oven thermostat in the oven and set the oven dial to 350°. If, after 10 to 20 minutes, the thermometer indicates a temperature differing by more than 100 degrees from the dial setting, have the thermostat replaced. If the error is less, pull the control knob off and turn the calibration screw to a lower or higher temperature. A quarter turn makes a change of about 25 degrees on most models, but recheck with the thermometer after adjustment. Do not touch the selector screw that adjusts for natural or LP gas.

Troubleshooting Gas Ranges

Problem	Possible Causes	Solution
Top burner will not light	Defective igniter system Pilot light out Clogged ports in burner or pilot	Replace igniter or module Relight pilot Clean ports with a pin *(page 289)*
Pilot flame goes out	Too much air in fuel mixture Too little gas reaching pilot	Partially close mixer plate *(page 289)* Adjust pilot to three-fourths-inch height *(page 289)*
Top burner flame yellow-tipped	Too little air in mixture	Partially open mixer plate *(page 289)*
Noisy, blowing flame	Too much air in mixture	Partially close mixer plate *(page 289)*
Burner flame too high	Too much air/gas mixture reaching burner	Reduce both air and gas *(page 289)*
Flame produces soot	Too much gas in mixture	Reduce gas in mixture *(page 289)*
Oven does not light	Defective glow bar Pilot light out	Replace glow bar Relight pilot
Oven does not maintain set temperature	Oven thermostat not calibrated properly	Test and recalibrate oven thermostat *(page 289)*, if necessary
"Gas" odor with all pilots lighted	Possible gas leak	Call utility company or serviceman; do not use range until it has been checked

The Electric Range

Benjamin Franklin cooked a turkey with electricity in 1749 in Philadelphia, but the first electric range was not built until 1896. Since then, many small refinements have been added, but its operating principle remains much like that of the heating element in an electric skillet *(page 235)*.

Although some ranges will include complex accessories such as rotisseries and meat-roasting probes, the only complicated standard parts are top-element controls *(page 292)*, which provide any desired degree of heat. All the heating elements in the electric range—including those for the oven and the broiler—are sealed units that are impervious to food and water spillage. But rough usage can cause a short circuit, and the element will fail to heat. They are easy to replace *(pages 292-293)*. Important: Before you work on the elements, turn off power to the range at the service panel.

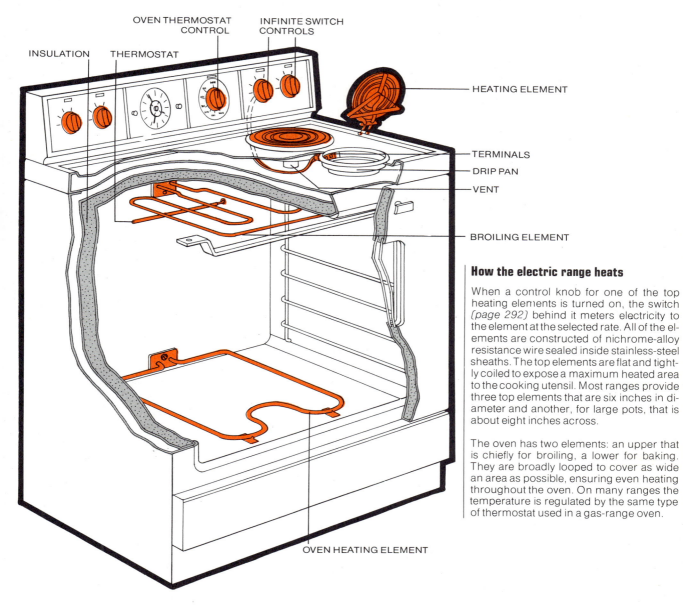

INSULATION

THERMOSTAT

OVEN THERMOSTAT CONTROL

INFINITE SWITCH CONTROLS

HEATING ELEMENT

TERMINALS

DRIP PAN

VENT

BROILING ELEMENT

OVEN HEATING ELEMENT

How the electric range heats

When a control knob for one of the top heating elements is turned on, the switch *(page 292)* behind it meters electricity to the element at the selected rate. All of the elements are constructed of nichrome-alloy resistance wire sealed inside stainless-steel sheaths. The top elements are flat and tightly coiled to expose a maximum heated area to the cooking utensil. Most ranges provide three top elements that are six inches in diameter and another, for large pots, that is about eight inches across.

The oven has two elements: an upper that is chiefly for broiling, a lower for baking. They are broadly looped to cover as wide an area as possible, ensuring even heating throughout the oven. On many ranges the temperature is regulated by the same type of thermostat used in a gas-range oven.

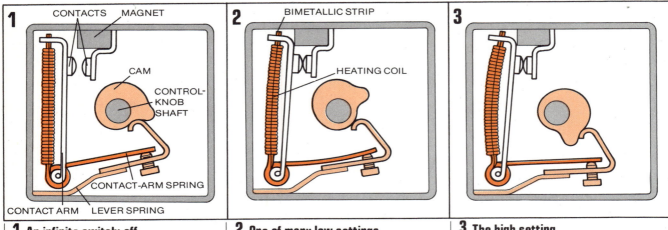

1 CONTACTS   MAGNET   CAM   CONTROL-KNOB SHAFT   CONTACT-ARM SPRING   CONTACT ARM   LEVER SPRING

2 BIMETALLIC STRIP   HEATING COIL

3

1 An infinite switch: off

With two springs, a magnet, a cam, and a bimetallic strip inside a heating coil, this infinite switch gives completely variable heat adjustment instead of a few settings. When the control knob is at the off position, the cam presses its slimmest part on a lever spring. The lever spring pushes up the contact-arm spring with maximum force, pivoting the contact arm left to open the circuit. The cam lets the springs push hard enough to hold the contacts apart despite the attraction of a magnet.

2 One of many low settings

As the knob turns, fatter parts of the cam bear on the lever spring, decreasing leverage. The magnet overcomes the spring, closing the contacts to the heating element. Current also flows through the heating coil around the bimetallic strip, heating and warping it slightly. The strip bends the arm against the magnetic attraction—adding more separating force to the spring leverage. At some point—depending on how the cam adjusts spring pressure—the magnet is overcome and the contacts open.

3 The high setting

When the knob is set to the high position, the thickest part of the cam bears on the lever spring, pressing it down so far that it exerts no leverage at all on the contact arm. The magnet holds the contacts together, and only the bimetallic strip exerts any sort of separating force. The strip bends, but by itself it is unable to warp the movable arm sufficiently to overcome the pull of the magnet and thereby open the contacts. At this setting, the element stays on and reaches its highest temperature.

Testing and replacing a top element

If a top element on an electric range does not heat properly, test it by removing the element from its terminal block. Also remove another element of the same size that is working properly. Ranges with infinite switches *(above)* usually have elements with two terminals. Some can simply be unplugged *(right)*; others have terminal wires held by screws *(left)*. Ranges with other types of switches often have elements with three or more wires; before disconnecting these, make a diagram showing which colored wire goes to which terminal.

Attach the suspect element to the terminal block of the properly operating element, and turn on the switch. If the element still does not heat, it should be replaced. If the element heats, its own terminal block, wiring or switch is faulty. Call a serviceman and have them checked.

WIRES FROM TERMINAL BLOCK

TERMINAL BLOCK

Removing an oven heating element

If the top burners work but the oven or broiler will not heat, the problem could be an element, the thermostat, the timer or even the wiring. Remove the element by taking off its front support bracket and un-screwing its rear mounting bracket from the back of the oven. Then pull on the element gently to drag out the wires leading to the terminals, and detach them.

Take the element to a repair shop for test-ing. If the element passes the test, the ther-mostat or the wiring is defective and must be replaced by a serviceman. If the element is faulty, you can replace it yourself. When connecting the new element, be sure to feed the wires carefully through the open-ings in the back of the oven.

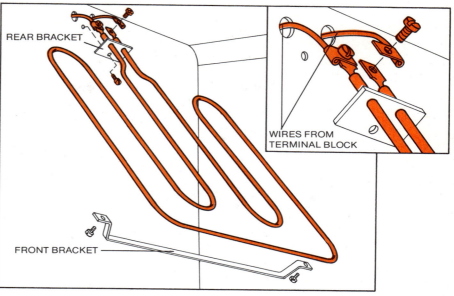

REAR BRACKET

WIRES FROM
TERMINAL BLOCK

FRONT BRACKET

Troubleshooting Electric Ranges

Problem	Possible Causes	Solution
No elements heat	Power not reaching range	Check fuse or circuit breaker
A top element does not heat	Defective top element	Test element (*opposite*) and replace if necessary
	Faulty terminal block, wiring or switch	Call a serviceman
One rear unit will not heat	Oven set for cleaning cycle	Because vapors vented during cleaning get a rear unit very hot, it will not function when the oven is set to clean
Oven does not heat	Faulty oven element	Remove element (*above*) and have it tested
	Automatic timer improperly set	Reset automatic timer to "MANUAL" and advance time-of-day clock 24 hours
	Defective thermostat or wiring	Call a serviceman
Broiler does not heat	Faulty broiler element	Remove element and have it tested
	Defective thermostat or wiring	Call a serviceman
Oven does not brown food	Faulty broiler element	Remove element and have it tested
Oven does not maintain set temperature	Oven thermostat improperly calibrated	Test and recalibrate oven thermostat (*page 289*)
Oven lamp will not light	Lamp burned out	Replace with bulb especially designed for use in oven

The Microwave Oven: Cooking by Radar

The fact that electromagnetic waves can generate heat has long been known; after all, sunlight, a form of electromagnetic energy, warms materials it shines on. But it was not until 1946 that the idea of cooking with radar first dawned on an engineer who proceeded to use the emissions of a radar tube to make popcorn.

Microwave ovens, unlike gas and electric ranges, which create heat and transfer it to the food, generate electromagnetic waves that oscillate much more rapidly than ordinary radio waves—closer to the frequency of light waves. These microwaves magnetically agitate the food molecules, causing them to heat faster than an ordinary oven can. Since the microwave-induced heat penetrates only about three quarters of an inch, many foods must stand briefly outside the oven after exposure to the microwaves to cook through, and may need browning by conventional cooking. Because microwaves can damage human tissue, follow manufacturers' precautions.

WAVE GUIDE

ANTENNA

CAPACITOR

STIRRER

LATCH

TRANSFORMER

COOLING FAN

FUSE

MAGNETRON

TIMER

Inside a microwave oven

The oven, turned on by setting the timer, starts only when the oven door has been closed and latched. House current flows to a transformer to boost the normal 120 volts to 4,000 volts. Then a capacitor—which, along with an element in the magnetron base, passes current in one direction only —changes the AC to DC. The current next enters the magnetron *(opposite)*, which generates high-frequency electromagnetic waves. From the magnetron, the waves go into a wave guide, a rectangular conduit that channels them toward the oven.

As the microwaves enter the oven, a fan-like mechanism called a stirrer bounces the waves down into the oven *(opposite)* where they are then absorbed by the food, causing it to cook.

The magnetron is protected from overheating by a fan and a thermostatic switch. A fuse in the power line protects against electrical overload.

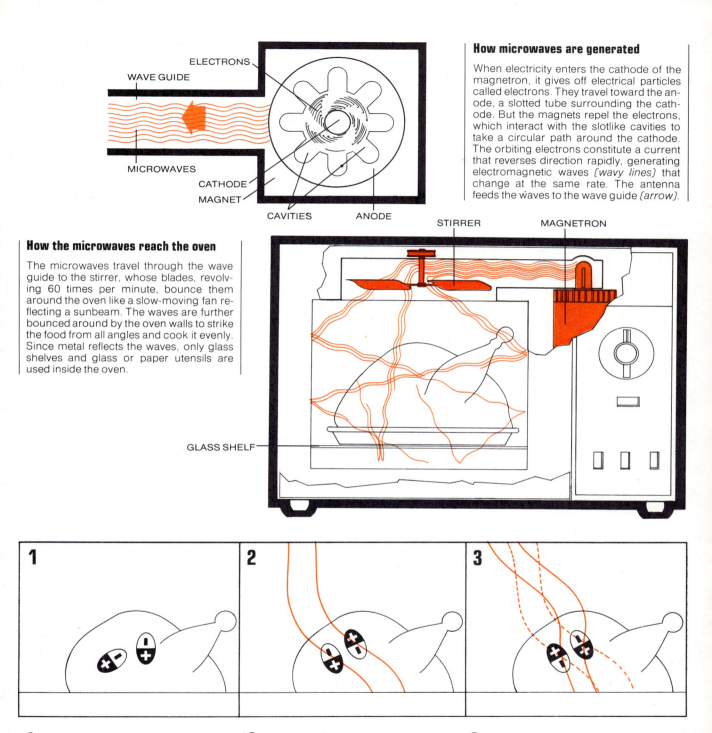

How microwaves are generated

When electricity enters the cathode of the magnetron, it gives off electrical particles called electrons. They travel toward the anode, a slotted tube surrounding the cathode. But the magnets repel the electrons, which interact with the slotlike cavities to take a circular path around the cathode. The orbiting electrons constitute a current that reverses direction rapidly, generating electromagnetic waves (*wavy lines*) that change at the same rate. The antenna feeds the waves to the wave guide (*arrow*).

ELECTRONS
WAVE GUIDE
MICROWAVES
CATHODE
MAGNET
CAVITIES **ANODE**
STIRRER **MAGNETRON**
GLASS SHELF

How the microwaves reach the oven

The microwaves travel through the wave guide to the stirrer, whose blades, revolving 60 times per minute, bounce them around the oven like a slow-moving fan reflecting a sunbeam. The waves are further bounced around by the oven walls to strike the food from all angles and cook it evenly. Since metal reflects the waves, only glass shelves and glass or paper utensils are used inside the oven.

1 Before cooking: random molecules

Ordinarily, the molecules (*black and white ovals*) in a turkey—or any other food—are arranged at random. They contain positive and negative electrical charges, however, which interact with the electromagnetism of microwaves, causing the molecules to turn and heat by friction.

2 Bringing molecules into order

When the oven is turned on, the positive and negative electric charges of the food molecules respond to the electromagnetism of the microwaves like iron filings to a bar magnet. The molecules line up so that their charges lie parallel to the lines of force in the magnetic field (*wavy lines*).

3 Turning molecules around

As the microwaves' magnetic field changes direction (*wavy solid and dashed lines*), the food molecules move to keep themselves lined up. The microwaves reverse direction 4.9 billion times a second; the food molecules oscillate equally fast, creating friction that causes them to heat.

Why You Should—and Can—
Adjust Your Own System

In all the world, no one has quite the same heating conditions that you do. Whether your house is too warm, too cold or just right, it is unique. Even identical houses in a tract, equipped with identical heating systems, heat differently. All sorts of things affect your comfort and the amount of fuel you consume to achieve it. The number of lights you keep on, for example. The amount of baking and cooking you do. The size of your family. The house location and exposure.

Even a computer could not take into account all the factors involved. So heating systems are designed by formula—and by some educated guesswork. When a heating contractor installs one, he considers the number of rooms and their size, and whether the house is insulated or not, but usually gives only a cursory glance at such factors as type of construction and window area. Then he consults a formula to determine how much heat the house needs. Heat is measured in British thermal units, or B.T.U.s —a B.T.U. being the amount of heat necessary to raise the temperature of one pound of water $1°F$. Heating plants are rated according to the number of B.T.U.s they can produce per hour. For a typical eight-room house, the heating-plant capacity may range, depending largely on the climate of the region, from 80,000 to 140,000 B.T.U.s per hour.

Most contractors are inclined to lean toward what they consider the safe side by installing a unit with higher capacity than the formula calls for. But an oversized heating plant is wasteful. It generates a lot of heat quickly and shuts off. While it is off, the combustion chamber and the pipes or ducts get cool; when it starts up again, it must use extra fuel to reheat these components. Heating is also uneven: rooms get too hot, then too cold.

The most efficient heating plant is one that has just the right hourly B.T.U. capacity and runs almost continuously. It provides an even flow of warmth to all parts of the system and, by not having to reheat itself intermittently, saves fuel. A plant with a woefully inadequate B.T.U. capacity is, of course, a homeowner's nightmare. His only recourse is to get a bigger plant or install auxiliary space heaters.

But even a heating system that is exactly the right size rarely heats all rooms equally. A perfect balance is impossible, but many systems can be regulated to achieve fairly uniform comfort. It takes a lot of living with any system to achieve this goal. Because of the many variables involved, it is up to you to determine whether the system is doing its job—unless you want a heating engineer for a house guest all winter. The first step toward diagnosing problems—and solving some yourself—is to get acquainted with the principal kinds of systems and their components.

Direct heat and central heat

Some 22 million American homes have a direct-heat system—a throwback to the era of fireplaces and potbellied stoves. The heating apparatus exudes warmth directly to the space where it is located. Electricity provides a particularly comfortable source of direct heat. Resistance wires, similar in principle to the elements in a toaster, run through baseboard units *(pages 324-325)* or may be strung inside walls, ceilings or floors; individual thermostats control the temperature in each room.

The great majority of homes, however, have central-heat systems. These systems are popular largely because they are more efficient and can be located in an out-of-the-way place, yet can heat the entire house. Central systems are made up of several distinct units:
■ HEAT PRODUCER. This may be an oil, gas or wood burner, an electric heater or a heat pump *(page 329)*, alone or in combination.

■ HEAT EXCHANGER. This unit is called a furnace if it heats air, a boiler if it heats water or makes steam. The air, water or steam goes through passageways inside the exchanger that keep it separated from the combustion gases of the burner; the gases are expelled through a flue. Any of these heat exchangers can be hooked up to any of the several kinds of heat producers.

■ HEAT DISTRIBUTOR. There are three types, one for each type of exchanger. In a warm-air system, the air is drawn into the exchanger by a large fan (a blower) and sent through ducts to warm-air registers. In a hot-water system, water is forced through the exchanger by a pump (a circulator) and sent through pipes to convectors, a type of radiator. Steam rises under its own pressure from the exchanger, going through pipes to radiators.
■ CONTROLS. Most homes have one thermostat in the living area to turn the heating plant on and off. But some achieve closer control with several, and a few installations sense outside temperature in order to respond more to weather changes.

The most common problem with central systems is uneven heat: rooms nearest the heat producer get too hot, those farther away never get warm enough. Since tinkering with one part of a system may affect other parts, adjustments may take days or weeks; so this is primarily a job for the homeowner.

Steam systems are least amenable to adjustment, but the heat of individual radiators can be regulated by turning the dial on each air vent *(page 323)*. If your vents are not adjustable, change them; they are not expensive.

Hot-water systems are frequently divided into zones for different parts of the house; temperature in each zone is regulated by a separate thermostat *(page 316)*. Other systems may have balancing valves in the basement piping; for a full flow of water, turn a screw in each valve so that the screw slot is parallel with the pipe; turn the screw at an angle to restrict flow. In some systems, the convectors in each room have water-inlet valves; open or close them in order to adjust the flow of warm water into the convector.

Warm-air systems offer the most possibilities for adjustment. The basic method is to position dampers inside the warm-air ducts to regulate air flow (page 312). Generally the damper controlling air flow to the most distant room is fully open, the one nearest the furnace almost closed. Adjust the air flow to all rooms by speeding up or slowing down the blower. On many units, this is done by adjusting the blower pulley to change the ratio between the motor drive and the blower (page 314). On other models, speed is regulated by moving a switch or by changing the blower's electrical connections. Lowering the temperature at which the blower turns on starts warm air circulating sooner and saves fuel by using all the furnace heat.

Improving the efficiency of any heating system is important in times of soaring fuel costs. Some of the most effective steps:
■ Insulate the attic. Six inches of insulation can cut fuel consumption up to 25 per cent. Ten inches will work even better in cold regions.
■ Weather-strip doors and windows.
■ Add storm doors and windows; in cold areas they will pay for themselves in a few years.
■ When a fireplace is not in use, keep the damper closed; an open chimney wastes heat.
■ Put heavy draperies on doors and windows, and keep them closed at night and when rooms are not occupied.
■ Lower your thermostat gradually, a degree at a time, to accustom yourself to a lower temperature. You may actually find that you are more comfortable with less heat.

What the Chimney Does

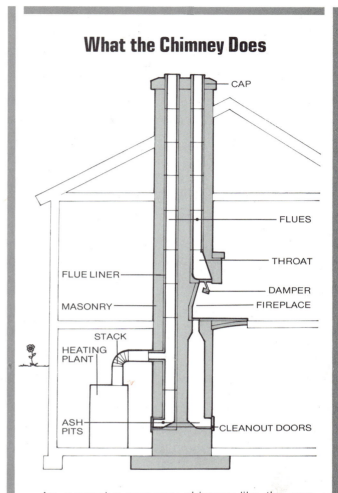

An expansive masonry chimney like the one above is a cheery anachronism in a modern heating system—metal stovepipes would be less durable but equally useful. The chimney flues dispose of combustion wastes—carbon dioxide, nitrogen, sulfur dioxide, water vapor and carbon monoxide. By channeling the warm, rising gases, the flues create a draft that pulls air over the fire. For the powerful draft an open fire needs, the fireplace requires a sloped back and a stepped throat controlled by a damper.

Each heat source needs its own flue, but one chimney can have several flues. A flue liner keeps fumes from seeping through surrounding masonry, which is protected from water by a cap. Ashes and soot are removed through cleanout doors.

THERMOSTATS

A house thermostat is a sly switch. Once it is set at the desired temperature, the thermostat keeps the room very close to that temperature by switching a heating system on and off—and by cheating. The cheating is necessary because at least a degree and a half separates the on and off temperatures. And after the system has been switched off, it continues to produce some heat, so that room temperature still rises. This inertia effect, when added to the temperature difference between on and off, can result, at times, in uncomfortably large swings in room temperature.

Cheating limits the swing by reducing both effects. When the thermostat starts the heating system, it also starts an electric heater, called an anticipator, near its temperature-sensing element. The anticipator heats the thermostat faster than the heating system heats the room. Before room temperature rises much, the temperature in the thermostat reaches the heating system's turnoff point —anticipating the room temperature's rise. The heat in the system continues to raise room temperature, but little over the desired level.

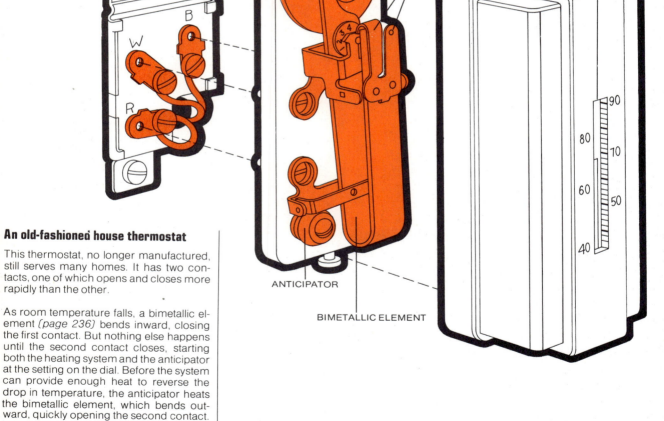

An old-fashioned house thermostat

This thermostat, no longer manufactured, still serves many homes. It has two contacts, one of which opens and closes more rapidly than the other.

As room temperature falls, a bimetallic element *(page 236)* bends inward, closing the first contact. But nothing else happens until the second contact closes, starting both the heating system and the anticipator at the setting on the dial. Before the system can provide enough heat to reverse the drop in temperature, the anticipator heats the bimetallic element, which bends outward, quickly opening the second contact. It does not open the first contact—to turn off the system—until the temperature is slightly above the dial setting.

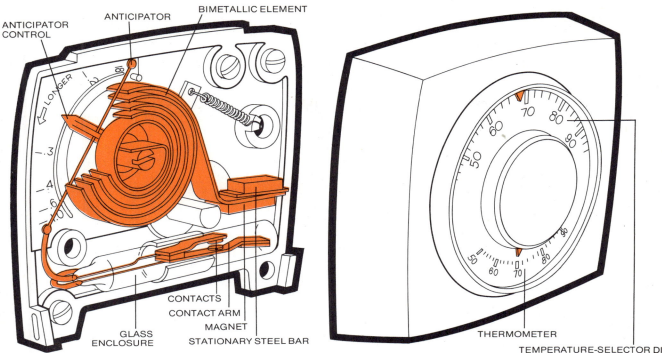

ANTICIPATOR
CONTROL

ANTICIPATOR

BIMETALLIC ELEMENT

LONGER

CONTACTS
CONTACT ARM
MAGNET
STATIONARY STEEL BAR

GLASS
ENCLOSURE

THERMOMETER

TEMPERATURE-SELECTOR DIAL

A modern house thermostat

Most thermostats currently manufactured have bimetallic elements in coil form and contacts sealed in glass to protect them from dirt. As the room cools, the bimetallic element in the thermostat shown above begins to uncoil, until, at the desired temperature, the uncoiling force breaks the hold between a stationary steel bar and a mag-

net on the end of the coil. The magnet drops near the glass enclosure, where it can abruptly pull up the contact arm inside the tube and close the contacts sharply. The closed contacts complete a circuit to the heating system and the anticipator. The anticipator heats the bimetallic element and it begins to coil. When the element's coiling force is strong enough to break the magnet's hold on the contact arm, the arm

drops to break the circuit and turn off the system. Simultaneously, the magnet snaps upward onto the stationary bar, which holds it in place, and keeps the contacts open until the room cools off again.

The anticipator control adjusts anticipation time by regulating the heat produced. It is a movable contact that determines how much resistance wire is in the circuit.

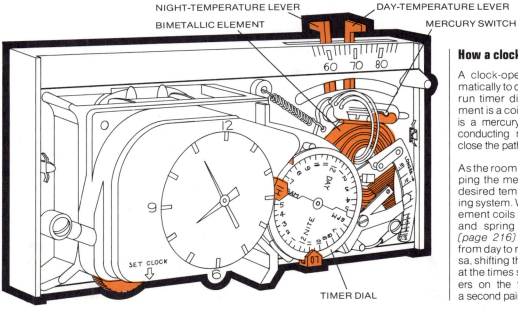

NIGHT-TEMPERATURE LEVER

DAY-TEMPERATURE LEVER

BIMETALLIC ELEMENT

MERCURY SWITCH

60 70 80

SET CLOCK

TIMER DIAL

How a clock thermostat works

A clock-operated thermostat shifts automatically to day or night settings as a clock-run timer dial rotates. The bimetallic element is a coil, like the one above. At its end is a mercury switch—a bulb of electricity-conducting mercury that tilts to open or close the path between two terminals.

As the room cools, the element uncoils, tipping the mercury-switch bulb until, at the desired temperature, it turns on the heating system. When temperature rises, the element coils and tips the switch off. A cam and spring connected to a clock-timer (page 216) automatically rotate the coil from day to night temperature and vice versa, shifting the switch position accordingly, at the times set by the "HI" and "LO" pointers on the timer. Some thermostats have a second pair of settings for daytime use.

Maintenance and Calibration

In old-fashioned thermostats *(page 300)* and some modern ones, the contacts are exposed to air and may become dirty. Dirt can prevent contacts from closing completely—and thus prevent a thermostat from turning on a heating system. If you have an exposed-contact thermostat, you should clean the contacts periodically. Even if contacts are kept clean, they wear after long service and no longer close properly; then the thermostat has to be replaced.

Because this older type of thermostat is no longer made, consult your heating-supply dealer about which modern model you need; it must be of the same voltage rating as the old, and adaptable to the burner's stack control *(pages 304-305)* or gas control *(pages 308-309)*. Procedures for cleaning and replacing old thermostats are described below.

The contacts of most thermostats now being made are sealed in glass enclosures and cannot become dirty. But the wall on which a thermostat is mounted may be jarred and the thermostat thrown out of calibration. In that event, the thermostat's contacts will not close when room temperature drops to the preset point. But with care, you can calibrate a modern thermostat yourself *(opposite)*.

DOLLAR BILL

CONTACT POINTS

Cleaning an open-contact thermostat

The points of an open-contact thermostat should be cleaned at the start of each heating season. The first step in the procedure is to loosen the body screw at the bottom of the thermostat. Then pull the thermostat cover toward you and lift it upward to remove it. Now lightly blow through the contact points, standing far enough away so that you will not deposit vapor from your breath on them. Then rub remaining dirt off the contact surfaces by sliding paper between them—a crisp dollar bill or an index card. Do not use sandpaper: its abrasiveness will wear down the contacts. Replace the cover and tighten the body screw.

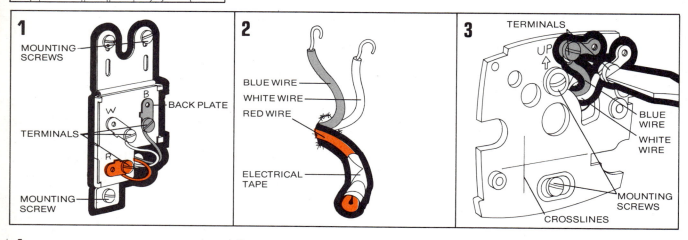

1 Replacing an old thermostat

Shut off power to the burner. Take off the thermostat cover. Remove the thermostat body by unfastening its mounting screws *(above)*. The back plate and wiring to the burner will be exposed. Commonly, there are terminals labeled "R," "W" and "B" for red, white and blue wires to the burner.

2 Preparing the wiring

Detach the wires and tape them temporarily to the wall. Unscrew the back plate. Cover the red wire's end with electrical tape, since you will not need it in wiring the new thermostat. Modern heating thermostats make use of only two wires.

3 Mounting the new thermostat

Mount the new back plate with the upper mounting screw. Attach the white and blue wires. Color coding can be ignored. Use a level to get the back plate crosslines exactly vertical and horizontal. Put in the lower mounting screw, mount the body, tighten the contact screws and snap on the cover.

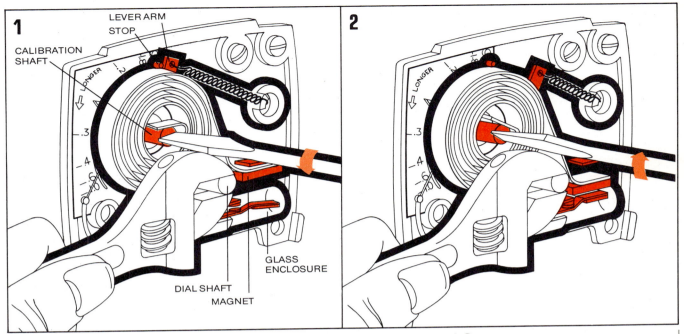

1 Calibrating a thermostat

Before calibration, the thermostat's internal temperature must be stabilized: the thermostat should be in the off position at least 10 minutes with no heat source nearby. Then set the temperature-selector dial at the room temperature. Remove the cover.

Hold the dial shaft with a wrench to make sure the shaft does not rotate. With a screwdriver, turn the calibration shaft counterclockwise until the lever arm touches the stop. Continue to turn the shaft counterclockwise until the magnet remains away from the glass enclosure when the screwdriver pressure is released.

2 Setting the snap-action point

Slowly turn the calibration shaft clockwise until the magnet snaps against the glass enclosure. The thermostat now is calibrated and, in operation, the magnet will snap against the glass to close the contacts at the set temperature. Replace the cover.

How to Check for a Defective Thermostat

If your room temperature drops 5° or more below the point at which you have set the thermostat and your heating system does not start, the first thing you should do is check the heating system (see instructions on pages 305, 309, 313, 315, 319, 323 and 325). If you find nothing wrong there, test the thermostat.

Remove the thermostat cover and body from the wall, leaving in place only the wiring leading to the burner, and the back plate. Check the thermostat body and the back plate to make perfectly sure that there are no broken wires and that all of the wires are tightly secured under their terminal screws. If your heating system has an open-contact thermostat, clean the contacts at this time.

If you still have not located the source of your trouble, take a five-inch length of insulated wire and strip half an inch of insulation from each end of it. Holding only the insulated portion of the wire, touch the bare ends to the terminals on the back plate. If the thermostat has a three-wire connection, carefully push the contacts closed with a block of wood. If the burner goes on, the thermostat is defective and must be replaced. But if the burner does not go on, the problem is elsewhere. Remount the thermostat and call your serviceman.

OIL BURNERS

Soon after World War I, the oil burner began to capture the attention of America with a promise of clean, dependable, fully automatic central heating —no coal to shovel, no dirty supply bin, no ashes to take out. By 1928, half a million homeowners had converted their coal furnaces to oil heat by adding a burner and rebuilding the combustion chamber. Many of those old conversion units still work faithfully and well—along with some 12 million oil burners of more modern design used in warm-air *(pages 310-315),* hot-water *(pages 316-321)* and steam *(pages 322-323)* systems.

The high-pressure burner used in most homes does not simply burn oil. It prepares a mixture of air and oil (usually about 16 parts of air to one part of oil), sets this mixture aflame with a powerful high-voltage spark, and burns it in an enclosed combustion chamber. In this chamber, a continuous swirl of yellow flame reaches temperatures as high as 3,200°, providing enough heat from a single gallon of oil to warm a small house for two hours in winter, or to make available a two-day supply of hot water in the summer.

An oil-fired heating plant

The oil burner mixes oil and air, ignites the mixture within an air tube *(opposite)* and burns it in the combustion chamber. To make the fuel mixture, the motor drives a fan that draws air through the air shutter, and a pump draws oil through a filtered fuel line. To ignite it, the normal 120-volt current is stepped up to 10,000 volts by a transformer. A master switch turns the burner on and off manually, but if ignition fails, a heat-sensitive device in the stack control or a light-detecting cell in the burner shuts off the motor. An automatic draft regulator monitors the flow of exhaust gases through the stack and up the chimney.

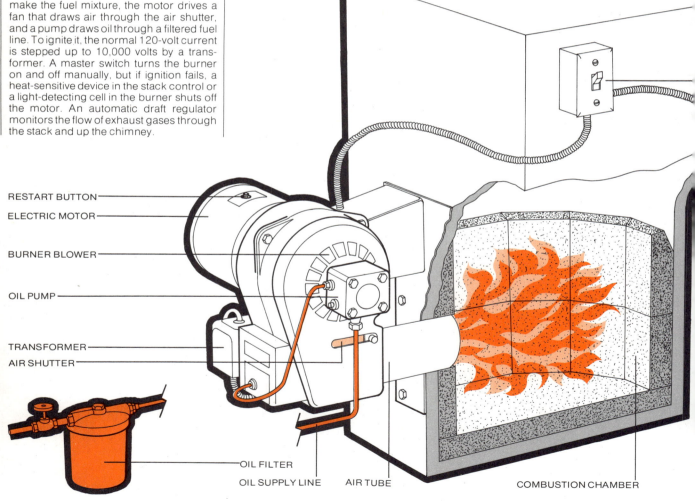

RESTART BUTTON
ELECTRIC MOTOR
BURNER BLOWER
OIL PUMP
TRANSFORMER
AIR SHUTTER
OIL FILTER
OIL SUPPLY LINE
AIR TUBE
COMBUSTION CHAMBER

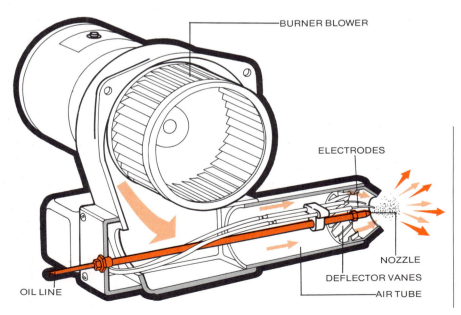

DRAFT REGULATOR

STACK

STACK CONTROL

RESET BUTTON

MASTER SWITCH

Starting a Balky Burner

If your oil burner stops when it should not or fails to start when it should, run through this checklist before calling in a serviceman.

■ Check the thermostat setting. As a temporary measure, try resetting it at least 5° higher than the room temperature.
■ Make sure the master switch is on. Important: Some burners have two master switches, one at the burner and another at a convenient spot like the head of the basement stairs; check both.
■ Check for either a burned-out fuse or a tripped circuit breaker.
■ Check your tank to be sure you are not out of oil; if it has no gauge, open the filler pipe and insert a long stick.
■ Press the reset button on the ignition safety control on the stack or the burner.
■ Press the restart button on the motor.
■ Refer to the appropriate troubleshooting chart for your type of heating system—warm-air *(pages 313, 315)*, hot-water *(page 319)* or steam *(page 323)*—for malfunctions that may affect your oil burner.

BURNER BLOWER

ELECTRODES

NOZZLE

DEFLECTOR VANES

AIR TUBE

OIL LINE

How the burner works

Outside air *(curved arrow)*, forced into the air tube by the burner blower, passes through deflector vanes that form the air stream into a rapidly swirling spiral. At the same time, the pump pulls oil from the tank through the oil line to the nozzle, from which it emerges in a cone-shaped spray. At the nozzle, the oil and air combine into a highly flammable mixture that is ignited when the burner first goes on by a high-voltage spark that flashes between two electrodes. The spark is required only for starting; thereafter the flame *(colored arrows)* continues on its own.

Burner Maintenance

An oil burner runs for about 1,500 hours during an average heating season, year in and year out. Breakdowns are rare. But steady operation may hide waste and inefficiency. Unless the burner and the related components of the heating system are properly adjusted, unnecessary fuel is consumed, soot is created, heat output is diminished—and even the electric bills are inflated.

An annual inspection and routine maintenance by a professional are almost essential before the start of each heating season, and this care is generally included in the service contracts most homeowners sign up for. The checklist opposite lists the chores that a serviceman can be expected to perform in the course of his annual inspection.

The checklist also includes some simple procedures the homeowner can perform between inspections to keep his oil burner running smoothly and to remedy such heat-wasting defects as an improperly adjusted draft regulator *(opposite)*, a leaky mounting plate *(below, left)* or a sooty stack control *(below, right)*.

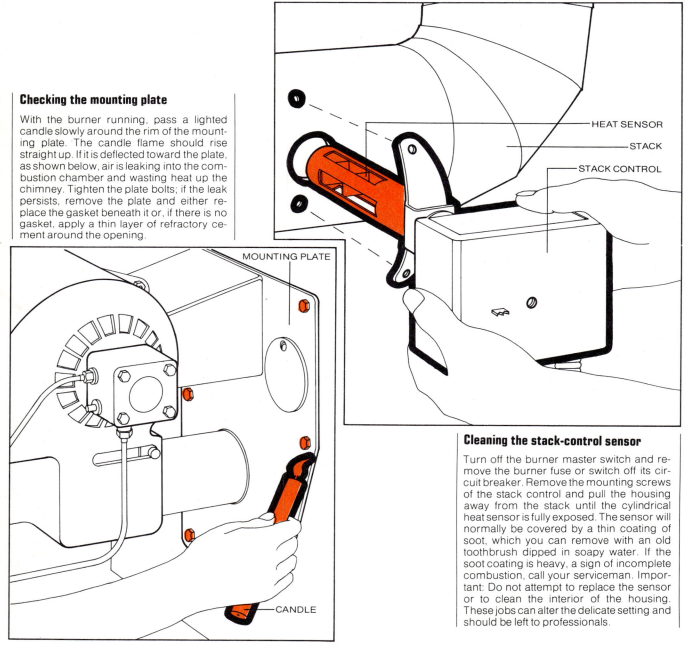

Checking the mounting plate

With the burner running, pass a lighted candle slowly around the rim of the mounting plate. The candle flame should rise straight up. If it is deflected toward the plate, as shown below, air is leaking into the combustion chamber and wasting heat up the chimney. Tighten the plate bolts; if the leak persists, remove the plate and either replace the gasket beneath it or, if there is no gasket, apply a thin layer of refractory cement around the opening.

MOUNTING PLATE

CANDLE

HEAT SENSOR

STACK

STACK CONTROL

Cleaning the stack-control sensor

Turn off the burner master switch and remove the burner fuse or switch off its circuit breaker. Remove the mounting screws of the stack control and pull the housing away from the stack until the cylindrical heat sensor is fully exposed. The sensor will normally be covered by a thin coating of soot, which you can remove with an old toothbrush dipped in soapy water. If the soot coating is heavy, a sign of incomplete combustion, call your serviceman. Important: Do not attempt to replace the sensor or to clean the interior of the housing. These jobs can alter the delicate setting and should be left to professionals.

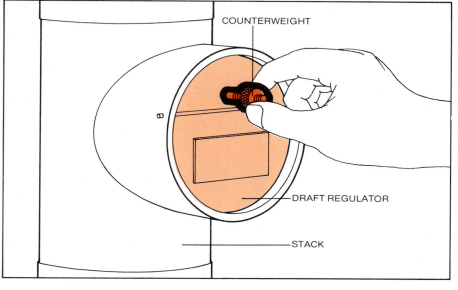

COUNTERWEIGHT

B

DRAFT REGULATOR

STACK

Adjusting the draft regulator

The draft regulator, normally closed when the burner is off, should automatically open an inch or two to admit air to the chimney when the burner is running. The serviceman will adjust the regulator as part of his yearly routine. But expansion-contraction movements and vibration during the heating season may throw it off.

Rattling or soot accumulations are signs of maladjustment—on this system, screw a counterweight inward to increase draft, outward to cut draft.

Oil-Burner Maintenance Checklist

You should have a serviceman inspect and adjust your oil burner once a year. Between his visits you can make certain routine checks and adjustments yourself, if necessary. The serviceman will generally do the following:

■ Clean or replace the burner nozzle and its attached oil strainer.

■ Clean or replace the oil-supply-line filter and its gasket seal.

■ Clean or replace the electrodes; adjust the electrode spark gap.

■ Clean the air tube and adjust the air shutter.

■ Clean the blower and its housing.

■ Clean the transformer terminals.

■ Lubricate the motor, if necessary.

■ Check and clean the oil pump.

■ Clean and test the stack control.

■ Check and adjust the draft regulator.

■ Check and adjust thermostats, and all boiler and furnace controls.

These are some additional maintenance steps that you can perform routinely between inspections or whenever you suspect a problem:

■ If the motor has oil cups, lubricate it between inspections at the intervals—usually twice yearly —called for by the owner's manual. Use a few drops of electric-motor oil—not all-purpose oil.

■ Clean the fan blower at least once between inspections. Turn off the master switch and remove dust from the blades by inserting a thin percolator brush through the air-intake openings. (NOTE: On some burners, the housing swings up to expose the blower for cleaning.)

■ Check for air leaks around the mounting plate *(opposite, left)* and seal if necessary.

■ Remove the stack control at least once between inspections and clean soot from the heat sensor *(opposite, right)*.

■ With the stack control removed, disassemble the stack and remove the soot and rust by rapping each section sharply against a floor covered with newspapers.

■ After you have replaced the stack and the stack control, reseal the chimney connection with refractory cement.

■ Step outside occasionally when the burner is running and look at your chimney. Black smoke is a sign of incomplete combustion. If you spot it, call your serviceman.

GAS BURNERS

It was not until after World War II that transcontinental pipelines brought natural gas to nearly all parts of the United States, but since then upward of 35 million gas burners have been installed for home heating systems—twice the number that have oil burners. As a fuel, gas is more expensive than oil in many areas. But a gas burner is less costly to install than an oil burner; gas heat pollutes less than oil heat; and gas delivery does not depend on a truck's ability to brave a blizzard.

Most gas burners consume natural gas mixed with air in the ratio of about 1 cubic foot of gas to 16 cubic feet of air. The efficiency of the burner depends on the mixture, which a serviceman should adjust. Most other problems involve the pilot and its thermocouple safety device; they can generally be corrected by the homeowner.

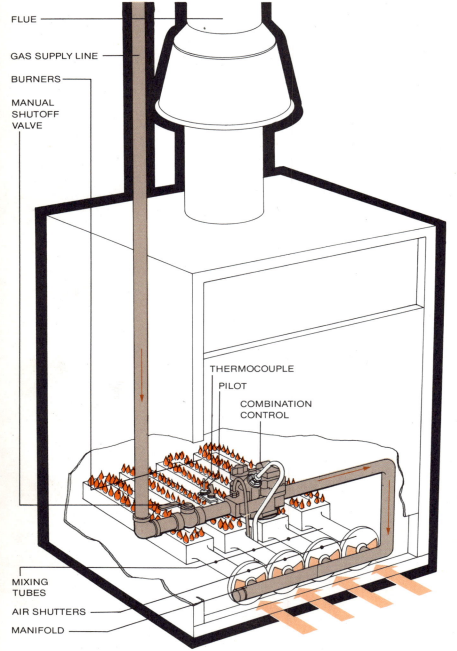

FLUE

GAS SUPPLY LINE

BURNERS

MANUAL
SHUTOFF
VALVE

THERMOCOUPLE

PILOT

COMBINATION
CONTROL

MIXING
TUBES

AIR SHUTTERS

MANIFOLD

How a gas burner works

When the contacts of a house thermostat close *(page 300)*, current runs to a solenoid *(pages 178-179)*, opening up a diaphragm valve in a combination control. Gas flows *(small arrows)* from a supply line past a manual shutoff, through a manifold, then to tubes that mix it with air *(broad arrows)*. The mixture goes to burners where, ignited by a pilot, it makes heat that a heat exchanger (not shown) turns to steam, hot water or warm air; wastes go up a flue. The thermocouple and another solenoid stop gas flow if the pilot goes out.

Adjusting the pilot flame

A thermocouple *(left and opposite, top left)* shuts off gas if the pilot light goes out. But the pilot will not stay lighted if it is too low to heat the thermocouple. In the model below, the pilot flame may be raised or lowered by taking off the screw cap and carefully turning the adjustment screw on the combination control to regulate flow *(arrow)* in the pilot supply line. Models vary: follow the manufacturer's manual. Pilot reignition procedures also vary; they are on a metal tag attached to, or near, a gas cock on the combination control *(below)*.

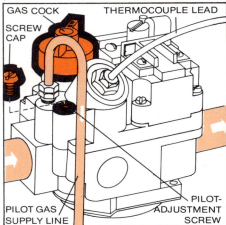

GAS COCK

SCREW
CAP

THERMOCOUPLE LEAD

PILOT GAS
SUPPLY LINE

PILOT-
ADJUSTMENT
SCREW

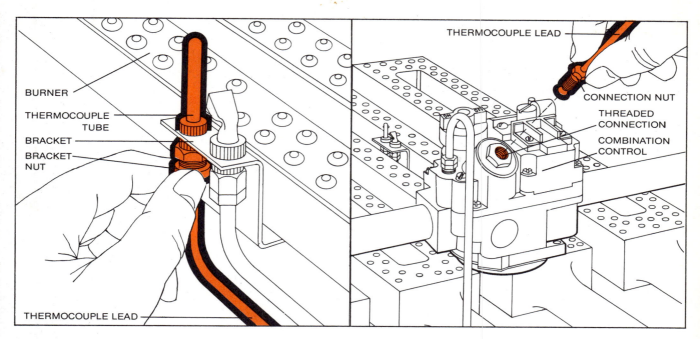

BURNER

THERMOCOUPLE TUBE

BRACKET

BRACKET NUT

THERMOCOUPLE LEAD

THERMOCOUPLE LEAD

CONNECTION NUT

THREADED CONNECTION

COMBINATION CONTROL

Replacing a thermocouple

If a pilot does not stay lighted after adjustment of the flame, the thermocouple may be at fault. A thermocouple *[page 259]* is a small electric generator contained in a steel tube that sits in the pilot flame *[above]*. Over several years, the end of the thermocouple in the steel tube may deteriorate from heat.

And the copper lead, which runs out of the pilot assembly into the combination control *[above, right]*, may become brittle and break when even slightly jarred.

To replace a faulty thermocouple, take off the lead to the thermocouple. Unscrew the connection nut inside the threaded connection to the lead at the combination control. Unscrew the bracket nut under the pilot bracket. Next, insert the steel tube of a new thermocouple in the bracket, then slide the bracket nut up the new lead and screw it tight. Clean and dry the combination control's threaded connection. Slide the connection nut to the end of the copper lead; screw it into the threaded connection. Tighten it a quarter turn past finger-tight.

Troubleshooting Gas Burners

Problem	Possible Causes	Solution
No heat	Power not reaching burner	Check for blown fuse or tripped circuit breaker
	Pilot out	Relight pilot following instructions on burner
Pilot does not light	Pilot opening dirty	Pull off pilot shield, and clean opening with thin copper wire
	Loose or defective thermocouple	Tighten connection nut — but not more than a quarter turn past finger-tight; if pilot does not stay lighted, replace thermocouple
Pilot does not stay lighted	Pilot flame too large or too small, and not heating thermocouple	Adjust pilot flame so that it extends outward and upward about one and a half inches *(left)*

FORCED-WARM-AIR SYSTEMS

Over half the central heating systems in American houses are the forced-warm-air type—29 million units. Unlike hot-water and steam systems, a forced-air system uses no water, so there is no danger of burst pipes, no need for filling or draining. It warms and recirculates air with a burner, a motor-driven fan—or blower—and a duct network.

Because it distributes warm air under draft, a forced-air system is more efficient than one that depends on the principle that warm air rises: it can send heat where needed and keep temperatures steady. So it provides comfort at lower furnace temperatures than its predecessor and burns less fuel. The furnace may use oil or gas *(pages 304-309)*, a heat pump *(page 329)* or an electric resistance coil.

Most forced-warm-air systems humidify, or can be modified to do so, and generally can be adapted to cool the house in summer. Cooling may be achieved simply by opening a panel to circulate basement air throughout the house or, more elaborately, by utilizing the ducts and blower in conjunction with a central air conditioner. Despite its versatility, the forced-warm-air system is so simple in construction and operation that the owner can deal with most of the problems that may occur.

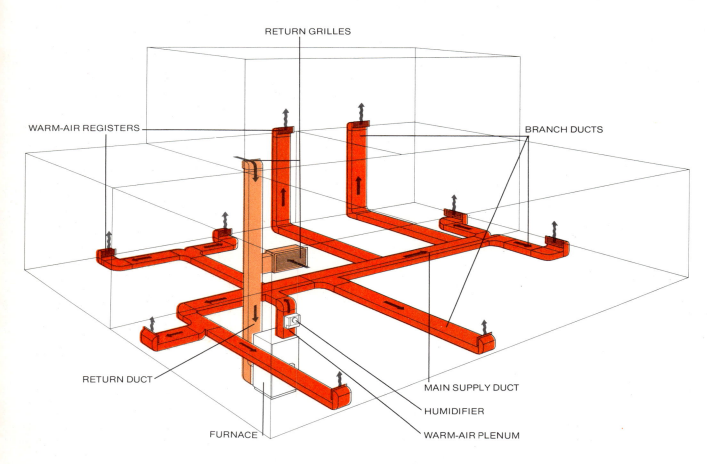

RETURN GRILLES

WARM-AIR REGISTERS

BRANCH DUCTS

RETURN DUCT

MAIN SUPPLY DUCT

HUMIDIFIER

FURNACE

WARM-AIR PLENUM

How warm air circulates

In this diagram of ducts *(above)* for a two-story house, arrows show the paths that warm air takes as it travels away from the furnace, and back to it, pushed by the blower. The furnace, containing both the burner and the blower, is topped by a chamber called the warm-air plenum. The plenum leads to a long main supply duct that feeds into branch ducts, which in turn supply openings called warm-air registers that release heated air into each room.

Dampers inside the main and branch ducts can be adjusted by lever handles to balance the flow, so that each register receives the desired quantity of warm air *(page 312)*. Each register also has a damper to regulate air flow. Warm air flows upward from these registers *(wavy arrows)*. Cooler, heavier air drops to the floor and flows through return air grilles to a return air duct leading back to the furnace. A small two-story house usually has one return grille per story. Larger homes may have return grilles in each room.

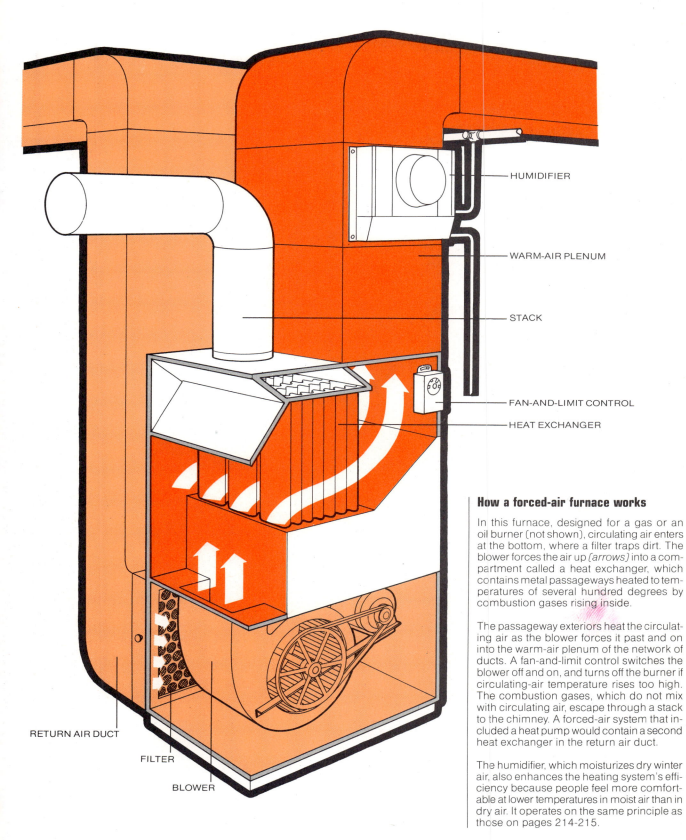

HUMIDIFIER

WARM-AIR PLENUM

STACK

FAN-AND-LIMIT CONTROL

HEAT EXCHANGER

RETURN AIR DUCT

FILTER

BLOWER

How a forced-air furnace works

In this furnace, designed for a gas or an oil burner (not shown), circulating air enters at the bottom, where a filter traps dirt. The blower forces the air up *(arrows)* into a compartment called a heat exchanger, which contains metal passageways heated to temperatures of several hundred degrees by combustion gases rising inside.

The passageway exteriors heat the circulating air as the blower forces it past and on into the warm-air plenum of the network of ducts. A fan-and-limit control switches the blower off and on, and turns off the burner if circulating-air temperature rises too high. The combustion gases, which do not mix with circulating air, escape through a stack to the chimney. A forced-air system that included a heat pump would contain a second heat exchanger in the return air duct.

The humidifier, which moisturizes dry winter air, also enhances the heating system's efficiency because people feel more comfortable at lower temperatures in moist air than in dry air. It operates on the same principle as those on pages 214-215.

Tuning a System

Two independent switches control a furnace in a forced-warm-air system. One is, as usual, the house thermostat, mounted on a wall in living quarters. The other is also a thermostatic type of switch; called a fan-and-limit control, it is on the furnace itself.

When temperature on the house thermostat falls to where you have set it (page 300), the furnace burner goes on. But no air comes through the ducts and registers until the furnace temperature reaches a point preset on the fan-and-limit control (bottom); then the blower starts. This time lag prevents the blower from sending cold air to the rooms.

The burner stays on until the house thermostat shuts it off. But the furnace still has usable heat, and to utilize it, the blower will run until the furnace cools to a second point that has been set on the fan control.

The ducts of many warm-air systems have dampers (below) that will permit temperature regulation in different parts of the house. Without dampers, all the regulating must be done at room registers or by the house thermostat, which only senses temperatures near it.

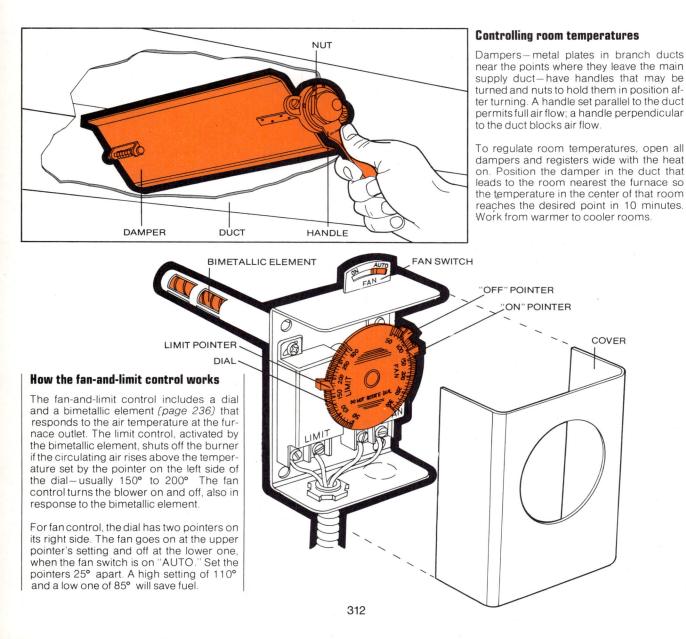

Controlling room temperatures

Dampers—metal plates in branch ducts near the points where they leave the main supply duct—have handles that may be turned and nuts to hold them in position after turning. A handle set parallel to the duct permits full air flow; a handle perpendicular to the duct blocks air flow.

To regulate room temperatures, open all dampers and registers wide with the heat on. Position the damper in the duct that leads to the room nearest the furnace so the temperature in the center of that room reaches the desired point in 10 minutes. Work from warmer to cooler rooms.

How the fan-and-limit control works

The fan-and-limit control includes a dial and a bimetallic element [page 236] that responds to the air temperature at the furnace outlet. The limit control, activated by the bimetallic element, shuts off the burner if the circulating air rises above the temperature set by the pointer on the left side of the dial—usually 150° to 200° The fan control turns the blower on and off, also in response to the bimetallic element.

For fan control, the dial has two pointers on its right side. The fan goes on at the upper pointer's setting and off at the lower one, when the fan switch is on "AUTO." Set the pointers 25° apart. A high setting of 110° and a low one of 85° will save fuel.

Troubleshooting Warm-Air Systems

Problem	Possible Causes	Solution
No heat	Power not reaching furnace	Check for blown fuse or tripped circuit breaker
	Burner not functioning	See troubleshooting chart for gas burners *(page 309)*, or checklist for oil burners *(page 305)*
	House thermostat not functioning	Check thermostat *(box, page 303)*; replace if necessary *(page 302)*
Insufficient warm-air flow	Air filter dirty	Clean or replace filter
	Heat-exchanger surfaces dirty	Shut off entire system at house service panel; clean exchanger surfaces with stiff brush
	Air leaks in main or branch ducts	Check for leaks *(page 306)*; stop leaks with duct tape
	Warm-air registers dirty	Clean register with brush or vacuum-cleaner suction tool
	Damper on warm-air register closed	Open damper
	Return-air grilles blocked by furniture or draperies	Remove blockage
	Blower not operating or running too slow	See troubleshooting chart for blowers *(page 315)* for additional causes
Large temperature differences between rooms	Branch-duct dampers improperly set	Reset dampers *(opposite)*
	Damper in branch duct or warm-air register closed	Open both damper and register; reset dampers in all branch ducts in order to eliminate any room-to-room temperature differences *(opposite)*
Dirt on walls or ceilings near registers	Blower filter dirty	Clean or replace filter
	Registers and grilles dirty	Clean with vacuum-cleaner suction tool
	Duct interiors have accumulation of dirt	Open ductwork in basement by pulling apart sections of the duct; vacuum dirt off with vacuum-cleaner suction tool

Bargain-Basement Air Cooling

A forced-air heating system may be used for summer cooling if the furnace is in the basement, as it almost always is. The idea is to employ the furnace blower to circulate the cool air of the basement through the house.

Open the furnace panel that permits access to the blower. Move the lever on the fan switch, which is usually mounted on the fan-and-limit control, from "AUTO" to "ON." With the lever at "ON," the blower runs continuously, picking up cool—but damp—basement air and sending it into the rooms above. If the fan-and-limit control has no separate fan switch, move the pointers on the fan control to their lowest settings: that will keep the blower going until you return the pointers to their normal positions.

Adjusting the Blower

A blower consists of a squirrel-cage fan *(page 333)* driven by a motor that may be mounted directly on the fan shaft but more often is connected through a V-belt and pulleys. The blower itself is usually trouble-free, but the belt and motor pulley need periodic checking and adjustment.

Excessive belt tension occurs if shafts are too far apart or pulleys are not aligned: wear and power loss result. Belt slippage develops if shafts are too close: a belt squeal or poor air flow—or both—results.

Blower speed, set by the belt position on the motor pulley, is critical. A blower running too fast is noisy and wastes power; a slow blower does not deliver sufficient air flow.

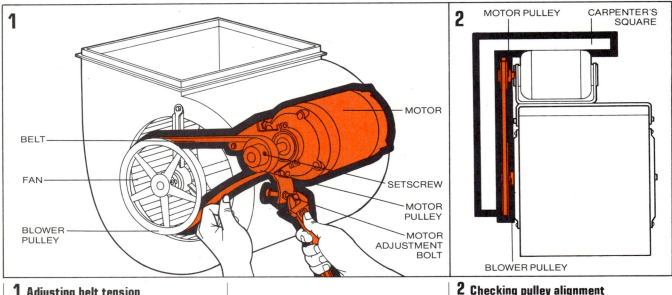

1 Adjusting belt tension

Press the belt midway between the pulleys; it should give three quarters of an inch to a full inch. In order to correct the tension, use a wrench to turn the motor-adjustment bolt, which in turn moves the motor toward or away from the blower.

2 Checking pulley alignment

With a carpenter's square check alignment of the pulleys. If they are not parallel in a line at right angles to the motor housing, loosen the inner setscrew on the motor pulley and shift the pulley. Retighten the screw, then recheck the belt tension.

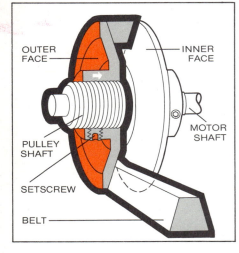

Changing blower speed

The motor pulley has two faces, discs that can be moved closer together or farther apart. The closer they are, the higher the drive belt rides on the pulley—in effect, increasing the diameter of the pulley and thus the speed of the blower. Widening the space between the faces lowers the belt's position to decrease the effective pulley diameter and slow down the blower.

To adjust blower speed, loosen the setscrew that locks the outer face of the pulley to the pulley shaft, and turn the pulley face counterclockwise to decrease the speed, clockwise to increase it. Tighten the setscrew, and if necessary, readjust the belt tension and the pulley alignment.

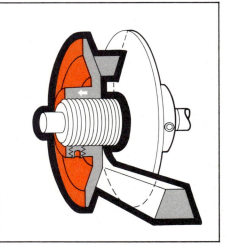

Troubleshooting Warm-Air Blowers

Problem	Possible Causes	Solution
Noisy blower	Moving parts need oil Belt worn	Put light machine oil in oil cups Replace belt (but first locate cause of wear, and correct—belt too loose or too tight, pulleys not aligned, dirt or grease on belt or pulleys); to install a new belt, move the motor toward the blower *(opposite)* until the belt can be stretched over the motor and blower pulleys. Do not snap it into place
	Belt too tight or too loose	Using motor-adjustment bolt, readjust tension *(opposite)*
	Pulleys loose on shafts	Position setscrews over flat areas of shafts, and tighten
	Pulleys warped or bent	Replace pulleys, first wiping with a clean rag to remove oil and dirt; after replacing, check tension and pulley alignment
	Blower running too fast Blower loose on shaft	Reduce blower speed *(opposite)* Position blower setscrews over flat area on shaft and tighten
	Cable to motor rubbing against metal surfaces	Move cable away from rubbed surface and anchor with tape
Insufficient air flow at warm-air registers	Blower not running	Check fuse or circuit breaker; if it fails repeatedly, call serviceman
	Belt too loose Blower loose on shaft	Increase belt tension *(opposite)* Position blower setscrews over flat area on shaft and tighten
	Blower running too slow	Increase blower speed *(opposite)*
Rushing noise or vibration in ducts	Air velocity too high	Reduce blower speed *(opposite)*
Dust on wall or ceiling near registers	Access panel to blower compartment loose or open Blower compartment is dirty	Keep door on panel closed unless working on blower Vacuum blower and housing with vacuum-cleaner suction tool at start of heating season

HOT-WATER SYSTEMS

Hot-water heating systems circulate and recirculate hot water at temperatures that are between 180° and 240°. The water stays warm for a considerable period after the thermostat has shut down the boiler, making for economic fuel consumption and the maintenance of even temperatures without drafts. The water, rising from a boiler, releases its heat in one of three devices: a convector, a radiator or a baseboard unit.

A convector is simply a housing containing a pipe with fins to help transfer heat to the air. Cool air enters at floor level; it is warmed as it rises through the fins, and is released through a grille at the top. Convectors are less expensive and better looking than radiators, which transfer heat to the air by passing the hot water through a series of looped pipes. Baseboard units are small but long convectors set at floor level. The system described on these and the following pages uses convectors.

Repairs on the piping require a plumber. But the homeowner can easily deal with the most frequent problem, caused by air in the system. And some repairs on the circulator *(pages 320-321),* which is another cause of difficulties, may be made by the homeowner without professional help.

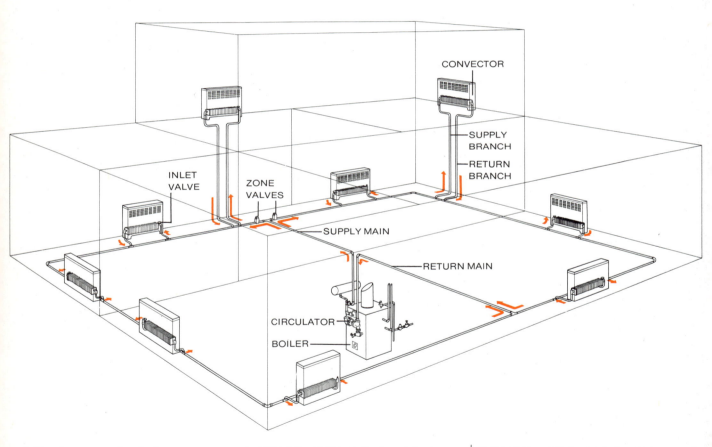

How hot water circulates

In this forced-hot-water system, a motor-operated pump called a circulator drives hot water through the piping as indicated by the arrows. From a boiler, the water goes to a pipe, one and a quarter inches in diameter, called a supply main. This pipe divides into two zone-supply pipes of three-quarter-inch size, which travel in different paths around the perimeter of the house just below the floor level of the first story. The two zone pipes recombine at a return main, which carries water back to the boiler. Motor-operated zone valves are controlled by separate thermostats, so that each zone can be kept at a different temperature or, if desired, closed off. Room convectors for both the first and second stories are, in effect, bypasses connected to the zone supply by a smaller pipe—usually one half inch in diameter—called a supply branch; a return branch leads from the convector outlet back to the zone-supply pipes. In most houses, each convector has an inlet valve that can be turned on and off without much effect on any other convector. But in houses where convectors are part of the supply pipes, no convector can be shut off without stopping the system.

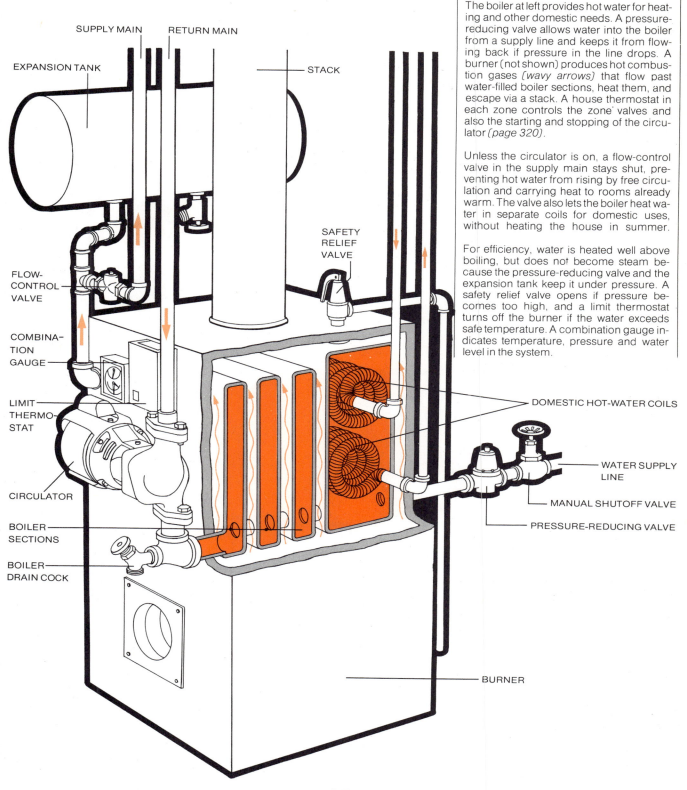

EXPANSION TANK

SUPPLY MAIN

RETURN MAIN

STACK

FLOW-
CONTROL
VALVE

SAFETY
RELIEF
VALVE

COMBINA-
TION
GAUGE

LIMIT
THERMO-
STAT

CIRCULATOR

BOILER
SECTIONS

BOILER
DRAIN COCK

DOMESTIC HOT-WATER COILS

WATER SUPPLY
LINE

MANUAL SHUTOFF VALVE

PRESSURE-REDUCING VALVE

BURNER

How a hot-water boiler works

The boiler at left provides hot water for heating and other domestic needs. A pressure-reducing valve allows water into the boiler from a supply line and keeps it from flowing back if pressure in the line drops. A burner (not shown) produces hot combustion gases *(wavy arrows)* that flow past water-filled boiler sections, heat them, and escape via a stack. A house thermostat in each zone controls the zone' valves and also the starting and stopping of the circulator *(page 320)*.

Unless the circulator is on, a flow-control valve in the supply main stays shut, preventing hot water from rising by free circulation and carrying heat to rooms already warm. The valve also lets the boiler heat water in separate coils for domestic uses, without heating the house in summer.

For efficiency, water is heated well above boiling, but does not become steam because the pressure-reducing valve and the expansion tank keep it under pressure. A safety relief valve opens if pressure becomes too high, and a limit thermostat turns off the burner if the water exceeds safe temperature. A combination gauge indicates temperature, pressure and water level in the system.

System Maintenance

Most problems in hot-water heating systems involve air and its interaction with water. Because water expands when heated and contracts when cooled, the water in a heating system rises into the expansion tank *(below),* where the volume of air in the tank presses like a soft cushion against the changing volume of water. The air cushion permits the water pressure, which is 12 pounds per square inch when the water is cold, to rise to almost 30 pounds when the water is heated. If the pressure rises higher, water is released through the safety relief valve. The pressure exerted by the expansion tank allows water temperature rise to 240° without turning the water to steam.

When water cools it absorbs air. If water absorbs too much of the air in the expansion tank, the pressure becomes too high when the water is heated again. Any fresh water added to the system will also contain air —when this fresh water is heated it sends air into the system. The air accumulates in a convector, blocking hot-water flow; unless the air is removed, the convector remains cold.

The combination gauge

Mounted on the side of the boiler, the combination gauge *(right)* has scales for water temperature, pressure and "altitude." The altitude actually refers to a pressure setting that is made when a hot-water heating system is first installed. With a closed expansion tank like the one shown below, this system is filled with cold water until the movable pointer stands at 12 pounds of pressure per square inch. Then the gauge rim and its glass are removed and the stationary pointer is set to match the position of the movable pointer. Thereafter, the stationary pointer serves as a reference point for the movable pointer; the latter registers any changes in pressure.

The movable pointer registers the pressure when the system is operating. A drop of the movable pointer below the stationary pointer indicates the system needs water. If your system does not refill automatically, check the gauge each month and refill as necessary *(box, opposite).*

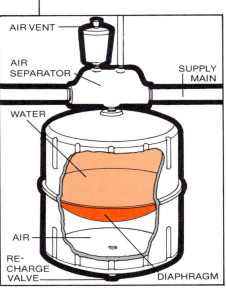

Draining the expansion tank

Without enough air in the expansion tank, high pressure forces hot water out the safety relief valve. The tank, full of water, feels hot all over. It needs draining. Shut off power to the boiler circuit at the service panel; close the water-supply shutoff valve; let the tank cool. A tank on newer systems *(above)* often has a combination valve to let water out and air in when it is open. Without this fitting, air will not enter unless the tank is fully drained. On older systems, close the valve between tank and boiler before draining the tank. Some systems have a tank *(right)* in which a rubber diaphragm separates air and water. An air separator and vent carry off excess air. If the pressure should fall below 12 pounds per square inch, the relief valve will spout and the tank will feel hot all over. Attach a bicycle pump to the air-recharge valve to add air.

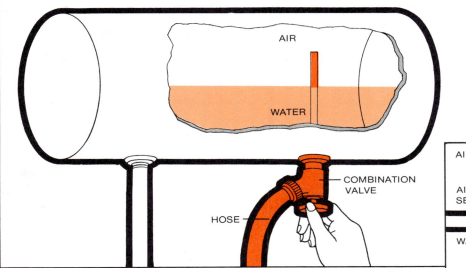

Troubleshooting Hot-Water Heating Systems

Problem	Cause	Solution
No heat	Electric power not reaching boiler	Check for blown fuse or tripped circuit breaker
Convectors are cold	Air in convectors	Purge air from convectors *(below, right)*
Water spilling from pressure-relief valve	Not enough air in expansion tank	Recharge expansion tank with air *(opposite)*
Loud clanking in circulator; motor runs, but water not circulating	Broken coupler	Replace coupler *(page 320)*
Circulator leaks	Damaged seal or worn impeller	Replace seal, impeller, or both *(page 321)*
Convector-valve stem leaks	Packing material worn	Drain system to level of the convector; repack the valve (see instructions for repacking faucets on page 75), then refill the system

Draining and Refilling the System

To drain a hot-water heating system—for repairs or to keep pipes from freezing in a winter power failure—shut off power to the boiler circuit at the service panel. Let the water cool to lukewarm. Close the water-supply shutoff valve *[page 317]*. Attach a hose to the boiler drain cock—with the other end of the hose in a drain below boiler level. Open the drain cock and air vents on the top convectors.

To refill the system, close the boiler drain and the air vents. Open up the water-supply shutoff valve. If there is a pressure-reducing valve, water will stop flowing automatically when the boiler is entirely filled. Otherwise, fill until the combination-valve gauge *(opposite)* shows 20 pounds per square inch. In either case, when water stops running into the boiler, vent air from each convector *[right]*. If pressure then drops below 12 pounds per square inch, add water; if pressure remains above 12, drain water.

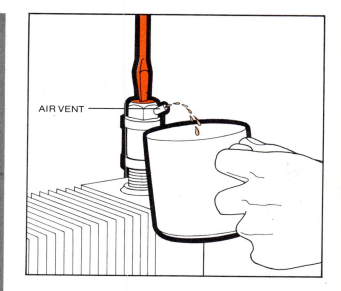

AIR VENT

Purging air from convectors

A vent for purging air is situated at the top of every convector. Some vents work automatically. Others are opened and closed with a screwdriver *[above]* or special vent key. When the vent is opened, a hissing indicates escaping air. After all the air has been discharged, water spurts out, so have a cup or a pan ready to catch it. Close the vent as soon as the spurting starts.

Circulator Problems

A hot-water heating system depends upon the circulator, which is primarily a motor-driven centrifugal pump. The motor shaft and the pump shaft have a flexible connection, called a coupler, which incorporates one or more springs.

The coupler has several functions. It keeps noise from the motor from traveling through the heating pipes into the house, it absorbs the shocks of starting and stopping, and it prevents excessive wear. Most impor-

tant of all, the coupler is designed to serve as a safety device: if the pump jams, the coupler springs break and sever the connection between the shafts, thereby protecting the motor from overheating. The coupler may also break if the motor mountings sag as a result of over-oiling (the motor needs lubricating at the beginning of each heating season with SAE 20 oil dripped into its oil cups).

Another trouble spot in the circulator is the pump seal. Water running out of the weep hole (exploded view, opposite) is a signal that the seal needs replacing.

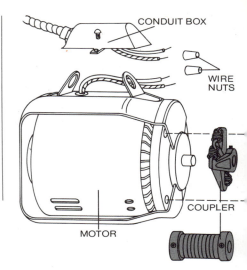

CONDUIT BOX

WIRE NUTS

COUPLER

MOTOR

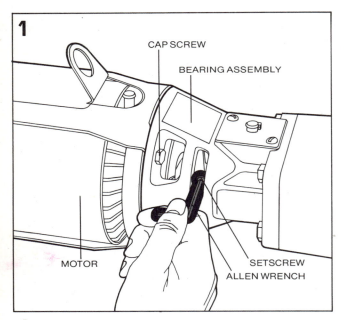

CAP SCREW

BEARING ASSEMBLY

MOTOR

SETSCREW
ALLEN WRENCH

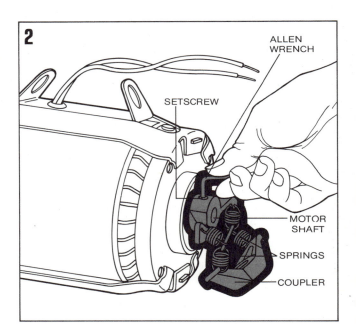

ALLEN WRENCH

SETSCREW

MOTOR SHAFT

SPRINGS

COUPLER

1 Servicing the circulator

Before removing the motor and coupler, cut off electricity to the boiler circuit at the service panel. Unless there are valves above and below the pump, close the valve on the water supply line and drain the system (page 319). Remove the conduit-box cover on the motor and disconnect the wires. Turn the motor until the setscrew on the pump shaft is visible. With an Allen wrench, loosen that screw. With an adjustable wrench, loosen the cap screws holding the motor to the bearing assembly. Slide the coupler off the pump shaft.

2 Replacing the coupler

With the motor separated from the bearing assembly, remove the damaged coupler from the motor shaft.

Turn the setscrews in the coupler at least three full turns. If the coupler sticks to the motor shaft, use a pry bar to get it off.

If any of the coupler arms or springs are worn or broken, you must remove and replace the whole coupler. Replacement of just one or two springs can unbalance the coupler and may even cause it to break.

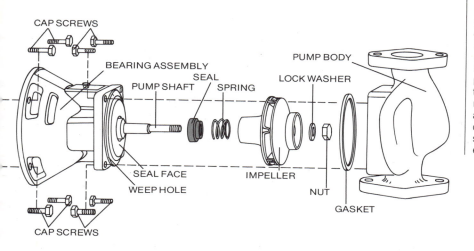

CAP SCREWS

BEARING ASSEMBLY

PUMP SHAFT   SEAL   SPRING

PUMP BODY

LOCK WASHER

SEAL FACE

WEEP HOLE

IMPELLER

NUT

GASKET

CAP SCREWS

How the circulator is disassembled

A typical circulator, shown at left in an exploded view, can be disassembled rather easily by removing eight cap screws holding together its three main sections—the motor, the bearing assembly and the pump body. The bearing assembly holds the pump shaft and impeller, and is mounted to the pump body by four cap screws. The motor, in turn, is mounted to the bearing assembly by four more cap screws. The coupler is fixed to the motor and pump shafts by setscrews, which fit into recesses on the shafts.

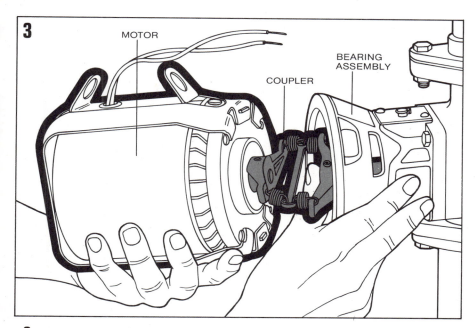

3

MOTOR

COUPLER

BEARING ASSEMBLY

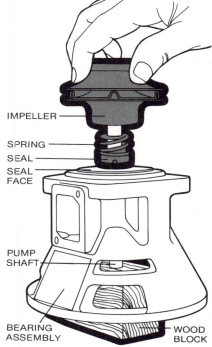

IMPELLER

SPRING

SEAL

SEAL FACE

PUMP SHAFT

BEARING ASSEMBLY

WOOD BLOCK

3 Remounting the coupler and motor

Slide the new coupler over the motor shaft and tighten the setscrews. Holding the motor in your left hand, use the thumb of your right hand to push the free half of the coupler onto the pump shaft, lining up the setscrews with the recess on the shaft. Then screw the motor to the bearing assembly. Tighten the setscrew, locking the coupler to the pump shaft.

Make sure that the oil caps on the motor face upward. Then reconnect the wiring and replace the cover on the conduit box.

Replacing the pump seal

With this type of circulator disassembled (left and above), remove the impeller nut and lock washer, and slide the impeller off the pump shaft, rapping the shaft with a screwdriver. Remove the spring. Pry off the brass ring. If the seal face is pitted or scored, replace the bearing assembly. In reassembling, place the pump shaft on a block of wood. Press firmly on the new seal with a screwdriver and reassemble the circulator. To replace some seals, impeller and shaft must be withdrawn from the rear of the bearing assembly.

STEAM SYSTEMS

Although steam heat has its charms—hisses and bangs that can be warm and reassuring sounds—the noise and its expensive plumbing have reduced its popularity, and today it survives mostly in older houses. In a steam heating system, a boiler in the basement converts water into steam, which rises under its own pressure through pipes and inlet valves to room radiators. The steam transfers its heat to the relatively cool metal of the radiators and condenses back to water, which flows under its own weight through the same valves it entered, and thence to pipes leading downward to the boiler again. There the water is reheated into steam that repeats its journey endlessly as long as the boiler's burner remains on.

The plumbing in a steam-heat system

Steam is generated in a boiler equipped with drains, a fill valve, a pressure gauge and safety devices, and a low-water cutoff switch. The steam rises through a large supply main to smaller branches and into the radiators. Air that is pushed ahead as steam rises is released through vents on the radiators. The return flow of water through the branches to the supply main runs off into a large vertical pipe called the return main, and from there into the boiler. The cross-connecting "Hartford loop" applies steam pressure to the last leg of the return, preventing boiler water from backing up when pressure gets too high.

Pressure measurement and control

A gauge *(below),* mounted to tubing atop the boiler, indicates steam pressure by measuring air pressure. Steam from the boiler forces condensate upward through a pigtail of curled pipe, and the condensate in turn compresses the air above it. The air operates the gauge and a pressure safety control, which shuts off the boiler when pressure exceeds a safe level. A safety valve releases dangerous pressures.

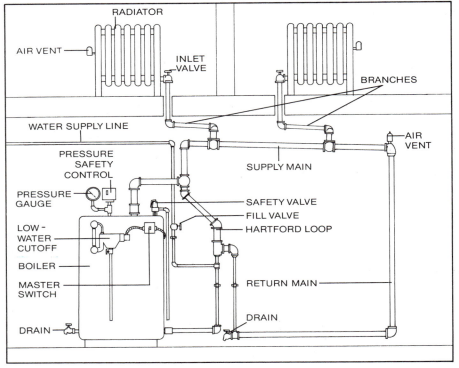

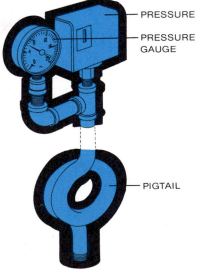

How to check and adjust water level

A gauge glass *(right)* indicates the water level in the boiler: when the water in the glass stands midway between the cocks, boiler water is at the proper operating level. A low-water cutoff actuated by a float shuts down the boiler when its water level falls dangerously low. Unless your system fills automatically, check the gauge glass at least weekly, and when necessary, fill the boiler to the midpoint on the glass by opening the fill valve *(above).* To keep the low-water cutoff clean of sediment, once a month open the blowoff valve and flush water through the discharge pipe until it runs clear; then refill the boiler.

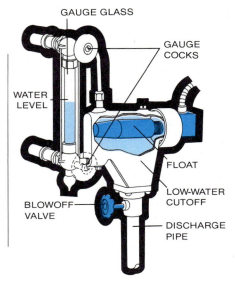

Troubleshooting Steam Heating Systems

Problem	Possible Causes	Solution
No heat	Power not reaching boiler	Check for blown fuse or tripped circuit breaker
	Water level in boiler too low	Open fill valve in the water line, and fill boiler to midpoint on the gauge glass
	Burner not functioning	See troubleshooting chart on page 309 for gas burners, and checklist on page 305 for oil burners
	Thermostat defective	See page 303
Individual radiator cold	Inlet valve closed	Open valve all the way; all inlet valves should be fully open
	Radiator not tilted toward inlet end	Increase the tilt if it is necessary *(below)*
Rooms unevenly heated	Air vents improperly adjusted	Open vents in radiators farthest from boiler and partly close vents nearer boiler *(below)*
Leaky inlet valve	Packing around valve stem worn	Shut off power to the boiler, let the radiator cool and repack the valve stem *(page 75)*
Hammering in a radiator	Radiator not tilted toward inlet end	Increase the tilt if it is necessary *(below)*
Hammering in pipes	Water trapped in pipes by settling of house so that pipes no longer form a downhill path to the return main	With a level, check slopes of supply main and branches, and reposition them if necessary so that they slope down toward the return main
Gauge glass cloudy or rusty, and cannot be read	Rust in boiler	Turn off power to boiler; allow it to cool to lukewarm; open the drains at the bottom of the boiler and in the return main; drain completely, refill the boiler and drain it again; repeat until water in the glass gauge is clear (Note: If rusty water drips from radiator air vents, call a professional repairman)

SCREWDRIVER SLOT
DIAL

How a radiator air vent works

An air vent *(left)* lets air out as steam enters a radiator. If a radiator stays cold, open the vent wider by using a screwdriver to turn the dial to a lower number.

How a radiator ejects water

Water flows by gravity out of a radiator via the inlet valve. If it does not, the radiator may be tilted so that water collects, blocking steam. Check the tilt with a carpenter's level. If necessary, raise the legs with wood blocks at the air-vent end.

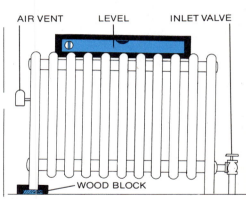

AIR VENT   LEVEL   INLET VALVE

WOOD BLOCK

ELECTRIC BASEBOARDS

Baseboard electric heating is a throwback to a by-gone era. With it, the house has no central heating system; instead, each room has its own heater, just as it did when homes were warmed by fireplaces or potbellied stoves. Because it needs neither air ducts nor plumbing, a baseboard electric system is especially easy to install—although more house insulation will be needed to retain the heat.

Baseboard units are mounted at floor level—one or more to a room, depending on the space to be heated—and wired directly into the house power supply. Models are made to use either 120 or 240 volts (120-volt wiring is shown here). The heaters are costly to operate, and relatively slow to respond to outdoor temperature changes; but they are simple to install, adapt to varied requirements, and produce clean, even heat.

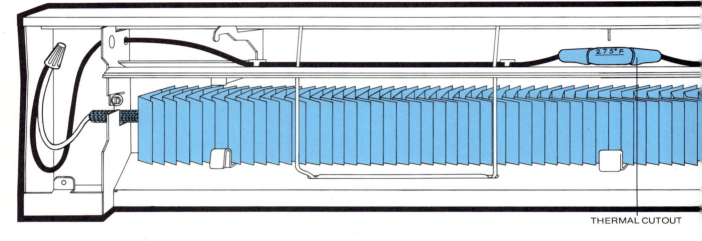

THERMAL CUTOUT

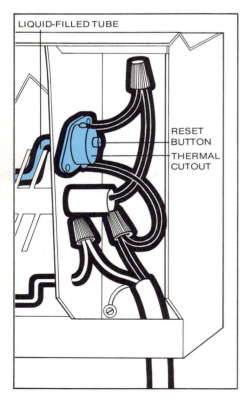

LIQUID-FILLED TUBE

RESET BUTTON

THERMAL CUTOUT

How a thermal cutout works

A thermal cutout *(left)* prevents overheating from blocked air flow. This one has a metal tube, filled with liquid, along the back of the heater. When heat passes a preset level, the liquid expands, pushing a brass diaphragm at the tube end to open contacts and shut off power. Pushing the reset button recloses the contacts.

Checking the thermal cutout

If a heater is cold when room temperature drops 5° below the thermostat setting, first press the thermal-cutout reset button. If no heat comes on, the cutout may be faulty. Turn off power to the circuit at the service panel. Using the method described on page 262, attach a voltage tester to the thermal-cutout terminals *(right)*.

Set the thermostat 5° above room temperature and turn the power on, being careful not to touch connections. If the tester fails to light, see the troubleshooting chart opposite. If it does, the cutout is defective. With power off, remove the tester and replace the cutout, following manufacturer's directions for dismantling the heating element and replacing the unit.

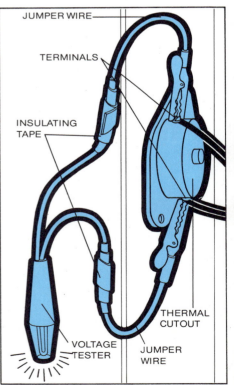

JUMPER WIRE

TERMINALS

INSULATING TAPE

THERMAL CUTOUT

VOLTAGE TESTER

JUMPER WIRE

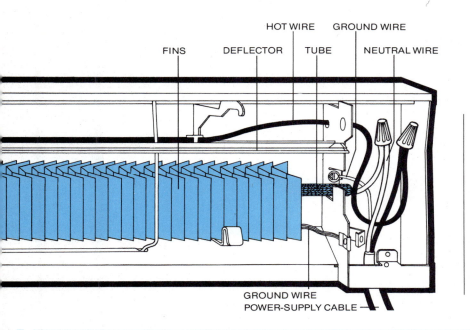

FINS   DEFLECTOR   TUBE   NEUTRAL WIRE

HOT WIRE   GROUND WIRE

GROUND WIRE
POWER-SUPPLY CABLE

How a baseboard heater works

In a typical 120-volt unit *(left)*, power flows from the hot (black) wire in a power-supply cable through a resistance wire *(page 234)* sheathed in a ceramic-and-metal tube and surrounded by heat-spreading fins. After passing through the protective thermal cut-out (similar in function to the one on the opposite page), current returns through the neutral (white) wire. The unit heats a room when cold air that enters through a gap in the bottom of a front panel (not shown) is warmed by the heating tube and fins. The air rises, guided by a deflector, and displaces colder air by convection.

Troubleshooting Baseboard Electric Heaters

Problem	Possible Causes	Solution
No heat	Blown fuse or tripped circuit breaker	Replace fuse or reset circuit breaker
	Drapery or furniture blocking air flow through heater	Move obstruction; if thermal cutout has a reset button, push it in
	Thermal cutout defective	Check cutout *(opposite, bottom right)*; before removing faulty cutout, diagram color of wires going to each cutout terminal
	Resistance wire in heating element defective	Turn off power at service panel; check resistance wire with continuity tester *(page 137)*; before replacing element, check voltage rating; old and new element ratings must match
	Heater wiring defective	Power off; check wiring visually and with continuity tester *(page 137)*
	Defective thermostat	Check thermostat *(box, page 303)*
	House wiring defective	Turn off power at service panel; attach and tape voltage tester to white and black supply-cable wires; set thermostat 5° above room temperature; turn power on; if tester does not light, call an electrician

Cooling

Air-Conditioning Your Home Comfortably and Efficiently

The summer of 221 A.D. was a scorcher in Rome. While most of the populace suffered, the Emperor Heliogabalus could command satisfying relief: he ordered a thousand slaves into the mountains to bring back a caravanload of snow to cool the imperial gardens.

Although the Emperor's way of beating the heat is an interesting sidelight in history books, he was not by any means the father of air conditioning. Centuries before him, Egyptians learned to store water in reservoirs on house roofs to wet down the outside walls. The dry desert winds evaporated the water, cooling the interiors. In India, almost everybody knew that a wet mat, hung in the wind across an open door, cooled the incoming breeze.

These rudimentary systems applied principles still useful today: first, as substances melt or evaporate, they absorb heat from whatever is nearby; second, comfort demands both temperature control and air circulation.

But, for most of civilization, a completely satisfactory way to make people comfortable in hot weather remained elusive. In 1833, a doctor named John Gorrie hit on a pleasing but still primitive way: he blew air over buckets of ice to soothe the fevers of malaria patients in Florida. Gorrie, among others, saw a market for a machine that could make ice. Around 1850, he and other inventors were at work on machines that put the cooling power of evaporation to work under controlled conditions.

In one typical design, ethyl ether, a refrigerant, was pressurized by a compressor and then released in coils, where it evaporated, freezing the water around the coils. This basic refrigeration cycle laid the foundation for the development of modern refrigerators (pages 282-287), as well as room and central air conditioners like those described on the following pages.

One major problem remained unsolved. Humidity control, it became apparent, was as crucial a factor in regulating interior climate as temperature and air circulation. Moisture carried by hot air condensed on the cold coils of early refrigerators, reducing humidity slightly; but no one could control it.

A young engineer, Willis Carrier, set out to solve this problem, and in 1902 he succeeded, devising a machine for a Brooklyn printer who had difficulty because his paper swelled on humid days. By controlling both the temperature of refrigerator coils and the volume of air moved by fans, Carrier found he could also control the humidity. He chilled the air, thus forcing most of its moisture to condense; then he mixed this chilly, dry air with uncooled air to release a comfortably cool and dry mixture. This system is the one universally used today.

The price of this comfort is measured by the electricity bills, which, as anyone who pays them knows, rise implacably. One way to conserve electricity is to match the capacity of air-conditioning units to cooling needs. Too small a unit cannot remove enough heat to cool a room. Yet, too large a unit quickly chills the air, but runs so briefly that the slower dehumidifying process cannot remove enough moisture to make the air comfortably dry.

B.T.U.s of cooling capacity

Air-conditioning capacity used to be described in tons. This method, which goes back to Gorrie's day, refers not to the weight of the unit, but to its cooling capacity compared with the amount of cooling provided by melting a ton of ice in 24 hours. Today, heat-removing capacity is usually measured in B.T.U.s per hour—the same units that gauge a heating system's ability to produce heat *(page 297)*.

If you think your room air conditioner may be too small, or large, you can figure what capacity you need with the Cooling Load Estimate Form, available from the Association of Home Appliance Manufacturers, 20 North Wacker Drive, Chicago, Illinois 60606.

Even if you install a unit that matches your needs, you can still lighten its load and shrink your electric bill. Exhaust fans, installed in kitchen, bathroom, laundry and attic, can help conserve electricity. They remove heat and humidity at points of highest accumulation.

You should also:
- Clean or replace filters monthly, since dirt reduces the efficiency of cooling fins and coils.
- Make sure air flow is unobstructed inside and outside. Drapes and furniture can deflect cold air back into the unit, causing it to shut off without cooling the room adequately.
- Turn off unneeded lights. Ninety per cent of the power that is used by incandescent lamps turns into heat.
- Leave storm windows on during the cooling season. They can cut your cooling load by as much as 20 per cent.
- Install awnings on the sunny side of the house, and draw blinds to block outdoor heat.
- Set the thermostat to cool less. Changing the setting five degrees can save as much as 15 per cent of cooling costs.

Another way to cut electricity use is to have an efficient unit. An air conditioner's efficiency is judged by its Energy Efficiency Rating, or E.E.R.—the number of B.T.U.s produced per watt. If a unit's E.E.R. is not marked on the nameplate (usually found behind the front panel), divide the B.T.U. rating by the wattage. The higher the number, the better the unit's E.E.R. A 6,000-B.T.U. unit requiring 600 watts has an E.E.R. of 10, a high efficiency level. At 1,200 watts, its E.E.R. is 5, a poor rating. (It makes sense to compare E.E.R.s only for units with the same capacity.) More efficient units need more efficient compressors and larger motors and coils, which cost more initially, but save electricity and money in the long run.

HEAT PUMPS

An air conditioner draws heat from warm indoor air and transfers it out of doors. A heat pump does the same thing, but it also has a special reversing valve so that it can work backward. It thus gains the ability to draw heat from outdoor air and transfer it indoors (even chilly air contains some heat that can be tapped).

Heat pumps are best suited to areas where winters are mild and where hot and humid summers make air conditioning a necessity. As long as winter temperatures remain moderate, heat pumps are much more economical to operate than traditional electric baseboard heaters because they merely move heat by means of electricity, rather than create it. But their efficiency goes down drastically as outdoor temperatures decline and the outer condenser coils frost over, thus insulating them from the source of their heat. At extremely low temperatures, an auxiliary resistance coil—a supplementary heater that adds heat when the condenser coils are defrosting (box, below)—must bear much or all of the heating burden, which it does at as high a cost as an electric baseboard.

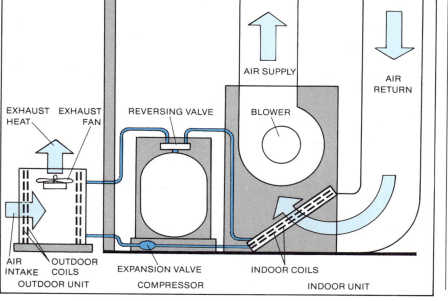

EXHAUST HEAT — EXHAUST FAN — REVERSING VALVE — BLOWER — AIR SUPPLY — AIR RETURN — AIR INTAKE — OUTDOOR COILS — EXPANSION VALVE — INDOOR COILS — OUTDOOR UNIT — COMPRESSOR — INDOOR UNIT

How a heat pump works

In the heating mode, cold refrigerant passes through the outdoor coils, drawing heat from the air. Next it is pulled through the reversing valve into the compressor, which makes it denser and hotter. The hot fluid is then pumped to the indoor coils, giving up its heat to the air circulating around the coils, which is then distributed through the house ducts. The fluid goes from the indoor coils into an expansion valve, where it cools, and then enters the outdoor coils to repeat the cycle. In the cooling mode, the direction of the flow is changed by the reversing valve. The refrigerant first flows to the indoor coils to pick up heat from the air. Following a route opposite that of the heating mode, the fluid then expels heat outside, aided by an exhaust fan.

In three-piece systems, as shown here, the compressor is located indoors in a separate cabinet and is connected by refrigerant pipes to the outdoor and the indoor coils. In one- and two-piece systems, the compressor is located outdoors.

Defrosting the Coils

During protracted stretches of extremely cold winter weather, the outdoor coils of a heat pump frost up like an old-fashioned ice-cream freezer. If the unit is functioning properly, it will defrost itself automatically by switching over to the cooling mode. Then heat from the warm air inside the house will be transferred to the coils and will melt the ice that covers them.

Occasionally, the defrost mechanism will fail to operate properly. The signs of such trouble are readily apparent on the outdoor coils of the unit: if the coils are sheathed by a heavy coat of ice rather than by mere frost, in all likelihood the control valve is not opening and closing as it should. You may be able to alleviate the problem manually by shifting the heat pump between the heating and cooling modes at 10-minute intervals for one hour. If this fails to restore the defrosting system to automatic operation, call a repair service.

ROOM AIR CONDITIONERS

An air conditioner installed in the window of a closed room turns the room into a giant walk-in refrigerator. The conditioner works on exactly the same principles found in all refrigeration systems *(pages 282-283),* and has the same basic mechanical components. Both appliances remove heat from inside an enclosed space and release it outside. But the air conditioner has one feature that most refrigerators lack. The conditioner not only cools the air, but also removes humidity and dumps it outside. The comfort of cool, dry air on hot, muggy days has made air conditioners basic appliances in millions of American homes.

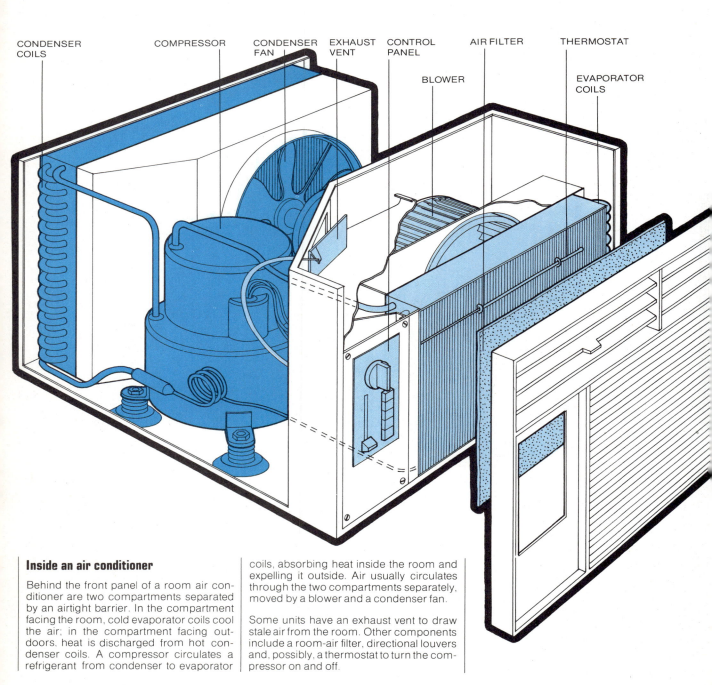

CONDENSER COILS   COMPRESSOR   CONDENSER FAN   EXHAUST VENT   CONTROL PANEL   AIR FILTER   THERMOSTAT   BLOWER   EVAPORATOR COILS

Inside an air conditioner

Behind the front panel of a room air conditioner are two compartments separated by an airtight barrier. In the compartment facing the room, cold evaporator coils cool the air; in the compartment facing outdoors, heat is discharged from hot condenser coils. A compressor circulates a refrigerant from condenser to evaporator coils, absorbing heat inside the room and expelling it outside. Air usually circulates through the two compartments separately, moved by a blower and a condenser fan.

Some units have an exhaust vent to draw stale air from the room. Other components include a room-air filter, directional louvers and, possibly, a thermostat to turn the compressor on and off.

The flow of air

Two separate currents of air flow continuously through an air conditioner. Hot and humid air, drawn in from the room by the blower *(far right)*, passes across the cold evaporator coils where it is both cooled and dehumidified *(below)*; the cool, dry air is blown back into the room through the louvers on the front panel.

At the same time, in the second circulation system, air is drawn into the unit through side vents located outside the room. The condenser fan then forces this outside air across the condenser coils, which contain refrigerant heated by the air inside the room. The air from the side vents cools off the condenser coils and carries their heat outside the house.

FRONT PANEL

LOUVERS

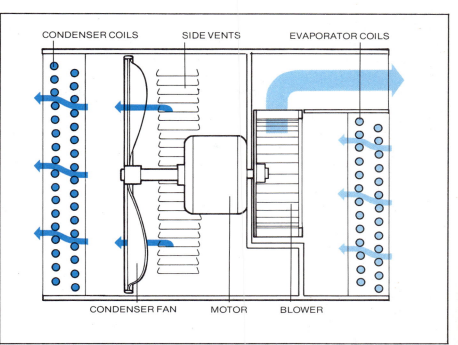

CONDENSER COILS   SIDE VENTS   EVAPORATOR COILS

CONDENSER FAN   MOTOR   BLOWER

How an air conditioner dehumidifies

An air conditioner will provide comfort as much by drying the air as by lowering its temperature. Hot, moist air not only cools as it passes over the evaporator coils, but also loses its ability to hold moisture. The air's water vapor condenses in droplets on the evaporator coils, drips into a collecting pan, and flows by gravity through tubes leading to a second collecting pan located under the condenser fan.

A rotating slinger ring, attached to the fan blades and partly immersed in the pan, whips the water up out of the pan, and the fan flings it across the hot condenser coils. The water helps to cool the coils, then passes outside the house in water droplets.

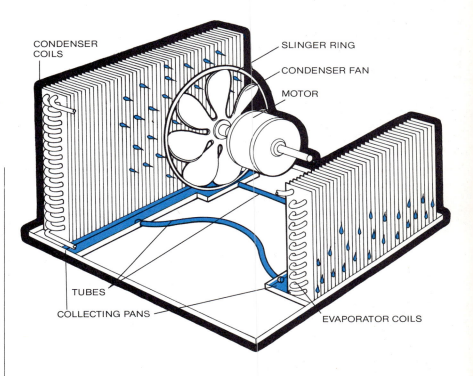

CONDENSER COILS

SLINGER RING

CONDENSER FAN

MOTOR

TUBES

COLLECTING PANS

EVAPORATOR COILS

Maintenance

Only an air-conditioning repairman has the tools and skills to test and fix the sealed, pressurized refrigeration system in your air conditioner, but some repairs, such as replacing a thermostat *(below),* are simple; and anyone can do all the maintenance work necessary to keep a unit operating efficiently. At the start of the cooling season, oil the fan motor bearings *(pages 194-195),* straighten bent coil fins *(bottom, right)* and remove dust and lint from the coils. Most important of all, clean or replace the air filter at the start of the cooling season and monthly during it: dirty filters cause more unnecessary calls to servicemen than any other problem. Central air conditioners *(pages 334-335),* although basically similar to room air conditioners, are more complicated mechanically, and are much more expensive; to protect their investment, many owners buy a service contract *(page 257)* that covers both the routine maintenance and emergency repairs.

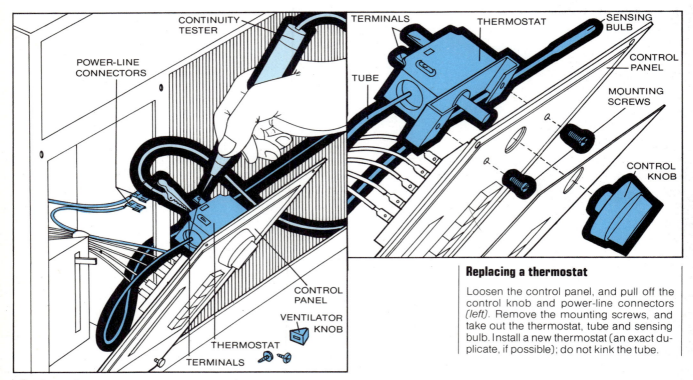

Replacing a thermostat

Loosen the control panel, and pull off the control knob and power-line connectors *(left).* Remove the mounting screws, and take out the thermostat, tube and sensing bulb. Install a new thermostat (an exact duplicate, if possible); do not kink the tube.

Testing a thermostat

If the compressor does not run or runs continuously, check the thermostat. Unplug the power cord, pull off the ventilator knob, remove the top screws of the control panel and loosen the panel's bottom screws so it opens. Pull off the two power-line connectors and attach a continuity tester *(page 137)* to their terminals. With the thermostat at its warmest setting, the tester lamp should not light. Turn the knob to the coldest setting; the tester lamp should light.

Straightening bent fins

Bent or dirty condenser and evaporator fins cut air flow, reducing cooling efficiency. Straighten bent fins with a fin comb sold at refrigeration-parts stores. Spacing of the comb teeth should match that of the fins on your coils—spacing is marked as fins per inch. Combs remove dirt from coils, but a vacuum cleaner does it better.

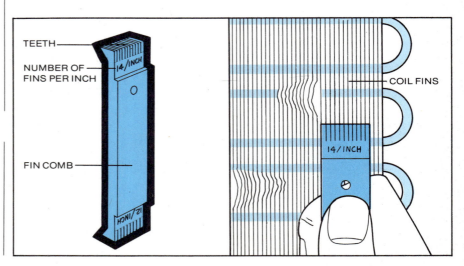

Troubleshooting Air Conditioners

Problem	Possible Causes	Solution
Unit does not run	Power not reaching unit Defective cord	Check plug, fuse or circuit breaker Check and replace cord *(pages 186-187)*
Fuses blow or circuit breaker trips repeatedly	Unit restarted too soon after use Wrong fuse Overloaded circuit	Wait five minutes before restarting Use time-delay fuse of correct rating Plug other appliances into a different circuit
Fan runs but air is not cooled	Defective thermostat Defective compressor	Replace thermostat *(opposite)* Call repairman
Compressor runs to cool air but fan does not circulate it	Blower or fan obstructed Fan-motor bearings dry Defective fan motor	Shut off power and clear obstruction Lubricate fan motor *(page 194)* Call repairman
Compressor turns on and off repeatedly	Cold air deflected into unit Unit restarted too soon Condenser air flow blocked Thermostat bulb out of position	Move curtains or furniture deflecting cold air Wait five minutes before restarting Vacuum-clean condenser coils Reposition bulb in return air flow but not touching evaporator coils
Unit does not cool sufficiently	Thermostat set too warm, or is defective Insufficient air flow Low outside temperature causing evaporator to ice over Cool air escaping Loose blower Unit too small for room size or weather conditions	Adjust thermostat; replace if necessary Clean or replace air filter; vacuum-clean both coils and straighten bent fins *(opposite)* Do not run unit when outside temperature is below 70° Close unit exhaust or ventilation doors; close heating-system registers; seal leaks around doors and windows Tighten screw holding blower on shaft Install unit with higher B.T.U. rating
Noisy operation	Loose or obstructed blower Dry bearings in fan motor Bent or dirty fan blades Vibrating refrigerant tubing Loose or insecure mounting	Tighten screw holding blower on shaft; remove obstructions Lubricate bearings Straighten and clean blades Carefully align tubing so it does not hit metal; tape tubing to solid support Tighten mounting or add additional supports
Water drips from inside unit	Improper installation Drain tube plugged	Tilt unit slightly toward outside Remove and clean with small brush
Water drips from outside unit	Extremely humid weather	Dripping is normal; if necessary, attach a pan and drain to carry water out of the way

Central Air Conditioners

The most convenient way to cool, dehumidify and filter air in a house is with a central air conditioner rather than with individual room units, and this extra comfort is being provided to about two million more homes each year. The systems generally used distribute the conditioned air through ducts, as warm-air heating systems do, and most are combined with warm-air furnaces. The cooling units, unlike room air conditioners, are made in two separate parts: the evaporator coil fits into the plenum chamber atop the furnace *(below),* and is connected by tubing to the condenser unit. The condenser unit —with its heat and noisy machinery—is located outside of the house *(opposite, bottom).*

Nearly all warm-air furnaces are now designed for the simple addition of such cooling units. But not all warm-air systems have ductwork adequate for air conditioning, since cooling requires more and perhaps larger ducts than heating does. For summer conditioning, large quantities of cold air have to be forced up and hot air pulled out, demanding —particularly to cool second-floor bedrooms—not only a blower that is powerful but also ducts that can handle the substantial air flow.

Cooling a house through a furnace

In the air-conditioning system at right, installed in a forced-air heating system with only minimum modification of the existing equipment, the air flow through the ductwork *(arrows)* remains the same as in the winter. Hot, humid air from the house flows to the basement through the return air duct and passes through the air filter. (Because of the increased air flow required to force cold air throughout the house, check the filter monthly and, if necessary, replace it or cleanse it of dust and pollen.)

The furnace blower, reset to operate at a high speed (instructions for such adjustment are on page 314), forces the filtered air across the evaporator coil. Located in the plenum chamber above the furnace, it is cooled by refrigerant from the condenser unit outside the house. Moisture condensing on the coil trickles down through a pipe to the floor drain, while the cooled and dehumidified air is pushed through the air-supply ducts to the rooms above.

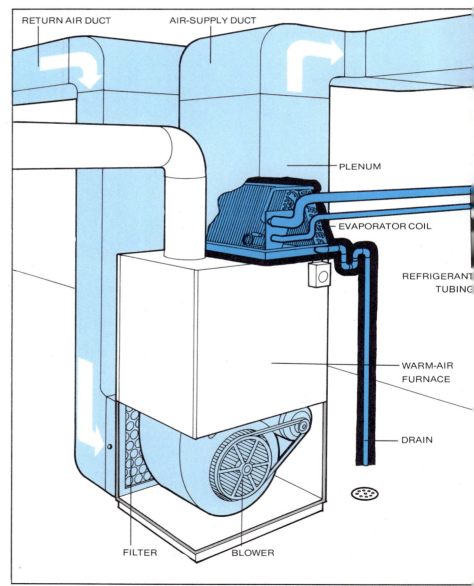

RETURN AIR DUCT

AIR-SUPPLY DUCT

PLENUM

EVAPORATOR COIL

REFRIGERANT TUBING

WARM-AIR FURNACE

DRAIN

FILTER

BLOWER

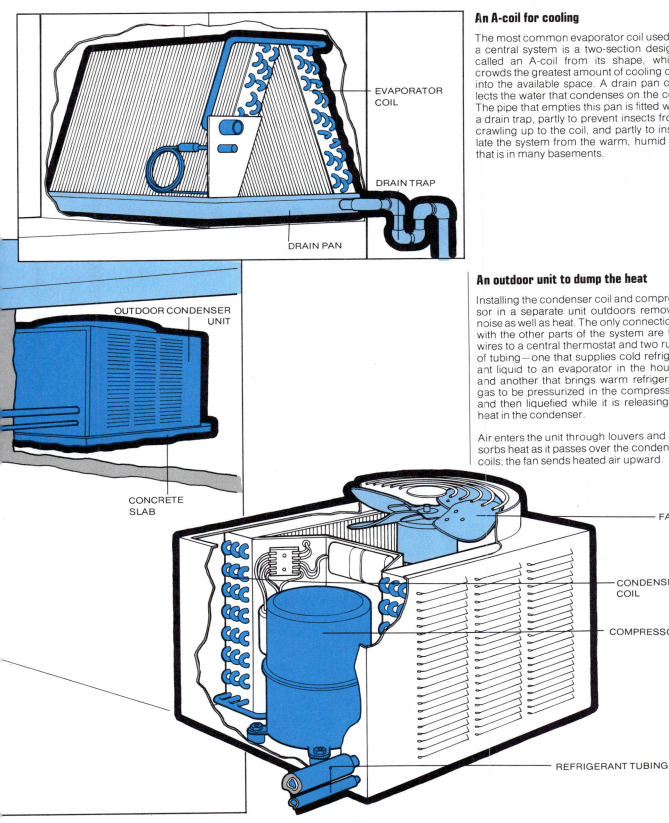

An A-coil for cooling

The most common evaporator coil used in a central system is a two-section design, called an A-coil from its shape, which crowds the greatest amount of cooling coil into the available space. A drain pan collects the water that condenses on the coil. The pipe that empties this pan is fitted with a drain trap, partly to prevent insects from crawling up to the coil, and partly to insulate the system from the warm, humid air that is in many basements.

EVAPORATOR COIL

DRAIN TRAP

DRAIN PAN

OUTDOOR CONDENSER UNIT

CONCRETE SLAB

An outdoor unit to dump the heat

Installing the condenser coil and compressor in a separate unit outdoors removes noise as well as heat. The only connections with the other parts of the system are the wires to a central thermostat and two runs of tubing—one that supplies cold refrigerant liquid to an evaporator in the house, and another that brings warm refrigerant gas to be pressurized in the compressor, and then liquefied while it is releasing its heat in the condenser.

Air enters the unit through louvers and absorbs heat as it passes over the condenser coils; the fan sends heated air upward.

FAN

CONDENSER COIL

COMPRESSOR

REFRIGERANT TUBING

VENTILATING FANS

Any air that moves can be a comfort, of course. When it is moved so that hot air is replaced with cooler air, dirty air with clean, the comfort is further increased. Even in an air-conditioned house, fans lighten the load on the cooling mechanism to give optimum comfort for less money. For all these purposes, a permanently installed fan—in attic, roof, wall or ceiling—can be matched to need.

Small exhaust fans *(pages 338-339)* remove heat, humidity, grease and odors from bathroom, kitchen or laundry. Larger fans, installed in attic or roof, take even greater advantage of the fact that hot air rises. A large attic fan *(below)* pulls cool air in at the bottom of a house and blows hot air out at the top. It alone will do a surprisingly effective job of cooling in a temperate climate. A roof fan *(bottom)* fulfills a more limited assignment: emptying hot air out of an attic and replacing it with cooler air drawn in through vents in the eaves.

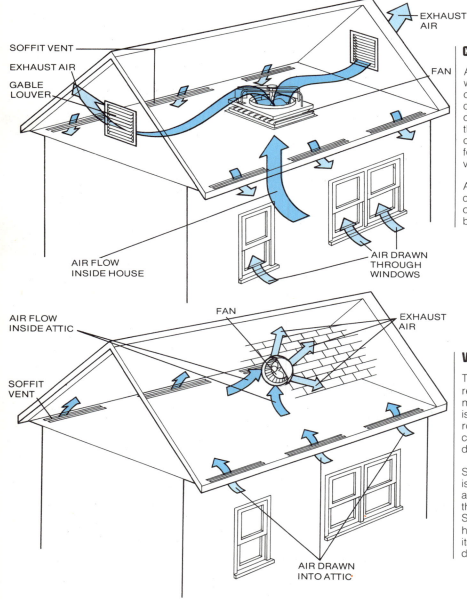

SOFFIT VENT
EXHAUST AIR
GABLE LOUVER
EXHAUST AIR
FAN
AIR FLOW INSIDE HOUSE
AIR DRAWN THROUGH WINDOWS

AIR FLOW INSIDE ATTIC
FAN
EXHAUST AIR
SOFFIT VENT
AIR DRAWN INTO ATTIC

Cooling with an attic fan

A home can be cooled at relatively low cost with a large fan installed in the attic, either on the floor *(left)* or in a gable wall. The fan, controlled by a timer or switch downstairs, does not actually cool indoor air. Rather, as the arrows show, it draws fresh air through open windows into rooms to be cooled and forces hot attic air out through gable louvers or screened soffit vents in the eaves.

An attic fan works best after sunset, when it can replace hot air in the house with cooler outdoor air; but it can be run at any time to blow hot air out of the attic.

Ventilating with a roof fan

The summer temperature in an attic can reach 130°, close to the upper limit of human endurance. Even when the attic floor is insulated, some of this heat radiates into rooms below, making heavy work for an air conditioner. As much as half this extra burden can be lifted with a roof fan.

Set into the roof near the ridgeline, the fan is controlled by a thermostat that turns it on at a selected level, say 100°, and off when the attic temperature drops to about 85°. Smaller than the attic fan above, this fan exhausts hot air only from the attic. But since its suction is limited to the attic, it does not draw dust or pollen into the living quarters.

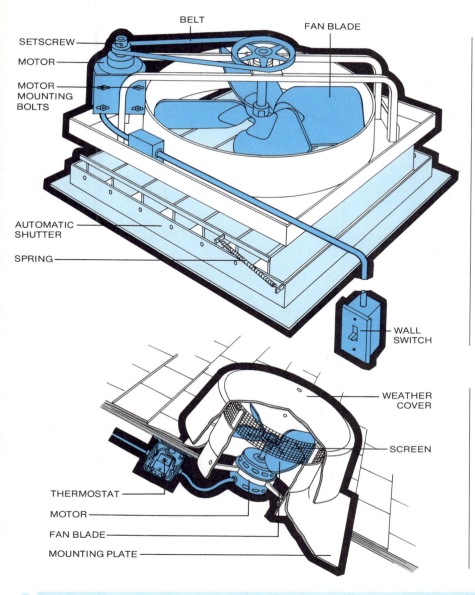

SETSCREW
MOTOR
MOTOR MOUNTING BOLTS
BELT
FAN BLADE
AUTOMATIC SHUTTER
SPRING
WALL SWITCH

THERMOSTAT
MOTOR
FAN BLADE
MOUNTING PLATE
WEATHER COVER
SCREEN

A large fan for the attic

To ventilate an average-sized home, a fan must move at least 5,000 cubic feet of air a minute. This job requires blades 24 inches in diameter or larger, driven through a belt and pulley by a one-third- or a one-half-horsepower electric motor that is connected to a separate 120-volt, 20-ampere circuit. When installed in an attic floor (opposite), the fan sits directly above a shutter fitted with blades that are pulled open by air pressure when the fan is running; when the fan stops, a spring pulls the shutter closed. The wall switch (or timer) that controls the fan can be installed in any convenient place. For a 24-inch fan, about 16 square feet of metal louvers are needed to handle the air moved by the fan.

At the start of the cooling season, clean the fan and shutter blades; lubricate the motor and shutter. Tighten screws and bolts, including those holding the motor pulley and the fan blades to their shafts. Tighten the belt—by repositioning the motor—so it will not slip. Replace a worn belt.

A fan that sits on the roof

Less expensive than an attic fan, the roof fan at left will still move 1,000 cubic feet of superheated air out of an attic each minute. The most common sizes use 14- or 16-inch blades that are turned by a one-tenth-horsepower direct-drive motor. The fan is mounted over a hole in the roof; a cover keeps rain out and a screen bars insects. The thermostat is near the fan.

Once a year, clean the motor housing and the fan blades. Oil the motor if it has oil holes, and remove any debris that might clog the screen.

Troubleshooting Attic Fans

Problem	Possible Causes	Solution
Fan does not run	Electricity not reaching motor Defective switch or loose wiring Defective motor	Check circuit breaker or fuse Replace switch; tighten connections Replace motor
Insufficient air flow	Slipping or worn belt Blocked air openings	Adjust tension or replace belt Clean shutters, louvers and vents
Excessive noise	Dry motor bearings Dirty or unbalanced blades Loose mounting	Lubricate bearings with motor oil Clean blades; straighten or replace Tighten all bolts and screws

Exhaust Fans

Bathrooms, laundry rooms and kitchens often need forced ventilation. Large amounts of heat and humidity are added to the air each time a hot shower is taken or clothing is washed and dried. A kitchen range will generate as much as 200 pounds of grease-laden moisture each year, as well as heat and odors.

Exhaust fans eliminate the discomfort of poor ventilation and help prevent rust and mildew damage. They also ease the air-conditioner or dehumidifier load by removing much heat and humidity at the source.

The typical exhaust fan illustrated below is installed through the exterior or wall of a room, eliminating the need for ducts. Other types are designed for ceiling installation; they are often used in bathrooms and may have long ducts leading to the outside. Some exhaust fans are controlled with a pull chain, others with a wall switch or timer.

The hooded fans on the opposite page, especially engineered for use above kitchen ranges, contain aluminum filters to trap grease. The ducted model exhausts heat, moisture, smoke and odors outdoors; the ductless hood cleans the air by circulating it through filters.

All of these fans require periodic cleaning for efficiency and safety. An accumulation of dirt and grease can be a fire hazard, and it may restrict the flow of air sufficiently to cause overheating of the motor. Cleaning procedures are outlined below and opposite; directions for replacing a defective switch are below.

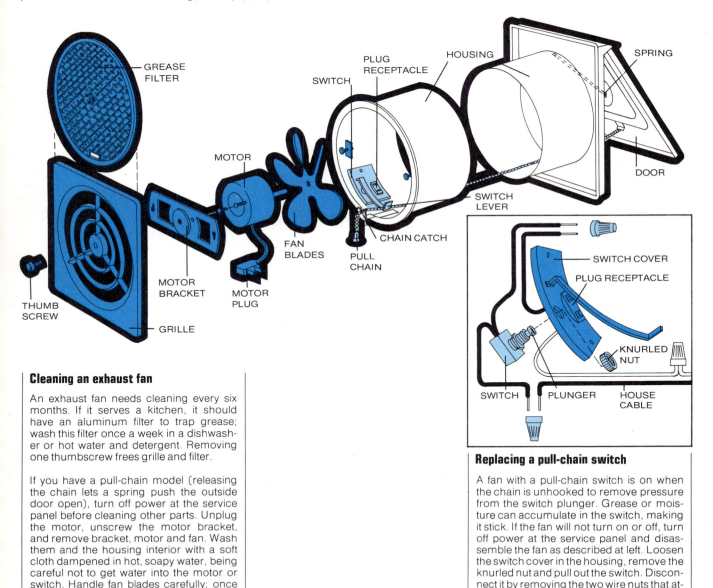

Cleaning an exhaust fan

An exhaust fan needs cleaning every six months. If it serves a kitchen, it should have an aluminum filter to trap grease; wash this filter once a week in a dishwasher or hot water and detergent. Removing one thumbscrew frees grille and filter.

If you have a pull-chain model (releasing the chain lets a spring push the outside door open), turn off power at the service panel before cleaning other parts. Unplug the motor, unscrew the motor bracket, and remove bracket, motor and fan. Wash them and the housing interior with a soft cloth dampened in hot, soapy water, being careful not to get water into the motor or switch. Handle fan blades carefully; once bent, they are noisy. If the motor has ports marked "OIL," put in a few drops of light oil before reassembling the fan.

Replacing a pull-chain switch

A fan with a pull-chain switch is on when the chain is unhooked to remove pressure from the switch plunger. Grease or moisture can accumulate in the switch, making it stick. If the fan will not turn on or off, turn off power at the service panel and disassemble the fan as described at left. Loosen the switch cover in the housing, remove the knurled nut and pull out the switch. Disconnect it by removing the two wire nuts that attach the switch to the house cable. Test the switch with a continuity tester (page 137). If it is defective, replace it.

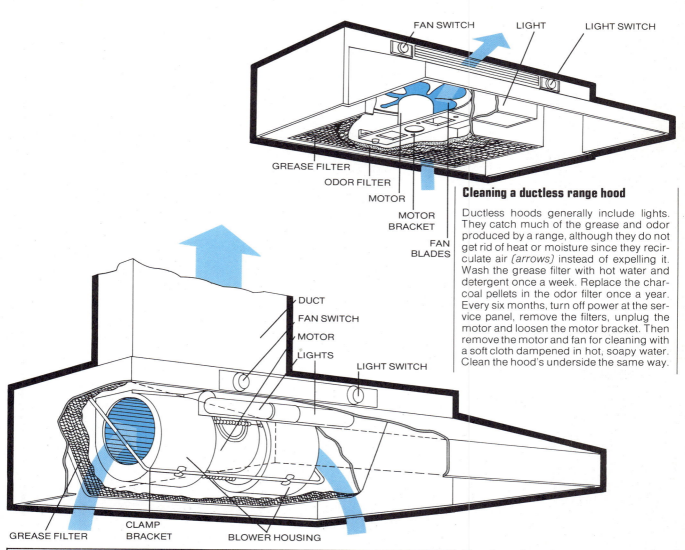

FAN SWITCH   LIGHT   LIGHT SWITCH

GREASE FILTER
ODOR FILTER
MOTOR
MOTOR BRACKET
FAN BLADES

DUCT
FAN SWITCH
MOTOR
LIGHTS
LIGHT SWITCH

GREASE FILTER   CLAMP BRACKET   BLOWER HOUSING

Cleaning a ductless range hood

Ductless hoods generally include lights. They catch much of the grease and odor produced by a range, although they do not get rid of heat or moisture since they recirculate air *(arrows)* instead of expelling it. Wash the grease filter with hot water and detergent once a week. Replace the charcoal pellets in the odor filter once a year. Every six months, turn off power at the service panel, remove the filters, unplug the motor and loosen the motor bracket. Then remove the motor and fan for cleaning with a soft cloth dampened in hot, soapy water. Clean the hood's underside the same way.

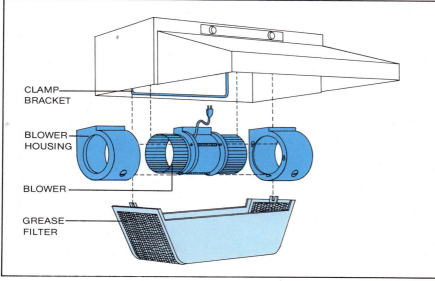

CLAMP BRACKET
BLOWER HOUSING
BLOWER
GREASE FILTER

Cleaning a ducted range hood

Ducted range hoods, the most efficient of kitchen ventilators, often have lights and blowers (enclosed fans with a squirrel-cage design rather than blades) that move large amounts of air *(arrows)*. But if not cleaned regularly, they accumulate grease and dirt that lower their efficiency. Once a week, remove the grease filter and wash it with hot water and detergent. Every half year, turn off power at the service panel and clean the whole unit.

Remove the filter, unplug the motor, and unsnap the swinging clamp bracket to remove the motor and blowers. Slip off the blowers' housings and carefully remove the blowers by loosening the setscrews that hold them on the motor shaft. Clean these parts in hot, soapy water. With a soft cloth dampened in soapy water, clean the cooling openings in the motor housing. Cleaning ductwork is a professional's job.

Getting the Most Out of Machines for Yard and Garden

Yards and gardens were the last bastions of manual labor around the home. Launderers had had their hands out of water and cooks had stopped carrying wood for the stove long before power lawn mowers for domestic use came on the market after World War II. Until then, mechanized lawn mowing was only for parks, big estates and golf courses.

Once rolling, however, the forces of mechanization advanced rapidly. In recent years, power mowers have all but supplanted manual models. Electric hedge trimmers began to replace manual shears in the 1960s. And subsequent development of efficient but small rechargeable batteries made feasible still another laborsaving device, the portable electric grass clipper. The latest addition to the homeowner's backyard arsenal is the small gasoline or electric chain saw, which speeds the pruning of trees and the cutting of wood for the fireplace. Other tools that are now weapons of the homeowner as well as the professional landscaper—such as gasoline-powered rototillers and whirling-line weed trimmers—are better rented than purchased. The lightweight models that are for sale at home centers do not measure up to the quality of the heavy-duty rental machines. And since they are needed only occasionally, it is more practical to leave their maintenance and repair to someone else.

Yard and garden jobs, more than others around the home, require powerful machinery. Riding mowers can have engines of 14 or even more horsepower. Everyday rotary mowers have engines of about three horsepower that propel the blade tips at 200 miles per hour.

The heavy-duty jobs that the outdoor power tools perform not only demand power but cause rapid wear. Parts loosen, cutting edges are blunted and engines balk. Correcting such faults when they occur not only makes machines perform more efficiently but extends their lives. Poor maintenance, on the other hand, results in machines that are dangerous, no matter how carefully used.

Some necessary maintenance is often overlooked. Sharpening is one example—although one tool, the hedge trimmer, with teeth of extremely hard steel, rarely needs such attention. But a lawn-mower blade keeps its edge only about half a season, and the many small blades of a chain saw should be filed after half an hour of cutting hardwood logs.

Symptoms of dullness are unmistakable. Grass clippers need sharpening when they begin to bend grass and trap it between the blades instead of snipping it off neatly. A chain saw cuts more slowly as it become dull, and the chain turns very hot; it may saw crooked or buck, trying to jump out of your hands. A lawn mower will shorten grass even if its blade is blunt; but the lawn will assume a brown cast after a couple of days because some grass blades have been ripped rather than cut.

The best tool for sharpening lawn-mower and grass-clipper blades is an ordinary flat file (page 28). By removing only small amounts of metal, it helps you avoid oversharpening blades. You can use a sharpening stone (page 28) after filing to hone the edges smooth.

When sharpening a blade, it is important to preserve the angle of the edge ground into the blade at the factory. Do not try to work freehand; lock the blade in a vise. A lawn-mower blade is sharpened by filing the upper side of the edge to form a narrow wedge (page 350). (Be careful to file both ends of the blade equally or the blade will be unbalanced and could vibrate enough to damage the mower.) When sharpening grass clippers (page 353), however, the idea is to shape abrupt corners on the edges of the two blades—clippers cut grass between the blades rather than slicing it.

Chain saws are an exception to the flat-file rule. Sharpening them requires a round file (page 356) and an angle guide—available from the dealer. File each cutter equally, and do not try to remove a deep nick or to reshape a break. If such damage occurs, take the chain apart and install a new cutter link (page 355)—a saw with cutters of unequal height or irregular shape is uncontrollable and dangerous to use.

Power-cord problems

Most other maintenance pertains to engines (pages 344-345) or motors (pages 190-195). But most electrically powered yard tools have one accessory that requires special attention: very long power cords. Even these long cords are seldom long enough to reach the farthest corner of the yard, so that an extension cord is generally necessary. And either the machine cord or its extension is easily cut through.

Just any extension cord will not do for an outdoor machine. Its motor may draw a heavy current, and that current may have to travel a long distance from house receptacle to machine. Both current load and distance affect the size of wire required (box, page 127); if the wire is too small, voltage will be reduced by the long transmission distance, downgrading performance or even damaging the motor.

If you sever the cord or extension, it is best to replace the whole thing. To avoid that expense, you can attach male and female plugs (page 187) to the cut ends and connect them together again. Ordinary plugs pull apart easily, but special connectors that twist together and lock are made for heavy-duty use; you will find them at an electrical-supply house that serves industrial customers.

One way to minimize extension-cord problems is to have outdoor cable laid from the house to receptacles around the yard. It is a fairly simple job for an electrician, and many homeowners do it themselves.

However you supply electricity to outdoor machines, make sure grounding connections are adequate. You ordinarily use these machines while standing in damp grass, which makes a good electrical contact between you and the earth so that a shock easily causes serious harm. Inspect your tools frequently and replace damaged cords and plugs promptly. The electrical code requires a ground-fault circuit interrupter (page 145) to be installed on any circuit with outdoor receptacles. It trips so fast that it prevents harm to you even if your tool becomes defective or the grounding system fails.

Bedding down your machines for the winter

Garden machines are unlike the others around the house in that they are seasonal tools and must be put away for the winter. Rust is the main enemy; it can freeze (that is, immobilize) a machine and make it difficult—or even impossible—to get it back in commission for the following season. For protection against rust, machines with electric motors require little preparation: just remove grass accumulations, which retain moisture, and lightly coat unpainted exterior metal parts, especially blades, with engine oil.

In gasoline engines, rust is more insidious; it can, in effect, weld the piston to the cylinder wall. Four-stroke engines, the kind usually found on lawn mowers, rust more easily than the two-stroke engines in chain saws because of the difference in their fuel supplies: the two-stroke type uses oil mixed with gasoline to lubricate the cylinder while the engine runs, and thus has built-in rust protection.

Before storing either kind of engine, drain leftover gasoline from the fuel tank to keep it from evaporating—it would leave gummy deposits in the carburetor or fuel line.

Start the engine and run it until it stops, thus using up any gasoline in the fuel line and carburetor. Drain the oil from a four-stroke engine and fill it with fresh oil. If your engine has a sediment bowl, remove the bowl from the carburetor, wipe it clean and reinstall it. Brush off the engine and lightly coat all unpainted metal parts with engine oil.

Remove the spark plug and pour a tablespoon of engine oil through the spark-plug hole. Replace the plug, and crank the engine several times by hand to distribute the oil evenly in the cylinder. Close the choke, and cover the air cleaner and exhaust pipe with cloths to keep debris out of the engine.

Cover all outdoor machine tools before putting them away, but do not give in to the temptation to seal them in plastic bags in the expectation that the plastic will keep moisture out. Plastic also traps moisture, and this humidity will cause severe rust over the winter. The best wraps are old newspapers or grocery bags. Store tools in a dry place where there is unimpeded air circulation.

Electric machines are generally ready to be plugged in when spring comes. Engine-driven ones, however, require preparation. When you take the mower or chain saw out of storage, check the spark plug (page 349) and replace it with a new one if necessary. Before installing the plug, crank the engine several times to expel any excess oil from the cylinder. Tighten screws and bolts. Uncover the air cleaner and exhaust pipe, pour fresh gasoline into the tank, connect the cable to the spark plug, and start the engine. The exhaust will emit dense blue smoke until the oil residue in the cylinder has been burned. If the engine turns out to be especially hard to start, take off the air cleaner and pour a couple of tablespoonfuls of fuel down the carburetor throat.

POWER LAWN MOWERS

Most lawn mowers depend for their muscle on a four-stroke gasoline engine—a collection of precision parts, working in close synchronism to harness violent explosions *(opposite)* to the task of cutting grass. For mowers, this type of engine has nearly replaced the simpler two-stroke engine still used on chain saws *(pages 354-357).*

All gasoline engines require periodic attention to keep them running smoothly, and all are made of similar parts, adjusted in similar ways (the exception is the chain saw's unique carburetor). Dull blades and broken starter ropes are common mower problems that you can fix at home.

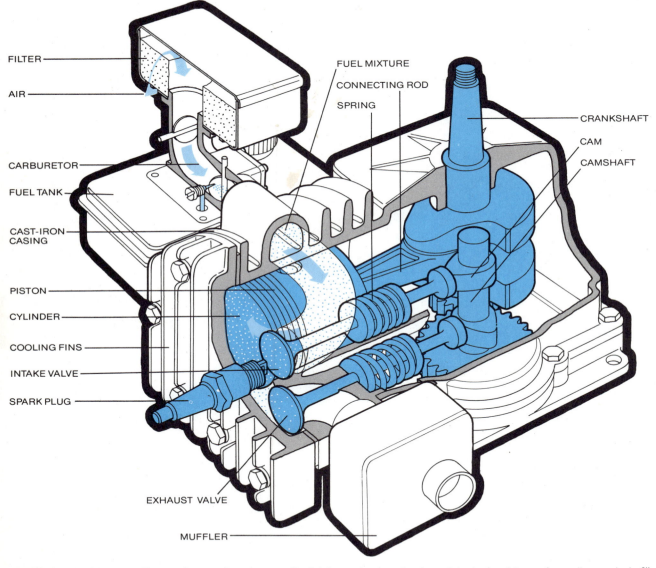

FILTER
AIR
CARBURETOR
FUEL TANK
CAST-IRON CASING
PISTON
CYLINDER
COOLING FINS
INTAKE VALVE
SPARK PLUG
EXHAUST VALVE
MUFFLER

FUEL MIXTURE
CONNECTING ROD
SPRING

CRANKSHAFT
CAM
CAMSHAFT

Inside and outside a gasoline engine

Within the cast-iron casing of a typical one-cylinder mower engine, a connecting rod converts back-and-forth motion of the piston into rotary motion of the crankshaft. A pair of gears links the crankshaft to a camshaft whose cams, with the help of stiff springs on the intake and exhaust valves, open and close the valves in time with the piston *(opposite page).*

Mounted outside the engine is a simple carburetor that uses a stream of air *(light blue arrows),* filtered through a layer of foam rubber, to atomize gasoline from the fuel tank. A mixture of gasoline and air *(light blue dots)* passes by way of the intake valve into the cylinder where it is ignited by a spark plug. Leaving the cylinder by the exhaust valve, waste gases go through a noise-reducing muffler. Heat, another by-product of combustion, is dissipated by cooling fins molded into the engine casing.

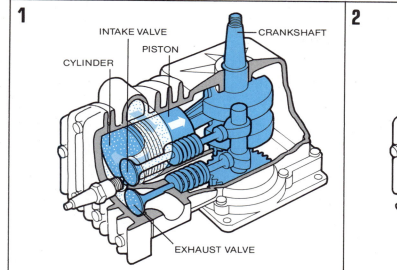

1 INTAKE VALVE
CRANKSHAFT
PISTON
CYLINDER
EXHAUST VALVE

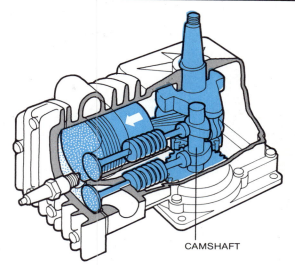

2 CAMSHAFT

SPARK PLUG

EXHAUST VALVE

1 The start of the cycle: intake

On the intake stroke, the exhaust valve is closed. Vaporized fuel mixture *(light blue dots)* rushes into the cylinder through the open intake valve *(light blue arrow)* to fill a partial vacuum created as the crankshaft pulls the piston right *(white arrows)*.

2 Compression

As the crankshaft continues to turn, it rotates the camshaft so that both valves are closed, and it forces the piston to the left. The piston compresses the fuel mixture to about one eighth its original volume and heats it to make it more explosive.

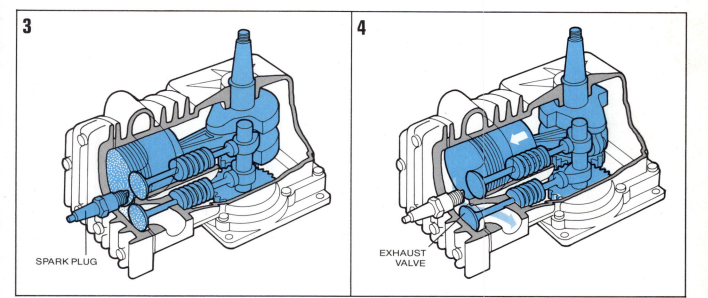

3 Ignition

Near the end of the compression stroke, the spark plug ignites the fuel mixture. The temperature inside the cylinder jumps to 2,000°, more than quadrupling the pressure, which shoves the piston to the right to turn the crankshaft.

4 Exhaust

Pushed leftward again by the crankshaft, the piston forces waste gases out the open exhaust valve. As the crankshaft turns, it will pull the piston to the right, the exhaust valve will close, and fuel and air will enter the cylinder to start the cycle again.

The Electric System

With even the simplest lawn mowers, the price of convenience is complexity—and complexity in this case demands proper maintenance of the machine. The lawn-mower blade requires only an occasional filing to keep it sharp. But the engine calls for more attention. The oil needs to be changed and the carburetor adjusted regularly. The spark plug has to be cleaned or replaced and its gap set with a round feeler-gauge. Contact points in the magneto also have to be adjusted, a job which requires a flat feeler-gauge. To uncover the points, the blower housing and the flywheel must be taken off. Many flywheels can be loosened with the help of a hammer blow; others are made to be removed with a special tool that is called a flywheel puller.

How a lawn mower works

A power lawn mover cuts grass with an edged, angled bar fastened to the engine crankshaft. As the blade rotates, its slightly raised rear edge creates a draft that lifts the grass for better cutting and also blows grass clippings out the discharge chute. A mower cuts grass to a length determined by the height of the blade, which can be adjusted by raising or lowering the wheels with height-adjustment levers. The lever and a cable on the handle control a combination choke and throttle on the carburetor. The engine can run only when the safety bar along the inside of the handle is raised and gripped. (Mowers made before 1983 lack this safety feature.) When the safety bar is released, a cable connected to it pulls a brake band tight against the flywheel, instantly stopping the spinning of the flywheel and magneto, and grounding out the electrical current to the spark plug. (The magneto is concealed beneath the flywheel and a blower housing that covers the flywheel cooling fins.)

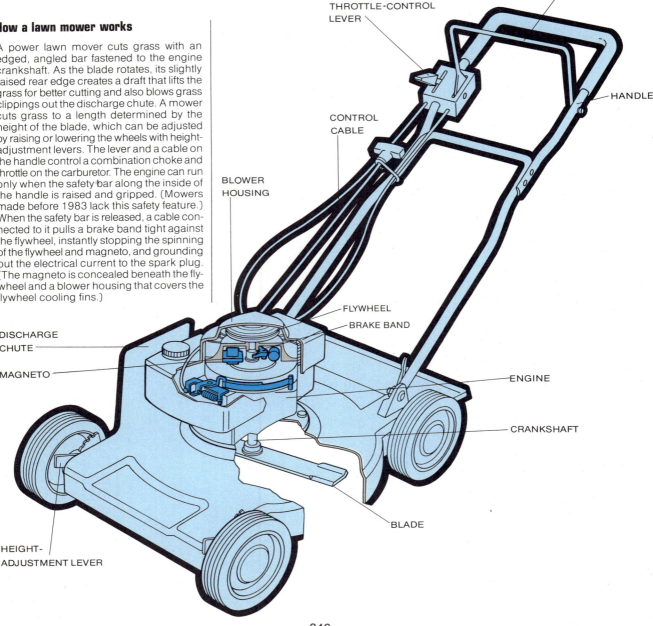

SAFETY BAR

THROTTLE-CONTROL LEVER

HANDLE

CONTROL CABLE

BLOWER HOUSING

FLYWHEEL

BRAKE BAND

DISCHARGE CHUTE

MAGNETO

ENGINE

CRANKSHAFT

BLADE

HEIGHT-ADJUSTMENT LEVER

How a magneto fires a spark plug

As the crankshaft turns a flywheel containing a permanent magnet past a transformer *(page 177)*, the moving magnet's field generates electricity in the transformer's primary coil, creating another magnetic field. A cam on the crankshaft then opens a pair of contact points—a kind of switch —that work with an electronic device called a condenser to interrupt the primary-coil circuit and cause the magnetic field to collapse. This new change in magnetism generates electricity in the secondary coil. Since the secondary has more turns of wire than the primary, the voltage produced is high. This high voltage jumps the spark-plug gap in a spark that ignites the fuel.

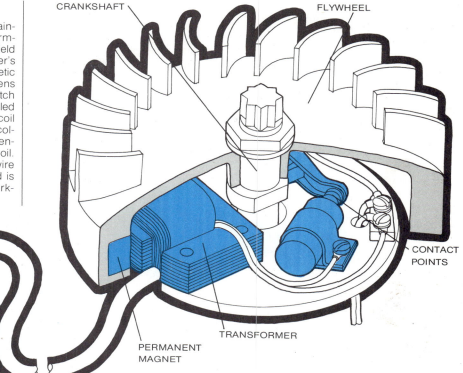

CRANKSHAFT

FLYWHEEL

CONTACT POINTS

SPARK PLUG

PERMANENT MAGNET

TRANSFORMER

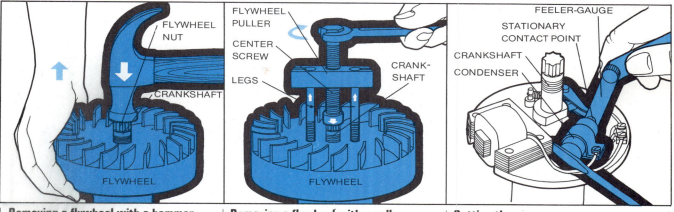

Removing a flywheel with a hammer

A hammer is used to loosen many flywheels. Disconnect the cable from the spark plug and remove the blower housing *(page 351)*. Hold the flywheel with one hand, and with a wrench, unscrew the nut to the top of the crankshaft; then loosen the flywheel by pulling up on it and striking the nut sharply with a hammer *(above)*. Take off the nut and remove the flywheel.

Removing a flywheel with a puller

Many flywheels require a flywheel puller for removal. They are designed with threaded holes in the top, into which you can screw the legs of the puller after you have completely removed the flywheel nut. Using a wrench to turn the puller center screw lifts the flywheel off the crankshaft.

Setting the gap

Turn the crankshaft until the contact points open as wide as possible. Place between the points a feeler-gauge of the thickness specified by your service manual. Loosen the stationary point—in this case attached to the condenser—and move it so that both points touch the gauge lightly. Tighten the stationary point, then remove the feeler-gauge and reassemble the lawn mower.

Lawn-Mower-Engine Maintenance

During a summer's operation, your lawn mower may stall in tall grass, stutter and stumble as you accelerate from idle to operating speed, or become exasperatingly hard to start. Almost invariably the cause is engine trouble—a worn or defective spark plug, or a carburetor setting thrown off by the engine's own vibration. An hour spent checking the spark plug and adjusting the carburetor will help keep your mower running smoothly until you store it for the winter.

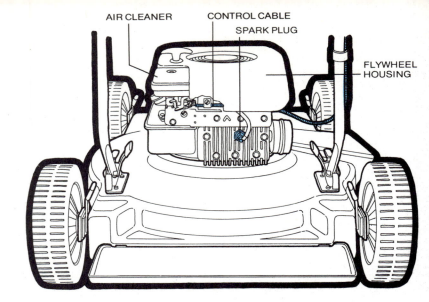

Locating the parts

A rear view of a power mower *(above)* shows two external components—the control cable and the spark plug—that need maintenance. But to work on the choke you must remove some parts *(below)*.

Adjusting the choke

Starting trouble often arises in the choke. Pull the spark-plug connector off the plug, so the engine cannot start accidentally. Move the throttle lever on the lawn-mower handle to "CHOKE." Unscrew the nuts securing the flywheel housing and pull it off, then unscrew the wing nut securing the air cleaner and set the cleaner aside. You can now see the carburetor's choke plate—a rotatable disc that controls air flow. It should be completely closed; but if it is not, loosen the screw of the control-cable clamp and slide the cable forward *(arrow)* until the plate closes. Hold the cable in place and tighten the clamp screw.

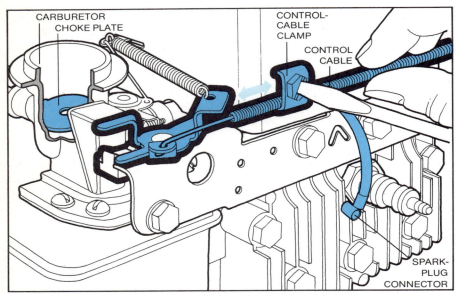

Adjusting the carburetor

Two separate adjustments of the carburetor—made with the engine running—set the correct gas mixture and idling speed. With the air cleaner and flywheel housing back in place and the spark plug connected, start the engine. If it will not start, close the needle valve by turning it clockwise until you feel slight resistance; do not tighten further or you will damage the valve. Then open the valve three quarters of a turn to one and a half turns, as specified in your service manual. You should now be able to start the engine. Run the engine at high speed two minutes to warm it up. Important: Do not touch the hot engine or bring a hand or foot near the whirling blade. Turn the needle valve clockwise one eighth of a turn. Wait a few seconds, then turn the valve another eighth of a turn. Continue turning clockwise in eighth-turn steps until the engine begins to slow. Now, counting the steps this time, turn it counterclockwise in eighth-turn steps until the engine begins to falter. The correct valve setting is halfway between the two extremes.

To set idling speed, move the throttle to "SLOW" and turn the adjustment screw until the sound of the engine indicates that it is running at about half its maximum speed. The correct idling speed may seem fast to you, but small gasoline engines are designed for high speed; slow idling may cause unburned fuel to foul the spark plug.

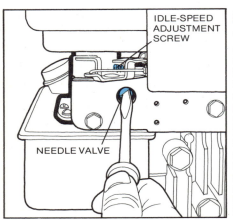

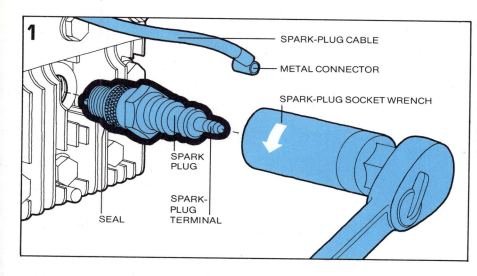

SPARK-PLUG CABLE

METAL CONNECTOR

SPARK-PLUG SOCKET WRENCH

SPARK PLUG

SPARK-PLUG TERMINAL

SEAL

1 Removing the spark plug

If an engine stutters or frequently misfires, check the spark plug. Remove the connector and examine it; if it seems too loose for the plug, squeeze it slightly with pliers until it fits snugly over the terminal, then take it off again. Wipe dirt from around the spark plug with a clean rag, then unscrew it with a spark-plug socket wrench. Reuse a plug that shows normal wear; replace a defective one (drawings, bottom).

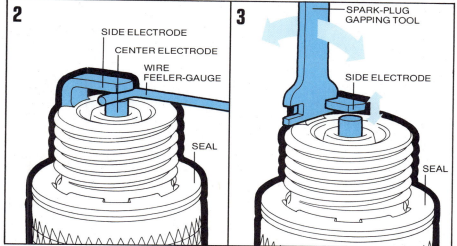

SIDE ELECTRODE

CENTER ELECTRODE

WIRE FEELER-GAUGE

SEAL

SPARK-PLUG GAPPING TOOL

SIDE ELECTRODE

SEAL

2 Checking the spark-plug gap

Check the gap of every plug, new or old, before installing it. Consult your service manual for the correct gap, and pull a wire feeler-gauge of that diameter between the electrodes. The gauge should fit snugly.

3 Adjusting the gap

If necessary, bend the spark plug's side electrode with a spark-plug gapping tool, narrowing or widening the gap until the gauge shows it is correct.

Before installing a plug, oil the threads; set the seal in place and screw the plug into the engine with your fingers; and then tighten the plug slightly with the socket wrench. Reattach the spark-plug cable.

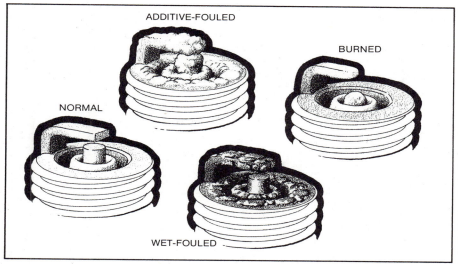

ADDITIVE-FOULED

BURNED

NORMAL

WET-FOULED

Analyzing a spark plug

The drawings at left show spark plugs in four distinct conditions. All but the normal one should be discarded—but the others can be used to diagnose engine trouble.

On a normal plug, electrodes show slight wear, with thin brown or tan deposits.

Additive-fouled electrodes are peppered with debris that can short-circuit the plug. Cause: fuel with high lead content.

Wet-fouled electrodes are coated with oil. Causes: clogged air filter, weak ignition system or excessive idling.

Burned plugs have light gray or chalky electrodes, worn by heat. Causes: dirty cooling fins, a carburetor set too lean, or an overloaded engine.

Blades and Ropes

There comes a time for nearly every lawn-mower owner when his mower begins to chop at his lawn instead of cutting it. Or when, trying to start the engine, he finds himself sitting down hard on the ground with one end of a broken starter rope in his hand. Sharpening a lawn-mower blade is simplicity itself—a few dozen strokes of a file, and the job is done. Replacing a starter rope is more complicated, but basically the procedure is the same for all mowers. The tricky part of the job is coiling the starter spring, which is stiff and sometimes obdurate. Important: Never work on a power mower until you disconnect the spark-plug cable.

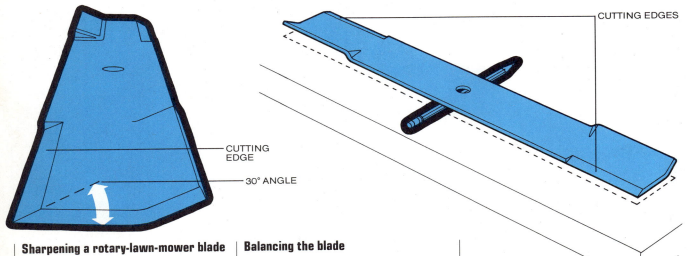

CUTTING EDGES

CUTTING EDGE

30° ANGLE

Sharpening a rotary-lawn-mower blade

Pull the cable off the spark plug, then remove the nut or screw that holds the blade to the crankshaft. Put the blade in a vise [page 353] and file the cutting edges to a 30° angle. Do not try to remove deep nicks in the blade. Nicks do not affect cutting appreciably, and removing them requires onerous filing of both cutting edges to keep the blade balanced.

Balancing the blade

Before reinstalling the blade, balance it on a pencil. A small difference in weight between the two halves of the blade can cause vibration, making the mower cut unevenly. If one end of the blade sinks, file the cutting edge until the blade remains level. Put the blade back on the crankshaft, cutting edges forward and facing the grass, then reconnect the spark-plug cable.

Troubleshooting Power Lawn Mowers

Problem	Possible Causes	Solution
Engine hard to start or runs erratically	Choke not completely closed Fouled or incorrectly gapped plug Contact-point gap incorrect Defective condenser Incorrect fuel-air mixture or idling speed	Adjust the choke (page 348) Clean or replace plug and adjust gap (page 349) Reset gap (page 347) Replace the condenser Adjust the carburetor (page 348)
Engine stalls	Fuel line or gas-cap vent clogged Engine overheating	Clean fuel line and vent with a wire Check oil level and brush dirt from between cooling fins
Grass not cut cleanly	Dull blade	Sharpen and balance blade
Excessive vibration	Blade out of balance	Balance blade (above)

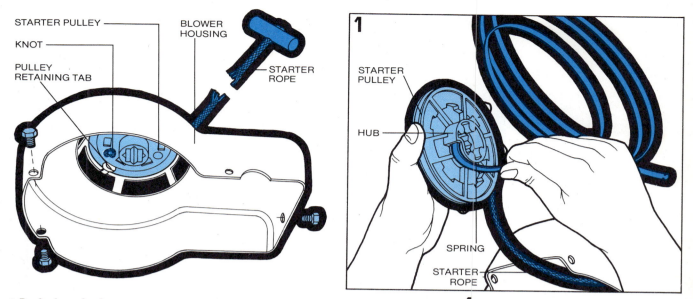

Replacing a broken starter rope

After disconnecting the spark plug, unbolt the starter-pulley housing to reach the pulley—on some mowers you must first remove the blower housing *(above)*. Lift the pulley from under the retaining tab and out of the housing. As the pulley comes out of the housing, a spring will uncoil. Detach the spring from the housing, and pull the old rope out of the pulley. Thread a new rope through holes in the blower housing and pulley. Tie a knot in the rope outside the pulley, but do not wind the rope around yet.

1 Coiling the spring

The spring sometimes comes out of the pulley hub while you attach the rope. If it has, insert the notched end of the spring into the slot in the hub; then begin coiling the spring around the hub in the same direction it comes out of the slot.

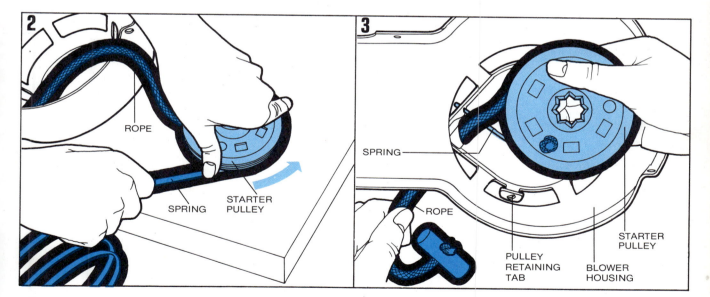

2 Winding the rope

Hold the pulley, hub down, on a flat surface; turn it to continue coiling the spring. When it is coiled, hold it against the face of the pulley and turn the pulley in the opposite direction to wind as much rope as possible into the pulley groove.

3 Reinstalling the pulley

Engage the spring end in the notch in the blower housing; pull on the starter handle to take up slack in the rope. Insert the pulley in the housing under the retaining tab. Release the pulley slowly to let the spring settle in place. Reattach the housing.

SHRUB AND GRASS CUTTERS

The difference in operation between the hedge trimmer *(below)* and the grass clipper *(right)* is that the trimmer's cutting blades move forward and back while the clipper's blades move side to side. More important to the user, however, is a dif- ference in power supplies. Most hedge trimmers have to be plugged into house current, which runs motors able to drive blades over 20 inches long. Grass trimmers use rechargeable batteries to run smaller motors driving three-inch-wide blades. Clipper blades need periodic sharpening *(opposite, bottom)*, but trimmer blades rarely do. If badly nicked, they should be replaced *(below)*.

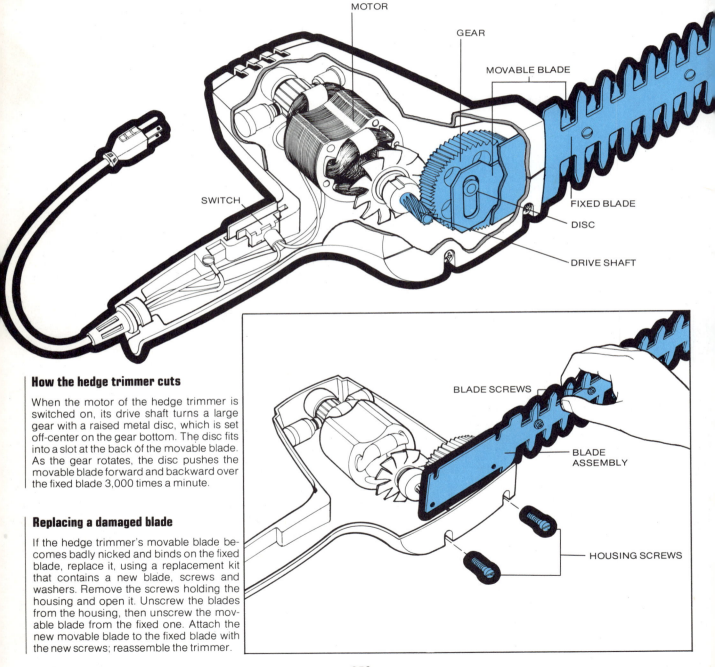

MOTOR

GEAR

MOVABLE BLADE

SWITCH

FIXED BLADE

DISC

DRIVE SHAFT

BLADE SCREWS

BLADE ASSEMBLY

HOUSING SCREWS

How the hedge trimmer cuts

When the motor of the hedge trimmer is switched on, its drive shaft turns a large gear with a raised metal disc, which is set off-center on the gear bottom. The disc fits into a slot at the back of the movable blade. As the gear rotates, the disc pushes the movable blade forward and backward over the fixed blade 3,000 times a minute.

Replacing a damaged blade

If the hedge trimmer's movable blade becomes badly nicked and binds on the fixed blade, replace it, using a replacement kit that contains a new blade, screws and washers. Remove the screws holding the housing and open it. Unscrew the blades from the housing, then unscrew the movable blade from the fixed one. Attach the new movable blade to the fixed blade with the new screws; reassemble the trimmer.

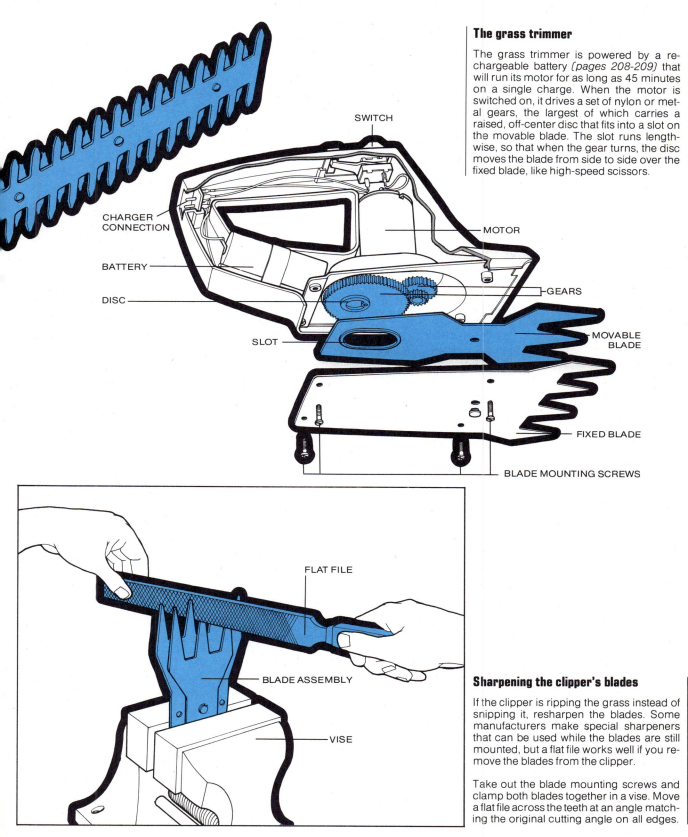

The grass trimmer

The grass trimmer is powered by a rechargeable battery *(pages 208-209)* that will run its motor for as long as 45 minutes on a single charge. When the motor is switched on, it drives a set of nylon or metal gears, the largest of which carries a raised, off-center disc that fits into a slot on the movable blade. The slot runs lengthwise, so that when the gear turns, the disc moves the blade from side to side over the fixed blade, like high-speed scissors.

SWITCH

CHARGER CONNECTION

BATTERY

DISC

SLOT

MOTOR

GEARS

MOVABLE BLADE

FIXED BLADE

BLADE MOUNTING SCREWS

FLAT FILE

BLADE ASSEMBLY

VISE

Sharpening the clipper's blades

If the clipper is ripping the grass instead of snipping it, resharpen the blades. Some manufacturers make special sharpeners that can be used while the blades are still mounted, but a flat file works well if you remove the blades from the clipper.

Take out the blade mounting screws and clamp both blades together in a vise. Move a flat file across the teeth at an angle matching the original cutting angle on all edges.

CHAIN SAWS

A chain saw uses the power of a gasoline engine or an electric motor to drive a chain studded with tiny cutting blades around an oval guide bar at up to 2,800 feet per minute. Electric chain saws (right) are smooth and relatively quiet, but they are limited in their use afield by the length of their extension cords. Gasoline-driven chain saws are noisy but offer more freedom of movement, and

range from the two-horsepower model below to eight-horsepower giants used by lumberjacks.

The gasoline-powered chain saw's magneto and rope starter can be fixed in the same way as those on the lawn mower (page 351). The engine's exhaust ports are easily cleaned (page 357). But the most common maintenance job is keeping its cutting chain sharp and at the correct tension (page 356). Important: Disconnect the spark plug before working on a gasoline-driven saw, and wear work gloves to handle the chain.

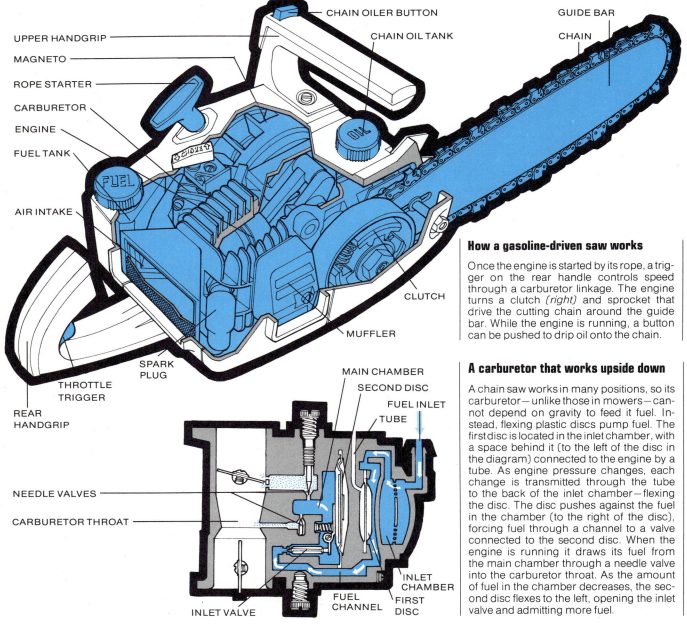

UPPER HANDGRIP
MAGNETO
ROPE STARTER
CARBURETOR
ENGINE
FUEL TANK
AIR INTAKE
THROTTLE TRIGGER
REAR HANDGRIP
SPARK PLUG

CHAIN OILER BUTTON
CHAIN OIL TANK
GUIDE BAR
CHAIN
CLUTCH
MUFFLER

NEEDLE VALVES
CARBURETOR THROAT
INLET VALVE
FUEL CHANNEL
FIRST DISC
INLET CHAMBER

MAIN CHAMBER
SECOND DISC
FUEL INLET TUBE

How a gasoline-driven saw works

Once the engine is started by its rope, a trigger on the rear handle controls speed through a carburetor linkage. The engine turns a clutch (right) and sprocket that drive the cutting chain around the guide bar. While the engine is running, a button can be pushed to drip oil onto the chain.

A carburetor that works upside down

A chain saw works in many positions, so its carburetor — unlike those in mowers — cannot depend on gravity to feed it fuel. Instead, flexing plastic discs pump fuel. The first disc is located in the inlet chamber, with a space behind it (to the left of the disc in the diagram) connected to the engine by a tube. As engine pressure changes, each change is transmitted through the tube to the back of the inlet chamber — flexing the disc. The disc pushes against the fuel in the chamber (to the right of the disc), forcing fuel through a channel to a valve connected to the second disc. When the engine is running it draws its fuel from the main chamber through a needle valve into the carburetor throat. As the amount of fuel in the chamber decreases, the second disc flexes to the left, opening the inlet valve and admitting more fuel.

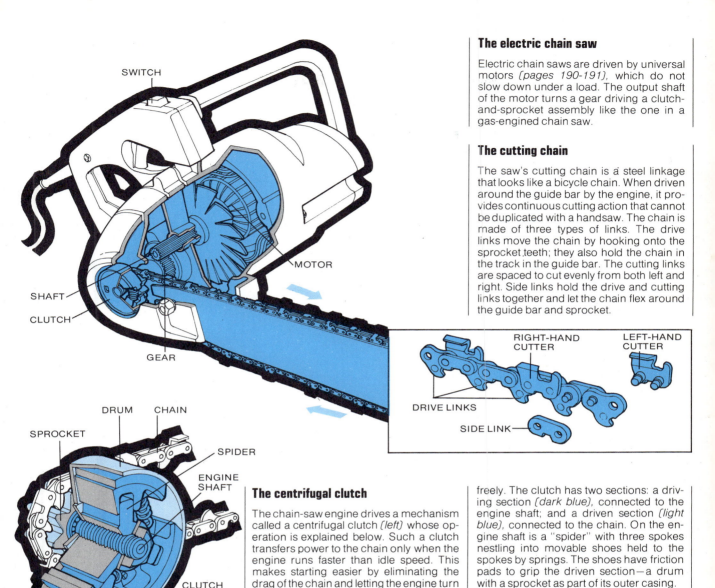

The electric chain saw

Electric chain saws are driven by universal motors *(pages 190-191),* which do not slow down under a load. The output shaft of the motor turns a gear driving a clutch-and-sprocket assembly like the one in a gas-engined chain saw.

The cutting chain

The saw's cutting chain is a steel linkage that looks like a bicycle chain. When driven around the guide bar by the engine, it provides continuous cutting action that cannot be duplicated with a handsaw. The chain is made of three types of links. The drive links move the chain by hooking onto the sprocket teeth; they also hold the chain in the track in the guide bar. The cutting links are spaced to cut evenly from both left and right. Side links hold the drive and cutting links together and let the chain flex around the guide bar and sprocket.

The centrifugal clutch

The chain-saw engine drives a mechanism called a centrifugal clutch *(left)* whose operation is explained below. Such a clutch transfers power to the chain only when the engine runs faster than idle speed. This makes starting easier by eliminating the drag of the chain and letting the engine turn freely. The clutch has two sections: a driving section *(dark blue)*, connected to the engine shaft; and a driven section *(light blue)*, connected to the chain. On the engine shaft is a "spider" with three spokes nestling into movable shoes held to the spokes by springs. The shoes have friction pads to grip the driven section—a drum with a sprocket as part of its outer casing.

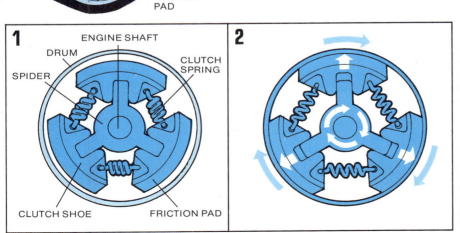

1 The clutch disengaged

When the engine is off or running at idle, the tension of the springs holds the clutch shoes firmly to the spider. The friction pads cannot touch the clutch drum and no power is transferred to the sprocket and chain.

2 The clutch engaged

When engine speed increases, the spider rotates quickly and its centrifugal force overcomes the springs holding the clutch shoes. The shoes slide out and press their pads against the drum, turning it and the sprocket. The clutch revolves as a unit and drives the chain around the guide bar.

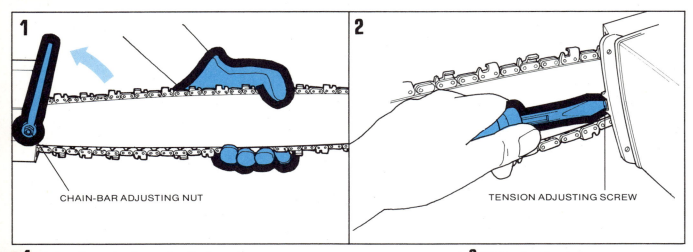

CHAIN-BAR ADJUSTING NUT

TENSION ADJUSTING SCREW

1 Chain adjustment: loosening the bar

A slack chain wears out its drive links and can damage the guide bar and sprocket. Tighten a new chain after a few minutes of use; check it often, and tighten it whenever it can be pulled easily around the bar. To reset the tension, loosen the chain-bar adjusting nut with a wrench. Support the bar in its horizontal position.

2 Tightening the chain

Increase the chain tension by turning the tension adjusting screw clockwise until the chain can be pulled around the bar with moderate resistance. Retighten the chain-bar adjusting nut—making sure that the bar remains horizontal—and check the chain tension again. If it is still not correct, repeat the procedure.

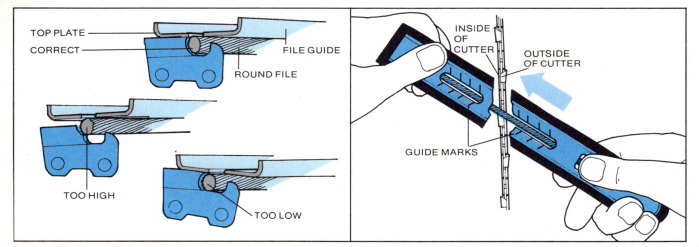

TOP PLATE
CORRECT
FILE GUIDE
ROUND FILE
TOO HIGH
TOO LOW

INSIDE OF CUTTER
OUTSIDE OF CUTTER
GUIDE MARKS

Placing a file for sharpening

To sharpen a chain, you need a round file and file guide of the type recommended for your model by the manufacturer. Hold the file and guide diagonally across the cutter so that the guide is flat against the top plate of the cutter you are sharpening *(top)*. If the guide is placed so that the file is too high *(center)*, it will dull the blade further. Placing it too low *(bottom)* will create a cutting shape that wears quickly.

Moving a file for sharpening

Turn the file guide so that the marks cut into it are parallel to the chain. File from the inside of each cutter to the outside, being careful to keep the guide flat on the blade's top plate and at the correct angle to the chain. File blades on one side of the chain first. Sharpen them all at the same point on the bar and use the same number of strokes on each one. Then file the blades on the other side of the chain the same way.

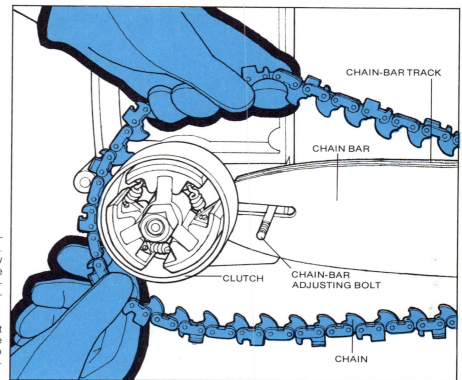

Replacing a chain

If the chain is badly worn or chipped, replace it by taking off the bar adjusting nut. Then loosen the tension adjusting screw and remove the cover that protects the clutch. Then take the chain off the sprocket, lift it out from behind the clutch and remove it from the chain bar.

Place the new chain around the sprocket and bar, making sure that the drive links are engaged to the sprocket teeth and set into the chain-bar track. Adjust the chain tension as described at left.

CHAIN-BAR TRACK

CHAIN BAR

CLUTCH

CHAIN-BAR ADJUSTING BOLT

CHAIN

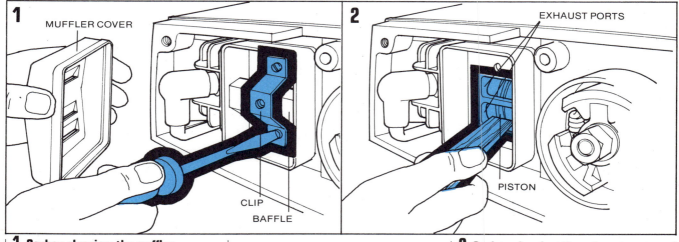

1 MUFFLER COVER

CLIP

BAFFLE

2 EXHAUST PORTS

PISTON

1 Carbon cleaning: the muffler

If your chain saw seems to be losing power, carbon may be clogging the muffler and exhaust ports. When the muffler is cool, pry off the muffler cover, and unscrew the clip and baffle. Then use a knife to scrape the carbon from every one of these three parts, taking special care to clean out the slots in the muffler cover.

2 Carbon cleaning: the exhaust ports

Before working on the ports, pull gently on the starting cord so that the piston moves until it completely covers the exhaust ports. This keeps carbon that is dislodged during cleaning from falling into the cylinder and damaging it. Scrape the carbon from the exhaust ports with a piece of soft wood, and replace the muffler assembly.

PICTURE CREDITS

BIBLIOGRAPHY

Althouse, Andrew D., Carl H. Turnquist, and Alfred F. Bracciano, *Modern Refrigeration and Air Conditioning*. The Goodheart-Wilcox Company, Inc., 1968.

Daniels, George:
Home Guide to Plumbing, Heating, and Air Conditioning. Popular Science Publishing Company, 1972.
How to Be Your Own Home Electrician. Popular Science Publishing Company, 1965.

Day, Richard:
The Practical Handbook of Electrical Repairs. Arco Publishing Company, Inc., 1969.
The Practical Handbook of Plumbing and Heating. Arco Publishing Company, Inc., 1969.

Emerick, Robert Henderson, *Troubleshooters' Handbook for Mechanical Systems*. McGraw-Hill Book Company, 1969.

Engineering Staff, Howard W. Sams and Company, Inc., *Basic Electricity and an Introduction to Electronics*. Howard W. Sams and Company, Inc., 1967.

Field, Edwin M., *Oil Burners*. Theodore Audel and Company, 1973.

Hertzberg, Robert:
Handyman's Electrical Repairs Handbook. Arco Publishing Company, 1962.
The Home Owner Handbook of Electrical Repairs. Bounty Books, 1974.

Meyerink, George, *Appliance Service Handbook*. Prentice-Hall, 1973.

Middleton, Robert G., *Practical Electricity*. Theodore Audel and Company, 1973.

Mix, Floyd M., *House Wiring Simplified*. The Goodheart-Wilcox Company, Inc., 1973.

Nielsen, Louis S., *Standard Plumbing Engineering Design*. McGraw-Hill Book Company, 1963.

Russell, Allen, *Getting Started in Heating and Air Conditioning Service*. Business News Publishing Company, 1973.

Safford, Edward L., *Electrical Wiring and Lighting for Home and Office*. Tab Books, 1973.

Strock, Clifford, and Richard L. Koral, eds., *Handbook of Air Conditioning, Heating and Ventilating*. Industrial Press, Inc., 1965.

Wheeler, Gershon J., *How to Repair Electrical Appliances*. Reston Publishing Company, 1972.

Periodicals
Air Conditioning, Heating and Refrigeration News, Business News Publishing Company, Birmingham, Michigan.
Consumer Reports, Consumers Union, Mount Vernon, New York.
Consumers' Research, Consumers' Research, Washington, New Jersey.
Popular Mechanics, The Hearst Corporation, New York City.
Popular Science, Popular Science Publishing Company, New York City.

Other Publications
Air Control for Hydronic Systems, Bell and Gossett, 1966.
Automatic Controls for Heating and Air Conditioning Systems, National Environmental Systems Contractors Association, 1966.
Central Heating Equipment Service Instructor's Manual, General Electric Company.
Code and Manual for the Design and Installation of Warm Air Winter Air Conditioning Systems and Year 'Round Air Conditioning Systems, National Environmental Systems Contractors Association.
Copper Tube Handbook, Copper Development Association.
Data Book, 1971, American Society of Plumbing Engineers, 1971.
Equipment Selection and System Design Procedures, National Environmental Systems Contractors Association, 1973.
Fundamentals of Gas Appliance Venting and Ventilation, American Gas Association, 1974.
Gas Appliances and Controls, Robertshaw Controls Company, 1972.
Home and Farm Water Supply Manual, The F. E. Myers and Brothers Company, 1972.
Hydronics Manual, Dunham-Bush, Inc., 1963.
Introduction to the Installation of Residential Ducted Heating and Air Conditioning Systems, National Environmental Systems Contractors Association, 1972.

Manual of Individual Water Supply Systems, U.S. Environmental Protection Agency, 1973.

Manual of Septic-Tank Practice, U.S. Department of Health, Education and Welfare, 1969.

Planning for an Individual Water System, American Association for Vocational Instructional Materials, 1973.

A Primer on Water Quality, U.S. Department of the Interior Geological Survey, 1965.

Service Training Guideline: Gas Heating Fundamentals, General Electric Company.

Servicing Air Conditioners and Refrigerators, Charous and Niebergall, Inc., 1972.

Servicing Portable Appliances, Books I-IV, Charous and Niebergall, Inc., 1972.

Simplified Electric Wiring Handbook, Sears, Roebuck and Company, 1969.

Small Engines, Volumes I and II, American Association for Vocational Instructional Materials, 1971.

Systems Handbook, 1973, American Society of Heating, Refrigerating and Air Conditioning Engineers, 1973.

The Total Comfort System Story, National Environmental Systems Contractors Association.

Water System and Treatment Handbook, Water Systems Council, 1966.

ACKNOWLEDGMENTS

For their help in the preparation of this book the editors would like to thank the following individuals: John C. Adams, Fedders Corporation, Edison, New Jersey; James R. Baldwin, the F. E. Myers and Brothers Company, Ashland, Ohio; Curtis B. Barnard, Carrier Corporation, Syracuse, New York; Simon Bayne, Eagle Electric Manufacturing Company, Inc., Long Island City, New York; Rix Beals, National Oil Fuel Institute, New York City; Don Beehler, Goulds Pumps, Inc., Seneca Falls, New York; Kevin Bingham and Tom O'Callaghan, Harrison Bros., Inc., Alexandria, Virginia; George M. Bliss III, United Association of Plumbers and Steamfitters, Washington, D.C.; Harry G. Brown, Mansfield Sanitary, Inc., Perrysville, Ohio; Richard C. Brusie, Air Conditioning and Refrigeration Institute, Arlington, Virginia; Ken J. Buck, Sloan Valve Company, Franklin Park, Illinois; Robert F. Bukowski, Schick, Inc., Lancaster, Pennsylvania; John C. Bumstead, State of New York Department of Health, Division of Sanitary Engineering, Albany; George Cain, Copper Development Association, Stamford, Connecticut; George W. Carter, Willis Mechanical Company, Inc., Bronx, New York; A. V. Cauhorn, Edco International Corporation, Detroit; Anthony Caviello, New York City; Joseph Childress, National Association of Plumbing, Heating, Cooling Contractors, Washington, D.C.; Joseph E. Cole, Cornwall Corporation, Boston; Donald R. Cozzolino, Stanley Tools, New Britain, Connecticut; Dale Curtis, Crane-Deming Pumps, Salem, Ohio; Timothy Cuthbert, The Whirlpool Corporation, Benton Harbor, Michigan; Joseph Della Rocca, North American Philips Corporation, New York City; E. S. Douglass, Electric Energy Association, New York City; Martin Dretel, D&S Pump and Supply Company, Inc., Brewster, New York; Dr. D. Dunning, Department of Health, Education and Welfare, Food and Nutrition Service, Washington, D.C.; Bert Dunphy, Editor, *Fueloil and Oil Heat*, Cedar Grove, New Jersey; Raymond Durazo, Plastics Pipe Institute, New York City; Brian F. Eckl, Water Treatment Division, Sta-Rite Industries, Inc., Deerfield, Wisconsin; George Einhart, Radiator Specialty Company, Charlotte, North Carolina; Michael Fain, New York City; Daniel Falone, New York City; Ralph Faust, Robertshaw Company, Morristown, New Jersey; George P. Glasser, The F. E. Myers and Brothers Company, Ashland, Ohio; Edward C. Grout, Water Treatment Division, Sta-Rite Industries, Inc., Deerfield, Wisconsin; Jean Hapwood, General Electric Company, New York City; M. Jay Harms, A. O. Smith Corporation, Kankakee, Illinois; Paul Hersch, American Waterworks Association, Denver; Les Heuton, Square D Company, Circuit Breaker Division, Cedar Rapids, Iowa; Ronald J. Hobel, Underwriters' Laboratories, Inc., Melville, Long Island; Derry Hollingsworth, The Franklin Institute, Philadelphia; John Houlihan, Water Systems Council, Chicago; Flynn E. Hudson, General Electric Wiring Device Business Department, Providence, Rhode Island; C. M. Jauch, Essex International, Inc., Belton, South Carolina; John Kaussner, American Standard, New Brunswick, New Jersey; Ken Kelton, Public Service Electric and Gas Company, Newark; Bertram York Kinzey, Richmond, Virginia; Barbara Kuehn, Home Ventilating Institute, Chicago; Frederick W. Kuo, All County Sewing Machine Center, Queens, New York; Neil L. Larsen, Honeywell, Inc., Minneapolis; Jay H. Lehr, National Water Well Association, Columbus, Ohio; John A. Lenhart, The Singer Company, Elizabeth, New Jersey; Donald T. Lideen, McCulloch Corporation, Los Angeles; Bob Lynch, National Oil Fuel Institute, New York City; George McNally, New York City; Barbara Mellman, Waste King Universal, Los Angeles; Patricia Mohs, New York City; B. P. Montagriff, Teledyne Company, Fort Collins, Colorado; Lawrence Murray, Philadelphia Electric Company, Philadelphia; John W. Newton, GTE Sylvania, Inc., Danvers, Massachusetts; Robert O'Connor, Roper, Inc., Kankakee, Illinois; Wes Parker, Sloan Valve Company, Franklin Park, Illinois; Richard Parrish, Litton Industries, Minneapolis; John H. Pomeroy, Farmers Home Administration, Washington, D.C.; Raymond and Richard Roes, Hasko Utilities Company, Inc., New York City; Dr. Robert Rosenberg, The Institute of Gas Technology, Chicago; August B. Russo, The Black and Decker Manufacturing Company, Hampstead, Maryland; Frances Saunders, The Brooklyn Union Gas Company, Brooklyn, New York; Fred E. Schmuck, Fluidmaster, Inc., Anaheim, California; Andrea F. Schoenfeld, Office of Consumer Affairs, Washington, D.C.; Robert Seaman, American Standard, New Brunswick, New Jersey; A. J. Shaffer, Bissell, Inc., Grand Rapids, Michigan; Bernie Shapiro, Rosetta Electric Company, Inc., New York City; Carle Shapiro, Rival Manufacturing Company, Kansas City, Missouri; Dr. Moris Shore, Department of Health, Education and Welfare, Food and Drug Administration, Rockville, Maryland; Norman Stoll, Hydronics Institute, Berkeley Heights, New Jersey; Robert M. Stone, Rival Manufacturing Company, Kansas City, Missouri; Chuck Tarshus, Corning Glass Works, Corning, New York; Bruno Valbona, Waring Products Division, Dynamics Corporation of America, New Hartford, Connecticut; William J. Whitsell, Environmental Protection Agency, Washington, D.C.; Robert S. Wyly, National Bureau of Standards, Washington, D.C.

The editors would also like to thank the following: The American Gas Association, Arlington, Virginia; Association of Home Appliance Manufacturers, Chicago; Delta Faucet Company, Greensburg, Indiana; Farberware Division of LCA Corporation, Yonkers, New York; McGraw-Edison Company, Toastmaster Division, Elgin, Illinois; Modern Faucet Manufacturing Company, Los Angeles; Proctor-Silex, Philadelphia; Rockwell International, Morgantown, West Virginia; Scovill Manufacturing Company, Hamilton Beach Division, Waterbury, Connecticut.

INDEX

Pressure, water. See Water pressure

Pressure flush valves, 102-103; diaphragm-type, 102, 103; piston-type, 102, 103. See also Toilets with pressure flush valves

Pressure switch connected to water pump, 110, 111, 112, 113, 114, 115; parts, 111; tubing to, 113; water pressure and, 111; working on, 116-117

Pressure tanks, 37, 106, 110, 111, 112, 113, 114, 115; precharged, for prevention of waterlogging, 106, 107; repair or replacement of, 117; repressurizing, 116; troubleshooting, 117; water-bag tank, 106; waterlogging in, 106, 107; waterlogging remedy for, 116. See also Water supply, independent; Waterlogging

Pressure-valve handle, 103; plunger unit of, 103; replacing parts of, 103

Prime in water pumps: loss or inadequacy of, 117; repriming pump, 117

Propane torch, 50, 51; flame spreader attached to, 66; proper use of, during soldering, 60-61; use of, to thaw frozen pipes, 66

Pump(s), water. See Water pumps

Pump house, diagram of, 112; electric heater for, 112

Putty, plumber's, 81, 83, 86, 87

Putty knife, 30

R

Raceway surface wiring, 174, 175; connection of, to existing receptacle, 175; description of, 175; installation of receptacles, 175

Radiators, 316, 319, 322, 323

Radios: kwh consumed, 131; light-duty extension cords for, 152

Range hoods, 339

Ranges, cooking, 288-293. See also Microwave ovens; Ranges, electric; Ranges, gas

Ranges, electric, 291-293; electric circuit for, 146; infinite switch and how it works, 292; kwh consumed, 131; life span of, 17; 120 volts and 240 volts in cable for, 130; receptacle for, 172; troubleshooting, 293

Ranges, gas, 288-290; gas leak in, 290; troubleshooting, 290

Reamer on tube cutter, 51; use of, 58

Receptacles, 172-175; extra, with surface wiring, 174-175; ground-fault circuit interrupter (GFCI), 173; grounding, types of, 145; grounding adapter for, 172, 173; 120-volt type, 172; outdoor, for yard tools, 342; replacement of, 172-173; three-slot grounded type, 172, 173; for 240-volt circuits, 130, 172; ungrounded, 172. See also Outlets

Receptacles, wiring of: at end of run, 172; in middle of run, 172; safety tests for, 142, 143, 172; split-circuit wiring, 173

Reciprocating piston pump. See Piston pumps

Refrigerator (or refrigerator-freezer), 282-287; early, 14-15; frost-free type, 282, 285; kwh consumed, 131; life span of, 17; self-defrosting, 282, 283, 284; troubleshooting, 287

Repair-service technicians, 16-18, 20, 23; of authorized agency, 16; dealing fairly with, 18, 20, 23; of factory-service outlet, 16; guides to finding, 16-17; "hot-line" numbers for emergencies, 16-17; need for, 16, 132, 274; owner's understanding with, before work begins, 18, 23

Repairs: basic, on small appliances, 184-187; determining cause of trouble, 183; finding hidden retaining screws, 43-44, 46, 72, 184-185; how to remove appliance housing, 184-185; keeping papers for all appliances, 16; kicking a balky machine, 14, 16; methodical approach to, 13-14, 16, 23; precautions, 182-183; repairing or replacing appliance cords, 186-187; savings on, 182; service contracts for, 17-18, 257; troubleshooting checklist, 23; warranties and, 16, 19; what to do about faulty appliances and unsatisfactory service, 20-22. See also Repair-service technicians; Troubleshooting charts

Resistance wire (nichrome): in appliance heating elements, 232, 234; in electric baseboard units, 298, 324-325

Retaining screws of appliance housing, hidden, 184-185

Reverse-pressure faucet stem, 71; assembly of, 73; replacing washers of, 72-73. See also Faucet stems; Stem faucets

Rings: compression rings, 59; restriction rings, 103; snap ring, 85. See also O-rings

Riser pipes, 39, 52-53; shutoff valves for, 39, 52-53

Roof fan, care of, 337

Rubber plunger, 50, 90, 101

Rust, protection against, 343

Rusted pipe connections, separation of, 47

S

"Sacrificial" anode, 258, 262

Safety, electrical, 142-143; tests, 143

Saws, 29; crosscut, 29; hacksaw, 29, 63; keyhole, 29

Screw(s): finding hidden screws, 43-44, 46, 72, 184-185; flathead, 31; handling washer screw with snapped-off head, 47; left-handed washer screw, 47; loosening tight screws, 47; metal, 31; setscrew, 72, 77, 78; terminal, 140, 152, 155; worn slot on, and correction of, 47

Screwdrivers, 26; flat-blade type, 26; Phillips, 26; proper use of, 25

Scum in septic tank, 107, 118, 120, 121; measuring level of, 107, 121

Sealant, silicone, 247. See also Tube sealants

Seat-dressing tool, 48, 49, 74

Seat wrenches, 49, 74; right-angled, 49, 74; straight or "pencil" tool

type, 49, 74

Seepage pit, 119

Septic tank, 37, 104, 107, 118-121; annual inspection, 120, 121; cleaning, 37, 107, 121; components of sewage in, 118, 120; garbage disposer and, 210; location marker, 120; measuring scum and sludge levels, 121; required capacity of, 118, 119. See also Drainage field

Service contracts, 17-18, 257, 336

Service panel, electrical, 128-129, 146, 148-149; fuses and circuit breakers in, 130; labeling circuits on, 135; making connections at, 132; tracing problems from, 135. See also Circuit breakers; Fuses

Service pipe (or main water line), 38, 52-53, 56

Service technicians. See Repair-service technicians

Sewage disposal: into main sewer lines, 37; into septic tank, 37. See also Septic tank

Sewage-disposal systems, 37-38, 107, 118-121; drainage-field system, 37, 118-119, 120; the "head" in, 37; precautions to ensure maximum life for, 118; seepage pit, 119. See also Drain system; Drains; Septic tank

Sewage in septic tank, components of, 118, 120; effluent, 107, 118, 120; gas, 118, 120; scum, 107, 118, 120; sludge, 107, 118, 120, 121

Sewer, house, 118, 119

Sewing machines, 222-227; kwh consumed, 131; life span of, 17; needle-thread tension, and its adjustment, 226; troubleshooting, 227

Shaded-pole motor, 189, 192-193; troubleshooting, 195; where used, 189, 192. See also Motor(s)

Shavers, electric, 228-229; curved-head type, 228; finding retaining screw, 185; flat-head type, 229; kwh consumed, 131; rotary-head type, 229

Sheathed cable, 139

Shocks, electrical, 142; prevention of, 142, 145, 343

Shopping for plumbing supplies, 44-45, 76; identifying replacement parts, 45; renting expensive tools, 42, 48-49, 50-51. See also plumbing tool kit

Short circuit, 130, 135, 148, 149; testing for, in heating element, 264

Shower plumbing, parts of, 92-93, 94-95. See also Bathtub and shower plumbing

Shutoff valves, 38, 52-53; attaching new faucet lines to, 81, 83; becoming familiar with plan of, 39-40; for branch runs and risers, 39, 52-53; care in use of, 39; for fixtures, 39, 52-53; gate valve used as, 55; joining copper tube to, 59; joining plastic tube to, 59; main valve, 38, 52-53, 67; use of, when making repairs, 13, 14, 42

Silicone: caulking, 31; gear grease, 201; sealant, 247; spray, 31

Single-lever faucets, 35, 76-79; copper